THE

THIRD PART

OF THE

Institutes of the Laws of England;

CONCERNING

HIGH TREASON,

AND OTHER PLEAS OF THE CROWN.

AND

CRIMINAL CAUSES.

ECCLES. viii. 11.

Quia non profertur cito contra malos sententia, absque timore ullo filii hominum perpetrant mala.

Inertis est nescire quod sibi liceat.

AUTHORE EDWARDO COKE, MILITE, *J. C.*

HÆC EGO GRANDÆVUS POSUI TIBI, CANDIDE LECTOR.

THE LAWBOOK EXCHANGE, LTD.
Clark, New Jersey

ISBN 978-1-58477-201-9

Lawbook Exchange edition 2001, 2012

The quality of this reprint is equivalent to the quality of the original work.

THE LAWBOOK EXCHANGE, LTD.
33 Terminal Avenue
Clark, New Jersey 07066-1321

Please see our website for a selection of our other publications and fine facsimile reprints of classic works of legal history:
www.lawbookexchange.com

Library of Congress Cataloging-in-Publication Data

Coke, Edward, Sir, 1552-1634.
The third part of the institutes of the laws of England: concerning high treason, and other pleas of the Crown and criminal causes / authore, Edwardo Coke.
p. cm.
Originally published: London: Printed for W. Clarke and Sons, 1817.
Includes bibliographical references.
ISBN 1-58477-201-8 (cloth: alk. paper)
1. Criminal law—England. I. Title.

KD7869 .C65 2001
345.42—dc21 2001045980

Printed in the United States of America on acid-free paper

THE

THIRD PART

OF THE

Institutes of the Laws of England;

CONCERNING

HIGH TREASON,

AND OTHER PLEAS OF THE CROWN.

AND

CRIMINAL CAUSES.

ECCLES. viii. 11.

Quia non profertur cito contra malos sententia, absque timore ullo filii hominum perpetrant mala.

Inertis est nescire quod sibi liceat.

AUTHORE EDWARDO COKE, MILITE, *J. C.*

HÆC EGO GRANDÆVUS POSUI TIBI, CANDIDE LECTOR.

LONDON:

PRINTED FOR W. CLARKE AND SONS, LAW BOOKSELLERS, PORTUGAL-STREET, LINCOLN'S INN.

1817.

A TABLE *of the ſeveral* CHAPTERS *of the* Third Part of the Inſtitutes, of the Pleas of the Crown.

MULTI MULTA, NEMO OMNIA NOVIT.

 28. *A plague*

63. *Councell*

98. *De*

THE TABLE.

DEO,

DEO,

PATRIÆ,

TIBI.

A PROEME

TO THE

THIRD PART *of the* INSTITUTES.

IN the Second Part of the Inftitutes we have fpoken only of acts of parliament, (viz.) of Magna Carta, and many ancient and other acts of parliament, which we have explained, and therein obferved which of them are declaratory of the ancient lawes of this realme, which are introductory of new, and which mixt: all of them (excepting a very few) concerning common pleas, and thefe two great pronouns, *meum* and *tuum*.

In this Third Part of the Inftitutes, we are to treat *de malo*, viz. of high treafon, and other pleas of the crowne, and criminall caufes, moft of them by act of parliament, and fome by the common law: in which cafes the law of all other is moft neceffary to be knowne, becaufe it concerneth the fafety of his majeftie, the quiet of the common-wealth, and the life, honour, fame, liberty, blood, wife, and pofteritie of the party accufed, befides the forfeiture of his lands, goods, and all that he hath: for it is truly faid of thefe laws, *Reliquæ leges privatorum hominum commodis profpiciunt, hæ regiæ majeftati, fubditorum vitæ, ac publicæ tranquillitati confulunt.* And that in thefe cafes the ancient maxime of the law principally holdeth, *Mifera fervitus eft, ubi jus eft vagum, aut incognitum.* And where fome doth object against

See the 1. part of the Inftitutes fect. 500.

Malum non habet efficientem, fed deficientem caufam. Evill hath not an efficient, but a deficient caufe, by reafon of the want of fome vertue or notable good.

Stamford.

againſt the lawes of England, that they are darke and hard to be underſtood, we have ſpecially in theſe and other parts of the Inſtitutes opened ſuch windowes, and made them ſo lightſome, and eaſie to be underſtood, as he that hath but the light of nature, (which Solomon calleth the candle of Almighty God, Prov. 20. 27.) adding induſtrie and diligence thereunto, may eaſily diſcerne the ſame. And that may be verified of theſe lawes, that *lex eſt lux*, Prov. 6. 23, the law itſelfe is a light. See Rom. 2. 14. And when we conſider how many acts of parliament (publiſhed in print) that have made new treaſons and other capitall offences, are either repealed by generall or expreſſe words, or expired: how many indictments, attainders of treaſons, felonies, and other crimes, which are not warrantable by law at this day: and how few book-caſes there have been publiſhed of treaſons, (though a ſubject of greateſt importance) and thoſe very ſlenderly reported: we in reſpect of the places which we have holden, and of our own obſervation, and by often conferences with the ſages of the law in former times concerning criminall cauſes or pleas of the crowne, have thought good to publiſh this third part of the Inſtitutes, wherein we follow that old and ſure rule, *Quod judicandum eſt legibus, et non exemplis.* A worke arduous, and full of ſuch difficultie, as none can either feele or beleeve, but he onely which maketh tryall of it. And albeit it did often terrifie me, yet could it not in the end make me deſiſt from my purpoſe; (eſpecially in this worke) ſo farre hath the love and honour of my country, to paſſe through all labours, doubts, and difficulties, prevailed with me.

This, as other parts of the Inſtitutes, wee have ſet forth in our Engliſh tongue, not onely for the reaſons in the preface to the firſt part of the Inſtitutes alledged, which we preſume may ſatisfie any indifferent and prudent reader: but ſpecially this treatiſe of the pleas of the crowne, becauſe, as it appeareth by that which hath been ſaid, it concerneth all the ſubjects of the realme more neerly by many degrees, then any of the other. Hereunto you may adde that which Robert Holcoth an Engliſh man

Bal. cent. 3. fo. 348.

man furnamed *Theologus magnus*, upon the fecond chapter of the book of Wifdome, in or about the 20. yeare of king E. 3. wrote to this effect. *Narrant hiftoriæ quod cum Willielmus dux Normannorum regnum Angliæ conquifiviffet, deliberavit quomodo linguam Saxonicam poffit deftruere, et Angliam, et Normanniam in idiomate accordari, et ideo ordinavit, quod nullus in curia regia placitaret nifi in Gallico, et iterum quod puer quilibet ponendus ad literas addifceret Gallicum, et per Gallicum Latinum, quæ duo ufque hodie obfervantur. Hæc ille.* But the ftatute of 35 E. 3. cap. 15. made not long after Holcoth wrote, 35 E. 3. ca. 15. hath taken thefe edicts of a conqueror away, and given due honour to our Englifh language, which is as copious and fignificant, and as able to expreffe any thing in as few and apt words, as any other native language, that is fpoken at this day. And (to fpeake what we think) we would derive from the Conqueror as little as we could.

When Henry the firft died, all the iffue male of the Conqueror, and of his fonnes were dead without iffue male.

The wife of king H. 1. was Mawde daughter of Malcolme king of Scotland firnamed Canmor, and of Margaret his wife, who was the granchild of Edmond Ironfide king of England, viz. the faid king Edmond had iffue Edward firnamed the Outlaw, becaufe he lived a long time beyond fea with Salamon king of Hungary out of the extent of the lawes of this realme. Edward had iffue the faid Margaret his eldeft daughter, famous for her piety and vertue; fhe had iffue Mawde wife of king H. 1. who by her had iffue Mawde, of whofe Englifh blood by Geffery Plantagenet earle of Anjou all the kings of England are lineally defcended.

We have in this Third Part of the Inftitutes cited our ancient authors, and bookes of the law, viz. Bracton, Britton, the Mirror of Juftices, Fleta, and many ancient records, never (that we know) before publifhed, to this end, that feeing the pleas of the crown are for the moft part grounded upon, or declared by

ftatute

ſtatute lawes, the ſtudious reader may be inſtructed what the common law was before the making of thoſe ſtatutes, whereby he ſhall know, whether the ſtatutes were introductory of a new law, declaratory of the old, or mixt, and thereby perceive what was the reaſon and cauſe of the making of the ſame, which will greatly conduce to the true underſtanding thereof.

We ſhall firſt treat of the higheſt, and moſt hainous crime of high treaſon, *Crimen læſæ majeſtatis*; and of the reſt in order, as they are greater and more odious then others.

CAP. I.

OF HIGH TREASON.

BY the ſtatute of 25 E. 3. *de proditionibus*, is declared in certaine particular caſes, what offences ſhall be taken to be treaſon, with this reſtriction, that if any other caſe ſuppoſed to be treaſon ſhould happen before any juſtices, the juſtices ſhould tarry without going to judgment of the treaſon, till the caſe be ſhewed before the king and his parliament, whether it ought to be adjudged treaſon or other felony: therefore we will lay our foundation upon, and begin with that act of parliament, the letter whereof *in proprio idiomate* enſueth.

25 E. 3. cap. 2.

Divers opinions. *Ad fait declariſement.*

Nota, This is a law for the moſt part declaratory, but addeth alſo divers things to the ancient law.

AVXINT pur ceo que divers opinions ount eſtre eins ceux heures qen caſe doit eſtre dit treaſon (1), *et en quel caſe nemi, le roy a le requeſt des ſeigniours et commons ad fait declariſment* (2) *que enſuiſt. Ceſtaſſavoire, quant home* (3) *fait compaſſer* (4) *ou imaginer* (5) *la mort* (6) *noſtre ſeignior* (7) *le roy* (8), *madame ſa compaigne* (9), *ou de lour fitzeigne et heire* (10), *ou ſi home violaſt la compaigne le roy* (11), *ou leigne file le roy nient marie* (13), *ou la compaigne leigne fitz* (12) *et heire le roy. Ou ſi home leve guerre encounter noſtre ſeignior le roy* (14) *en ſon realme, ou ſoit aidant as enemies noſtre dit ſeignior le roy en ſon realme, donnant a eux aid, ou comfort en ſon roialme, ou per aylours* (15), *et de ceo provablement ſoit attaint de overt fact per gents de lour condition* (16). *Et ſi home counterface le grand* (17), *ou privie ſeale le roy, ou ſa monye* (18). *Et ſi home apport faux money en ceſt roialme counterfait al mony dangliterre, ſicome la mony appelle * Luſheburgh, ou auter ſembleble a la dit mony dangliterre, ſachant le money eſtre faux* (19) *pur merchander ou payment faire en diſceite noſtre dit ſeignior le roy et de ſon people. Et ſi home tuaſt chancellor, treaſurer, ou iuſtices noſtre ſeignior le roy del un banke ou del auter, iuſtices in eire et daſſiſes, et touts auters iuſtices aſſignes de oier et terminer* †, *eſteaunts en lour places en feſants lour offices. Et ſoit a entendre que les caſes ſuiſnomes doit eſtre adjudge treaſon, que ſe extent a noſtre ſeigniour le roy et ſa roiall majeſtie: Et de tiel manner de treaſon la forfeiture des eſcheates appertenont a noſtre ſeignior le roy, cibien des terres et tenements tenus des auters, come de luy meſme* (20).

* Luſheburghs, alias Luxenburghs were a kinde of baſe coine to the likeneſſe of our Engliſh money, ſo called, becauſe they were coined in Luſheburgh, which ſometime was an earledome, and after a dukedome. See Chaucer in the Prologue to the Monk's Tale, the hoſt ſpeaking to a luſty monk, ſaith, *God wot, no Luſhburghes pay ye*, that is (upon the coherence of the verſe) No payment make ye that is not full and currant.

† *Injuria illata judici ſeu locum tenenti regis videtur ipſe regi illata, maxime ſi fiat, in exercente officium.*

Item, WHEREAS divers opinions have been before this time, in what case treason shall be said, and in what not; the king at the request of the lords and of the commons, hath made a declaration in the manner as hereafter followeth: that is to say, when a man doth compasse or imagine the death of our lord the king, of my lady his queene, or of their eldest sonne and heire: or if a man doe violate the kings compagnion, or the kings eldest daughter unmarried, or the wife of the kings eldest sonne and heire: or if a man doe levie warre against our lord the king in his realme, or be adherent to the kings enemies in his realme, giving to them aide and comfort in the realme or elsewhere, and thereof be provably attainted of open deed by people of their condition. And if a man counterfeit the kings great or privie seale, or his money: and if a man bring false money into this realme counterfeit to the money of England, as the money called Lusheburgh, or other like to the said money of England, knowing the money to be false, to merchandize or make payment, in deceipt of our said lord the king and of his people. And if a man slay the chancellor, treasurer, or the kings justices of the one bench or the other, justices in eire, or justices of assize, and all other justices assigned to heare and determine, being in their place doing their offices. And it is to be understood, that in the cases above rehearsed, it ought to be judged treason, which extend to our lord the king and his royall majestie; and of such treason the forfeiture of the escheates pertaineth to our lord the king, as well of the lands and tenements holden of others, as of himself.

And albeit nothing can concerne the king, his crowne, and dignity, more then *crimen læsæ majestatis*, high treason: yet at the request of his lords and commons, the blessed king by authority of parliament made the declaration, as is above-said: and therefore, and for other excellent lawes made at this parliament, this was called *benedictum parliamentum*, as it well deserved. For except it be Magna Charta, no other act of parliament hath had more honour given unto it by the king, lords spirituall and temporall, and the commons of the realme for the time being in full parliament, then this act concerning
1 H. 4. cap. 10. treason hath had. For by the statute of 1 H. 4. cap. 10. reciting that where at a parliament holden 21 R. 2. divers paynes of treason were ordained by statute, in as much as there was no man did know how to behave himselfe, to doe, speak, or say, for doubt of such paines: It is enacted by the king, the lords and commons, that in no time to come any treason be judged otherwise, then it was ordained by this statute of 25 E. 3.
1 E. 6. cap. 12. The like honour is given to it by the statute of 1 E. 6. cap. 12.
1 Mar. cap. 1. and by the statute of 1 Ma. cap. 1. sess. 1. different times,
Sess. 1. but all agreeing in the magnifying and extolling of this blessed act of 25 E. 3. Of this act of 1 Mariæ, we shall speak more hereafter.

hereafter. But to proceed to give a light touch how other acts of parliament have been called. The parliament holden at Oxford, *an.* 42. H 3. was called *insanum parliamentum.* 12 E. 2. the parliament of whitebands, *albarum fibularum* or *metellarum.* 5 E. 3. *parliamentum bonum.* 10 R. 2. *parliamentum quod fecit mirabila*, that wrought wonders. 21 R. 2. *magnū parliamentū.* 6 H. 4. *parliamentū indoctū*, lack-learning parliament. 4 H. 6. *parliamentū fustiū*, the parliament of bats. The session of parliament in *an.* 14. H. 8. called the black parliament. The act of 1 E. 6. was called *parliamentū pium*, the pious parliament. And the said act of 1 Mar. *parliamentū propitium*, the merciful parliament. The parliaments of queen Elizabeth stiled *pia*, *justa*, *et provida.* The parliament holden *anno* 21 of king James, called *fœlix parliamentum*, the happy parliament. And the parliament holden in the third yeare of our soveraigne lord king Charles, *benedictum parliamentum*, the blessed parliament. The severall reasons of these former appellations appeare of record and in history, and the latter are yet fresh in memory. At the making of the statute of 25 E. 3. the high courts of justice were furnished with excellent men, *viz.* Sir William Shardshill knight (shortly written in bookes Shard) lord chiefe justice of the kings bench, and his compagnions justices of that court; Sir John Stonor knight, commonly written in books Stone, lord chief justice of the court of common pleas, and his compagnions justices of that court; and Gervasius de Wilford, lord chiefe baron of the exchequer, men famous in their profession, and excellent in the knowledge of the lawes. At the making of the statute of 1 H. 4. were Sir Walter Clopton knight, lord chiefe justice of the kings bench, and his compagnions justices of that court; and Sir William Thirning knight, lord chief justice of the court of common pleas, and his compagnions justices of that court; and Sir John Cassie knight, lord chiefe baron of the exchequer; men equall to any of their predecessors in the knowledge of the lawes. At the making of the statute of 1 E. 6. were Sir Richard Lister knight, lord chiefe justice of the kings bench, and his compagnions justices of that court; and Sir Edward Montague knight, lord chiefe justice of the court of common pleas, and his compagnions justices of that court; and Sir Roger Cholmeley knight, lord chiefe baron of the exchequer; men of that excellency, as they were worthy of the name of The worthies of the law. At the making of the statute of 1 Mar. were Sir Thomas Bromley knight, lord chiefe justice of the kings bench, and his compagnions justices of that court; and Sir Richard Morgan, knight, lord chiefe justice of the court of common pleas, and his compagnions justices of that court; and Sir D. Brook knight, lord chiefe baron of the exchequer, men renouned for their great knowledge and judgement in their profession. All these we have named in the honour of [3]

 them,

them, and of their families and poſterities, for that they in their ſeverall times were great furtherers of theſe excellent lawes concerning treaſon. *In memoria æterna erit juſtus.* And all this was done in ſeverall ages, that the faire lillies and roſes of the crowne might flouriſh, and not be ſtained by ſevere and ſanguinary ſtatutes. But let us come to the act it ſelfe, and for the better underſtanding thereof, and of the book-caſes, and other records grounded upon the ſame: let us divide this act concerning high treaſon into ſeverall claſſes or heads, and then proſecute the ſame in order.

The firſt concerneth death,
- By compaſſing or imagining the death of the { King, Queene, Prince, } and declaring the ſame by ſome overt deed.
- By killing and murdering of the { Chancellor. Treaſurer. Juſtices of the one Bench or other. Juſtices in eyre. Juſtices of aſſize. Juſtices of oier and terminer, &c. } In their places doing their offices.

The ſecond concerneth, violation, that is, to violate or carnally to know
- the kings conſort, or queene.
- the kings eldeſt daughter unmarried.
- the princes wife.

The third is levying war againſt the king.

[4] The fourth is adhering to the kings enemies within the realme, or without, and declaring the ſame by ſome overt act.

The fifth is counterfeiting of
- the great ſeale.
- the privie ſeale.
- the king's coyne.

The ſixth and laſt, by bringing into this realme counterfeit money to the likeneſſe of the kings coine, &c.

So as treaſon is *membrum diviſum*, and theſe ſeverall claſſes or heads are *membra dividentia.* And if the offence be not within one of theſe claſſes or heads, it is no treaſon.

(1) *Treaſon*] is derived from [*trahir*] which is treacherouſly to betray. *Trahue*, betrayed, and *trahiſon, per contractionen*, treaſon, is the betraying it ſelfe.

> *Detegit imbelles animos, nil fortiter audens*
> *Proditio.*

Inter leges Canuti, fo. 118. ca. 61. *Proditiones* (Hlaꝼoꞃd ꞅpice) *numera-*

numerabantur inter ſcelera jure humano inexpiabilia. Treaſon is divided into two parts, *viz.* high treaſon, *alta proditio*, and into petit treaſon, *proditio parva.* The Latin word uſed in law is *proditio (à prodere)* and thereof cometh *proditorie*, which of neceſſity muſt be uſed in every indictment of treaſon, and cannot be expreſſed by any other word, periphraſis, or circumlocution.

(2) *Ad fait declariſement.*] This law is for the moſt part declaratory of the ancient law, and therefore this word *(declariſement)* is uſed. But yet the ſtudious reader ſhall obſerve, that in divers clauſes it addeth to the former law, whereunto this word *(declariſement)* will ſufficiently extend.

(3) *Quant home*, &c.] This extendeth to both ſexes, *homo* including both man and woman. This act is generall, and therefore extendeth to ſome perſons which claimed a priviledge to be exempted from ſecular juriſdiction. (For example,) [a] Adam de Orleton biſhop of Hereford was indicted of high treaſon for aiding the Mortimers, &c. with men, and armour againſt king E. 2, &c. Whereupon he was arraigned, and alledged *ſe abſque offenſa Dei, et ſanctæ eccleſiæ, et abſque licentia domini ſummi pontificis non poſſe nec debere reſpondere in hac parte.* And thereupon the archbiſhop of Canterbury, York, and Dublin, and their ſuffragans came to the barre, claimed his priviledge, and took him away; and he was ſo far from puniſhment, as he was after tranſlated to Worceſter, and after to Wincheſter. But this ſtatute (to cleare all doubts) extendeth to all perſons, * as well eccleſiaſticall as temporall, and ſo hath it ever ſince been put in execution, as hereafter in divers caſes it appeareth. See hereafter cap. Murdre et Larceny.

A man that is *non compos mentis*, as ſhall be ſaid more fully hereafter in the next ſection, or an infant within the age of diſcretion is not *(un home)* within this ſtatute; for the principall end of puniſhment is, that others by his example may feare to offend, *ut pœna ad paucos, metus ad omnes perveniat:* but ſuch puniſhment can be no example to mad-men, or infants that are not of the age of diſcretion. And God forbid that in caſes ſo penall, the law ſhould not be certaine; and if it be certaine in caſe of murder and felony, *à fortiori*, it ought to be certaine in caſe of treaſon.

If a man commit treaſon or felony and confeſſeth the ſame, or be thereof otherwiſe convict, if afterward he become *de non ſane memorie (qui patitur exilium mentis)* he ſhall not be called to anſwer: or if after judgement he become *de non ſane memorie*, he ſhall not be executed, for it cannot be an example to others.

And all aliens that are within the realme of England, and whoſe ſoveraignes * are in amity with the king of England, are within the protection of the king, and doe owe a locall obedience to the king, (are *homes* within this act) and if they commit high treaſon againſt the king, they ſhall be puniſhed as traytors, but otherwiſe it is of an enemy, whereof you may reade at large, lib. 7. Calvin's caſe, fol. 6, &c. and 17, &c.

(4) *Fait compaſſer.*] Let us ſee firſt what the compaſſing or imagining the death of a ſubject was before, and at the time of the making of this ſtatute, [a] when *voluntas reputabatur pro facto.* And [b] Bracton ſaith, that *ſpectatur voluntas et non exitus, et nihil intereſt utrum quis occidat, aut cauſam mortis præbeat.* So as when the law was ſo holden, he muſt *cauſam mortis præbere*, that is, declare the ſame

[a] Rot. Romana. 17 E. 2. m. 6. Rot. Clauſ. 1 E. 3. part 1. memb. 13. Artic. Cleri. 9 E. 3. cap 15, & 16. Tr. 21 E. 3. coram rege Rot. 173.

Privilegium ſeculare non competit ſeditioſo equitanti cum armis, &c. ſecundum leges eccleſiæ.

25 E. 3. ſtat. 1. cap. 4. which was before this act. Mich. 31 E. 3. coram rege Rot. 55. Buck. Abbot de Miſſeny. See in the Chap. of Clergy in what caſes the priviledge of clergy is taken away.

* To perſons eccleſiaſticall and temporall.

Bract. lib. 3. 120, 121. 134, 135. Britton, 5. 18. Fleta, cap. 23. 30. Mirror, cap. 1. cap 2. § 11. de appeale de homicide, 3 E. 3. cor. 383. 25 E. 3. 42. cor. 139. 26 aſſ. 27. 3 H. 7. cap. 1. 3 H. 7. 1. 12. 21 H. 7. 31. 1. Mar. Dier. 104. Tr. 32 E. 1. Coram rege. 15. 8 E. 2. Corone. 369. 395. Cuſtum. de Norm. cap. 79. fo. 94, 95. 33 H. 8. cap. 20. 1 & 2 Mar. c. 10. To aliens.

* [5]

[a] See hereafter, cap. 73.

Where and how *voluntas reputabatur pro facto*, by the ancient law and the change thereof.

[b] Bracton, fol

same by some open deed tending to the execution of his intent, or which might be cause of death, as justice [c] Spigurnel reporteth a case adjudged; that a man's wife went away with her avowterer, and they [d] compassed the death of the husband, and as he was riding towards the sessions of oier and terminer and gaole-delivery, they assaulted him and stroke him with weapons, that he fell downe as dead, whereupon they fled; the husband recovered and made hue and cry, and came to the sessions and shewed all this matter to the justices, and upon the warrant of the justices, they were taken, indicted, and arraigned; and all this speciall matter was found by verdict; and it was adjudged that the man should be hanged, and the woman burnt. And Sir William Beresford, chiefe justice of the common pleas said, that before him and his compagnions justices of oier and terminer and gaole-delivery, a youth was arraigned, for that he would have stolne the goods of his master, and came to his masters bed, where he lay asleepe, and with a knife attempted with all his force to have cut his throat; and thinking that he had indeed cut it, he fled, whereupon the master cried out, and his neighbours apprehended the youth; and all this matter being found by special verdict, in the end he was adjudged to be hanged, &c. *Quia * voluntas reputabitur pro facto.* So as it was not a bare compassing or plotting of the death of a man, either by word, or writing, but such an overt deed, as is aforesaid, to manifest the same. So as if a man had compassed the death of another, and had uttered the same by words or writing, yet he should not have died for it, for there wanted an overt deed tending to the execution of his compassing. [e] But if a man had imagined to murder, or rob another, and to that intent had become *insidiator viarum*, and assaulted him, though he killed him not, nor took any thing from him, yet was it felony, for there was an overt deed. But in those days, in the case of the king, if a man had compassed, or imagined the death of the king (who is the head of the commonwealth) and had declared his compassing, or imagination by words or writing, this had been high treason, and a sufficient overture by the ancient law. And herewith agree all our ancient books. Glanvil saith, *cum quis de morte regis, &c. infamatur, &c.*

Bracton in the title *de criminibus læsæ majestatis. Ipse accusatus præloquutus fuit mortem regis.* And Britton. fol. 16. *grand treason est a compasser nostre mort.* and fo. 39. b. *cyface lencusor son appeale &c. que il cya mesme cēi John pur parler tiel mort, ou tiel treason &c.* And Fleta saith in his title *de crimine læsæ majestatis, si quis mortem regis ausu temerario machinatus fuerit &c. quamvis voluntatem non perduxit ad effectum.* And the Mirror saith, *crime de majestie est un peche horrible fait al roy &c. p. ceux q. occirent le roy, ou compassant a faire.* And it will delight you (in respect of reverend antiquity) to heare a president of an appeale (which then and after was in use) of high treason, *en pleine pliam. &c. en temps roy Edmond en cestes parolx. Rocelyn icy dit vers Waligrot illonq. q. a tiel iour tiel anne del raigne de tiel roy, en tiel lieu vient celuy Waligrot a cēi Rocelyn, et luy trova destre en compa y, et en aide ensemblement ove Atheling, Thurkild, Ballard, et autres de faire prisoner, ou en tache pur occire nrē seignior le roy Edmond, ou en auter manner p. coupe feloniousment, et a ceo faire fuer' entreinres a ceo counsel celer, et a ceo felony issint fornit solonq. lour poier.* By all which it is manifest, that compassing, machinating, counselling, &c. to

[c] 15 E. 2. tit. Cor. 383.

[d] Note this word [compassed.]

* *Sed hæc voluntas non intellecta fuit de voluntate nudis verbis, aut scriptis propalata, sed mundo manifestata fuit per apertum factum, Id est, cum quis dederat operam, quantum in ipso fuit, ad occidendum, et sic de similibus.*

[e] *Insidiator viarum.* See hereafter, cap. 5. De Heresie.

25 E. 3. 42. 27. ass. p. 38. 4 H. 4. ca. 2. 13 H. 4. 7. per Gascoign. But see 9 E. 4. fo. 26. *Insidiator viarum* without taking of somewhat, resolved to be no felony. V. lib. 11. fo. 29. b. Al. Poulter's case. Vid. postea cap. 16. Robbery, in fine.

Glanvil, lib. 14. cap. 14. lib. 1. c. 2. Bract. lib. 3. f. 118. Britton, fol. 16 & 39. b. Note the word *Compasse.* Fleta, lib. 1. c. 21. Mirr. cap. 1. § 5. cap. 2. § 11. Note this word *Compasse* Mirror, c. 2. § 11. De lappeale de majestie.

Rot. pat. 25 E. 3. part 1. m. 16. Vide Mic. 4 H. 4. Coram rege. Rot. 22. See hereof more in the 57 cha. of Appeales.

Bracton, Britton, Fleta, &c.

to kill the king, though it hath no other declaration thereof but by words, was high treaſon by the common law. And ſee hereafter, *verb. per overt fait, et de ceo provablement, &c.*

(5) *Fait compaſſer ou imaginer.*] So as there muſt be a compaſſing or imagination, for an act done *per infortunium*, without compaſſing, intent, or imagination, is not within this act, as it appeareth by the expreſſe words thereof. *Et actus non facit reum, niſi mens ſit rea.* And if it be not within the words of this act, then by force of a clauſe hereafter, *viz. Et pur ceo que p'uſors auters, &c.* It cannot be adjudged treaſon, untill it be declared treaſon by parliament, which is the remedie in that caſe, which the makers of the law provided in that caſe. This compaſſing, intent, or imagination, though ſecret, is to be tryed by the peers, and to be diſcovered by circumſtances precedent, concomitant, and ſubſequent, with all endeavour evermore for the ſafety of the king. This was the caſe of Sr. Walter Tirrel a French knight, who the firſt day of Auguſt *ann.* 13 Williel. 2. *ann. dom.* 1100 being a hunting with the king in the new foreſt, was commanded by the king to ſhoot at a hart, *exiit ergo telum volatile, et obſtante arbore in obliquum reflexum faciens, per medium cordis regem ſauciavit, qui ſubito mortuus corruit.*

Regula.

Mat. Par. pa. 51. Holling. pa. 26. b. Mat. Weſtm. W. Malmeſbury.

It appeareth alſo by the Cuſtumer of Normandy, treating of treaſon, and the expoſition of the ſame, that this act was not treaſon. To calculate or ſeek to know by ſetting of a figure or witchcraft, how long the king ſhall raigne or live, is no treaſon, for it is no compaſſing, or imagination of the death of the king, within this ſtatute of 25 E. 3. and this appeareth by the judgment of the parliament in 23 Eliz. whereby this offence was made felony during the life of queen Eliz. which before was puniſhable by fine and impriſonment.

Cuſtum. de Nor. cap. 14. Vide inter Indictamenta de 17 E. 4. de Th. Burdit. al. ſed judicandum eſt legibus, et non exemplis. 23 Eliz. cap. 2.

The ancient law was, that if a mad man had killed or offered to kill the king, it was holden for treaſon; and ſo it appeareth by king Alfred's law before the conqueſt, and in lib. 4. in Beverlyes caſe. But now by this ſtatute and by force of theſe words, *fait compaſſer ou imaginer la mort*, he that is *non compos mentis* and totally deprived of all compaſſings, and imaginations, cannot commit high treaſon by compaſſing or imagining the death of the king: for *furioſus ſolo furore punitur:* but it muſt be an abſolute madneſſe, and a totall deprivation of memorie. And this appeareth by the ſtatute of 33 H. 8. for thereby it is provided, that if a man being *compos mentis* commit high treaſon, and after accuſation, &c. fall to madneſſe, that he might be tryed in his abſence, &c. and ſuffer death, as if he were of perfect memory: for by this ſtatute of 25 E. 3. a mad man could not commit high treaſon. It was further provided by the ſaid act of 33 H. 8. that if a man attainted of treaſon became mad, that notwithſtanding he ſhould be executed; * which cruell and inhuman law lived not long, but was repealed, for in that point alſo it was againſt the common law, becauſe by intendment of law the execution of the offender is for example, *ut pœna ad paucos, metus ad omnes perveniat*, as before is ſaid: but ſo it is not when a mad man is executed, but ſhould be a miſerable ſpectacle, both againſt law, and of extreame inhumanity and cruelty, and can be no example to others.

* *Inter leges Alvredi*, cap. 4. lib 4. fo. 124. Beverlie's caſe. Ovid. *Scilicet in ſuperis etiam fortuna luenda eſt. Nec veniam leſo numine, caſus habet.*

33 H. 8. cap. 20. * 1 & 2 Ph. and Mar. ca. 10. [a] Bract. lib. 3. fo. 118. Britton, cap. 8. a diſheriter. Glanv. lib. 1. cap. 2. Fleta, lib. 1. cap. 21. Mirror, ca 1. § 5 *Vers roy de la tre.*

 (6) *Mort.*

a 13 Eliz. cap. 1. nota declared. Brook, tit. treason, 24. b 1 H. 4. 1. 19 H. 6. 47. 13 H. 8. 12. *vide infra verb.* (16) *Per overt fait.*

(6) *Mort.*] [a] He that declareth by overt act to depose the king, is a sufficient overt act to prove, that he compasseth and imagineth the death of the king. And so it is to [b] imprison the king, or to take the king into his power, and manifest the same by some overt act, this is also a sufficient overt act for the intent aforesaid. But peruse advisedly the statutes of 13 Eliz. cap. 1. 2. & 14 Eliz. cap. 1.

(7) *Nrē seignior le roy.*] These words extend to all his successors, as it hath been alwayes taken.

3 Mar. Dier. 131. pl. 7.

[7]

(8) *Le roy.*] Is to be understood of a king regnant, and not of one that hath but the name of a king, or a nominative king, as it was resolved in the case of king Phillip, who married queen Mary, and was but a nominative king, for queen Mary had the office and dignity of a king, so as she that wanted the name of a king, but had the office and dignity, was within this act of 25 E. 3. And hee that had the name, and not the office and dignity of the king was not within it. And therefore an act was made, that to compasse or imagine the death of king Phillip, &c. during his marriage with the queen, was treason. A queen regnant is within these words *(nrē seignior le roy)* for she hath the office of a king.

1 & 2 Phi. and Mar. cap. 10.

Vide 11 H. 7. c. 1.

This act is to be understood of a king in possession of the crowne, and kingdom: for if there be a king regnant in possession, although he be *rex de facto, et non de jure*, yet is he *seignior le roy* within the purvien of this statute. And the other that hath right, and is out of possession, is not within this act. Nay if treason be committed against a king *de facto, et non de jure*, and after the king *de jure* commeth to the crowne, he shall punish the treason done to the king *de facto*: and a pardon granted by a king *de jure*, that is not also *de facto*, is voyde.

4 E. 4. 1. 9 E. 4. 1. 2.

If the crown descend to the rightfull heire, he is *rex* before coronation: for by the law of England there is no *interregnum*: and coronation is but an ornament or solemnity of honour. And so it was resolved by all the judges Hil. 1 Ja. in the case of Watson and Clarke seminary priests: for by the law there is alwayes a king, in whose name the lawes are to be maintained, and executed, otherwise justice should faile. Divers kings before the conquest voluntarily renounced their kingly office: and so did king H. 2. in the 16. yeare of his reigne, and Henry his sonne was created and crowned.

Hil. 1 Ja. in the case of Watson and Clark seminary priests. 9 E. 4. 1. b.

It appeareth by Britton, that to compasse the death of the father of the king, is treason, and so was the law holden long after that: for after king E. 2. had dismissed himselfe of his kingly office, and duty, and his sonne by the name of E. 3. was crowned, and king regnant, those cursed caitifs, Thomas Gourny, and William Ocle, and others were attainted of high treason for murthering the king's father, who had been king by the name of E. 2. and had judgement to be drawne, hanged, and quartered.

See the preamble, *Auxint pur ceo que divers opinions eunt estre eins ceux heures, que qen case doit estre dit treason, et in quel case nemi.* Rot. parliam. 4 E. 3. num. 5. * Eodem rot. num. 3. and 4.

* The like judgement was given against Sir John Matrevers knight, and others, as being guilty of the death of the king's uncle, Edmond earl of Kent, which at that time (being so neer of the bloud royall) was by some holden also treason. But now this act of 25 E. 3. hath restrained high treason in case of death *(al nrē seignior le roy, sa compaigne, et al eigne fitz, et heire le roy.*

Nicholas de Segrave was charged in open parliament *in præsentia dni. reg. comitum, baronum, et aliorum de consilio regis tunc ibi existent'*, that

Plac. in parliam. E. 1. *anno regni sui*, 33 North. Rot. 17. & 22.

that the king in the warre of Scotland being amongſt his enemies, Nicholas Segrave his liege man, and holding of the king by homage, and fealty, ſerved him for his aid in that warre, did maliciouſly move contention and diſcord without cauſe, with John de Crombewell, charging him with many enormous crimes, and offered to prove it upon his body. To whom the ſaid John anſwered, that he would anſwer him in the king's court, as the court ſhould conſider, &c. and thereupon gave him his faith. After Nich. withdrew himſelfe from the king's hoſt, and from the king's aid, leaving the king amongſt his enemies, *in periculo hoſtium ſuorum*, and adjourned the ſaid John to defend himſelf in the court of the king of France, and prefixed him a certaine day, *et ſic quantum in eo fuit, ſubjiciens, et ſubmittens dominium regis, et regni ſubjectioni dni. regis Franciæ, ad hoc faciendum, iter ſuum arripuit uſque Dovoriam, ad transfretandum, &c.* All which the ſaid Nich. confeſſed, *et voluntati dni. regis de alto et baſſo inde ſe ſubmiſit. Et ſuper hoc dns. rex volens habere aviſamentum comitum, baronum, magnatum, et aliorum de conſilio ſuo, injunxit eiſdem in homagio, fidelitate, et ligeantia quibus ei tenentur, quod ipſum fideliter conſulerent, qualis pœna pro tali facto ſic cognito fuerit infligenda: qui omnes, habito ſuper hoc diligenti tractatu, et aviſamento, conſideratis, et intellectis omnibus in prædicto facto contentis, &c. dicunt quod hujuſmodi factum meretur amiſſionem vitæ et membrorum, &c.* So as this offence was then ſolemnely in parliament adjudged high treaſon. But this is taken away by this act of 25 E. 3. being not under any of the claſſes, or heads ſpecified in this act. [8]

40 Aſſ. 25.

So piracy by any of the king's ſubjects upon another, was taken to be treaſon before this act, for ſo is the book to be intended, becauſe a pirat is *hoſtis humani generis*. But by this act it is not now to be judged treaſon. See hereafter in the chapter of Piracy.

One doth marie a queen regnant, if the huſband compaſſe the death of the queene, and declare the ſame by overt act, he is guilty of treaſon, and puniſhable by this act, for to this and many other purpoſes ſhe is a diſtinct perſon by the common law. And ſo if a queene wife of a king regnant, compaſſe the death of the king, and declare the ſame by overt act, ſhe is guilty of treaſon, and puniſhable by this act. So as (that we may ſpeak it once for all) by theſe and many others that might be cited, (ſome whereof ſhall hereafter be touched) the preamble of this act appeareth to be true, that divers opinions had been before the making of this act, what offences ſhould be adjudged high treaſon, and what not.

Britton, cap. 8. and other ancient authors *ubi ſupra*.

Rot. parlia. 3 R. 2. num. 18. See placita coram rege Hill. an. 3 R. 2. (Cavendiſh) rot. 8. London Holl. cron. 3 R. 2. pa. 422. 60. b. &c.

This ſtatute having reſtrained the compaſſing, &c. of death to the king, queen, and prince, it came to paſſe after the making of this act, that in 3 R. 2. two citizens of London, John Kerby, mercer, and John Algore, grocer conceiving malice againſt John Imperiall Janevois of S. Mary in Genoa that came as ambaſſadour from the ſtate of Genoa to the king (under the king's letters of ſafe conduct, for alliance to be had betweene the king and the duke and comminalty of Genoa aforeſaid) for that the ſaid John Imperiall had obtained a * monopolie to furniſh this land (keeping his ſtaple at Southampton) of all ſuch wares as came from the Levant, ſo plentifully as was to be had in all the weſt parts of Chriſtendome, the ſaid John Imperiall was killed by them, as more at large appears by the record. And albeit the ſaid John Imperiall was an ambaſſadour

* Monopoly.

nota his end.

fadour under the king's fafe conduct, and the killing of him was *jufti belli caufa*, yet the killing of him was no treafon, becaufe it was not under any of the faid claffes or heads, until it was at that time declared by parliament in thefe words, *quel cafe examine et difpute inter les feigniors, et commons, et puis nre. al roy en pleine parliament, eftoit illonques devant nre. feignior le roy declares, determinus et affentus, que tiel fait, et coupe eft treafon, et crime de royall majeftie blemye, en quel cafe il ne doit allower a nulluy priviledge del clergie*, and accordingly the faid Kerby and Algore were attainted of high treafon in the king's bench, Hill. 3 Rich. 2. *ubi fupra:* but this declaration is taken away by the ftatute of 1 Mariæ, as hereafter fhall be faid, and yet of this declaration we fhall make much ufe hereafter.

2Regum, cap. 10. 4. 12. 31. The killing of a foreine ambaffadour. *Honor legati, honor mittentis eft, et proregis dedecus redundat in regem.*

22 Aff. p. 49. *Mort dun ambaffad. le roy.*

In the 22 yeare of E. 3. which was about 3 yeares before the making of this act, one John at Hill had murdered A. de Walton the king's ambaffadour, *nuncium dni. regis miff. ad mandatum regis exequendum:* this was adjudged high treafon, for which he was drawne, hanged, and beheaded, &c. For true it is, *quod legatus ejus vice fungitur, a quo deftinatur, et honorandus eft ficut ille cujus vicem gerit, et legatos violare contra jus gentium eft.* But by this act of 25 E. 3. it is reftrained to the death *de nre. feignior le roy*, and therefore *prorex* is not within this ftatute.

(9) *Sa compaigne.*] This word *compaigne*, (which is all one with confort or wife) was ufed, that compaffing, &c. muft be during the marriage with the king, for after the king's death fhe is not *fa compaigne*, and therefore it extendeth not to a queene dowager, and for this caufe this word *compaigne* was ufed in this act.

Britton *ubi fupra.*

(10) *Le fitz eigne et heire le roy.*] The eldeft fonne and heire of a queen regnant is within this law. Before this ftatute fome did hold, that to compaffe the death of any of the king's children, was treafon. But by this act it is reftrained to the prince, the king's fonne, being heire apparant to the crowne for the time being: and he need not be the firft begotten fonne, for the fecond after the deceafe of the firft begotten without iffue, is *fitz eigne* within this ftatute, *et fic de cæteris.* If the heire apparant to the crowne be a collateral heire apparant, he is not within this ftatute, untill it be declared by parliament, as it was in the duke of York's cafe.

[9]

Roger Mortimer, earle of March, was in *anno domini* 1487 (11 R. 2.) proclaimed heire apparant. *Anno* 39 H. 6. Richard duke of York was likewife proclaimed heire apparant. And fo was John de la Poole earle of Lincolne, by R. 3. And Henry marquiffe of Exeter, by king Henry the eighth. But none of thefe or of the like, are within the purvieu of this ftatute. And now that we have handled compaffings and imaginations, let us proceed to the refidue which concerne acts and deeds.

Heire is here taken for heire apparant, for he cannot be heire in the life of the father.

Mirror, ca. 1. § 5. Brit. c. 23. fo. 43. a.

(11) *Si home violaft la compaigne le roy.*] The Mirror faith, *Crime de majeftie vers le roy p. ceux avowterors q. fpergiffent la feme le roy.* Whereby it appeareth that this was high treafon by the common law.

33 H. 8. cap. 21.

Violare is here taken for *carnaliter cognofcere*; and it is no treafon, unleffe it be done during the marriage with the king, and extendeth not to a queen dowager, as hath been faid. And if the wife

of

of the king doth yeeld and conſent to him that committeth this treaſon, it is treaſon in her.

(12) *Ou la compaigne de lour fitz et heire.*] This alſo extendeth to the wife of the prince during the coverture betweene them, and not to a dowager, and if the wife yeeld and conſent to him that commits this treaſon, it is treaſon in her.

Heire.] Here is taken *ut ſupra*, for heire apparant.

(13) *Ou leigne file nient marie.*] (That is,) eldeſt daughter not married at the time of the violation, albeit there had been an elder daughter then ſhe, who is dead without iſſue. * The Mirror. *Avowterors q. ſpergiſſent la file le roy eignes legittime, avant ceo q. el ſoit marie.*

And the reaſon that the eldeſt only is here mentioned, is, for that for default of iſſue male, ſhe only is inheritable to the crowne.

(14) *Ou ſi home leva guerre enconter noſtre ſeignior le roy.*] [a] This was high treaſon by the common law, for no ſubject can levie warre within the realme without authority from the king, for to him it only belongeth, See F. N. B. 113. a. *Le roy de droit doit ſaver et defender ſon realme vers enemies, &c.*

[b] A compaſſing or conſpiracy to levie war, is no treaſon, for there muſt be a levying of war *in facto*. But if many conſpire to levie war, and ſome of them do levie the ſame according to the conſpiracy, this is high treaſon in all, for in treaſon all be principals, and war is levied.

If any levie war to expulſe ſtrangers, to deliver men out of priſons, to remove counſellors, or againſt any ſtatute, or to any other end, pretending reformation of their own heads, without warrant; this is levying of war againſt the king: becauſe they take upon them royall authority, which is againſt the king. There is a diverſity betweene levying of war and committing of a great riot, a rout, or an unlawfull aſſembly. [c] For example, as if three, or foure, or more, doe riſe to burne, or put down an incloſure in Dale, which the lord of the manor of Dale hath made there in that particular place; this or the like is a riot, a rout, or an unlawfull aſſembly, and no treaſon. But if they had riſen of purpoſe to alter religion eſtabliſhed within the realme, or laws, or to go from town to town generally, and to caſt downe incloſures, this is a levying of war (though there be no great number of the conſpirators) within the purvien of this ſtatute, becauſe the pretence is publick and generall, and not private in particular. And ſo it was reſolved in the caſe of Richard Bradſhaw, miller, Robert Burton, maſon, and others of Oxfordſhire, whoſe caſe was, that they conſpired and agreed to aſſemble themſelves with ſo many as they could procure at Enſlowe-hill in the ſaid county, and there to riſe, and from thence to go from gentlemans houſe to gentlemans houſe, and to caſt downe incloſures, as well for inlargement of high-wayes as of errable lands. And they agreed to get armour and artillery at the lord Norrys his houſe, and to weare them in going from gentlemans houſe to gentlemans houſe for the purpoſe aforeſaid, and to that purpoſe they perſwaded divers others: and all this was confeſſed by the offenders. And it was reſolved, that this was a compaſſing and intention to levie war againſt the queen, becauſe the pretence was publick within the ſtatute of 13 Eliz. cap.

Paſch. 28 H. 8. in Spilman's Reports in caſe of Queen Anne.
33 H. 8. ubi ſupra, in caſe of Queen Katherine.
* Mirror, ca. 1. § 5.
See Brit. cap. 23. fo. 43, 44. and cap. 29. fol. 71.
1 Mar. Parl. 2. c. 1.
a Glanvil, lib. 1. cap. 2. l. 14. c. 1.
Bracton, lib. 3. fol. 118.
Britton, f. 16, &c.
Fleta, li. 1. ca. 21.
Mir. ca. 1. § 5.
b 1 Mar. 98. b. Dier. in Sir N. Throgmorton's caſe.
See 21 E. 3. 23.
21 R. 2. cap. Repeale.
1 H. 4. cap. 3.
8 E. 3. 20.
See hereafter, cap. 73 againſt going or riding armed.
c See Rot. Parl. in Cro. Epiphan. 20 E. 1. Rot. 23. Humfrey de Bohun's caſe. 4 Eliz. 210. b. Dier.
See the ſtatute of 1 Mar. ca. 2. By which, grand riots in ſome caſes be made felony.

[10]

Paſch. 39 Eliz. by all the judges of England, I being attourney-generall, and preſent.

cap. 1. (the letter whereof herein ſhortly followeth,) and the offenders were attainted and executed at Enſlowe-hill.

And this diverſity is proved by a latter branch of this act. *Et ſi per caſe aſcun home de ceſt realme chimancha arme diſcovert ſecretment ove gents armes, contre aſcun autre, pur luy tuer, ou diſrober, ou pur luy prender, ou retayner tanq. il face fine, ou ranſome pur ſa deliverance, neſt lentention le roy et de ſon counſell, q. en tiel caſe ſoit adjudge treaſon, mes ſoit adjudge felony, ou treſpaſſe, ſolonq. le ley del tre. auncientment uſe.* Whereby it appeareth, that bearing of armes in warlike manner, for a private revenge or end, is no levying of war againſt the king within this ſtatute. So that every gathering of force is not high treaſon. And ſo it was reſolved in parliament, in 5 H. 4 rot. parliam. nu 11. & 12. the earle of Northumberland's caſe.

Rot. Parl. 5 H. 4. nu. 11, 12.

13 Eliz. cap. 1. b. The indictments and attainders of treaſon by force of this ſtatute are not more to be followed, becauſe the ſtatute which made them good, is expired. Dier, 3 & 4 Ph. and Mar. 144. 10 E. 4. 6. 1 Mar. Treaſon, Br. 24. Ter. Mic. 8 H. 8. Mich. 7 H. 5. Coram rege. Heref. Rot. 20.

By the ſaid ſtatute of 13 Eliz. cap. 1. it is enacted, declared, and eſtabliſhed, that during the naturall life of queene Elizabeth, if any within the realme or without, ſhould compaſſe, imagine, invent, deviſe, or intend to levie war againſt her majeſty, within this realme, or without, and the ſame declare by writing, or word, &c. that it ſhould be high treaſon: ſo during the life of the queen, a conſpiracy to levie war was high treaſon, though no war were levied; and upon that law, Bradſhaw, Burton, and others, were attainted of high treaſon, for conſpiracy only to levie war. But it was reſolved by all the juſtices, that it was no treaſon within the ſtatute of 25 E. 3. as hath been ſaid. The words in this law are [*levie guerre*] an actuall rebellion or inſurrection is a levying of war within this act, and by the name of levying war is to be expreſſed in the indictment. If any with ſtrength and weapons invaſive, and defenſive, doth hold and defend a caſtle or fort againſt the king and his power, this is levying of war againſt the king within this ſtatute of 25 E. 3.

It was reſolved by all the judges of England in the reigne of king H. 8. that an inſurrection againſt the ſtatute of labourers, for the inhanſing of ſalaries and wages, was a levying of war againſt the king, becauſe it was generally againſt the kings law, and the offenders took upon them the reformation thereof, which ſubjects by gathering of power ought not to do. It was ſpecially found, that divers of the kings ſubjects did miniſter and yeeld victuals to Sir John Oldcaſtle, knight, and others, being in open war againſt the king, and that they were in company with them in open war; but all this was found to be *pro timore mortis, et quod receſſerunt, quam cito potuerunt:* and it was adjudged to be no treaſon, becauſe it was for feare of death. *Et actus non facit reum, niſi mens ſit rea.* And therefore this in them was no levying of war againſt the king within this act.

(15) *Ou ſoit adherent as enemies noſtre ſeigniour le roy, a eux donant aide et comfort en ſon roialme et aylors.*]

[a] Rot. Parl. 20 E. 1. nu. 2. John de Brittaine's caſe. Rot. Parl. 33. E. 1. Rot. 6. Rob. de Ros de Werke's caſe. 8 E. 3. 20. 38 E. 3. 31. a. Parl. 4 R. 2. nu. 17, 18, &c. 5 R. 2. Triall 54. Hil. 18 E. 3. coram rege. Rot. 145. Eborum, 43. Aſſ. 28. 42. Aſſ. 19. Gilbert de M. was a Scot. Rot. Parl. 7 R. 2. nu. 15. 17. 24. 7 H. 4. 47. Cuſt. de Norm. ca. 73.

[b] *Vid.* 13 Eliz. Dier. 298.

Adherent.] [a] This is here explained, viz. in giving aide and comfort to the king's enemies within the realme or without: delivery or ſurrender of the king's caſtles or forts by the kings captaine thereof to the kings enemie within the realme or without for reward, &c. is an adhering to the kings enemy, and conſequently treaſon declared by this act. [b] A. is out of * the realme at the time of a rebellion within England, and one of the rebels flye out of the

* [11]

the realme, whom A. knowing his treason doth aide or succour, this is no treason in A. by this branch of 25 E. 3. because the traytor is no enemy, as hereafter shall be said; and this statute is taken strictly.

See hereafter, 35 H. 8. cap. 2.

As enemies.] *Inimicus* in legall understanding is *hostis*, for [c] the subjects of the king, though they be in open war or rebellion against the king, yet are they not the king's enemies, but traytors; for enemies be those that be out of the allegiance of the king. If a subject joine with a foraine enemy, and come into England with him, he shall not be taken prisoner here and ransomed, or proceeded with as an enemy shall, but he shall be taken as a traytor to the king.

[c] 43 Ass. 28, 29. 33 H. 6. 1. 19 E. 4. 6. a. and b. 4 Mar. Treason. Br. 32. 1 Mar. ibid. 24. 21 E. 3. 23. 22 Ass. p. 49. 13 El. Dyer, 298. Ex libro de Griffin de Perkin Werbeck.

[d] An enemy coming in open hostility into England, and taken, shall be either executed by marshall-law, or ransomed; for he cannot be indicted of treason, for that he never was within the protection or ligeance of the king, and the indictment of treason saith, *contra ligeantiam suam debitam.*

[d] Dier, 4. Mar. fo. 145. a. Lib. 7. fo. 6. b. Calvin's case.

[e] David prince of Wales levied war against E. 1. this was treason, for that he was within the homage and ligeance of the king, and had judgement given against him as a traytor, and not as an enemy. And albeit in many presidents of indictments, subjects that be rebels, and traytors, &c. be called *proditores et inimici*; yet within this statute they are not *inimici.*

[e] Fleta, lib. 1. c. 16.

[f] In the duke of Norfolk's case the question was, a league being between the queene of England and the king of Scots, whether the lord Herise and other Scots *in aperto prælio* burning and wasting divers townes in England without the assent of the king, were enemies in law within this statute, and resolved that they were. [g] See more hereafter in this third part of the Institutes. cap. 49. of Piracy, &c. upon the statute of 28 H. 8. cap. 15.

[f] Mich. 13. & 14. Eliz. per Justice. 19 E. 4. 6. b. 18 H. 6. ca. 4. 20 H. 6. cap. 1.

[g] 27 E. 3. cap. 13. 31 H. 6. cap. 4. 7 E. 4. 14. 13 E. 4. 9. 21 E. 3. 16, 17. Regist. 129. Fit. N. B. 114.

Ou per ailors.] That is to say, out of the realme of England. But then it may be demanded, how should at this time this forraigne treason be tried? And some [h] of our books doe answer, that the offender shall be indicted and tried in this realme where his land lyeth, and so it was adjudged in 2 H. 4. But now by the statute of 35 H. 8. cap. 2. (which yet remains in force) all offences made or declared, or hereafter made or declared treasons, misprisions of treason, and concealements of treason, committed out of the realme of England, shall be inquired of, heard, and determined, either in the king's bench or before commissioners in such shire as shall be assigned by the king. If it be before commissioners, it hath been commonly used, that the king doth write his name in the upper part of the commission. But in the case of Patrick o'Cullen an Irishman, the queene did put her signature to the warrant to the lord keeper, and not to the commission: * and it was holden by the justices that the one way and the other was a sufficient assignement by the king within the statute of 35 H. 8.

[h] 4 Ass. p. 15. 5 R. 2. *ubi supra.* 19 E. 4. 6. b. Dier. 3. Mar. 132. Pasch. 2 H. 4. *coram rege.* Rot. 8. Wallia. 35 H. 8. cap. 2. 3 Mar. *ubi supra.* 13 Eliz. Dier. 298. Stanford Pl. Cor. fo. 90. a. and b. See the first part of the Institutes, 440.

* Hil. 36 Eliz. in the case of Patrick o'Cullen, for a treason at Brussels *in partibus marinis.*

[i] It was resolved by all the judges of England, that for a treason done in Ireland the offender may be tryed by the statute of 35 H. 8. in England, because the words of the statute be, all treasons committed out of the realme of England, and Ireland is out of the realme of England. And so it was resolved in Sir John Parrot's case. And our word here [*per ailors*] is as much as out of the realme

[i] 33 El. in Orrick's case. lib. 7. f. 23. Calvin's case. *Vid.* Dier. Mich. 19 & 20 Eliz. fo. 360. lib. 11. fo. 63. in Doct. Foster's case.

k28 H. 8. ca. 15. This act concerning treasons is not taken away by the statute of 35 H. 8. cap. 2. *Vide infra* cap. 49. fo. 181. of Piracy, &c. Vid. 5 Eliz. c. 5.

realme of England. See Pasch. 2 H. 4. *coram rege rot.* 8. Salop. Treason in Wales.

[k] All treasons done upon the sea shall be inquired, heard, and determined in such shires and places of the realme as shall be limited by the king's commission, in like forme and condition, as if the same had been done upon the land, &c. after the common course of the lawes of this land. And by the preamble it appeareth, that it could not be tryed by the common law, but by the civill law before the lord admirall. See hereafter in the exposition of the statute of 28 H. 8. cap. 15. *et infra*, cap. 49.

[12]

g See 1 E. 6. ca. 12. the last clause. 5 E. 6. ca. 11. 1 & 2 Ph. & Mar. ca. 10. and 11. 1 Eliz. cap. 6. 13 Eliz. cap. 1. Stanf. pl. Cor. 89. and 164. Br. coron. 4 Mar. 220. Dier. 2 Mar. fo. 99.

(16) *Et de ceo provablement soit attaint per overt fait per gents de lour condition.*] In this branch four things are to be observed, [g] first this word [*provablement*] provably, that is, upon direct and manifest proof, not upon conjecturall presumptions, or inferences, or straines of wit; but upon good and sufficient proofe. And herein the adverb [*provablement*] provably, hath a great force, and signifieth a direct and plain proof, which word the king, the lords, and commons in parliament did use, for that the offence was so hainous, and was so heavily, and severely punished, as none other the like, and therefore the offender must provably be attainted, which words are as forcible, as upon direct and manifest proof. Note, the word is not (probably) for then *commune argumentum* might have served, but the word is [*provably*,] be attainted.

* Rot. parl. an. 33 E. 1. Rot. 6. Jo. Salvyn's case. h 43. Ass. 28. 8 E. 3. 20. 7 H. 4. 27. 34 E. 3. cap. 12. Lib. 4. fo. 57. the Sadler's case.

2. This word *(attaint)* necessarily implyeth that he be proceeded with, and attainted according to the due course, and proceedings of law, and not by absolute power, or by other meanes, * as in former times had been used. [h] And therefore if a man doth adhere to the enemies of the king, or be slaine in open warre against the king, or otherwise die before the attainder of treason, he forfeiteth nothing, because (as this act saith) he is not attainted: wherein this act hath altered that, which before this act, in case of treason, was taken for law. And the statute of 34 E. 3. cap. 12. saves nothing to the king, but that which was in *esse*, and pertaining to the king at the making of that act. And this appeareth by a judgement in parliament in *anno* 29 H. 6. cap. 1. that * Jack Cade being slaine in open rebellion could no way be punished, or forfeit any thing, and therefore was attainted by that act of high treason.

* 29 H. 6. cap. 1.

Vide supra verbo ¶ Mort. fo. 6. Vide 21 R. 2. cap. 3. but it is repealed by 1 H. 4. ca. 3. * Hill, 36 Eliz. Doctor Lopes case, 13 Eliz. c. 1. Brooke, Treason, 24.

3. *Per overt fait,*] *per apertum factum.* This doth also strengthen the former exposition of the word *(provablement,)* that it must be provably, by an open act, which must be manifestly proved. As if divers doe conspire the death of the king, and the manner how, and thereupon provide weapons, powder, * poison, assay harnesse, send letters, &c. or the like, for execution of the conspiracy. Also preparation by some overt act, to depose the king, or take the king by force, and strong hand, and to imprison him untill he hath yeelded to certaine demands, this is a sufficient overt act to prove the compassing, and imagination of the death of the king: for this upon the matter is to make the king a subject, and to dispoyle him of his kingly office of royall government. And so it was resolved by all the judges of England. Hill. 1 Jac. *regis*, in the case of the lo. Cobham, lord Gray, and Watson and Clarke seminary priests: and so had it been resolved by the justices, Hill. 43. Eliz. in the case of the earles of E. and of S. who intended to goe to the court

Hill. 1 Ja. R. Lo. Cobham's case.

court where the queen was, and to have taken her into their power, and to have removed divers of her counsell, and for that end did assemble a multitude of people; this being raised to the end aforesaid was a sufficient overt act for compassing the death of the queen. And so by woful experience in former times it hath fallen out, in the cases of king E. 2. R. 2. H. 6. and E. 5. that were taken, and imprisoned by their subjects. And this is made more plain by the legall forme of an inditement of treason: for first it is alledged according to this act, *quod* * *proditorie compassavit, et imaginatus fuit mortem et destructionem dni. regis, et ipsum dom. regem interficere, &c.* in the second part of the inditement is alledged the overt act, *et ad illam nephandam, et proditoriam compassationem, imaginationem, et propositum suum perficiend' et perimplend'* and then certainly to set downe the overt fact for preparation to take, and imprison the king, or any other sufficient overt act, which of necessity must be set downe in the inditement. Hereby it appeareth how insufficient many inditements were of high treason, wherein it was generally alledged, that *per apertum factum compassavit et imaginatus fuit mortem dom. regis, &c.* * For example *termo. Mic. anno* 5 E. 6. Edward duke of Somerset was indited before commissioners of oyer and terminer in London, *quod ipse deum præ oculis suis non habens, sed instigatione diabolica* ‡ *seductus, apud Holborne in parochia Sancti Andreæ infra civitatem London, viz.* 20 *die Aprilis anno regni domini regis Edw. sexti quinto, et diversis diebus et vicibus antea et postea falso, maliciose, et proditorie* * *per apertum factum circumivit, compassavit, et imaginavit cum diversis aliis personis prædictum dominū regem de statu suo regali deponere et deprivare, &c.* Which indictment, and all others of like forme were against law, as hath been said, and of the matter of this indictment that noble duke was by his peers found not guilty. But then it may be demanded, for what offence he had judgement of death, and 2. what law made it an offence. The offence appeareth in his indictment, for the former part thereof contained high treason, whereof he was acquitted, and the latter part contained one only offence of felony (whereof he was found guilty) in these words, *et ulterius juratores præd. præsentant, quod præfatus Edwardus dux Somerset deū præ oculis suis non habens, sed instigatione diabolica seductus* 20 *Maii an. regni dicti dom. regis Edwardi sexti quinto supradicto, ac diversis aliis diebus et vicibus antea et postea apud Holborn in præd. paroch. Sancti Andreæ in civitate London, et apud diversa alia loca infra civitatem London præd. felonice ut felo dicti dom. regis per aperta verba et facta procuravit, movit, et instigavit complurimos subditos ipsius domini regis ad insurgendum, et apertum rebellionem et insurrectionem infra hoc regnum Angliæ movend' contra ipsum dominum regem, et ad tunc et ibid. felonice ad capiendum et imprisonandum prænobilem Johannem comitem Warwick de privato consilio domini regis ad tunc existen', contra pacem dicti domini regis coronam et dignitatem suam, et contra formam statuti in hujusmodi casu editi et provisi.* The statute whereupon this indictment was intended to be grounded, was the branch of the statute of 3 and 4 E. 6. by which it is provided, "That if any person or persons by ringing of any bel, &c. or by malicious speaking or uttering of any words, or making any outcry, &c. or by any other deed or act shall raise or cause to be raised or assembled any persons to the number of 12 or above, to the intent that the same persons should

* In ancient time *traditiose, et felonice.* parl. 33 E. 1. rot. 6. Robert de Ros his case, but now *proditorie* is necessarily required.

Vide Britton, fo. 16. et 19.

1 Mar. Br. treason. 24.

* Ter. Mic. 5 E. 6. Lib. Intr. Coke, fo. 482.

Sanguinis O maledicta sitis, &c.

‡ [13]

* Per apertum factum.

Vid. hereafter ca. 5. de Heresie, generall indictments against Lolards, &c.

The residue of the indictment of the duke of Somerset.

To take and imprison one of the privie councell.

Contra formam statut.

3 & 4 E. 6. cap. 5.

should do, commit, or put in ure any of the acts and things above mentioned (whereof to take and imprison any of the kings most honourable privie counsell was one) and the persons to the number of 12 or above so raised and assembled after request and commandement (in such sort as in that act is prescribed) shall make their abode and continue together, as is aforesaid, (in the act) or unlawfully perpetrate, doe, commit, or put in ure any of the acts or things abovesaid, that then all and singular persons by whose speaking, deed, act, or any other the meanes above specified any persons to the number of 12 or above, shall be raised or assembled for the doing, committing, or putting in ure any of the acts or things above mentioned, shall be adjudged for his so speaking or doing a felon, and suffer execution of death as in case of felony, and shall lose his benefit of sanctuary and clergy." Hereby it doth manifestly appeare, that the truth concerning this nobleman's attainder, and execution in divers things, is contrary to the vulgar opinion, and some of our chronicles, and in some points contrary to law. First, that for the felony made by the said branch of the said act he could not have had his clergie, for clergy in that case is expresly ousted by the said act. 2. That he was not indicted for going about, &c. the death of the earle of Warwick then of the kings privie counsell, but only for his taking or imprisonment, and therefore could not be indicted upon the statute of
3H. 7. ca. 14. 3 H. 7. as some have imagined. 3. That the indictment is altogether insufficient, for it pursueth not the words or matter of the said branch of the said act, as by comparing of them it manifestly appeareth; which (we being desirous that truth may appeare in all things) we have thought good upon this occasion to adde for
Lib. 9. fo. 114. in seignior Sancher's case. advancement of truth. 4. That being but attainted of felony, he could not by law be beheaded, as elsewhere we have shewed. And this act that created the felony saith, that such a felon shall suffer execution of death, as in case of felony. 5. Lastly, this
1 Mar. cap. 12. 1 Eliz. ca. 16. 7 E. 6. ca. 12. whole act was justly holden to be a doubtful and dangerous statute, and therefore was deservedly repealed. And after the fall of this duke, see the preamble of the statute of subsidie of 7 E. 6.

[14] And now to returne to cases of high treason. If a man be arraigned upon an indictment of high treason, and stand mute, he shall have such judgement, and incurre such forfeiture, as if he had been convicted by verdict, or if he had confessed it. For this standeth well with this word *provablement*, for *fatetur facinus, qui judicium fugit:* but otherwise it is in case of petit treason, murder, or other felony.

13 Eliz. Dier, 298. 13 Eliz. cap. 1. *Nota bene. Vide supra verbo* Mort. If a subject conspire with a foraine prince beyond the seas to invade the realme by open hostility, and prepare for the same by some overt act, this is a sufficient overt act for the death of the king, for by this act of parliament in that case there must be an overt act. * *Qui capiti, aut saluti regis perfidiose sive solus, sive servis aut sicariis mercede conductis stipatus insidiabitur, vita et fortunis ejus omnibus privator.* So as thereby an overt act was required.

* Inter leges Alveredi, cap. 4.

The composition and connexion of the words are to be observed, viz. [thereof be attainted by overt deed.] † This relateth to the severall and distinct treasons before expressed), and specially to the compassing and imagination of the death of the king, &c. for that it is secret in the heart) and therefore one of them cannot be

† So resolved by the justices Pasc. 35 Eliz. which we heard and observed.

be an overt act for another. As for example: a conſpiracy is had to levie warre, this (as hath been ſaid and ſo reſolved) is no treaſon by this act untill it be levied, therefore it is no overt act or manifeſt proofe of the compaſſing of the death of the king within this act: for the words be *(de ceo, &c.)* that is, of the compaſſing of the death. For this were to confound the ſeverall claſſes, or *membra dividentia, et ſic de cæteris, &c.*

[a] Divers latter acts of parliament have ordained, that compaſſing by bare words or ſayings ſhould be high treaſon; but all they are either repealed or expired. And it is commonly ſaid, that bare words may make an heretick, but not a traytor without an overt act. And the wiſdome of the makers of this law would not make words only to be treaſon, ſeeing ſuch variety amongſt the witneſſes are about the ſame, as few of them agree together. But if the ſame be ſet downe in writing by the delinquent himſelfe, this is a ſufficient overt act within this ſtatute.

[b] Cardinall Poole, albeit he was a ſubject to H. 8. and of the kings blood, (being deſcended from George duke of Clarence, brother to king E. 4.) yet he in his booke of the ſupremacy of the pope, written about 27 H. 8. incited Charles the emperour, then preparing againſt the Turke, to bend his force againſt his naturall ſoveraigne lord and countrey; the writing of which booke was a ſufficient overt act within this ſtatute: and to move the emperour the rather in that book, he made H. 8. almoſt as ill as the Turk, in theſe words, *in Anglia ſparſum nunc eſt hoc ſemen, ut vix à Turcico internoſci queat, idque authoritate unius coaluit.*

[c] In the preamble of the ſtatute of 1 Mar. concerning the repeale of certaine treaſons, &c. It is agreed by the whole parliament, that lawes juſtly made for the preſervation of the common-wealth without extreame puniſhment, are more often obeyed and kept, then lawes and ſtatutes made with great and extreame puniſhments: and in ſpeciall, ſuch lawes and ſtatutes ſo made: whereby not only the ignorant and rude unlearned people, but alſo learned and expert people minding honeſty, are oftentimes trapped and ſnared, yea, many times * for words only, without other fact or deed done or perpetrated: therefore this act of 25 E. 3. doth provide, that there muſt be an overt deed. But words without an overt deed [d] are to be puniſhed in another degree, as an high miſpriſion.

Per gents de lour condition.] That is, *per pares*, or their equals, whereof we have ſpoken before in the expoſition of the [e] 29 chapter of Magna Carta. verb. *per judicium parium ſuorum*, and more ſhall be ſaid hereafter. This branch *(per gents de lour condition)* extendeth only to a conviction by verdict, whereof the ſtatute particularly ſpeaketh; but yet where the party indicted confeſſeth the offence or ſtandeth mute, he ſhall have judgement as in caſe of high treaſon. For this branch being affirmative, is taken *cumulative* and not *privative*. And therefore ſeeing upon confeſſion, or ſtanding mute, the judgment in caſe of high treaſon was given at the common law, this act being, as it hath been ſaid, affirmative, taketh not away the ſame: and (to ſay once for al) the clauſe hereafter of reſtraint of like caſes, &c. extends onely to offences, and not to tryalls, judgements, or executions.

[a] 26 H. 8. cap. 13. 1 E. 6. cap. 13. 1 & 2 Ph. and Mar. cap. 9, 10. 1 Eliz. cap. 6. 13 Eliz. ca. 1, &c. 14 Eliz. cap. 1.

[b] See the fourth part of the Inſtitutes, ca. 26. Brook, treaſon 24 writing of letters.

[c] 1 Mar. ceſſ. 1. c. 1. See the ſtatute of 3 H. 7. hereafter, cap. 4. directly in the point by the judgement of the parliament. *Nota*, this act of 25 E. 3. faith, *per overt fait, per apertum factum*, and not *per apertum dictum*, by word or confeſſion. See 25 H. 8. c. 12. Eliz. Barton, Edw. Locking, and others attainted by parliament for divers words and conſpiracies which being not within this act without an overt act they could not be attainted by the common law.

* Nota.

[d] See in the chapter of Miſpriſion.

[15]

[e] Mag. Car. ca. 29.

Bract. l. 3. fo. 118. Brit. fo. 10, &c. Bract. l. 5. fo. 414. Fleta, l. 1. ca. 21. Mirror, ca. 1. § 6. de fausonerie.

(17) *Si home counterface le grand seale.*] All our ancient authors agree that this was high treason by the common law, and for this offence his judgement was to be drawn, hanged, and quartered, at the common law, as in other cases of high treason, (the counterfeiting of the kings mony excepted.) See the second part of the Institutes. W. 1. cap. 5.

29 Ass. pa. 49. * 1 E. 3. tit. Chre. F. 13. 22 Ass. Pl. 49.

* In ancient time every treason was comprehended under the name of felony, but not *è contra:* and therefore a pardon of all felonies was sometime allowed in case of high treason. But the law is, and of long time hath been otherwise holden: and if the inditement were *felonicè*, and not *proditoriè*, (for the king may lessen the offence, if it please him) then the pardon of felonies is good at this day, for no inditement can be of high treason without this word (*proditoriè:*) and *in qualibet proditione implicatur felonia, quia in quolibet brevi de exigendo super quolibet indictamento de proditione proclamator facit sic*, I. B. an exigent on thy head of treason and felony.

2 R. 3. 9.

3 H. 7. 10. a.

A compassing, intent, or going about to counterfeit the great seale is no treason, but there must be an actuall counterfeiting, also it must be to the likenesse of the kings great seale, the words be, *counterface le grand seale le roy.*

Now it is to be seen what shall be said a forging, or counterfeiting of the great seale. If the lord chancellor, or lord keeper put the great seale to a charter &c. without warrant, this is no treason, because the great seale is not counterfeited. But it seemeth by Briton fo. 10. b. that it was treason at the common law, and of that opinion is Fleta fo. 29. a. but it is no treason now (without question) by the negative clause of this act.

If a man take wax lawfully imprinted with the great seale from one patent, and fix it to a writing purporting a grant from the king, there have been divers opinions in this case what the offence is, which we will rehearse.

40 Ass. p. 33.

In 40 Ass. which was about 15 years after the making of this act, it was not holden high treason, but a great misprision, for that it is no counterfeiting of a new, but an abuse of the true great seale.

Rot. Claus. 42 E. 3. nu. 8. in coro.

In 42 E. 3. the abbot of Bruer caused Rob. Rigge his commoigne to rase a charter of R. 1. and put out the mannor of Fisfetruda, and in place thereof put in Elleghe. And this offence was heard, and sentenced before the king and his counseil in the star-chamber, as a great offence and misprision: for if it had been high treason, it should have had another tryall, and yet this was a great abuse of the great seal.

2 H. 4. fo. 25.

2 H. 4. The taking of the great seale from one patent and fixing it to a commission to gather mony, &c. was adjudged to be such an offence, as the offender had judgement to be drawne, and hanged. The record of which case we have perused, and the effect thereof is this. The partie is indited generally for counterfeiting of the great seal, whereunto he pleaded not guilty, and the jury found him not guilty of the counterfeitting of the great seale, as was supposed by the inditement, and found further specially, that he tooke the great seale from one patent, and put it to the commission, and that the party put the same in execution, and there judgement was given, that he should be drawne and hanged: which (whatsoever the offence was) ought not to have been given upon this

Errores ad sua principia referre, est refellere. To bring errors to their beginning, is to see their last.

this verdict, the jury finding him not guilty of the offence alledged in the inditement: and befides the judgement is fuch, as is given in cafe of petit treafon, and not of high treafon. Hereby it appeareth how dangerous it is for any to report a cafe by the ear, fpecially concerning treafon, unleffe he had advifedly read the record: for (as I take it) the mifreport of this cafe hath hatched errors, and he miftooke the judgment, if it had been high treafon, for then it fhould have been drawne, hanged, and quartered.

[16]

37 H. 8. Br. tit. Treafon. A chaplain had fixed fuch a great feale to a patent of difpenfation with non-refidence, and this was holden a mifprifion, and not high treafon, for it was an abufe of the great feale, and no counterfeiting of it. Stanford faith that it was adjudged in his time according to the book of 2 H. 4. *et fic ex errore fequitur error.*

37 H. 8. Br. Treafon.

Stanf. Pl. Coron. fo. 3. c.

G. Leak a clark of the chancery joyned two cleane parchments fit for letters patents fo clofe together with mouth glew, as they were taken for one, the uppermoft being very thinne, and did put one labell through them both, then upon the uttermoft he writ a true patent, and got the great feale put to the labell, fo the labell and the feale were annexed to both the parchments, the own written, and the other blanck: he cut off the glewed fkirts round about, and tooke off the uppermoft thinne parchment (which was written, and was a true and perfect patent) from the labell, which with the great feale did ftill hang to the parchment, then he wrote another patent on the blancke parchment, and did publifh it as a good patent. Hereupon two queftions were moved. 1. Whether this offence be high treafon or no. 2. If it be high treafon, then whether he may be indited generally for the counterfeiting of the great feale, or els the fpeciall fact muft be expreffed. And upon conference had between the judges, upon great advifement and confideration it was in the end, concerning the firft point, refolved by the juftices (faving a very few) upon the authorities aforefaid, and for that it was no counterfeiting of the great feale within this ftatute, that this offence was neither high treafon, nor petit treafon, becaufe it is not within either of the branches of this ftatute, but it is a very great mifprifion, and the party delinquent liveth at this day. As to the 2. point it was refolved, that if the fpeciall matter had amounted to counterfeiting of the great feale in law within this act, then he might have been generally indited of high treafon for counterfeiting the great feale. As if a man in an affray kill a conftable that comes to keep the kings peace without any expreffe malice prepenfed, this is murder in law, and yet the delinquent may bee generally indited of murder by malice prepenfed.

Bracton agreeth with it. *Ubi fupra.* Leak's cafe. Hil. 4 Ja. R.

40 Aff. 33. 42 E. 3. Rot. Cl. *Ubi fupra.* 37 H. 8. Br. dev.

And [a] Fleta who wrote before this act telleth us, that *crimen falfi dicitur, cū quis illicitus (cui non fuerit ad hoc data authoritas) de figillo regis rapto vel invento, et brevia cartafque confignaverit.* But whatfoever offence it was before the making of this ftatute, it is after this ftatute no high treafon, becaufe it is no counterfeiture of the great feale, but a mifufor thereof.

[a] Fleta, l. 1. ca. 22. Britton, fo. 10. b. See before, fo. 15.

Qui [b] *convictus fuerit pro falfatione figilli dom. regis, quòd tradatur epifcopo Sarum, qui eum petiit ut clericum fuum fub pœna et in forma qua decet, quia videtur concilio quod in tali cafu non admittenda eft purgatio, &c.* Hereby it fhould appeare that in thofe dayes a man might have had his clergie for this offence, and therefore as fome hold, it

[b] Rot. Parl. Hil. 18 E. 1. fo. 92. nu. 125.

was not then holden to be high treaſon, and herein alſo is the preamble of this act, concerning divers opinions in caſe of treaſon, verified.

This ſtatute naming the great ſeale and privie ſeale, the forging and the counterfeiting of the privie ſignet, or of the ſigne manuell was not within this ſtatute. But by the [c] ſtatute of 1 Mar. it is made high treaſon in both caſes. Albeit that in this act there is no mention made of * ayders and conſenters to this counterfeiting, yet they are within the purvieu of this ſtatute, for there be no acceſſaries in high treaſon.

(18) *Ou ſa* [d] *monye.*] [e] This was treaſon by the common law, as it appeareth by all the ſaid ancient authors, *ubi ſupra (verbo, ſi home counterface le grand ſeale)* and therefore the opinion in 3 H. 7. is holden for no law, that it was but felony before this act. [f] The forging of the kings coine, is high treaſon, without utterance of it, for by this act the counterfeiting is made high treaſon. See the ſecond part of the Inſtitutes. W. 1. cap. 15. [g] See Thom. Walſingham. *Hypodigme Neuſtrie. an. dom.* 1278. *judæi pro tonſura monetæ in magna multitudine ubique per Angliam ſuſpenduntur, &c.*

[h] *Si ipſe qui facit monetam authoritate regis, &c. illam facit minus in pondere vel allaiata, viz. alcumino vel alio falſo metallo contra ordinationem, &c.* This is there holden to be high treaſon, and by that book taken for a counterfeiter of the kings money within the purvien of this ſtatute. [a] And herewith agreeth Britton, who ſaith, *des fauceres q. ount noſtre monye counterfet ou pluis de allaye miſe in noſtre monye, q. nuſter, ne ſerroit ſolonq. le forme et uſage de noſtre realme.*

[b] *Ordeine fuit q. nul roy de ceſt realme ne puit changer ſa money, ne impairer, ne amender, ne auter monye faire q. de ore et argent, ſans laſſent de touts les counties.* It was ordained, that no king of this realme might not change his money, nor impaire, nor amend the ſame, nor other money make then of gold or ſilver, without aſſent of parliament.

[c] Clipping, waſhing, and filing of the money of this realme, was no counterfeiting of it within this act. And therefore being a like caſe, it was declared by parliament in anno 3 H. 5. cap. 6. to be high treaſon: but that act being repealed by 1 *Mariæ* the ſtatute of 5 Eliz. cap. 11. hath [d] declared, that clipping, waſhing, rounding, or filing, for wicked lucre and gaine, &c. to be high treaſon. And by the ſtatute of [e] 18 Eliz. it is declared, that if any perſon for wicked lucre or gaines-ſake, ſhall by any art, wayes, or meanes whatſoever, impaire, diminiſh, falſifie, ſcale, or lighten the kings money, &c. it is high treaſon, for being a like caſe, it was to be declared by parliament.

Forging [f] or counterfeiting of foraine money, which is not currant within the realme, is miſpriſion of treaſon, and the offender ſhall forfeit, as for concealement of high treaſon.

Sa money] [g] This extendeth only to the kings money coyned within this realme; and therefore after this ſtatute, if a man had counterfeited the money of another kingdome, though it were currant within this realme, it was no treaſon, untill it was ſo de-

[c] 1 Mar. cap. 6. 1 & 2 Ph. and Mar. ca. 11.

* 19 H. 6. 47. 3 H. 7. 10. Stanf. Pl. Coron. 3. vide poſtea, cap. 64. *principall and acceſſ.* See Mich. 13 & 14 Eliz. Dier, 296. Conier's caſe.

[d] See Mat. Par. *anno* 34 H. 3. pag. 753. *de pecunia approbata et reprobata.* Et Walſingham, 28 E. 1. *anno Dom.* 1300. ſtat. 31 E. 1. *de weights et meaſures.* Raſt. 7.

[17]

[e] Vet. Magna Chart. ca. Itin. fo. 151. a. 22 Aſſ. p. 49. 3 H. 7. 10. 25 E. 3. 42. b. Coro. 130.

[f] 6 H. 7. 13. 1 R. 3. 1.

[g] Walſ. Hyp. Neuſtrie, pa. 69. 1278. 6 E. 1.

[h] 3 H. 7. 10. a. b.

[a] See inter leges Athelſtani, ca. 14. Canuti, cap. 61. Britton, cap. 5. fo. 10. b. See the Mirror, ca. 1. § 6. De la mony falſifie acc' with 3 H. 7. and ca. 5. § 1. and Fleta, ca. 22. acc.

[b] Mirr. ca. 1. § 3. inter Artic. perviels royes ordeinus. Rot. Par. 17 E. 3. nu. 15. Vide hic poſtea, cap. 31. 45 E. 3. ca. 13. 9 H. 5. cap. 11. Stat. 1.

See the ſecond part of the Inſtitutes, ca. 20. Artic. ſuper Cart. and the expoſition upon the ſame. [c] 3 H. 5. ca. 6. 1 E. 6. cap. 12. 5 Eliz. cap. 11. [d] *Nota*, for wicked lucre and gain. [e] 18 Eliz. cap. 1. [f] 14 Eliz. cap. 3. [g] See hereafter, cap. Principall and Acceſſory.

clared

clared by parliament [h] in an. 1 Mariæ, and in an. 1 & 2 Ph. and M. and the faid acts of 5 Eliz. & 18 El. do extend to forrain coyne currant within this realme. And it is holden, that at the making of this ftatute of 25 E. 3. there was no money currant within this realme, but the kings own coyne. [i] See the ftatute called *ftatutum de moneta magnum, et ftatutum de moneta parvum.* And it is to be knowne, that if any doe counterfeit the kings coyne contrary to this ftatute of 25 E. 3. [k] he fhall have the punifhment of his body, but as in cafe of petit treafon, that is, to be drawne and hanged till he be dead, but the forfeiture of his lands is as in other cafes of high treafon, for this ftatute is but a declaration of the common law, and the reafon of his corporall punifhment is, for that in this cafe he was only drawne and hanged at the common law, but a woman in that cafe was to be burnt.

[h] 1 Mar. cap. 6. 1 & 2 Ph. and Mar. cap. 11.

[i] Vet. Mag. Carta, part 2. fol. 38, 39, 40.

[k] Fleta, lib. 1. c. 22. who wrote before this ftatute, which is but a law declaratory, as it appeareth before. 23 Aff. p. 2. Dier, 6 Eliz. Term. Tr. MS. *pro tonfura monete trahe et pend.* Tr. 24 H. 8. in Juftice Spilmans Reports accord.

[l] The abbot of Miffenden in the county of Buckingham for counterfeiting and refection of the kings money, was adjudged to be drawne and hanged, and not quartered. The want of obfervation of the faid diftinction hath made fome to erre in their judgement. Nota. This act of 25 E. 3. maketh no expreffion of the judgement, therefore fuch judgement as was at the common law either in cafe of high treafon or petit treafon muft be given.

[l] Mich. 31 E. 3. coram rege. Rot. 55. Buck. within fix yeares after making of our ftatute.

But if one be attainted for diminifhing of the kings mony upon any of the ftatutes made in queen Maries time, or in the time of queen Elizabeth, becaufe it is high treafon newly made, the offender fhall have judgement as in cafe of high treafon, which judgement you may fee in the firft part of the Inftitutes. Sect. 747.

[m] And when a woman commits high treafon and is quick with childe, fhe cannot upon her arraignment plead it, but fhe muft either pleade not guilty, or confeffe it: and if upon her plea fhe be found guilty, or confeffe it, fhe cannot alleage it in arreft of judgement, but judgement fhall be given againft her: and if it be found by an inqueft of matrons that fhe is quick with childe, (for *privinment enfent* will not ferve) it fhall arreft, and refpite execution till fhe be delivered, but fhe fhall have the benefit of that but once, though fhe be againe quick with childe: fo as this refpite of execution for this caufe is not to be granted, only in cafe of felony, whereof juftice Stanford fpeaketh, but in cafe of high treafon, and petit treafon alfo.

[m] 25 E. 3. 42. b. Cor. 130. 23 Aff. p. 2. 22 Aff. p. 71. 22 E. 3. Cor. 253. 12 Aff. p. 11, 8 E. 2. Cor. 410.

[18]

Stanford, f. ult. b.

(19) *Si home port faux money en ceft roialme, counterfeit au money dangliterre, et fachant le money eftre faux, &c.*] By this branch fix things are to be obferved. Firft, that the bringing in of counterfeit money, and not the counterfeiting is expreffed in this word [*apport.*] Secondly, that it muft be brought from a foraine nation, and not from Ireland, or other place belonging to, or being a member of the crowne of England, and fo it hath been refolved, fo wary are judges to expound this ftatute concerning treafon, and that in moft benigne fenfe: for albeit Ireland be a diftinct kingdome, and out of the realme of England to fome purpofes, as to protections and fines levied, &c. as hath been faid: yet to fome intent it is accounted as a member of or belonging to the crowne of this realme. And therefore a writ of error is maintainable here in the kings bench of a judgement given in the kings bench in Ireland, fo as the judges did conftrue this ftatute not to extend to falfe money brought out of Ireland, Thirdly, it muft be to the fimilitude of the

Vid. hereafter, cap. 30. Rot. Parl. 17 E. 3. nu. 15.

7 H. 7. 10.

Lib. 7. Calvin's cafe, *ubi fupra.*

the money of England. Fourthly, that the bringer of it into this realme, must know it to be counterfeit. Fifthly, uttering of false money in England, though he know it to be false and counterfeit to the likenesse of the coyne of England, is no treason within this statute, unlesse he brought it from a foraine nation, for the words be, *si home apport faux money en cest realme.* But if money false or clipped be found in the hands of any that is suspicious, he may be imprisoned untill he hath found his warrant, *per statutum de moneta magn' vet. Mag. Cart.* fo. 38. 2 *parte.* Lastly, he must merchandize therewith, or make payment thereof, expressed in these words, *pur merchandizer, ou paiment faire in deceipt nostre seignior le roy et son people.* See more, *de moneta regis*, and of the derivation thereof in the second part of the Institutes, *in artic' super cartas*, cap. 20.

3 H. 7. 10.

Si home tuast chancelour, tresurer, ou justice nostre seigniour le roy del. un banke ou del auter, justice in eire, ou dassises et touts auters justices assignes doier et terminer esteant en lour place feasant lour office.

In this case albeit one intend to kill any of these here named in their place, and doing their office, and thereupon strike or wound any of them, this is no treason; for our statute saith, *si home tuast chancelor, &c.* If a man kill the chancellour, &c. For if it be treason, death must ensue. And the reason wherefore it is treason in these cases is, because sitting judicially in their places, (that is, in the kings courts) and doing their office in administration of justice, they represent the kings person, who by his oath is bound that the same be done. And this act extends only to the persons here particularly named, and to no other: and therefore extendeth not to the court of the lord steward, or of the constable and marshall, nor to the court of the admiralty, or any other, nor to any ecclesiasticall court. Nay, it extends not to the high court of parliament, if any member of the lords house, or house of commons be slaine in his place, and doing his office, because it is *casus omissus*, and not mentioned in this act. But in all those cases it is wilfull murder, for the law implyeth malice.

Et soit assavoire q. in les cases suisnomes doit ee adjudge treason q. se extenda a nostre seignior le roy et sa royall majestie: et de tiel treason le forfeiture des escheates appertient a nostre seignior le roy cibien des tres. et tenements tenus des auters, come de luy mesme.

(20) [a] *Des tres. et tenements tenus des auters come de luy mesme.*] This is an affirmance of the common law, and the reason thereof is, for that the offence is committed against the soveraigne lord the king, who is the light and the life of the common-wealth: and therefore the law doth give to the king in satisfaction of his offence, all the lands, &c. which the offender hath, and that no subject should be partaker of any part of the forfeiture for this offence.

[a] Rot. Parliam. 20 E. 1. nu. 2. John de Britain's case. 3 Reg. 21. 15. See *inter leges Alveredi*, cap. 4. *ubi supra. Vita et fortunis omnibus privator.* Cust. de Norm. ca. 14. 22 lib. Ass. pl. 49.

[19]

And where the words be [lands and tenements holden, &c.] yet the forfeiture extends to * rents charges, rents seck, commons, corrodies, and other hereditaments which are not holden, for in case of high treason the tenure is not materiall.

* Brook, Esch. 9. See hereafter. *Verbo. Et de tiel manner de treason, &c.* Otherwise it is in case of petit treason and felony

This clause hath 7. limitations. First, this act extends not [b] to lands in tayle, (saving only for the life of tenant in tayle) but the forfeiture of escheats is to be understood of such lands and tenements, as he might lawfully forfeit. And these generall words take not away the

[b] 7 H. 4. 27. See hereafter in the title of *Premunire. Verb.* (des tres, &c.) Vid. 26 H. 8. cap. 13.

the ftatute of *donis conditional'* [c] but latter ftatutes give the forfeiture of eftates in tail. 2. Nor doth this act extend to ufes, but * latter ftatutes doe name ufes. 3. [d] Nor to rights of actions, where the entrie is taken away, and fo is the law cleerly holden at this day. 4. Nor to any conditions, but by a [e] latter ftatute conditions, unleffe they be infeparably knit to the perfon, be given to the king. 5. Nor to rights of entry, where any was in the lands [f] by title before the treafon committed, but fuch a right of entry is fince given by latter ftatutes. 6. Nor to lands or tenements, or rights [g] *in auter droit*, as in the right of the church, nor to lands in the right of a wife, but only during the coverture, and it extendeth to land which the offender hath [h] for life, for the forfeiture of the profits during his life. 7. It extendeth not to * a founderfhip of an houfe of religion *in free almoign*, for that is annexed to the bloud of the founder. Here goods and chattels be not named, but the forfeiture of them is implyed in the judgement.

[i] *Nota* lector, the faid acts of 26 H. 8. 33 H. 8. 5. and 6 E. 6. doe yet remain in force, notwithftanding the faid ftatute of 1 Mar. as it hath been often adjudged and refolved, and namely Mich. 21. Ja. in the exchequer chamber, in a writ of error, upon a judgement given in the exchequer, between Ratcliffe, and the lord Sheffeild, by all the judges of England, and is agreeable to common experience.

See more of high treafon in the next chapter following, cap. 2. verbo. *Et pur ceo que plufors auters cafes, &c.*

[c] 26 H. 8. ca. 13. in fine. 33 H. 8. ca. 20. 5 & 6 E. 6. cap. 11. lib. 7. fo. 12, 13.

* 23 H. 8. ca. 20. 5 E. 6. ca. 11.

[d] Lib. 3. fo. 210. 7 H. 4. 6, &c.

[e] 33 H. 8. c. 20. lib. 7. fo. 11. Englefield's cafe.

[f] Englefield's cafe. *Ubi fupra.*

[g] 5 E. 6. *ubi fupra.* 1 Mar. Dier, 123. Dier, 12 El. 289. Temps. H. 8. Br. Coron. 5.

[h] 1 Mar. Dier, 108.

* 24 E. 3. 33. 72. Corody, Br. 5. Temps. H. 8. Efcheat, 239.

[i] 12 El. Dier, 289. Lib. 3. fo. 10. 35. Lib. 7. fo. 33. 34. lib. 8. 72. 166. lib. 9. fo. 140. Stanf. Pl. Corone, 187. a.

CAP. II.

OF PETIT TREASON.

ET ovefque ceo il y ad un auter manner de treafon, ceftaffavoir, quant un fervant tua fon maifter (1) *ou un feme tua fon baron* (2), *ou quant home feculer ou de religion tua fon prelate a que il doit foye et obedience* (3). *Et de tiel manner de treafon la forfeiture des efcheats appertenont a chefcun feignior de fon fee proper, &c.*

Britton, ca. 8. and cap. 22.

And moreover there is another manner of treafon, that is to fay, when a fervant flayeth his mafter, or a wife her hufband, or when a man fecular or religious flayeth his prelate to whom he oweth faith and obedience. And of fuch treafon the efcheats ought to pertain to every lord of his own fee, &c. [20]

It was called high or grand treafon in refpect of the royall majefty againft whom it is committed, and comparatively it is called petit treafon (whereof now this ftatute fpeaketh) in refpect it is committed againſt ſubjects and inferiour perſons, whereof this act doth enumerate three kinds.

(1) *Quant un ſervant tua ſon maiſter.*] This was petit treaſon by the common law, for ſo it appeareth by the [a] book of 12 Aſſ. that a woman ſervant killed her miſtris, wherefore ſhe had judgement to be burnt, which is the judgement at this day of a woman for petit treaſon. And herewith agreeth 21 E. 3. where the reader muſt know, that in ſtead of *mere* in that caſe you muſt read maiſter.

[a] 12 Aſſ. p. 30. 21 E. 3. 17. F. coron. 447. Statham, tit. cor. 21 E. 3. 22 Aſſ. p. 49.

[b] And upon this act, if the ſervant kill the wife of his maſter, it is petit treaſon, for he is ſervant both to the huſband and wife.

[b] 19 H. 6. 47. Pl. Com. 86. b. Dier, 3 Mar. 128. 7 El. 235.

[c] If the child commit parricide in killing of his father or mother (which the law-makers never imagined any childe would doe) this caſe is out of this ſtatute, unleſſe the childe ſerved the father or mother for wages, or meat, drink or apparell, for that it is none of theſe three kinds ſpecified in this law. And yet the offence is far more hainous and impious in a child then in a ſervant, for *peccata contra naturam ſunt graviſſima:* but the judges are reſtrained by this act, to interpret this act, *à ſimili*, or *à minore ad majus*, as hereafter ſhall be ſaid. And * ſome ſay that parricide was petit treaſon by the common law.

[c] Exodus, c. 21. v. 15. 17. Lev. 20. v. 9. 1 Mar. per Bromley and Portman of the report of Juſtice Daliſon. vid. 1 R. 3. 4. *In culeo paricidæ cum ſimia, cane, gallo, et ſerpente incluſi mari olim mergebantur: ſed nos non habemus talem conſuetudinem.*

* 22 E. 1. Math. Par. 874.

[d] A ſervant of malice intended to kill his maſter, and lay in wait to doe it whileſt he was his ſervant, but did it not till a year after he was out of ſervice, and it was adjudged petit treaſon within this act.

[d] 33 Aſſ. p. 7. Li. 1. f. 99. Shelly's caſe. 10 H. 6. 47. pl. com. 260.

(2) *Un feme tua ſon baron.*] [e] This was petit treaſon by the common law, as it appeareth in our books. If the wife procure one to murder her huſband, and he doth it accordingly, in this caſe the wife being abſent is but acceſſory, and ſhall be hanged and not burnt, becauſe the acceſſory cannot be guilty of petit treaſon, where the principall is not guilty but of murder: and the * acceſſory muſt follow the nature of the principall: but if he that did the murder had been a ſervant of the huſband, it had been treaſon in them both, and the wife ſhould have been burnt. And ſo it is in the caſe before of a ſervant, and in the caſe hereafter of a clerk.

[e] 15 E. 2. Coron. 383. 19 H. 6. 47. See c. Pr. & Acc' Dier, 34 H. 8. 50. Dier, 16 El. 332. Saunders' caſe. Paſch. 32 E. 3. Rot. 62. coram rege. Ph. Clifton's caſe.

* 40 Aſſ. p. 15.

If the wife and a ſtranger kill the huſband, it is petit treaſon in the wife, and murder in the ſtranger, and ſo it is in the caſe of the ſervant next before, and of the clerk next after.

Before this ſtatute it was petit treaſon, *ſi quis falſaverit ſigillum domini ſui de cujus familia fuit.* Britton agreeth herewith. But theſe are taken away by this act, and all other ſaving theſe, that are here expreſſed.

Fleta, li. 1. ca. 22. Britt[illegible], fo. 16.

(3) *Quant home ſeculer ou de religion tua ſon prelate a que il doit foy et obedience.*] This clauſe is underſtood only of an eccleſiaſticall perſon, be he ſecular, or regular, if he kill his prelate, or ſuperiour, to whom he oweth faith, and obedience, it is petit treaſon: and ſo it was at the common law. And petit treaſon doth preſuppoſe a truſt, and obedience in the offender, either civill, as in the wife and ſervant, or eccleſiaſticall, as in the eccleſiaſticall perſon.

19 H. 6. 47.

Aidors, abettors, and procurers of any of theſe petit treaſons, are within this law.

40 Aſſ. ubi ſupra. et 16 El. ubi ſup.

If the ſervant kill his miſtris, viz. his maſters wife, this is treaſon (as hath been ſaid) not by equity, for that is denied as well in

19 H. 6. 47. by all the judges.

petit treaſon, as high treaſon, but it is within the letter of this ſtatute, for ſhe is a maſter.

In high treaſon there is no acceſſories, but all be principalls, and therefore whatſoever act or conſent will make a man acceſſory to a felony, before the act done, the ſame will make him a principall in caſe of high treaſon. But in caſe of petit treaſon, there may be acceſſories, either before, or after the act done, as in caſe of murder or homicide. [21]

Here it appeareth that acts of parliament may bind men of the church, ſecular, or regular, and no benefit of clergy allowed unto them in caſe of treaſon: but [a] hereof you ſhall read at large in the expoſition of the 15. chapter of *Articuli cleri.*

[a] See the 2. pt of the Inſtitutes. Artic. cleri. ca.15.Hil.3.R.2. coram rege Rot. 8. London. Jo. Imperial's caſe.

(3) *Et de tiel manner de treaſon forfeiture des eſcheats apperteinont a cheſcun ſeignior de ſon fee proper.*] See hereof hereafter in the chapter of forfeiture. [b] If a man ſeiſed in fee of a fair, market, common, rent charge, rent ſeck, warren, corrody, or any other inheritance, that is not holden, and is attainted of felony, the king ſhall have the profits of them during his life: but after his deceaſe, ſeeing the blood is corrupted, they cannot deſcend to the heir, * nor can they eſcheat becauſe they be not holden, they periſh and are extinct by act in law: for in eſcheats for petit treaſon or felony, a tenure is requiſite, as well in the caſe of the king, as of the ſubject.

For eſcheats ſee the 1. part of the Inſtitut. ſect. 1. ſo. 13. a.

[b] See before, cap. 1. verbo, des terres et tenements, &c.

* See 1 pt. of the Inſtitutes, fo. 13. verb. Avera la terre per eſcheat.

An approver in caſe of felony, refuſing the combate with the appellee, ſhall have like judgment that is for petit treaſon, *probator recuſans duellum adjudicatur ſuſpendi, et trahi in odium falſæ accuſationis:* but yet it is not petit treaſon, becauſe it is none of the three ſpecified in this act.

Mic. 4 H. 4. coram rege. Rot. 22. Anglia.

The caſe which Shard reciteth in 40 Aſſ. that a Norman being leader of an Engliſh ſhip, who had Engliſh men with him, and robbed divers upon the ſea, and were taken and found guilty: and as to the Norman it was but felony (becauſe Normandy was loſt by king John, and was out of the ligeance of E. 3.) and as to the Engliſh it was adjudged treaſon, and the offenders drawn and hanged, which was the judgement of petit treaſon: but this caſe muſt be intended to fall out before this ſtatute of 25 E. 3. for it is none of the petit treaſons mentioned in this act.

40 Aſſ. 25. Vide 2 H. 5. cap. 6.

Et pur ceo que pluſors auters caſes de ſemblables treaſon (1) *purront eſcheer en temps avener, queux home ne purra penſer ne declarer en preſent: aſſentu eſt, que ſi autre caſe ſuppoſe* (2) *treaſon* (3), *que neſt eſpecifie paramount* (4), *aviegne de novel devant aſcun juſtice, demoerge le juſtice ſans aler a judgment de treaſon, tanque per devant noſtre ſeignior le roy en ſon parliament* (5) *ſoit le caſe mre. et declare* (6), *le que le ceo doit eſtre adjudge treaſon, ou auter felony.*

Rerum progreſſus oſtendunt multa, quæ initio prævideri non poſſunt.

And becauſe that many other like caſes of treaſon may happen in time to come, which a man cannot think nor declare at this preſent time: it is accorded, that if any other caſe ſuppoſed treaſon, which is not above ſpecified, doth happen before any juſtice, the juſtice ſhall tarry without going to judgement of the treaſon, till the cauſe be ſhewed and declared before

before the king and his parliament, whether it ought to be judged treason or other felony.

(1) *Semblable treason.*] In this case, the judges shall not judge *à simili*, or by equity, argument, or inference of any treason, high or petit, for no like case shall be adjudged treason, &c. And note this branch extendeth (as hath been said) to the offence, viz. treason, and not to tryall, judgement, or execution.

(2) *Si auter case suppose treason.*] No other case, though of as high or higher nature, &c. shall be adjudged treason high or petit, as before it appeareth in the case of paricide, *anno* 1 *Mariæ, ubi supra.*

(3) *Treason.*] Either high treason, or petit treason, so as this branch extendeth as hath been said to the offence of treason only.

[22] (4) *Que nest specifie paramount.*] This word [*specifie*] is to be specially observed, for it is as much to say, as particularized, or set downe particularly: so as nothing is left to the construction of the judge, if it be not specified and particularized before by this act. A happy sanctuary or place of refuge for judges to flye unto, that no mans blood and ruine of his family do lie upon their consciences against law. And if that the construction by arguments *à simili*, or *à minori ad majus* had been left to judges, the mischiefe before this statute would have remained, viz. diversity of opinions, what ought to be adjudged treason, which this statute hath taken away by expresse words: and the statute of 1 Mar. doth repeale all treasons, &c. but only such as be declared and expressed in this act of 25 E. 3. wherein this word [expressed] is to be observed.

See the exposition upon the statute, *de frang. prisonam.* 1 H. 6. 5. 9 E. 4. 26, &c. See 1 Mar. of Justice Dalison's report, ubi supra.

1 Mar. cap. 1.

In the parliament holden *anno* 5 H. 4. the earle of Northumberland came before the king and lords in parliament, and by his petition to the king, acknowledged to have done against his allegiance: and namely, for gathering of power and giving of liveries, whereof he prayeth pardon: and the rather, that upon the kings letters he yeelded himselfe, and came to the king unto Yorke, where he might have kept himselfe away. The which petition the king delivered to the justices by them to be considered. Whereupon the lords made protestation, that the order thereof belonged to them, as peers of the parliament, to whom such judgement belonged in weighing of this statute of 25 E. 3. &c. and they judged the same to be no treason, nor felony, but only trespasse finable at the kings will. And the opinion in 27 Ass. is denied, that if one of the indicters discover the counsell of the king, that it should be treason; because it is not specified before in this act, and therefore neither high treason, nor petit treason.

Rot. Parl. 5 H. 4. nu. 11, 12. See nu. 15. Ibid.

27 Ass. p. 63.

(5) *Tanque per devant le roy et son parliament.*] By this it is apparent, that any like or other case ought to be declared by the whole parliament, (and not by the king and lords of the upper house only, or by the king and the commons, or by the lords and commons.) And so was it done by the whole court of parliament in 3 R. 2. *ubi supra.* 5 Eliz. 18 Eliz. *ubi supra*, and many other acts of parliament.

John duke of Gwyen and of Lancaster, steward of England, and Thomas duke of Glocester, constable of England, the kings uncles,

Rot. Par. 17 R. 2. nu. 20.

uncles, complained to the king, that Thomas Talbot knight, with other his adherents, confpired the death of the faid dukes in divers parts of Chefhire, as the fame was confeffed and well knowne, and prayed that the parliament might judge of the fault (which petition was juft, and according to this branch of the ftatute of 25 E. 3.) but the record faith further: whereupon the king and lords in the parliament adjudged the fame fact to be open and high treafon: which judgement wanting the affent of the commons, was no declaration within this act of 25 E. 3. becaufe it was not by the king and his parliament according to this act, but by the king and lords only.

(6) *Soit le cafe monftre et declare, &c.*] This declaration may be abfolute, or *fub modo*, for a time. 13 El. cap. 1, 2. 14 El. ca. 1, 2. &c.

By this which hath been faid it manifeftly appeareth, what damnable and damned opinions thofe were concerning high treafon, of Trefilian chiefe juftice of the kings bench, Sir Robert Belknap chiefe juftice of the common bench, Sir John Holt, Sir Roger Fulthorp, and Sir William Burghe, knights, fellowes of the faid Sir Robert Belknap, and of John Lockton one of the kings ferjeants, that were given to king R. the 2. at Nottingham, in the eleventh yeare of his reigne. But more deteftable were the opinions of the juftices in 21 R. 2. and of Hanckford and Brinchley the kings ferjeants, (and the rather, becaufe they took no example by the punifhment of the former) which affirmed the faid opinions to be good and lawfull, faving Sir William Thirning chiefe juftice of the common bench gave this anfwer: That declaration of treafon not declared belongeth to the parliament; but to pleafe, he faid, that if he had been a lord or a peer of parliament, if it had been demanded of him, he would have made the like anfwers. Thefe juftices and ferjeants being called in queftion in the parliament holden *anno* 1 H. 4. for their faid opinions, anfwered as divers lords fpirituall and temporall did) that they durft no otherwife do, for feare of death. It was thereupon enacted, that the lords fpirituall and temporall, or juftices, be not from thenceforth received to fay, that they durft not for feare of death to fay the truth. Which opinions being fo manifeftly againft our faid act of 25 E. 3. afterwards in the parliament holden 1 H. 4. it is affirmed by authority of parliament, that in the faid parliament of 21 R. 2. divers ftatutes, judgements, ordinances, and ftablifhments were made, ordained, and given, erronioufly and dolefully in great difherifon and finall deftruction and undoing of many honourable lords, and other liege people of this realme, and of their heires for ever. And therefore not only that parliament of 21 R. 2. and the circumftances and dependances thereupon, are wholly reverfed, revoked, voided, undone, repealed, and adnulled for ever, but alfo the parliament holden in 11 R. 2. by authority of which parliament, Trefilian, Belknap, and the reft of thofe falfe juftices and ferjeants aforefaid were attainted, is confirmed, for that it was (as there the parliament affirmeth) for the great honour and common profit of the realme.

Anno 21 R. 2. in Latin.

11 R. 2. ca. 1. and 4.

[23]

Rot. Parl. 1 H. 4. nu. 97.

Melius eft omnia mala pati quam malo confentire.

1 H. 4. ca. 3.

See the confequence of erroneous opinions in cafe of high treafon.

1 H. 4. cap. 4.

Et fi per cafe afcun home de ceft roialme chivache armee, &c.] And if percafe any man of this realme ride armed, &c. For expofition hereof, fee the chapter hereafter againft riding or going armed.

For

1 Mar. cap. 1. *Seſſione prima.* The like ſtatute was made, *anno* 1 E. 6. ca. 12. See the ſtatute of 1 H. 4. cap. 10. to the like effect.

For the better inſtruction of the reader to diſcerne what offences be high treaſon or petit treaſon at this day, it ſhall be neceſſary to adde hereunto the ſtatute of 1 Mar. whereby it is enacted, [That no act, deed, or offence, being by act of parliament or ſtatute made treaſon, petit treaſon, or miſpriſion of treaſon, by words, writing, ciphering, deeds, or otherwiſe whatſoever, ſhall be taken, had, deemed, or adjudged to be high treaſon, petit treaſon, or miſpriſion of treaſon, but only ſuch as be declared and expreſſed to be treaſon, petit treaſon, or miſpriſion of treaſon, in or by the act of parliament or ſtatute made in the 25 yeare of the raigne of the moſt noble king of famous memory, king Edward the third, touching or concerning treaſon, or the declaration of treaſon, and none other, &c. any act or acts of parliament, ſtatute, or ſtatutes, had or made at any time heretofore or after the ſaid 25 year of king E. 3. or any other declaration or matter to the contrary in any wiſe notwithſtanding.]

Inter leges Canuti, cap. 1. *Inprimis juſtæ leges ut efferantur injuſtæ deprimantur.* Aliter in antiquo MS. *Inprimis ut juſtæ leges erigantur, injuſtæ ſubvertantur.*

Before this act ſo many treaſons had been made and declared by act of parliament ſince this act of 25 E. 3. ſome in particular, and ſome in generall, and in ſuch ſort penned, as not only the ignorant and unlearned people, but alſo learned and expert men were many times trapped and ſnared: and ſometimes treaſons made or declared in one kings time, were abrogated in another kings time, either by ſpeciall or generall words: ſo as the miſchief before 25 E. 3. of the uncertainty what was treaſon, and what not, became to be ſo frequent and dangerous, as the ſafeſt and ſureſt remedy was, by this excellent act of 1 Mar. to abrogate and repeale all, but only ſuch as are ſpecified and expreſſed in this ſtatute of 25 E. 3. By which law, the ſafety both of the king and of the ſubject, and the preſervation of the common-weale is wiſely and ſufficiently provided for, in ſuch certainty, as *nihil relictum eſt arbitrio judicis.* And certainly the two rules recited in the preamble of the ſaid act of 1 Mariæ, are aſſuredly true. The firſt, [that the ſtate of a king ſtandeth and conſiſteth more aſſured by the love and favour of the ſubject toward their ſoveraigne, then in the dread and fear of lawes made with rigorous pains and extreme puniſhment for not obeying their ſoveraigne.] And the other, [that lawes juſtly made for the preſervation of the common-weale without extreme puniſhment or penalty, are more often, and for the moſt part better obeyed and kept, then lawes and ſtatutes made with great and extreme puniſhment.] *Mitiùs imperanti melius paretur.*

[24]

Seneca.

In which act five notable things are to be obſerved. Firſt, it extendeth (without exception) to all high treaſons made by any act of parliament ſince the ſaid act of 25 E. 3. Secondly, to all declarations of high treaſons by any act of parliament ſince the ſaid act of 25 E. 3. (as of the ſaid declaration in 3 R. 2. of killing an ambaſſadour and the like.) Thirdly, to all petit treaſons made or declared by any act of parliament ſince the ſaid act of 25 E. 3. Fourthly, albeit miſpriſion of treaſon is not mentioned in the act of 25 E. 3. yet every miſpriſion of any treaſon made or declared ſince that act by any act of parliament, is abrogated. Fifthly, no offence to be treaſon, petit treaſon, or miſpriſion of treaſon, but only ſuch as be declared and expreſſed to be treaſon, petit treaſon, or miſpriſion of treaſon by the ſaid act of 25 E. 3. Here three things are to be obſerved: firſt, that this word [expreſſed] excludeth all implications

implications or inferences whatsoever. Secondly, here misprision of treason is taken for concealement of high treason or petit treason, and only of high treason or petit treason specified and expressed in the act of 25 E. 3. Thirdly, that no former judgement, attainder, president, resolution, or opinion of judges or justices of high treason, petit treason, or misprision of treason, other then such as are specified and expressed in the said act of 25 E. 3. are to be followed or drawne to example: for the words be direct and plaine, [that from henceforth, no act, deed, or offence, &c. shall be taken, had, deemed, or adjudged to be treason, petit treason, or [a] misprision of treason, but only such as be declared and expressed in the said act of 25 E. 3. &c. any act of parliament or statute after 25 E. 3. or any other declaration or matter to the contrary notwithstanding.] So as there is no high treason, petit treason, or misprision of any treason made or declared by any act of parliament or otherwise since the act of 25 E. 3. but only such as have been made since the said act of 1 Mariæ, and of those only such as were made [b] perpetuall, and not during the life of queen Mary or of queen Elizabeth, whereof there be divers which now are expired, which you may reade being all in print. But there wanted nothing to the perfection of the statute of 25 E. 3. but a limitation of some certaine time wherein the offender should be accused. [c] *Post intervallum temporis accusator non erit audiendus, nisi docere potest se fuisse justis rationibus impeditum.*

Or the declaration of treason, &c. [d] Declarations made during the naturall life of queen Elizabeth ceased by her death: for declarations may have limitations as well as statutes introductory of new lawes.

There is another excellent branch of a statute made [e] in 1 & 2 Ph. & Mar. in these words. [And be it further enacted by the authority aforesaid, that all trials hereafter to be had, awarded, or made for any treason, shall be had and used only according to the due order and course of the common law.]

All trials.] [f] Upon these words many things have been observed by others. First, that the letter of this act extendeth only to triall of high treasons, or petit treasons, and not to misprision. Secondly, foraine treasons are to be tried by the statute [g] of 35 H. 8. cap. 2. and so it was resolved by all the justices of England in Orurks case, and had been so resolved before. But for trials of treasons to be had in Wales, or where the kings writ runneth not, in such shires as the king shall assigne by his commission by the * statute of 32 H. 8. ca. 4. are abrogated by this act, because they are triable by the law.

[h] It hath been holden, that upon the triall of misprision of treason there must be two lawfull witnesses, as well upon the triall, as upon the indictment, as it was resolved by the justices in the lord Lumleyes case, Hil. 14. Eliz. reported by the lord Dier, under his own hand, which we have seen, but left out of the print, which for other purposes is cited hereafter. Thirdly, it hath beene holden, that this act extendeth not to the indictment of any treason, but to the triall by peers, if the offender be noble: or by freeholders, if the offender be under the degree of nobility: and therefore upon the indictment which is in manner of an accusation, by the statutes of 1 E. 6. and 5 E. 6. two lawfull witnesses are requisite;

[a] That is, of such treason, high or petit, as is expressed in the act of 25 E. 3. and of no other treason.

[b] 1 Mar. cap. 6. 1 & 2 Ph. and Mar. cap. 11. 5 Eliz. ca. 1. and 11. 18 Eliz. cap. 1. 13 Eliz. cap. 2. 23 Eliz. cap. 1. 27 Eliz. cap. 2. 3 Jac. cap. 4.

[c] Bracton, lib. 3. fol. 118. b.

[d] 13 Eliz. cap. 1. 14 Eliz. cap. 1. and cap. 2.

[e] 1 & 2 Ph. and M. cap. 10.

[f] See the second part of the Institutes, Mag. Carta, cap. 29. Verbo (per judicium parium.)

[g] 35 H. 8. cap. 2. 3 Mar. Dier, 132. lib. 7. fol. 23. in Calvin's case. Pasch. 33 Eliz. Orurk's case.

* 32 H. 8. cap. 4.

[h] 1 E. 6. cap. 12. 5 E. 6. cap. 11. Both which are mentioned in the next section. Hill. 14 Eliz. Dier, MS. *Nota.* This is the last resolution of the judges in this point. At this time Catlin and Dier were chief justices, and Sanders chiefe baron, &c.

[25]

1 E. 6. cap. 12. 5 E. 6. cap. 11. See 13 El. cap. 1. See before verb. [*De ceo provablement soit attaint.*]

quisite: the words of the statute of 1 E. 6. in the last branch be, [that none shall be indicted, arraigned, condemned, or convicted for any treason, petit treason, misprision of treason, or for any words before specified to be spoken, after the said first day of February, for which the same offender or speaker shall in any wise suffer pains of death, imprisonment, losse or forfeiture of his goods, chatels, lands, or tenements, unlesse he be accused by two sufficient and lawfull witnesses, or shall willingly without violence confesse the same.

Nota that [before specified] doe refer to the words mentioned before in the act. 1. It is manifest by the connexion of the words, viz. [for any words before specified to be spoken, &c.] 2. The treasons in 25 E. 3. were mentioned before. 3. The first words be [for any treason, petit treason, misprision of treason, &c.]

See 1 El. cap. 6. Stanf. Pl. Coron. 89. and 164. 4 Mar. Coron. Br. 220. Dier, 2 Mar. 99. and 3 Mar. 132.

* Nota the generality of these words. *Regula. verba generalia generaliter sunt intelligenda.* See hereafter c. 49. of Piracy, &c.

And by 5 E. 6. ca. 11. it is provided by the last clause save one, [that none shall be indicted, arraigned, condemned, convicted, or attainted for any of the treasons or offences aforesaid, or for any * other treasons that now be, or hereafter shall be, which shall hereafter be perpetrated, committed, or done, unlesse the same offender be thereof accused by two lawfull accusers, &c. unlesse the said party arraigned shall willingly, without violence confesse the same.] Here two things are to be observed. 1. The particular penning of both these acts, viz indicted, arraigned, convicted, &c. and the words of 1 & 2 of Ph. & Mar. extend to tryalls only, and not to the indictment. 2. Two lawfull accusers in the act of 5 E. 6. are taken for two lawfull witnesses, for by two lawfull accusers, and accused by two lawfull witnesses (as it is said 1 E. 6.) is all one: which word (accusers) was used, because two witnesses ought directly to accuse, that is, charge the prisoner, for other accusers have we none in the common law, and therefore lawfull accusers must be such accusers as law allow. And so was it resolved in the Lo. Lumleys case by the justices: for if accusers should not be so taken, then there must be two accusers, by 5 E. 6. and two witnesses by 1 E. 6. And the strange conceit in 2 Mar. that one may be an accuser by hearsay, was utterly denied by the justices in the Lo. Lumleys case. And this word (awarded) in the statute of 1 & 2 Ph. and Mar. extendeth to the tryall upon the arraignment, and not to the indictment, for that is not said to be awarded.

Hil. 14 El. Lo. Lumley's case. Ubi supra. 2 Mar. Dier, 99, 100. Thomas' case.

[a] Mich. 13 & 14 El. Rolston's case.

And it was resolved by all the justices in [a] Rolstons case upon the rebellion in the north, that these words [shall willingly without violence confesse the same] are to be understood where the party accused upon his examination before his arraignment, willingly confessed the same without violence, that is, willingly without any torture: and is not meant of a confession before the judge, for he is never present at any torture, neither upon his arraignment was ever any torture offered. And here commeth another [b] statute made in 1 & 2 Mar. to be considered, by which it is provided, that treason for the counterfeiting and impairing of the coin currant in this realm, &c. the offender therein, &c. shall be indicted, arraigned, tried, convicted, or attainted by such like evidence, and in such manner and form, as hath been used and accustomed within this realm, at any time before the first year of king E. 6. &c.

[b] 1 & 2 Ph. and Mar. c. 11. supra.

Wherein

Wherein the fpeciall penning of this act is to be obferved, which in cafe of treafon concerning the counterfeiting or impairing of coin, &c. hath by particular words reftored the evidence requifite by the common law, before the ftatute of 1 E. 6. as well upon the indictment as the triall. But the act of 1 & 2 Ph. and Mar. cap. 10. extends to trials only in other cafes of high treafon, and therefore that act extendeth not to the indictment of other high treafons. Alfo it is moft neceffary (as many doe hold) that there fhould be two lawfull accufers, that is, two lawfull witneffes at the time of the indictment, for that it is commonly found in the abfence of the party accufed, and it may be when the party fufpected is beyond fea, or in remote parts, and may be outlawed thereupon; and therefore feeing the indictment is the foundation of all, it is moft neceffary to have fubftantial proof in a caufe fo criminall, where *probationes oportent effe luce clariores*. Laftly, * if the indictment were part of the tryall, then ought he that is noble, and a lord of parliament be indicted of high treafon, &c. by his peers: for the tryall of him (without queftion) muft be by his peers: but the indictment of peers of the realm is always by free-holders, and not by their peers, as hereafter fhall appear. We have been the longer herein in refpect of fome variety of opinion (for want of due and intire confideration had of all and every part of that which hath been faid) upon ferious ftudy touching this point, without refpect of a common wandring opinion.

1 & 2 Ph. and Mar. cap. 10.

*[26]

See Magna Cart. c. 29. and the expofition thereupon.

And it feemeth that by the ancient common law one accufer, or witneffe was not fufficient to convict any perfon of high treafon: [a] for in that cafe, where is but one accufer, it fhall be tried before the conftable and marfhall by combat, as by many records appeareth. [b] But the conftable and marfhall have no jurifdiction to hold plea of any thing, which may be determined or difcuffed by the common law. And that two witneffes be required, appeareth by our [c] books, and I remember no authority in our books to the contrary: and the common law herein is grounded upon the law of God expreffed both in the old and new Teftament: [d] *in ore duorum aut trium teftium peribit qui interficietur: nemo occidatur uno contra fe dicente teftimonium.*

[a] Pat. 25 E. 3. part 1. nu. 16. Rot.Parl.21R.2. nu. 19. 21. the D. of Norff. cafe. Rot. Pat. 3 H. 4. Balleshul's cafe. Rot. Vafcon. 9 H. 4. nu. 14. John Bolemer's cafe. Rot. Parl. 2 H. 6. nu. 9. the earl of Ormond's cafe. Rot. Pat. 8 H. 6. pt. 2. m. 7. between Upton and Dowy. Vide the 4. part of the Inftitutes. cap. the Court of Chivalry, &c. See Bract. lib. 3. fo. 119. a.

[b] 13 R. 2. cap. 2.

[c] Mirror, ca. 3 §. ordenance de attaint. Bract. l. 5. f. 354. 48 E. 3. 30. 35 H. 6. 46. Fort. ca. 32. 15 E. 4. f. 1. Pl. Com. fo. 8.

And this feemeth to be the more clear in the triall by the peers, or nobles of the realm, becaufe they come not *de aliquo vicineto*, whereby they might take notice of the fact in refpect of *vicinitie*, as other jurors may doe.

[d] Deu. 17. 6. 19. 15 Mat. 18. 16. John 18. 23. 2 Cor. 13. 1. Heb. 10. 28.

Having now rehearfed what others have faid and holden, we upon due confideration had of the whole matter will fet down our own opinion, and reafons, in thefe four points following. Firft, that the ftatute of [e] 5 E. 6. cap. 11. is a generall law, and extends to all high treafons, as well by the common law declared by the ftatute of 25 E. 3. as to any other ftatute made or to be made, the negative words of which ftatute be: [no perfon fhall be [f] indicted, arraigned, convicted, condemned, or attainted for any treafon, that now is, or hereafter fhall be, &c.] Which words without all queftion are generall, and fo to be taken. The words of that ftatute be further, [unleffe the fame offender be accufed by two lawful accufers,] thefe two lawful accufers are in judgement of law taken for two lawful witneffes, and that for two caufes: firft, they muft be lawful, that is, allowed by the laws of the realm; and by the law, upon

[e] And fo I hold the ftatute of 1 E. 6. c. 12. to be a generall law, and to extend to all high treafons, &c.

[f] Nota as well upon the indictment as the arraignment of treafon there ought to be two accufers. See Dier, 2 & 3 Ph. and Mar. 132.

upon the arraignment of the prisoner upon the indictment of treason, no other accuser can be heard, but witnesses only. Secondly, the words of the statute are [which said accusers at the time of the arraignment of the party accused, if they be then living, shall be brought in person before the party so accused, and avow, and maintain that which they have to say to prove him guilty of the treason, unlesse the party arraigned shall willingly without violence confesse the same,] as by that act it appeareth. Now to avow and maintain that which they have to say to prove him guilty of the treason, is the proper office and duty of witnesses, and so it is said in the statute of [g] 1 E. 6. c. 12, in the last clause (by two lawful witnesses.) See the statute of 5 El. c 1. where it is said [accused by good and sufficient testimony:] and to the same intent, the statute of 1 & 2 Ph. and Mariæ, cap. 11. for the word [accused.]

[g] 1 E. 6. cap. 12. the last clause. 5 El. cap. 1. 1 & 2 Ph. and Mar. cap. 11. Bract. li. 3. f. 118. *Qui accusat integræ famæ sit, et non criminosus.*

[i] Stat. de Kenelw. secunda parte, Vet. Mag. Cart. cap. 16.

[k] See the first part of the Institutes. sect. 194. See Fortescue, cap. 26, 27. Juries ought to be informed by evidences, and witnesses.

1. *Puniantur accusatores penes dominum regem, quòd amodò rex eis de facili non credat: et talis pœna fiat eis, qualis debeat fieri illis, qui injuste fideles dni. regis exhæredari et destrui fecerunt, &c.*

2. That this act of 5 E. 6. extend as well to petit treason, as high treason, for the words be [any treason] and so doth the statute of 1 E. 6. cap. 12.

3. That the statute of 1 & 2 Ph. and Mar. cap. 10. doth not abrogate the said act of 1 E. 6. or of 5 E. 6. For that act of 1 & 2 Ph. and Mar. extends only to trialls by the verdict of twelve men *de vicineto*, of the place where the offence is alleadged, and [k] the indictment is no part of the triall, but an information or declaration for the king, and the evidence of witnesses to the jury is no part of the triall, for by law the tryall in that case is not by witnesses, but by the verdict * of twelve men, and so a manifest diversity between the evidence to a jury, and a tryall by jury. And the word [awarded] in that statute doth prove that that act extended only to the *venire facias* for trial, for neither the indictment nor the evidence can be said to be awarded: *veritas quæ minime defensatur, opprimitur, et qui non improbat, approbat. Et sic liberè animam meam liberavi.*

*[27]

[a] 27 E. 3. cap. 8. 28 E. 3. cap. 18. 8 H. 6. cap. 29. 1 Mar. fo. 144. Shirley's case, and so it was resolved by all the judges, Hil. 36 El. in the case of doctor Lopez, Emanuel Loysie, and Stephen Ferreira de Gama.

[a] The tryall against an aliennee, that lived here under the protection of the king, and amity being between both kings, for high treason, shall by force of this act of 1 & 2 Ph. & Mar. be tried according to the due course of the common law, and therefore in that case he shall not be tried *per medietatem linguæ*, as he shall be in case of petit treason, murder, and felony, if he prayeth it.

[b] 33 H. 8. c. 23. 3 Mar. Dier, 132. Dier, 12 El. 286. b. li. 11. fo. 63. a. in doctor Foster's case.

[c] 27 Ass. p. 1. 21 Ass. p. 12. W. 1. c. 3. &c. Mic. 25 & 26 El. per les justices in Somervile's and Arden's case. Dier 12 El. 286. b. All this was resolved, Mic. 1 Ja. in Sir Walter Raleigh's case. Pl. Com. 388. Count de Leicester's case.

4. [b] That a tryall in a forein county upon examination before three of the councell, &c. by the statute of 33 H. 8. cap. 23. is abrogated by this act of 1 & 2 Ph. and Mar. being a tryall contrary to the due course of the common law, which is to have it tryed by jurours of the proper county, [c] but the indictment being found in the proper county, it may be by speciall commission heard and determined before commissioners in any forein county, but the tryall must be by jurours of the proper county; and this is warranted by the course of the common law. And albeit when the term begins, all commissions of oier and terminer in the county where the kings bench sit, be suspended during the term, yet if an indictment be found before such commissioners before the tearm, there may be a speciall commission made to commissioners in the same county, sitting the kings bench in that county, to

to hear and determine the ſame during the tearm: for the kings bench hath no power to proceed thereupon, till the indictment be before them. And it is the better, if the ſpeciall commiſſion bear teſte after the beginning of the tearm. Note a diverſity between generall commiſſions of oier and terminer, and ſuch a ſpeciall commiſſion; and the court of kings bench may be adjourned, and in the mean time the commiſſioners may ſit there.

[d] And where it is provided by the ſtatute of 33 H. 8. cap. 23. that peremptory challenge ſhould not from thenceforth be admitted or allowed in caſes of high treaſon, or miſpriſion of treaſon: [e] this branch is abrogated by the ſaid act of 1 Mar. For the end of challenge is to have an indifferent tryall, and which is required by law; and to bar the party indicted of his lawfull challenge, is to bar him of a principall matter concerning his tryall: and all acts of parliament concerning incidents to tryalls contrary to the courſe of the common law, are abrogated by the ſaid words, [and that all trialls hereafter, &c.] but all this is to be underſtood of perſons under the degree of nobility; for in caſe of a triall of a noble man, lord of parliament, he cannot challenge at all any of his peers.

[f] Henry Garnet ſuperiour of the jeſuites in England upon his arraignment for the powder treaſon, did challenge Burrel a citizen of London peremptorily, and it was allowed unto him by the reſolution of all the judges; [g] ſo as in caſe of high treaſon, or miſpriſion of high treaſon, a man may challenge 35. peremptorily, which is under three juries, but more he cannot.

Laſtly, all ſtatutes made before the ſaid act of 1 & 2 Ph. & Mar. for tryall of high treaſon, petit treaſon, or miſpriſion of treaſon, contrary to the due courſe of the common law, are abrogated by the ſaid act of 1 & 2 Ph. & Mar. and tryalls by the due courſe of the common law, with challenges incidents in thoſe caſes are reſtored.

[h] If a man be indicted of high treaſon, he may at this day plead a forein plea, as he might doe by the common law, and ſhall be tryed in the forein county; but otherwiſe it is in caſes of petit treaſon, murder, or felony, for there it ſhall be tryed in the county where the indictment is taken.

And foraſmuch as the proceeding againſt a noble peer of the realm, being a lord of parliament in ſome points agrees, and in other points differeth from the proceeding againſt a ſubject under the degree of nobility: it ſhall be neceſſary to ſhew wherein they agree, and wherein they differ.

[d] 33 H. 8. c. 23.

[e] And ſo it was reſolved. an. 1 Ja. in Sir Walter Raleighs caſe, by all the judges and had been reſolved ſo before. Stan. pl. cor. 157.

[f] 3. Ja. R. in Garnets caſe. And ſo it was reſolved, M. 25 & 26 El. in Somerviles and Ardens caſe.

[g] Br. tit. Challenge, 217.

[h] 22 H. 8. c. 14. 32 H. 8. c. 3. See 4 H. 8. c. 2. and 22 H. 8. c. 2. pleading, &c. for being taken out of ſanctuary in a forain county in caſe of murder or felony. See hereafter, cap. Sanctuary, all ſanctuaries taken away: and note that the ſtat. of 22 H. 8. &c. extend only to indictments and not to appeals.

[28]

1. The noble peer of the realme muſt be indicted before commiſſioners of oier and terminer, or in the kings bench, if the treaſon, miſpriſion of treaſon, felony, or miſpriſion thereof be committed in that county where the kings bench ſit, as it was reſolved in the caſe of Tho. d. of N. in an. 13. Eliz. And this is common to both degrees to be indicted by jurors of that county where the offence was committed. 1 H. 4. 1.

2. When he is indicted, then the king by his commiſſion under the great ſeale conſtitutes ſome peer of the realme, to be *hac vice*, ſteward of England: for his ſtile in the commiſſion, is, (*Seneſchallus Angliæ*) who is judge in this caſe of the treaſon or felony, or of the miſpriſion of the ſame committed by any peer of the realm. 1 H. 4. 1. 10 E. 4. 6. b. 13 H. 8. 12.

This commiſſion reciteth the indictment generally as it is found: and power given to the lord ſteward to receive the indictment, &c. and to proceed, *ſecundum legem et conſuetudinem Angliæ*. And a commandement is given thereby to the peers of the realme, to be attendant and obedient to him: and a commandement to the lieutenant of the Tower to bring the priſoner before him.

3. A *certiorari* is awarded out of the chancery to remove the indictment it ſelfe before the ſteward of England *indilatè*, which may either beare date the ſame day of the ſtewards commiſſion, or any day after.

4. The ſteward directs his precept under his ſeale to the commiſſioners, &c. to certifie the indictment ſuch a day and place.

5. Another writ goeth out of the chancery directed to the lieutenant of the Tower, to bring the body of the priſoner before the ſteward at ſuch day and place as he ſhall appoint.

6. The lord ſteward maketh a precept under his ſeale to the lieutenant of the Tower, &c. and therein expreſſeth a day and place when he ſhall bring the priſoner before him.

7. The ſteward maketh another precept under his ſeale to a ſerjeant at armes, to ſummon *tot et tales dominos, magnates, et proceres hujus regni Angliæ prædicti R. comitis E. pares, per quos rei veritas melius ſciri poterit, quòd ipſi perſonaliter compareant coram prædicto ſeneſchallo apud Weſtm. tali die et hora, ad faciend. ea quæ ex parte domini regis forent facienda, &c.* Wherein four things are to be obſerved. Firſt, that all theſe precepts moſt commonly beare date all in one day. Secondly, that no number of peers are named in the precept, and yet there muſt be twelve or above. Thirdly, that the precept is awarded for the returne of the peers before any arraignment or plea pleaded by the priſoner. Fourthly, that in this caſe the lords are not *de vicineto*, and therefore the ſitting and triall may be in any county of England. And herein are great differences between the caſe of a peer of the realme, and of one under the degree of nobility.

8. At the day, the ſteward with ſix ſerjeants at armes before him takes his place under a cloth of eſtate, and then the clerk of the
1 H. 4. 1. crown delivereth unto him his commiſſion, who redelivereth the ſame unto him. And the clerk of the crown cauſeth a ſerjeant at armes to make three oyes, and commandement given in the name of the lord high ſteward of England to keep ſilence: and then is the
1 H. 4. 1. commiſſion read. And then the uſher delivereth to the ſteward a white rod, who re-delivereth the ſame to him againe, who holdeth it before the ſteward. Then another oyes is made, and commandement given in the name of the high ſteward of England, to all juſtices and commiſſioners to certifie all indictments and records, &c. Which being delivered into court, the clerk of the crown readeth the return. Another oyes is made, that the lieutenant of the Tower, &c. returne his writ and precept, and to bring the priſoner to the bar: which being done, the clerk reads the retorne. Another oyes is made, that the ſerjeant at armes return his precept with names of the barons and peers by him ſummoned, and the return of that is alſo read. Another oyes is made, that all earles, barons and peers (which by the commandement of the high ſteward be ſummoned)
[29] anſwer to their names, and then they take their places and ſit down, and their names are recorded: and the entry of the record is, that they

they appear, *ad faciendum ea quæ ex parte domini regis eis injungentur.* And when they be all in their places, and the prisoner at the bar, the high steward declares to the prisoner the cause of their assembly, and perswades him to answer without feare, that he shall be heard with patience, and that justice shall be done. Then the clerk of the crown reades the indictment, and proceeds to the arraignment of the prisoner, and if he plead not guilty, the entry is, *et de hoc de bono et malo ponit se super pares suos, &c.* Then the high steward giveth a charge to the peers, exhorting them to try the prisoner indifferently according to their evidence. 1 H. 4. 1.

9. The peers are not sworn, but are charged, *super fidelitatibus, et ligeantiis domino regi debitis:* for so the record speaketh.

10. Then the kings learned councell give evidence, and produce their proofes for the king against the prisoner.

11. But the prisoner, when he pleadeth not guilty, whereby he denieth the fact, he needs have no advice of councell to that plea. But if he hath any matter of law to plead, as Humfrey Stafford in 1 H. 7. had, viz. The priviledge of sanctuary, he shall have councell assigned to him to plead the same, or any other matter in law: as to plead the generall pardon, or a particular pardon, or the like. And after the plea of not guilty, the prisoner can have no councell learned assigned to him to answer the king's councell learned, nor to defend him. And the reason thereof is, not because it concerneth matter of fact, for *ex facto jus oritur:* but the true reasons of the law in this case are: First, that the testimonies and the proofs of the offence ought to be so clear and manifest, as there can be no defence of it. * Secondly, the court ought to be in stead of councell for the prisoner, to see that nothing be urged against him contrary to law and right; nay, any learned man that is present may inform the court for the benefit of the prisoner, of any thing that may make the proceedings erroneous. And herein there is no diversity between the peer and another subject. And to the end that the triall may be the more indifferent, seeing that the safety of the prisoner consisteth in the indifferency of the court, the judges ought not to deliver their opinions before-hand of any criminall case, that may come before them judicially. And we reade, that in the case of Humfrey Stafford that arch-traytor, Hussey chief justice, besought king Henry the seventh, that he would not desire to know their opinions before-hand for Humfrey Stafford, for they thought it should come before them in the kings bench judicially, and then they would do that which of right they ought: and the king accepted of it. And therefore the judges ought not to deliver their opinions before-hand upon a case put, and proofs urged of one side in absence of the party accused: especially in cases of high nature, and which deserve so fatall and extreme punishment. For how can they be indifferent, who have delivered their opinions before-hand without hearing of the party, when a small addition, or substraction may alter the case: And how doth it stand with their oath, who are sworn, That they should well and lawfully serve our lord the king and his people in the office of a justice? and they should do equall law, and execution of right to all his subjects, &c. See more of this matter in the 13 section here following.

In Scotland in all criminall cases, yea in cases of high treason, *pars rea* may have councell learned. Vide hereafter upon the statute of 31 Eliz. concerning witnesses.

*See more hereof cap. 63. Councell learned in Pleas of the Crown.

1 H. 7. fo. 26.

18 E. 3.

12. There be alwayes either all, or some of the judges ever atten-

dant upon the high steward, and sit at the feet of the peers, or about a table in the middest, or in some other convenient place.

13. After all the evidence given for the king, and the prisoners answers, and proofs at large, and with patience heard: then is the prisoner withdrawn from the bar to some private place under the custody of the lieutenant, &c. And after that he is withdrawn, the lords that are tryers of the prisoner go to some place to consider of their evidence: and if upon debate thereof, they should doubt of any matter, and thereupon send to the high steward, to have conference with the judges, or with the high steward, they ought to have no conference, either with the judges or the high steward, but [30] openly in court, and in the presence, and hearing of the prisoner; as it was resolved by all the justices of England in the reign of king H. 8. in the case of the lord Dacres of the North. And this was a just resolution; for when the lords should put a case, and ask advice thereupon, the prisoner ought by law to be present, to see that the case or question be rightly put: and therefore that nothing be done in his absence, untill they be agreed on their verdict. Hereupon it followeth, that if the peers of the realm, who are intended to be indifferent, can have no conference with the judges, or with the high steward in open court in the absence of the prisoner: *à fortiori*, the king's learned counsell should not in the absence of the party accused, upon any case put, or matter shewed by them, privately preoccupate the opinion of the judges: and upon so just a resolution the case succeeded well, for the peers found the lord Dacres not guilty.

Pasch. 26 H. 8. in the case of the lord Dacres of the North, reported by justice Spilman, which we have seen.

14. A noble man cannot waive his triall by his peers, and put himselfe upon the triall of the country, that is, of twelve freeholders: for the statute of Magna Carta is, that he must be tried *per pares*. And so it was resolved in the lord Dacres case, *ubi supra*.

Mag. Cart. cap. 29.

15. * The peers ought to continue together (as juries in case of other subjects ought to do) until they be agreed of their verdict: and when they are agreed, they all come again into the court, and take their places, and then the lord high steward publicly in open court, beginning with the puisne lord, (who in the case of the lord Dacre was the lord Mordant,) said unto him; My lord Mordant, is William lord Dacre guilty of the treasons, whereof he hath been indicted or arraigned, or of any of them? And the lord standing up said, Not guilty: and so upward of all the other lords *seriatim*: who all gave the same verdict: In which case the entry is, *super quo W. Comes E. & cæteri antedicti pares instantes super fidelitatibus & legeantiis dicto domino regi debitis, per præfatum senescallum ab inferiori pare usq; ad supremum separatim publice examinati dicunt quòd W. dominus Dacre non est culp. &c.*

* Resolved by all the judges. Mich. 13 & 14 El. in the case of Tho. duke of Norff. 1 H. 4. fo. 1. 10 E. 4. 6. b. 13 H. 8. fo. 12. Tr. 26 H. 8. Spilman's report.

16. The peers give their verdict in the absence of the prisoner, and then is the prisoner brought to the bar again: and then doth the lord steward acquaint the prisoner with the verdict of his peers, and give judgement accordingly, either of condemnation or acquitall. But it is not so in the case of another subject: for there the verdict is given in his presence.

17. Every lord of parliament, and that hath voice in parliament, and called thereunto by the king's writ, shall not be tried by his peers, but only such as sit there *ratione nobilitatis*, as dukes, marquisses,

Rot. Roman. 17 E. 2. m. 6. Adam Orleton B. of Hereford.

marquisses, countes, viscounts or barons, and not such as are lords of parliament, *ratione baroniarum, quas tenent in jure ecclesiæ*, by reason of their baronies which they hold in the right of the church, as arch-bishops, and bishops, and in time past some abbots and priors, but they shall be tried by the countrey, that is, by freeholders, for that they are not of the degree of nobility.

2 H. 4. Marks. B. of Carlisle. Stanf. Pl. Coron. li. 3. ca. 62. fo. 153. in Temps H. 8.

18. [a] No noble man shall be tried by his peers, but only at the suit of the king upon an indictment of high treason, or misprision of the same, petit treason, murder, or other felony, or misprision of the same. But in case of a premunire or the like, though it be at the suit of the king, he shall not be tried by his peers, but by freeholders. And so in an appeale at the suit of the party for petit treason, murder, robbery, or other felony, he shall be tryed by freeholders. See more hereof in the second part of the Institutes, Magna Carta, cap. 29.

[a] 10 E. 4. 6. b. Mag. Cart. c. 29.

19. [b] And albeit a man be noble, and yet no lord of the parliament of this realm, (as if he be a nobleman of Scotland, or of Ireland, of France, &c.) he shall be tried by knights, esquires, or others of the commons. And so it is of the sonne of a duke, marquisse, earle, &c. he is noble, and called lord: and yet because he is no lord of parliament, he shall be tried as one under the degree of a peer, and lord of parliament.

[b] 11 E. 3. bre. 473. 8 R. 2. proces. pl. ultimo. 20 E. 4. 6. 20 El. Dier, 360. 38 H. 8. Br. treason. Seignior Sancras case. Lib. 9. fo. 117.

20. No peer of the realm, or any other subject shall be convicted by verdict, but the said offences must be found by above four and twenty, viz. by twelve, or above, at his indictment, or by twelve peers, or above, if he be noble, and by twelve, and not above, if he be under the degree of nobility.

[31]

21. A peer of the realme being indicted of treason, or felony, or of misprision, as is aforesaid, and duly transmitted to the lords, may be arraigned thereof in the upper house of parliament, as frequently in parliament rolls it doth appeare: but then there must be appointed a steward of England, who shall put him to answer: and if he plead not guilty, he shall be tried *per pares suos*, and then the lords spiritual must withdraw, and make their proxies: but no appeal of treason can be in parliament, [a] but is ousted by the statute of 1. H. 4. cap. 14.

10 E. 4. 6. Rot. par. 21. R. 2. Countee de Arundels case. Rot. Parliam. 5 H. 4. nu. 11, 12. 31 H. 6. nu. 49. Countee de Devons case. 28 H. 6. nu. 19. Duke of Suff.

22. [b] And as the beginning (viz. the finding of the indictment by freeholders) is equall to them both: so the most extreme and heavy judgement, if they be found guilty, is equal to both, &c. which you may reade in the first part of the Institutes, Sect. 147.

[a] 1 H. 4. cap. 14.

[b] 1 H. 4. 1. Stanf. Pl. Coron. 182. E. K. See hereafter. cap. Judgement and Execution.

23. [c] And though the commission of the lord steward be only in these latter times *hac vice*, yet may the same be adjourned, as other commissioners *hac vice* may. And so it was holden in the lord Dacres case. And so it was done by the steward of England in the case of R. earle of S. and of F. his wife, who adjourned his commission until the next day.

[c] Pasch. 26 H. 8. ubi supra. L. 5 E. 4. 33. 12 H. 4. 20.

24. If execution be not done according to the judgement, then the high steward in the case of a peer of the realm, or the court or commissioners in case of another subject, may by their precepts under their seales command execution to be done according to the judgement: but in case of high treason, if all the rest of the judgement (saving the beheading, which is part of the judgement) be pardoned, this ought to be under the great seale of England.

25. And when the fervice is performed, then is an oyes made for the diffolving of the commiffion; and then is the white rod, which hath been borne and holden before the fteward, by him taken in both his hands, and broken over his head.

Laftly, the indictments together with the record of the arraignment, triall, and judgement, fhall be delivered into the king's bench, there to be kept and inrolled.

Hitherto we have fpoken when a noble man doth appear, and plead not guilty, and put himfelf upon his peers: Now let us fee what fhall be had againft him when he is indicted and appears not, and cannot be taken: and generally he fhall be outlawed, *per judicium corronatorum*. But how doth that ftand with Magna Charta, *nec fuper eum ibimus, nec fuper eum mittemus, nifi per legale judicium parium fuorum?* That is to be intended, when he appears and pleads not guilty, and puts himfelf upon his peers: but when he abfents himfelf, and will not yeild himfelf to the due tryall of his peers, then he fhall be outlawed *per judicium coronatorum*, or elfe he fhould take advantage of his own contumacy, and flying from judgement. [d] For proces to be awarded upon the indictment or appeal of treafon, felony, or trefpafs, either againft a nobleman or any other, fee the ftatute of 6 H. 6. and 8 H. 6. and if the proces and order prefcribed by thofe ftatutes be not purfued, the outlawry may be reverfed by writ of error, which writ ought to be granted to him *ex merito juftitiæ*, as it was adjudged in Ninian Menvils cafe: and thofe ftatutes doe extend as well to the kings bench, as to other courts having by commiffion power to hear and determine the fame, and very few outlawries of treafon or felony, are of force and validity in law, for that thefe acts are not purfued.

Mag. Cart. ca. 29.

[d] See hereafter in the chapter of Judgement and Execution concerning reverfing of outlawries. 6 H. 6. c. 1. 8 H. 6. ca. 10. Mich. 26 and 27 Eliz. in bre. de error coram Rege in Ninian Menvills cafe. Utlary de haut treafon reverfe in bank le roy.

And thefe acts are well expounded by our * books, and therefore they fhall not need to be recited at large. This is neceffary to be added, that the opinion of Stanf. Pl. Cor. 182. l. upon the ftatute of 33 H. 8. c. 20. is, where the attainder is not erroneous, but lawfull by the courfe of the law: and fo it was refolved, Tr. 28 Eliz. and thereupon [e] the ftatute of 28 Eliz. ca. 2. was made, that no attainder that then was for any high treafon fhould be reverfed for error where the party was executed. But that act extendeth only to attainders before that act, and where the party attainted fuffered pains of death, as hath been faid.

* 19 H. 6. fo. 1. 2. 11 H. 6. 54. 1 E. 4. 1. 30 H. 6. proces. 192. 31 H. 6. 11. Vide F. N. B. 115. l. Li. Intr. R. f. 122. Stanf. Pl. cor. 68, 69. 182 l.

[e] 28 El. ca. 2.

[32]

But admitting the proces be awarded according to thefe ftatutes, and the truth is, that the party indicted of high treafon (be he noble or other) at the time of the outlawry pronounced, is out of the realm, &c. whether may he avoid the fame by writ of error? The anfwer is, that he might have avoided the fame by writ of error at the common law: but now in cafe of high treafon he is barred of his writ of error by the ftatutes of 26 H. 8. and 5 E. 6. which ftatutes are expounded to extend generally to all treafons, but thofe ftatutes extend not to any other offence than high treafon only, and therefore all other offences remain as they did at the common law for that point.

See the firft part of the Infti. fect. 26 H. 8. cap. 13. 5 E. 6. cap. 11. 12 El. Dier 287.

Now for that all indictments for any offence whatfoever, as well of noblemen, as of any under the degree of nobility, ought by the common law of the realm to be by perfons duly returned, and by * lawfull liege people, indifferent as they ftand unfworn, and without any denomination of any: a good and profitable law was

* Artic. fup. cart. cap. 9. 28 E. 1. 20 E. 3. cap. 6. 34 E. 3. c. 4. 42 E. 3. c. 11. Regift. 178. Raft. pl. 117

* was made in that behalf at the parliament holden 11 H. 4. in thefe words. *Item* becaufe that now of late [a] inquefts were taken at Weftm' of perfons named to the [b] juftices, without due return of the fherif, of which perfons fome were [c] outlawed before the faid juftices of record, and fome fled to fanctuary for treafon, and fome for felony, there to have refuge; by whom as well many offenders were indicted, as other lawfull liege people of our lord the king, not guilty by confpiracy, abetment, and falfe imagination of other perfons for their fpeciall advantage and fingular lucre, againft the courfe of the common law ufed and accuftomed before this time. Our faid lord the king for the greater eafe and quietneffe of his people, will and granteth, that the fame indictment fo made, with all the dependance thereof be [d] revoked, adnulled, void, and holden for none for ever. And that from henceforth no indictment be made by any fuch perfons, but by enqueft of the king's lawful [e] liege people, in the manner, as was ufed in the time of his noble progenitors, returned by the fherifs, or baylifs of franchifes, without any [f] denomination to the fherifs, or baylifs of franchifes before made by any perfon of the names, which by him fhould be impanelled, except it be by the officers of the faid fherifs or baylifs of franchifes fworn and known to make the fame, [g] and other officers to whom it pertaineth to make the fame according to the law of England. And if any indictment be made hereafter in any point to the contrary, that the fame indictment be alfo void, revoked, and for ever holden for none.

* 11 H. 4. ca. 9.
[a] Stanf. pl. cor. 87. e.
[b] Rot Parl. 11. H. 4. nu. 15. in the kings bench.
[c] Vid. 11 H. 4. fo. 41. 21 H. 6. 30. 9 E. 4. 16. 3 H. 6. 55. 26 Aff. 28.
[d] 11 H. 4. 41.
[e] 14 H. 4. 19.
[f] 21 E. 3. 5. 15 E. 3. chal. 113. 27 Aff. pa, 65. 28 Aff. 24. 22. 49 E. 3. 1. 49 Aff. 1. 28. 43 E. 3. chall. 94. 6 R. 2. chall. 102. 7 H. 4 10. 21 E. 4. 74. 19 H. 6. 9. 21 H. 6. 22. 14 H. 7. 1.
[g] Nota.

The body of this act confifteth upon two diftinct purviens or branches, the one to remedy a mifchief paft, the other to provide for the time to come. The firft branch confifteth of a preamble, and a purvien: and the preamble containeth thefe eight parts. Firft, it fheweth divers inquefts had been taken at Weftminfter by perfons named to the juftices. Secondly, without due return of the fherif. Thirdly, of which fome were outlawed before the faid juftices of record. Fourthly, fome fled to fanctuary for treafon, and fome for felony. Fifthly, by whom many offenders were indicted. Sixthly, fome not guilty. Seventhly, by confpiracy, &c. Eighthly, that all this was againft the courfe of the common law. By the body of the act, it is enacted that the fame indictment, with all the dependance thereof, be revoked, and made void. Then followeth the fecond branch or purvien for the time to come, and this purvien confifteth of divers parts: Firft, in defcribing by what perfons indictments ought to be found, and therein 1. *privativè*, that is, not by any fuch perfons, having reference to the preamble, which perfons we have before particularly diftinguifhed. 2. *Pofitivè*, that all indictments muft be found by perfons of thefe qualities. 1. They muft be the kings lawfull liege people. 2. Returned by fherifs, or baylifs of franchifes, and other officers to whom it pertaineth. 3. Without any denomination to the fherifs, baylifs, or other officers: and this purvien is in affirmance, and declaratory of the common law.

The fecond part of the purvien is introductory of a new law, viz. that if any indictment be made hereafter in any point to the contrary, that the fame indictment be void, revoked, and holden for none. Wherein thefe two things are to be obferved: 1. That this [33] is a generall law, and extendeth to all indictments for any crime, default,

fault, or offence whatsoever: for the words be [if any indictment] generally without naming of any court, or before whom. 2. If the indictment be found by any persons that are outlawed, or not the kings lawfull liege people, or not lawfully returned, or denominated by any, viz. by all or any of these, that then the indictment is void, for the words be, [if any indictment be made hereafter in any point to the contrary, &c.] Upon this statute in the case of Robert Scarlet before the justices of assize at Bury in the county of Suffolk, in sommer vacation, 10 Ja. R. these points were resolved and adjudged: First, where at the sessions of the peace holden at Woodbridge in the said county of Suffolk, Robert Scarlet by confederacy between him and the clerk, that was to read the pannell of the grand jury returned by the sherif, (whereof he was none, albeit he laboured the sherif to have returned him) that the clerk should read him as one of the pannell, which was done accordingly, and he sworn. It was resolved and adjudged that this case was within the statute, for that he was not returned by the sherif. Secondly, that where the rest of the great inquest giving faith to him indicted seventeen honest and good men upon divers penall statutes, which was done by the said Robert Scarlet maliciously. It was resolved and adjudged, that albeit he * alone was sworn without the return of the sherif, and all the rest duly returned, yet this case was within this statute, and all the indictments found by him and the rest were void by this statute: for hereby it appeared what mischief such a one might doe. Thirdly, that Robert Scarlet upon this case had offended against the said act, and might be indicted thereupon: and accordingly he was upon sufficient proof of the fact, as aforesaid, indicted upon the said act, and pleaded not guilty, and was found guilty. Fourthly, that this act extended not only to indictments of treason and felony, but of all other offences and defaults whatsoever, according to the generality of the words. Fifthly, consideration was had of the act of 3 H. 8. cap. 12. and resolved clearly that this statute had not altered the act of 11 H. 4. in any thing concerning the offence of Scarlet, as upon that, which shall be said of the act of 3 H. 8. shall appear. And upon hearing of councell learned what they could say in arrest of judgement, at last judgement was given, that he should be fined and imprisoned, and ordered by the court that no proces should goe out upon the said indictments found by the said great inquest, whereof Scarlet was one.

* 47 E. 3. 1. 7 H. 4. 10. 21 E. 4. 74.

3 H. 8. ca. 12.

But notwithstanding this good law, through the subtilty, and untrue demeanor of sherifs, and their ministers, great extortions and oppressions be and have been committed and done to many of the kings subjects by means of returning at sessions holden within counties and shires for the body of the shire, the names of such persons as for the singular advantage, &c. of the said sherifs and their ministers, will be wilfully forsworn and perjured by the sinister labour of the said sherifs and their ministers, by reason whereof many substantial persons, the king's true subjects have been wrongfully indicted of murders, felonies, and misdemeanours: and sometime by labour of the said sherifs and their ministers, divers great felonies and murders have been concealed, &c. For remedy of which mischiefs it is enacted by the said statute of 3 H. 8. cap. 12. That the justices of gaol delivery, or justices of peace, whereof

whereof one to be of the quorum, in their open ſeſſions may reform the panell returned by the ſherif to inquire for the king, by putting to and taking out the names of the perſons ſo impanelled by the diſcretion of the ſaid juſtices, &c. and that the ſherif ſhall return the panells ſo reformed. This act extends only to juſtices of gaol delivery, and of the peace: the body of the act for offences is generall and evident. *Vide* 11 H. 7. cap. 24. Vid. 11. H. 7. ca. 24.

Nota Lector, that the aforeſaid parliament of 11 H. 4. begun in *quindena Hillarii*, anno 11 H. 4. and the ſame tearm, viz. Hil. 11 H. 4. fo. 41. it was according to the ſaid act of 11 H. 4. reſolved by Gaſcoign chief juſtice, and all the reſt of the juſtices, that an indictment of felony found by an inqueſt before 5 H. 4. whereof one was outlawed of felony, and another was acquitted by the generall pardon, ſo as they were not *probi et legales homines* to enquire as the law willeth, and after the party had pleaded not guilty to the felony, it was awarded, that all the indictments by them found, were adnulled and made void. Herewith agreeth Stanford in his pleas of the crown, fo. 87. and 88. Vide F. tit. Indictment 25. and Coron. 89. and Brook tit. Indictment 2. Note the act ſaith, that they were outlawed before themſelves, ſo as the court may take knowledge thereof of themſelves, or of any other, as *amicus curiæ*: but the ſafeſt way for the party indicted is to plead, upon his arraignment, the ſpeciall matter given unto him by the ſtatute of 11 H. 4. for the overthrow of the indictment, with ſuch averments, as by law are required, (agreeable to the opinion of the Lord Brook. *Ubi ſupra.*) and to plead over to the felony, and to require councell learned for the pleading thereof, which ought to be granted, and alſo to require a copy of ſo much of the indictment, as ſhall be neceſſary for the framing of his plea, which alſo ought to be granted. And theſe laws made for indifferency of indicters, ought to be conſtrued favourably, for that the indictment is commonly found in the abſence of the party, and yet it is the foundation of all the reſt of the proceeding.

Hil. 11 H. 4. f. 41.

[34]

Stanf. Pl. cor. 87, 88. F. tit. Indictment 25. and Coron. 89. Br. tit. indict. 2.

Vid. le ſtatutes de 1 R. 3. ca. 4. 33 H. 6. c. 2. W. 2. ca. 13. 1 E. 3. ſtat. 2. ca. 17. All tending that indictments may be duly had.

To draw to an end concerning tryals: it is regularly true, that by the common law the tryall ſhall be in the county, where the indictment is taken: and by the aforeſaid act of 35 H. 8. treaſons and miſpriſions of treaſons committed or done out of the realm, &c. ſhall be enquired of, heard, and determined before the juſtices of the king's bench, &c. Now the caſe fel out upon this ſtatute to be thus: * one was indicted before the juſtices of the kings bench, at the tearm holden at Hertford, by a jury of the county of Hertford, for divers high treaſons committed out of this realm, and after the tearm was adjourned to Weſtm. in the county of Midd. The queſtion was, by which of the counties the party indicted ſhould be tried: and it was reſolved, that he ſhould be tried by men of that county where the indictment was taken. But otherwiſe it is upon the ſtatute of 5 El. ca. 1. the caſe being, that Horn biſhop of Winch. tendred to Edmond Bonner late biſhop of London, in the county of Surrey, within his dioces the oath of ſupremacy according to the act 1 Eliz. which Bonner refuſed, and this was certified by the biſhop of Winch. into the kings bench, then ſitting at Weſtminſter in the county of Midd. Now, by the ſtatute of 5 El. he that refuſeth the oath is to be indicted of a premunire by a jury of Midd. as a jury of that county might doe for any offence done in that

Dier 3 Mar. 131, 132. Stanf. pl. cor. 90. 35 H. 8. ca. 2.

* Mich. 35 & 36 El. in the caſe of Francis Dacres.

5 El. cap. 1.

Mich. 6 & 7 El. Dier fo. 234. Bonner's caſe.

that county, and extendeth only to the indictment, where the words of the act of 35 H. 8. be, [shal be enquired of, heard, and determined,] the question upon the statute of 5 Eliz. was, if Bonner should appear and plead not guilty, by what county he should be tried, whether by a jury of Midd. where the indictment was, or by a jury of Surrey, where the offence was committed; and resolved that he should be tried by a jury of Surrey: for the statute of 5 El. extendeth to the indictment only, and leaveth the triall to the common law, which appointeth the tryall to be, where the offence is committed, and so a manifest diversity between the two cases: for regularly by the common law in all pleas of the crown, *debet quis juri subjacere, ubi deliquit.*

Bract. lib. 3. fo. 154. b. *Vincula qui sensit, didicit succurrere vinctis.* Bract. lib. 3. fo. 105. a. Stanford 78. Bract. li. 3. f. 137. Note Shackells about the feet ought not to be, but for fear of escape. Mirror, c. 2. §. 9.

It is now necessary to be known, how prisoners (to speak once for all) committed for treason, or any other offence ought to be demeaned in prison. Bracton saith, *solent praesides in carcere continendos damnare, ut in vinculis contineantur, sed hujusmodi interdicta sunt à lege, quia carcer ad continendos, non ad puniendos haberi debeat:* And in another place he saith, *Cum autem taliter captus coram justic. est producendus, produci non debet ligatis manibus, (quamvis interdum gestans compedes propter evasionis periculum,) et hoc ideo, ne videatur coactus ad aliquam purgationem suscipiendam.*

[a] Brit. c. 5. fo. 14. [b] Cap. 11. fo. 17. W. 2. c. 1. after judgement. Lib. 3. fo. 44. Lib. 8. fo. 100. 24 H. 8. Dier. 249. Pl. Com. 360. a. [c] Fleta li. 1. ca. 26. [d] Mirror c. 5. §. 1. [e] 8 E. 2. cor. 432. [f] Tr. 7 E. 3. coram rege Rot. 44.

[a] If felons come in judgement to answer, &c. they shall be out of irons, and all manner of bonds, so that their pain shall not take away any manner of reason, nor them constrain to answer, but at their free will. [b] And in another place he saith, and of prisoners we will that none shall be put in irons, but those †, which shall be taken for felony, or trespass in parks or vivaries, or which be found in arerages upon account, and we defend that otherwise they shall not be punished nor tormented. [c] *Omnes autem attachiabiles licet vicecomiti in prisona custodire, &c. non tamen ad puniend', sed ad custodiend', &c.* [d] It is an abuse that prisoners be charged with irons, or put to any pain before they be attainted.

† [35]

[e] *Quidam sacerdos arraniatus de felonia posuit se super patriam, & stetit ad barram in ferris, sed per praeceptum justic. liberatur à ferris.* And there is no difference in law, as to a priest and a lay man, as to irons.

* 1 E. 3. c. 7.

[f] *Presentat quod ubi quidam Robertus Bayhens de Tanesby captus fuit, & in prisona castri Lincoln detentus pro quodam debito statut. mercatorii in custodia Tho. Boteler constabularii castri de Lincoln ibi praed. Tho. le Boteler posuit ipsum Robertum in profundo gaole inter lenones in vili prisona contra * formam statut. &c. et eodem profundo detinuit, quousque idem Robertus fecit finem cum eo de 40 s. quos ei solvit per extorsionem.*

So as hereby it appeareth, that where the law requireth that a prisoner should be kept in *salva & arcta custodia,* yet that that must be without pain or torment to the prisoner.

Tortures, the rack, &c.

Hereupon two questions do arise, when and by whom the rack or brake in the Tower was brought in.

Rot. Par. 26 H. 6. Rot. Parl. 28 H. 6. nu. 30.

To the first, John Holland earl of Huntingdon, was by king H. 6. created duke of Exeter, and anno 26 H. 6. the king granted to him the office of the constableship of the Tower: he and William de la Poole duke of Suffolk, and others, intended to have brought in the civill lawes. For a beginning whereof, the duke of Exeter being constable of the Tower first brought into the Tower the

the rack or brake allowed in many cases by the civil law: and thereupon the rack is called the duke of Exeter's daughter, because he first brought it thither.

Hollenshed. pa. 670. &c. Innocentem cogit mentiri dolor.

To the second upon this occasion, Sir John Fortescue chiefe justice of England, wrote his book in commendation of the lawes of England, and therein preferreth the same for the government of this countrey before the civill law; and particularly that all tortures and torments of parties accused were directly against the common lawes of England, and shewed the inconvenience thereof by fearfull example, to whom I refer you being worthy your reading. So as there is no law to warrant tortures in this land, nor can they be justified by any prescription being so lately brought in.

Fortescue. ca. 22. fo. 24.

And the poet in describing the iniquity of Radamanthus, that cruell judge of hell, saith,

Castigatque, auditque dolos, subigitque fateri. Virgil.

First, he punished before he heard, and when he had heard his deniall, he compelled the party accused by torture to confesse it. But far otherwise doth Almighty God proceed *postquam reus diffamatus est.* 1. *Vocat.* 2. *Interrogat.* 3. *Judicat.* To conclude this point, it is against Magna Carta, cap. 29. *Nullus liber homo, &c. aliquo modo destruatur, nec super eum ibimus, nec super eum mittemus, nisi per legale judicium parium suorum, aut per legem terræ.* And accordingly all the said ancient authors are against any paine, or torment to be put or inflicted upon the prisoner before attainder, nor after attainder, but according to the judgement. And there is no one opinion in our books, or judiciall record (that we have seen and remember) for the maintenance of tortures or torments, &c.

Luke 16. 1, 2. &c. John 7. 51. Nunquid lex nostra judicat hominem nisi prius audierit ab ipso?

Proditor illudit verbis, dum verbera cudit.

And now, to conclude this chapter of treason. It appeareth in the holy scripture, that traytors never prospered, what good soever they pretended, but were most severely and exemplarily punished: As [a] Corah, Dathan, and Abiram, by miracle: *dirupta est terra sub pedibus eorum, et aperiens os suum devoravit illos, &c.* [b] Athalia the daughter of Amri, *interfecta est gladio.* [c] Bagatha and Thara against Assuerus, *appensus est uterq; eorum in patibula.* [d] Absolon against David. *Suspensus in arbore, et Joab infixit tres lanceas in corde ejus.* [e] Achitophel with Absolon against David. *Suspendio interiit,* he hanged himselfe. [f] Abiathar the traiterous high priest against Solomon. *Abiathar sacerdoti dixit rex, &c. Et quidem vir mortis es, sed hodie te non interficiam, &c. Ejecit ergo Solomon Abiathar, ut non esset sacerdos.* [g] Shemei against David, *gladio interfectus.* [h] Zimri against Ela, who burnt himselfe. [i] Theudas *(qui occisus est, et circiter* 400 *qui credebant ei, dispersi sunt et redacti ad nihilum)* and Judas Galilæus, *ipse periit, et omnes quotquot consenserunt ei, dispersi sunt.* Lastly, [k] Judas Iscariot, *secundum nomen ejus vir occisionis,* the traytor of traytors. *Et hic quidem possedit agrum de mercede iniquitatis suæ, & suspensus crepuit medius, et diffusa sunt omnia viscera ejus.*

[a] Numb. 16. 31, 32. & 27. 3.
[b] 2 Regum, 11. 16.
[c] Esth. 12. 2,3.
[d] 2 Sam. 18. 9. 14.
[e] 2 Sam. 17. 23.

[36]

[f] 1 Reg. 2. 26,27.
[g] 2. Sam. 16. 5,6. 1 Reg. 2. 8. &c. 46.
[h] 1 Regum 16. 9. &c. 18.
[i] Act. Apost. 5. 36,37.
[k] Act. Apost. 1. 18. Math. 27. 5. laqueo se suspendit. *Qui molitur insidias in patriam, id facit quod insanus nauta perforans navem in qua ipse vehitur.*

Peruse over all our books, records, and histories, and you shall finde a principle in law, a rule in reason, and a trial in experience, that treason doth ever produce fatal and final destruction to the offender, and never attaineth to the desired end, (two incidents inseparable thereunto.) * And therefore let all men abandon it, as the most poisonous bait of the devill of Hell, and follow the precept in holy

* *Felix quem faciunt aliena pericula cautum.* Prov. 24. 21.

holy ſcripture, Fear God, honour the king, and have no company with the ſedicious.

See more of treaſon in the next chapter of Miſpriſion, &c. and in Principall and Acceſſory, in the title of Judgement and Execution: and the chapter of *Monomachia*, Single Combat, &c. the reſidue of this act of 25 E. 3.

CAP. III.

OF MISPRISION OF TREASON.

Miſpriſio proditionis. See Bract. lib. 3. fo. 118. b. & 119. a.

MISPRISIO commeth of the French word *meſpris* which properly ſignifieth neglect or contempt: for [*mes*] in compoſition in the French ſignifieth *mal* as *mis* doth in the Engliſh tongue: as miſchance, for an ill chance, and ſo *meſpriſe* is ill apprehended or known. In legall underſtanding it ſignifieth, when one knoweth of any treaſon or felony, and concealeth it, this is miſpriſion, ſo called, becauſe the knowledge of it is an ill knowledge to him, in reſpect of the ſevere puniſhment for not revealing of it: for in caſe of miſpriſion of high treaſon he is to be impriſoned during his life, to forfeit all his goods, debts, and duties for ever, and the profits of his lands during his life: and in caſe of felony, to be fined and impriſoned. And in this ſenſe doth the ſaid ſtatute of 1 & 2 Ph. and Mar. ſpeak, when it ſaith, Be it declared, and enacted, by the authority aforeſaid, that concealement or keeping ſecret of any high treaſon be deemed and taken only miſpriſion of treaſon, and the offenders therein to forfeit and ſuffer, as in caſes of miſpriſion of treaſon hath heretofore been uſed. * But by the common law concealment of high treaſon was treaſon, as it appeareth in the caſe of the lord Scrope, an. 3 H. 5. and by Bracton, lib. 3. fo. 118. b. and 119 a.

See hereafter ca. 65. of miſpriſions, &c. See hereafter in Theftbote, ca. 61. 1 & 2 Ph. & Mar. Ubi ſupra. See 1 E. 6. c. 12. and 1 El. ca. 6. 25 H. 8. ca. 12.

* Hil. 14. El. cited by the lo. Dier in the lo. Lumley's caſe. MS.

[a] 14 El. ca. 3.

[a] It is miſpriſion of high treaſon, for forging of money, which neither is the money of this realme of England, nor currant within the ſame.

[b] 13 El. ca. 2.

[b] Miſpriſion of high treaſon in concealing of a bull, &c. See the ſtatute.

[c] 2 R. 3. fo. 9. Stanf. 57. c.

[c] It is ſaid in 2 R. 3. that every treaſon or felony includeth in it a miſpriſion of treaſon or felony. Therefore if any man knoweth of any high treaſon, he ought with as much ſpeed as conveniently he may to reveale the ſame to the king, or ſome of his privie councell, or any other magiſtrate. And miſpriſion in a large ſenſe is taken for many great offences which are neither treaſon nor felony, whereof we ſhall ſpeak more hereafter, being in this place reſtrained to miſpriſion of treaſon.

See John Coniers caſe, Dier 296. That the receiving of one that hath counterfeited the king's coine, and comforting of him knowing him to have counterfeited the king's coine, is but miſpriſion.

See more of Miſpriſion of Treaſon in the chapters of High Treaſon, and of Principall and Acceſſory.

CAP.

CAP. IV.

Felony by compaſſing or conſpiring to kill the King, or any Lord, or other of the King's Counſell.

NEXT hereunto we have thought good to ſpeak of the ſtatute of 3 H. 7. the letter of which law enſueth. 3 H. 7. cap. 14.

Item, FORASMUCH as by quarrels made to ſuch as have been in great authority, office, and of counſell with kings of this realme, hath enſued the deſtruction of kings, and the undoing of this realme; ſo as it hath appeared evidently, when compaſſing of the death of ſuch as were of the kings true ſubjects was had, the deſtruction of the prince was imagined thereby: and for the moſt part it hath growne, and been occaſioned by envie, and malice of the kings own houſhold-ſervants; as now of late ſuch a thing was likely to have enſued: * and for ſo much as by the law of this land, if actuall deeds be not had, there is no remedy for ſuch falſe compaſſings, imaginations, and confederacies had againſt any lord, or any of the kings counſell, or any of the kings great officers in his houſhold, as ſteward, treaſurer, and comptroller: and ſo great inconveniencies might enſue, if ſuch ungodly demeaning ſhould not be ſtraitly puniſhed before that actuall deed were done. Therefore it is ordained by the king, the lords ſpirituall and temporall, and the commons of the ſaid parliament aſſembled, and by authority of the ſame, That from hence forward, the ſteward, treaſurer, and comptroller of the kings houſe for the time being, or one of them, have full authority and power to enquire by twelve ſad men, and diſcreet perſons of the chequer roll of the kings honourable houſhold, if any ſervant admitted to be his ſervant ſworne, and his name put into the chequer roll of his houſhold, whatſoever he be, ſerving in any manner, office, or roome, reputed, had and taken, under the ſtate of a lord, make any confederacies, compaſſings, conſpiracies, or imaginations with any perſon or perſons, to deſtroy or murder the king, or any lord of this realme, or any other perſon ſworne to the kings counſell, ſteward, treaſurer, or comptroller of the kings houſe; that if it be found before the ſaid ſteward for the time being, by the ſaid twelve ſad men, that any ſuch of the kings ſervants as is aboveſaid, hath confederated, compaſſed, conſpired, or imagined, as is aboveſaid, that he ſo found by that inquiry, be put thereupon to anſwer. And the ſteward, treaſurer, and comptroller, or two of them have power to de-

* Nota.

termine

termine the ſame matter according to the law. And if he put him in triall, that then it be tried by other twelve ſad men of the ſame houſhold: and that ſuch miſdoers have no challenge, but for malice. And if ſuch miſdoers be found guilty by confeſſion, or otherwiſe, that the ſaid offence be judged felony, and they to have judgement and execution as felons attainted ought to have by the common law.

[38] This act divideth itſelf into two generall parts, viz. the preamble, and the body of the act. In the preamble three things are to be obſerved.

1. That by quarrels made to ſuch, as are in great authority, office, and of counſell with the kings of the realm, have enſued the deſtruction of the kings, and the undoing of the realm, as in the records of parliament, and hiſtories of king E. 2. R. 2. king H. 6. &c. you may read. And as king William Rufus was ſlain in the new foreſt by the glance of an arrow, ſo the overthrow of the king, &c. hath followed by glances, and conſequents, when the tow of deſtruction hath been aimed at the overthrow of thoſe, who were in great authority neer about, and dear to the king, not daring in direct manner to aim at the king himſelf. Therefore, the firſt concluſion is, that when the compaſſing of the death of ſuch, as were of the king's true ſubjects was had, the deſtruction of the prince was imagined thereby.

2. That for the moſt part, it hath grown by envy and malice by the king's own houſhold ſervants: and the reaſon thereof is, for that they being of the kings houſhold, have greater and readier means either by night, or by day to deſtroy ſuch as be of great authority, and neer about the king: and ſuch an attempt and conſpiracy was before this parliament made by ſome of this kings houſhold ſervants, and great miſchief was like thereupon to have enſued, which was the cauſe of the making of this act.

See before in the chapt. of High Treaſon. Verb. Overt Act.

3. The concluſion of the preamble is, that by the law of the land, if actuall deeds be not had, there is no remedy for ſuch falſe compaſſings, &c. This is a true declaration: for the bare conſpiracy of the death of any lord or other of the king's councell, or of the ſteward, treaſurer, or comptroller, unleſſe they had been ſlain indeed, was no felony before this act, and ſo reſolved upon the contempt and conſpiracy aforeſaid.

In the body of this act, ſix things are enacted. Firſt, that the offender muſt have three qualities. 1. He muſt be the kings ſervant ſworn. 2. His name muſt be put in the cheque roll of the kings houſhold. 3. He muſt be under the ſtate of a lord: and if he conſpire with any other, that is not of the kings houſhold, yet is the conſpiracy within this act, but he of the king's houſhold is only the felon within the purvien of this ſtatute, as it appeareth by the words of the ſtatute.

See before in the chapt. of high treaſon. Ubi ſup.

Secondly, againſt what perſons the offence made felony by this act is to be committed: and in number they be four. 1. To deſtroy or murder the king. By this act it expreſly appeareth by the judgement of the whole parliament, that beſides the confederacy, compaſſing, conſpiracy, or imagination, there muſt be ſome other overt act or deed tending thereunto, to make it treaſon within the ſtatute of 25 E. 3. And therefore the bare confederacy, compaſſing, conſpiracy, or imaginations by words only, is made felony by this act. But if the conſpirators doe provide any weapon, or other thing, to accompliſh their deviliſh intent; this and the like is an overt act to make it treaſon. 2. Any lord of this realme being ſworn of the kings councell: for by the purvien of this act, he muſt be alſo of the kings councell: this is underſtood of the kings privy councell, and ſo throughout the act. 3. Any other of the kings councell (that is, the kings privy councell) being under the degree of a lord. 4. The ſteward, treaſurer, and comptroller of the kings houſhold, being great officers, though they be not of the king's councell.

Thirdly, the third generall part expreſſeth the perſons to whom power is given to enquire and determine this felony. The ſteward, treaſurer, and comptroller, or any one of them may enquire. And they or two of them have power by this act to hear and determine the ſame: and though the words be for the inquiry, that they three, or any of them, &c. yet an indictment taken before two of them is good, becauſe it is for advancement of juſtice. And this act is in nature of a commiſſion to them, for other commiſſion they need not to have: and this you may ſee in divers other acts of parliament of like nature. If any the houſhold ſervants conſpire the death of the ſteward, treaſurer, and comptroller, yet by force of this act they are judges of the cauſe, and none other can be, and in that caſe, they will aſſiſt themſelves for their direction, with ſome grave and learned men in the laws. But if the death of any one of them be compaſſed, then it is more convenient that it be heard and determined before the other two.

18 E. 3. 1.
23 Aſſ. 17.
27 H. 6. 8.
27 H. 8. 13.

[39]

Fourthly, the fourth part ſetteth forth, firſt, how the inquiry, and after, the trial ſhall be made, that is, that the inquiry muſt be made by twelve ſad men and diſcreet perſons of the cheque roll of the kings houſhold: and when the offender hath pleaded not guilty, the tryall ſhall be by the like perſons. And here though this act limiteth the inquiry to be by twelve, yet if it be inquired of by more than twelve, the preſentment is good, but the tryall muſt be by twelve only.

Fifthly, no challenge ſhall be made, but for malice.

Sixthly, by the context of the whole act, the conſpiracy, that is to be heard and determined by this act, muſt be plotted to be done within the kings houſhold.

Vide lib. Plac. Coke fo. 482.

The offender againſt this ſtatute ſhall have the benefit of his clergy: for whenſoever felony is made by any ſtatute, and the benefit of clergy is not expreſsly taken away, the offender ſhall have his clergy.

See the ſtatute of 3 & 4 E. 6. whereby amongſt other things in ſome caſe it was high treaſon, and in ſome caſe felony, to intend, or goe about to kill, or impriſon any of the kings privy councell, &c. from which felony, the benefit of ſanctuary, and clergy was taken away: but theſe treaſons and felonies are repealed by the ſtatute of 1 Mar.

3 & 4 E. 6. ca. 5.

CAP.

CAP. V.

OF HERESIE.

CONCERNING herefie five things fall into confideration. Firft, who be the judges of herefie. Secondly, what fhall be adjudged herefie. Thirdly, what is the judgement upon a man convicted of herefie. Fourthly, what the law alloweth him to fave his life. Fifthly, what he fhall forfeit by judgement againft him.

[a] Bract. l. 3. fo. 123. & 124. in Conc' Oxon. Newburg. li. 2. ca. 13. 6 H. 3. Stow. Holl. 203. 2 H. 4. Rot. Parl. nu. 29 Sautries cafe.

Touching the firft, an heretique may be convicted [a] before the archbifhop and other bifhops, and other the clergy at a generall fynod, or convocation, as it appeareth both by our books, and by hiftory. See the ftatute of 25 H. 8. cap. 19. revived by 1 El. cap. 1.

[b] And the bifhop of every dioces may convict any for herefie, and fo might he have done before the ftatute of 2 H. 4. ca. 15. as it appeareth by the preamble of that act in thefe words.

Fitz. N. B. 269. a. 1 El. ca. 1. [b] Vid. 23 H. 8. ca. 9. F. N. B. Ubi fupra. 5 El. ca. 23. 10 H. 7. 17. b. Doct. & Stud. lib. 2. ca. 29. Br. 2. Mar. tit. Herefy 1.

Whereas the diocefans of the faid realme cannot by their jurifdiction fpirituall, without aid of the faid royall majefty, fufficiently correct the faid falfe and perverfe people, (i. heretiques named before) becaufe the faid falfe and perverfe people doe goe from dioces to dioces, and will not appear before the faid diocefans, but the fame diocefans and their jurifdiction fpirituall, and the keys of the church with the cenfures of the fame, doe utterly contemn and defpife.

Now that ftatute doth provide, that the diocefan of the fame place, fuch perfon or perfons, &c. may caufe to be arrefted, and under fafe cuftody in his prifons to be detained. From this act and other acts and authorities quoted in the margent, thefe two conclufions are to be gathered. Firft, that the diocefan hath jurifdiction of herefy, and fo it hath been put in ure in all queen Elizabeth's reign: and accordingly it was refolved by Flemming chief juftice, Tanfield chief baron, Williams, and Crook juftices, Hil. 9. Ja. R. in the cafe of Legate the heretique, and that upon a conviction before the ordinary of herefy, the writ of *de hæretico comburendo* doth lie. Secondly, that without the aid of that act of 2 H. 4. the diocefan could imprifon no perfon accufed of herefy, but was to proceed againft him by the cenfures of the church. And now feeing, that not only the faid act of 2 H. 4. but 25 H. 8. c. 14. are repealed, the diocefan cannot imprifon any perfon accufed of herefy, but muft proceed againft him, as he might have done before thofe ftatutes, by the cenfures of the church, as it appeareth by the faid act of 2 H. 4. c. 15. Likewife the fuppofed ftatute of 5 R. 2. c. 5. and the ftatutes of 2 H. 5. c. 7. 25 H. 8. c. 14. 1 & 2 Ph. and Mar. c. 6. are all repealed, fo as no ftatute made againft heretiques ftandeth now in force;

[40] Mat. Hammond Anno 21 El. Holl. 1579. Stowe. 1161. Hil. 9. Ja. Regis Legates cafe.

Vide 1. E. 6. c. 21. 1 El. c. 1.

force: and at this day no perfon can be indicted, or impeached for herefy before any temporall judge, or other, that hath temporall jurifdiction, as upon perufall of the faid ftatutes appeareth.

Every archbifhop of this realme may cite any perfon dwelling in any bifhops dioces within his province for caufes of herefy, if the bifhop, or other ordinary immediate thereunto confent, or if that the fame bifhop, or other immediate ordinary, or judge doe not his duty in punifhment of the fame. 23 H. 8. ca. 9.

2. Touching the fecond point, if any perfon be charged with herefy before the high commiffioners, they have no authority to adjudge any matter or caufe to be herefy, but only fuch, as hath been fo adjudged by the authority of the canonicall fcripture, or by the firft four generall councells, or by any other generall councell, wherein the fame was declared herefie by the expreffe and plain words of the canonicall fcripture, or fuch as fhall hereafter be determined to be herefy by parliament, with the affent of the convocation: for fo it is expreflly provided by the faid act of 1 El. And albeit this provifo extendeth only to the faid high commiffioners, yet feeing in the high commiffion, there be fo many bifhops, and other divines, and learned men, it may ferve for a good direction to others, efpecially to the diocefan, being a fole judge in fo weighty a caufe.

No manner of order, act, or determination for any matter of religion, or caufe ecclefiafticall, had or made by the authority of the parliament in *anno* 1 El. fhall be accepted, deemed, interpreted, or adjudged herefy, fchifm, or fchifmaticall opinion, any order, decree, fentence, conftitution, or law (whatfoever the fame be) notwithftanding. 1 El. ca. 1.

There was a ftatute fuppofed to be made in 5 R. 2. that commiffions fhould be by the lord chancellor made, and directed to fherifs, and others, to arreft fuch as fhould be certified into the chancery by the bifhops, and prelates, * mafters of divinity, to be preachers of herefies, and notorious errors, their fautors, maintainers, and abetters, and to hold them in ftrong prifon, until they will juftifie themfelves to the law of holy church. By colour of this fuppofed act, [a] certaine perfons, that held, that images were not to be worfhipped, &c. were holden in ftrong prifon, until they (to redeem their vexation) miferably yeelded before thefe mafters of divinity to take an oath, and did fwear to worfhip images, [b] which was againft the morall and eternall law of Almighty God. We have faid (by colour of the faid fuppofed ftatute, &c.) not only in refpect of the faid opinion, but in refpect alfo, that the faid fuppofed act, was in truth never any act of parliament, though it was entred in the rolls of the parliament, for that the commons never gave their confent thereunto. And therefore in the [c] next parliament, the commons preferred a bill reciting the faid fuppofed act, and conftantly affirmed, that they never affented thereunto, and therefore defired that the faid fuppofed ftatute might be anienti\ed, and declared to be void: for they protefted, that it was never their intent to be juftified, and to bind themfelves and their fucceffors to the prelates, more then their anceftors had done in times paft: and hereunto the king gave his royall affent in thefe words, *Y pleift au roy*. And mark well the manner of the penning the act: for feeing the commons did not affent thereunto, the words of the act be,

5 R. 2. ftat. 2. cap. 5. repealed by 1 E. 6. c. 12. & 1 Eliz. ca. 1.
* *In diebus illis* Mafters of divinity (and batchelors of divinity) now doctors of divinity and batchelors.
[a] Rot. clauf. 19 R. 2. m. 17. in Dorf.
[b] Exod. 20. 4. Levit. 26. 1. Deut. 5. 8. & 16. 22. Pfal. 97. 7. 1 John 5. 21.
[c] Rot. Parl. 6 R. 2. nu. 62. *Vide* 7 H. 4. nu. 62. Rot. Parl.

[41]

It is ordained and affented in this prefent parliament, that, &c. And fo it was, being but by the king and the lords.

It is to be known, that of ancient time, when any acts of parliament were made, to the end the fame might be publifhed, and underftood, efpecially before the ufe of printing came into England, the acts of parliament were ingroffed into parchment, and bundled up together with a writ in the king's name, under the great feal to the fherif of every county, fometime in Latin, and fometime in French, to command the fherif to proclaim the faid ftatutes within his bayliwick, as well within liberties, as without. And this was the courfe of parliamentary proceedings, before printing came in ufe in England, and yet it continued after we had the print, till the reign of H. 7.

Now at the parliament holden in 5 R. 2. John Braibrook bifhop of London being lord chancellor of England, caufed the faid ordinance of the king and lords to be inferted into the parliamentary writ of proclamation to be proclaimed amongft the acts of parliament: which writ I have feen, the purclofe of which writ, after the recitall of the acts directed to the fherif of N. is in thefe words. *Nos volentes dictas concordias, five ordinationes in omnibus et fingulis fuis articulis inviolabiliter obfervari, tibi præcipimus quòd prædictas concordias, five ordinationes in locis infra balivam tuam, ubi melius expedire volueris, tam infra libertates, quam extra, publicè proclamari, et teneri facias juxta formam prænotatam. Tefte rege apud Weftm. 26 May, anno regni regis R. 2. 5.* But in the parliamentary proclamation of the acts paffed in *anno* 6 R. 2. the faid act of 6 R. 2. whereby the faid fuppofed act of 5 R. 2. was declared to be void, is omitted: and afterwards the faid fuppofed act of 5 R. 2. was continually printed, and the faid act of 6 R. 2. hath by the prelates been ever from time to time kept from the print.

Coram Rege Hil. 1 H. 5. Rot. 4. & 5.

Certain men called Lollards were indicted for herefy, upon the faid ftatute of 2 H. 4. for thefe opinions, viz. *Quod non eft meritorium ad Sanctum Thomam, nec ad Sanctam Mariam de Walfingham peregrinari. 2. Nec imagines crucifixi et aliorum fanctorum adorare. 3. Nulli facerdoti confiteri nifi foli Deo, &c.* Which opinions were fo far from herefy, as the makers of the ftatute of 1 Eliz. had great caufe to limit what herefy was.

Indictment generall. *Vide fupra* ca. 1. *Verbo, per overt fait.* *Lollardi et falfi hæretici.*

And afterwards they thought not good to contain thefe opinions in any indictment, but indicted them in general words, one of which indictments as to lollardry and herefy followeth. *Jurati dicunt fuper eorum facramentum, quod A. R. E. D. Lollardi et falfi hæretici die Jovis poft hebdomadam Pafchæ, anno regni regis H. 6. poft conqueftum nono, apud Abendon in com' Berks infra villg. falfò et proditoriè ut communes proditores, et infurrectores confpiraverunt, imaginati fuerunt, et ad invicem confœderaverunt cum quamplurimis proditoribus illis affociatis, et felonibus de eorum comitiva, et eorum falfa malitia præcogitata, ut communes infidiatores altarum viarum, ad fidem catholicam deftruendam, et ibidem falfò et proditoriè ut communes proditores, et felones dicti d'ni regis fecerunt, et fcripferunt diverfas falfas billas, et fcripturas feditiofas, et nonnulla fidei et doctrinæ Chriftianæ contraria continentes, et eas populo domini regis publicandas et credendas falfò, damnabiliter in diverfis locis, viz. in civitatibus London, Sarum, et villis de Coventria et Marleburgh, nequiter pofuerunt, fixerunt, et projecerunt, ac indies fic fcribere, affigere et projicere et ponere non ceffant, nec formidant, in graviffimam*

Communes infidiatores viarum. *Vide* fup. c. 1. f. 5. *Ad fidem catholicam deftruendam. Diverfas falfas billas et fcripturas, &c.*

mam majeftatis, et coronæ dignitatis regis noftri offenfam, et Chriftianæ fidei ludibrium, et pacis dicti domini regis perturbationem, et omnium Chrifti fidelium injuriam et contemptum. Which generall indictment, and all other of like form were utterly infufficient in law: for albeit the words of the ftatute be generall, yet the indictment muft contain certainty, whereunto the party indicted may have an anfwer. Alfo where the parties are indicted, *ut communes infidiatores viarum*, that alfo is infufficient, as it appeareth by the ftatute 4 H. 4. ca. 2.

John Keyfer was excommunicated by the greater excommunication before Thomas archbifhop of Canterbury, and legate of the apoftolique fee, at the fuit of another, for a reafonable part of goods, and fo remained eight months: the faid Keyfer openly affirmed that the faid fentence was not to be feared, neither did he fear it. And albeit the archbifhop, or his commiffary hath excommunicated me, yet before God I am not excommunicated: and he faid that he fpake nothing but the truth, and it fo appeared; for that he the laft harveft ftanding fo excommunicate, had as great plenty of wheat, and other grain, as any of his neighbours, faying to them in fcorn (as was urged againft him) that a man excommunicate fhould not have fuch plenty of wheat. The archbifhop denying thefe words to be within the faid act of 2 H. 4. did by his warrant in writing comprehending the faid caufe, by pretext of the faid act commit the body of the faid Keyfer to the gaol at Maidftone, for that (faith he) in refpect of the publifhing of the faid words, *dictum Iohannem non immeritò habemus de hærefi fufpectum.* By reafon whereof the faid John Keyfer was imprifoned in Maidftone gaol, and in prifon detained under the cuftody of the keeper there, untill by his counfell he moved fir John Markham then chief juftice of England, and other the judges of the king's bench, to have an *Habeas corpus*, and thereupon (as it ought) an *Habeas corpus* was granted: upon which writ the gaoler returned the faid caufe, and fpeciall matter, and withall, according to the writ, had his body there. The court upon mature deliberation perufing the faid ftatute, (and upon conference with divines) refolved, that upon the faid words Keyfer was not to be fufpect of herefy, within the faid ftatute, as the archbifhop took it. And therefore the court firft bayled him, and after he was delivered: for that the archbifhop had no power by the faid act for thofe words to commit him to prifon.

[42] Mich. 5 E. 4. Rot. 143. Coram Rege. In rationabili parte bonorum.

Hillary Warner being an inhabitant within the parifh of S. Dunftans in the Weft, held opinion and publifhed there, and in divers other places, *quòd non tenebatur folvere aliquas decimas curatori five ecclefiæ parochiali ubi inhabitabat.* Whereupon Richard bifhop of London commanded Edward Vaughan and others to arreft the faid Hillary Warner: by force whereof they did arreft him, and detained him in prifon a day and a night, and then he efcaped. Hillary Warner brought his action of falfe imprifonment againft Edward Vaughan and others: in bar whereof the defendants pleaded the ftatute of 2 H. 4. and that the plaintif held and publifhed the opinion aforefaid; which opinion was, *contra fidem catholicam, feu determinationem fanctæ ecclefiæ*, and that the defendants, as fervants to the faid bifhop, and by his commandment did arreft the plaintif, and juftified the imprifonment: whereupon Hillary Warner the plaintiff demurred in law, and after long and mature deli-

Mich. 11. H. 7. Rot. 327. In communi banco.

beration it was by Brian chief juftice, and the whole court of common pleas adjudged, that the faid opinion was not within the faid ftatute of 2 H. 4. for that it was an error, but no herefy. Which I have the rather reported, for that the reporter of this cafe did not only mifreport the time of the bringing of the action, but the ftatute, which was the ground of the matter in law, and leaveth out the judgement. The record it felf is worthy the reading.

Hil. 10 H. 7. f. 17.

Upon that which hath been faid touching the faid ftatute of 2 H. 4. four conclufions doe neceffary follow. Firft, that feeing, that many opinions were by the bifhops taken to be herefy, which in troth had no fhadow of herefy, and fo miftaken, and unjuftly extended by the bifhops further than the purvien, and true intention thereof, as by that which hath been, and might be faid, appeared, the makers of the faid act of parliament of 1 El. had great reafon to limit (as hath been faid) what opinions fhould be judged herefy by authority of that commiffion grounded upon that act. Secondly, that if any ecclefiafticall judge or commiffioner fhall by pretext of any ftatute, or other caufe, commit any man to prifon, upon motion in court on the behalf of the party imprifoned, the judges of the common law ought to grant an *Habeas corpus* for him: upon the retorn of which writ, if it fhall appear to the judges, that the imprifonment is well warranted by law, the party fhall be remanded: and if the imprifonment be without warrant of law, then the party ought to be delivered. Thirdly, if the imprifonment be not warranted by law, the party imprifoned may have his action of falfe imprifonment, and recover his damages. Fourthly, that when an act of parliament is made concerning matter meerly fpirituall, as herefie, &c. yet that act being part of the lawes of the realm, the fame fhall be conftrued and interpreted by the judges of the common lawes, who ufually confer with thofe that are learned in that profeffion. But let us now defcend to the third point.

See in the fecond part of the Inftitutes, the expofition upon the ftatute of *Artic. Cleri*, the refolution of all the judges of England to the 21 and 22 articles, or objections.

[43]

3. To the third. [a] It appeareth by Bracton, Britton, Fleta, Stanford, and all our books, that he that is duly convict of herefie, fhall be burnt to death.

4. To the fourth. [b] The ecclefiafticall judge at this day cannot commit the perfon that is convict of herefie to the fheriffe, albeit he be prefent, to be burnt; but muft have the king's writ *de hæretico comburendo*, according to the common law: for now all acts of parliament (as hath been faid before) againft hereticks are repealed. And the reafon wherefore herefie is fo extremely and fearfully punifhed, is, for that *gravius eft æternam, quam temporalem lædere majeftatem:* and *hærefis eft lepra animæ.* [c] The party duly convicted of herefie, may recall, and abjure his opinion, and thereby fave his life, but a relapfe is fatall: for as in cafe of a difeafe of the body, after recovery, recidivation is extremely dangerous: fo in cafe of herefie (a difeafe of the foule) a relapfe is irrecoverable. And as he that is a leper of his body, is to be removed from the fociety of men, left he fhould infect them, by the king's writ *de leprofo amovendo:* fo he that hath *lepram animæ*, that is, to be convicted of herefie, fhall be cut off, left he fhould poyfon others, by the king's writ *de hæretico comburendo.* But if the heretick will not after conviction abjure, he may by force of the faid writ [d] *de hæretico comburendo* be burnt without abjuration.

3. As to the fifth. [e] The ftatute made in the 2 year of H. 5. cap.

[a] Mir. cap. 4. de Majeftie. Bracton, ubi fupra. Britton, cap. 9. Fleta lib. 1. ca. 35. Regifter. F. N. B. 269.

[b] F. N. B. 269. Rot. Par. 2 H. 4. nu. 29. Sautryes cafe. Bre. de hæretico comburendo per regem & concilium in parliamento.

[c] 2 Mar. tit. herefie, Br. 7.

[d] 2 Mar. ubi fupra.

[e] Vid. Doct. et Stud. lib. 2. ca. 29.

cap. 7. whereby the forfeiture of lands in fee-simple, and goods, and chattels was given in case of heresie, standeth repealed by the act of 1 Eliz. cap. 1. The books that speak of this forfeiture are grounded upon the said act of 2 H. 5. which then stood in force, saving 5 R 2. which was before that statute: for there, though Belknap swore, *per ma foy si home soit miscreant, sa terre est forfeitable, et le seigniour avera ceo p. voy descheate;* yet was his opinion never holden for law: for neither lands, nor goods [f] before the making of that statute of 2 H. 5. were forfeited by the conviction of heresie, because the proceeding therein is meerely spirituall, *pro salute animæ*, and in a court that is no court of record. And therefore the conviction of heresie worketh no forfeiture of any thing that is temporall, viz. of lands or goods. [g] For what cause the said hereticks were called Lollards you may read in Caudries case, and Linwood thereto agreeth. * And it is to be observed, that in proceeding against Lollards, the prelats, besides their opinions, did charge them with hainous offences: as conspiracy with multitudes of people, insurrection, rebellion, or some other treason, or great crimes.

Br. tit. Forfeiture 112. Stan. pl. cor. 35. I. 2 Mar. Br. tit. Heresie.

[f] Vid. hereafter in case of piracy.

[g] Lib. 5. Caudries case, fol. 25. b.

* 1 H. 5. fo. 6. a. Rot. Parl. 5 H. 5. nu. 11. in the case of Sir *John Oldcastle*. Pasch. 9 H. 6. *John Sharps case*, &c. Rot. Parl. 7 H. 4. nu. 67. 11 H. 4. nu. 29. 3 H. 5. nu. 39. 1 H. 6. nu. 20.

We have spoken thus much of this argument, because there be divers wandring opinions concerning some of these points, that are not agreeable to the law, as it standeth at this day. See the fourth part of the Institutes, cap. Chancery, in the articles against Cardinal Woolsey, artic. 44.

CAP. VI.

Of Felony by Conjuration, Witchcraft, Sorcery, or Inchantment.

THE first act of parliament that made any of these offences felony, was the statute [a] of 33 H. 8. which was repealed by the statutes of 1 E. 6. cap. 12. and 1 Mariæ. But [b] before the conquest it was severely punished: sometimes by death, sometimes by exile, &c. [c] And after, it was made felony by the statute of 5 Eliz. and againe by 1 Jac. which repealeth 5 Eliz.

[a] 33 H. 8. ca. 8. 1 E. 6. cap. 12.

[b] Inter leges Alveredi, fo. 23. Edwardi et Guthruni, cap. 11. Ethelstani, ca. 6. Canuti, 4, 5.

[c] 5 Eliz. ca. 16. 1 Jac. cap. 12.

A conjurer is he that by the holy and powerfull names of Almighty God invokes and conjures the devill to consult with him, or to do some act.

A conjurer described.

A witch is a person that hath conference with the devill, to consult with him or to do some act.

A witch described.

An inchanter, *incantator*, is he, or she *qui carminibus, aut cantiunculis dæmonem adjurat*. They were of ancient time called *carmina*, because in those dayes their charmes were in verse.

An inchanter described.

Carminibus Circe socios mutavit Ulyssis.
By charmes in rhyme (O cruell fates!)
Circe transform'd Ulysses mates.

And again. *Carmina de cœlo possunt detrudere lunam.*
By rhymes they can pul down full soon,
From lofty sky the wandring moon.

* A sorcerer, *sortilegus, quia utitur sortibus in cantationibus dæmonis.*

* A sorcerer described.

Exod. cap. 22. 17. Deut. ca. 18. 10, 11, 12. Num. ca. 23. 23. 1 Reg. ca. 15. 23.

monis. Thou ſhalt not ſuffer a witch to live. *Non eſt augurium in Jacob, nec divinatio in Iſrael.* And the Holy Ghoſt hath compared the great offence of rebellion to the ſinne of witchcraft.

And here it juſtly may be demanded, what puniſhment was againſt theſe deviliſh and wicked offenders before theſe ſtatutes, which were made of very late time.

[d] Linwood de officio arch-preſb. § Ignorantia.

* Mir. cap. 1. §. 5. & cap. 2. § 12. & cap. 4. § De majeſtie. Brit. fo. 16 b. & 71. F. N. B. 269. b.

And it appeareth by our ancient [d] books that theſe horrible and deviliſh offenders, which left the everliving God, and ſacrificed to the devill, and thereby committed idolatry, in ſeeking advice and aide of him, were puniſhed by death. * The Mirror ſaith, *Que ſorcery et devinal ſont members de hereſie.* And there he deſcribeth hereſie. *Hereſie eſt un mauvaſe et faux creance ſurdant de error en la droit foy Chriſtien:* and after ſaith, *Le judgement de hereſie eſt dec arſe in cendre.* And herewith agreeth Britton: *Sorcerers, ſorcereſſes, &c. et miſcreants ſoient arſes.* And Fleta: *Chriſtiani autem apoſtatæ, ſortilegi, et hujuſmodi detractari debent, et combari.* And burning then was, and yet is the puniſhment for hereticks. So as the conuſance of theſe offences, if they be branches of hereſie, (as the law was then taken) belonged (as to this day hereſie doth) to eccleſiaſticall judges. In which caſe when they have given ſentence, there lieth a writ *de hæretico comburendo.*

[e] Int. leges Edw. ca. 11. fo. 55. & Ethelſtani ca. 6. fo. 60. & Canuti cap. 5. fo. 5.

45 E. 3. 17. b.

I have ſeen a report of a caſe in an ancient Regiſter, that in October *anno* 20 H. 6. Margery Gurdeman of Eye, in the county of Suffolk, was for witchcraft and conſultation with the devill, after ſentence and a relapſe, burnt by the king's writ *de hæretico comburendo.* [e] And this agreeth with antiquity, for witches, &c. by the laws before the conqueſt were burnt to death.

*Some think that this ſhould be the oath of allegiance, *Que il ſerra foiall et loiall, &c.* Vid. 25 E. 3. 42. B. Coron. 131. See hereafter ca. 74. of perjury, verb. That as well the judge, &c.

[45]

A man was taken in Southwark with a head and a face of a dead man, and with a book of ſorcery in his male, and was brought into the king's bench before Sir John Knevett then chief juſtice: but ſeeing no indictment was againſt him, the clerks did ſwear him, that from thenceforth * he ſhould not be a ſorcerer, and was delivered out of priſon, and the head of the dead man and the book of ſorcery were burnt at Tuthill at the coſts of the priſoner. So as the head and his book of ſorcery had the ſame puniſhment, that the ſorcerer ſhould have had by the ancient law, if he had by his ſorcery praied in aid of the devill.

1 Chron. chap. 10. v. 13, 14. 1 Reg 15. 23. * Nota. 1 Reg. 28. 8.

The holy hiſtory hath a moſt remarkable place concerning the reprobation and death of king Saul. *Mortuus eſt ergo Saul propter iniquitates ſuas, eò quòd prævaricatus ſit mandatum Domini, et non cuſtodierit illud,* * *ſed inſuper Pythoniſſam conſuluerit, nec ſperaverit in Domino, propter quod interfecit eum, et tranſtulit regnum ejus ad David filium Iſai.* So Saul died for his tranſgreſſion which he committed againſt the Lord, even againſt the word of the Lord which he kept not: and alſo for aſking counſell of one that had a familiar ſpirit, to enquire of it, and enquired not of the Lord; therefore he ſlew him, and turned the kingdome unto David the ſonne of Iſai.

Therefore it had been a great defect in government, if ſo great an abomination had paſſed with impunity. And this is the cauſe, that we have proved how and in what manner conjuration, witchcraft, &c. were puniſhed by death, &c. before the making of the ſaid late ſtatutes.

1 Jac. cap. 12.

But now let us peruſe the ſtatute made in the firſt year of king

James, which only ſtandeth in force, and divideth itſelf into five ſeverall branches.

1. If any perſon or perſons ſhall uſe, practiſe, or exerciſe any invocation or conjuration of any evill and wicked ſpirit.

Here the devill by the holy, and powerfull names of Almighty God is invoked (as hath been ſaid:) and this invocation, or conjuration of a wicked ſpirit is felony, without any other act or thing, ſave only the apparition of the ſpirit. See W. 1. cap. 41. in the oath of the champion, &c.

2. Or ſhall conſult, covenant with, entertaine, employ, feed, or reward, any evill or wicked ſpirit, to, or for any intent or purpoſe.

By this branch, if any conſult, &c. (howſoever the wicked ſpirit appeareth and commeth) theſe actions (here mentioned) with or to that wicked ſpirit, to or for any intent or purpoſe, is felony without any other act or thing.

3. Or take up any dead man, woman, or childe, out of his, her, or their grave, or any other place where the dead body reſteth, or the ſkin, bone, or any part of a dead perſon, to be imployed or uſed in any manner of witchcraft, ſorcery, charme, or inchantment.

Albeit the offender that commits theſe barbarous and inhumane dealings with the bodies of the dead, do not actually imploy or uſe them in witchcraft, ſorcery, charme, or inchantment: yet if he did them of purpoſe to uſe therein, it is felony, for the words of this branch be, [to be imployed or uſed in any manner of witchcraft, &c.]

4. Or ſhall uſe, practiſe, or exerciſe any witchcraft, inchantment, charme or ſorcery, whereby any perſon ſhall be killed, deſtroyed, waſted, conſumed, pined, or lamed, in his, or her bodie, or any part thereof.

By this branch, no other witchcraft, inchantment, charme, or ſorcery (then is before ſpecified) is felony, unleſſe by means thereof ſome perſon be killed, deſtroied, waſted, conſumed, pined or lamed, &c. Which words have reference only to this laſt generall clauſe.

5. That then every ſuch offender or offenders, their aiders, abetters, and counſellors, being of any the ſaid offences duly and lawfully convicted, and attainted, ſhall ſuffer paines of death, as a felon, or felons, and ſhall loſe the priviledge, and benefit of clergie, and ſanctuary.

Albeit accessories before be here specially named, yet accessories after may be of this felony, as afterwards is said upon the statute of 3 H. 7. for taking away of women, and upon the statute of 8 H. 6. for stealing of records.

The second part of this act concerneth felony in a second degree; and the branches thereof are also in number five.

[46] 1. If any person or persons take upon him or them by witchcraft, inchantment, charme, or sorcery, to tell or declare, in what place any treasure of gold or silver should or might be found, or had in the earth, or other secret places.

The mischiefs before this part of the act was: That divers impostors, men and women would take upon them to tell, or do, these five things here specified, in great deceipt of the people, and cheating and cousening them of their money, or other goods. Therefore was this part of the act made, wherein these words [take upon him or them] are very remarkable. For if they take upon them, &c. though in truth they do it not, nor can do it, yet are they in danger of this first branch.

2. Or where goods, or other things lost, or stoln should be found or become.

Herein they become offenders, if they take upon them as aforesaid. And note, the taking upon them, to tell and declare, governe both these branches.

3. Or to the intent to provoke any person to unlawfull love.

Herein also they become offenders, by taking upon them, as is aforesaid. Here is the change of a new verbe, viz. [to provoke] so as the sense is, if any person or persons shall take upon him or them by witchcraft, inchantment, charme or sorcery, to the intent, to provoke any person to unlawfull love.

4. Or whereby any cattel or goods of any person shall be destroyed.

The letter of this branch is this: If any person shall take upon him by witchcraft, inchantment, charm, or sorcery, whereby any cattell or goods of any person should be destroyed. Although this be not sententious, yet the meaning thereof is to be taken, by supplying these words after sorcery [any thing] and not to turn [destroyed] into the infinitive mood, as the rest be; for then it satisfied not the meaning of the makers: for a taking upon them to destroy cattel, &c. if they be not destroyed, is not within the danger of this act, and therefore must be supplied as is aforesaid.

5. Or to hurt or destroy any person in his or her body, although the same be not effected or done.

As

As in the caſe of cattel or goods, the deſtruction muſt be (as is aforeſaid) effected and done: ſo in caſe of the perſon of man, woman, or childe, though the hurt be not effected, or done; yet is the taking upon him, &c. to hurt or deſtroy any perſon, &c. within this branch.

Being therefore lawfully convicted.

Here [convicted] is taken in a large ſenſe for attainted, and the rather, for that after in this act the words be [lawfully convicted and attainted, as is aforeſaid.]

Shall for the ſaid offence, &c.

Here are expreſſed the puniſhments inflicted upon theſe impoſtors, mountebanks, and cheating quackſalvers, viz. 1. To ſuffer impriſonment by the ſpace of a whole year without bail or mainprize. 2. Once every quarter of the year theſe mountebanks are to mount the pillory, and to ſtand thereupon in ſome market towne ſix houres, and there to confeſs his or her error, and offence.

And if any perſon being once convicted of the ſame offences, &c.

Here is alſo [convicted] taken for attainted, for he ſhall not be drawn in queſtion for the ſecond offence, to make it felony, till judgement be given againſt him for the firſt; for the indictment of felony recites the former attainder, and the ſecond offence muſt be committed after the judgement. And ſo it is in the caſe of forgery upon the ſtatute of 5 Eliz. and in caſe of conveighing of ſheep alive out of this realme, and ſome others. 5 Eliz. cap. 14. 8 Eliz. cap. 3.

Saving to the wife of ſuch perſon as ſhall offend in any thing contrary to this act, her title of dower, and alſo to the heire and ſucceſſor of every perſon, his or their titles of inheritance, ſucceſſion, and other rights, as though no ſuch attainder of the anceſtor or predeceſſor had been made.] [47]

The judgement againſt a felon is, that he be hanged by the neck until he be dead: and albeit nothing elſe is expreſſed in the judgement, yet by the common law many things are therein implied; as the loſſe of his wives dower, the loſſe of his inheritance, corruption of his blood, forfeiture of his goods, &c. Now a ſaving will ſerve for any thing, that is implied in the judgement, as in this caſe for the wives dower, and alſo for the heirs inheritance, and for all the reſt of the things implied in the judgement. But a ſaving will not ſerve againſt the expreſſe judgement in caſe of felony, for that ſhould be repugnant; as ſaving the life of the offender ſhould be void, becauſe it is repugnant to the expreſſe judgement, viz. that he be hanged by the neck until he be dead. Alſo where the ſaving is to the heir, it is well ſaved by the name of the heir, becauſe notwithſtanding the forfeiture implied in the judgement, his inheritance is ſaved, and by conſequent the blood not corrupted, for if

See the 1. part of the Inſtitutes. ſect. 747.

Vide lib. 1. in the caſe of Alton Woods. fo.

if the blood were corrupted, he could not inherit as heir, but notwithstanding this ſaving the lands are forfeited during his life.

5 El. cap. 14.

The ſtatute of 5 Eliz. for preſervation of the wives dower, and the heirs inheritance, in caſe of forgery, is penned in this form. Provided alway, that ſuch attainder of felony ſhall not in any wiſe extend to take away the dower of the wife of any ſuch perſon attaint: nor to the corruption of blood, or diſheriſon of any heir or heirs of any ſuch perſon attaint.

8 El. ca. 3.

The words of the ſtatute of 8 Eliz. be, Provided always that this act ſhall not extend to corruption of blood, or be prejudiciall or hurtfull to any woman claiming dower by or from any ſuch offender, &c. Wherein it is to be obſerved, that by the avoidance of corruption of blood, the inheritance is impliedly ſaved. See the manner of the penning of the act of 31 Eliz. concerning this matter and divers others.

31 El. ca. 4.

See the ſtatute of 3. Ja. ca. 4.

And ſurely it is very convenient that when new felonies be made by act of parliament, that ſuch ſavings or proviſions be made both for the wives dower, and the heirs inheritance, as were had and made in theſe preſidents.

CAP. VII.

OF MURDER.

[a] See the 1. pt. of the Inſtit. for the word Murder, ſect. 287. and for Felony, ſect. 500 & 745. See the 2. part of Inſtit. Marlbr. ca. 25. Cuſt. de Norm. cap. 68.

HAVING [a] now paſſed High Treaſon, Petit Treaſon, Miſpriſion of Treaſon, Felony by the ſtatute of 3 H. 7. Hereſy, and Conjuration, Witchcraft, &c. we are next in order to treat of felonies in general: and of all felonies, murder is the moſt hainous. *Inter leges Canuti*, ca. 61. fo. 118. *Cædes manifeſtæ numerantur inter ſcelera nullo humano jure expiabilia.* See here, ca. Pardon. And of all murders, murder by poyſoning is the moſt deteſtable. Therefore firſt of murder. *Murdrum* is derived of the Saxon word *mord.*

[b] *The definition of murder.* Vid. devant. ca. Treaſon. verb. Quant home, &c. Bract. l. 3. fo. 120, 121, 134, 135. Brit. fo. 5. 18. Fleta, lib. 1. cap. 23. & 30. Mirror, cap. 1. §. ca. 2. § 11. de Appeal de homicide. Tr. 32 E. 1. Coram Rege Rot. 15. 25 E. 3. 28. 26 Aſſ. p. 27. 3 E 3. cor. 383. 3 H. 7. ca. 1. 3 H. 7. 1. 12. 21 H. 7. 31. E. 2. Coron. 389. 1 Ma. Dier, 104. b. See the firſt part of the Inſtit. 104.

[b] Murder is when a man of ſound memory, and of the age of diſcretion, unlawfully killeth within any county of the realm any reaſonable creature *in rerum natura* under the king's peace, with malice fore-thought, either expreſſed by the party, or implied by law, ſo as the party wounded, or hurt, &c. die of the wound, or hurt, &c. within a year and a day after the ſame.

Hereof we will ſpeak, together with ſome things concerning the acceſſories to the ſame, and leave the reſidue to others, that have written thereof. Now let us examine the principal parts of this deſcription.

[48]

Tr. 31. E. 3. Coram rege. Rot. 54. per morſ. canis.

Killing.] As by poyſon, weapon ſharp or blunt, gun, croſsbow, cruſhing, bruiſing, ſmothering, ſuffocating, ſtrangling, drowning, burning, burying, famiſhing, throwing down, inciting a dog, a dog, or bear, &c. to bite, or hurt, &c. whereof death ensueth, laying a sick man in the cold, &c.

Poyson, (*Venenum, à venis, quia à venis permeat*) is, as hath been said, the most detestable of all, because it is most horrible, and fearfull to the nature of man, and of all others can be least prevented, either by manhood, or providence: and that made Fleta to say, *Item nec per patriam se defendere debet quis de veneno dato, sed tantum per corpus suum, eo quod initium facti non fuit tam publicum, quod sciri poterit à patria, &c.* but that is not holden for law at this day.

Bract. l. 3. f. 121. Brit. fo. 14. See lib. Intr. Coke 25. lib. 4. fo. 44. Vauxes case. Lib. 9. fo. 81. Agnes Gores case.

[a] This offence was so odious, that by act of parliament it was made high treason, and inflicted a more grievous and lingring death then the common law prescribeth, viz. That the offender should be boyled to death in hot water: upon which statute [b] Margaret Davy a young woman was attainted of high treason for poysoning of her mistris, and some others were boyled to death in Smithfield the 17 day of March in the same yeer. But this act was too severe to live long, and therefore was repealed by 1 E. 6. cap. 12. and 1 Mar. cap. 1.

Deut. 28. 24. Cursed is he that smiteth his neighbour secretly.

[a] 22 H. 8. ca. 9. Read the statute. Dier, 33 H. 8. fol. 50. a. Saccombes case.

All the ancient authors, *ubi supra*, of old time defined murder to be, *occulta hominis occisio, &c.* when it was done in secret, so as the offender was not known: but now it is taken in a larger sense.

[b] Anno 33 H. 8.

Britton mentioneth another kind of murder (which is not holden for murder at this day) when he saith: *Ceux auxi que fauxement pur lower, ou en auter manner eunt ascun home damne ou fait damner au mort, &c.* yet this is murder before God. And David killed Uriah with his pen, and these men with their tongue.

Britton, fo. 14.

Within any county of the realm.] [c] If two of the kings subjects goe over into a forain realm and fight there, and the one kill the other, this murder being done out of the realm, cannot be for want of triall heard and determined by the common law: [d] but it may be heard and determined before the constable and marshall.

[c] 13 H. 4. 5 & 6. Stanf. pl. cor. 65. Mic. 25 & 26 El. so resolved in Dowties case.

[d] 13 R. 2. ca. 2. 1 H. 4. c. 14. Rot. Parl. 8 H. 6. nu. 38.

If A. give B. a mortal wound in a forain country, B. commeth into England and dieth: this cannot be tried by the common law, because the stroak was given there, where no *visne* can come, but the same shall be heard and determined before the constable and marshall: for the words of the statute of 13 R. 2. be: To the constable it pertaineth to have conusance of contracts, concerning deeds of arms, or of war out of the realm, and also of things that touch arms, or war within the realm, which cannot be determined or discussed by the common law.

13 R. 2. ca. 2.

If a man be strucken upon the high sea, and dieth of the same stroke upon the land, this cannot be inquired of by the common law, because no *visne* can come from the place, where the stroke was given (though it were within the sea pertaining to the realm of England, and within the liegeance of the king) because it is not within any of the counties of the realm. Neither can the admirall hear and determine this murder, because though the stroke was within his jurisdiction, yet the death was *infra corpus comitatus*, whereof he cannot inquire: neither is it within the statute of 28 H. 8. because the murder was not committed on the sea. But by the said act of 13 R. 2. the constable and marshall may hear and determine the same. And before the making of the statute of 2 E. 6. if

Lib. 2. fo. 93. Tr. 25 Eliz. in Lacyes case. Fortescue, ca. 32. fo. 38.

28 H 8. ca. 13.

2 E. 6. ca. 24.

a man

a man had been feloniously stricken, or poysoned in one county, and after had died in another county, no sufficient indictment could thereof have been taken in either of the said counties, because by the law of the realm, the jurors of one county could not inquire of that, which was done in an other county. It is provided by that act that the indictment may be taken, and the appeal brought in that county, where the death doth happen. Before the

[49]
18 E. 3. 32.
9 H. 6. 63.
3 H. 7. 12.
4 H. 7. 18.
6 H. 7. 10.

making of this statute, the appeal might have been brought in either of the said counties, but the triall must have been out of both: but when both counties could not joyn, then both appeal and indictment failed at the common law.

But here be two things to be observed: first, that in case of treason or misprision thereof, or of felony, or misprision of the same within the realm, the party ought to be indicted within the same county, where the fact is done, and it cannot be alledged in any other county, then in truth where it was done. And therefore in the case above said, neither the stroke, nor poysoning, nor the death, though they be transitory, can be alledged in the indictment or appeal, but where in truth they were done. Secondly, the statute of 2 E. 6. extendeth not where one is stricken or poysoned on the sea, or in any forain kingdome, and dieth in England, but where one is stricken or poysoned in one county, and dieth in another.

This act extendeth, where the murder, or felony is done in one county, and another shall be accessory in another county: whereof you may read at large in the lord Sanchar's case.

Lib. 9. fo. 117, 118. &c.

Mich. 13 Jac. regis. Sir Thomas Overburies case. See hereafter. ca. 62. of Indictments more of this case.

Richard Weston being Sir Thomas Overburies keeper in the Tower of London, did poyson him in that part of the Tower which is within London. R. earl of S. and F. his wife, James Franklin and Anne Turner were accessories before the fact in the county of Midd. and Sir Gervase Helwys lieutenant of the Tower was accessory before the fact in London. Now upon this statute of 2 E. 6. ca. 24. divers questions were resolved: first, if the accessory be in Midd. where the kings bench sit, and the principall is attainted in another county, the kings bench may try the accessory, as it was resolved in the lord Sanchars case, *ubi supra*. 2. If the indictment of the accessory be taken in the kings bench, the justices shall not by force of the statute of 2 E. 6. write in their own names, *quia placita sunt coram rege, & non coram justiciariis*, but remove the record by the kings writ of *certiorari*. 3. Divers presidents were shewn, that where accessories before the fact were in Midd. where the kings bench did sit, &c. and the attainder of the principall had been in another county, the justices of the kings bench have removed the attainder by writ of *certiorari* before them. See the lord Sanchars case, *ubi supra*, and another case where the principall was attainted in the county of Oxon, before justices of oier and terminer, and the accessory was in Midd. where the kings bench sate. 4. Richard Weston being attainted as principall in the city of London, proceeding was to be had against James Franklin and Anne Turner in the kings bench where they were indicted. The question was, if the kings bench should remove the record of the attainder of the principall by *certiorari* before them, and after the said earl and his wife should be tried by their peers before the lord steward, whether the Lord steward might write to the kings bench for the record of the attainder: for the words of 2 E. 6. be, Shall write to the *custos rotulorum*, or keepers of the record where

such

ſuch principall ſhall hereafter be attainted or convict. And to prevent all doubts, a ſpeciall writ was directed according to the words of the act, to the commiſſioners of oier and terminer, to certifie whether the principall was attainted, convicted, or acquitted, and they made a particular certificate accordingly: ſo as the record of the attainder remained ſtill with the commiſſioners of oier and terminer in London. 5. It was reſolved upon conſideration had of the whole act, that the words of the act being, the juſtices of gaol delivery, or of oier and terminer, or other there authorized, ſhall proceed, &c. the ſame extend to the high ſteward to write, &c.

The indictment of Richard Weſton was, that he 9 *die Maii anno* 11 *regis Jacobi, &c.* gave to Sir Thomas Overbury a poyſon called roſeacre in broth, which Sir Thomas Overbury not knowing it, received, *et ut idem Ri. Weſton præfatum Thomam Overbury magis celeriter interficeret, et murdraret*, 1 *Junii anno* 11 *Jac. regis*, gave unto him another poyſon called white arſenick. And that Richard Weſton, 10 *Julii, anno* 11. *Jac. regis*, gave unto him poyſon, called mercury ſublimat, in tarts, &c. *ut præd. Thomam magis celeriter interficeret, & murdraret.* And that a perſon unknown, by the procurement, and in the preſence of Richard Weſton, 14 Septemb. 11. *ſupradicto*, gave to the ſaid Thomas a glyſter with poyſon in it, called mercury ſublimat, &c. *ut præd. Thomam magis celeriter interficeret et murdraret. Et prædict. Thomas Overbury de ſeparalibus venenis prædict. et operatione inde à prædict. ſeparalibus temporibus, &c. graviter languebat uſque* 15 *diem. Septemb. anno* 11. *ſupradicto, quo quidem* 15 *die Septembris, &c. prædictus Thomas de ſeparalibus venenis prædictis obiit venenatus.* And this was reſolved to be a good indictment by all the juſtices of the king's bench, although it doth not appeare in particular, of which of the ſaid poyſons he died. For the ſubſtance of the indictment was, whether he was poyſoned or no, by the ſaid Richard Weſton. And upon this indictment he was arraigned, pleaded not guilty, and had judgement given againſt him. And afterward Anne Turner, Sir Gervaſe Helwys lieutenant of the Tower, and Richard Franklin the phyſitian, were indicted as acceſſories before the fact, and arraigned, and pleaded not guilty: and it fell out in evidence, that Franklin had prepared divers other poyſons, then were contained in the indictment, as the powder of diamonds, the powder of ſpiders, lapis cauſticus, and cantharides, over and beſides the poyſons in the indictment. And it was reſolved, that any of theſe was ſufficient to prove the indictment; for the ſubſtance of the indictment was poyſoning, which (as hath been ſaid) is ſecret: ſee Machallis caſe *ubi ſupra*, and after verdict, judgement was given againſt all theſe acceſſories. And after, the ſaid earle and the counteſſe his wife were indicted as acceſſories before the fact, and were arraigned before the lord chancellor of England, and *hac vice*, lord high ſteward of England: and upon the arraignment of the counteſſe, ſhe confeſſed the indictment: and when the clerk of the crown did aſk her, What ſhe could ſay why judgement of death ſhould not be given againſt her? ſhe ſaid, That ſhe could ſay much againſt her ſelfe, but nothing for her ſelfe. And then the lord ſteward gave judgement of death againſt her, viz. That ſhe ſhould be hanged by the neck till ſhe were dead: and adjourned his commiſſion, (as it was reſolved he might do by law) untill the next day; and then the [50] the ſaid earle was arraigned, and pleaded not guilty, and put himſelf upon his peers, who found him guilty: and thereupon the lord ſteward gave the like judgement againſt him. Which caſe we have recited the more largely for two cauſes. Firſt, for that we remember not any of the nobility of this realm to have been attainted in former times for poyſoning of any. Secondly, for that it is the firſt caſe that fell out upon the ſaid act of 2 E. 6. in caſe of triall by peers of any that was noble, and the proceeding herein was by great adviſement. But now let us return where we left.

Reaſonable creature, in rerum natura.] As man, woman, childe, ſubject born, or alien, perſons outlawed, or otherwiſe attainted of treaſon, felony, or premunire, Chriſtian, Jew, Heathen, Turk, or other Infidel, being under the kings peace.

[a] Chro. de Dunſtabl, Holl. 252. Coram Juſtic. Itiner. in Com. Kanc. 18 E. 1. See the ſecond part of the Inſt. cap. Stat. de Judaiſmo.

[a] A maſter of a ſhip and divers mariners, &c. were attainted of murder before juſtices in eire, for drowning of many Jewes within the county of Kent.

[b] 22 E. 3. Coron. 263. 8 E. 2. Cor. 418. Stan. p. cor. 21. c.

[c] 1 E. 3. 23, 24. 3 Aſſ. p. 2.

[d] Bract. li. 3. f. 21. Fleta, lib. ca. 23.

[b] If a woman be quick with childe, and by a potion or otherwiſe killeth it in her wombe; or if a man beat her, whereby the childe dieth in her body, and ſhe is delivered of a dead childe, this is a great miſpriſion, and no murder: but if the childe be born alive, and dieth of the potion, battery, or other cauſe, this is murder: for in law it is accounted a reaſonable creature, *in rerum natura*, when it is born alive. And the [c] book in 1 E. 3. was never holden for law. And 3 Aſſ. p. 2. is but a repetition of that caſe. And ſo horrible an offence ſhould not go unpuniſhed. And ſo was the law holden [d] in Bractons time, *Si aliquis qui mulierem praegnantem percuſſerit, vel ei venenum dederit, per quod fecerit abortivum, ſi puerperium jam formatum fuerit; et maximè ſi fuerit animatum, facit homicidium.* And herewith agreeth Fleta: and herein the law is

[51]

Geneſis, c. 6. v. 6.

Dier. 3. Eliz. fol. 186.

grounded upon the law of God, which ſaith, *Quicunque effuderit humanum ſanguinem, fundetur ſanguis illius, ad imaginem quippe Dei creatus eſt homo.* If a man counſell a woman to kill the childe within her wombe, when it ſhall be born, and after ſhe is delivered of the childe, ſhe killeth it; the councellor is an acceſſory to the murder, and yet at the time of the commandement, or councell, no murder could be committed of the childe *in utero matris*: the reaſon of which caſe proveth well the other caſe.

Malice prepenſed.] Firſt let us ſee what this malice is.

Malice prepenſed is, when one compaſſeth to kill, wound, or beat another, and doth it *ſedato animo*. This is ſaid in law to be malice forethought, prepenſed, *malitia praecogitata*. This malice is ſo odious in law, as though it be intended againſt one, it ſhall be extended towards another. * *Si quis unum percuſſerit, cum alium percutere vellet, in felonia tenetur.*

Dier. 3 Mar. 128. Pl. Com. 474, 475, 476. Lib. 9. fol. 81. Agnes Gores caſe.

* Bracton, lib. 3. fol. 155.

Mandata recipiunt ſtrictam interpretationem, ſed illicita latam et extenſivam. But herein there is a diverſity between the principall and the acceſſory. For if A command B, to kill C, and B by miſtaking killeth D in ſtead of C, this is murder in B becauſe he did the act: and it ſprang out of the root of malice, and the law ſhall couple the event to the cauſe: but A is not acceſſory, becauſe his commandement was not purſued; and his conſent, which muſt make him acceſſory, cannot be drawne to it, for he never commanded the death of D. But where death enſueth upon that act which is commanded,

commanded, though death it ſelfe be not commanded, there he is acceſſory to it, for there the commandement is the cauſe of death. As if A command B to beat C, and he beat him, whereof he dieth: the commander is acceſſory, and therefore the diverſity is apparent, as to the acceſſory. Where death is purſuant, and followeth upon the act commanded, there the conſent of the commander may well be drawn to it, for that the commandement is the mean of the death. But where death enſueth upon another diſtinct cauſe, there the conſent of the acceſſory cannot be drawn to it, *et ſic de cæteris.*

Another diverſity there is, when the commandement extends expreſly to the killing of another, and for the better accompliſhment thereof preſcribeth a mean; that is, to kill him by poyſon, and he killeth him with a gun, he is acceſſory: for the commandement was to kill, which enſued, though the mean was not followed, *et finis rei attendendus eſt.* And the ſubſtance of the commandement, viz. [to kill] is purſued: and the ſame offence that was commanded, is committed. But otherwiſe it is, if the ſame offence which is commanded be not committed. As if one command one to rob the vintners man of plate, as he is to come to a gentlemans chamber to his ſupper with wine; and he breaketh the taverne in the night, and ſtealeth the plate there; the commander is not acceſſory to this burglary, for this is another offence then he commanded, and the conſent of the acceſſory muſt be drawn to the murder or felony committed.

2. It muſt be malice continuing untill the mortall wound, or the like be given. Albeit there had been malice between two, and after they are pacified and made friends, and after this upon a new occaſion fall out, and the one killeth the other; this is homicide, but no murder, becauſe the former malice continued not.

If A command B to kill C, and before the act be done, A repenteth and countermand his commandement, and charge B not to do it: if B after killeth him, A is not acceſſory to it: for the malicious minde of the acceſſory ought to continue to do ill untill the act done. Pl. Com. ubi ſup.

If two fall out upon a ſudden occaſion, and agree to fight in ſuch a field, and each of them go and fetch their weapon, and go into the field, and therein fight, the one killeth the other: here is no malice prepenſed, for the fetching of the weapon and going into the field, is but a continuance of the ſudden falling out, and the blood was never cooled. But if they appoint to fight the next day, that is malice prepenſed.

Malice implyed, is in three caſes.] Firſt, in reſpect of the manner of the deed. As if one killeth another without any provocation of the part of him, that is ſlain, the law implieth malice: whereof you may read lib. 9. fol. 67. Mackallyes caſe. Alſo the poyſoning of any man, whereof he dieth within the year, implieth malice, and is adjudged wilfull murder of malice prepenſed. One may be poyſoned four manner of ways: *guſtu* by taſte, that is by eating, or drinking, being infuſed into his meat or drink: *anhelitu*, by taking in of breath, as by a poyſonous perfume in a chamber, or other room: 3. *contactu*, by touching: and laſtly, *ſuppoſitu*, as by a glyſter or the like. Now for the better finding out of this horrible offence, there be divers kindes of poyſons, as the powder of diamonds,

[52]

Lib. 9. fo. 67. b. in Mackallies caſe.

1 E. 6. c. 12

diamonds, the powder of ſpiders, *lapis cauſticus*, (the chief ingredient whereof is ſoap) cantharides, mercury ſublimate, arſenick, roſeacre, &c.

Lib. 9. fo. 68.

2. In reſpect of the perſon ſlain. As if a magiſtrate or known officer, or any other, that hath lawfull warrant, and in doing, or offering to doe his office, or to execute his warrant, is ſlain, this is murder, by malice implied by law, as the ſherif, juſtice of the peace, underſherif, chief conſtable, petit conſtable, or any other miniſter of the king. If a man kill a watchman doing his office, it is murder: ſo it is, if any, that come in aid of the kings officer, &c. to doe his office, be ſlain, it is murder.

Mackallies caſe. Ubi ſupra. Lib. 4. fo. 40. b. 41. a. Youngs caſe.

3. In reſpect of the perſon killing. If A aſſault B to rob him and in reſiſting A killeth B this is murder by malice implied, albeit he never ſaw or knew him before. If a priſoner by the dures of the gaoler, commeth to untimely death, this is murder in the gaoler, and the law implieth malice in reſpect of the cruelty. And this is the cauſe, that if any man dieth in priſon, the coroner ought to ſit upon his body, to the end it may be inquired of, whether he came to his death by the dures of the gaoler, or otherwiſe: all which appeareth in Britton: and this ſitting of the coroner continueth till this day.

Mackallies caſe. Ubi ſupra.

Brit. ca. 11. De priſons fo. 18. a. See the Mirror cap. 2. § 11. De homicide. 5 H. 6. 58. 27 Aſſ. p. 41.

If the ſherif, or other officer, where he ought to hang the party attainted, according to his judgement and his charge, will againſt the law, of his own wrong, burn or behead him, or *è converſo*; the law in this caſe implieth malice in him. Neither can the king by any warrant under the great ſeal alter the execution, otherwiſe then the judgement of law doth direct: for it is a maxime in law, *non alio modo puniatur quis, quam ſecundum quod ſe habeat condemnatio*.

Bract. l. 3. fo. 104.

And it is to be known, that in caſe of treaſon and felony, there is an expreſſe judgement, and an implied judgement: expreſſe, when upon appearance, &c. an expreſſe judgement is given againſt him, *quòd ſuſpendatur per collum*. Implied, when the offender makes default, and is outlawed, where the judgement is, *ideo utlagetur*; or in caſe of abjuration, *quia abjuravit regnum*: and yet the like execution ſhall be in caſe of outlawry or abjuration, as in caſe of an expreſſe judgement: and ſo it was adjudged in caſe of a perſon outlawed for felony, he ought to be hanged untill he be dead, and cannot be beheaded, * and the like is in caſe of abjuration. But in caſe of high treaſon, becauſe beheading is parcell of the judgement, the king may pardon all the reſidue of the execution except that: for ſeeing the king may pardon the whole execution, he may pardon any part, or all, ſaving part. If a lieutenant, or other that hath commiſſion of marſhall authority, in time of peace hang, or otherwiſe execute any man by colour of marſhall law, this is murder, for this is againſt Magna Charta cap. 29. and is done with ſuch power and ſtrength, as the party cannot defend himſelf; and here the law implieth malice. *Vide* Paſch. 14. E. 3. in Scaccario the abbot of Ramſeys caſe in a writ of error in part abridged by Fitzh. tit. Scire fac. 122. for time of peace.

See hereafter in the title of Sanctuary for Abjuration. Paſch. 20 R. 2. Coram Rege Linc. Ro. 58. * Mich. 1 R. 2. Coram Rege. Rot. 1. Bedf. See hereafter cap. Judgement and Execution.

[a] Thom. countee de Lancaſter being taken in an open inſurrection, was by judgement of marſhall law put to death, in *anno* 14 E. 4. This was adjudged to be unlawfull, *eò quòd non fuit arrainiatus*,

[a] Paſch. 39 E. 3. Coram Rege Rot. 92. Wiltes. Similie Paſch. 28 E. 3. Coram Rege Rot. 37. In caſe de Mortimer, who was put to death anno 1 E. 3. Vide Rot. Brevium anno 1 E. 3. part. 1.

rainiatur, seu ad responsionem positus tempore pacis, eò quòd cancellaria, et aliæ curiæ regis fuerunt tunc apertæ, in quibus lex fiebat unicuique, prout fieri consuevit, quòd contra cartam de libertatibus cum dictus Thomas fuit unus parium et magnatum regni non imprisonetur, &c. Nec dictus rex super eum ibit, nec super eum mittet, nisi per legale judicium parium suorum, &c. tamen tempore pacis absque arraniamento, seu responsione, seu legali judicio parium suorum, &c. adjudicatus est morti. [53]

Within a year and a day.] How this year and a day shall be accounted, is to be seen. If the stroke, or poyson, &c. be given the first day of January, the year shall end the last day of December: for though the stroke, or poyson, &c. were given in the afternoon of the first day of January, yet that shall be accounted a whole day, for regularly the law maketh no fraction of a day: and the day was added, that there might be a whole year at the least after the stroke, or poyson, &c. for if he die after that time, it cannot be discerned, as the law presumes, whether he died of the stroke or poyson, &c. or of a natural death; and in case of life the rule of law ought to be certain. But seeing the year and day in the case of murder and homicide, must be accounted *apres le fait*, after the deed, if a man be stricken or poysoned, &c. the first of January, and he dieth of that stroke or poyson the first day of May, whether shall the year and day be accounted after the stroke or poyson given, or after the death? and it shall be accounted after the death, for then the man was murdered, and not after the stroke or poyson given, &c. both in the indictment at the suit of the king, and in the appeal at the suit of the party. And so it hath been often adjudged contrary to the opinion of justice Stanford. A murderer half a year after the murder is received, and aided by another, this accessory may be indicted or appealed within the year after he became accessory, though it be after the year, that the murder was committed, and shall be tryed when the principall is attainted.

See the statute of Gloucest. 6 E. 1. ca. 9. 3 H. 7. ca. 1. 3 E. 3. Cor. 303. Lib. 5. fo. 1. in Cleytons case.

Lib. 4. fo. 41, 42. in Heydons case.

Stanf. Pl. Cor. 63.

26 Ass. p. 52.

If a murder be committed in the day time in a town not inclosed, and the murderer not apprehended, the township shall be amercied, but if inclosed, whether the murder be in the night, or day, the town shall be amercied. They that are present when any man is slain, and doe not their best indeavour to apprehend the murderer, or manslayer shal be fined and imprisoned. What judgment a felon attainted shall have, and what he shall forfeit; see the first part of the Institutes, sect. 747. and here, cap. Judgement and Execution.

3 H. 7. c. 1. stat. 1. 3 E. 3. cor. 299. 8 E. 2. cor. 391. Inter leges regis Edw. cap. 6. Æthelstani cap. 1. Ed. cap. 6. &c.

* Nota that before the reign of H. 1. the judgement for felony was not always one, but king H 1. ordained by parliament, that the judgement for all manner of felonies should be, that the person attainted should be hanged by the neck till he be dead, which continueth to this day. See more for murder in the chapter of Monomachia.

* 9 H 1. Hovanden, anno 1108. Simon Dun. Rad. and Floren. Wigorn. Hollengsh. 45.

CAP. VIII.

OF HOMICIDE.

HOMICIDIUM ex vi termini comprehendeth petit treason, murder, and that which is commonly called manslaughter: for *homicidium est hominis cædium*, and *homicidium est hominis occisio ab homine facta*. Therefore the right division of homicide is; that of homicides, or manslaughter, some be voluntary, and of malice forethought; as petit treason, and murder of another, and murder of himself. Of the two former we have spoken; and of murder of himself we shall speak hereafter. Of manslaughters, some be voluntary, and not of malice forethought: of these some be felony (as shall be shewed hereafter) and some be no felony; of which, some be in respect of giving back inevitably in defence of himself, upon an assault of revenge: and some without any giving back; as upon the assault of a thief or robber upon a man in his house, or abroad: Some upon the assault of one, that is under custody; as the sherif, or gaoler assaulted by his prisoner. Some in respect that he is an officer or minister of justice, without any assault in execution of his office, or lawfull warrant. And lastly, some homicides, that be no felony, be neither forethought, nor voluntary; as manslaughter by misadventure, *per infortunium*, or *casu*. And some of these, that be no felony, are causes of forfeiture of a man's goods, and some be not: and of these several branches in their order. And first of murder of a man's self, who commonly is called *felo de se*.

3 E. 3. cor. 290. 289. 312. Britton cap. 7.

Felo de se.

Felo de se is a man, or woman, which being *compos mentis*, of sound memory, and of the age of discretion, killeth himself, which being lawfully found by the oath of twelve men, all the goods and chattels of the party so offending are forfeited.

Regula.

Now let us peruse the severall branches of this description, *majus est delictum seipsum occidere, quam alium.*

[a] Rot. Clauf. 1 E. 1. m. 7. Rot. Clauf. 6 E. 1. Alma filia Roberti de Keston. 3 E. 3. cor. 324. Rot. Escheat. anno 47 E. 3. nu. 17. Ricus Algate.

[b] 8 E. 2. cor. 412. 22 E. 3. cor. 244. Pl. Com. 260.

Being compos mentis.] [a] If a man lose his memory by the rage of sicknes or infirmity, or otherwise, and kill himself while he is not *compos mentis*, he is not *felo de se*: for, as he cannot commit murder upon another, so in that case he cannot commit murder upon himself. [b] If one during the time that he is *non compos mentis* give himself a mortall wound, whereof he, when he hath recovered his memory, dieth, he is not *felo de se*: because, the stroke which was the cause of his death, was given when he was not *compos mentis: et actus non facit reum, nisi mens sit rea.* If a man give himself a wound, intending to be *felo de se*, and dieth not within the year and day after the wound, he is not *felo de se*.

Of the age of discretion.] Hereof we have spoken before treating of murder.

[c] 44 E. 3. 44. [illegible]

Kill himself.] [c] And this is often voluntary, and sometime not voluntary. If A. give B. such a stroke as he felleth him to the ground, B. draweth his knife, and holds it up for his own defence:

fence: A. in haſt meaning to fall upon B. to kill him, falleth upon the knife of B. whereby he is wounded to death, he is *felo de ſe*: for B. did nothing but that which was lawfull in his own defence.

Lawfully found.] [d] No goods be forfeited, untill it be lawfully found by the oath of twelve men, that he is *felo de ſe*: and this doth belong to the coroner *ſuper viſum corporis*, to inquire thereof: and if it be found before the coroner *ſuper viſum corporis*, that he was *felo de ſe*, [a] the executors or adminiſtrators of the dead ſhall have no traverſe thereunto. And this is the reaſon, that no man can preſcribe to have felons goods, becauſe they are not forfeited, until it be found of record, that he is *felo de ſe*.

[d] Pl. Com. 360. b.

[55]

[a] Stanf. pl. cor. 183. d.

[b] If a man be *felo de ſe*, and is caſt into the ſea, or otherwiſe ſo ſecretly hidden, as the coroner cannot have the view of the body, and by conſequence cannot inquire thereof: in this caſe it may be inquired thereof by the juſtices of peace of that county; for they have power by their commiſſion to inquire of all felonies. But if it be found before them, the executors or adminiſtrators of the dead may have a traverſe thereunto, but not to the indictment taken before the coroner *ſuper viſum corporis*, as before is ſaid: and ſo hath it been reſolved. And ſo in the caſe aboveſaid may the kings bench enquire thereof, if the felony be committed in the county where the kings bench ſit, and the executors or adminiſtrators of the dead may traverſe the ſame.

[b] Hil. 37 Eliz. in the kings bench by the whole court, in the caſe of one Laughton of Cheſhire. See 8 E. 2. cor. 412. 3 E. 3. cor. 312. fi e. Stanf. pl. cor. 184.

Are forfeited.] Albeit [c] Bracton was of opinion, that if a man that was *reus alicujus criminis captus ſit pro eodem, utpote pro morte hominis, vel cum furto manifeſto, vel quod utlegatus ſit, et metu pœnæ imminentis mortis mortem ſibi conſciverit, hæredem non habebit, quia ſic convincitur felonia prius facta*, viz. *furtum, mors hominis, vel hujuſmodi, et conſcientiæ metus in reo pro confeſſo habetur. Aliud erit ſi non ſit in crimine deprehenſus, &c. non debet in aliquo caſu exhæredatio fieri, niſi præcedat crimen, propter quod periculum mortis vel membrorum ſuſtineri debet, &c.* But the law makes no ſuch diverſity: [d] for *felo de ſe*, whatſoever offence he hath committed (whereof he was not in his life time attainted) ſhall forfeit no lands, but his goods and chattels only. [e] And ſo ſaith Britton, *En caſe ou home eſt felon de ſoy meſme, ſoient ſes chateux judges nous come chateux de felon, le heritage ne quident remaine as heires.* For no man can forfeit his land without an attainder by courſe of law.

[c] 8 E. 2. cor. 426. 44 E. 3. 44. 22 E. 3. cor. 259. 3 E. 3. cor. 301. 3 E. 3. 3. cor. 362. 5 Mar. Dier. 160. 9 Eliz. Dier. 262. Bract. lib. 3. f. 150. Fleta, lib. 2. c. 34.

[d] Pl. com. 261. a. & b. per touts les juſtices.

[e] Britton, cap. 7. Cuſtum. de Norm. cap. 21.

A [f] villain giveth himſelfe a mortall wound, the lord ſeiſeth his goods, the villain after dieth of the wound within the year and the day, the goods are forfeit.

[f] Pl. com. 260. b.

And herein [g] there is a diverſity between chattels perſonels in action, and in poſſeſſion: for if a debt be owing to two, unleſſe it be in caſe of two joint merchants, and the one is *felo de ſe*, he doth forfeit the whole: but otherwiſe it is of goods in poſſeſſion, for there he forfeiteth but his part.

[g] 8 E. 4. 4. Pl. com. 259. b.

A leaſe [h] is made for years to the huſband and wife, the huſband drowneth himſelf, the leaſe is forfeited, as you may read at large in Plowdens Commentaries.

[h] Pl. com. 260. Dier, 2 Mar. 108.

Now let us purſue the branches into which bloody homicide did ſpend and empty itſelfe.

Some manſlaughters be voluntary, and not of malice forethought, upon ſome ſudden falling out. *Delinquens per iram pro-*

vocatus puniri debet mitius. And this for distinction sake is called manslaughter. There is no difference between murder, and manslaughter; but that the one is upon malice forethought, and the other upon a sudden occasion: and therefore is called chance-medley. As if two meet together, and striving for the wall the one kill the other, this is manslaughter and felony. And so it is, if they had upon that sudden occasion gone into the fields and fought, and the one had killed the other: this (as hath been said) had been but manslaughter, and no murder; because all that followed, was but a continuance of the first sudden occasion, and the heat of the blood kindled by ire was never cooled, till the blow was given, *et sic de similibus.*

Manslaughter [i] is felony, and hereof there may be accessories after the fact done: but of murder, there may be accessories, as well before, as after the fact.

Some be [k] voluntary, and yet being done upon an inevitable cause are no felony. As if A. be assaulted by B. and they fight together, and before any mortall blow given A. giveth back, untill he commeth unto a hedge, wall, or other strait, beyond * which he cannot passe, and then in his own defence, and for safeguard of his owne life killeth the other: this is voluntary, and yet no felony, and the jury that finde, it was done *se defendendo*, ought to finde the speciall matter. [a] And yet such a precious regard the law hath of the life of man, though the cause was inevitable, [b] that at the common law he should have suffered death: and though the statute of Glocester save his life, yet he shall forfeit all his goods and chattels. [c] Hereof there can be no accessories, either before or after the fact, because it is not done *felleo animo*, but upon inevitable necessity *se defendendo*. If A. assault B. so fiercely and violently, and in such a place, and in such manner, as if B. should give back, he should be in danger of his life, he may in this case defend himselfe; and if in that defence he killeth A, it is *se defendendo*, because it is not done *felleo animo*: for the rule is, when he doth it in his own defence, upon any inevitable cause, *Quod quis ob tutelam corporis sui fecerit, jure id fecisse videtur.*

Some without any giving back to a wall, &c. or other inevitable cause. [d] As if a thiefe offer to rob or murder B. either abroad, or in his house, and thereupon assault him, and B. defend himselfe without any giving back, and in his defence killeth the thief, this is no felony; for a man shall never give way to a thief, &c. neither shall he forfeit any thing. [e] And so it is declared by the statute of 24 H. 8. Likewise [f] if a prisoner assault the gaoler, the gaoler is not by law inforced to give back: but if in defence of himselfe he kill the prisoner, this is no felony.

[g] So if any officer, or minister of justice, that hath lawfull warrant, and the party assault the officer or minister of justice, he is not bound by law to give back, but to carry him away: and if in execution of his office he cannot otherwise avoid it, but in striving kill him, it is no felony. And in that case the officer or minister of justice shall forfeit nothing, but the party so assaulting or offering to flye away, and is killed, shall forfeit his goods and chattels.

[h] *Vicecomes seu balivus domini regis, qui interficit duos latrones non permittentes*

[i] Lib. 4. fol. 44. Bibithes case

[k] 15 E. 3. cor. 116. 15 Ass. p. 7. 43 Ass. 31. See the stat. of Gloc. cap. 39. 3 E 3. cor. 184. 286. & 297. 305. & 361. See hereafter, ca. 101. of Judgement and Execution. Verb. Of death of a man se defendendo.

*[56]

[a] 43 Ass. 31. Rot. Parl. 3 R. 2. nu. 18. Iohn Imperials case.

[b] 21 E. 3. 17. Gloc. cap. 9. 4 H. 7. 2.

[c] Lib. 4. fo. 44. Bibiths case. Bracton.

[d] Lib. 5. fo. 91. Semayns case. 26 Ass. p. 23. 32. 29 Ass. p. 23. 3 E. 3. cor. 305. & 330. 22 E. 3. cor. 261. 21 H. 7. 39.

[e] 24 H. 8. cap. 5.

[f] 22 Ass. p. 55.

[g] 3 E. 3. cor. 290. 22 E. 3. cor. 261. M. 22 E. 3. coram rege Rot. 181. Eborum. Rot. libert. anno 1 & 2 E. 1. m. 2.

[h] Pasch. 16 E. 3. Coram rege. Rot. 131. Norff.

permittentes se justiciari in sui defensionem, et non ex felonia, seu malitia, acquietatur.

[i] If at a just or turnement, or at the play with sword and buckler by the kings commandement, one doth kill another, this is no felony. [k] In the reigne of king H. 2. it was enacted, that if in such case one was slaine, it should be no felony, for that in friendly manner they contended to try their strength, and to be able to doe the king service in that kinde, as occasion should be offered.

[i] 11 H. 7. 22. Vid. hereafter. cap. Against riding and going armed.

[k] Mirror, cap. 1. § 13. Des adventures.

There is an homicide, that is neither forethought, nor voluntary. [l] As if a man kill another *per infortunium, seu casu*, that is homicide by misadventure. *De amputatore arborum, qui cum ramum projiceret, inscius occidit transeuntem: aut cum quis pilam percusserit, &c. ex cujus ictu occisus est, tales de homicidio non tenentur.* Homicide by misadventure, is when a man doth an act, that is not unlawfull, which without any evill intent tendeth to a man's death.

[l] Bract. lib. 3. fo. 136. b. See the stat. of Gloc. ca. 9. Marl. cap. 25. Bract. lib. 3. 120. Brit. ca. 7. fo. 15. Fleta, lib. 1. ca. 30. Mir. ca. 1. § 9.

Unlawfull.] [m] If the act be unlawful it is murder. As if A. meaning to steale a deere in the park of B, shooteth at the deer, and by the glance of the arrow killeth a boy that is hidden in a bush: this is murder, for that the act was unlawfull, although A. had no intent to hurt the boy, nor knew not of him. But if B. the owner of the park had shot at his own deer, and without any ill intent had killed the boy by the glance of his arrow, this had been homicide by misadventure, and no felony.

[m] Bract. lib. 3. 120. b. Sed erit distinguendum utrum quis dederit operam rei licitæ vel illicitæ, &c.

[n] So if one shoot at any wild fowle upon a tree, and the arrow killeth any reasonable creature afar off, without any evill intent in him, this is *per infortunium*: for it was not unlawful to shoot at the wilde fowle: but if he had shot at a cock or hen, or any tame fowle of another mans, and the arrow by mischance had killed a man, this had been murder, for the act was unlawfull.

[n] 3 E. 3. cor. 354. 2 H. 4. 18. 11 H. 7. 23. a.

[57]

Without any evil intent.] If a man knowing that many people come in the street from a sermon, throw a stone over a wall, intending only to feare them, or to give them a light hurt, and thereupon one is killed, this is murder; for he had an ill intent, though that intent extended not to death, and though he knew not the party slaine. For the killing of any by misadventure, or by chance, albeit it be not felony, *quia voluntas in delictis, non exitus spectatur*; yet he shall forfeit therefore all his goods and chattels, to the intent that men should be wary so to direct their actions, as they tend not to the effusion of mans blood,

Marlbr. ca. 25.

Nec veniam effuso sanguine casus habet.

Nota, Homicide is called chancemedley, or chancemelle, for that it is done by chance (without premeditation) upon a sudden brawle, shuffling, or contention: for meddle or melle (as some say) is an ancient French word, and signifieth brawle, or contention. But I take it that the French word is *mesle*, which signifying shuffling or contending, and by corruption we changing the S to D, doe call it *medle*, the S being not pronounced, whereof we have made *medletum*. So as killing of a man by chance-medle, is killing of a man upon a sudden brawle or contention by chance, for the word [*medle* or *melle*,] whereof we have made a Latin word *medletum or melletum*, see Glanvill, lib, 1. cap. 2. *cognoscere de medletis, de verberibus, de plagis:* that is, of brawling, or brabling, of battery,

D. Medletis.

battery, of wounding: the first in words, the other two in strokes, &c. in ancient time expressed by these two Saxon words, viz. *flit*, a *flitan*, to brawle; and *fiht*, which we retaine still to fight when it proceeds to blowes. *Unde flitwit, flichwite, fightwite, &c.*

And thus much of homicide committed by man. See in the next chapter of deodands, of another kinde of killing of a man.

CAP. IX.

OF DEODANDS.

[a] 8 E. 2. Cor. 403. 8 E. 2. Ibid. 189. A mill wheel. Fleta lib. 1. ca. 25. quicquid mobile sit in molendino. Mirror c. 1. § 13. 12 R. 2. Cor. 20. a masse of earth in a mine.

[b] Bract. lib. 3. fo. 120. b. á bove, cane, &c.

[c] Bracton, lib. 3. fo. 122. a. Britton, fo. 6. 15. Mirror, cap. 1. § 3. Fleta, li. 1 ca. 25. 45 E. 3. 2. b. Vide 4 E. 1. stat. officium coron. 6 E. 6. Dier, 77. b. 61. a. Quæ movent ad mortem sunt Deo danda. 2 Mar. ibid. 107. b. Kelway, 21 H. 7. fo. 8.

[d] Lib. 5. fo. 110. b. Foxleys case accord. And this is the reason they cannot be claimed by prescription. 45 E. 3. ubi supra. Fleta ubi sup.

[e] 8 E. 2. cor. 389.

[f] Exod. 2. 28.

*[58]

Doct. & Stud. lib. 2. 156. b. Br. Forfeit. 112. All our ancient authors ubi supra Rot. Parl. 51 E. 3. nu. 73.

DEODANDS when any [a] moveable thing inanimate, or [b] beast animate, doe move to, or cause the untimely death of any reasonable creature by mischance [c] in any county of the realm (and not upon the sea, or upon any salt water) without the will, offence, or fault of himself, or of any person. [d] They being so found by lawful inquisition of twelve men, being *precium sanguinis*, the price of blood, are forfeited to God, that is to the king, Gods lieutenant on earth, to be distributed in works of charity for the appeasing of Gods wrath.

And it is to be observed, that there is a diversity, as concerning the deodand, when the party slain is within the age of discretion, viz. of 14. years, and when he is above the age of discretion. For when he is slain by fall from a cart, horse, mill, &c. and is within the age of discretion, there is no deodand, as it is adjudged [e] in 8 E. 2. tit. coron. 389. But otherwise it is, if an oxe, horse, bull, or the like, doe kill any within the age of discretion, there the same are deodands.

And this law concerning deodands, is grounded upon the law of God, Exodus 2. vers. 28. *Si bos cornu percusserit virum, aut mulierem, et mortui fuerint, lapidibus obruetur.* See justice Stanford, lib. 1. cap. 12. which need not here to be recited. If A. killeth a man with the sword of B. the sword shall be forfeit to the king * as a deodand, because *movet ad mortem*, and for default of safe keeping of the same by the owner.

But now that we have cited, and referred you to our books of law already known, and published: let us cast our eye upon some records of parliament concerning deodands, of, or out of ships or other vessels upon rivers, or waters, fresh or salt, the law being clear, that in *aqua dulci* there may be deodands, but in the sea, or in *aqua salsa*, being any arm of the sea, though it be in the body of the county, there can be no deodand of the ship, or any part thereof, though any be drowned out of it; because, though the arm of the sea be within the body of the county, the ship or other vessel is subject to such dangers upon the raging waves in respect of the wind and tempest. And this diversity doth notably appear in the parliament roll. Amongst the petitions in parliament it is desired, that if it happen any man, or boy to be drowned by a fall out of any ship, boat, or vessel, they shall be no deodands. Whereunto the king upon great advice, and conference with his judges and councell

councell learned (as always the king doth to petitions in parliament) made anſwer, The ſhip, boat, or veſſel being upon * the ſea ſhall be adjudged no deodand, but being upon a freſh river, it is a deodand, but the king will ſhew favour.

* The arm of the ſea is included herein.

See the like petitions in other rolls of parliament *anno* 1 R. 2. nu. 106. 4 R. 2. nu. 33. 1 H. 5. nu. 35. &c. but never obtained more, then the common law gave in theſe caſes.

CAP. X.

Of BUGGERY, or SODOMY.

IF any perſon ſhall commit buggery with mankind, or beaſt; by authority of parliament this offence is adjudged felony without benefit of clergy. But it is to be known, (that I may obſerve it once for all) that the ſtatute of 25 H. 8. was repealed by the ſtatute of 1 Mar. whereby all offences made felony or premunire by any act of parliament made ſince 1 H. 8. were generally repealed, but 25 H. 8. is revived by 5 Eliz.

25 H. 8. ca. 6. 5 Eliz. ca. 17.

1 Mar. ubi ſup.

Buggery is a deteſtable, and abominable ſin, amongſt chriſtians not to be named, committed by carnall knowledge againſt the ordinance of the Creator, and order of nature, by mankind with mankind, or with brute beaſt, or by womankind with bruite beaſt.

Horrendum illud peccatum. 5 El. ca. 17.

Bugeria is an Italian word, and ſignifies ſo much, as is before deſcribed, *pæderaſtes* or *paidereſtes* is a Greek word, *amator puerorum*, which is but a ſpecies of buggery, and it was complained of in parliament, that the Lumbards had brought into the realm the ſhamefull ſin of ſodomy, that is not to be named, as there it is ſaid. Our ancient authors doe conclude, that it deſerveth death, *ultimum ſupplicium*, though they differ in the manner of the puniſhment. Britton ſaith, that ſodomites, and miſcreants ſhall be burnt, and ſo were the ſodomites by Almighty God. Fleta ſaith, *pecorantes et ſodomitæ in terra vivi confodiantur:* and therewith agreeth the Mirror, *pur le grand abhomination*, and in another place he ſaith, *Sodomie eſt crime de majeſtie, vers le roy celeſtre.* But (to ſay it once for all) the judgement in all caſes of felony, is, that the perſon attainted be hanged by the neck, untill he, or ſhe be dead. But in ancient times, in that caſe, the man was hanged, and the woman was drowned, whereof we have ſeen examples in the reign of R. 1. And this is the meaning of ancient franchiſes granted *de furca, et foſſa*, of the gallows, and the pit, for the hanging upon the one, and drowning in the other, but *foſſa* is taken away, and *furca* remains.

Rot. Parl. 50 E. 3. nu. 58.

Britton ca. 9. Gen. 19. 9. Rom. ca. 1. 17. F. N. B. 269. a. Fleta li. 1. ca. 37. Mirror ca. 4. §. de majeſty, ca. 1. § 15. & cap. 2. ſect. 11.

[59]

Cum maſculo non commiſcearis coitu fœmineo, quia abominatio eſt. Cum omni pecore non coibis, nec maculaberis cum eo: mulier non ſuccumbet jumento, nec miſcebitur ei, quia ſcelus eſt, &c.

Levit. 18. 22, 23. 1 Tim. 1. 10.

The act of 25 H. 8. hath adjudged it felony, and therefore the judgement for felony doth now belong to this offence, viz. to be hanged by the neck till he be dead. He that readeth the preamble of this act, ſhall find how neceſſary the reading of our ancient authors is: the ſtatute doth take away the benefit of clergy from the delinquent. But now let us peruſe the words of the ſaid deſcription of buggery.

Deteſtable and abominable.] Thoſe juſt attributes are found in the act of 25 H. 8.

Amongſt Chriſtians not to be named.] Theſe words are in the uſuall indictment of this offence, and are in effect in the parliament roll of 50 E. 3. *ubi ſupra*, nu. 58.

By carnal knowledge, &c.] The words of the indictment be, *contra ordinationem creatoris, et naturæ ordinem, rem habuit veneream, dictumque puerem carnaliter* * *cognovit, &c.* So as there muſt be *penetratio*, that is, *res in re*, either with mankind, or with beaſt, but the leaſt penetration maketh it carnall knowledge. [a] See the indictment of Stafford, which was drawn by great advice for committing buggery with a boy, for which he was attainted and hanged.

[b] The ſodomites came to this abomination by four means, viz. by pride, exceſſe of diet, idleneſſe, and contempt of the poor. *Otioſus nihil cogitat, niſi de ventre et venere.* Both the agent and conſentient are felons: and this is conſonant to the law of God. [c] *Qui dormierit cum maſculo coitu fœmineo, uterque operatus eſt nefas, et morte moriatur.* And this accordeth with the ancient rule of law, *agentes et conſentientes pari pœna plectentur.*

Emiſſio ſeminis maketh it not buggery, but is an evidence in caſe of buggery of penetration: and ſo in rape the words be alſo, *carnaliter cognovit*, and therefore there muſt be penetration; and *emiſſio ſeminis* without penetration maketh no rape. *Vide* in the chapter of Rape. If the party buggered be within the age of diſcretion, it is no felony in him, but in the agent only. When any offence is felony either by the common law, or by ſtatute, all acceſſories both before and after, are incidently included. [d] So if any be preſent, abetting and aiding any to do the act, though the offence be perſonall, and to be done by one only, as to commit rape, not only he that doth the act is a principall, [e] but alſo they that be preſent, abetting, and aiding the miſdoer, are principalls alſo, which is a proof of the other caſe of Sodomy.

Or by woman.] This is within the purvien of this act of 25 H. 8. For the words be, if any perſon, &c. which extend as well to a woman, as to a man, and therefore if ſhe commit buggery with a beaſt, ſhe is a perſon that commits buggery with a beaſt, to which end this word [perſon] was uſed. And the rather, for that ſomewhat before the making of this act, a great lady had committed buggery with a baboon, and conceived by it, &c.

There be four ſins in holy ſcripture called *clamantia peccata*, crying ſins, whereof this deteſtable ſin is one, expreſſed in this diſtichon.

Sunt vox clamorum, vox ſanguinis, et ſodomorum,
Vox oppreſſorum, merces detenta laborum.

* This is grounded upon the word of God. viz. Gen. 19. 4, 5. Judges, 19. 22. Ut cognoſcamus eos.

[a] Coke, lib. Intr. 352. Mich. 5 Ja. Coram rege.

[b] Ezek 16. 49. Gen. 18. 29. Deut. 29. 23. Eſay, 13. 19. Jer. 23. 14. 49. 18. 50. 4. Luke, 17. 28, 29. 2 Pet. 2. 6. Jud. verſ. 7. Rom. 1. 26, 27. Sapient. 10. 6, 7.

[c] Levit. 20. 13. 1 Cor. c. 6. v. 10.

[d] 3 & 4 P. & Mar. juſtice Daliſons Reports. Stanf. Pl. cor. Pl. com. 97.

[e] 11 H. 4. 13. See the 2. part of the Inſtitutes in the expoſition upon the ſtatute of W. 1. ca. 13. and W. 2. ca. 34.

CAP. XI.

OF RAPE.

RAPE is felony by the common law, declared by parliament for the unlawfull and carnall knowledge and abuse of any woman above the age of ten years against her will, or of a woman child under the age of ten years with her will, or against her will, and the offender shall not have the benefit of clergy.

What offence this was at the common law, and what acts of parliament have been enacted concerning the same; see in the second part of the Institutes in the exposition upon the statute of W. 1. ca. 13. and W. 2. ca. 34. and the first part of the Institutes, sect. 190. 7 H. 6. 2. 22 E. 4. 22. 6 H. 7. 4. b.

[a] The doubt that was made in 14 Eliz. at what age a woman child might be ravished, was the cause of the making of the [b] act of 18 Eliz. ca. 6. for plain declaration of the law. [That if any person should unlawfully know and abuse any woman-child under the age of ten years, every such unlawful and carnall knowledge should be felony, and the offender therein being duly convicted, shall suffer as a felon without allowance of clergy.]

[c] Although there be *emissio seminis*, yet if there be no penetration, that is, *res in re*, it is no rape, for the words of the indictment be, *carnaliter cognovit, &c.*

[d] In the parliament rolls we read what detestation hath been had of this hainous offence. At the petition of Isabell late the wife of John Botiler of Beausie in the county of Lancaster knight, which Isabell one William Pull of Wirrall in the county of Chester gent, shamefully did ravish. It is enacted by authority of parliament, that if William Pull doe not yeeld himself after proclamation made against him, that he shall be taken as a traitor attainted.

[e] The same Isabell by another petition shewed, how the said William by dures and menace of imprisonment inforced her to marry him, and by colour thereof ravished her, for the which she prayeth her appeal, which to her is granted.

[f] Margaret late the wife of sir Thomas Malefant knight, made the like complaint against one Lewis Leyson alias Gethey a Welchman. Against whom the like order is taken, as was for the said Isabell: onely where the rape was committed in Wales, it is enacted, that the same shall be tried in Somersetshire.

[g] Upon complaint of Henry Beamont son and heir of sir Henry Beamont knight, and Charles Vowell esquire, &c. against one Edward Lancaster of Skipton in Craven esquire, for taking away dame Joan Beamont the late wife of the said Sir Henry, being lawfully married to the said Charles, and for that the said Edward married the said dame Joan against her will, and ravished her. Against Edward Lancaster and others, remedy is given by appeal, and further [h] upon occasions happening thereupon, the statute

Deut. 22. 25. Inter leges Alveredi, cap. 25. & Canuti 49, 50. See W. 2. c. 34. W. 1. ca. 13. Rot. Parl. 8. E. 2. & Rot. Claus. 8 E. 2. m. 3. Quia in casu quando aliquis, &c. 6 R. 2. ca. 6. 18 Eliz. cap. 6. Lib. 11. fo. 29. Alexander Poulters case. See the 1. part of the Institutes. sect. 190. Mich. 19 E. 3. Coram rege. Rot. 159. London quod ipsam de puellagio suo felonicè et totaliter defloravit. 7 H. 6. 2. 22 E. 4. 22. 6 H. 7. 4. b.

[a] Di. 14 El. f. 304.

[b] 18 El. ca. 6.

[c] See before in the next preceding chapter of buggery.

[d] Rot. Parl. 15 H. 6. nu. 14.

[e] In the same roll nu. 15.

[f] Rot. Parl. 18 H. 6. nu. 28.

[g] Rot. Parl. 31 H. 6. nu. 72.

[h] 31 H. 6. ca. 9.

ſtatute of 31 H. 6. was made, which giveth remedy to a woman enforced to be bound by ſtatute or obligation, as by the act it appeareth.

It is read in ſtory, that chaſt Lucretia being raviſhed, ſhe was found in extreme heavineſſe, and it was demanded of her, *Salvan?* ſhe anſwered, *Quomodo mulier ſalva eſſe poteſt læſa pudicitia?* and yet thereof it is truly ſaid, *Duo fuerunt, et unus commiſit adulterium.*

Gen. 34. In the holy hiſtory you ſhall read, *Dinam cum vidiſſet Sichem filius Hemor Hevei princeps terræ illius, adamavit et rapuit, &c.* Obſerve well what followed thereupon. Likewiſe, *Ammon prevalens viribus ſuis oppreſſit Thamar ſororem ſuam, et cubavit cum ea, &c. quæ aſpergens cinerem capiti ſuo, ſciſſa talari tunica, impoſitis manibus ſuper caput ſuum ibat ingrediens et clamans &c.* And obſerve alſo the end of the offender.

2 Sam. 13. 14. 19.

[61]

CAP. XII.

Felony for carrying away a Woman againſt her Will, &c.

Exod. 21. 16. Deut. 24. 7. * 1 Tim. 1. 10.

WE have thought good next after Buggery and Rape, to ſpeak of the ſtealing of women, becauſe the * apoſtle doth rank, after the ſodomite, him that is plagiarius, ſo called, becauſe *lege Flavia plagis damnaretur.* And we will begin with the ſtatute of 3 H. 7. cap. 2.

3 H. 7. c. 2. 39 El. cap. 9.

Where women, as well maidens, as widows and wives, having ſubſtances, ſome in goods moveable, and ſome in lands and tenements, and ſome being heirs apparant unto their anceſtors, for the lucre of ſuch ſubſtances, been oftentimes taken by miſdoers, contrary to their will, and after married to ſuch miſdoers, or to other by their aſſent, or defoyled, to the great diſpleaſure of God, and contrary to the kings laws, and diſparagement of the ſaid women, and utter heavineſſe, and diſcomfort of their friends, and to the evill enſample of all other: it is therefore ordained, eſtabliſhed, and enacted by our ſoveraign lord the king, by the advice of the lords ſpirituall and temporall, and the commons in the ſaid parliament aſſembled, and by authority of the ſame, That what perſon or perſons from henceforth that taketh any woman ſo againſt her will unlawfully, that is to ſay, maid, widow, or wife, that ſuch taking, procuring, and abetting to the ſame, and alſo receiving wittingly the ſame woman ſo taken againſt her will, and knowing the ſame, be felony. And that ſuch miſdoers, takers, and procurators to the ſame, and receytors, knowing the ſaid offence in form aforesaid, be henceforth reputed and judged as principall felons. Provided alway that this act extend not to any person taking any woman, only claiming her as his ward, or bondwoman.

This act on the offenders part doth extend to all degrees, and to all persons, but extendeth not to all women: for on the womans part four things are necessarily required to make the offence felony. First, that the maid, wife, or widow have lands or tenements, or moveable goods, or be an heir apparent. Secondly, that she be taken away against her will. Thirdly, that she be married to the misdoer, or to some other by his consent, or be defiled, (that is, carnally known) for if these concurre not, the misdoer is no felon within this statute, but otherwise to be punished. And so it was resolved, 3 & 4 Ph. and Mar. And after resolved by all the judges of England upon advised consideration of this act of 3 H. 7. and upon consultation, and conference between them, as the lord Dier hath reported under his own hand, which I have seen, but the report thereof is omitted in the print; and the indictments grounded upon this statute, are according to this resolution. Fourthly, that she be not ward, or bondwoman to the person that taketh her, or causeth her to be taken only as his ward, or bondwoman.

3 & 4 Ph. and Mar. justice Dalisons report. Mich. 26 Eliz. Dier manuscript. And so resolved by parliament. in anno 39 El. cap. 9.

By this act, not only the takers, but the procurers, abetters of the felony, and receivers of the said woman wittingly, knowing the same, be all adjudged as principall felons: the like whereof we finde not in any other statute, that we remember. But by a construction of the common law, they that receive the misdoers, and not the woman, are accessories; for this act maketh the receivers of the woman, &c principals.

Nota, quia raro.

[62]

For the odiousnesse of this offence, the benefit of clergie is taken away from all the offenders against the said act. Vid. Kelway, and Stanford.

39 Eliz. cap. 2. Kelway, 81. b. Stanf. pl. cor. 37. b.

See a good and profitable statute made for such as take away maidens or women children, &c. within the age of sixteene yeares (though it be not against their will) without consent of parents, &c. and a penalty imposed for deflowring, or contracting matrimony with such maids or women-children; and further, the forfeiture which such maid or woman-childe undergoe, which consent to such contract, &c. But because we are now to speak of felonies, whereunto that act extends not, we refer the reader to the statute itselfe. Only we will adde a case which we find in the parliament roll.

4 & 5 Ph. and Mar. cap. 8. Hil. 34. Eliz. lib. 3. fo. 37. Ratcliffes case.

The Lady Nevill of Essex complained in parliament, that John Brewse and others brake her house at London, and violently took thereout Margerie the daughter of John Nierford her sonne (by her first husband) and carried the said Margerie away to the house of Sir Robert Howard knight; and they kept away the said Margerie, to the end she should not pursue in court christian, for the annullation of a contract of matrimony, against the said John Brewse. This was holden so great an offence, as the said Sir Robert was committed by the lords to the Tower of London, and he after found surety, and promised to do his uttermost to bring forth the said Margery by a day prefixed, or else to yield himself prisoner to the

Rot. Parl. 2 R. 2. nu. 34.

Tower

Tower againe: but it seems the maid was restored to her mother againe, &c. for I find no further prosecution of that cause. See hereafter, cap. 45, *in fine*. 43 Eliz. cap. 13.

CAP. XIII.

Of Felonie for cutting out of Tongues, and putting out of Eyes, &c.

3 H. 4. ca. 5.

IF any man doe cut out the tongue, or put out the eyes of any of the kings lieges, of malice prepensed, it is felony.

The mischiefe before this statute was, that when one had been beaten, wounded, maimed, or robbed, &c. the misdoers, to the end that the party grieved might not be able to accuse them, did cut out their tongues, or put out their eyes, pretending the same to be no felony: and therefore it is ordained and established to be felony by this act.

Here it is to be observed, that where it doth appear by the preamble of this law, that this offence had been before this act daily done: this law did so terrifie offenders, as we remember not, that we have read in any book or record, any to be indicted, &c. upon this law, above one at the most. And of all statutes these are to be preferred, which prevent offences before they be done, before those which punish them after they be done. And therefore in the making of this law there was *salutaris severitas, et beata securitas.*

Malice prepensed.] That is,voluntary and of set purpose, though it be done upon a sudden occasion: for if it be voluntary, the law implyeth malice.

Bract. lib. 3. fo. 144. b.

We read in Bracton, that the cutting off of a mans privie members was felony by the common law: for he saith, *Quid dicitur si quis alterius virilia absciderit, et illum libidinis causa vel convitii castraverit? tenetur sive hoc volens fecerit, vel invitus, et sequitur pœna aliquando capitalis, aliquando perpetuum exilium cum omni bonorum ademptione.* And agreeable thereunto, I finde a record in Bracton's time to this effect: *Henricus Hail et A. uxor ejus capti et detenti sunt in prisona de Evilchester, eò quòd rectati fuerunt quòd ipsi absciderunt virilia Johannis Monachi, quem idem Henricus deprehendit cum prædicta A. uxore ejus, &c.* Fleta saith, *Si quis castratus fuerit, talis pro mahemiato poterit adjudicari.* And, therewith agreeth old justice Sennal in the Mirror; and so is the law holden at this day. And in the Appeale and Indictment of Mayhem it is said, *felonicè mayhemavit:* whereof we shall speak more hereafter in his proper place. Cutting off of eares is no felony, as it appeareth by the statute of 37 H. 8. Vid. Stanf. Pl. cor. 27. a. The offender shall have the benefit of his clergie.

Rot. Clauf. anno 13 H. 3. m. 9.

[63]

Fleta, lib. 1. ca. 38. Mir. ca. 1. § 9. De homicidio. See hereafter ca. 53. of Mayhem. 37 H. 8. cap. 6. Mir. cap. 4. De artic. de Eire.

CAP.

CAP. XIV.

OF BURGLARIE.

A BURGLAR (or the perſon that committeth burglary) is by the [a] common law a felon, that in the night breaketh and entreth into a manſion houſe of another, of intent to kill ſome reaſonable creature, or to commit ſome other felony within the ſame, whether his felonious intent be executed or not. We call it in Latin *burglaria:* and in *ſtatuto de officio coronat.* the offenders are called *raptores domorum.*

This word [b] *burglar*, is derived of theſe two words, viz. *burgh*, ſignifying an houſe, and *laron* ſignifying a thief, as it were an houſe-thiefe. [c] The Saxons called it huſbrec, *inter ſcelera inexpiabilia.* And aptly was it derived from *latro:* for,

[d] *Ut jugulent homines, ſurgunt de nocte latrones.*

[e] Britton calleth him a *burgeſſor.* Then let us peruſe the branches of this deſcription.

In the night.] [f] The word in the indictment or appeale, is, *noctanter, id eſt, noctu.* The natural day is divided *in lucem*, light, which is *dies ſolaris*, and *in tenebras*, which is night. [g] And therefore as long as the day-light continues, whereby a mans countenance may be diſcerned, it is called day: and when darkneſſe comes and day-light is paſt, ſo as by the light of day you cannot diſcerne the countenance of a man, then it is called night. [h] *Poſuiſti tenebras, et facta eſt nox, in qua pertranſeunt beſtiæ ſilvæ; ſol oritur et congregatæ ſunt, exit homo ad opus et operationem ſuam, et redit veſpere.* This doth aggravate the offence, ſith the night is the time wherein man is to reſt, and wherein beaſts runne about ſeeking their prey.

In ancient records *crepuſculum* was ſignified, when it was ſaid *Inter canem et lupum:* for when the night begins, the dog ſleeps, and the wolf ſeeks his prey. For ſo we finde the entry oftentimes in the raigne of E. 1. as taking one example for many. [i] *Margeria filia Nicolai de Okele appellat Johannem Choſe pro raptu, et pace regis fracta, die Martis, &c. inter canem et lupum, id eſt, inter diem et noctem, vel in crepuſculo, Anglicè* twylight.

[k] *In placito de domo combuſta malitioſè hora veſpertina, ſcilicet inter canem et lupum venerunt malefactores, A. B. &c.*

[l] *Ignitegium, à tegendo ignem,* i. coverle fue, *hora octava poſt meridiem.*

[m] Bracton ſaith, *Si quis furem nocturnum occiderit, ita demum impune foret, ſi parcere ei ſine periculo ſuo non potuit; ſi autem potuit, aliter erit, in manibus enim regis ſunt vita et mors hominum, ſicut coram rege apud Windeſore de quodam homine de Cocham, coram Gulielmo de Ralegh tunc juſticiario, cui dominus rex in tali caſu perdonavit mortem.* Agreeable hereunto was the law of the Twelve Tables, *Si noctu furtum factum ſit, jure cæſus eſt.*

Break

[a] Inter leg. Edm. cap. 6. fo. 76. 22 Deut. 2.

[b] Lib. 4. fo. 39. Brooke's caſe.

[c] Inter leges. Canuti, fo. 118. cap. 61. Lamb.

[d] Horace lib. 1. epiſt.

[e] Britton, fo. 17.

[f] 4 E. 6. Br. cor. 185. Stanf. pl. cor. fo. 30.

[g] 3 E. 3. cor. 293.

[h] Pſal. 164. Lib. 7. fo. 6. b. Milborns caſe.

[i] Tr. 7 E. 1. coram rege, Rot. 12 Gloc.

[k] Placita corone apud novum caſtrum, anno 24 E. 1. Rot. 6. in dorſo.

[l] Hil. 3. R. 2. coram rege Rot. 8. London. John Imperials caſe.

[m] Bract. lib. 3. fo. 144. b. Pardon.

1 Mar. Dier 99. *Break and enter.*] The words of the indictment be, *Fregit et intravit:* and this is understood of an actuall breaking of the house, and not of a breaking in law: for every entry into the house by a trespasser, is a breaking in law: but in case of a burglary, every entry is not a breaking of the house, for the words of the indictment be, *Felonicè et burglariter fregit, &c.* As if the doore of a mansion house stand open, and the thief enter into the house with a purpose to steale, this is a breaking of the house in law, and yet no burglary, because there must be an actuall breaking. So it is if the window of the house be open, and a thiefe with a hook or other engine draweth out some of the goods of the owner: this is no burglary, because there is no actuall breaking of the house. But if the thiefe breaketh the glasse of the window, and with a hook or other engine draweth out some of the goods of the owner, this is burglary, for there was an actuall breaking of the house. It is deemed an entry, when the thiefe breaketh the house, and his body, or any part thereof, as his foot, or his arme, is within any part of the house: or when he putteth a gun into a window which he hath broken, or into an hole of the house which he hath made, of intent to murder or kill; or as hath been said, a hook or other engine into any part of the house which he hath broken, of intent to steale: this being put by him into the house, is an entry and breaking of the house. But if he doth barely break the house without any such entry at all, that is no burglary, for it must be *fregit et intravit.*

Stanf. pl. cor. 30. a. Dier 1 Mar. 99. a. 22 Ass. p. 39. 95.

* 13 H. 4. 13.

* If divers come in the night to do a burglary, and one of them break and enter, the rest of them standing neere to the doore, or about other parts of the house, or at a lanes end, or some orchard gate, or field gate, or the like, to watch that no help shall come to defend and aide the owner or dweller; this is burglary in all.

That which is done *in fraudem legis*, the law giveth no benefit thereof to the party. As if thieves come in the night with hue and cry, pretending that they be robbed, and shall require the constable to search for the felons, and whilest he goeth with them into some mans house, they binde and rob the constable, and dweller, this is burglary; for in judgement of law it is their act.

Into a mansion house.] The indictment saith, *Domus mansionalis*, a mansion or dwelling house.

[a] 2 E. 6. Br. cor. 180. Britton, fo. 17.

[a] *Domus mansionalis* is divided into two branches, viz. to inset edifices, as hall, parler, buttry, kitching, and lodging chambers, &c. and the outset buildings, as barnes, stables, cowhouses, dairies, &c. all these are parcels of the mansion-house, and will passe by the name of *domus mansionalis*. And albeit every mansion-house hath not all these buildings, yet every house for the dwelling and habitation of man is taken to be a mansion-house, wherein burglary may be committed.

[b] Lib. 4. fo. 40. in Brocks case. Hil. 38 Eliz. per les justices, ibid.

[b] If a man hath a mansion house, and upon some accident he and all his family some part of the night are out of the house, and in the mean time a thief break and enter into the house, of intent to steale; this is burglary, although neither the owner nor any of his family is in the house: for the indictment of burglary is, *domum mansionalem, &c. fregit, &c.* and this is *domus mansionalis.* [c] See hereafter the statutes of 23 H. 8. and 5 E. 6.

[c] 23 H. 8. cap. 1. 5 E. 6. cap. 9. See *inter leges Alvcredi*, c. 6.

If

[d] If a man do break and enter a church in the night, of intent to steale, &c. this is burglary, for *ecclesia est domus mansionalis omnipotentis Dei.* [e] *Frustra legis auxilium invocat, qui in legem committit.* [f] *Domus mea domus orationis vocabitur, vos autem fecistis illam speluncam latronum. Sacrilegium derivatur à sacro et legere, id est, furari.*

A tent or booth in fair or market, is not *domus mansionalis*, but of another name or kind; [g] but that is provided for by the statute of 5 E. 6. cap. 9. whether the robbery be done in the night, or in the day, the owner, &c. being within the same, sleeping or waking. But a shop wherein any person doth converse being parcell of a mansion-house, or not parcell, is taken for a mansion-house.

Likewise a chamber or room, be it upper or lower, wherein any person doth inhabit or dwell, is *domus mansionalis*, in law. [65]

Our ancient authors and old records did expresse burglary under this word, *hamsuckne*, or *hamsokne*. The first is derived from two Saxon words, viz. of *ham*, that signifieth a mansion-house, *domus mansionalis*, which to this day we call our home: and *suckne* or *succen*, that is, *seeken*, as much to say, as to seek a man in his house to slay or rob him.

It is to be noted that our ancient authors, nor our old bookcases do distinguish between the day and the night, when the offence should be committed in the house, save only the Mirror.

Si quis hamsockne, *quæ dicitur invasio domus contra pacem domini regis in domo sua se defenderit, et invasor occisus est, impersecutus et inultus remanebit, si ille quem invasit aliter se defendere non potuit: dicitur enim quòd non est dignus habere pacem, qui non vult observare eam.* And the Mirror saith, *Hamsockne de auncient ordinance est peche mortel, car droit est que chescun eyt quiet en son hostel, q. a la ley est.*

Others derive *hamsockne* from *ham*, which of both sides is confessed to be a mansion-house, and *sockne* which signifies a court, as much to say, as to have jurisdiction, or to hold plea of offences done to a man in his house.

One was indicted, *Quod clausum I. S. fregit, &c. ad ipsum interficiendum.* This is not felony without any act done, though it were *noctanter:* for the appeale and indictment of burglary is *quod domum mansionalem, &c. fregit et intravit.* So as neither close nor any other place, but the mansion-house only is required to make burglary. But burglary may be committed as well in the outset buildings, as in the inset, for all are parts of the mansion-house, and he that breaketh any of the outset buildings doth break *domum mansionalem*, as well as he that breaks the inset.

Of intent to kill.] If a man be indicted, that he in the night time did feloniously break the house of I. S. *ad verberandum ipsum I. S.* this is no burglary, because it was but to beat, and not to kill. But if it were *ad interficiendum I. S.* then it is burglary, though he never touched him; for the intent must be to commit felony, and not trespasse, or other thing that is not felony, the words of the appeale or indictment being, *Quod felonicè et burglariter fregit, et intravit, &c.* so as there must be a felonious and burglarious intent.

Or to commit some other felony.] They be burglers which break any house or church in the night, although they take away nothing:

[d] Britton. fo. 17. Dier, 1 Mar. 99. 22 E. 3. tit. cor. 264. 22 Ass. p. 95. 26 Ass. 19.

[e] 27 Ass. 42. 20 E. 2. Cor. 283. 12 E. 3. Cor. 120. Rot. Claus. 3 E. 3. m. 2 & 18. the ordinary may allow clergy for sacriledge. Lib. 11. fo. 29.

[f] Matth. 21. 23.

[g] 5 E. 6. cap. 9.

Bracton, lib. 3. fo. 144. b. Britton, fo. 33. Statut. Walliæ, fo. 6. ter. de Snoden. Mirr. cap. 1. § 11. de Hamsockne. Exposit. vocab. inter statuta. Fleta, lib. 1. ca. 42.

13 H. 4. fol. 7. tit. cor. 229.

13 H. 4. ubi sup.

22 E. 3. cor. 264. 22 Ass. 39. & 95.

thing: otherwiſe it is of robbery, as ſhall be ſaid hereafter. See Stanf. Pl. Cor. 30. b.

23 H. 8. cap. 1. 5 E. 6. ca. 9.

The ſtatutes of 23 H. 8. cap. 1. and 5 E. 6. cap. 9. do not define what burglary is, but take away the benefit of clergy from certaine kindes of burglary. As when an actuall robbery is done, and when the owner or dweller, &c. is put in fear, &c. or when the owner or dweller, &c. is ſleeping or waking within any place within the precinct of the ſame houſe; theſe circumſtances do aggravate the burglary: and therefore the makers of thoſe ſtatutes took away the benefit of clergie not in all caſes of burglary, but in thoſe particular caſes where a robbery is done, &c. But the ſtatute of 18 Eliz. cap. 6. hath taken away the benefit of clergie in all caſes of burglary: and hereby a good and equall proportion is kept in all caſes of this nature. And both acts of parliament, and the reſolution of judges do well agree together, which ſome not well obſerving have publiſhed manifeſt errours, which being in caſe of life are fit to be reformed.

Clergie. 18 Eliz. cap. 6.

35 Eliz. ca. 15.

If any man ſhall break a houſe by day, and take away thence money or goods to the value of five ſhillings or more, in any part of a dwelling houſe, or outhouſe belonging to the ſame, though no perſon be therein, for this felony he ſhall loſe the benefit of his clergy, ſo as for this offence the party ſhall ſuffer death, as in caſe of burglary.

[66]

CAP. XV.

Of BURNING of HOUSES.

De Incendiariis inter leges Æthelſtani, cap. 6. fo. 61. Et Canuti, cap. 61. fo. 118. *Huſbærnet* numeratur inter ſcelera inexpiabilia.

HAVING now ſpoken of burglaries, and felonies concerning houſes, there reſteth one other of that kind, wherewith we will conclude this diviſion, and that is, Burners of houſes: which being a felony by the common law, let us ſee what our ancient authors, and old parliaments, and records have left unto us thereof.

[a] Cap. Itineris.

[a] The ancient article of the eire was, *De incendiariis nocturnis vel diurnis, et combuſtionibus tempore pacis nequiter perpetratis.*

[b] Bract. l. 3. 146. b.

[b] Hereof Bracton ſaith, *Si quis turbata ſeditione incendium fecerit nequiter et in felonia, vel ob inimicitiam, vel alia de cauſa, capitali ſententia punietur. Nequiter dico, quia incendia fortuita, vel per negligentiam facta, et non mala conſcientia, non ſic puniuntur, quia civiliter agitur contra tales.*

Brit. fo. 16.

Britton ſaith, *Soit inquiſe de ceux que feloniouſment en temps de peace aient auters blees, ou auters meaſons arſes, et ceux que ſerr' de ceo attaint, ſoient arſes, iſſint que ils ſoient punies per meſme le choſe dont ilz pecherent.*

Fleta li. 1. ca. 35. De combuſtionibus.

Fleta ſaith, *Si quis ædes alienas nequiter ob inimicitiam, vel prædæ cauſa tempore pacis combuſſerit, et inde convictus fuerit per appellum, vel ſine, capitali debet ſententia puniri.*

Mirror ca. 1. § 8. De Ardours cap. 2. § 11. De Appeal darſon. & § 12. cap. 3. § Al arſon.

The Mirror, *Ardours ſont, que ardent citie, ville, maiſon home, maiſon beaſt, ou auters chateux, de lour felonie en temps de pace pur hame haine ou vengeance, &c.* In Appeal *de arson. Issint ico dise, &c. Que Sebright illonque est defamy, &c. de ceo que a tiel jour, &c. en tiel meason,* * *ou biens, mist le feu, &c.* And afterwards *en respons al arson. Al arson poit il dire, que la venture avient de mischance, et nient de felony purpense.* * Ou biens. W. 1. ca. 15.

So hainous was this offence, that in anno 3 E. 1. it was declared by parliament, *Que ceux queux sont prises pur arson feloniousment fait, ne soient en ascun manner replevisablis. Adjudicantur suspendi, qui ex malitia præcogitata combusserunt magnam partem de Lynne in com. Norff.* Hil. 7 E. 2. Corã rege Rot. 24. Norff.

Upon dispersing of bills, threatning burning of houses, &c. was made high treason, whereof more hereafter: but that act is repealed by 1 E. 6. cap. 12. and 1 Mar. Now upon that which hath been said, our purpose is to frame a description of this felony, as may also be warranted by our year-books, and the common opinion and experience at this day. 8 H. 6. ca. 6. See 15 H. 6. nu. 23.

Burning is a felony at the common law, committed by any that maliciously and voluntarily, in the night or day, burneth the house of another.

Now let us peruse this description, by all his materiall parts. All the ancient authors.

Burning.] Putting of fire into any part of a house, whereby that part burneth. For it is necessary, that there be a burning, but it is not necessary, that all or any part be wholly burnt, nor that the fire hath any continuance, but the intent only sufficeth not. As if one put fire into any part of a house, and it burneth not, this is no felony, for the words of the indictment be, *incendit, et combussit.* Again, if it doth burn, though it goeth out of it itself, it is felony. 3 H. 7. 10. 11 H. 7. 1. 23 H. 8. ca. 1. 25 H. 8. ca. 3. 5 & 6 E. 6. ca. 9. 4 & 5 Ph. & Mar. cap. 4. Lib. 11. fo. 35. Alexander Poulters case.

By the common law.] This is proved by all the ancient authors, acts of parliament, and books aforesaid. And the reason thereof is, for that burning of houses being an hostile action, is presumed in law to be done maliciously for revenge, and as an enemy, to consume the same by fire in time of peace. It was made in speciall manner high treason, (as before is said) viz. if any threatned by casting of bils, to burn an house, if money be not laid in a certain place, and after did burn the house: but this treason is repealed by 1 E. 6. ca. 12. and 1 Mar. but yet the felony remaineth still: for *in proditione* (as hath been said) *implicatur felonia.* 3 H. 7. ubi supra. [67] 8 H. 6. ca. 6. 3 H. 7. 10. per Brian. High treason. Nota.

Maliciously and voluntarily. Proved also by the words of the indictment, which be, *voluntariè, ex malitia sua præcogitata, et felonicè.* For if it be done by mischance, or negligence, it is no felony, as before it appeareth.

The law doth sometime imply, that the house was burnt maliciously and voluntarily. As if one intend to burn the house of A only, and not the house of B. and yet in burning the house of A. the house of B. is burnt; in this case the burning of the house of B. is felony, because it proceeded of the malicious and voluntary burning of the house of A. and the event shall be coupled to the cause, which was voluntary, and malicious: and therefore in the indictment for the burning of the house of B. it shall be said, *voluntariè ex malitia sua præcogitata, et felonicè, &c.* Pl. Com. fo. 475.

The house of another.] This is not only intended of inset houses, parcell of the mansion-house, but to the outset also, as barn, stable, cow-houſe, ſheephouſe, dairy houſe, millhouſe, and the like, parcell of the manſion houſe: but burning of a barn, being no parcell of a manſion houſe, is no felony: and yet if there be corn or hay within it, the burning thereof is felony, though the barn be not part of a manſion houſe. * But the offender is not ouſted of his clergy, but where he burns ſome part of a manſion houſe, or a barn with corn.

Tr. 44 Eliz. Coram rege. Ro. 20. 229. Lib. Int. Coke, fo. 25. b. lib. 4. fo. 20. Barhams caſe.

* Pl. Com. 475.

Note the ancient authors extended this felony, further then houſes, viz. to ſtacks of corn, wayns or carts of cole, wood or other goods. And it is ſaid in 3 H. 7. *ubi ſupra*, *Certum eſt quòd crematio domorum felonicè fuit felonia per communem legem.*

3 & 4 E. 6. c. 5.

The attempt to burn a ſtack of corn, was made felony by the ſtatute of 3 and 4 E. 6. but this is repealed by 1 Mariæ.

37 H. 8. ca. 6.

Burning of the frame of a houſe, was made felony by the ſtatute of 37 H. 8. becauſe the frame of a houſe is no houſe: but that is repealed by 1 E. 6. ca. 12. and 1 Mariæ.

43 El. ca. 13.

43 El. ca. 13. It is felony if any within the counties of Cumberland, Northumberland, Weſtmerland, or the B. of Dureſme wilfully, and of malice burn or cauſe to be burnt any barn or ſtack of corn or grain, without benefit of clergy.

Bract. lib. 3. fo. 146. b.

Note a diverſity between the indictment of burglary and burning; for the indictment of burglary muſt ſay (as hath been ſaid) *domum manſionalem*, but ſo need not the indictment of burning, but *domum*, viz, a barn, &c. malt houſe, or the like.

[68]

CAP. XVI.

OF ROBBERY.

See the 1. part of the Inſtitutes. Sect. 501. Cuſtum. de Norm. cap. 71.

[a] Int. leges Canu. cap. 61. fo. 118. Lamb.

[b] Bracton, li. 3. fo. 146.

ROBBERY is a felony by the common law, committed by a violent aſſault, upon the perſon of another, by putting him in fear, and taking from his perſon his money or other goods of any value whatſoever. [a] See *inter leges Canuti*, *apertæ compilationes numerantur inter ſcelera hominum inexpiabilia.*

Robbery.] [b] It is derived *de la robe*, both becauſe in ancient times (as ſometime yet is done) they bereave the true man of ſome of his robes or garments, and alſo for that his money or other goods are taken from his perſon, that is, from or out of ſome part of his garment, or robe about his perſon. And is ranked in this place, for that it concerneth not only the goods, but the perſon of the owner. We call it, *roberia et rapina*, and the theef *raptor.*

Bracton, lib. 3. fo. 150. b. Britton, fo. 22. Fleta, lib. 1. ca. 37. Mirror cap. 1. §. 10.

Whereof Bracton ſaith, *Eſt enim quaſi furtum rapinæ, quæ idem eſt, quantum ad nos, quod roberia, et eſt genus contrectationis contra voluntatem domini, et ſimilis pœna ſequitur utrunque delictum, unde prædo dicitur fur improbus: quis enim magis contrectat rem alienam invito domino, quam ille qui rapit?*

Britton & Fleta Ubi ſupra. 14 E. 3. cor. 115.

Felony by the common law.] This is agreed of, of all, both ancient and late, without any queſtion. And it is deemed in law to be amongſt the moſt hainous felonies, *crimen improbiſſimum.*

Violent

Violent assault.] This agreeth with the indictment, *violenter et felonicè cepit, &c.* Bract. li. 3. fo. 150. b.

By putting him in fear.] This agreeth also with the indictment: and this circumstance maketh the difference between a robber and a cutpurse: both take it from the person, but this takes it *clam et secretè*, without assault or putting in fear, and the robber by violent assault, and putting in fear. If one cut a purse, with money in it above twelve pence, he shall be hanged, and the benefit of clergy is taken from him. But of ancient time the punishment was otherwise. *S. captus in London cum bursa quam scidit cum tribus solidis, et hoc non potuit dedicere, et ideo amittat dextrum pollicem.* Britton saith, *Des cinsors des burses, voylens que celuy que la burse coupa, si auter maviese ne eyt fait, eyt judgement de pillory; et silz eyent emble auter chose meinder de 12 deniers, perdent un oraile, et si le chose passe 12 deniers, eyent judgment de mort.* 10 H. 3. cor. 434. Britton, fo. 24. b.

By taking.] The words of the indictment be, *violenter et felonicè cepit. Hic opus est interprete.* For it must be understood, that there is an actuall taking in deed, and a taking in law, and that may be, when a thief receiveth, &c. For example: if thieves rob a true man, and find but little about him, take it, this is an actuall taking; and by menace of death, compell him to swear upon a book to fetch them a greater sum, which he doth, and deliver it unto them, which they receive, this is a taking in law by them, and adjudged robbery: for fear made him to take the oath, and the oath, and fear continuing, made him bring the money, which amounteth to a taking in law, and in this case there need no speciall indictment, but the generall indictment *(quòd violenter et felonicè cepit,)* is sufficient. And so it is, if at the first, the true man for fear deliver his purse, &c. to the thief. 44 E. 3. 14. 4 H. 4. 2.

This word [*cepit*] necessarily implieth, that the thief must be in possession of the thing stoln: for example, if the bag or purse of the true man be fastned to his girdle, &c. and the thief the more easily to take the bag or purse, doe cut the girdle, whereby the bag or purse falleth to the ground, this is no taking, for the thief had never any possession thereof, *et sic de similibus:* but if the thief had taken up the bag, or purse, and in striving had let it fall, and never took it again, this had been a taking, because he had it in his possession; for the continuance of his possession is not required by law. [69]

From his person.] The words of the indictment be, *à persona, &c.* If the true man seeking to escape, for the safeguard of his mony, cast it into a bush, which the thief perceiving, takes it; this is a taking in law from the person, because it is done at one time. If the true man had cast off his surcote, or other uppermost garment, and the same lying in his presence, a thief assault him, &c. and take the surcote, this is robbery; for that which is taken in his presence, is in law taken from his person: and so it is of the horse of a true man, which stands by him, *et sic de similibus.* 14 E. 3. cor. 115.

In ancient authors and records, in pleas of the crown, you shall read of *sakebere, &c.* whom we will derive and explain. *Sakebere, sacbere,* or *sacburgh, sac,* or *sak* is an ancient French word, and signifieth a bag, purse, or powch. So that *sackbere* is he that did bear the bag, &c. and in legall understanding, is he that was robbed of his mony in his bag. And this agreeth with the interpretation thereof

Bract. lib. 3. fo. 150. b. of by Bracton, viz. *Furtū verò manifestū est, ubi latro deprehensus est seisitus de aliquo latrocinio, viz.* hondhabende, and bacberende, *et insecutus fuerit per aliquē cujus res illa fuerit, qui dicitur* sacaburth. And herewith agreeth Fleta, lib. 1. c. 42. § *Sunt autem*, &c. And Britton, fo. 22. b. & 72. b. agreeth herewith, and calleth him *sakebere;* and so doth justice Stanford, Pl. Cor. fo. 28. term him, which (as we take it) is his right name derived of these two words, *sac*, and *bere*, that is, he that did bear the bag, &c.

Fleta, l. 1. ca. 42. Britton fo. 22. b. & 72 b. Stanf. fo. 28.

14 E. 3. cor. 115. 22 Ass. p. 39. 27 Ass. 38. 24 E. 3. 42. 13 H. 4. 7. 9 E. 4. 28.

Of what value soever.] Though it be under the value of twelve pence, that is taken; (as to the value of a penny or two pence) it is robbery, but somewhat must be taken, for the assault only to rob without taking some money or goods is no felony, and such opinions, as seem to the contrary were maintained by that, which then was anciently holden, *Quòd voluntas reputabatur pro facto.* See before, cap. High Treason, fo. 5. *insidiator viarum.*

CAP. XVII.

In what Cases Breakers of Prisons are Felons.

In the second part of the Institutes upon the statute of 1 E. 2. De frangentibus prisonam.

WE have spoken sufficiently hereof in his proper place, in the exposition of the statute of 1 E. 2. *de frangentibus prisonam.* Only this is to be added, that in case of felony, the offender shall have the benefit of clergy, for the breach of prison.

[70]

CAP. XVIII.

Where Escape Voluntary is Felony.

WE have also spoken somewhat hereof in the exposition of the said act of 1 E. 2. And the voluntary escape can be no felony in the gaoler, unlesse the prisoner be under custody by lawfull warrant expressing the offence, which you may see there at large.

2. There must be a felony done at the time of the escape: for a relation which is but a fiction in law, shall never make a man a felon, as likewise there it appeareth. See Stanford, lib. 1. cap. 26, &c.

CAP.

CAP. XIX.

Of Felonie by ſtealing, carrying away, withdrawing or avoiding of Records, &c.

SI aſcun record (1) *ou parcel dicel, breif, retorne, pannell, proces, ou garrant d'attorney* (2) *en les courts le roy* (3) *de chancery* (4) *eſchequer, lun banke, ou lauter, ou ſa treaſorie* (5) *ſoit voluntarement emblee, emport, retreit, ou avoide* (6) *per aſcun clerke ou auter perſon* (7), *a cauſe de quel aſcun iudgement* (8) *ſoit reverſe* (9): *que tiel embleor, emporter, retraher, et avoider, lour procurators, councellors, et abettors* (10) *ent endites* (11) *et ſur proces ſur ceo fait, ont duement convicts per lour proper confeſſion, ou per enqueſts prender des loiall homes, (dont la moitye ſoit des homes daſcun court* (12) *de meſme les courts, et lauter moitye des auters) ſoient adjudges pur felons, et encorgent la paine de felony, et que les iudges de les courts de lun banke, ou de lauter eyent power de oier et terminer, tielz defaults devant eux, et ent fait punition, come devant eſt dit* (13). 8 H. 6. cap. 12.

IF any record or parcell of the ſame, writ, retorne, panell, proceſſe or warrant of attorny in the kings courts of chancery, exchequer, the one bench or the other, or in his treaſury be willingly ſtolne, taken away, withdrawne, or avoided by any clerk, or by other perſon, becauſe whereof any judgement ſhall be reverſed: that ſuch ſtealer, taker away, withdrawer, or avoyder, their procurators, counſellors, and abettors, thereof indicted, and by proces thereupon made thereof duly convict, by their own confeſſion, or by inqueſt to be taken of lawfull men, (whereof the one halfe ſhall be of the men of any court of the ſame courts, and the other halfe of others) ſhall be judged for felons, and ſhall incurre the paine of felony. And that the judges of the ſaid courts, of the one bench or of the other, have power to hear and determine ſuch defaults before them, and thereof to make due puniſhment, as afore is ſaid. [71]

The miſchiefe before this ſtatute was, That whereas records are of ſuch high nature and credit, as they import in themſelves abſolute verity without contradiction; to the end, that there might be an end of contention and controverſie, and men might reſt in ſafety and repoſe, certaine clerks and other perſons did oftentimes imbeſell records, or ſome parcell of them, and ſometime a

 writ,

writ, retorne, panell, proces, or warrant of attorney; or rase or vitiate the same; by reason whereof divers judgements were avoided, or reversed, whereby no man (as the statute saith) had any thing in surety. This was a great misprision, for the which the offenders therein might be punished, either at the suit of the king by indictment, or at the suit of the party by an action upon his case. See the record concerning this matter following. *Placita coram justiciariis de banco termino Trinitatis anno* 19 *E.* 1. *Rot.* 57. *indors.*

Radulphus de Greshope communis attornatus de com. Westmerland malitiose rotulum excurtavit et abscidit, et ideo per annum et diem committitur turri London, postea anno 20 *E.* 3. *per mandatum regis liberatur et per justiciarios ei est inhibitum ne de cætero in eadē curia de aliquibus negotiis se intromittat.*

Which remedie and punishment were thought too weak against clerks and other persons, which (committing such things) commonly were of small ability: therefore this act, considering the danger of the offence, maketh the same felony, as by the letter thereof appeareth.

* See the first part of the Institutes sect. 117. for this word.

(1) *Si ascun * record.*] A record is regularly a monument or act judiciall before a judge, or judges, in a court of record, entred in [a] parchment in the right roll. It is called a record, for that it recordeth or beareth witnesse of the truth, and is derived of the verb *recordor*, whereof the poet speaketh,

[a] 9 E. 4. 3. b. 16 Eliz. Dier, 330. a.

Virgil.

Si rite audita recordor.

It hath this soveraigne priviledge, that it is proved by no other but by itselfe. *Monumenta (quæ nos recorda vocamus) sunt vetustatis et veritatis vestigia.* And albeit the cause adjudged be particular, yet when it is entred of record, it is of great authority in law, and serves for perpetuall evidence, and therefore ought to be common to all, yea, though it be against the king: as it is declared by act of parliament in *anno* 46 E. 3. which you may reade in the preface to the third book of my reports.

Rot. Parl. 46 E. 3. 9 H. 7. 16. See the preface to the third book.

(2) *Breife, retorne, panel, proces, ou garr' d'attornie.*] All these are sufficiently known, and yet have we treated of the same in the first part of the Institutes.

(3) *En les courts le roy.*] Here are expressly named four of the kings courts, viz. the chancery, the exchequer, the kings bench, and the court of common pleas, and hereunto is added the kings treasury: so as this act extendeth not to any other court or place, then is here named.

(4) *Chancery.*] This must be understood of the court of chancery, which proceedeth according to the course of the common law, as in case of priviledge, of *scire facias* upon recognizances, traverses of offices, and the like: for as to these it is a court of record, but as to the proceeding by English bill in course of equity, it is no court of record, for thereupon no writ of error lieth, as in the other cases.

37 H. 6. 14.

(5) *Ou sa treasorie.*] The kings treasury is called *thesauraria regis*, the place where the kings treasure is kept. This treasure is twofold, viz. his money or coine: and another, that is far more precious and excellent, and those be the sacred judgements, records, and other judiciall proceedings under the safe custody of the treasurer,

[72]

treasurer, and chamberlains of the exchequer. And this treasury is partly in the exchequer, and partly in the towre of London: for there be ancient rolls of the treasury remaining in the towre. And therefore this act intending to include both the one, and the other, saith generally, *en sa treasorie*. Register. F. N. B. 244. d.

(6) *Soit voluntarement emblee, emport, retreit, ou avoide.*] In the indictment upon this statute besides *felonicé*, this word [*voluntarié*] must of necessity be used, to agree with this act. Here be four words used, *emblee* stolne, *emport* carried away, *retreit* withdrawne, *ou avoide* or avoided. So as the sense is, if any record or part of it, writ, retorne, panell, proces, or warrant of attorney, &c. be stolne, carried away, withdrawn, or avoided, &c. And this word [avoided] is a large word, and doth include, rasing, or clipping, or cutting off of the side, or other part of the roll, or any other kind of avoiding the same. 2 R. 3. 10.

(7) *Per ascun clerk ou auter person.*] This act doth not extend to any judge of the court; both because it beginneth with a clerk, &c. and for that by the statute of 8 R. 2. a penalty is inflicted upon a judge, &c. for making any false entry, rasing any roll, or changing any verdict. See the statute; for it extendeth also to clerks. Only this is to be observed in that statute, that where it is said [the king and his councell,] it is intended of the court of justice where the matter dependeth: for the judges are the kings councell for judicature and proceedings according to law and justice. 2 R. 3. 10. 8 R. 2. cap. 4. 2 R. 3. 10.

Justice Ingham paid in the raigne of E. 1. eight hundred marks for a fine, for that a poore man being fined in an action of debt at thirteen shillings foure pence, the said justice moved with pity caused the roll to be rased, and made it six shillings eight pence. 2 R. 3. 10.

This case justice Southcot remembred, when Catlyn chiefe justice of the kings bench in the raigne of queen Elizabeth, would have ordered a rasure of a roll in the like case, which Southcot, one of the judges of that court, utterly denied to assent unto, and said openly, that he meant not to build a clock-house: for (said he) with the fine that Ingham paid for the like matter, the clock-house at Westminster was builded, and furnished with a clock, which continueth to this day.

(8) *A cause de quel ascun judgement soit revers.*] This act extendeth only to records, whereupon judgement is given. But whether judgement be given in causes criminall at the suit of the king upon an indictment, or at the suit of the party in an appeale, or in actions, reall, personall, or mixt, or of the like nature, this act extends thereunto, if judgement be afterwards given, and to outlawries, for there judgement is given *per judicium coronatorum*. For it is not materiall whether the act be done against this statute, either before or after judgement, so judgement be given. 2 R. 3. 10.

(9) *Revers*] is here taken, not only where the judgement is made erroneous, and to be reversed by writ of error, but where the judgement is so annihilated, and made voide, as it bindeth not, or may be reversed or avoided by plea. See the book in 2 R. 3. fol. 10. which expoundeth well this statute.

(10) *Que ticl embleor, emporter, &c. lour procurers, counsellors et abettors, &c.*] This act expresly extendeth to accessories before, and leaveth accessories after to the construction of law, yet may

Vide 3 & 4 Ph. and Mar. Justice Dalisons Report, ubi sup.

there be accessories after the fact: for whensoever an offence is made a felony by act of parliament, there shall be accessories to it both before and after, as if it had been a felony by the common law, and therefore though this act expresseth accessories * before, yet it taketh not away accessories after, but leaveth them to the law, contrary to the opinion of justice Stanford. See before the exposition of 3 H. 7. for taking away of women against their will.

Stanf. pl. cor. 44. b.
3 H. 7. cap 2.
2 R. 3. fo. 10.

(11) *Ent endites.*] If the acts that make this felony, be committed in two counties, the indictment faileth, as hath bin said before upon the statute of 2 & 3 E. 6. cap. 24. And this case of felony rising in two counties, is not holden by any statute yet made.

(12) *Dont la moity soit des hommes dascun court.*] Here is a party jurie, the one halfe to be of the officers and clerks of the court, &c. for their knowledge, and for the better information of the others.

(13) *Et que les judges des dits courts de lun bank ou de lauter eyent power de oier et terminer tiels defaults devant eux, et ent faire punition, come est avant dit.*] This clause is in nature of a commission to the justices of either bench, if the offence be committed in the county where the benches do sit. And the justices of either bench have a concurrent authority, and which of them enquire first shall proceed: but if the felony be committed in another county, then where the benches sit (as for example in Surry, Hertfordshire, &c.) there the justices ought to have a commission. But if the bench sit in Middlesex, and the felony is done in London, in which case a commission is requisite, as is aforesaid. But then some have said, that by the charters of London confirmed by parliament, the major ought to be principall in the commission, and the major is none of the judges authorized by this act to heare and determine this felony, but the justices of the one bench or the other; and therefore the statute being penall, and to be taken strictly, no proceeding can be. *Sed salva res est:* for the charters of the city of London extend only to such offences committed in London, whereof the major with others by commission may enquire of, heare, and determine, and not to such offences so annexed by authority of parliament to other persons (as in this case to the justices of the one bench or the other) as the major is not warranted by the said act to enquire, &c. And therefore a commission in this case may be made to the justices of the one bench or the other, omitting the major, *ne curia regis deficeret in justitia exhibenda.*

2 R. 3. 10.
2 R. 3. 11.

And albeit this kinde of felony is an heinous offence, yet may the offenders therein have their clergy: for untill the raign of H. 7. (that we may note it once for all) the benefit of clergy was not taken away by any act of parliament in case of felony. As for the statute of *bigamis* made in 4 E. 1. it was but an exposition and allowance of the constitution made at the generall councell at Lyons concerning the same, as before hath been said. But (as we remember) the first statute making a new felony that took away the benefit of clergy was the statute of 7 H. 7, concerning souldiers. *Vide* lib. 8. fol. 160. & lib. 11. fol. 11.

4 H. 7. cap. 13.
22 H. 7. cap. ult.
7 H. 7. cap. 1.

CAP.

CAP. XX.

Of Felony in ſuch as uſe the Craft of Multiplication.

NONE from henceforth ſhall uſe to multiply gold or ſilver, or uſe the craft of multiplication (1): and if any the ſame doe, he ſhall incur the pain of felony. 5 H. 4. ca, 4.

This is the ſhorteſt act of parliament that we remember; before the making whereof, divers of the nobility, gentry, and others did waſt and conſume a great part of their inheritance, and wealth, about the art of multiplication, by the ſubtile and ſiniſter perſwaſion of certain impoſtors, and deceivers, which took upon them to be ſkilfull therein, and to be able to multiply gold and ſilver, being themſelves for the moſt part very poor and indigent perſons, of whom it was ſaid, *Quòd pollicentur aliis ingentes divitias, et ipſi petunt parvas drachmas.* See Chaucer our Engliſh poet, who wrote about the time of the making of this act, in the tale of the Channons Yeoman, fo. 63. *(in libro meo,)* that the end of this ſliding and curſed craft (ſo full of impoſture and deceit) is extream beggery: he is worth the reading, for he diſcovereth the ſecrets of this craft, as our act tearms it.

Now ſeeing the end of this feigned art of multiplication is meer deceit, and tendeth to the undoing of many; at this parliament the uſe of this craft of multiplication is made felony. For the better underſtanding of that which ſhall be ſaid, it is to be known, that there are ſix kinds of metalls, viz. *aurum, argentū, æs, ſive cuprum (quia inventum fuit in Cypro) ſtannum, plumbum, et ferrum.* That is to ſay, gold, ſilver, copper, tynne, lead, and iron; for *chalybs* ſteel is but the harder part of iron, and *orichalcum, aurichalcum,* viz. lattyn or braſſe, is compounded of copper and other things.

(1) *The craft of multiplication.*] That is, to change other metals into very gold or ſilver. And this they pretend to doe by a *quint eſſence,* or a fifth eſſence. Four eſſences, or elements we know, fire, aire, water, and earth, but ſay they, this *quint eſſence* is a certain ſubtill, and ſpirituall ſubſtance extracted out of things by ſeparation from the four elements, differing really from their eſſence, as *aqua vitæ,* the ſpirit of wine, or the like, and this is called *elixar,* or the philoſophers ſtone, and it is part of alchemie, or chemie, in Latine *ars chemica.* The offenders therein are called multipliers, chemiſts, alchemiſts, &c. There * may be acceſſories to this new felony, both before and after. King Henry the ſixth, by his letters patents, *de concilii ſui deliberatione deputavit Willm. Cautelo et alios cives civitatis London ad inveſtigandam veritatem ſuper hiis quæ in ſcriptis erunt eis monſtrata, pro multiplicatione nuniſmatis,*

* 7 E. 6. Dier, 88 Rot. Pat. 34 H. 6. m. 13.

[a] Ro. Pat. 35 H. 6.

[b] Ro. Pat. 34 H. 6. m. 7. Hanc artem ſophiſticam impoſturam nominat *Melancthon.* Mentiendi et fallendi artem. *Petrarch. Eraſ.* in Colloquio Dæmonis præſtigias. *Peucerus Chaucer* ubi ſupra. The curſed and ſliding craft. *Vertitur in fumum quicquid ineptus agit.* See *Pancirollus.* Int. nova reperta tit. 7. fo. 357.

nummiſmatis, tam de auro, quam argento, et quicquid in præmiſſis egerint, cum eorum opinione referrent in ſcriptis regi et concilio ſuo.

The like [a] letters patents *anno* 35 H. 6. *pro Thoma Harvie et aliis.*

Rex [b] *ex ſua regali prærogativa, &c. dedit licentiam Johanni Faceby et aliis ad inveſtigandum, proſequendum et perficiendum quandam precioſiſſimam medicinam, quintam eſſentiam, lapidem philoſophorum nuncupatum, nec non poteſtatem faciendi et exercendi tranſmutationes metallorum in verum aurum, et argentum,* with a *non obſtante* of this ſtatute of 5 H. 4. By theſe letters patents this act is more explained, then by any record we have ſeen.

Vide Stanf. pl. cor. 37. b.

How theſe ſeveral kinds of metalls, as is ſuppoſed, proceed originally from ſulphur * and quickſilver, as from their father and mother, and other things concerning the ſame, you may at your leiſure read in George Agricola, lib. 10. ca. 1. Encelms, li. 1. ca. 1. Pl Com. 339.

Gen. c. 1. v. 9. cap. 2. v. 11.

Almighty God in the fourth day created the earth, and no mention is made of metals, for that they were as parts of the earth.

The fatall end of theſe five are beggery; this kind of alchemiſt, the monopoliſt, the concealer, the informer, and poetaſters.

Sæpe pater dixit, ſtudium quid inutile tentas?
Mæonides nullas ipſe reliquit opes.

*[75]

I could give examples (of mine own obſervation) of all theſe, if it were pertinent to our purpoſe.

CAP. XXI.

Of Felony in Hunters in the Night, or with painted Faces, in any Foreſt, Park, or Warren.

1 H. 7. ca. 1.

AT every ſuch time as information ſhall be made of any unlawfull huntings in any foreſt, park, or warren (3) by night, or with painted faces (1) to any of the kings councell (4) or any the juſtices of the kings peace (5) in the county where any ſuch hunting ſhall be had, of any perſon to be ſuſpected (2) thereof, it ſhall be lawfull to any of the ſame councell, or juſtices of peace, to whom any ſuch information ſhall be made, to make a warrant (6) to the ſherif of ſuch county, or to any conſtable, bailif, or other officer within the ſame county, to take and arreſt the ſame perſon and perſons of whom ſuch informations ſhall be made, and to have him, or them before the maker of the ſame warrant, or any other (7) of the kings ſaid councell, or his juſtices of peace of the ſame county. And that the ſaid counſellor or juſtice of peace, before whom ſuch perſon, or perſons ſhall be brought, by his diſcretion have power to examine him or them ſo brought, of the

the ſaid hunting, and of the ſaid doers in that behalf (8): and if the ſame perſon * wilfully conceal the ſame huntings, or any perſon with him defective therein (9), that then the ſame concealment be againſt every ſuch perſon ſo concealing felony, and the ſame felony to be enquired of and determined, as other felonies within this realm have uſed to be: and if he then confeſſe the truth, and all that he ſhall be examined of, and knoweth in that behalf (10), that then the ſaid offences of huntings by him done, be againſt the king our ſoveraigne lord, but treſpaſſe finable, by reaſon of the ſame confeſſion, at the next generall ſeſſions of the peace to be holden in the ſame county, by the kings juſtices of the ſame ſeſſions, there to be ſeſſed. And if any reſcous, or diſobeiſance be made to any perſon having authority to doe execution, or juſtice by any ſuch warrant, by any perſon, the which ſo ſhould be arreſted, ſo that the execution of the ſame warrant thereby be not had, that then the ſame reſcous and diſobeyſance be felony (11), inquirable and determinable, as is aforeſaid. And over this, it is enacted and ſtabliſhed, that if any perſon or perſons hereafter be convict of any ſuch huntings with painted faces, viſors, or otherwiſe diſguiſed, to the intent they ſhould not be known, or of unlawfull hunting in time of night, that then the ſame perſon or perſons ſo convict, to have like punition, as he or they ſhould have, if he or they were convict of felony (12).

* See the expoſition of this word [conceal] hereafter in this chap.

[76]

Now let us peruſe the words of this new and ill penned law.

(1) *By night, or with painted faces.*] That is to ſay, either by night, or in the day with painted faces, for that doth equall the caſe of the night, in reſpect the offenders cannot be known, or diſcerned, in regard of ſuch diſguiſings. And albeit the body of the act ſpeaketh only of painted faces, yet it extendeth to viſors and other diſguiſings, for thoſe words are in the preamble rehearſing the miſchief, and the remedy muſt be appliable thereunto, and the laſt branch of this act doth make this point clear.

(2) *As information ſhall be made, &c. of any perſon to be ſuſpect.*] Hereby it appeareth, that a bare information without ſhewing juſt cauſe of ſuſpition at the leaſt, is not ſufficient to ground a warrant according to this act, for the words be, [of any perſon to be ſuſpected.] And this act is generall, and extends to all perſons of what eſtate or degree ſoever, and as well to women, as to men: for the words be [if any perſon] and *generalia verba ſunt generaliter intelligenda.* And it is neceſſary for him that taketh the information, to take it in writing, becauſe it is the ground of his warrant.

(3) *Of any unlawfull huntings in any foreſt, park, or warren.*] This act doth not extend to any chaſe of the king, or of any other perſon, neither doth it extend to any foreſts, parks, or warrens in uſe or reputation, and which are not foreſts, parks, or warrens in law. See the 1. part of the Inſtitutes, ſect. 378. what a foreſt, a chaſe, and a park, &c. is. 21 E. 1. tit. Foreſts. Raſt. 19.

(4) *To any of the kings councell.*] This is underſtood of the kings privy councell; and any one will ſerve, but he muſt be dwelling in the county where ſuch offence is committed.

(5) *Or*

(5) *Or to any the justices of the kings peace, &c.*] And likewise any one justice of the peace will serve.

(6) *Warrant.*] This warrant ought to be in writing under the seal of him that maketh it.

(7) *Before the maker of the same warrant, or any other, &c.*] So as the officer may carry the party arrested before any privy counsellor, or justice of peace within that county, and to that effect must the warrant be made.

(8) *By his discretion have power to examine him or them so brought of the said hunting, and of the doers in that behalf.*] So as the examination must consist upon two parts. First, of the hunting by the party himself. Secondly, of other doers in that behalf.

D. Haward tempore H. 1. fo. 24. Vide Hotl. 10 R. 1. 153. Vide Camden Brit. 210. (9) *And if the said person wilfully conceal the said hunting, or any person with him defective therein.*] This branch being in the disjunctive, if he conceal either his own offence, or of the other misdoers with him therein, the letter of this act is that it is felony, but by construction * upon the whole statute, it is no felony: and a hunting without killing of any game, is within the danger of this statute.

*[77]

This act is to be taken strictly; for it is the first law that was made for the making of any hunting felony, against that excellent and equall branch of *carta de foresta. Nullus de cætero vitam vel membra pro venatione nostra, &c.* See the statutes of 21 E. 1. 1 E. 3. stat. 1. cap. 8. 7 R. 2. ca. 4. Westm. ca. 8. Regist. fol. 9. F. N. B. fo. 67. Vet. N. B. 41. 45 E. 3. 7. 33 H. 8. Dier. 50.

Cart. de Forest. cap. 10.

Rot. Parl. 9 H. 4. nu. 40. The old statutes concerning the forests are called the good old laws, and customes, and commanded to be observed; and therefore this new act of H. 7. is too severe for beasts that be *feræ naturæ*, whereof there can be no felony by the common law, and that in case of the forests, parks, &c. of subjects, which never was before: and therefore the judges have made a favourable construction, as hereafter in this chapter you shall find.

(10) *And if he confess the truth, and all that he shall be examined of, and knoweth in that behalf.*] That is of his own guiltinesse, and of other misdoers with him, then this act makes it no felony, but trespasse finable, as it was before: but it must be a wilfull concealment; therefore if he knew not the names of the other misdoers, or knew not whether they were there or no, it is no offence, for the concealment must be wilfull. And seeing there is no time limited by this act, and the concealment ought to be wilfull, it were reason, that the information should be made in convenient time after the fact done.

(11) *And if any rescous or disobeisance be made to any person having authority to do execution of justice by any such warrant by any person, the which so should be arrested, so that execution of the same warrant be not had, that then the same rescous and disobedience be felony.*] Here it is to be observed that the hunting being as yet no felony, the rescous could not be felony, if this branch had not been. Herein two things are to be considered; first, that it extendeth not but to the rescous, or disobeysance, that is committed by the party himself, that is to be arrested, and not to any other. Secondly, that if the party rescue himself, yet if he be pursued and taken, so as execution of the warrant be had, it is no felony, as it is manifest by the letter of this branch.

(12) *And*

(12) *And over this be it enacted, &c. That if any person or persons hereafter to be convict of any such huntings with painted faces, visors, or otherwise disguised, &c. or of unlawfull hunting in the night,* * *that then the same person or persons so convict, to have like punition, as he or they should have, as if they were convict of felony.*]

* Nota [that the] &c. So as before such conviction there is no felony.

Gerrard the queens attorney general (who was a grave and reverend man) said openly in the kings bench, that it had been resolved by the justices upon this statute, that if a man in the night, or by day with painted face doe hunt, &c. and being examined according to the act and concealeth it, this is (upon the construction of the whole act) no felony; for the first clause concerning concealment, and this clause which now we handle, must be coupled or joyned by construction together, viz. if any person be convict of such hunting with painted face, or of unlawfull hunting in the night, this conviction must be upon not guilty pleaded, which the justices expounded to be the * concealment intended in the first branch, for they held that it ought to be a judiciall concealment, and not an extrajudiciall concealment, before one of the privy councell, or a justice of peace which may lie in averment, so as before it be felony, he must be convicted of such hunting, &c. upon not guilty pleaded first: and after such conviction then must he be indicted again, *super tota materia*, that he *felonicè* did conceal, &c. against the form of the statute: and if the offender upon the first indictment confesseth the indictment, then it is such a judiciall confession as this act intendeth, and no felony within this statute. And this we heard the attorney report, and then observed it, which concurring with our own opinion we thought good to publish, and the rather for that in master Lambards book of Justice of Peace amongst his precedents of indictments an erroneous precedent of an indictment is of felony for the concealment, &c. upon examination before justices of peace.

Mic. 19 & 20 El. In the kings bench a report of the resolution of the justices upon this branch.

* Concealment expounded.

[78]

It is said in 33 H. 8. that chasing in parks is made felony, (intending this statute) notwithstanding it may be made tresspasse at the pleasure of the party, which we think is the clearest way.

Dier, 33 H. 8. fol. 50. a.

Now what time shall be adjudged night, see before in the chapter of Burglary. For this felony the delinquent may have his clergy: see Stanford, 37. b.

CAP.

CAP. XXII.

Of Felony for imbesiling the Kings Armour, Ordnance, &c. or Victuall, to the Value of Twenty Shillings, provided for Souldiers.

31 El. cap. 4. BE it enacted by the authority of this present parliament, that if any person, or persons, having at any time hereafter the charge or custody of any armour, ordnance (1), munition, shot, powder or habillements of war (2) of the queens majesties, her heirs, or successors, or of any victuals provided for the victualling of any souldiers, gunners, mariners, or pioners, shall for any lucre, or gain, or wittingly, advisedly, and of purpose to hinder or impeach her majesties service, imbesill, purloin, or convey away any the same armour, ordnance, munition, shot, or powder, habillements of war, or * victualls, to the value of twenty shillings, at one or severall times: that then every such offence shall be judged felony, and the offender and offenders therein to be tried, proceeded on, and suffer as in case of felony. Provided always, and be it enacted by the authority aforesaid, that none shall be impeached for any offence against this statute, unlesse the same impeachment be prosecuted or begun within the year next after the offence done. And that this act, nor any thing therein contained, nor any attainder nor attainders of any person or persons for any offence made felony by this act, shall in any wise extend, or be adjudged, interpreted, or expounded to make the offender or offenders to forfeit, or lose any lands, tenements, or hereditaments any longer, then during his or their life or lives, or to make any corruption of blood to any the heir or heirs, of any such offender or offenders, or to make the wife of any such offender to lose or forfeit her dower, or title of dower of or in any lands
[79] tenements, or hereditaments, or her action or interest to the same: any thing in this act contained, or any attainder or attainders hereafter to be had for any offence made felony by this act to the contrary notwithstanding. And that such person and persons, as shall be impeached for any offence made felony by this statute, shall by vertue of this act be received, and admitted to make any lawfull proofe that he can, by lawfull witnesse or otherwise, for his discharge and defence in that behalfe, any law to the contrary notwithstanding.

* Nota for victualls.

This is a necessary law, and so penned, as it requireth no curious exposition.

(1) *Ordnance.*] That is guns or artillerie so called, of an order, or

or ordinance anciently made, of what bore, size, or bulk the same should be. And albeit the ordinance (that we can finde) is not extant, yet the name remaineth.

(2) *Habillements of warre.*] Habillement is properly apparell or clothing: but in legall understanding it doth not only extend to harnesse and armour, but to all utensils that belong to war, without which men have not ability to maintain war.

This act making a new felony, hath five excellent provisions, worthy to be imitated in all like cases of new felonies. First, that none shall be impeached for this new felony, but within a year after the offence done. Secondly, that the offender should not lose his lands any longer than during his life. Thirdly, this act makes not any corruption of blood, but that his heire shall inherit. Fourthly, not to make the wife lose her dower. Fifthly, that such persons as shall be impeached for any offence made felony by this act, shall be admitted to make any lawfull proofe [a] by witnesse, or otherwise for his discharge and defence in that behalfe.

Bonum est scire et sequi.

Vid. hereafter, cap. of felony for any having a plague sore a more speciall provision.

[a] Nota.

In the statute of 4 *Jacobi regis*, there is also a good president, viz. [All which trials (viz. in cases of felony in that act before mentioned) [b] first for the better discovery of the truth, and secondly, for the better information of the consciences of the jurie and justices, there shall be allowed to the party so arraigned the benefit of such witnesses only to be examined upon oath, that can be produced, for his better clearing and justification]: that as witnesses are produced and sworne against him, so he may have witnesses produced and sworne for him, for *jurato creditur in judicio.* And to say the truth, we never read in any act of parliament, ancient author, book case, or record, that in criminall cases the party accused should not have witnesses sworne for him; and therefore there is not so much as *scintilla juris* against it. And I well remember when the lord treasurer Burleigh told queen Elizabeth, Madame, here is your attorney generall (I being sent for) *qui pro domina regina sequitur*, she said she would have the forme of the records altered; for it should be *attornatus generalis qui pro domina veritate sequitur.* And when the fault is denied, truth cannot appear without witnesses.

4 Jac. regis cap. 1.

[b] Nota, two excellent means for advancement of justice.

Hobelarius (*id est*, a light-horseman) *electus in Scotiam recepit armaturas et denarios, ibidem servitурus, postea non proficiscitur per mandatum regis, et recusavit reddere armaturas, et denarios, &c. per juratores est culp. et committitur mareschallo, et finivit regi* 10 *li. et invenit securitatem ad armaturas redeliberandas, &c.*

Hil. 16 E. 3. coram rege. Rot. 129. Norff.

CAP.

CAP. XXIII.

Of Felonie in ſuch as paſſe the Sea to ſerve Forain Princes, &c. or do ſerve Forain Princes, &c. without taking the Oath of Obedience.

3 Jac. cap. 4.

EVERY ſubject of this realm (1) that ſhall goe or paſſe out of this realm to ſerve (2) any foraign prince (3), ſtate (4), or potentate (5), or ſhall paſſe over the ſeas, and there ſhall voluntarily ſerve (6) any ſuch foraine prince, ſtate, or potentate, not having before his or their going or paſſing, as aforeſaid, taken the oath of obedience (7) (preſcribed by that act) before the cuſtomer and controller of the port, haven, or creek, or one of them, or their or either of their deputy or deputies, ſhall be a felon.

Some have objected, that the going or paſſing out of this realm, to ſerve, &c. cannot be tried; for that offences done out of the realme, cannot without a ſpeciall proviſion be tried within the realme. And it is a ſure rule, that in criminall cauſes concerning life or member, *ubi deliquit, ibi punietur:* the offence is locall, and cannot be tried, but where it is committed, nor cannot be alleaged to be in any other place then where in truth it was done. To this it is anſwered, that by a latter clauſe in this act, this felony ſhall be tried in the town wherein the haven or port is, wherein he went or paſſed over; which clauſe is, And be it further enacted, that all and every offence to be committed or done againſt this preſent act, ſhall and may be inquired of, heard, and determined before the juſtices of the kings bench, juſtices of aſſize and gaole-delivery in their ſeveral aſſiſes; and all offences, other than treaſon, ſhall be inquired of, heard, and determined before the juſtices of peace in their quarter ſeſſions, to be holden within the ſhire, diviſion, limit, or liberty, where ſuch offence ſhall happen. So as by the purvien and meaning of the makers of this act, this felony muſt be tried in the county where he went or paſſed over, and conſequently in that town where part of the act was done. And theſe words [and wherein ſuch offence ſhall be committed] muſt be conſtrued in this caſe, where part of the offence is committed. For *ſic interpretandum eſt, ut verba accipiantur cum effectu:* and by the expreſſe words, all and every offence to be committed or done againſt this preſent act muſt be inquired of, heard, and determined, &c. And therefore the felony cannot paſſe away with impunity, and that which is done out of the realme ſhall be proved to the jury in evidence. Note where a forain treaſon by this act is made, it is enacted to be tryed where the offender is taken.

See 33 H. 8. ca. 7. Simile.

(1) *Every*

(1) *Every subject of this realme.*] This branch extends to all persons of what estate, degree, or profession soever.

(2) *To serve.*] Albeit the party did not serve, yet if the offender went or passed over to serve without taking the oath, he is in danger of this statute. And this extendeth to any kind of service, either in campe or army, or in house or otherwise.

(3) *Any foraine prince.*] [*Princeps*] Prince is here taken for the person that is *primus*, i. e. *Qui primum locum, et gradum obtinet*, whether he be king, or any other that hath soveraigne authority, by what name or title soever. The word hath other significations, but not pertinent to the exposition of this act. Prince. [81]

(4) *State.*] The former word [prince] includeth any, that is a monarch, or in nature of a monarch, or an absolute prince. This word [state] extends to any state, either aristocraticall, where few be in authority, or democraticall, where the people have the chiefe government without any superiour, saving such as they elect and choose. State.

(5) *Potentate.*] This is a large word, and extendeth to potentates, as well ecclesiasticall as temporall. Potentate.

(6) *Or shall passe, &c. and there shall voluntarily serve.*] Although he went not over of purpose to serve, but upon some other occasion: yet if he after voluntarily serve any such foraine prince, state, or potentate, and have not taken the oath, he is a felon.

(7) *The oath of obedience.*] This is particularly set downe in the said act.

And that if any * gentleman or person of higher degree, or any person or persons, which have borne, or shall beare any office or place of captaine, lieutenant, or any other place, charge, or office in campe, army, or company of souldiers, or conducter of souldiers, shall after goe or passe voluntarily out of this realme to serve any such foraine prince, state, or potentate, or shall voluntarily serve any such prince, state, or potentate, before he and they shall become bound by obligation with two such sureties, as shall be allowed by the officers, &c. shall be a felon.

* Vid. hereafter cap. 34. in fine. Second part of the Institutes. The statute of additions. 1 H. 5. cap. 5.

By this branch, if he be a gentleman, or of higher degree, or any such military man, as here is described; because he is able to do more harme, if he be so disposed, he must not only take the oath by the former branch, but he must become bound by this branch with two sureties, &c. The forme of the obligation is set downe in this act. The exposition of the former branch giveth light to the understanding of the residue of this clause.

There is a proviso, that no attainder of felony, made felony by this act, shall take away dower, nor make, or work, any corruption of blood, or disherison to the heire. The offenders in any of the said cases of felony may have the benefit of their clergie.

CAP. XXIV.

Of Felonie in Purveyors.

See in the fourth part of the Inſtitutes, cap. Chancery. Articles againſt Cardinal Woolſey. Artic. 33, 35, 36.

[a] Artic. ſup. Cart. cap. 2: 18 E. 2. cap. ult. 5 E. 3. cap. 4.

[b] 5 E. 3. cap. 2. 25 E. 3. cap. 1.

[c] 25 E. 3. cap. 15.

[d] 36 E. 3. cap. 2. Vid. Stanf. pl. cor. 37. b.

[e] 27 H. 8. cap. 24.

SEE the ſtatutes of Artic. ſuper Cartas, anno 28 E. 1. cap. 2. 18 E. 2. ca. ult. 5 E. 3. cap. 2. 25 E. 3. cap. 1. & 15. 27 E. 3. cap. 1. 36 E. 3. cap. 2. And before in the ſecond part of the Inſtitutes, in the expoſition of the ſtatute of Artic. ſuper Cartas, cap. 2. you ſhall finde in what caſe a purveyor may be charged with felony, which briefly may be reduced to theſe four heads. Firſt, [a] if any that take upon him to be a purveyor, or his deputy or ſervant make purveyance of any thing above twelve pence without warrant. Secondly, [b] or make purveyance of any thing above twelve pence without teſtimony and appriſement of the conſtable, and four honeſt men, and without delivery of tales. Thirdly, [c] or take any ſheep with their woolles between Eaſter and Midſummer, and carry them to his own houſe and ſheer them. Fourthly, [d] or make any takings or buyings, or take any carriage in other manner then is contained in their commiſſions, they ſhall have puniſhment of life and member: and this act remains ſtill in force without alteration. The offenders may have the benefit of their clergie.

[e] By this ſtatute it is enacted, that purveyors aſſigned by commiſſion ſhall make purveyance of victuals, corne, and other things, as well within liberties and franchiſes, as without, any grant, allowance, or other thing to the contrary, or let thereof notwithſtanding: but the purveyors ſhall obſerve the ſtatutes for them provided in every behalfe, as by that act appeareth. [f] Upon this act it was holden, that if the diſcharge of purveyance were by letters patents, this act makes it of no force: but if the diſcharge were by ſtatute, then the purveyor is bound to obſerve the ſtatute, as by the ſtatute of 14 E. 3. cap. 1. *pro clero*, eccleſiaſticall perſons are diſcharged by ſtatute, which the purveyor is bound to obſerve. See the ſtatutes of 25 E. 3. ſtatut. 5. cap. 21. & 43 E. 3. cap. 3. in what manner and in what time the kings butler or his lieutenant ſhall take wines, &c.

[f] Trin. 40. Eliz. coram rege. In a quo warrant. the lord Darcies caſe.

See more of purveyors in the fourth part of the Inſtitutes cap. of the Counting houſe or Green cloth.

See lib. 8. fo. 45, 46. in Evans caſe, a commiſſion for taking up of boyes for the kings chappell, the generall words well expounded.

Rot. Parl. anno 28 E. 3. nu. 34.

By an act of parliament not in print, it is enacted that no purveyor arreſted for any miſdemeanour ſhall have any privy ſeal, to cauſe ſuch as arreſted him to come before the councell to anſwer to the king, but have his remedy by the common law.

At a parliament holden 4 Jacobi regis.

Upon a grievous complaint made at the parliament holden in the fourth year of our late ſoveraign lord king James, by the commons of the realm concerning many grievances ſuffered by his ſubjects in the execution of a commiſſion granted to certain perſons for getting of ſalt-peter, his majeſties anſwer (amongſt other things) was,

was, that he had never an intention to make any application of his prerogative therein, further then might ſtand with the lawfull, and neceſſary uſe thereof. And further his majeſty was pleaſed out of his gracious care, and goodneſſe to revoke and annull all commiſſions, or grants made to any perſon or perſons, for and concerning digging, and working of ſalt-peter, intending to conſider of ſuch a courſe afterwards, as the ſame might be made without any juſt cauſe of complaint, as by the ſaid royall anſwer (amongſt other things) more at large appeareth. In purſuance whereof, by the ſaid kings commandment, Popham chief juſtice, and all the juſtices of England, and barons of the exchequer, were aſſembled at Serjeants-Inne in Fleetſtreet, in December, in the ſaid fourth year, to reſolve and certifie, what prerogative the king had for digging, and taking of ſalt-peter in the houſes, buildings, or grounds of his ſubjects, that thereupon a new commiſſion might be made accordingly, who upon often conferences, and mature conſideration reſolved as followeth.

Salt peter, *quaſi*, ſalis petræ, colligitur aut ex materia quam veteres muri, rupes, et ſaxa exſudant, aut ex terra ſalſuginoſa et puta, quæ in ſtabulis animalium urinam ad multos annos excepit, Latine *nitrum*.

[83]

Firſt, where it was objected, that gunpowder was invented in Germany, within time of memory, in the reign of king E. 3. ſo as the king could not claim it by preſcription: and that before the 31 year of the reign of queen Eliz. (which was the yeer after the Spaniſh invaſion) we, as yet, find not any commiſſion or licence granted by any king or queen of this realm to any for the digging or taking of ſalt-petre: and in the ſaid 31 year of the ſaid late queen, two commiſſions or licences were granted, the one particular, to George Conſtable eſquire, to dig, open, and work during the ſpace of eleven years for ſalt-peter within the counties of York, Nottingham, Lancaſter, Northumberland, Cumberland, and the biſhoprick of Durham, as well within our own lands, grounds, and poſſeſſions, as alſo within the lands, grounds, and poſſeſſions of any of our loving ſubjects within the counties aforeſaid; and the conſideration of the grant was, that he ſhould deliver a great quantity of powder to be made by the ſaid George Conſtable, and provided for the ſtore of the queens majeſty at a lower rate, then was paid for it before, with this further clauſe; [And further our will and pleaſure is, that the ſaid George Conſtable ſhall at his own proper coſts and charges erect, make up, and lay all mud walls, ſtables, and grounds whatſoever ſo digged up;] whereupon it was inferred that no other buildings could be digged up by force of that commiſſion, but only ſtables. The other commiſſion was generall, made unto George Evelyn, Richard Hils, and John Evelyn, and extended throughout the realms of England and Ireland, and all other the dominions of the ſame, as well within our own proper lands, grounds, and poſſeſſions, as alſo within the lands, grounds, and poſſeſſions of any of our ſubjects, with the like clauſe of the erection and reparation, as is aforeſaid, without naming of manſion houſes by expreſſe words, and without any prohibition to the ſubject to dig for ſalt-peter in their own buildings or grounds.

In the accounts, &c. from the 21 of April 18 E. 3 for one year following anno Domini 1344. under the title of artificers and workmen (inter alios.) Gunners 6. And of their wages and ſtipends per diem, it is ſaid (amongſt others) gunners ſix pence. *Latine* bombardæ, tormenta, ſclopi.

Paſch. 49 E. 3. Coram rege rot. 27. Oxon. diverſi malefactores venerunt ad manerium, &c. cum arcubus, ſagittis, baliſcis et goons.

Vide Rot. Parl. 1 R. 2. nu. 38. William captain of the caſtle of Catherick, being charged for delivering it to the enemy, in the reign of E. 3. without commiſſion, anſwered (inter alia) that the enemies brought to battery thereof nine peeces des groſſes cannons.

Hollingſh. fo. 453.

Walſing. 10 R. 2. 1366.

Pol. Virg. De invent' rerum. fo. 2. ca. 11.

Pancerollus Nova reperta. Tit. 18. pag. 679. anno Domini 1378.

John More, pag. 196. anno Domini. 1382.

Purveyance of salt-peter. See the 1. part of the Institutes. Magna Carta cap. 21.

As to the first, it was resolved by all, that forasmuch as the taking of salt-peter, was for the necessary defence, and safety of the realm that the king had a right of purveyance of it; and should not be driven to buy it in forain parts, which forain princes might restrain, and so this realm might want sufficient for the defence thereof, to the great perill, and hazard of the same: but the king was to take it, for the necessary defence of the realm, according to the limitations hereafter expressed; and it is no prejudice to the owners of the soyl, for the place that is digged must be made up
2. again, and repaired in as good plight as it was beefore. Secondly, that this taking of salt-peter in the buildings or grounds of the subject, being a purveyance as is aforesaid, is an incident inseparable to the crown, and cannot be granted, demised, or transferred to any other, but ought to be taken only by the kings ministers, as other purveyances ought, and cannot be converted to any other use, then for the defence and safety of the realm, for which purpose only the law doth give to the king this prerogative; and it is not like to a mine of gold or silver in the ground of the subject, for there the king hath an interest in those metals, and not purveyance only. And if the powder which is so made by the kings ministers begin to decay, as it will doe within two or three years, then this either ought to be changed for other, or sold, and the money thereof comming to be employed for powder for the defence of the realm, and the kings ministers ought to make great provision of salt-peter, for that will last a long time, and when
[84] need is to make thereof gun-powder, which will be made before
3. the navy can be put in readinesse, &c. Thirdly, the ministers of the king cannot in digging for salt-peter undermine, weaken, or impair any of the walls or foundations of any of the houses of the subject, be they mansion houses, or out-houses, as barns, stables, dove-houses, mills, or the like, neither can they dig the floor of any mansion-house, which serves for the habitation of man, because his mansion is the safest place of refuge, and safety of himself and his family, as well in sicknesse, as in health, and his defence, as well in the night, as in the day, against felons, and misdoers, neither can the kings ministers dig the floor of any barn of the subject employed for the safe keeping of corn, hay, &c. for the floor of a barn cannot be made dry, or serviceable again in a long time, but they may dig in the floors of stables, and oxehouses, so that they leave sufficient room there for the horses, and other beasts of the owner, and so that they repair the same again in convenient time, as well as it was before. They may also dig in the floors of cellers, and vaults, so that the wine, beer, or other necessary provision of the owner be not removed, or in any sort impaired: and they may dig any mud wals, which be not the wals of any mansion house, and in the ruines and decayes of any houses which be not preserved for the
4. necessary habitation of man. Fourthly, they ought to make the places as well, and commodious for the owner, as they were be-
5. fore. Fifthly, they ought not to work in the possessions of the subject, but between the rising of the sun, and the going down of the same, so as the owner may make fast the doors of his house,
6. and put it in defence against misdoers. Sixthly, they ought not to place or fix any furnace, vessell or other necessaries in any house or building of the subject, without his consent, nor so neer any mansion as he by it may receive any prejudice or disquiet. Seventhly,

venthly, they ought not to continue in one place above a convenient time, nor return thither but after a long time. 7. Laſtly, that 8. the owner of the ſoyle cannot be reſtrained from digging, or taking of ſalt-peter, for the property thereof is in the owner of the ſoyl, and the king hath but the purveyance thereof, and that every man might work that would, and then there ſhould be more plenty of powder, and at a cheaper rate. And theſe reſolutions are agreeable with that maxime, * That the common law hath ſo admeaſured the prerogatives of the king, that they ſhould neither take away nor prejudice the inheritance of any. And theſe monopolies being *malum in ſe*, and againſt the common laws, are conſequently againſt the prerogative of the king, for * the prerogative of the king is given to him by the common law, and is part of the laws of the realm. Which reſolutions were delivered in writing by Popham chief juſtice unto the kings privy councell, as the unanimous reſolution of all the judges, and barons of the exchequer, and were by his majeſties privy councell well allowed of, and approved, as Popham chief juſtice reported. Upon theſe reſolutions theſe conſequents do follow. Firſt, if a man of his own authority, or by colour of any commiſſion, licence, or grant, doth take upon him to take any ſalt peter in the buildings, or grounds of any other ſubject to make thereof gunpowder, in any ſort to his own uſe, albeit he covenanteth, or agreeth to ſerve the king of ſo many laſts of powder: yet ſeeing it is but a purveyance, he cannot ſell any powder thereof made to any of the kings ſubjects, or make any private benefit thereof: and if he doe, he may be indicted of digging, and taking of the ſalt-peter at the kings ſuit, and be grievouſly fined and impriſoned, for that it is a grand treſpas with an high hand. Secondly, the party grieved may have his action of treſpaſſe, and recover damages for the treſpaſſe, &c. according to the quality of the treſpaſſe.

* Pl. Com. 236.

* Stanf. Pl. Cor. 162. a. Stanf. Prer. 5. b.

[a] Complaints made againſt purveyours in parliament.

[b] By the ſtatute of 9 R. 2. all ſtatutes made concerning purveyors be confirmed, and to be put in execution, and that juſtices of peace have power to hear and determine their offences. See the fourth part of the Inſtitutes, cap. 8. art. 33. 35. 36. againſt Cardinall Woolſey.

[a] Rot. Parl. 4 H. 4. nu. 111. Eodem anno 81. 9 H. 4. 15.

[b] Rot. Parl. anno 9 R. 2. nu 31. not in print

CAP. XXV. [85]

Of Felony in wandring Souldiers and Mariners.

1. ALL idle and wandring ſouldiers or mariners, or idle perſons wandring as ſouldiers or mariners, ſhall be reputed felons, and ſuffer as in caſe of felony. 39 El. ca. 17.

So as not only he that is a ſouldier, or mariner in deed, but he that is an idle wanderer, and takes upon him to be a ſouldier or or mariner, though in troth he be none, is in danger of this law; for, as the preamble ſaith, they abuſe the name of that honourable profeſſion.

2. Every idle, and wandring ſouldier or mariner, which comming from his captain from the ſeas, or from beyond the ſeas, that ſhall not have a teſtimoniall under the hand of ſome one juſtice of peace of, or neer the place where he landed, ſetting down therein the time and place when, and where he landed, and the place of his dwelling and birth, unto which he is to paſſe, and a convenient time therein limited for his paſſage, is by this act adjudged a felon.

3. Or if he hath ſuch a teſtimoniall, and ſhall exceed the time therein limited above fourteen days, he is by this act a felon, unleſſe he fall ſick by the way, ſo as after his recovery he ſetleth himſelf in ſome lawfull courſe of life, or reſort to the place where he was born, or was laſt abiding: but in both theſe two caſes he muſt be a ſouldier or mariner in deed.

4. If any ſuch idle, and wandring ſouldier, or mariner, or other idle perſon wandring as ſouldier or mariner, ſhall forge or counterfeit ſuch teſtimoniall, he is by this act a felon.

5. Or if he ſhall have with him or them any ſuch teſtimoniall forged or counterfeit, knowing the ſame to be counterfeit or forged, he is alſo by this act a felon. And in both theſe laſt caſes, as well he that is a ſouldier or mariner in deed, as he that is none, is in danger of this act.

And the offender againſt any of the articles of this ſtatute ſhall not have the benefit of his clergie.

Juſtices of aſſiſe, juſtices of gaole delivery, and juſtices of peace, have power by this act to heare and determine the ſaid felonies.

But if ſome honeſt perſon valued in the laſt ſubſidie to ten pounds in goods, or forty ſhillings in lands, or ſome honeſt freeholder, as by the ſaid juſtices ſhall be allowed, will be contented before ſuch juſtices to take him or them into his ſervice for one whole yeare, and will become bound by recognizance, as the ſtatute doth appoint, then they ſhall not proceed any further againſt him, unleſſe ſuch perſon retained depart within the year, without the licence of him, that ſo retained him; and then he is to be indicted, tried, and judged as a felon, and not to have the benefit of his clergie.

CAP.

CAP. XXVI.

Of Felonie in Souldiers that depart from their Captaines without License.

THIS ſtatute is become of little force or uſe: for the ancient manner of retainer of ſouldiers whereunto that act referreth, is utterly altered: for then knights or gentlemen expert in war, and of great revenues and livelihood in their countrey, covenanted with the king to ſerve him in his war for ſuch a time with ſuch a number of men: and the ſouldiers made their covenant with their leaders or maſters, and then they were muſtered before the kings commiſſioners, and entred of record before them; and that was certified into the * exchequer, and thereupon they took their wages of the king, as it appeareth by many preſidents of the exchequer, and may be gathered by the preamble and body of the act, and by the Regiſter, where it appeareth, that a writ was framed upon that ſtatute directed to a ſerjeant at armes *ad capiend' conductos ad proficiſcend' in obſequium, &c.* And this was thought an excellent military policy, that the ſouldiers, (part whereof were of their own tenants) ſhould be choſen and led by knights and gentlemen of quality of their owne countrey, with whom they muſt fight in war, and live withall in peace, when they returned into their countrey, in reſpect whereof, the ſouldier would the more cheerfully and obediently follow his leader, and the leader would the more reſpectfully and lovingly uſe his ſouldier when he is abroad. See the ancient forme of commiſſions for arraying and muſtering of men in 5 H. 4.

18 H. 6. cap. 19. 5 Eliz. cap. 5. extendeth it to mariners and gunners.

* By the ſtatute of 5 R. 2. cap. 11.

See the writ in the Regiſter 191, directed to the ſerjeant at armes. 5 R. 2. cap. 10. Rot. Parl. 5 H. 4. nu. 29. the like for keeping of caſtles and forts.

Rot. Parl. 5 H. 4. nu. 24, 25.

By this act the benefit of clergie was not taken away from the delinquent.

The ſtatute of 2 E. 6. cap. 2. extendeth only when the ſouldier departs after that he hath ſerved the king in his war: and ſuch an offender ſhall not enjoy the benefit of his clergie.

2 E. 6. cap. 2. renued 4 & 5 Ph. and Mar. cap. 3. 1 Ja. cap. 25.

If any ſoldier being no captain, immediately retained with the king, which ſhall be in wages and retained, or take any preſt to ſerve the king upon the ſea, or upon the land beyond the ſea, depart out of the kings ſervice without licence of his captain (1), that ſuch departing be taken, deemed, and adjudged felony. And that all the juſtices in every ſhire of England, where any ſuch offenders be taken (2), have power to enquire of the ſaid offences, and the ſame to hear, and determine, as they doe and may doe of felony, &c. expreſſed in the kings commiſſion to them made, as though the ſame offences were done in the ſame ſhire; and alſo that the departing of ſuch ſoldiers, and alſo their retainers, if it be traverſed, be

7 H. 7. cap. 1. 3 H. 8. cap. 5.

tried in the same shire, where they be for such a cause arrested, and arraigned.

Lib. 6. fo. 27. Case de souldiers. Dier 4 Eliz. 211.

Both these acts of 7 H. 7. and 3 H. 8. are perpetuall acts, for this word [king] includeth all his succession.

(1) *Without licence of his captain.*] The statute of 3 H. 8. is without licence of the kings lieutenant there.

[87]

(2) *That all the justices in every shire of England, where any such offenders be taken, &c.*] This act of 7 H. 7. extends to all the kings justices in every shire, viz. justices of assise, gaol delivery, oier and terminer, and of the peace. And if the offender be taken in the county where the kings bench set, he may be indicted, &c. there: but this clause in 3 H. 8. is restrained to justices of peace. This clause in both the said statutes is cumulative, and for more speedy proceeding with the offender. But admit the offender be never taken, yet may he be indicted of felony in the county where the departure was, and if he appear not, he may be outlawed, for by the first clause, the offence is made felony, and the second clause is affirmative, and not privative.

See Stanf. Pl. cor. fo. 168. c.

He or they so offending shall not enjoy the benefit of his clergy.

This branch in the act of 7 H. 7. is generall, but in the act of 3 H. 8. there is an exception out of the like branch, viz. of men being within orders of holy church. So as it differeth much, whether he be indicted upon the one statute, or the other.

Lamb. Inter. léges Edovardi fo. 136. Hoven. Annal. 35. Pœna Hereslitæ.

But observe what punishment the ancient law of England inflicted upon the souldier that departed from the kings host, both before, and since the conquest. *Item qui fugiet à domino, vel socio suo pro timiditate belli, vel mortis, in conductione heretochii sui in expeditione navali, vel terrestri, perdat omne quod suum est, et suam ipsius vitam, et manus mittat dominus ad terram quam ei antea dederat.* For the exposition of *Heretochius* and *Hereslite*, see the fourth part of the Institutes, cap. *Court de Chivalry.*

Now concerning armour, arms, charges of souldiers, mustering of them, &c. See the statutes in print of Confirmat. Cart. 25 E. 1. Vet. Magna Cart. 2. parte, fol. 35. 1 E. 3. cap. 5. 18 E. 3. ca. 7. 25 E. 3. cap. 8. 4 H. 4. cap. 13. 11 H. 7. cap. 7. and 3 H. 8. ca. 5. and 4 & 5 Ph. & Mar. cap. 3. for appearing at musters, &c. But 4 & 5 Ph. and Mar. cap. 2. an act for having of horse, armour, and weapon is repealed by the statute of 1 Ja. ca. 25.

An act not in print, Rot. Parl. *anno* 5 H. 4. nu. 24, 25. for araying and mustering of men, for watching of beacons, &c.

Records of parliament, 4 H. 4. nu. 48. 7 H. 4. nu. 124. 1 H. 5. nu. 17.

Book cases. 48 E. 3. 3, 4. 21 E. 4. 17. per Catesby. 9 E. 4. 26. lib. 7. fo. 7, 8.

See the second part of the Institutes, Confirmat. Cart. cap. 5. *ubi supra.*

Vide Pasch. 16 E. 2. Phelip Master del Hospit. de S. Katherins case, *in libro meo*, fo. 83. b.

CAP.

CAP. XXVII.

Of Felony to marry a ſecond Huſband or Wife, the former Huſband or Wife living.

IF any perſon (1), or perſons within his majeſties dominions of England and Wales, being married (2), doe at any time after marry any (3) perſon or perſons, the former huſband or wife being alive, that then every ſuch offence ſhall be felony, &c. 1. Ja. cap. 11.

This is the firſt act of parliament that was made againſt polygamy. *Polygamia eſt plurium ſimul virorum, uxorumve connubium.*

The difference between bigamy, or trigamy, &c. and polygamy is, *quia bigamus ſeu trigamus, &c. eſt qui diverſis temporibus, et ſucceſſive duas, ſeu tres, &c. uxores habuit. Polygamus, qui duas vel plures ſimul duxit uxores.*

(1) *If any perſon.*] This law is generall, and extendeth to all perſons, of what eſtate, or degree ſoever.

If the man be above the age of fourteen, which is his age of conſent, and the woman above the age of twelve, which is her age of conſent, though they be within the age of one and twenty, are within the danger of this law, which appeareth by this, that this act extendeth not to a former marriage made within the age of conſent, as hereafter ſhall appear. See the 1. part of the Inſtitutes. ſect. 104.

Being married, &c.] This extendeth to a marriage *de facto*, or voydable by reaſon of a precontract, or of conſanguinity, or of affinity, or the like: for it is a marriage in judgement of law untill it be avoided, and therefore though neither marriage be *de jure*, yet they are within this ſtatute.

(3) *Doe at any time marry.*] This ſecond marriage is meerly void, and yet it maketh the offender a felon.

And the party and parties ſo offending, ſhall receive ſuch and the like proceeding, triall and execution in ſuch county, where ſuch perſon or perſons ſhall be apprehended, as if the offence had been committed in ſuch county, where ſuch perſon or perſons ſhall be taken or apprehended.

See before the expoſition of the ſtatutes of 7 H. 7. and 3 H. 8. concerning departing of ſouldiers, &c.

Out of the generality of this law, there be five exceptions: Firſt, it extendeth not to any perſon or perſons, whoſe huſband or wife be continually remaining beyond the ſeas, by the ſpace of ſeven years together. By this branch notice is not materiall, in reſpect of the commorancy beyond ſea. See 22 E. 4. Conſultation. 5. The opinion of the doctors. Pains caſe lib. 9. fo. 72.

Secondly, it extends not, when the huſband or wife ſhall abſent him or herſelf, the one from the other, by the ſpace of ſeven years in any parts within his majeſties dominions, the one of them not knowing

knowing the other to be living within that time. Here notice is materiall, in respect the commorance is within the realm.

* Thirdly, nor to any person or persons, that at the time of such marriage be divorced by any sentence had in the ecclesiasticall court.

There be two kinds of divorces, the one that dissolveth the marriage *à vinculo matrimonii*; as for precontract, consanguinity, &c. and the other *à mensa et thoro*; as for adultery, because that divorce by reason of adultery, cannot dissolve the marriage *à vinculo matrimonii*, for that the offence is after the just and lawfull marriage. This branch in respect of the generality of the words, priviledge the offender from being a felon, as well in the case of the divorce *à mensa et thoro*, as where it is *à vinculo matrimonii*, and yet in the case of the divorce *à mensa et thoro*, the second marriage is void, living the former wife or husband. And if there be a divorce *à vinculo matrimonii*, and the adverse party appeal, which is a continuance of the former marriage, and suspend the sentence, yet after such a divorce, the party marrying is no felon within this statute, in respect of the generality of this branch, although the marriage be not lawfull.

Fourthly, nor to any person or persons, where the former marriage is by sentence in the ecclesiasticall court declared to be void and of no effect.

Fifthly, nor to any person or persons, for or by reason of any former marriage made within age of consent: hereby it appeareth that the makers of the law intended that this act should extend to every person above the age of consent.

If the man be above fourteen, and the wife under twelve, or if the wife be above twelve, and the man under fourteen, yet may the husband or wife so above the age of consent, disagree to the espowsals, as well as the party that is under the age of consent; for the advantage of disagreement must be reciprocal. And so it was resolved by the judges and civilians, Trin. 42 Eliz. in the kings bench, in a writ of error between Babington and Warner. So as if either party be within age of consent, it is no former marriage within this act.

Trin. 42 Eliz. Coram rege. Inter Babington and Warner.

The offender against this statute may have the benefit of his clergy.

If he be a nobleman and lord of parliament, he shall be tried by his peers, albeit there be no provision speciall for it: for of common right, (that we may say it once for all) in case of treason, felony, and misprision of treason or of felony (as hath been said before) he is to be tried by his peers.

Marriage in some sort felony by the common law.

I find that by the ancient law of England, that if any Christian man did marry with a woman that was a Jew, or a Christian woman that married with a Jew, it was felony, and the party so offending should be burnt alive.

Contrahentes cum Judæis, Judæabus, pecorantes, et sodomitæ in terra vivi confodiantur, &c. Fleta lib. 1. ca. 35. §. *Contrahentes.*

CAP.

C A P. XXVIII.

Of Felony for any having a Plague ſore upon him, contrary to Commandment goeth abroad, &c.

IF any perſon infected with the plague, commanded (by ſuch perſons as are appointed by the act) to keep houſe, ſhall contrary to ſuch commandment wilfully and contemptuouſly goe abroad, and ſhall converſe in company, having any infectious ſore upon him uncured, ſuch perſon ſhall be adjudged a felon. 1 Jac. ca. 31.

This is felony, albeit no other perſon by ſuch means be infected, for this ſtatute was made to prevent the moſt horrid and fearfull infection of the plague. The law was generall, and extended to all eſtates and degrees whatſoever, and was grounded upon the law of God: and the reaſon of the law of the realme is, that the infectious ſick ſhould be removed from the whole. The party offending might have had the benefit of his clergy. Levit. cap. 13. Numb. cap. 5. Regiſt. F. N. B. 234. Bre. de leproſo amovendo Bract. lib. 5. f. 421. a. Brit. fo. 39. 88. Fleta, li. 6. ca. 39. 22 E. 3. Rot. Clauſ. 2. parte, nu. 14.

Here is a rare proviſo, That no attainder of felony by vertue of this act, ſhall extend to any attainder, or corruption of blood, or forfeiture of goods, chattels, lands, tenements, or hereditaments.

In this proviſo theſe things are to be obſerved: firſt, that by the avoyding of the corruption of blood, the wives dower is impliedly ſaved: for where the heir ſhall inherit, the wife ſhall be endowed againſt the heir. Secondly, that there ſhall be * no forfeiture of goods, or chattels, which is rare, and the like we have not obſerved before, and by conſequent the offender may make his will and teſtament, and if he doe not, the ordinary ought to grant adminiſtration of the goods and chattels, as he ought to doe in other caſes. * Nota.

Theſe words [to any attainder or] muſt be omitted, and the ſenſe to be, to any corruption of blood, for (as it is printed) it is, that no attainder of felony ſhall extend to any attainder, &c.

This act is become of no force for want of continuance, and is expired ſince we wrote this chapter, therefore to be put out of the charge of the juſtices of peace.

CAP. XXIX.

Of Felonie in Jaylers by Dures of Imprisonment, &c. by Statute, and by the Common Law.

14 E. 3. ca. 10. Geol in French is a prison. Geolier a keeper of a prison. Anglice, a jayl, or jayler.
* An approver.
3 E. 3. Cor. 295.

IF it happen that the keeper of the prison, or underkeeper (1) by too great dures of imprisonment (2), and by pain make any prisoner that he hath in his ward to become an * appellor (3), against his will (4), and thereof be attainted, he shall have judgement of life and member (5).

18 E. 3. Cor. 272.

* 1 E. 3. ca. 14. 20 E. 3. cap. 5. 1 R. 2. ca. 4. W. 1. cap. 36. 11 H. 4. 2. 91. 22 E. 3. 15. See the exposition of W. 1. c. 28.

[a] Mich. 7 Jacobi in curia stellat. Sir John Hollis case.

Before the making of this statute, if a jayler had by dures of imprisonment made his prisoner become an approver, to appeal honest men for his own private, of intent to have of their goods, when they were committed to his custody, and to retain them in prison without being let to mainprise, and the appellees upon his appeal be hanged: this is felony in the jayler by the common law: but if the appellees were acquitted, then it was no felony, but a great misprision in the jayler, which was one of the causes of the making of this act: for by this act, if the prisoner become an approver against his will, whether the appellees be acquited, or attainted, or after the approvement not proceeded with, and whether the approvement be true or false, so it be by dures of imprisonment, and against the will of the prisoner, it is felony. * For it is not lawfull for any man to excite or stir any other to a just accusation, complaint or lawfull suit, for *culpa est se immiscere rei ad se non pertinenti*; (and so was [a] it resolved Mich. 7. Ja. in the star-chamber, in sir John Hollis his case, by the whole court) much more to doe it by dures of imprisonment, most of all by a jayler, who hath the custody of the prisoner committed to him, to enforce him by dures to become an approver. And therefore this law hath made it felony in the jayler or under-jayler.

11 H. 4. 73. simile. 13 E. 3. bar. 253. simile.

(1) *Keeper of the prison, or under-keeper.*] If he be keeper, or under-keeper, *de jure*, or *de facto*, by right or by wrong, he is within the purvien of this statute.

* W. 2. cap. 34. 28 E. 3 ca. 3. 13 R. 2. stat. 2. cap. 3. 1 E. 2. De frang. prisonam.

(2) *By too great dures of imprisonment.*] Every imprisonment is taken and deemed in law *duritia, dures:* a little addition to it by the jayler is too great dures in this case.

(3) *To become an appellor.*] That is an approver.

9 E. 4. fo. 26. Br. Cor. 203.

(4) *Against his will.*] That is, when the prisoner never would have done it of his own will, if the jayler, or under-jayler had not enforced him thereunto.

[b] Britton, fo. 18. Fleta, lib. 1, c. 26. versus finem. Mirror cap. 1. §. 9 De homicidio.

(5) *Judgement of life or member.*] * These words doe imply felony. For this offence, the offender shall have the benefit of his clergy.

[b] If the jayler keep the prisoner more straitly then he ought of right, whereof the prisoner dyeth, this is felony in the jayler by the

the common law. And this is the cause, (as before hath been said) that if a prisoner die in prison, the coroner ought to sit upon him. See before cap. Petit Treason, fo. 34. how prisoners are to be demeaned.

How gaoles are rejoyned and united to the office of sherifs, see this statute of 14 E. 3. ca. 10. 19 H. 7. ca. 10. lib. 4. fo. 34. Muttons case. Adde thereunto Rot. Parl. 18 E. 3. nu. 43. and so was it decreed in Fortescues case, in the exchequer chamber, *anno* 2. Car. regis. [92] 14 E. 3. ca. 10. 19 H. 7. c. 10. Li. 4. fo. 34. Muttons case. Parl. 18 E. 3. nu. 43. 2 Car. Regis in the exchequer chamber, Fortescues case.

CAP. XXX.

Of Felony by bringing in, Payment, or Receipt of certaine Money.

IT is felony to make, coin, buy, or bring in, and put in payment, &c. any galley half pence, suskyn, or dotkyn. 3 H. 5. cap. 1. Stat. 1. Rast. Abb. tit. Money nu. 27.

The reason of this law was, for that these moneys were base, and not of the allay of sterling, which was (amongst others) the cause of the making of the generall law of 9 H. 5. cap. 6. stat. 2. 9 H. 5. c. 6. Stat. 2.

It is felony to pay, or receive for payment any money called blanks. 2 H. 6. ca. 9 For the better understanding of this statute, it is to be known, that these blanks were white money coyned by king H. 5. in France after his victory at Agincourt, and league with France, whose style then was, *rex Angliæ, regens et hæres Franciæ*. And they were called blanks or whites in respect of the colour, because at the same time he coyned also a salus in gold, the salus, being of the value of twenty two shillings, was of the allay of sterling: but the blanks, which were much more common, being each of them valued at eight pence, were not of the allay of sterling, and therefore they only were decried by the said act of 2 H. 6.

See the second part of the Institutes. Artic. super Cartas cap. 20.

For either of these offences of felony the offender may have his clergy.

CAP.

CAP. XXXI.

Of Felony for Transportation of Silver, or Importation of false or evill Money, &c.

Mirror, c. 1. §. 3. Inter les articles de viels roys ordeins. Rot. Parl. 17 E. 3. nu. 15. not printed.

DEFENDUE fuit que nul argent ſerra tranſport hors del realm.

This was the ancient law of England long before the conqueſt.

At the parliament holden *anno* 17 E. 3. as well the tranſportation of ſilver, as the importation of falſe and evill money, is enacted by authority of that parliament to be felony. And alſo if the ſearchers mentioned in the act be aſſenting to the bringing in of falſe money, or willingly ſuffering ſilver or money to be tranſported, it is alſo made felony. But becauſe this act was never printed nor tranſlated into Engliſh, and for that there be other things obſervable, enacted thereby, worthy to be known, we will tranſcribe the ſame, *de verbo in verbum in proprio idiomate.*

[a] See Britton cap. 5. fo. 10. b. Ceſt allay eſt ſolonque le forme et uſage del realm. Mirror. ca. 1 §. 3. before the conqueſt. & cap. 1. §. 6. & cap. 5. §. 1. See inter leges Æthelſtani. c. 14. Canuti ca. 8. Fleta, lib. 1. ca. 22. Glanv. li. 14. c. 7. Of what weight and allay the kings money ſhall be. 25 E. 3. ca. 13. 9 H. 5. ca. 11. See before cap. Treaſon. Verb. *Sa monye.* See the ſecond part of the Inſtitutes. Artic. ſuper cartas cap. 20.

[b] This is felony. See the like in the ſecond part of the Inſtitutes. 1 E. 2. De frangentibus priſonam. 14 E. 3. 10. &c.

[c] The reward of the ſearchers if they be diligent, &c.

* Le parliament tenus a Weſtm. a la quinzeme de Paſch. du raign noſtre ſeignior. le roy Edward tiers apres le conqueſt dys et ſeptiſme.

ITEM accorde eſt de faire une monoie des bones eſterlings en Engleterre du pois et del [a] alay del auncient eſterling, que avera ſon cours en Engleterre entre les grandz et la comune de la terre, et la quele ne ſerra portes hors du royalme dengleterre en nulle manere, ne pur quecunque cauſe que ceo ſoit. Et en caſe que les Flemings voillent faire bone monoie dargent groſſes ou autres accordant en alay es bones eſterlings, que tiel monoie eit cours en Engleterre entre merchand et merchand et autres qi la vodroient reſceuire de lour bone gree, iſſint que nul argent ſoit portes hors du roialme.

Item eſt accordes et aſſentus, que bones gents et loialx ſoient aſſignes es ports de miere, et ailours, ou mieſter ſerra, de faire la ſerche que nul argent ſoit portes hors du roialme en monoie n'autrement, forſpris que les grandz quant ils vont per dela qils penſent aver veſſeals dargent pur ſervir lour hoſtels: Et que nul ſoit cy hardy [b] de porter fauſſe et malvois monoie en roialme, ſur paine de forfeiture de vie et de membre, et a faire eſchanges a ceux qi paſſeront la miere d'or pur lour bones Eſterlings a la value.

Item aſſentus eſt et accordes, que les dits ſercheours, per cauſe qils ferront lour offices plus diliagement et plus loialment, [c] ils eient la tierce partie de tote la fauxe monie, qils purront trover portee

portee deins le roialm a lour proffit demeen : et en meſme la manere eient la tierce partie de la bone monoie quele ilz troveront en la miere paſſent hors de la terre. Et en caſe qils ſoient troves negligents ou rebealx a tieux ſerches faire, [d] *que lour terres et tenements, biens et chateux ſoient ſeiſes en la main le roy, et lour corps pris, et detenus tanque ils eient fait fine au roy pur lour diſobeiſance. Et en caſe quils ſoient* [e] *aſſentants de porter tiels fauxe monoie, et de ſueffrire ſachantement largent ou monoie autrement, (forſpris que les grandz quant ilz vont per dela qils penſent aver veſſeals dargent pur ſervir lour hoſtels come de ſuis eſt dit) eſtre meſnes hors du roialme, eient judgement de vie et de membre.*

[d] the puniſhment of them if they be negligent, &c.

[e] Their aſſent to the bringing in of falſe money, or wittingly to ſuffer ſilver, or money, &c. to be tranſported, is felony.

Item, IT is accorded to make money of good ſterling in England of the weight and allay of the ancient ſterling, which ſhall be currant in England between the great men and commons of the land, and the which ſhall not be carried out of the realm of England in any manner, nor for any cauſe whatſoever. And in caſe, that the Flemings will make good money of ſilver groſſe or other, according, in allay [94] of good ſterling, that ſuch money ſhall be currant in England between merchant and merchant, and others, who of their own accord will receive the ſame, ſo that no ſilver be carried out of the realm.

Item, It is accorded and aſſented, That good and lawfull men be aſſigned in the ports of the ſea, and elſewhere, where need ſhall be, to make ſearch, that no ſilver be carried out of the realm in money or otherwiſe, (except that the great men may when they goe out of the realm, have ſilver veſſels to ſerve their houſes) and that none be ſo hardy to bring falſe and ill money into the realm upon pain of forfeiture of life and member, and to make exchanges with them, that ſhall paſſe the ſea, of gold for their good ſterling to the value.

Item, It is aſſented and accorded, that the ſaid ſearchers, becauſe they may doe their offices more diligently and more lawfully, ſhall have the third part of all the falſe money that they can find to be brought into the realme for their own benefit; and in the ſame manner they ſhall have the third part of the good money which they ſhall find upon the ſea paſſing out of the realm. And in caſe they ſhall be found negligent or diſobedient in making ſuch ſearches, that their lands and tenements, goods and chattels ſhall be ſeiſed into the kings hands, and their bodies taken and detained untill they have made fine to the king for their diſobedience. And in caſe they ſhall be aſſenting to the bringing in of ſuch falſe money, or wittingly ſhall ſuffer ſilver or money (except veſſels of ſilver for the great men when they goe out of the kingdome to ſerve in their houſes, as before is ſaid) to be tranſported out

out of the realme, they ſhall have judgement of life and member.

The offenders in caſe of felony made by this act may have the benefit of their clergy.

[95]

CAP. XXXII.

Of Felonie for carrying of Wooll, Woolfels, Leather, or Leade out of the Realme.

27 E. 3. cap. 3. the ſtatute of the Staple.

Mirror, cap. 1. § 3. Inter les artic. per vieles royes ordeins. Defendu que nul de ameſnaſt leyne hors del realme.

NO merchant, Engliſh, Welch, or Iriſh, ſhall carry any manner of wools, leather, woolfels or lead, out of the ſaid realme and lands, upon paine of forfeiture of life and member, nor ſhall tranſport any of the ſaid wares or merchandizes in the name of merchant ſtrangers, nor ſhall ſend or hold their ſervants, &c. in the parts beyond the ſea to ſurvey the ſale of the ſaid wares or merchandizes, or to receive the money coming of the ſale of the ſame, nor take payment of gold or ſilver, nor of any other thing in recompence or commutation, or in the name of payment in the parts beyond the ſea out of the realme and lands aboveſaid of merchandizes ſold in England, Ireland, or Wales, touching the ſtaple, but that all ſuch payment ſhall be made in gold or ſilver, or merchandizes in England, Ireland, or Wales, where the contract was made, upon paine of life and member.

Cap. 11. That no merchant privie nor ſtranger, nor any other, of what condition that he be, go by land or by water towards wines, or other wares or merchandizes coming into our ſaid realme or lands, in the ſea, nor elſewhere to foreſtall or buy the ſame, or in other manner to give earneſt upon them, before that they come to the ſtaple, or to the port where they ſhall be diſcharged; nor enter into the ſhips for ſuch cauſe, till the merchandizes be ſet to land to be ſold, upon paine of loſſe of life and member.

Cap. 12. No merchant privie, ſtranger, or other ſhall carry out of our realme of England, wools, leather, or woolfels to Barwick upon Twede, nor elſewhere, nor into Scotland upon the like paine, nor that any merchant, nor any other ſell his wools, woolfels, or leather, to any of Scotland, nor to any other to carry into Scotland: upon the like paine.

Cap. 18. If the merchants or other people of Ireland or Wales, after they be in the ſea with their merchandizes, do paſſe to any place, other then to the ſtaples in England: it is felony.

No

No merchant, or other ſhall make any conſpiracie, confederacy, &c. or ill device in any point, that may turn to the impeachment, diſturbance, defeating, or decay of the ſtaples, &c. and if any do, and be thereof attainted before the major and miniſters of the ſtaple, or other whom the king ſhall aſſigne, he ſhall incurre the paine of loſſe of life and member. Cap. 25.

Item, *ou auterfoitz fuit orden en * leſtatuts de leſtaple que nul Englois paſſera la mere ove leynes, quire, pealtz lanuts, ne per auter, ſur peine de forfeiture de vie et member, terres et tenements, biens et chateux: eſt accord que la forfeiture de vie et member ſoit ouſte de tout en leſtatute de leſtaple, et que nul home ſoit impeach por tiel forfeiture de vie et member, cibien in temps paſſe come avenir, la forfeiture des terres et tenements, biens et chateux eſteant en ſa force.* The ſame in Engliſh. 38 E. 3. cap 6. 27 E. 3. ca. 3, &c. ſtat. Stapulæ. [96]

Alſo, where heretofore it was ordained in the ſtatutes of the ſtaple, that no Engliſh man ſhould paſſe the ſea with wools, leather, woolfels, nor by other, upon paine of forfeiture of life and member, lands and tenements, goods and chattels. It is accorded that the forfeiture of life and member be ouſted in the whole in the ſtatute of the ſtaple, and that no man be impeached by ſuch forfeiture of life and member, as well in times paſt, as to come, the forfeiture of the lands and tenements, goods and chattels, being in his force.

By the expreſſe letter of the body of this law, the forfeiture of life and member is ouſted *de tout* in the ſtatute: therefore it is holden, that the felony is taken away throughout the ſtatute, but the forfeiture of lands and goods remaineth by the expreſſe letter of this act.

By the ſtatute of 18 H. 6. no man ſhall carry wool, or woolfels, out of this realme to other places, then to the ſtaple at Callice, without the kings licenſe, upon paine of felony, &c. And that as well commiſſioners aſſigned, as the juſtices in every county where ſuch wools and woolfels ſhall be ſo carried out, have power and authority to enquire of the premiſes, and them to hear, and determine, &c. 18 H. 6. cap. 15. Stanf. Pl. Cor. 37. b.

But this act extendeth not to wools which ſhall paſſe the ſtrait of Marroke. And this is a perpetuall law, and cannot be expired, as it is ſuppoſed in the laſt impreſſion of the ſtatutes at large, but it extendeth only to wools and woolfels. The offender herein may have his clergie.

And for the better underſtanding of ancient ſtatutes and records concerning wools, it is neceſſary to explaine certaine words and termes. By the ſtatute of 25 E. 3. cap. 9. a ſack of wool containes but twenty ſix ſtone, and every ſtone fourteen pound, where before it was [a] twenty eight ſtone.

Pochet of wool, *unde pochettum*, that is, a little poke or ſack containing halfe a ſack of wool. Sarpler, *unde ſarpleia*, is alſo halfe a ſack, and is derived from the French word *ſarpillier*, which ſig-

[a] Compoſ. de ponderibus vet. Mag. Carta, 2 part. fo 31. Saccus anæ, Rot. Parl. 27 E. 3. nu. 53.

nifieth a wrapper, within which wrapper halfe a ſack is contained.

[b] Compoſit. de ponderibus, ubi ſupra.

[b] A weigh of wool, *unde waga*, is halfe a ſack.

A tod or toit of wool, *unde toddum lanæ*, containeth two ſtone, and is derived from the French word *toilet*, which is a wrapper, within which by uſage two ſtone of wooll is foulded: ſome fetch it from the Flemmiſh word *dodderem*, which ſignifieth *nectere*, to weave, becauſe it is woven into cloth. *Petra lanæ* is a ſtone of wooll, ſo called, becauſe the weight, being a ſtone, containes fourteen pound.

[97]

CAP. XXXIII.

Againſt Tranſportation of Iron, Braſſe, Copper, Latten, Bell-metall, Pan-metall, Gun-metall, or Shroofe-metall, (Tinne and Lead only excepted.)

28 E. 3. cap. 5. 33 H. 8. cap. 7. 2 E. 6. cap. 37. See the penalties in the ſtatutes themſelves, which are thought to be too weak. Ferrum a feriendo. Timber is a Saxon word, in old French, Marem, unde Maremium, Latine, ligni materia, vel lignum ædificatorium. * Terra fullonica.

THE tranſportation of theſe are prohibited by divers acts of parliament upon the penalties therein expreſſed. And hereby is prohibited the tranſportation of any gunnes whatſoever, a neceſſary law, and worthy of due execution.

And we have obſerved, that God hath bleſſed this realme with things for the defence of the ſame, and maintenance of trade and traffick, that no other part of the Chriſtian world hath the like: viz. Iron to make gunnes, &c. more ſerviceable and perdurable then any other. Secondly, timber for the making and repairing of our navie, and eſpecially of the knees of the ſhips, better then any other. Thirdly, * our fullers earth is better for the fulling of our cloth, then any other. Fourthly, our wooll makes better cloth, and more laſting and defenſible againſt winde and weather, then the wooll in any nation out of the kings dominions; and many other ſpeciall gifts of God.

But here will we ſtay, and pray, that none of theſe may be tranſported for many inconveniencies, that will follow thereupon.

CAP. XXXIV.

Of Felony for ſtealing of a Faulcon.

37 E. 3. cap. 19.

EVERY perſon (1) that findeth (2) any falcon (3), tercelet (4), lannner, or laneret (5), or any other falcon, that is loſt of his lords (6), that forthwith he ſhall bring it to the ſherif of the county, and that the ſherif make proclamation (7), &c. and if any ſteal any hawk (8), and the ſame carry

carry away not doing the ordinance aforesaid, it shall be done of him as of a thief that stealeth a horse (9) or other thing.

The statute of 34 E. 3. inflicted the penalty for the concealing and taking away of the hawk, two years imprisonment, and the price of the hawk to the lord, if he hath wherewith, and if not, he shall the longer abide in prison. This act of 37 E. 3. maketh the offence felony. 34 E. 3. cap. 22.

The new printed book of the statutes at large, in stead of these words, (or any other falcon) hath, or any other hawk. Printed for the society of stationers, 1618.

I have seen some manuscripts (in these words) in the original tongue, wherein the statute was published. *Que quecunque person que trove faucon, tercelet, lanier, ou lanyret, austor ou auter faucon.* And both these differ from the truth of this law. For the first extendeth this act to any hawk whatsoever. And the manuscript to *austor* or *autor*, a goshawk, whereas in truth, this law extendeth only to such as be of the kinde of faulcons, being long winged hawks, which many times by flying far off are lost, and not to any short-winged hawk, as the goshawk, the tercel of the goshawk, the sparhawk, &c. And in the body of the act this word (faulcon) is ever used, and not this word (hawk) as hereafter appeareth. We would have been glad to have cleared this point by the record of the parliament roll, but the roll of this act is not to be found, and yet being a generall law, the judges are to take notice thereof: and that which I have set down, as the words of the law, agreeth with the first impression thereof, and with all succeeding impressions saving the last. See hereafter, cap. Larceny, verb. Personall goods, &c. [98] Lib. 8. fo. 27, 28. In casu principis.

(1) *Every person.*] This is a generall law, and extendeth to all persons of what degree or sex soever.

(2) *That findeth.*] Note by the common law the felonious taking of any hawk long-winged, or short-winged, from the peark, &c. or from the person of any man, with a mind to steal her, is robbery: but the finding of a faulcon, though he concealed, denied, or sold her, was no felony, but by this act.

(3) *Any faulcon.*] By this and the last words, or any other faulcon, it appeareth that only faulcons are within this law, as besides those that are here named, the gerfaulcon, *girofalco*, or *ardearius*, and the tercell, which is called a jerkin; and the lanner is called *falcunculus*. But the merlyn, which is called *æsalo*, and the hobby which is called *alaudaria*, though they be long-winged hawks, yet being not of the kind of faulcons they are not within this statute, neither is any short-winged hawk, as the goshawk, the tercell of the goshawk, or the sparhawk, &c. as has been said, within this act.

(4) *Tercelet.*] This is the tercell of the faulcon, called a tercell gentill, the male of the faulcon called *terciolus, quia tertia parte minor sit femella*, because the tercell is a third part lesse then the female.

(5) *Lanner and laneret.*] These (as hath been said) are of the kind of faulcons, which appeareth not only by the name *falcunculus*, but by the words of the act, for having named the lanner and laneret, it is said, or any other faulcon.

Albeit these hawks, that shall be so lost, have no vervels, yet must the finder carry them to the sherif, for vervels are not required by this act. The only thing that the finder is to doe, to save himself from felony, is forthwith (the word in the originall is *maintenant)* after his finding to carry the hawk to the sherif.

(6) *That is lost of his lords.*] Lords are taken here for the owners, the word in the original is *seignior*, which signifieth as well a proprietary, as a lord.

10 E. 4. 1. 7 R. 2. barre 241. Lib. 5. fo. 108 Sir Hen. Constables case.

(7) *To prove reasonably*] This is not intended according to the generall sense of this word (proof) that is, by a jury of twelve men, but (reasonably,) that is, by vervels, or by marks, or by other proof to the sherif.

(8) *And if any steal any hawk, &c.*] The concealing and carrying away of the hawk, not bringing the same to the sherif according to this ordinance, is adjudged a stealing by this act. And yet if a man finde goods, and conceal or deny them, it is no felony.

14 El. Dier, 307. Fines case. Lib. 7. fo. 17. in case de Swans.

(9) *As of a thief that stealeth a horse.*] But yet by the common law one hath not as good and absolute a property in hawks, being *ferœ natura*, and reclaimed for delight and pleasure (for they may become wild again, and return to their naturall liberty) as in a horse, or any other thing of profit: but the concealing and carrying away of the hawk reclaimed, being found was no felony before this statute, no more then any thing of profit, because the party came to the hawk by finding. See more hereof in the chapter of larceny. A hawk that is not reclaimed is *nullius in bonis*, but *occupanti conceditur*, and he that first getteth the hawk enjoyeth it.

[99]

In this act four things are to be observed. First, that the sherif must make proclamation in all the good towns of the county that he hath such a faulcon in keeping. Secondly, if none come to challenge the faulcon within four months, if the finder be under the degree * of a gentleman (which here is called *un simple home)* the sherif shall have the falcon, paying reasonable costs, &c. Thirdly, if the finder be a gentleman, and no challenge by the owner within four months, then he shall have the faulcon, paying reasonable costs, &c. Fourthly, it is to be observed, that in these two latter branches, the last printed book hath this word (hawk :) but in the originall, and all the other printed books, the word is (falcon) under which word, all the rest mentioned in this act are included.

* Who shall be accounted in law a gentleman; see the second part of the Institutes the statute of Additions. 1 H. 5. c. 5. See before c. 23. 3 Jac. ca. 4. verb. And that if any gent.

For this offence of felony the offender shall have the benefit of his clergy, for at the time of the making of this act he that had stoln a horse should have had his clergy. See Stanf. Pl. Coron. fo. 37.

CAP.

C A P. XXXV.

Congregations, &c. by Maſons in their generall Chapters, &c.

3 H. 6. ca. 1.

IT is ordained and eſtabliſhed that no congregations and confederacies ſhall be made by maſons in their generall chapters and aſſemblies, whereby the good courſe and effects of the ſtatutes of labourers are violated and broken, in ſubverſion of law; and if any be, they that cauſe ſuch chapters and congregations to be aſſembled and holden, ſhall be adjudged felons.

2 E. 3 de ſervientibus, ca. 1. &c. 25 E. 3. De ſervientibus c. 1. &c. 5 El. ca. 4.

Ceſſante cauſa ſeu ratione legis ceſſat ipſa lex. 14 H. 7. 11. Per Fineux ſimile. 27 H. 8. 4. b. Aide ſimile 10 E. 3. 8. Acount per Shard. 26 H. 6. Examination 14.

The cauſe wherefore this offence was made felony, is, for that the good courſe and effect of the ſtatutes of labourers were thereby violated and broken. Now all the ſtatutes concerning labourers before this act, and whereunto this act doth refer are repealed by the ſtatute of 5 Eliz. cap. 4. whereby the cauſe and end of the making of this act is taken away, and conſequently this act is become of no force or effect: *ceſſante ratione legis, ceſſat ipſa lex.* And the indictment of felony upon this ſtatute muſt contain, that thoſe chapters and congregations were to the violating and breaking of the good courſe and effect of thoſe ſtatutes of labourers, which now cannot be ſo alledged, becauſe thoſe ſtatutes be repealed. Therefore this would be put out of the charge of juſtices of peace written by * maſter Lambard.

* Lambard, page 227. vide Stanf. 37. b.

C A P. XXXVI.

[100]

Of Felony by bringing in of Buls of Excommunication, &c.

13 R. 2. Stat. 2. cap. 3.

IF any man (1) bring or ſend into this realm, or the kings power, any ſommons, ſentence, or excommunication (2) againſt any perſon of what condition that he be, for the cauſe of making motion, aſſent, or execution of the ſtatute of proviſors (3), he ſhall be taken, arreſted, and put in priſon, and forfeit all his lands and tenements, goods and chattels for ever, and incur the pain of life and member (4). And if any prelate make execution (5) of ſuch ſommons, ſentence, or excommunication, that his temporalties be taken, and abide in the kings hand till due redreſſe and correction be thereof made.

And if any perſon of leſſe eſtate then a prelate, &c. make ſuch execution, he ſhall be taken, arreſted, and put in priſon, and have impriſonment, and make fine and ranſome by the diſcretion of the kings councell.

By the common law when any perſon, either eccleſiaſticall or temporall, ſhould by pretext of forain power impugne or attempt to fruſtrate any of the laws of the realm, there lieth a writ called *ad jura regia:* if it were by an eccleſiaſticall perſon beneficed within this realm, then the writ is.

Regiſt. fo. 61. b. *Rex, &c. ſalutem. Turbamur, nec immerito, et movemur dum illos qui ſub noſtro degunt dominio, et ibidem beneficiis et redditibus honorantur, quo prætextu in defenſione, et tuitione jurium regiæ coronæ noſtræ ipſos nos aſſiſtere condeceret, eadem jura erectis contra nos cervicibus conſpicimus ſatagentes pro viribus impugnare, &c.*

Ibidem, 60. b. Ibid. 61. b. & 62. The general writ is, *Rex, &c. ad jura coronæ noſtræ integra et illæſa pro viribus conſervanda, eo amplius curam et operam adhibere nos convenit ſtudioſam quòd ad hoc eſt debito aſtringimur vinculo juramenti, et alios conſpicimus, ad ipſorum jurium enervationem anhelare:* and particularly againſt proviſions. So as proviſions, &c. were, as by theſe writs it appeareth, againſt the common law of the realm, but ſufficient puniſhment was not thereby inflicted: therefore this, and other ſtatutes were made.

And here it is worthy of conſideration, how the laws of England are not derived from any forain law, either cannon, civil, or other, but a ſpecial law appropriated to this kingdome, and moſt accommodate and apt for the good government thereof, under which it hath wonderfully flouriſhed, when this law hath been put in due execution: and therefore as by ſituation, ſo by law it is truly ſaid,

*Et penitus toto * diviſos orbe Britannos.*

* Diviſos { orbe & legibus.

(1) *If any man.*] Though theſe words be generall, yet they extend not to eccleſiaſticall perſons, becauſe there is ſpeciall proviſion for them after in the act.

(2) *Any ſommons, ſentence, or excommunication.*] Hereby are prohibited the popes buls of any ſentence or excommunication, &c. and proces of ſummons.

[101]

11 E. 3. Certif. 6. 30 Aſſ. p. 3. 19 E. 3. Quare non admiſit. 7. Brook. Premunire 10. 11 H. 4. 69. 76. 14 H. 4. 14. 7 E. 4. 14. 20 H. 6. 1. 35 H. 6. 42. F. N. B. 64. f. Lib. 5. fo. 12. in Caudries caſe.

It appeareth by our books that the bringing of any bull of excommunication into the realme againſt a ſubject, was againſt the common law of England, in reſpect it gave way to foraine authority. And ſo it was holden in the time of E. 1. and E. 3. &c. long before this act, and ever ſince.

(3) *Or execution of the ſaid ſtatute of proviſors.*] viz. 25 E. 3. *de proviſoribus.* See 25 E. 3. cap. 22. 27 E. 3. cap. 1. 38 E. 3. ſtat. 2. cap. 1. & 4.

(4) *Incurre the paine of life and member.*] [a] That is, of felony as hath been often ſaid before. This puniſhment is altered by the ſtatute of 13 Eliz. cap. 2. as hereafter in this chapter ſhall appeare.

[a] W. 2. cap. 24. 1 E. 2. de frang. priſonam. 28 E. 3. cap. 3. 13 R. 2. ſtat. 2. ca. 3. 9 E. 4. 26. Br. Cor. 203.

(5) *And if any prelate make execution, &c.*] This and the next following branch extend to eccleſiaſticall perſons. The puniſhment in both theſe branches, and in the former alſo is altered by the ſtatute of 13 Eliz. cap. 2. For thereby this offence is made high trea-

* ſon,

ſon, [b] as well in perſons eccleſiaſticall, as temporall: which act, and the cauſe of the making thereof you may reade in the caſe *de jure regis eccleſiaſtico, ubi ſupra.* [b] Lib. 5. f. 35, 36, &c. De jure regis eccleſ.

CAP. XXXVII.

Of Felony in receiving a Jeſuite, Seminary Prieſt, &c.

27 Eliz. cap. 2.

EVERY perſon which ſhall wittingly and willingly receive, relieve, comfort, or maintaine any jeſuite, ſeminary prieſt, or other prieſt, deacon, or religious, or eccleſiaſticall perſon (made by authority from the ſee of Rome ſince the feaſt of Saint John Baptiſt, an. 1 Eliz. borne within this realme) being at liberty and out of hold, knowing him to be a jeſuite, &c. ſhall for ſuch offence be adjudged a felon without benefit of clergie. Clergie taken away.

The cauſe of the making of this ſtatute of 27 Eliz. againſt jeſuites and ſeminary prieſts, &c. and their receivers, you may reade at large, lib. 5. fol. 38, 39, in the caſe *De jure regis eccleſiaſtico.*

CAP. XXXVIII. [102]

Of Felony in Recuſants concerning Abjuration.

35 Eliz. cap. 1.

IF any recuſant) other then a Popiſh recuſant or a feme covert) which by the tenor and intent of this act is to be abjured, ſhall refuſe to make abjuration, or after ſuch abjuration made ſhall not goe to ſuch haven, and within ſuch time, as is by this act appointed, and from thence depart out of the realme, according to this preſent act, or after his departure ſhall returne into any of her majeſties realmes or dominions, without her majeſties ſpecial licenſe in that behalfe firſt obtained; that then every ſuch perſon ſo offending, ſhall be adjudged a felon.

If any offender againſt this act before he or they be required to make abjuration, repaire to ſome pariſh church, on ſome Sunday or feſtivall day, and then and there heare divine ſervice, and make ſuch ſubmiſſion as by the act is preſcribed: then the ſaid offender is cleerly to be diſcharged.

The offender ſhall forfeit his goods and chattels, and his lands during his life only, the offence ſhall work no loſſe of dower or corruption of blood, and the heire to inherit. The offender ſhall not have the benefit of his clergie.

CAP. XXXIX.

Of Felonie in Egyptians, &c.

1 & 2 Ph. and Mar. cap. 4. 5 Eliz. cap. 20.

IF any outlandiſh people, calling themſelves, or being called Egyptians, ſhall remaine in this realme, or in Wales, one moneth, at one or ſeverall times: and if any perſon being fourteene yeares old, which hath been ſeen or found in the fellowſhip of ſuch Egyptians, or which hath diſguiſed him or herſelfe like to them, ſhall remaine here or in Wales by the ſpace of one moneth, either at one or ſeverall times, it is felony.

The offender ſhall not have the benefit of his clergie.

[103]

CAP. XL.

Of Felonie in dangerous Rogues.

39 Eliz. cap. 4. 1 Jac. cap. 7. 25.

IF any dangerous rogue that was baniſhed the realme or adjudged perpetually to the gallies, have returned into the realme without lawfull licenſe or warrant, it is felony: the felony to be tried where the offender is apprehended.

The offender may have the benefit of his clergie.

39 Eliz. cap. 4. 1 Jac. cap. 7.

If any rogue after he hath been branded in open ſeſſions with a Roman R. upon the left ſhoulder, or ſent to the place of his dwelling where he laſt dwelt by the ſpace of a yeare, or the place of his birth, to be placed in labour, have offended againe in begging, or wandering contrary to the ſaid ſtatutes, it is felony, to be tried in the county where the offender ſhall be taken.

The offender againſt this branch ſhall not have the benefit of his clergie.

Deut. ca. 15. v. 4. Mirr. cap. 1. § 3. Inter les Art. per viels royes ordeins.

Mendicus non erit inter vos, there ſhall be no begger among you.

Ordeine fuit que les povres fuiſſent ſuſteinus per les parſons, rectors, et les parochians cy que nul ne moruſt per default de ſuſteinance.

Sec

See an ancient ordinance in 50 E. 3. concerning ribauds and ſturdy beggers, that they be driven to their occupations or ſervices, or to the place from whence they came. Rot. Par. 50 E. 3. nu. 61. Brit. 49. b.

CAP. XLI.

Of Felonie by Forgerie in the ſecond Degree.

IF any perſon or perſons being once condemned of any of the forgeries mentioned in the act, ſhall after ſuch his, or their condemnation, eſt-ſoones commit or perpetrate any of the ſaid offences in forme in the ſaid act mentioned, that then every ſuch ſecond offence ſhall be adjudged felony. But no attainder of this felony ſhall extend to take away dower, nor to corruption of blood, or diſherifon of the heire. 5 Eliz. cap. 14.

In 43 Eliz. Markham was attainted of felony upon this branch in the kings bench for a ſecond forgery of many of the mannors and lands late of Sir Thomas Greſham knight, and was executed therefore. Markhams caſe coram rege. 43 Eliz.

* This felony is to be heard and determined before juſtices of oier and terminer, and juſtices of aſſiſe in their circuit. And albeit that juſtices of peace have power to heare and determine felonies, treſpaſſe, &c. yet are they not included under the name of juſtices of oier and terminer: for juſtices of oier and terminer are known by one diſtinct name, and juſtices of peace by another. But the juſtices of the kings bench are juſtices of oier and terminer within this ſtatute. Hil. 30 Eliz. coram rege. Lib. 9. fo. 118. b. Smiths caſe. 3 Mar. Br. tit. Oier & Term. 8.

The offender ſhall not have the benefit of his clergie.

See hereafter in the expoſition of this ſtatute for the firſt offence, where incidently there ſhall be more ſaid concerning the ſecond offence.

CAP. XLII. [104]

Of Felony for conveying of any Sheep alive out of the Realm in a ſecond Degree.

NO manner of perſon ſhall bring, deliver, ſend, receive, or take, or procure to be brought, delivered, ſent, or received into any ſhip, or bottome any rams, ſheep, or lambs, or any other ſheep alive, to be carried and conveyed out of this realm of England, Wales, or Ireland, or out of any of the queens dominions, upon pain that every ſuch perſon, their aiders, abetters, procurers, and comforters, ſhall for his 8 El. cap. 3. See the ſtatute of 3 H. 6. cap. 2.

His left hand cut off.

his and their first offence, forfeit all his goods, and suffer imprisonment one whole year without bayl or mainprise; and at the years end in some market town in the fulnesse of the market, have his left hand cut off, &c. And that every person est-soons offending against this statute shall be adjudged a felon, &c.

But this act shall not extend to any corruption of blood, or losse of dower. This felony is to be heard and determined before justices of oier and terminer, justices of gaol-delivery, and justices of peace. And the offender may have the benefit of his clergy, as well in case of the cutting off his hand as in case of felony. See Stanford, 37. b.

CAP. XLIII.

Of Felony in Servants that imbesill their Masters Goods after their Decease.

33 H. 6. cap. 1.

[a] This extends to the lord keeper of the great seal.

[b] This extends to the administrators, and also, if there be but one executor or administrator.

[c] Attainted by force of this act of parliament upon default. See the like many times in the parliament rolls. Rot. Parl. 15 H. 6. nu. 14. & 15. Rot. Parl. 18 H. 6. num. 28.

IF any of the houshold servants of any person shall after the decease of their lord or master violently and riotously take and spoil the goods which were their said lords or masters, and the same distribute amongst them, that upon full information [a] to the chancelour of England for the time being by the [b] executors or two of them, of such riot, taking, or spoil made, the chancelour by the advice of the chief justices, and chief baron, or two of them, shall have power to make so many and such writs to be directed to such sherifs, as to them shall seem necessary, to make open proclamation in such sort, as by the act is prescribed, to appear in the kings bench, &c. and if any such writ be retorned, &c. then if the said person or persons make default, then he or they making default shall be [c] attainted of felony.

The offenders shall have the benefit of their clergy.

CAP. XLIV.

Of Felony in Servants that imbesill their Masters Goods committed to their Trust above Forty Shillings.

EVERY servant to whom any caskets, jewels, money, goods, or cattels of his or their master, or mistris, shall be delivered to keep, that if any such servant or servants withdraw him or them from their said masters or mistrisses (1), and goe away with the said caskets, jewels, money, goods, or cattels, or any part thereof to the intent to steal the same, contrary to the trust and confidence in him or them put, &c. Or else being in service of his said master or mistris, without the assent and commandment of his master or mistris, imbesill the same or any part thereof, or otherwise convert the same to his own use, with like purpose to steal it: if the caskets, jewels, money, goods or cattels be of the value of forty shillings or above, shall be deemed and adjudged felony.

21 H. 8. ca. 7.
27 H. 8. ca. 17.
28 H. 8. ca. 2.
1 E. 6. ca. 12.
5 El. ca. 10.

Concerning the value, (to speak it once for all) *tantum bona valent, quantum vendi possunt.*

This act extendeth not to any apprentice or apprentices, nor to any servant within the age of eighteen years, at the time of the offence committed.

Vide Dier, 25 H. 8. fol. 5.

Dier, 25 H. 8. f. 5.

By the statute of 27 H. 8. the offender was ousted of his clergy, but that act is repealed by 1 E. 6. cap. 12. So as at this day the offender may have the benefit of his clergy.

1 E. 6. ca. 12.

(1) *Shall be delivered by his or their master or mistris.*] If the master deliver an obligation to his servant to receive the money thereby due, and the servant receive the money of the obligee, and goeth away with the same with intent to steal the same, this is no offence within this statute, because he had not the money of the delivery of his master: and if he had gone with the obligation with intent, *ut supra*, it had been also out of this act, because it was a chose in action. So if the master deliver to his servant wares or merchandises to sell, and selleth the same and goeth away with the money as before, this is no offence within this statute for the cause aforesaid. See Stanford, 37. b.

Dier, 26 H. 8. fo. 5. a. & b. See the form of the indictment upon this stat. Lamb. inter Praesidentes.

CAP.

CAP. XLV.

Of Felony to cut down or break up the Powdike in Marſhland in Norff.

22 H. 8. ca. 11. 2 & 3 Ph. and Mar. cap. 19.

EVERY perverſe and malitious cutting down and breaking up of any part of the new dike called the Powdike in Marſhland in the county of Norff. or of the broken dike called Oldfield Dike by Marſhland in the Iſle of Ely in the county of Cambridge, or of any other bank being parcell of the Rinde, and uttermoſt part of the ſaid country is adjudged felony.

The juſtices of peace have power to enquire of, and to hear and determine this felony. The offender may have the benefit of his clergy.

Some ſay that this is a private act, but it is *publicum in privato*, for the danger is publike though the place be private, and doth concern multitudes of people, and the ſea is ſuch an immenſe creature, as who can withſtand it without length of time, infinite dammage, and loſſe, and extream charge and coſt.

43 El. cap. 13. * See before cap. 12. fo. 61, 62. 3 H. 7. cap. 2. Vide 1 H. 5. c. 6. ſimile de Gales. * Blackmail is explained by the act it ſelf.

See the ſtatute of 43 El. cap. 13. whereby in the counties of Cumberland, Northumberland, Weſtmerland and the B. of Dureſme * carrying away or detaining of any perſon againſt his will, or impriſoning him or them to ranſome them or to ſpoil them, upon deadly feud or otherwiſe, or ſhall receive or carry * blackmail, or give black mail for protection, &c. is made felony without benefit of clergy.

CAP. XLVI.

Of one of the Grand Enqueſt being one of the Indictors of any Perſon or Perſons of Treaſon or Felony, and diſcover openly what Perſons were ſo indicted, &c.

THIS by ſome opinion in our books was holden for treaſon, or felony, and hereof divers reaſons were yeelded.

Stanf. fo. 36. a.

Firſt, that ſuch diſcovery was againſt his oath, but that could not be the reaſon, for perjury was neither treaſon nor felony.

Secondly, others did hold, that by this diſcovery the parties indicted of treaſon or felony might flee, or eſcape, but that can be no reaſon;

reason; for this discovery without more, can neither make him principall nor accessory.

Thirdly, others that endeavour to confesse and avoid the authorities in this case in law, are of opinion, that in those times the intent of a man, *in criminalibus*, was much respected, in as much as *in criminalibus voluntas reputabatur pro facto*, and that by this open discovery, &c. his intent appeared, that they might flee or escape. And now it is agreed on all parts, that at this day such discovery is neither treason nor felony: and the rather, for that no person ever died for such discovery. In Georges case, in *anno* 27 lib. Ass. upon his indictment he was acquited. But certaine it is, that such discovery is accompanied with perjury, and a great misprision to be punished by fine and imprisonment. 18 E. 3. Cor. 272. 27 Ass. p. 63. Georges case. [107]

CAP. XLVII.

Of Larceny or Theft by the Common Law.

HAVING thus far proceeded, we are now come to larceny, which commeth from *latrocinium*, and from *latrocinie*, by contraction, or rather abuse, to larceny.

The Mirror first describeth larceny, and then explaineth it. *Larcine est prise d'autre moeble corporelle trecherousment contre la volunt de celuy a q. il est p. male egaigne de la possession, ou del use.* Then doth he explaine and shew the reason of the principall words thereof. Mirror, cap. 1. § 10. De Larcenie.

Prise est dit, car baile nest my title de laroun, ne livery en le case.

Moeble corporelle est dit pur ceo q. en biens nient moebles, ou nient corporels, sicome de tre', rents, et des advowsons de esglises, ne se fait nul larcenie.

Trecherousment est dit pur ceo q. si lesloignour entende les biens estre siens, et que il les poet bien prender, en tiel case ne se fait my ceste peche, nec en case ou len prent l'autrui p. la ou len entend, que il pleist al seigniour des biens, que il les prendera, mes a ceo covient enseigner apparant presumption et evidence.

Et sciendum, quod furtum est, secundum leges, contrectatio rei alienæ fraudulenta, cum animo furandi, invito illo domino, cujus res illa fuerat. And then he also explaineth it. *Cum animo dico, quia sine animo furandi non committitur.* Bracton useth not the word *latrocinium*, but *furtum*, and so doth Granvile. See Britton a whole chapter *de Larcyns.* And Fleta hath it thus, *Est autem furtum contrectatio rei alienæ fraudulenta cum animo furandi invito dno. cujus res illa fuerit*, following Bracton *totidem verbis.* These descriptions are generally of theft, comprehending robbery, burglary, when any thing is taken, and all other latrocinies. But here larceny for distinction sake is taken in a narrower sense, viz. for single theft or thievery, and may be described thus. Bracton, lib. 3. fol. 150. Glanvil. lib. 7. c. 17. & lib. 10. cap. 15. Britton, cap. 15. de Larcyns. fo. 22. Fleta, lib. 1. ca. 36.

Larceny, by the common law, is the felonious and fraudulent taking and carrying away by any man or woman, of the meere personall goods of another, neither from the person, nor by night in the house of the owner. Larcenie defined.

Now

Now let us peruſe the principall parts of this deſcription.

See tit. Piracy, &c. Butlers caſe, 28 Eliz. *Felonious taking.*] Firſt it muſt be felonious, *id eſt*, *cum animo furandi*, as hath been ſaid. *Actus non facit reum*, *niſi mens ſit rea.* And this intent to ſteale muſt be when it cometh to his hands or poſſeſſions: for if he hath the poſſeſſion of it once lawfully, though he hath *animum furandi* afterward, and carrieth it away, it is no larceny: but this receiveth ſome diſtinction, as hereafter ſhall appeare.

2 E. 3. 1. Secondly, it muſt be an actuall taking: for an indictment, *quod felonice abduxit equum*, is not good, becauſe it wanteth, *cepit*. By taking, and not bailment or delivery, for that is a receipt, and not a taking: and therewith agreeth Glanvil. Glanvil. lib. 10. cap. 13. *Furtum non eſt ubi initium habet detentionis per dominum rei.*

13 E. 4. 9. But herein the law doth diſtinguiſh. For if a bale or pack of merchandize be delivered to carry to one to a certaine place, and he goeth away with the whole pack, this is no felony: but if he open the pack, and take any thing out *animo furandi*, this is larceny. Likewiſe if the carrier carry it to the place appointed, and after take the [108] whole pack *animo furandi*, this is larceny alſo: for the delivery had taken his effect, and the privity of the bailement is determined. And ſo it is of a tun of wine, or the like, *mutatis mutandis.*

Charge. Alſo there is a diverſity betweene a poſſeſſion, and a charge; for when I deliver goods to a man, he hath the poſſeſſion of the goods, 3 H. 7. 12. 21 H. 7. 15. and may have an action of treſpaſſe, or an appeale, if they be taken or ſtolne out of his poſſeſſion. But my butler or cook, that in my houſe hath charge of my veſſel or plate, hath no poſſeſſion of them, nor ſhall have an action of treſpaſſe or an appeale, as the bailee ſhall: and therefore if they ſteale the plate or veſſel, it is larceny. And ſo it is of a ſhepherd, for theſe things be *in onere, et non in poſſeſſione promi, coci, paſtoris, &c.*

13 E. 4. 9. If a taverner ſet a piece of plate before a man to drink in it, and Speciall uſe. he carry it away, &c. this is larceny: for it is no bailement, but a ſpeciall uſe to a ſpeciall purpoſe.

22 Aſſ. pl. 99. Thirdly, nor by trover or finding. If one loſe his goods, and 22 E. 3. cor. 265. another finde them, though he convert them, *animo furandi*, to his own uſe, yet is it no larceny, for the firſt taking is lawfull. So if one finde treaſure trove, or waife, or ſtray, and convert them *ut ſupra*, it is no larceny, both in reſpect of the finding, and alſo for that *dominus rerum non apparet.*

See cap. de Treaſon. Verb. quant. home, &c. Et cap. Murder. Felonious implyeth, that though the taking be actuall, yet muſt it be done by ſuch perſons as may commit felony. A mad man that is *non compos mentis*, or an infant that is under the age of diſcretion, cannot commit larceny, as in another place we have ſaid.

27 Aſſ. 40. 2 E. 3. cor. 160. Lex Inæ cap. 50. accord. Stanf. 26. c. 15 E. 2. Cor. 383. A feme covert committeth not larceny, if it be done by the coertion of her huſband: but a feme covert may commit larceny, if ſhe doth it without the coertion of her huſband: and there it appeareth, that a man may be acceſſary to his wife, but the wife cannot be acceſſary to her huſband, though ſhe know that he committed larceny, and relieve him, and diſcover it not: for by the law divine, ſhe is not bound to diſcover the offence of her huſband.

Mic. 37 E. 3. coram rege. Rot. 83 Lincolne. Felons came to the houſe of Richard Dey, and Margery his wife; the wife knew them to be felons, but the huſband did not, and both of them received them, and entertained them, but the wife conſented not to the felony. And it was adjudged, that this made not the wife acceſſary, *Quia ipſa in vita mariti ſui de aliquo receptamento*

ceptamento in præsentia viri sui, cui contradicere non potuit, occasionari non debet.

Uxor furi desponsata non tenebitur ex facto viri, quia virum accusare non debet, nec detegere furtum suum, nec feloniam, cum ipsa sui potestatem non habet, sed vir. Bracton, lib. 3. fol. 151. b.

La feme nequedent al felon poit dire q. tout scavoit ele del mauvaste son baron, pur ceo ne le poet ele my encuser, ne devoit, tant come ele fuit de luy covert, &c. Briton. cap. 24, fo. 47.

Uxor autem furis non teneatur pro delicto viri, pœna enim suos debet tenere authores, uxor autem virum accusare non debet, nec feloniæ suæ consentire, &c. Fleta, lib. 1. ca. 36.

Felonious and fraudulent taking.] If a man seeing the horse of B. in his pasture, and having a minde to steale him commeth to the sheriffe, and pretending the horse to be his, obtaineth the horse to be delivered unto him by a replevyn, yet this is a felonious and fraudulent taking, as it was resolved by the judges, as Catlin chiefe justice reported in the kings bench, Pasch. 15 Eliz. for the Replevyn was obtained *in fraudem legis.* Pasch. 15 Eliz. Vide statutum.

Carrying away.] For the indictment saith, *felonice cepit et asportavit.* The removing of the things taken, though he carry not them quite away, satisfieth this word *asportavit.* As if a guest take the coverlet or sheets of his bed, and rising before day, take the coverlet or sheets out of the chamber, where he lay, into the hall, to the intent to steal them, and went to the stable to fetch his horse, and the ostler apprehended him, and this was adjudged larceny: and the coverlet or sheets were carried away being removed from the chamber to the hall, albeit they were still in the house of the owner. 22 Ass. pl. 39. [109]

So if a mans horse be in his close, and one taketh him, and as he is carrying him away, he is apprehended, before he getteth out of the close, yet this is sufficient to make it larceny. Justice Dalizons Report.

Of mere personall goods.] It is said (mere) for though they be personall goods, yet if they savour any thing of the realty, no larceny can be committed of them; as any kind of corn or grain growing upon the ground is a personall chattell, and the executors of the owner shall have them, though they be not severed, but yet no larceny can be committed of them, because they are annexed to the realty. So it is of grasse standing on the ground, or of apples, or any other fruits upon trees, or bushes, or of woods growing; but if the owner cut the grasse, or gather the fruit, or cut the wood, then larceny may be committed of them. 12 E. 3. Cor. 199. 22 E. 3. Ibid. 256. lib. 4. fo. 19.

So it is of a box or chest with charters, no larceny can be committed of them, because the charters concern the realty, and the box or chest though it be of great value, yet shall it be of the same nature the charters be of: *et omne majus dignum trahit ad se minus.* 10 E. 4. 14. lib. 8. fo. 33. b. Caleys case.

No larceny can be committed by taking, and carrying away of a ward, or of a villain, because they are in the realty.

It appeareth by all our ancient authors *ubi supra,* and by the statute of W. 1. that there is grand larceny, and petit larceny, distinguished so by the value: for if the personall goods stoln amount to above the value of twelve pence, then is it grand larceny, and if it be under the value of twelve pence, then it is petit larcency, for which W. 1. ca. 15. See the exposition thereof. 27 H. 8. 22. Coriū foris facere or perdere Sax. *tholiz, his hide* is to be whipt. Mirror ca. 4. §. De crime de robbery.

which he shall forfeit all his goods, and suffer some corporall punishment, as whipping, &c.

And this was the ancient law before the conquest, for the Mirror saith, *Et tout soit que la ley ne eyt regard forsque al ceures des peuchers nequident linit le quantitie del robbery et larceny en cest manner, cestassavoir que nul ad judgement de la mort, si non larceny, &c. ne passont* 12 *deniers de sterlings.*

Lib. 7. fo. 18. In case de Swans.

a Vide verb (of another) next following. 12 H. 8. 39. 14 H. 8 3. 4. 18 H. 8. 2. 2 E. 2. distres 20 leveret. 2 E. 2. Avowry. 182. ferret. 38 E. 3. 10. 47 E. 3. 10. 5 H. 5. 1. 9 H. 6 2. F. N. B. 87. a. and 88. I. 86. l.

A man hath a mere property in some things that are tame by nature, and yet in respect of the baseness of their nature, a man shall not commit any larceny, great or small, though he steal them, as of mastifs, bloud-hounds, or of other kind, dogs or of cats, nor of some things that be [a] wild by nature, and made tame, as bears, foxes, apes, monkies, polcats, ferrets, and the like, and yet no manner of felony can be committed on them, in respect of their wild and savage nature, and therefore no person shall die for them: and likewise it is of their whelps, or calves, or young; for it is a rule in law, that if no felony can be committed of any thing that is *ferum natura*, and of age being reclaimed, or made tame, that no felony can be of the young in the nest, kennell or den.

b Mirror c. 1. § 10. Dier 14 El. 306, 307. 18 E. 4. 8. 16 E. 4. 11. 14 H. 8. 4. Vide before. 37 E. 3. fo. 37. F. N. B. 86. l.

[b] So as a man may have property in many things, and yet in respect of their nature there can be no felony of them. On the other side, of some things that be *ferae natura*, being reclaimed, felony may be committed in respect of their noble and generous nature and courage, serving *ob vitae solatium* of princes, and of noble, and generous persons, to make them fitter for great employments: As all kind of faulcons, and other hawks, if the party, that steals them know they be reclaimed.

c 18 H. 8. 2. b. Doct. & Stu. 9. b. Britton, 74, 75. Bract. l. 2. fo. 9. 8 E. 4, 5. d 11 H. 7. ca. 17. 31 H. 8. ca. 12.

Of another.] [c] No larceny can be committed of wild beasts, or of fowls that be wild, or of fishes that be at their naturall liberty in rivers, or great waters, because these be *nullius in bonis:* but larceny may be committed of young pigeons in dovehouses, or of young hawks in the nest. But if any person upon the ground of any other, doe take the egs of any faulcon, goshawk, lanner, or swan out of the nest, this is not felony, [d] but he shall be imprisoned by the space of a year and a day, and fined at the kings will, the one half to the king, and the other to the owner of the ground. But larceny may be committed of the egs of such as be *domitae natura*, as of hens, turkies, pehens, and the like. [a] And larceny may be committed of fishes in a trunk or pond, because they are not at their naturall liberty, but as it were beasts in a pownd.

[110]

a Stanf. 25. c. 12 E. 4. 4. 18 E. 4. 8. 22 H. 6. 59. 43 E. 3. 24. Vide before, verb. (Of meer personall goods) 3 H. 6. 55. lib. 5. fo. 104. b. lib. 7. fo. 16, 17. b 10 E. 4. 14.

[b] But if such as be wild, that serve for the food of man, be made tame, as deer, wild bore, conies, cranes, phesant, partridge, or the like, larceny may be committed of them, so as he that stealeth them know that they be tame. But the deer, &c. being wild, yet when he is killed larceny may be committed of the flesh, and so of phesant, partridge, or the like: and so note a diversity between such beasts as be *ferae natura*, and being made tame, serve for pleasure only, and such as be made tame and serve for food, &c. which diversity being not observed, hath made many men to erre.

7 E. 4. 14. Stanf. 25.

A man may be indicted, *Quare bona capellae in custodia, &c.* and so in time of vacation, *bona domus ecclesiae.*

At

At the aſſiſes at Leiceſter, in Lent, *anno* 10 Jac. the caſe was this, one William Hain had in the night digged up the graves of divers ſeverall men, and of one woman, and took the winding ſheets from the bodies, and buried the bodies again: and I adviſing hereupon for the rareneſſe of the caſe, conſulted with the judges at Serjeants Inne in Fleetſtreet; where we all reſolved, that the property of the ſheets was in the executors, adminiſtrators or other owner of them, for the dead body is not capable of any property, and the property of the ſheets muſt be in ſome body: and according to this reſolution, he was indicted of felony at the next aſſiſes, but the jury found it but petit larceny, for which he was whipped, as he well deſerved. 10 Jac. regis. Hains caſe. Furtum inauditum.

Nota. A felonious taking muſt be of the poſſeſſion, and not of the property removed from the poſſeſſion.

If a man doth bail, or lend his goods to another, although he hath the generall property of them, yet may he commit larceny of them, by the felonious taking and carrying them away, and in judgement of law he is ſaid in this caſe to take the goods of another: for the bailer hath *jus proprietatis,* and the bailee hath *jus poſſeſſionis,* or a ſpeciall property. 7 H. 6. 43.

The wife cannot ſteal the goods of her huſband, for they be not the goods of another, for the huſband and wife are one perſon in law, *duæ animæ in carne una.* 21 H. 6. Cor. 455. Abbridge daſſ 63.

Vide Stanf. Pl. Coron. fo. 24, 25.

To ſpeak it here once for all, if any perſon be indicted of treaſon, or of felony, or larcency, and plead not guilty, and thereupon a jury is retorned, and ſworn, their verdict muſt be heard, and they cannot be diſcharged, neither can the jurors in thoſe caſes give a privy verdict, but ought to give their verdict openly in court.

Macegriefs, fleſhmongers, ſuch as buy and ſell ſtollen fleſh, knowing the ſame to be ſtollen. Vide *Lamb. inter leges Edw. regis* fol. 140. b. *De Machecariis* derived of *mace* an old word for fleſh, and *grief,* wrong or injury. Britton, fo. 71.

CAP. XLVIII. [111]

De Anno Die et Vaſto.

Of the Year Day and Waſt.

HEREOF we have treated at large, in the ſecond part of the Inſtitutes in his proper place upon the expoſition of Magna Carta, cap. 22. where it appeareth, that at this day the king ſhall have but the profits for a year and a day in lieu and ſatisfaction of the waſt which the common law gave to the king in deſpite and deteſtation of the offence, as there you may read at large: and there it appeareth how neceſſary it is, ancient authors to be read, all which need not here to be rehearſed: * and Mirror, cap. 1. §. 3. and cap. 4. §. *Et le roy in remembrance,* &c. Lege quia optime, Glanv. li. 7. cap. 17. Bracton, lib. 3. fo. 129. 137. Britton, c. 5. f. 14. Fleta, lib. 1. c. 28. § *Cauſa vero,* &c. 17 E. 2. Prær. Regis cap. ultimo. Regiſt. 165. Mag. Cart. cap. 22. 3 E. 3. Cor. 356. 327. 310. 290. * 42 E. 3. ca. 1.

 that

that if any ſtatute be made to the contrary of Magna Carta, it ſhall be holden for none. And therefore if *prærogativa regis anno* 17 E. 2. cap. *ultimo*, be contrary thereunto, it is repealed as to the waſt.

CAP. XLIX.

Of Piracy, Felonies, Robberies, Murders, and Confederacies committed in or upon the Sea, &c.

HAVING now treated of felonies, &c. that are committed and done upon the land, we will conſider of piracies, and felonies, &c. done on the ſea, which by an act of parliament are to be enquired of, heard, and determined according to the courſe of the common law, as if they had been done upon the land.

Rot. Parl. 8 H. 6. nu. 42.

28 H. 8. ca. 15.

All treaſons (2), felonies, robberies, murders and confederacies committed in or upon the ſea, or in any other haven, river, creek, or place, where the admirall hath, or pretends to have power, authority, or juriſdiction (3), ſhall be enquired, tried, heard, determined, and judged in ſuch ſhires, and places in the realm, as ſhall be limited by the kings commiſſion under the great ſeal in like form and condition, as if any ſuch offence had been committed upon the land (5), to be directed to the lord admirall, or to his lieutenant, deputy, or deputies, and to three or four ſuch other ſubſtantiall perſons, as ſhall be named by the lord chancellour of England (4), for the time being, &c.

Vid. 27 E. 3. c. 13. del ſtaple. 31 H. 6. cap. 4. Vide 2 R. 3. fo. 2. Vide Palaches caſe.

And ſuch as ſhall be convict of any ſuch offence by verdict, confeſſion, or proces by authority of any ſuch commiſſion, ſhall have and ſuffer ſuch pains of death, loſſes of lands, goods and chattels, as if they had been attainted of any treaſon, felony, robbery, or other the ſaid offences done upon the land.

See before in the chap. of Hereſy.

The offenders not to be admitted to have the benefit of clergy.

[112]

The miſchief before this ſtatute was (as it appeareth by the preamble) that traitors, pirates (1), thiefs, robbers, murderers, and confederators upon the ſea many times eſcaped unpuniſhed, becauſe the common law of this realm extended not to theſe offences, but were judged, and determined before the admirall, &c. after the courſe of the civill laws, the nature whereof is, that before any judgement of death be given againſt the offenders, either they muſt plainly confeſſe their offences (which they never will do without torture or pains) or

See 40 Aſſ. pl. 25.

or by * witnesse indifferent, such as saw their offences committed, &c. which in these cases cannot be gotten but by chance, or very rarely: for this cause, the commons petitioned in [a] parliament in 8 H. 6. that the justices of peace might enquire of all piracies: but the kings answer was, That he would be advised.

* Concerning treason, see before cap. 2. verb. *All trials*. fo. 25. 1 E. 6. ca. 12. 5 E. 6. ca. 11. &c.

[a] Rot. Par. 8 H. 6. nu. 42.

This statute requires a considerate and just interpretation, wherein, for that it concerneth the life of man, the safest way is, to follow the resolutions of all the judges formerly had upon due consideration of all the parts of this act, and upon divers conferences, and in the end, when I was atturney generall, resolved by them unanimously as followeth:

Hil. 2. Ja. regis, at Serjeants Inne in Fleetstreet, the resolution of the justices.

Where divers did in the reign of the late queen Elizabeth commit piracy and robbery upon the high sea, of divers merchants of Venice, in amity with the said queen, and after the pirats, being not known, obtained a pardon, granted at the coronation of king James, whereby the king pardoned them all felonies *(inter alia)* First, that before this statute piracy, or robbery on the high sea was no felony, whereof the common law took any knowledge, for that it could not be tried, being out of all towns and counties, but was only punishable by the civill law, as by the preamble it appeareth; the attainder by which law wrought no forfeiture of lands, or corruption of bloud. Secondly, that this statute did not alter the offence, or make the offence felony, but leaveth the offence as it was before this act, viz. felony only by the civil law, but giveth a mean of triall by the common law, and inflicteth such pains of death, as if they had been attainted of any felony, &c. done upon the land. But yet (as hath been said) the offence is not altered, for in the indictment upon this statute, the offence must be alledged upon the sea; so as this act inflicteth punishment for that, which is a felony by the civill law, and no felony, whereof the common law taketh knowledge. Thirdly, although the king may pardon this offence, yet being no felony in the eye of the law of the realm, but only by the civill law, the pardon of all felonies generally extendeth not to it, for this is a speciall offence, and ought to be specially mentioned.

Three points resolved.

Vide similia. 19 E. 3. Cor. 124. 8 H. 4. 2. 9 E. 4. 28.

Upon this resolution these consequents do follow. 1. That by the attainder upon this act, though there be forfeiture of lands, and goods, yet there is no corruption of blood. 2. Seeing the offence is not made felony by the laws of this realm, there can be no accessory of any felony by the laws of the realm in this case, either before or after the offence, because the principall is no felon by our law, neither doth this act speak of any accessory. 3. If there be an accessory upon the sea to a piracy, that accessory may be punished by the civill law before the lord admirall, but cannot be punished by this act, because it extendeth not to accessories, nor makes the offence felony. * Lastly, the statute of 35 H. 8. ca. 2. taketh not away this statute for treasons done upon the sea for the cause aforesaid. Which resolution I have thought good to report, because it openeth the windows of this statute.

* See the fourth part of the Institutes, cap. High Treason.

In Trin. 18 Eliz. in lord Diers manuscript, there is a quære made, what offence it is to lodge and entertain upon the land a pirat, knowing him to be a pirat, and whether this accessory upon the land shall be tried by this statute, which is only of principalls in piracy. And it was thought by the two chief justices, that the surest way, was to have the commission in the county where the accessory

5 El. cap. 5. Vide supra, cap. High Treason. Verbo *Ou par ailors*, f. 11.

accessory offended, and there both the principall and the accessory may be indicted, and tried, *ut per statutum, anno* 5 & 6 E. 6. quære. *Hæc * ille.* So as this quære is now cleared by the resolution of the judges: and questionlesse the statute (intended of 2 & 3 E. 6. for there is none such in 5 & 6 E. 6.) extendeth only, when a murder or felony is committed in one countie, and another person is accessorie in another countie (as hath been said before:) but in that case the offence was committed upon the sea, and not in any countie, and so out of that statute: and therefore this part of the manuscript of the lord Dier was not thought fit to be printed.

2 & 3 E. 6. ca. 24.

Vid. lib. 2. fo. 93. Binghams case. See the lord Sancars case, lib. 9. 117, 118.

Anno 28 Eliz. Butlers case.

Butler and other pirats in summer vacation robbed divers of her majesties subjects, upon the coast of Northfolk, upon the high sea; and brought divers of the goods so taken into the county of Northfolke, and there were apprehended with the goods: The question moved to Wray chiefe justice, and justice Peryam, justices of assise in Northfolk, was, whether they might be indicted of felony in Northfolk, as if one steale goods in one county and carry them into another county, he may be indicted in either county? and it was resolved by them, that they could not be indicted for felony in Northfolk; because the originall taking was no felony, whereof the common law took conusance, because it was done upon the sea, out of the reach of the common law: and therefore not like the case, where one stealeth in one county and carrieth the goods into another, for there the originall act was felony whereof the law took conusance.

But now let us peruse the words of the statute.

(1) *Where traytors, pirats.*] This word pirat, in Latine *pirata*, is derived from the Greek word πειράτης, which againe is fetched from πειρᾶν, *à transeundo mare*, of roving upon the sea: and therefore in English, a pirat is called a rover and a robber upon the sea.

(2) *Treason, &c.*] Note, treason done out of the realme, is declared to be treason by the statute of 25 E. 3. and yet at the making of this act of 28 H. 8. it wanted triall, (as by the preamble of this statute it is rehearsed) at the common law. And therefore to establish a certainty therein, the statute of 35 H. 8. was made, as is aforesaid in the exposition of the statute of 25 E. 3. See Pasch. 43 Eliz. lib. 5. fo. 107. Sir Henry Constables case.

25 E. 3. cap. 1. 40 Ass. p. 25.

Before the statute of 25 E. 3. if a subject had committed piracie upon another (for so is the book to be intended upon a fact done before 25 E. 3.) this was holden to be petit treason, for which he was to be drawne and hanged: because *pirata est hostis humani generis*, and it was *contra ligeanciæ suæ debitum*: but if an alien, as one of the Normans, who had revolted in the reigne of king John, had committed piracy upon a subject, this offence could be no treason, for though he were *hostis humani generis*, yet the crime was not *contra ligeanciæ suæ debitum*, because the offender was no subject, but since the statute of 25 E. 3. this is no treason in the case of a subject.

(3) *Upon the sea, or in any other haven, river, creek, or other place, where the admirall hath, or pretends to have power, authority, or jurisdiction.*] These words [or pretends to have, &c.] are thus to be understood, between the high-water-mark, and the low-water-mark: for though the land be *infra corpus comitatus*, at the reflow; yet

yet when the sea is full, the admirall hath jurisdiction *super aquam* as long as the sea flowes: so as of one place there is *divisum imperium* at severall times: but extend not to any haven, river, creek, or other place, that is *infra corpus comitatus:* for offences there committed were triable by the common law, and out of the mischiefe and purvien of this statute: for in the preamble, the sea is only mentioned, and in the body of the act it is said, in like forme and condition, as if any such offence had been committed upon the land.

(4) *As shall be named by the lord chancellor of England.*] A nomination by the lord keeper of the great seale of England was taken to be * within this act by the greater opinion of the justices: but the statute of 5 Eliz. hath made a declaration of the common law concerning the power and authority of the lord keeper of the great seale, which hath cleared that, and all other like questions.

(5) *To heare and determine such offences after the common course of the lawes of this land used for treasons, felonies, &c. done and committed upon the land.*] If the offender upon his arraignment before commissioners by force of this statute stand mute, he shall have judgement *de peyne fort et dure*, by force of this generall branch, but it is out of the latter words of the act, viz. and such as shall be convict of any such offence by verdict, confession, or proces. For he that standeth mute is not convict of the offence, but suffereth for his contumacy. Also it is neither by verdict, confession, or proces.

For *peine fort et dure:* see in the second part of the Institutes, in the exposition upon the statute of W. 1. cap. 12.

8 E. 2. cor. 399. 46 E. 3. Conusance 36. Stanf. pl. coron. 51. k. Regist. 129. 13 R. 2. ca. 5. 2 H 4. cap. 11. Pl. com. 37. 2 R. 3. fo. 12. 19 H. 6. 7. 30 H. 6. 6. per Prisott. Fortescue, ca. 32. 5 Eliz. cap. 18.

*[114]

Trin. 7 Eliz. Dier 241. the case of Brook *alias* Cobham.

CAP. L.

OF CLERGIE.

WHAT person shall have his clergie, for what offences, in what suits, who is judge thereof, and at what time clergie is to be demanded, you may reade at large in Alexander Poulters case in the eleventh part of my reports: where also is resolved the diversity betweene a clerk convict, and a clerk attaint; what a clerk convict which hath his clergie shall forfeit, and at what time; and that none that hath his clergie allowed ought to make any purgation at this day; and that the king may pardon the burning of the hand, as well in an appeale, as upon an indictment.

[a] If the principall hath his clergie before attainder, the accessory either before or after ought to be discharged.

[b] You may adde to the former report a record in rot. Clauf. an. 3 E. 3. m. 2. & 18. That for sacriledge the ordinary may allow clergie. So as it is in the election of the ordinary, either to allow or disallow clergie in that case.

[c] See a notable record Trin. 21 E. 3. coram rege, Rot. 173. Hertford, that *privilegium clericale non competit seditioso equitanti cum armis platis, et cotearmuris, per leges Angliæ.*

Lib. 11. fo. 29, 30, &c. Alexander Poulters case. Lib. 5. 26, 27. in Caudries case. Vid. lib. 5. fo. 50. Biggens case, & fo. 110, Hestons case. 18 Eliz. cap. 6.

[a] Lib. 4. fo. 43, 44. Syers case. ib. Bibiths case. 2 E. 3. 27. 22 E. 3. cor. 260. 7 H. 4. 16. 10 H. 4. 5. 3 H. 7. 1. 3 H. 7. cor. 53. 4 E. 6. Br. cor. 184. 3 Aff. 14. 5 Aff. 5. 11 H. 4. 93.

[b] Rot. cl. 3 E. 3. m. 2. 18.

[c] Tr. 21 E. 3. cor. rege, Rot. 173. Hertford.

[d] 25 H. 8. cap. 3. 32 H. 8 cap. 3. Vid. 1 E. 6. ca. 12. 5 E. 6. ca. 10.

[d] It is provided by the ſtatute of 25 H. 8. that if any perſon be indicted of felony for ſtealing of any goods or chattels in any county, and thereupon arraigned, and be found guilty, or ſtand mute, or challenge peremptory above the number of twenty perſons, &c. they ſhall loſe the benefit of their clergie, in like manner as they ſhould have done, if they had been indicted and arraigned, and found guilty in the ſame county, where the ſame robbery or burglary was done or committed, if it ſhall appear to the juſtices, &c. by evidence given before them, or by examination, that for ſuch robbery or burglary in the ſame ſhire where they were committed or done, they ſhould have loſt the benefit of their clergie by force of the ſaid ſtatute, viz. of 23 H. 8. cap. 1.

Any perſon indicted.] This act extendeth not to appeales by writ or bill, nor to the appeales of the approvors.

[e] Poulters caſe. Ubi ſupra fo. 31.

Or by examination.] [e] By theſe words though the offender confeſſe the indictment, or ſtand mute, or challenge above twenty, &c. yet if by examination before the juſtices, the truth of the caſe appeareth, he may be put from his clergie.

[115]

By force of the ſaid ſtatute.] Viz. 23 H. 8. ſo as if for any burglary or robbery in one county he were not ouſted of his clergy by the ſtatute of 23 H. 8. but ſome later ſtatute, then the delinquent ſhall have his clergie in the county where the goods are carried: for example, if the robbery be done in a dwelling houſe, the owner or dweller, his wife, his children, or ſervants then being within the houſe, and put in feare and dread by the ſame, and the goods be carried into another county, he ſhall not have his clergy: but if the robbery in the dwelling houſe be not done with all the circumſtances mentioned in this act of 23 H. 8. (which circumſtances are not required by the ſtatute of 5 E. 6. cap. 9.) he ſhall not be ouſted of his clergie in the other county. And ſo of all like caſes.

Vid. Stanf. pl. cor. fo. 123, &c. De Clergie.

See 1 Jac. cap. 8. clergie taken from him which do ſtab another that hath not drawne a weapon, nor ſtricken firſt.

CAP. LI.

Of Abjuration and Sanctuary.

Cuſt. de Norm. cap. 24 & 8. Inter leges Inæ. cap. 5.

ABJURATION by the courſe of the common law may be thus deſcribed. When a man or a woman had committed felony, and the offender for ſafeguard of his or her life had fled to the ſanctuary of a church or churchyard, and there before the coroner of that place within forty dayes had confeſſed the felony, and took an oath for his or her perpetuall baniſhment out of the realm into a foraine countrey, chooſing rather *perdere patriam, quam vitam.* But that foraine countrey, into which he was to be exiled, muſt not be amongſt infidels. And this was the ancient law of this realme, which was, *prohibemus autem ne Chriſtiana fide tinctus quiſpiam à regno procul amandetur, neve ad eos qui nondum Chriſto fidem adjunxerunt relegetur, ne eorum aliquando fiat animorum jactura, quos propria Chriſtus vita redemit.*

Inter leges Canuti, fo. 105. ca. 3.

The foundation of the abjuration was the sanctuary of the church or church-yard. For he or she, that was not capable of this sanctuary, could not have the benefit of abjuration. [a] And therefore it is said, that he that committed sacriledge, because he could not take the priviledge of sanctuary, could not abjure. For the forme of abjuration see the statute of abjuration, Vet. Magna Carta, part 1. fol. 167. b. The [b] common law herein was very ancient, and had saved the life of many a man; and continued without change untill an act made in the twenty second year of H. 8. cap. 14. whereby it was provided, that the party abjured should not be banished out of the realm, but to some other sanctuary within this kingdom: [c] and to say the troth, abjuration was exceedingly intricated and perplexed by the said act of 22 H. 8. cap. 14. and other statutes: for which causes all statutes made before the thirty fifth yeare of queen Elizabeth, concerning abjured persons, stand repealed by the statute of 1 Jac. cap. 25. whereby the ancient common law concerning abjuration for felony was revived.

[d] But by an act made in the twenty first year of king James it is enacted, that no sanctuary or priviledge of sanctuary should be admitted or allowed in any case. By which act, such abjuration as was at the common law, founded (as hath been said) upon the priviledge of sanctuary, is wholly taken away: and the writ in the Register 69. a. *De restitutione extracti ab ecclesia* is become of no use.

[e] And yet the abjuration by force of the statute of 35 Eliz. ca. 1. before justices * of peace, or justices of assize, or by force of an act made at the same parliament, cap. 2. before two justices of peace or the coroner by a recusant, remaineth still; because such abjuration hath no dependancie upon any sanctuary. Which being sufficient to shew how the law standeth at this day, both concerning sanctuary and abjuration, might suffice.

But yet he that is desirous to reade the generall learning of abjuration the branch, and of sanctuarie the root, let him reade the Mirror, ca. 1. §. 13. & cap. 5. §. 1. where he may reade the right use of abjuration by the ancient law of England. Et inter leges Edwardi, nu. 10. Custum. de Normandie, cap. 24. Officium coronatorum, tit. Abjuration, Rast. pl. 2. Bracton, li. 3. fo. 135. & 136. Britton, cap. Abjuration, fo. 24. & cap. Coroners, fo. 7. And Fleta, lib. 1. cap. 29. 8 E. 2. ubi supra. 3 E. 3. Coron. 313. 335. 21 E. 3. 17. 29 Ass. p. 34. Rot. Pat. 25 E. 3. part. 3. m. 16. Hil. 43 E. 3. Rot. 10. Coram Rege Buck. Hil. 26 E. 3. Coram Rege Rot. 20. *Quando aliquis abjuravit regnum, crux ei deliberat' fuit in manu sua portanda in itinere suo per semitas suas, et vocatur vexillum sanctæ ecclesiæ.* Rot. Parl. 2 R. 2. nu. 28. the right use of sanctuary. 6 H. 4. 2. 8 H. 4. 2. 11 H. 4. 40. 7 H. 6. 8. 27 H. 6. 7. 2 E. 4. 17. 21. 9 E. 4. 29. 12 E. 4. 1, 2. 3 H. 7. Coron. Fitz. 54. 1 H. 7. 23. 25. 8 H. 8. Kelway. 188, 189, 190, 191. Fitz. Justice of Peace, fol. 202. Stanf. pl. cor. cap. Abjuration, fo. 116, 117, &c. *et ibidem* Sanctuary, cap. 38. Dier, 13 Eliz. fo. 296. lib. 5. fo. 12. 26. lib. 6. fo. 9. lib. Intrat. tit. Abjuration and Sanctuary.

[a] 8 E. 2. cor. 420.

[b] Sir Thomas Weyland Chiefe Justice of the Common Pleas, anno 17 E. 1. Vid. inter placita parl. an. 19 E. 1. apud Ashring in Cro. Epiphaniæ.

[c] 50 E. 3. cap. Artic. Cleri, 9 E. 2. c. 10. 1 R. 2. cap. 9. 7 H. 7. cap. 7. 21 H. 8. cap. 2. 22 H. 8. ca. 14. 26 H. 8. ca. 13. 28 H. 8. cap. 1. 33 H. 8. cap. 15. 1 E. 6. cap. 12. 2 E. 6. ca. 2. & 33. 5 E. 6. cap. 10 13 Eliz. ca. 7. 1 Jac. ca. 25.

[d] 21 Jac. in the continuance of statutes, &c.

[e] 35 El. ca. 1. & 2.

* [116]

CAP. LII.

De Hutesio et Clamore.

Of HUE and CRY.

THE one being an expression of the other. For *huer* in French *(unde hutesium)* is to hoot or shoute; in English to crie.

There be two kindes of hues and cries, the one by the common law, and the other by statute. Thereupon there are two pursuits, the one for the king, the other for the party by private suit.

Hue and cry by the common law, or for the king, is, when any felony is committed, or any person grievously and dangerously wounded, or any person assaulted and offered to be robbed either in the day or night; the party grieved, or any other may resort to the [a] constable of the town, and acquaint him with the causes, describing the party, and telling which way the offender is gone, and require him to raise hue and cry. And the duty of the constable is, to raise the power of the towne, [b] as well in the night as in the day, for the prosecution of the offender, and if he be not found there, to give the next constable warning, and he the next, untill the offender be found, and this was the law before the conquest. [c] *Si quis latroni obviam dederit eumque nullo edito clamore abire permiserit, quanticunque fuerit latronis vita æstimata extremum solvat denariolum, aut pleno, perfectoque jurejurando de facinore se nihil habuisse cogniti confirmato. Sin quis proclamantem exaudierit, neque vero fuerit insequutus, suæ in regem contumaciæ (ni omnem criminis suspicionem diluerit) pœnas dato.*

[a] Rot. Parl. an. 6 E. 3. num. 6. Constable of the town to make hue and cry.
[b] 2 E. 4. 8. b. & 9. a.
[c] Inter leges Canuti, fo. 110. ca. 26. See inter leges Edw. Conf. ca. 21.
For Oversamessa, See lib. Rub. c. p. 36. Bracton, li. 3. fo.

In antiquo M. S. si quis furi obviaverit, et sine vociferatione gratis eum dimisit, emendet secundum weram ipsius furis, vel plena lada se adlegiet, quòd cum eo falsum nescivit: si quis audito clamore supersedit, reddat oversamessa regis aut plene se laidiet. Bracton who wrote before any act of parliament concerning hue and cry, saith, *omnes tammilites, quam alii qui sunt* 15 *annorum* † *et amplius, jurare debent quòd utlagatos, murditores, robbatores, et burglatores non recipient, &c. Et si hutesium vel clamorem de talibus audiverint, statim audito clamore sequantur cum familia, &c.* and herewith agreeth Britton.

†[117]
Britton, fo. 15. & 19.
Fleta, li. 1. c. 24.
See the 2. part of the Institutes.

The statute of W. 1. cap. 9. being in affirmance of the common law, provideth, *Que touts communement soient prests a les somons des viscounts, et au crie de pais de suer et arrester felons, quant mister serra, auxibiens deins franchises come dehors.*

W. 1. ca. 9.
4 E. 1. de officio coronatoris.
See the statute of Winch. 13 Ed. 1.

And the statute of 4 E. 1. declareth the law *similiter de omnibus homicidiis, burglar', occisis, seu* * *periclitantibus levetur hutesium, &c. et omnes sequantur hutesium, et vestigium si fieri potest: et qui non fecerit, et super hoc convictus fuerit, attachietur quòd sit coram justiciariis de gaola, &c.* And by that act it appeareth that so it is in case of rape, and therewith agreeth, [a] Bracton also.

* 7 E. 3. fo. 16. 22 Ass. 57. 38 E. 3. fo 6. assaulted to be robbed. 9 E. 4. 26. See the Custum' of Norm. ca. 24.
[a] Bracton, li. 2. fo. 28 E. 3. ca. 11.

The life of hue and cry is fresh suit.

[b] Thamar the daughter of king David being violently ravished by her brother Amnon, the text saith of her, *quæ aspergens cinerem capiti*

[b] 2 Regum, c. 13. vers. 19.

capiti suo, scissa talari tunica, impositisque manibus super caput suum ibat ingrediens, et clamans.

[c] They which levy not hue and cry, or pursue not upon hue and cry, shall be punished by fine and imprisonment. [d] Also if a man be present when a man is murdred, or robbed, and doth not endeavour to attach the offender, nor levy hue and cry, he shall be fined and imprisoned.

[c] Bract. li. 3. fo. 118. b. Ca. Itin. m. c. 155. 3 E. 3. cor. 333.

[d] See 8 E. 2. cor. 395.

Of hue and cry by force of acts of parliament in five cases. [e] First, if a watchman doth arrest a night walker, and he disobey and fly, the watchman may make hue and cry.

[e] Stat. de Winc. watch. 4 H. 7. fo. 2. 18.

2. [f] *Si quis forestarius, parcarius, aut warrennarius in baliva sua malefactores aliquos invenerit vagantes ad damnum ibidem faciend', et qui se forestariis aut warennariis illis post clamorem et hutesium levatum ad pacem regis ad standum recte reddere noluerint, immo ad malitiam suam exequend' et continuand' et pacem regis diffugiend' fugam fecerit, et vi et armis se defenderint, licet forestarii, parcarii et warrennarii illi, aut alii quicunque ad pacem domini regis existentes in comitativa forestariorum, parcariorum, aut warrennariorum illorum venientes ad tales malefactores sic inventos arrestand' seu capiend', aliquem seu aliquos hujusmodi malefactorum interfecerint, non propter hoc occasionentur coram domino rege, et justiciariis quibuscunque aut aliis balivis domini regis, aut aliorum quorumcunque infra libertatem aut extra: nec propter hoc amittant vitam, aut membrum, aut alium pœnam subeant, immo firmam pacem domini regis inde habeant. Sed bene caveant forestarii, parcarii, warrennarii, et alii quicunque, ne occasione contentionis, discordiæ, contumeliæ, aut alicujus malevolentiæ, seu odii præhabit' aliquibus per balivas suas transeund' malitiose imponant, quod occasione malefaciendi in balivis suis intrant, cum hoc non fecerint, nec ipsos vagantes ut malefaciant, nec malefacientes invenerint, nec causam malefaciendi quærentes, et sic eos occidant. Quod si fecerint, et de hoc fuerint convicti, fiat de morte sic interfectorum, prout aliorum ad pacem domini regis existentium, et prout de jure et secundum consuetudinem regni fuerit faciend.*

[f] Statutum de anno 21 E. 1. Magna Cart. fo. 118. Foresters.

3. Welshmen outlawed, or indicted of treason or felony, that fly into Herefordshire, shall be apprehended, &c. or else pursued by hue and cry, and a forfeiture upon those that do not pursue. 23 H. 6. ca. 5. Vid. 17 H. 8. c. 26. Welshmen.

4. Hue and cry shall be levied upon takers of carriage within the vierge of the staple of that which pertaineth to the staple. 27 E. 3. ca. 4. staple.

5. Where a man is robbed: upon hue and cry, &c. what remedy he shall have against the hundred, &c. and how and in what manner the hue and cry shall be made in that case, see the statutes, and lib. 7. fo. 6. & 7. the statutes well expounded. And this robbery must be done in the day time, and not in the night, otherwise the party grieved shall not have his action. And so note a diversity between a hue and cry at the common law, or for the king, and a hue and cry by statute where the party grieved is to have his remedy by private action. Note also a diversity in the prosecution at the common law, or for the king, and by the statutes which give the party remedy, for a prosecution to the next constable is good by the common law, but so it is not by the said statutes which give the party grieved his action. See lib. 7. fo. 7. & 8. 22 El. Dier, 370. So the prosecution at the common law is a good excuse upon an indictment at the kings suit, but note that it is no bar to the parties action.

Winch. 13 E. 1. 28 E. 3. c. 11. 27 El. c. 13. 38 El. ca. 25.

[118]

Lib. 7. fo. 7, 8. 22 El. Dier 370.

Where hue and cry either by the common law, or by force of any statute is levied upon any person, the arrest of such person is lawfull,

29 E. 3. 9. 38 E. 3. 6. See 5 H. 7. 5. a. 21 H. 7. 28. a.

lawfull, although the cause of the hue and cry be feigned, and if the cause be feigned, he that levy the same shall also be arrested, and shall be fined and imprisoned. But common fame and voice is not sufficient to arrest a man in case of felony, unlesse a felony be done in deed.

Stat. de 18 E. 2.

It is an article of the leet, to enquire of hues and cries levied and not pursued.

De civitate London capienda in manum regis pro hutesio non levato. Rot. Claus. 30 H. 3. m. 5.

Mandatum est Guilielmo de Haverhull thesaurario regis, quòd civitatem London capiat in manum regis, eo quòd cives ejusdem civitatis non levaverunt hutesium et clamorem pro morte magistri Guidonis de Arretio et aliorum interfectorum secundum legem et consuetudinem regni. Teste rege apud Wndestok 22 die Augusti.

CAP. LIII.

OF MAYHEM.

OF mayhem you may read at large in the [a] first part of the Institutes sect. 194. & 502. and in justice Stanford. And where (as it is there cited) he saith, *Castratio verò, quam vis latens sit, adjudicatur mahemium.* Hereof we find an example.

[b] *H. Hull indictatus fuit de mayhemio, eo quòd abscidit virilia Johannis monachi, &c. quem idem H. deprehendit, &c. cum A. uxore sua.* Of the like accident you may read in Camden.

[c] *Dominus Robertus Nevil (cum numerosam prolem ex uxore suscepisset) ignotus in adulterio deprehensus, et ab adulteræ marito in vindictam genitalibus mutulatus, brevi vi doloris expiravit.*

Vide inter leges Alveredi. cap. 40 *de vulneribus, fo.* 43.

[d] By the ancient law of England, he that maimed any man, whereby he lost any part of his body, the delinquent should lose the like part, as he that took away another mans life, should lose his own.

And it is truly said, that *duellum est mahemium inceptum*, and *mahemium est homicidium inchoatum.* And therefore in the appeal or indictment it is said *felonice mayhemavit.*

[a] First part Institutes §. 194. 502. Stanf. Pl. Cor. 38. b. Cust. de Norm. ca. 79. Mehaimus. Bracton, lib. 3. 144, 145. Fleta, li. 1. ca. 38.
[b] Rot. Claus. anno 13 H. 3. nu. 9. See before, ca. 13. for cutting out of tongues, &c.
[c] Camden Brit. page 593.
[d] Bract. lib. 3. fo. 148. nu. 4. Mirror, cap. 4. §. De pains in divers manners. Brit. fo. 48. b. Fleta, li. 1. ca. 38. Membrum pro membro. 18 E. 3. 20. a. Vide 28 E. 3. fo. 94. 8 H. 4. 20, 21. Coron. 458.

CAP. LIV.

OF PREMUNIRE.

PRIMERMENT pur ceo que monstre est a nostre seigniour le roy per grevouses et clamouses pleints des grandees et communes avant ditz, coment plusors gents sont, et ount estre treits hors de realme a responder des choses dount la conusans apperteint a la court nostre seigniour le roy ; et auxint que les judgements rendus in mesme le court sont empeache en autre court, in prejudice et disherison nostre dit seigniour le roy et de sa corone, et de tout le people de son dit realme, et in defeasance et anientisment de la common ley de mesme le realme use de touts temps. Sur quoy ewe bone deliberation ove les grandees et auters de dit councell, assentus est et accord per nostre dit seigniour le roy, et les grandees et communes suisditz. Que touts gents de la ligeance le roy, de quel conditione que ilz sont, que trahent nulluy hors de realme (1) *en plea dont le conusance appertient a la court le roy, ou des choses dont judgement soit rendus* (2) *en le court le roy ; ou que suent en autri court a defaire ou impeacher les judgements rendue in le court le roy* (3) *eient jour, &c.* (4) In English thus.

27 E. 3. cap. 1. The print being examined agreeth with the record. See the first part of the Institutes, sect. 199.

The statute of 16 R. 2. cap. 5. saith, In curia Romana, vel alibi.

FIRST because it is shewed to our lord the king by the grievous and clamorous complaints of the great men and commons aforesaid, how that divers of the people be, and have been drawne out of the realme to answer of things, whereof the cognisance pertaineth to the kings court: and also that the judgements given in the said court be impeached in another court in prejudice and disherison of our lord the king, and of his crowne, and of all the people of his said realme ; and to the undoing and destruction of the common law of the same realme at all times used. Whereupon, upon good deliberation had with the great men and other of his said councell, it is assented and accorded by our lord the king, and the great men and commons aforesaid, that all the people of the kings ligeance, of what condition that they be, which shall draw any out of the realme in plea, whereof the cognisance pertaineth to the kings court, or of things whereof judgement is given in the kings court, or which doe sue in any other court to defeat or impeach the judgements given in the kings court, shall have day, &c.

The effect of the statute of 16 R. 2. is, if any pursue or cause to be pursued in the court of Rome, or elsewhere, any thing which toucheth the king, against him, his crowne and regality, or his

16 R. 2. cap. 5.

his realme, their notaries, procurators, &c. fautors, &c. shall be out of the kings protection.

Fourth part of the Institutes, cap. 8. artic. 1. Die Decemb. anno 21 H. 8. against cardinall Woolsey. Vet. N. B. 143.

* In this act is declared the soveraignty, prerogative, and freedome of the crowne of England, and the first article exhibited by the lords of the councell, (whereof sir Thomas More chancellor was one) and the principall judges concerning this matter, is worth your reading.

This offence is called a premunire of the words of the writ, grounded upon this and other statutes for punishment thereof. For the words of the writ be, *Rex vicecomiti, &c. Præmunire fac.* A. B. &c. And rightly it is so called, for he that is *præmonitus* is *præmunitus*.

Before the making of this statute of 27 E. 3. there were three great mischiefs. First, that the kings subjects have been drawn out of the realme, to the answer of things, whereof the conusance pertained to the kings court. Secondly, of things whereof judgements have been given in the kings courts. And thirdly, that after judgements given in the kings courts of the common law, of matters determinable by the common law, suits were commenced in other courts within the realme, to defeat or impeach those judgements. And these three mischiefs had three unsufferable effects: first, the prejudice and disherison of the king and of his crowne. Secondly, the disherison of all his subjects. And thirdly, the undoing and destruction of the common law of this realm: all which appeare in the preamble of this act.

They are called (other courts,) either because they proceed by the rules of other lawes, as by the canon or civill law, &c. or by other trials, then the common law doth warrant. For the triall warranted by the law of England for matters of fact, is by verdict of twelve men before the judges of the common law of matters pertaining to the common law; and not upon examination of witnesses in any court of equity: so as *alia curia*, is either that which is governed *per aliam legem*, or which draweth the party *ad aliud examen*. For if the freehold and inheritances, goods, and chattels, debts, and duties, wherein the king or subject hath right or property by the common law, should be judged *per aliam legem*, or be drawne *ad aliud examen*, the three mischiefs aforesaid expressed in the preamble and in this act should follow, viz. disherison of the king and of his crowne, the disherison of all his people, and the undoing and destruction of the common law at all times used: by which words of this act it appeareth, that all these mischiefs were against the ancient common lawes at all times used. And that also appeareth by the ancient writs of the common law, called *ad jura regia*, whereof some touch hath been given before, and which are worthy the reading: and also by divers acts of parliament; as the statute of Carlile, *anno* 35 E. 1. whereof we have treated before in the second part of the Institutes: and by the statute of 25 E. 3. *De provisoribus*. And it is observed, that in 29 E. 3. within two yeares after the said act of 27 E. 3. that they that were called in question upon the statute of premunire, *invenerunt manucaptores sufficientes, et sacramentum præstiterunt, quòd non attemptabunt, citra mare vel ultra, quod in præjudicium regis, legum, seu coronæ, seu judiciorum in curia regis reddit', tendere valeat quoquo modo, &c.* Whereby, and many other like records it appeareth, that judgements

Regist. 61, 62, &c.

Mic. 29 E. 3. coram rege. Rot. 44. Cornub. V. 46 E. 3. 13, 14. Nota, citra mare.

judgements ought not to be queſtioned *citra mare*, in any court, unleſſe it be according to the courſe of the lawes of the realme.

By the ſtatute of 4 H. 4. cap. 23. it is ordained and ſtabliſhed, that after judgement given in the courts of our lord the king, the parties and their heirs ſhall be thereof in peace, untill the judgement be undone by attaint, or by error, if there be error, as hath been uſed by the lawes in the times of the kings progenitors. 4 H. 4. ca. 23.

[a] Alſo that which hath been ſaid appeareth by our books and ancient records, as hereafter ſhall appeare. [a] 10 H. 4. 1, 2. 18 H. 6. 6. b.

[b] 5 E. 4. fol. 6 where the ſtatute of 16 R. 2. cap. 5. ſaith, *In curia Romana vel alibi*, eccleſiaſticall courts within the realme are within this word [*alibi.*] [b] 5 E. 4. 6. b. 44 E. 3. 36.

[c] Mich. 11 H. 7. it was adjudged by the whole court, that a ſuit in the eccleſiaſticall court within the realme for a temporall cauſe, was in caſe of premunire. [c] 11 H. 7. Premunire. Fitz. 15 H. 7. 9. acc'. lib. Intr. Raſt. 468.

[121]

[d] A preſident of a premunire, for ſuing in the eccleſiaſticall court for a debt. [d] Raſt. pl. 429. b. & 430.

[e] It was reſolved, that he that ſued in the eccleſiaſticall court for the forgery of a laſt will and teſtament, incurred the danger of a premunire, becauſe the party grieved might have his remedy by the common law. And in the ſame year of 17 H. 7. juſtice Spilman alſo reporteth, that one Turbervile, as well as for the king, as for himſelfe, did ſue a premunire againſt a perſon for ſuing for tithes in the eccleſiaſticall court, alledging the ſame to be ſevered from the nine parts, and judgement given againſt the defendant. [e] 17 H. 7. of the report of juſtice Spilman.

Alſo it appeareth that the admirals court is within this word [*alibi*] if he hold plea of any thing, which is not done *ſuper altum mare*, but *infra corpus comitatus*.

[f] Richard Beuchampe eſquire and Thomas Pauncefoot eſquire, and others, are charged with the offence of premunire, for that they ſued John Creſſey eſq; before Henry duke of Exeter admirall of England, for taking away a croſſe of gold and other goods, ſuppoſing the ſame to be taken *ſuper altum mare*, where in truth they were taken at Stratford in the county of Eſſex; where the ſtatute of 16 R. 2. is recited, that none ſhould ſue *in curia Romana ſeu alibi*, &c. and that the conuſance of this plea belonged to the common law, and not to the court of the admirall. And ſo it is of the conſtable and marſhall, if they hold plea of a matter determinable by the common law. [f] Mic. 38. H. 6. coram rege.

[g] Iſabel Winnington exhibited a bill of premunire againſt William Powdich upon the ſtatute of 16 R. 2. cap. 5. for ſuing in the admirall court before John earle of Huntington, admirall of England, for a cauſe which belonged to the common law, whereunto the defendant pleaded not guilty. [g] Mic. 9 H. 7. coram rege. Raſt. pl. 23. but this cauſe is entred. Trin. 9 H. 7. Rot. 37. coram rege.

And the reaſon of all theſe caſes is, becauſe they draw matters triable by the common law, *ad aliud examen*, and to be diſcuſſed *per aliam legem*.

But ſome have made a queſtion, whether ſince the eccleſiaſticall juriſdiction was acknowledged to be in the crowne, an eccleſiaſticall judge holding plea of a temporall matter belonging to the common law, doth incurre the danger of a premunire. Though hereof there is no queſtion at all, yet leſt any man might be led into an errour in a caſe ſo dangerous, we will clear this point by reaſon, preſident,

president, and authority. The reason holdeth still to draw the matter *ad aliud examen*, &c. And the like question might be made for the admirall court, which is, and ever was, the kings court, but governed *per aliam legem:* and so likewise of the court of the constable and marshall.

At a convocation holden *anno* 22 H. 8. by a publick instrument made by all the bishops and the whole clergie of England, the king was acknowledged to be supreame head of the church of England.

[h] 24 H. 8. tit. premunire, Brook 16.

[h] After this, viz. 24 H. 8. it appeareth that the statute of premunire remained in force against ecclesiasticall judges, for holding of pleas meerly determinable by the common law.

Hil. 25 H. 8. coram rege, Rot. Rich. Nick Bishop of Norwich his case.

In 25 H. 8. Richard Nick bishop of Norwich was attainted in a premunire at the kings suit, and his case was this. Within the towne of Thetford there then was a custome, that all ecclesiasticall causes arising within the said towne should be determined before the deane there, having a peculiar ecclesiasticall jurisdiction, and that no inhabitant of the same town should be drawn before any other ecclesiasticall judge, and that every person suing contrary to that custome, the same being presented before the maior of Thetford, should forfeit six shillings eight pence; and that an inhabitant of Thetford for an ecclesiastical cause rising within Thetford, sued another before the bishop of Norwich within his consistory court at Norwich: and this was presented before the maior of Thetford according to the custome, whereby he forfeited six shillings eight pence. The said bishop cited the said maior for taking of the said presentment *pro salute animæ* to appear before him at his house at Hoxon in Suffolke, where the maior appeared, and there the bishop *ore tenus* injoyned him, upon pain of excommunication to adnull the said presentment before a day. And for this offence he was attainted in a premunire upon his confession before Fitz James chief justice, and the court of kings bench, upon

[122]

the statute of 16 R. 2. the record whereof we have seen. By which judgement two points are cleared: first, that the statute of premunire extends to ecclesiasticall courts within the realme. Secondly, that after the king was in possession of his supremacy, the bishops incurred the danger of premunire.

Trin. 36 H. 8. coram rege. Rot. 9. the B. of Bangors case.

The bishop of Bangor was attainted in a premunire for holding plea of an advowsion, and of tithes severed from the nine parts.

D. & St. lib. 2. ca. 24. fo. 106. b. Lib. 2. ca. 23.

Saint Germin in his book of Doctor and Student, who wrote after 26 H. 8. holdeth: that if a man maketh a promise for a temporall thing, and swear to perform it, and doth it not; if he be sued for perjury in the spirituall court, a prohibition or a premunire lyeth in that case. Also he saith; if a man be excommunicate in the spirituall court for trespasse, or such other thing, as belongs to the kings crown and his royall dignity, &c. the party, if he will, may have a premunire fac. against him.

Br. tit. Premunire. 21. Temps. E. 6.

Brook reporteth, that Barloe bishop of Bath and Wels, in the reign of king E. 6. deprived the dean of Wels, which deanry was a donative: and thereby incurred the danger of a premunire.

1 Eliz. cap.

By the statute of 1 Eliz. (which restoreth the ancient jurisdiction ecclesiasticall to the crown) the act of 1 & 2 Ph. and Mar. cap. 8. is repealed. But there is a speciall proviso in that act of 1 Eliz. that it should not extend to repeale any clause, matter, or sentence contained or specified in the said act of 1 & 2 Ph. and Mar. which doth

doth concerne matter of premunire, but that so much of that which concerneth any matter or cause of premunire, should stand in force and effect. And that clause of the statute of 1 and 2 Ph. and Mar. is this. That whosoever shall by any proces obtained out of any ecclesiasticall court, within the realme or without, by pretence of any spirituall jurisdiction, or otherwise, contrary to the lawes of the realme, inquiet or molest any person, &c. for any mannors, &c. parcell of the possessions of any religious house, &c. shall incurre the danger of the act of premunire, in *anno* 16 R. 2.

See the statute of 25 H. 8. which also hath reference to the said act of premunire, and is revived by 1 Eliz. 25 H. 8. ca. 20.

Thomas Stoughton parson of N. in Suffolke, brought a writ of premunire against R. T. upon this statute of 27 E. 3. for suing in the court of audience of the archbishop of Canterbury, to impeach a judgement given in a *quare impedit*, before the justices of assize in the county of Suffolk, &c. the defendant pleaded not guilty, &c. And this (omitting many other things for this matter) shall suffice. And now let us peruse the body of the act. Trin. 29 Eliz. in communi banco Rot. 747. Tho. Stoughtons case

(1) *Trahe nulluy hors de realme.*] Of this there is no question, being against the ancient law of the realme always in use; as by this act appeareth. And this was a remedie for the first mischiefe.

(2) *Ou des choses dont judgements fuer' rendus, &c.*] This branch prohibiteth all forain suits, viz. in the court of Rome, &c. for any thing whereof judgement was given in the kings court. And this was a remedie for the second mischiefe.

(3) *Ou que suont en autre court a defaire ou impeacher les judgements rendue in le court le roy.*] This is a remedy for the third mischief. For having by the second branch provided against forain suits to undoe, or impeach judgements in the kings court, this branch doth (as hath been said) extend to all courts, which proceed by the rule of another law, or draw the party *ad aliud examen*, and therefore this branch doth extend to ecclesiasticall courts, to the court of the constable, and marshall, to the court of the admiralty, and to the court of equity proceeding in course of equity: for it had been to no effect to have provided against forain suits, which were troublesome, tedious, and chargeable, and to have suffered the party to have attempted and prosecuted any thing at home within this realm, to the prejudice and disherison of the king, and his crown, [123] and all his subjects, and to the subversion of the common law. And first we will speak of the court of equity. This court cannot proceed in course of equity after judgement at the common law, for three reasons. First, for that it draweth the matter triable, and determinable by the common law, *ad aliud examen*, viz. to a triall by witnesses, which (as hath been said) is contrary to the ancient law of the realm, and against the purview of this statute. Secondly, after judgment the parties ought to be at peace and quiet, for *judicia sunt tanquam juris dicta*, and if the party against whom judgement is given, might after judgement given against him at the common law, goe into court of equity for matter in equity, there either should be no end of suits, or every plaintif would leave the common law, and begin in the court of equity, whither in the end he must be brought, and that should tend to the utter subversion of the common law, as it is said in the act. Thirdly, the court of equity in the proceeding in course of equity is no court of record, 37 H. 6. 14.

cord, and therefore it cannot hold plea of any thing, whereof judgement is given, which is a judiciall matter of record. And this is the ancient law at all times used, as this act speaketh. As taking some few examples for many, both before, and after this statute.

Anno 6 E. 1. the earl of Cornwals case. Lancefton in Thesaur.

In the case of Edmond earl of Cornwall in *anno* 6 E. 1. it appeareth, that after judgement given before Roger Loveday and Walter Winborn justices of oier and terminer, against Walter bishop of Exeter and his tenants, the said bishop procured the bishop of Landaff in the parish churches of Cornwall and Devonshire to pronounce sentence of excommunication by the sentence of the archbishop of Canterbury (which sentence was had by the procurement of the said bishop of Exeter) against all persons of what estate, degrees or dignity soever, that dealt in the proceedings, &c. against the said bishop and his tenants before the said justices: and in this part of the record being in French, it is said *La corone, et la dignity nostre seigniour le roy ne doit per autre estre justice ne guyne, &c. Et les choses que sont passes en sa court per judgement, ou en auter manner, ne devient estre en autri court recrecees, &c.* Out of this record we may observe three things. First, what the ancient law of this realm was, before the making of this act. Secondly, that [*en autri court*] which are the words of this act, was taken to be another court within the realm. Thirdly, that the mischief before this act, was for suits in other courts within this realm, after judgements given in the kings courts. Read the whole record, which beginneth thus. *Cornub. dominus rex mandat, &c.*

Mich. 13 E. 3. In communi banco. Rot. 40. Inter Johannem de Dingle and Mich. de Englis Bedf.

And in 13 E. 3. there was a suit in the court of Rome after judgement in the kings court, and in that record it is said, *In regi contemptum, et coronæ suæ præjudicium, ac judicii prædicti enervatione manifestam, &c. Ac quòd judicia in curia regis rite reddita frustra redderentur, nisi debitum sortirentur effectum.*

[a] Fleta li. 6. ca. 36. Trin. 19 E. 3. Rot. 50. Coram rege John Boltons case. Mich. 19 E. 3. Rot. 16 & Rot. 29. Alan de Conesburghs case. F. N. B. 169. f. 20 E. 3. essoin. 24. 21 E. 3. 40. b.

[a] Fleta who wrote before this statute, saith, *Judicia debent rata permanere, et firma consistere, usque ad condignam satisfactionem inviolabiliter observentur.*

And as a maxime of the common law in the judiciall Register, fo. 12. 35. 41, &c. it is often said, *Ea quæ in curia domini regis rite acta sunt, debitæ executioni demandari debent.*

[b] 4 H. 4. ca. 23. [c] Pasc. 5 E. 4. Coram rege inter Cobbe and Nore. [d] Rot. Parl. simile. 3 H. 5. nu. 44. & 3 H. 6. nu. 22. [e] 22 E. 4. 37.

Now let us see what hath been done since the act. [b] The statute of 4 H. 4. cap. 23. hath been recited before, which is a judgement of parliament. [c] A judgement was obtained by covin and practice against all equity and conscience in the kings bench: for the plaintif retained by collusion an attorney for the defendant, (without the knowledge of the defendant, then being beyond sea) the attorny confesseth the action, whereupon judgment was given; [d] the defendant sought his remedy in parliament, and by authority of parliament power was given to the lord chancellor by advise of two of the judges to hear, and order the case according to equity: which proveth that the chancellour could not do it of himself without higher authority.

[e] No injunction after verdict at the common law is to be granted in chancery, and if the lord chancellor should grant an injunction in that case the judges said, that if the chancelor imprisoned the party

[124]

party for breach of the injunction, they would grant an *habeas corpus* and deliver him.

Amongſt the articles preferred to the king by Sir Thomas Moore lord chancellor of England, and all the privy councel, and by Fitz James chief juſtice, and juſtice Fitz-Herbert againſt cardinall Woolſey, one is in theſe words, [And the ſaid lord cardinall hath examined divers and many matters in the chancery, after judgement thereof given at the common law, in ſubverſion of your laws, and made ſome perſons to reſtore again to the other party condemned that, that they had in execution by vertue of the judgement of the common law] which I have ſeen in parchment under all their hands, and is yet to be ſeen. 1 Decemb. 21 H. 8. Art. 20.

If judgements given in the kings courts ſhould be examined in chancery, before the kings councell, or any other place, the plaintif or demandant ſhould ſeldome come to the effect of their ſuit, nor the law ſhould never have end, &c. See the Diverſity of Courts ca. Chancery. Doct. and Stud. ca. 18. the book of Diverſity of Courts.

Ralph Heydon gent. was indicted of a premunire upon the ſtatute of 27 E. 3. for procuring of Sir Nicholas Bacon lord keeper of the great ſeal, to grant an injunction in chancery after judgement given in an *ejectione firme* of lands in Hertfordſhire. And the record ſaith, *Quod predictus Radus machinatus eſt antiquas leges, et conſuetudines regni ſubvertere.* Mich. 8 & 9 El. in the kings bench.

A writ of premunire upon the ſaid ſtatute of 27 E. 3. by Richard Beans againſt Richard Lloyd, for ſuing before the preſident and councell in Wales, after judgement given in the court of common pleas, in an action of debt for forty and two pound ten ſhillings, *in ſubverſionem legum antiquarum, &c.* Trin. 21 El. in communi banco Rot. 319.

Peter Dewſe was indicted for procuring of Sir Thomas Bromly then lord chancelor, to grant an injunction in the chancery after a judgement given in an *ejectione firme.* Paſch. 27 El. in the kings bench.

John Heal of the Inner Temple London eſquire, was indicted of a premunire, for procuring a ſuit in chancery after a judgment given at the common law, contrary to the ſtatute of 27 E. 3. And the councell of Heal took two exceptions, one, that the court of chancery was not within the ſtatute of 27 E. 3. another, that one of the parties to the ſuit in chancery was named in one place by one name of baptiſme, and in another part of it by another. The court reſolved that the court of chancery was within the ſtatute of 27 E. 3. but found the other exception concerning miſnaming to be true. And therefore they quaſhed the indictment, but made a memorandum indorſed upon the back of the indictment, that it was overthrown for miſtaking a name, and not for the matter. Trin 30. El. in the kings bench. Diverſity of Courts, ca. Chancery.

Thomas Throckmorton exhibited a bill in the chancery againſt Sir Moyl Finch after judgement given againſt him in the court of exchequer upon apparent matter of equity. Upon which bill the defendant demurred in law, and for that Sir Thomas Egerton then lord keeper inclined to rule over the demurrer, ſaying that he would not meddle with the judgement, but puniſh the corrupt conſcience of the defendant, in relieving the plaintif in equity: upon a petition to queen Eliz. (who ever favoured the due proceeding of her laws,) ſhe referred the conſideration of the demurrer to all the judges of England, who hearing councell learned on Mich. 39 & 40 El. See the fourth part of the Inſt. cap. Court of Chancery.

both parts, and upon view of preſidents in the time of H. 8. and ſince of injunctions granted after judgements, and finding very few of them to warrant that which had been affirmed, and none of them to be done by the advice of any of the judges, they all after divers hearings, and conferences, and conſideration had of the laws and ſtatutes of the realm, unanimouſly reſolved, that the lord keeper could not after judgement given relieve the party in equity, although it appeared to them, that there was apparant matter in equity. And amongſt others, the judges gave this reaſon, that if the party againſt whom judgement was given, might after judgement given againſt him at the common law, draw the matter into the chancery, it would tend to the ſubverſion of the common law, for that no
[125] man would ſue at the common law, but originally begin in chancery, ſeeing at the laſt he might be brought thither, after he had recovered by the common law, and thereupon they all certified, that the demurrer was good, and that Sir Moyl Finch the defendant ought not to anſwer.

Hil. 12. Ja. regis coram rege.

An information upon this ſtatute of 27 E. 3. againſt Sir Anthony Mildmay, for that he and other commiſſioners of ſewers did impeach a judgement in the kings bench: he purchaſed a pardon from the king, and pleaded it.

See a privy ſeal bearing teſte 18 Julii, anno domini 1616, to the contrary, obtained by the importunity of the then lord chancellor being vehemently affraid: *ſed judicandum eſt legibus*, and no preſident can prevail againſt an act of parliament. And beſides, the ſuppoſed preſidents (which we have ſeen) are not authenticall, being moſt of them in torn papers, and the reſt of no credit.

44 E. 3. 7. 36. 39 E. 3. 7. 7 E. 4. 2. 27 H. 6. 5. 36 H. 6. 30. * 43 E. 3. 6. 42 E. 3. 7. 2 R. 3. 17. 27 H. 6. 5. 22 H. 8. tit. Præm. Br. 1. Tr. 39 E. 3. Rot. 95. Coram rege. 39 E. 3. 37. 30 E. 3. 11. 44 E. 3. 36. Forebys caſe. a 8 H. 4. 6. Lib. 11. fo. 34. b. in Alex. Poulters caſe.

(4) *Eient jour contenant le ſpace de 2 moys per garniſhment a faire a eux, &c.*] By this it appeareth that a premunire lyeth as well for the party, as for the king, and they both may join in one writ.

* If the defendant come not at the day, &c. by the expreſſe letter of the law judgement ſhall be given againſt him according to this act. This ſuit need not be againſt them by originall writ, but if the defendant be *in cuſtodia mareſchalli*, the ſuit may be againſt him by bill, becauſe the end of the giving of the two months was, that they ſhould have notice, which is ſatisfied, and therewith agreeth the preſidents; and the defendant cannot be ſued in any other court, when they are *in cuſtodia mareſchalli*. See the ſtatute of 18 El. cap. 5. but that ſtatute extends to common informers, and not when the ſuit is commenced by the party grieved.

a But if the defendant appear and plead, and the iſſue be found againſt him, or if he demur in law, &c. judgement ſhall be given againſt him, that he ſhall be out of protection, &c. And ſo hath this ſtatute been interpreted, and judgement given accordingly. Peruſe well the words of this act for this point, and ſee the book in 8 H. 4. 6.

39 E. 3. 7. 9 E. 4. 2. 15 H. 7. 9. F. N. B. 26. m.

By the ſtatute of 38 E. 3. cap. 2. the defendant ought to appear in perſon, and therefore he cannot appear by attorny without a ſpeciall writ out of the chancery: and this act doth bind as well thoſe that are lords of parliament as others.

27 H. 6. 5. 2 R. 3 10.

Avant le roy et ſon councell.] Here councell cannot be taken, as moſt commonly it is, for his judges of his courts of juſtice, who are ſaid to be of his councell for proceedings in courts of juſtice, becauſe the courts of juſtice are hereafter in this act named: neither

ther doth it intend the kings privy councell, but the king, and the lords of parliament in parliament, which is a court of justice.

See the first part of the Institutes, sect. 164. *Veigne les burgesses al parlement.* There is *commune concilium*, *magnum concilium*, *privatum seu continuum concilium*, and *concilium justiciariorum*, *le councel des justices.* The king is armed with divers councells.

Ils, lour procurators, attornies, executors, notaries, et mainteynors.] Note by this act the procurers, attornies, executors, notaries, and maintainers shall have the same punishment, that the principall shall have. Note in the statute of 2 R. 2. this word (fautors) crept in, a word (derived *à favendo*) of a large extent, as it was construed in the reign of H. 8.

The plaintif may choose whether he will make them all principals, or the one principall, and the other accessories, but the damages shall be severally taxed. Stanf. pl. cor. 44. f. 44 E. 3. 7. 36 H. 6. 30. 42 E. 3. 7.

He that procures one to sue to the court christian, shall forfeit as much as he that sueth, and is principall as well as the other, and are in equall degree of premunire: but if they both be indicted, the one of the act, and the other of the procurement, and he that is charged with the procurement is found guilty, and the other by an other enquest is found not guilty, judgement shall never be given against him, which was indicted of the procurement, because he cannot be an offender, but in respect of the offence of the other. 8 R. 2. Prem. 12. 8 H. 4. 6. pl. com. 97. b.

[126]

Hors de la protection le roy.] By these words the persons attainted in a writ of premunire are disabled to have any action or remedy by the kings law, or the kings writs; for the law and the kings writs are the things whereby a man is protected and aided, so as he that is out of the kings protection, is out of the aid and protection of the law. See Littleton sect. 199. and the 1. part of the Institutes the same sect. Lib. 7. fo. 14. in Calvins case.

But by the statute of 25 E. 3. it is provided, that he that purchaseth provisions to abbies, or priories shall be out of the kings protection, and that a man may do with him, as with the enemies of the king and his realm, and that he, that shall commit any thing against such provisors in body or goods, or other possessions, shall be excused against all people. 25 E. 3. ca. 2. See 5 El. ca. 1.

Et lour terres, biens, et chateux forfait au roy.] This is intended of the lands that he hath in fee-simple, or for life, which the delinquent might lawfully forfeit, and not lands in tail: for tenant in tail shall forfeit only for term of his life, for that was all he could lawfully forfeit at the making of this statute, either in case of treason or felony. And so it was resolved by the judges in the case of Trudgyn of Devonshire, who was attainted of a premunire upon the statute of 13 El. cap. 2. 34 H. 8. forfeit. Br. 101. Pasch. 21 El. resolution of the judges in Trudgyns case. Dier, manuscript. Vide before. 25 E. 3. Verb. Et soit assavoir.

Nota, this is a new kind of forfeiture given by this law, and is penall, and cannot by equity extend further then the records, and therefore this act extendeth not to the forfeiture of fairs, markets, rents charges, rent seck, warrens, annuities, or any other hereditament that is not within this word (*terre.*)

Lour corps imprison, et rents al volunt le roy.] The greatnesse of these punishments doe shew the greatnesse of the offence.

It is to be observed, that the said statute of 16 R. 2. is strictly 16 R. 2. ca. 5.

 penned

Examples of these are quoted before.

penned againſt offenders. For firſt it extendeth to all perſons of what quality, or ſex ſoever, the words be [if any]. 2. To all courts of what juriſdiction ſoever, and whether holden by right or wrong, *in curia Romana*, *ſeu alibi*, which word (*alibi*) is a word of a large extent, as before it appeareth. 3. To all things whatſoever. [Where any thing,] which words be as generall as can be. 4. Not only againſt the king, his crown and dignity, but againſt the kingdome alſo: againſt the king, his crown, and regalty, or realm. 5. This act extendeth not only to procurers, abetters, maintainers, counſellors, &c. which are known words in law, but to favourers, *fautores*, which word was largely extended in the reign of H. 8. whereby it is to be obſerved how dangerous it is to bring new or unuſuall words into any act of parliament, eſpecially into ſuch as be ſo penned: for there it appeareth that Cliff being a parſon of a church granted to the cardinall an annuity, ſo long as he ſhould be legate, *ut decentius et ſublimius ſe gereret in authoritate ſua legantina*, which the cardinall had by bull, and paid to him ten marks in name of ſeaſon, and he was adjudged a *fautor*. But ſuch evaſions were found out of this and other ſtatutes, as were made againſt uſurpations and incrochments upon the good and ancient common law, as divers and many ſtatutes were made from time to time to meet with ſuch evaſions, which being many, (and others which concern the offence of premunire) we will but name, and leave the reader to peruſe the ſame at large, wherein (as we conceive it) he ſhall find a great light, by that which hath been ſaid, viz. 25 E. 3. ca. 22. 25 E. 3. Statut. de proviſoribus. 38 E. 3. ca. 1, 2, 3, 4. 3 R. 2. cap. 3. 7 R. 2. ca. 12. 12 R. 2. ca. 15. 13 R. 2. Stat. 2. ca. 2. 16 R. 2. cap. 5. 2 H. 4. cap. 3. & 4. 6 H. 4. cap. 1. 7 H. 4. ca. 6. & 8. 9 H. 4. ca. 8. 3 H. 5. cap. 4. 24 H. 8. ca. 12. 25 H. 8. ca. 19, 20, 21. 26 H. 8. cap. 15. 28 H. 8. cap. 10. 35 H. 8. ca. 1. Note, queen Mary repealed all offences made to be in the caſe of premunire ſince the firſt day of the firſt year of H. 8. but ſome of them are revived by the ſtatute of 1 El. ca. 1. But in all queen Maries time, the ſtatutes made concerning the offences of premunire before the reign of H. 8. were neither repealed nor altered, but (as hath been ſaid) allowed of in queen Maries time. 1 & 2 Ph. and Mar. ca. 8. 1 El. ca. 1. 5 El. ca. 1. 13 El. cap. 1, 2. 8. 27 El. ca. 2. 21 Jac. ca. 3.

Vide juſtice Spilmans Report. Mich. 21. H. 8. Cliffs caſe.

[127]

1 Mar. ca. 1.

And where the ſtatute of 25 E. 3. de proviſoribus provideth, that certain offenders againſt that act, ſhall before they be delivered, make full renunciation, &c. becauſe we deſire that our ſtudent may in all things underſtand what he reads: it is to be known, that as well before that ſtatute, viz. in the reigns of E. 1. and E. 2. as after, the form of renunciation was to this effect. I renounce all the words compriſed in the popes bull to me made of the biſhoprick of A. (or the like) the which be contrary, or prejudiciall to the king our ſoveraign lord, and to his crown, and of that I put my ſelf humbly in his grace, praying to have reſtitution of the temporalties of my ſaid church, &c. Whereby it may appear what the law was in that caſe before 25 E. 3. And albeit theſe laws be very ſevere, eſpecially againſt the buls, &c. of the pope, and forain juriſdiction, and though queen Mary reſtored his ſupremacy in ſuch ſort as hereafter appeareth, yet would ſhe not repeal the ſaid ſta-

Dier manuſcrip. Hil. 1 El. le caſe de Chriſtoforſon Eveſque de Chicheſter.

tutes

tutes of provision and premunire, but provided that they should stand in force. See the statute of 1 & 2 Ph. and Mar. whereby it is enacted, That whosoever should by any proces obtained out of any ecclesiasticall court within this realm, or without, or by pretence of any spiritual jurisdiction, * or otherwise, contrary to the laws of this realm, inquiet, or molest any person, &c. should incur the danger of the act of premunire made in the sixteenth year of the reign of king R. 2. &c. And by another branch in the same act it is enacted, That all buls, dispensations, and privileges not containing matter contrary, or prejudiciall to the authority, dignity or preheminence royall of the realm. or to the laws of this realm now being in force, and not in this present parliament repealed, may be put in execution. And lastly, by the same act, it is declared and enacted, That neither any thing contained in the body of the said statute, or in the preamble thereof, shall be construed, or expounded to diminish, or take away any of the liberties, priviledges, prerogatives, preheminences, authorities or jurisdictions which were in the imperiall crown of this realm, or belonged to the same before the twentieth year of H. 8. and the popes holines to have such authority, preheminence, and jurisdiction, as his holinesse used, or might lawfully have used by authority of his supremacy the said twentieth year of H. 8. within this realm of England, without diminution or enlargement of the same, and none other. Whereby it appeareth how carefull the state was in queen Maries time to preserve the prerogative of the crown, and the ancient laws of the realm, and did at that time so cautiously restore the supremacy of the pope, *secundum quid*, but not *simpliciter*, and bounded his supremacy within strait and legall limitations, as by the said act appeareth.

1 & 2 Ph. and Mar. ca. 8.

* Nota.

See the statutes which inflict the punishment of premunire, viz. 2 R. 2. c. 12. 3 R. 2. ca. 3. 7 R. 2. ca. 12. 24 H. 8. ca. 12. 25 H. 8. ca. 19, 20. 1 El. cap. 1. 26 H. 8. cap. 15. 28 H. 8. ca. 16. 1 & 2 Ph. and Mar. cap. 1. 8 El. cap. 1. 5 El. ca. 1. 13 El. ca. 2. 8. 39 El. ca. 18. 27 El. ca. 2. See the fourth part of the Institutes, cap. Chancery, the articles at large against Cardinall Woolsey, artic. 7.

We have been the longer concerning cases of premunire. First, for that they be matters of great weight, and necessary to be known, and we wish that the offence may never be committed. And secondly, for that master Stanford hath in effect but named a premunire.

Stan. pl. cor. 44. f.

CAP. LV.

OF PROPHESIES.

33 H. 8. cap. 14. 1 E. 6. cap. 12. Nota. 1 Mar. ſtat. unicum, Seſſione prima. 5 Eliz. cap. 15. Mitius imperanti melius paretur. * Nota. The like act was made, 3 & 4 E. 6. ca. 15. expired.

PROPHESIES upon declaration of armes, fields, names, cogniſances, or badges, were made felony without the benefit of clergy: but this act is twice repealed by generall words of all felonies made by any ſtatute ſince the firſt year of H. 8.

In anno 5 Eliz. a more moderate ſtatute was made againſt propheſies by writing, ſinging, or other open ſpeech, or deed, by the occaſion of any armes, fields, beaſts, badges, or other like things accuſtomed in armes, cogniſances, or ſignets; or by reaſon of any time, year, or day, name, bloodſhed or warre, * to the intent thereby to make any rebellion, inſurrection, diſſention, loſſe of life, or other diſturbance within this realm, or other the queens dominions. For the firſt offence, impriſonment of his body by the ſpace of a year without baile, and forfeit to the queene and informer, ten pound. And for the ſecond offence impriſonment during life without baile, and forfeit to the queen all his goods and chattels, reall and perſonall: but he muſt be therefore impeached or accuſed within ſix moneths next enſuing the offence by him done. A juſt and neceſſary limitation, and the rather, for that the offence may be committed by bare words. This offence is to be heard and determined before juſtices of aſſiſe, juſtices of oier and terminer, and juſtices of peace.

See hereafter the chapter of Newes, and the ſecond part of the Inſtitutes, W. 1. cap. 33. He that hath read our hiſtories ſhall finde, what lamentable and fatal events have falne out upon vain propheſies carried out of the inventions of wicked men, pretended to be ancient, but newly framed to deceive true men; and withall, how credulous and inclinable our countreymen in former times to them have been, we will ſet down the truth concerning the ſame.

Auguſt. in lib. Retract.

Certaine it is, that to foretell of things to come, is a prerogative appropriated to the Holy Ghoſt; and that the devill cannot *prædicere*, foretell of things to come, which notwithſtanding, S. Auſtin did ſometime hold that he could. But afterwards juſtly retracted it in theſe words, *Rem dixi occultiſſimam audaciore aſſertione, quam debui, &c. certiſſimum eſt dæmones non præſcire.*

Now for the predictions and foretellings of the Sibyls being Gentiles, ſo long before the incarnation of our Saviour Chriſt; and more directly and particularly, of thoſe high myſteries of the incarnation and paſſion of Chriſt, the coming of Antichriſt, the ſubverſion of Rome, and the end of the world, they are by the true prophets of Almighty God, who ſpake by the Holy Ghoſt, well diſcovered; that while the church was in her cradle, theſe predictions were invented and fathered upon the Gentiles; to the intent to make the doctrine of the ſaid high myſteries of the goſpel the more credible amongſt the Gentiles. And if any ſuch predictions had been by the ſaid Sibyls, out of queſtion thoſe great lights of nature amongſt the Gentiles, Plato, Ariſtotle, Theophraſtus, or ſome fome other of thofe great philofophers, that with great alacrity dived into the fecrets of all kinds of learning, would have found them out, and made fome mention of them. But befides the faid [a] difcovery, fuch predictions by the Gentiles and heathen perfons are [b] againft the word of God.

Alfo predictions either of the time or end of the world, or that it is at hand, is not lawfull. For the firft, [c] fee the firft of the Acts, It is not for us to know the times and feafons which the Father hath put in his own power, &c. For the fecond, fee the fecond epiftle to the Theffalonians. I befeech you brethren, &c. that you be not fhaken in mind, or troubled, &c. as though the day of Chrift were at hand, let no man deceive you by any means.

We have the rather faid hereof thus much, for that we have heard divers men boldly and confidently upon their numerall calculation to have erred herein.

[a] Cafaubone Exercit 1. ad apparatum Annalium, cap. 10. [b] Ephef. c. 3. v. 9. Col. cap. 1. v. 26. Rom. ca. 16. v. 25.

[129]

[c] Acts ca. 1. v. 7. Mat. 24. 36. Mark 13. 32. 2 Theff. c. 2. v. 1, 2.

CAP. LVI.

OF APPROVER.

APROVER, or approver, in Latin *probator*, is a perfon indicted of treafon or felony in prifon for the fame, and not difabled to accufe: he may [a] upon his arraignment, before any plea pleaded and before competent judges [b] confeffe the indictment, and take a corporall oath to reveale all treafons and felonies, that he knows, and pray a coroner, before whom he is to enter his appeale or accufation againft all thofe that are *participes criminis*, or of his fociety in committing of treafon or felony contained in the indictment, thofe partners being within the realme: and if upon his appeale [c] all thofe partners be convicted, the king *ex merito justitiæ*, is to pardon him. But it is in the difcretion of the court, either to fuffer him to be an approver, or after his approvement to refpite judgement and execution, untill he hath convicted all his partners.

Aprover.] [d] He is by Bracton called *probator*, by Britton, *provor*, by the Mirror *provor* and *approver*: and his name putteth him in minde of his duty, viz, to prove and approve his accufation or appeale in every point, for [e] any fayler of truth difableth him *in omnibus*. And as he muft affirme the truth, and the whole truth, before the coroner in his appeale: fo in the rehearfall of the appeale before the juftices, it muft agree with the appeale, 26 Aff. p. 19. and Bracton *ubi fupra*. [f] In one record I finde him called *appellator*.

Perfon.] This extendeth not to a peer or a lord of parliament, for it is againft Magna Carta, cap. 29. for him to pray a coroner.

[g] A man attainted of treafon or felony cannot become an approver, becaufe (as the book faith) he is *hors de la ley*. Alfo though he be indicted, yet if he be out of prifon, he cannot approve.

Parl 28. E. 1. ca. Nota, for confronting. [a] 9 H. 5. cor. 440. 21 E. 3. 18. 19 H. 6. 47. 2 H. 7. 3. 12 E. 4. 10. 3 H. 6. 50, 51. [b] 1 H. 5. cor. 441. 3 H. 6. 50, 51. in bank le roy. Pafch. 2. H. 4. coram rege pl. 6. [c] 21 H. 6. 29. b. & 34. b. [d] Bract. lib. 3. fo. 122. b. & 152, &c. Britton. fo. 7. 11. 17. 48. Mir. cap. 1. § 13. cap. 3. exec. al provors, cap. 5. [e] 25 E. 3. 42. 21 H. 6. 34. 22. E. 3. cor. 460. 26. Aff. p. 19. [f] Pafch. 2 H. 4. coram rege. 6 [g] 11 Aff. pl. 17. 21 E. 3. 18.

19 E 2. cor. 387. 19 E. 3. ibid. 443. 17 E. 3. 13.

h Mir. ca. 1. § 13. Stanf. pl. cor. 140. d.

[h] The Mirror ſaith, that women, infants, idiots, lepers, or profeſſors in order of religion, or clerks, or perſons attainted of felony, or *non compos mentis*, cannot be approvers: and Stanford added men above the age of 70, or maymed: becauſe ſome of them cannot take an oath, and none of them can wage battell.

i 40 Aſſ. 39. 15 E. 3. cor. 113. 11 H. 7. 5.

k 25 E. 3. 39.

Indicted.] [i] For in any appeale either by writ or bill the defendant ſhall not become an approver: and before indictment, no perſon can approve, becauſe if his approvement be falſe, no judgement (whatſoever he confeſſed) can be given againſt him, unleſſe he be indicted, [k] and no judgement can be given againſt him if his appeale be falſe, but of the offence contained in the indictment, and ſo are the books to be underſtood.

l 8 H. 5. cor. 442.

[l] If one be indicted and approve, if after an appeale be ſued againſt him, the approvement ceaſeth.

m 19 H. 6. 4. 12 E. 4. 10. 6 H. 6. cor. 131. 19 E. 2. cor. 387.

Of treaſon or felony.] And that is only of that treaſon or felony that is contained in the indictment, as hath bin ſaid. [m] See Trin. 3 H. 4. Rot. 19. coram rege Hertford. *Probator in duello devicit appellat', de alta proditione,* * *pro quo devictus ſuſpenditur, decapitatur, et quarteria ſua dividuntur, et ſimile ibid. Anglia.*

* [130]

a 6 H. 6. ubi ſup. 21 E. 3. fo. 18. V. 3 H. 6. 51, 52.

b Bract. ubi ſup. 9 H. 4. 1. 2 H. 4. 19. 44 E. 3. 44. Lib. 10. fo. 76. b.

In priſon.] [a] Albeit he be indicted, yet if he be at large, and not in priſon, he cannot approve as before is ſaid.

Competent judge.] [b] As juſtices of the kings bench, juſtices of oier and terminer, and of gaole delivery, but not juſtices of peace, becauſe they have no authority by their commiſſion to aſſigne a coroner. And by the ſame reaſon the lord high ſteward of England cannot aſſigne a coroner in caſe of treaſon or felony.

12 E. 4. 10. 21 H. 6. 34, 35.

Corporall oath.] Though the oath be generall of all treaſons and felonies, yet in courſe of law no approvement can be, but of the offence contained in the indictment as hath been ſaid. And this oath and the accuſation of himſelf make his appeale or accuſation of another of the ſame crime, to amount in law to an indictment.

40 Aſſ. 39. 10 E. 4. 14.

Particeps criminis.] For it cannot be of another treaſon or felony then is contained in the indictment.

1 E. 3. 17. 1 Aſſ. p. 2.

Within the realme.] For if it be out of the realme, it wanteth triall, and therefore the accuſation or appeale not to be allowed.

26 Aſſ. 19. 8 H. 5 cor. 459. 21 H. 6. 34. 12 E. 4. 10.

Ex merito juſtitiæ.] And the reaſon is, for that he riddeth the countrey of wicked and hurtfull miſdoers: whereby the kings peace is kept, and the ſubject enjoyeth his own quiet. And therefore the king doth in the meane time give him wages.

Mich. 39 E. 3. coram rege Rot. 97. Suff.

7 E. 3. 7. 11 H. 4. 91. b. Of battell ſee more here, cap. Single combat, and the ſecond part of the Inſtitutes, Weſtm. 1. cap. 40.

A man became an approver and appealed five, and every of them joyned battell with him. *Et duellum percuſſum fuit cum omnibus, et probator devicit omnes quinque in duello, quorū quatuor ſuſpendebantur, et quintus clamabat eſſe clericum, et allocatur; et probator perdonatur:* ſo as the approver did and ought to fight in that caſe with all the appellees. But if there be two or more approvers againſt one man of one felony, and he joyne battell with them all, and vanquiſh the firſt, he is acquited againſt the other. Concerning the proces upon an approvement and other incidents, you may reade in Mr. juſtice Stanford, which need not here to be rehearſed.

* 47 E. 3. 5.

* If the appellee joyne battell, or plead not guilty, and after the

the king pardoneth the approver, the appellee ſhall be diſcharged, and ſhall not be arraigned at the ſuit of the king.

Convicted.] The appellee may chooſe either to wage battell with the approver, or to put himſelf upon the countrey; and if the appellee be found guilty by verdict, it ſerveth as well for the approver, as if he had been overcome by battell. And therefore the book in 19 H. 6. 35. is miſprinted, or miſreported: and the note of Fitzh. in abridging the caſe, tit. Coron. pl. 6. in the end, is againſt law. *Vid.* Rot. Parl. 17 E. 3. nu. 36.

Stanf. pl. cor. 142.

19 H. 6. 35. a. Rot. Parl. 17 E. 3. nu. 36.

CAP. LVII. [131]

OF APPEALS.

OF appeals we have ſpoken in the firſt and ſecond parts of the Inſtitutes, and you may reade thereof in my reports, lib. 4. fo. 40, 41, 42, &c. lib. 5. fo. 105. 111. lib. 6. fo. 44. 86. lib. 7. fo. 13. 30. lib. 9. fo. 13. 119. Whereunto we will adde a [b] caſe which was adjudged in an appeal, where the caſe, as touching the point of the appeal, was thus. Thomas Burghe, brother and heire of Henry Burghe brought an appeale of murder againſt Thomas Holcroft, of the death of the ſaid Henry: the defendant pleaded, that before the coroner he was indicted of manſlaughter, and before commiſſioners of oier and terminer, he was upon that indictment arraigned, and confeſſed the indictment, and prayed his clergie, and thereupon was entred *curia adviſare vult*, and concluded, and demanded judgement, if that appeal the plaintife againſt him ought to maintain: whereupon the plaintife demurred in law. And in this caſe three points were adjudged by ſir Chriſtopher Wray, ſir Thomas Gawdie and the whole court.

Firſt part of the Inſtitutes. § 189, 500, 501. Second part of the Inſtitutes, in Mag. Cart. ca. 34. W. 1. ca. 14. fo. 460. Cuſt. de Norm. cap. 68.

[b] Paſch. 20 Eliz. in the k. bench. Tho. Holcrofts caſe, and after, viz. Mich. 33. & 34 Eliz. between Kath. Wrote, late the wife of Rob. Wrote, pl. in an appeale againſt Tho. Wiggs def. coram rege, for the death of her huſband, reſolved againe accordingly.

Firſt, that the matter of the barre had been a good barre of the appeale by the common law, as well as if the clergie had been allowed: for that the defendant upon his confeſſion of the indictment had prayed his clergy, which the court ought to have granted, and the deferring of the court to be adviſed, ought not to prejudice the party defendant, albeit the appeale was commenced before the allowance of it.

The ſecond point adjudged was, that this caſe was out of the ſtatute of 3 H. 7. for that the words of that act are.

> If it fortune that the ſame felons and murderers, and acceſſories ſo arraigned, or any of them to be acquited, or the principall of the ſaid felony, or any of them to be attainted, the wife or next heire of him ſo ſlaine, &c. may have their appeal of the ſame death and murder againſt the perſons ſo acquited, or againſt the ſaid principals ſo attainted, if they be alive, and that the benefit of his clergie thereof before be not had.

3 H. 7. cap. 1.

And

And in this cafe the defendant Holcroft, was neither acquited nor attainted, but convicted by confeffion, and the benefit of clergy prayed,[q] as is aforefaid. So as the ftatute being penall concerning the life of man, and made in reftraint of the common law, was not to be taken by equity, but is *cafus omiffus*, and left to the common law.

As to the third it was objected, that every plea ought to have an apt conclufion, and that the conclufion in this cafe ought to have beene, *Et petit judicium fi prædict. Thomas Holcroft iterum de eadem morte, de qua femel convictus fuit, refpondere compelli debeat.* But it was adjudged that either of both conclufions was fufficient in law: and therefore that exception was difallowed by the rule of the court.

11 H. 4. 11. Pl. com. 306. b.

Nota, the ancient law was, that when a man had judgement to be hanged in an appeal of death, that the wife, and all the blood of the party flaine fhould draw the defendant to execution, and Gafcoigne faid, *Iffint fuit in diebus noftris.*

Trin. 10 E. 1. in Banco, Rot. 30. Norff.

Richardus de Crek appellat quinque pro felonia, et offert difratiocinare per corpus fuum contra quemlibet eorum feparatim. Ipfi petunt fe allocari, quod ubi appellans dicit in appello fuo, quod ipfi fregerunt oftium Bracini, et non fpecificat ex parte domus illius prædictum oftium fcitum fuit, et petunt judicium. Et Joh. Wanton unus defendent' defendit feloniam, et totum, et paratus eft defendere per corpus fuum ficut curia confideraverit.

[132]

Ricus dicit quòd non poteft pugnare contra prædictum Johannem eo quod ipfe mahematus eft in humero fuo dextro. Et prædictus Johannes petit judicium de ficut prædictus Ricus appellando ipfum optulit difrationare prædictum Robertum verfus ipfum tanquam felonem prout cur' confider' per corpus fuum, et nullam fecit mentionem de aliquo mahemio, unde petit judicium de appello ifto. Et ideo confiderat' eft tam ad calumpniam prædicti Henr. et aliorum, quàm prædicti Johannis, quòd appellum ejus nullum. Set pro rege inquiratur rei veritas, &c.

Nota how the conclufion of the appeal of felony ought to be when the plaintif is mayhemed and cannot make tryall by battail.

* See before c. 1. high treafon, fo. 6. 1 H. 4. ca. 14. Glanv. li. 14. c. 1. Bracton, lib. 3. fo. 118, 119. Britton cap. 16 Mich. 4 H. fol. 122.

* There lay an appeal of high treafon by the common law either in parliament before the ftatute of 1 H. 4. ca. 14. or in fuch of the kings courts as have jurifdiction thereof triable by battail or verdict: and this appeareth by all our ancient authors, and divers records, and fee in Bracton, fo. 119. a. What pleas the defendant in the appeal of treafon may have, to difable the plaintif to maintain his appeal, fee Fleta ubi fupra, and Britton ubi fupra.

8 & 29. Fleta lib. 1. ca. 21. The Mirror cap. 2. § 11. Pat. 25 E. 3. part. 1. m. 4. coram rege Rot. 22. &c. 8 H. 6. ca. 10. F. N. B. 115. Lib. Intrat. Raft.

C A P.

CAP. LVIII.

OF TREASURE TROVE.

Thesaurus inventus.

TREASURE trove is when any gold or silver, in coin, plate, or bullyon hath been of ancient time hidden, wheresoever it be found, whereof no person can prove any property, it doth belong to the king, or to some lord or other by the kings grant, or prescription.

Custum. de Nor. ca. 18.

The reason wherefore it belongeth to the king, is a rule of the common law; that such goods whereof no person can claim property belong to the king, as wrecks, strays, &c. *Quod non capit Christus, capit fiscus.* It is anciently called * *fynderinga*, of finding the treasure. And now let us peruse this description.

* Inter leges H. 1. ca. 11.

Gold or silver.] For if it be of any other metall, it is no treasure; and if it be no treasure, it belongs not to the king, for it must be treasure trove.

It is to be observed, that veyns of gold and silver in the grounds of subjects belong to the king by his prerogative, for they are royall mines, but not of any other metall whatsoever in subjects grounds.

Pl. Com. in case de Mines per totum.
Vid. Bract. li. 2. fo. 222. Auri fodina, et argenti fodina.
Fleta, lib. 4. ca. 19. Rot. Parl. 3 R. 2. nu. 42.
27 Ass. p. 19.

Wheresoever.] [a] Whether it be of ancient time hidden in the ground, or in the roof, or walls, or other part of a castle, [b] house, building, ruines, or elsewhere, so as the owner cannot be known.

Whereof no person can prove any property.] For it is a certain rule, [c] *Quod thesaurus non competit regi, nisi quando nemo scit qui abscondit thesaurum.*

Of ancient time hidden.] [d] *Est autem thesaurus vetus depositio pecuniæ, &c. cujus non extat modo memoria, adeo ut jam dominum non habeat.*

Belong to the king.] [e] Where of ancient time it belonged to the finder, * as by the said ancient authors it appeareth. And yet I find that before the conquest, *Thesauri de terra domini regis sunt, nisi in ecclesia, vel cœmeterio inveniantur; et licet ibi inveniatur auru, regis est, et medietas argenti est medietas ecclesiæ, ubi inventum fuerit, quæcunque ipsa fuerit, vel dives, vel pauper.*

By the kings grant or prescription.] 21 H. 6. tit. Prescription. 4. 22 E. 3. cor. 241. 1 H. 7. 33. 9 H. 7. 20. 46 E. 3. 16. Stanf. pl. cor. 39. b. lib. 5. fo. 109. b.

The punishment of him that concealeth, &c. it.] It appeareth by Glanvill, and Bracton also, that *occultatio thesauri inventi fraudulosa* was such an offence, as was punished by death. But it hath been resolved, that the punishment for concealment of treasure trove, is by fine and imprisonment, and not * of life and member.

[a] Bract. l. 1. fo. 10. li. 3. 120. Britton, fo. 3. b. 7. b. 26. b. 71. b. Mir. ca. 1. § 3. & § 13. ca. 3. §. isto. Glanv. l. 1. ca. 1. li. 14. ca. 2.

*[133]

[b] In bundell inquisit. 32 E. 3. in Abbathia Sanctæ Mariæ Eborum. Bract. ubi supra. Non refert in quo loco hujusmodi thesaurus inveniatur.

[c] 22 H. 6. Cor. 446.

[d] Bract. ubi supra, and the other ancient authors agree thereunto.

[e] Glanv. li. 1. c. 1. li. 14. ca. 2. 8 E. 2. Cor. 436. 22 E. 3. ibid. 241. Glanvil, ubi sup. Bracton and the other authors ubi supra.

* 22 Ass. p. 99.

To

The ancient authors ubi supra, agree hereunto.

To whom the charge thereof belongeth.] It belongeth to the coroner, as appeareth by the statute *de officio coronatoris, anno* 4 E. 1.

CAP. LIX.

OF WRECK.

SEE the second part of the Institutes W. 1. cap. 2. and the exposition upon the same.

CAP. LX.

Of False Tokens, or Letters in other Mens Names.

33 H. 8. ca. 1.

IF any person falsly and deceitfully obtain into his hands any moneys, goods, chattels, jewels, or other things of any person or persons, by colour or means of any false or privy tokens, or counterfeit letters made in any other mans name, &c. he shall suffer such correction by punishment of his body, setting upon the pillory, or other corporall pain (except pains of death) as shall be to him adjudged by the person and persons before whom he shall be convicted, with a saving to the party grieved by such deceit, such remedy by way of action, or otherwise, as he might have had by the common law.

Here it is to observed, that upon this statute, for this offence the offender cannot be fined, but corporall pain only inflicted.

[134]

CAP. LXI.

OF THEFTBOTE.

Stat. Wall. anno 12 E. 1. Vet. Mag. Cart. pt. 2. fo. 6.

THEFTBOTE (described by act of parliament) *est emenda furti capta sine consideratione curiae domini regis:* and so much the word signifieth, *bote* being taken for amends: *theftbote*, that is, amends for theft.

See Rot. clauf. an. 1 E. 1. m. 7. 42 Ass. p. 5.

This offence is more then misprision of felony, for that is not a concealment of his bare knowledge only: but theftbote is when the owner

owner not only knowes of the felony, but taketh of the thief his goods again, or amends for the same to favour or maintain him, that is, not to prosecute him, to the intent he may escape: but in that case, if he receive the thief himself, and aid and maintain him in his felony, then is he accessory to the felony. And so note a diversity, *quando proprietarius recipit latrocinium, et quando latronem*, But if a man take his goods again that were stollen, it is no offence, unlesse he favour the thief, as is aforesaid.

Mir. ca. 2. § 12. 3 E. 3. Cor. 353. Stanf. pl. coron. 40. b. 42 Ass. ubi supra.

The punishment of theftbote is ransome and imprisonment: and seeing the punishment of theftbote, which is greater then concealment of felony, is but ransome and imprisonment, it standeth with reason, that the punishment of * misprision of felony should be but fine and imprisonment. Theftbote is sometimes taken *pro ipso latrocinio*, for the thing itself stollen from you.

3 E. 3. Cor. 353.

* See before in the chapter of Misprision of Treason, ca. 3.

You shall read in ancient authors of redoubbors, addoubors, derived of the French word *addoubeur*, they are in law patchers, botchers, or menders of apparell, that take * theftbote of cloth (and change it into another fashion) and are dwelling out of burghs and cities; because in those days burghs and cities were so well governed, as such offenders were soon discoverd: for they were not then commended, for that they were populous, but for that the governors were provident in preventing of offences.

Mir. ca. 1. §. 17. Britton, fo. 33.

* That is, stoln cloth.

CAP. LXII.

OF INDICTMENTS.

CONCERNING Indictments we have spoken somewhat in the first part of the Institutes. Sect. 194. 208. And you may read in my Reports many resolutions concerning indictments, viz. lib. 4. fo. 40, 41, 42. &c. lib. 5. fo. 120, 121, 122, 123. li. 7. fo. 5, 6. 10. li. 8. fo. 57. 36, 37. li. 9. fo. 62, 63. 116. 118.

See the 1 pt. of the Institutes, sect. 194, 195.

We will add one point adjudged in the case between Burgh and Holcroft before mentioned in the chapter of Appeals, which was, that where it is provided by the statute *de Artic super Cartas*, cap. 3. *En case de mort del home (deins le verge) ou office del coroner appent as views, et enquests de ceo faire, soit maunde al coroner del pais que emsembliment ove le coroner del hostel le roy face loffice que appent, &c.* And in that case one man was coroner both of the kings house, and of the county, and the indictment of manslaughter was taken before him as coroner both of the kings house, and of the county. And it was adjudged that the indictment was good, because the mischief expressed in the statute was remedied, as well when both offices was in one person, as when they were in divers: and therefore in this case the rule did hold, *Quando duo jura concurrunt in una persona, æquum est, ac si esset in diversis.*

Holcrofts case. Artic. super Cart. ca. 10. The same was again resolved in Wrots case, ubi supra.

[135]

Richard Weston, yeoman, late servant of Sir Gervase Elwys, lieutenant of the Tower, and under the lieutenant, keeper of Sir Thomas Overbury then prisoner in the Tower, was indicted: for that he the said Richard the 9 day of May *an.* 11. *Ja. regis*, in the

Sir Tho. Overburies case. Mich. 13 Jac. See before, ca. 7. Of murder more of this case.

the Tower of London, gave to the said Sir Tho. Overbury poyson called roseacre in broth, which he the said Sir Thomas received. *Et ut idē Rich. Weston præfatum Tho. Overbury magis celeriter interficeret et murdraret, 1 Junii anno* 11 *Ja. regis supradict.* gave to him another poyson called white arsenick, &c. and that 10 *Julii an.* 11. *suprad.* gave to him a poyson called mercury sublimat' in tarts, *ut prædict' Tho. Overbury magis celeriter interficeret et murdraret:* and that a person unknown in the presence of the said Richard Weston, and by his commandment and procurement, the 14 of Septemb. *anno* 11. *supradict.* gave to the said Sir Thomas a glyster mixt with poyson called mercury sublimat, *ut prædictum Thomam magis celeriter interficeret et murdraret. Et prædictus Thomas Overbury de seperalibus venenis prædictis et operationibus inde, à prædictis seperalibus temporibus, &c. graviter languebat usque ad* 15 *diem Septemb. anno* 11. *supradicto, quo die dictus Thomas de prædictis seperalibus venenis obiit venenatus, &c.* And albeit it did not appear of which of the said poysons he died, yet it was resolved by all the judges of the kings bench, that the indictment was good; for the substance of the indictment was, whether he was poysoned or no. And upon the evidence it appeared, that Weston within the time aforesaid had given unto Sir Thomas Overbury divers other poysons, as namely the powder of diamonds, cantharides, lapis causticus, and powder of spiders, and aqua fortis in a glyster. And it was resolved by all the said judges, that albeit these said poysons were not contained in the indictment, yet the evidence of giving them was sufficient to maintain the indictment: for the substance of the indictment was (as before is said) whether he were poysoned or no. But when the cause of the murder is laid in the indictment to be by poyson, no evidence can be given of another cause, as by weapon, burning, drowning, or other cause, because they be distinct and several causes: but if the murder be laid by one kind of weapon, as by a sword, either dagger, styletto, or other like weapon is sufficient evidence, because they be al under one classis or cause. And afterwards, Ann Turner, Sir Gervase Helwys, and Richard Franklyn a physitian, (purveyor of the poysons) were indicted as accessories before the fact done: And it was resolved by all the said judges, that either the proofs of the poysons contained in the indictment, or of any other poyson were sufficient to prove them accessories: for the substance of the indictment of them as accessories was, whether they did procure Weston to poyson Sir Thomas Overbury: and because that not only Ann Turner, and Richard Franklyn, but some of the degree of nobility were indicted as accessories in another county, viz. in the county of Midd. divers notable points were resolved upon the statute of 2 E. 6. First, if the accessory be in the county of Midd. where the kings bench is, and the principall did the felony, &c. in another county, that the court of the kings bench is within the words of that act, viz. (and that the justices of gaol-delivery, or oier and terminer, or two of them, &c.) for the causes and reasons given in the lord Zanchers case, lib. 9. fo. 117, 118. &c. Secondly, if the indictment be taken in the kings bench, then the justices shall not write in their own names, *quia placita sunt coram rege.* Thirdly, divers presidents were shewed where the accessory was in the county of Midd. where the kings bench sat, and the principall was attainted in another county, that the

Vid. li. 9. fo. 67. Mackallies case acc.

2 E. 6. cap. 24.

the juftices of the kings bench have removed the record of the attainder of the principall before them by *certiorari*, and fo it was done in the lord Zanchers cafe, *ubi fupra*. The like prefident was fhewed in a cafe where the principall was attainted in the county of Oxon, and the acceffory was in Midd. and the kings bench fitting there, the juftices of the fame court removed the attainder before them by *certiorari*. Fourthly, it was refolved, that the lord fteward of England, who is a judge in cafe of high treafon, or felony committed by any of the peers of the realm, is within thefe words, juftices of gaol-delivery, or oier and terminer, becaufe he is a juftice of oier and terminer, for his authority is by commiffion, and the words of his commiffion be after divers recitals, *Et fuperinde, audiend', examinand', et refpondere compellend', et fine debit' terminand.*: fo as he hath power to heare and determine. And where the words be [or any two of them] that is to be intended, where there be two or more juftices, and yet where there is but one, it extendeth to him. As the ftatute of Merton, cap. 3. power being given to the fheriffe in cafe of rediffeifin, the words be, *affumptis tecum coronatoribus placitorum coronæ, &c.* in the plurall number. And yet where there is but one coroner in the county the ftatute extends thereunto, and the fheriffe fhall take that one. Alfo the words of the ftatute are further, That then the juftices of gaol-delivery or of oier and terminer, or other there authorized: within which words, [or other there authorized] the lord fteward is included. Fifthly, if the record of the attainder were by writ of *certiorari* removed out of London into the kings bench, then there arofe another doubt upon the faid ftatute, if afterward any proceeding fhould be had againft any peer, for that the words of the ftatute be, The juftices, &c. fhall write to the cuftos rotulorum or keeper of the record where fuch principall fhall hereafter be attainted; and the attainder in this cafe was in London, and the kings bench was in Middlefex: fo as if the record fhould be removed into the kings bench in Middlefex, the record fhould not be where the attainder was had; and confequently, the lord fteward could not write to the kings bench. And therefore to prevent all queftions, it was refolved, that in this cafe of the lord fteward, no *certiorari* fhould be granted, but a fpeciall writ fhould be directed according to the words of the faid act to the commiffioners of oier and terminer in London, to certifie whether the principall was convict or acquitted: and they made a particular certificate accordingly, fo as the record of the attainder of the principall, did notwithftanding that certificat, remain with the commiffioners of oier and terminer in London: fo as if any further proceeding fhould be had, the lord fteward might write to them, as after he did in the cafe of R. earl of S. and F. his wife.

[136]

39 H. 6. 42. 23 Aff. p. 7.

And it is to be obferved, that the ancient wall of London (a mention whereof doth yet remain) extended through the Tower of London; and all that which is on the weft part of the wall, is within the city of London, viz. in the parifh of All Saints Barking, in the ward of the Tower of London: and all that is on the eaft part of the wall is in the county of Middlefex; and the chamber of Sir Thomas Overbury was within the Tower on the weft part of the faid wall, and therefore Wefton was tried within the city of London.

And

[a] Mag. Cart. ca. 29. 5 E. 3. ca. 9. 25 E. 3. c. 4. stat. 5. 28 E. 3. ca. 3. 37 E. 3. cap. 18. 38 E. 3. cap. 9. 42 E. 3. cap. 3.
[b] Rot. claus. 18 H. 3. m. Rot. Parl. 15 E. 3. nu. 9, 10. & 15. 42 E. 3. nu. 29. Sir John A Lees case. 17 R. 2. nu. 37. 2 H. 4. nu. 60.

And where it is often said in many [a] acts of parliament, [b] records, and [c] book cases, that the king cannot put any man to answer, but he must be apprised by indictment, presentment, or other matter of record. True it is, in pleas of the crown or other common offences, nusances, &c. principally concerning others, or the publick, there the king by law must be apprised by indictment, presentment, or other matter of record: but the king may have an action for such wrong as is done to himselfe, and whereof none other can have any action but the king, without being apprised by indictment, presentment, or other matter of record, as a [d] *quare impedit*, [e] *quare incumbravit*, a writ of [f] attaint, [g] of debt, [h] detinue of ward, [i] escheat, [k] *scire fac. pur repealer patent*, *&c.*

[c] 7 E. 3. fo. 26. 50. Vide 6 E. 3. fo. 33. & 8 E. 3. 30. 26 E. 3. 74. tit. Rescous 21. 43 E. 3. 32. per Knivet. 2 E. 3. fo. 7. John de Britains case, 3 E. 3. 19. 45 E. 3. Decies tantum 12. [d] 5 E. 2. Quar. Imp. 167. 33 E. 3. Bre. 916. [e] 17 E. 3. 50. 74 F. N. B. 48. f. 13 E. 3. Jurisd. 23. [f] 42 E. 3. 26. F. N. B. 107. D. [g] 19 H. 6. 47. 34 H. 6. 3. &c. [h] 39 H. 6. 26. 1 H. 4. 1. 15 E. 3. Corody 4. [i] Regist. fo. 165. a. F. N. B. fo. 7. b. 21 H. 3. Bre. 882. Britton fo. 28. b. cap. 18. [k] 16 E. 3. Bre. 651.

[137]

CAP. LXIII.

Of Councell learned in Pleas of the Crowne.

See before cap. 2. Petit Treason. fo. 29. 34. 9 E. 4. 22. Stanf. pl. cor. 151. b. otherwise it is in an appeale which is the suit of the party.

WHERE any person is indicted of treason or felony, and pleadeth to the treason or felony, not guilty, which goeth to the fact best known to the party; it is holden that the party in that case shall have no councell to give in evidence, or alleage any matter for him: but for as much as *ex facto jus oritur* it is necessary to be explained, what matters upon his arraignment, or after not guilty pleaded, he may alleage for his defence, and pray councell learned to utter the same in forme of law.

1. And first upon the arraignment what advantage he may take in case of high treason by the common law. If it be for compassing the death of the king, he may alleage, that in the indictment there is no such overt or open act set down in particular, as is sufficient in law or the like. For it is to be observed, that in no case the party arraigned of treason or felony, can pray councell learned generally, but must shew some cause.

1 H. 7. 22.

2. Secondly, in case of high treason by force of any statute, he may alleage, that the indictment being grounded upon a statute, the statute is either mistaken or not pursued.

3. Thirdly, of what matters he may take advantage equally concerning them both. He may alleage, that there was not at the time of the indictment of high treason, two lawfull accusers, that is, two lawfull witnesses.

4. Fourthly, of what matters he may generally take advantage in all cases of treason and felony. He may alleage, that the offence is not certainly alleaged in respect of the matter, time, and place, or that he

he is not rightly named, or have not a right addition, or that the offences were done before the laſt generall pardon.

Fifthly, after he hath pleaded not guilty, what advantage he may take upon the evidence: he may alleage, that he ought to have two lawfull witneſſes in caſe of high treaſon to prove the fact againſt him. 5.

Sixthly, he may take advantage in arreſt of judgement, if the verdict be found againſt him, that the triall came not out of the right place: as it fell out in Arundels caſe, convicted by a jury of wilfull murder; he informed the court that the jury that tried him came out of a wrong place, and thereupon he had councell learned aſſigned him; who indeed found, that the *venire facias* was miſ-awarded, and the court thereof by the councell being informed, judgement was ſtayed. And that the priſoner may alleage theſe or the like matters, it is evident, becauſe for every matter in law riſing upon the fact, the priſoner ſhall have councell learned aſſigned him. Alſo it is lawfull for any man that is in court, to informe the court of any of theſe matters, leſt the court ſhould erre, and the priſoner unjuſtly for his life proceeded with. And the reaſon wherefore regularly in caſe of treaſon and felony, when the party pleads not guilty, he was to have no counſell, was for two cauſes. Firſt, for that in caſe of life, the evidence to convince him ſhould be ſo manifeſt, as it could not be contradicted. Secondly, the court ought to ſee, that the indictment, triall, and other proceedings be good and ſufficient in law; otherwiſe they ſhould by their erroneous judgement attaint the priſoner unjuſtly. 6. Lib. 6. fo 14. Arundels caſe. 9 E. 4. 22. Stanf. ubi ſup. 7 H. 4. 34, &c. See before fo. 19.

Robert Chirford counſelled the prior of the priory of Binham in Norfolke, that John of Leiceſter the kings ſerjeant at armes, comming to the priory with the kings writ of privie ſeale, ſhould not be admitted to the priory: for which counſell he was indicted in the kings bench, and depending the proces upon the indictment, the king doth pardon him: and in the pardon is contained a *ſuperſedeas* to the juſtices, commanding them to proceed no further. Rot. clauſ. 14 E. 2. 17. 27 Octob.

CAP. LXIV. [138]

Of Principall and Acceſſory.

ALBEIT juſtice Stanford hath well collected the books concerning principall and acceſſory, yet *diverſa deſiderantur*: and neceſſary it is, that ſome things touching the ſame ſhould be added, which are very neceſſary to be knowne.

It is a ſure rule in law, that *in alta proditione nullus poteſt eſſe acceſſorius, ſed principalis ſolummodo.* This rule being well underſtood, will open the reaſon of divers caſes, which yet are involved in darkneſſe.

High treaſon is either by the common law, or by act of parliament: we will ſet downe examples (which ever do illuſtrate) of both.

Mich. 12 & 13 Eliz. 296. Dier, Coniers cafe.

A. doth counterfeit the kings coine, viz. fhillings, and C. knowing the fame doth receive A. and comfort and aide him: this counterfeiting is high treafon by the common law in A, as hath been faid: and yet it hath beene holden that in this cafe C. hath not committed treafon: for fay they, in cafe of felony, a receiver of a felon after the felony done, knowing him to be a felon, is no principall, but an acceffory: and for that there is no acceffory in treafon, therefore C in the cafe before committeth no treafon; for then in judgement of law he muft be a counterfeiter of the kings coine within our ftatute of 25 E. 3. which he is not: and therefore they fay, this is *cafus omiffus*, and not within any of the claffes or heads of the faid act of 25 E. 3. But all agree, that procurors of fuch treafon to be done before the fact done, if after the fact be done accordingly, in cafe of treafon, are principals, for that they are *participes criminis* in the very act of counterfeiting.

[a] 19 H. 6. 47. 3 H. 7. 10. Stanf. fo. 3. See before cap. Treafon. Verb. Si home counterface le grand feale.

[a] But faving reformation we hold, that if any man committeth high treafon, and thereby becommeth a traytor, if any other man knowing him to be a traytor, doth receive, comfort, and aide him, he is guilty of treafon, for that there be no acceffories in high treafon. [b] And fo it was refolved in the cafe of Abingdon, who received, comforted, and aided Henry Garnet fuperior of the jefuits, knowing him to be guilty of the powder treafon, and accordingly Abingdon was indicted and attainted of high treafon.

[b] Pafch. 4. Jac. Abingdons cafe refolved by the juftices.

[c] M. 12 & 13 El. ubi fupra. See before ca. 3. Of Mifprifion of Treafon.

[c] And where it is faid, that the faid offence in Conyers cafe was mifprifion of treafon, that cannot be, becaufe there was a confent, and not a concealment only: otherwife, high treafon being the higheft offence, fhould have more favour, then felony: for the receiver and comforter in cafe of felony is punifhed by death, and fo is not he that committeth mifprifion of treafon. And laftly, this is no new treafon, but a partaking and a maintaining of the old.

[d] 7 H. 4. 27. 21 E. 4. 71. 13 H. 7. 10. Pl. com. Lib. 4. fo. 42. in Heydons cafe. Lib. 9. fo. 67. Mackallyes cafe. & lib. 11. fo. 5.

[e] Lib. 4. fo. 44. Vauxes cafe. Pl. com. fo. 474. Saunders cafe. Lib. 9. 81. Agnes Gores cafe. See Pafc. 32. E. 3. coram rege rot. 62. Ph. Cliftons cafe.

In cafe of felony there are principals and acceffories, and acceffories be of two forts, either before the offence be committed, or after. See the fecond part of the Inftitutes, W. 1. cap. 14. And concerning this, there be alfo certaine rules, [d] *Nullus dicitur felo principalis, nifi actor, aut qui præfens eft abettans, aut auxilians actorem ad feloniam faciendam.* But this rule hath his exception: for [e] in cafe of poyfoning, if one layeth poyfon for one, or infufe it into broth, or the like, albeit he be not prefent when the fame is taken; and either the party intended, or any other is poyfoned, yet is he a principall: and in that cafe, both the principall and procurer, or acceffory may be abfent. See the bookes aforefaid for acceffories before the felony committed, and where and in what manner the procurement fhall be faid in law to be purfued: the learning whereof is fo plainly fet downe, as the fame need not herein to be repeated. [f] *Nullus dicitur acceffarius poft feloniam, fed ille qui novit principalem feloniam feciffe, et illum receptavit * et comfortavit.* [a] And therefore if a man write letters for his deliverance, or in favour of him, or the like; he is no acceffory, for that he received not the felon.

[f] 25 E. 3. 39. b. cor. 126. 26 Aff. 47. 9 H. 4. 1. 7 H. 6. 42.

*[139]

[a] 26 Aff. ubi fup.

[b] Mic. 7 R. 2. coram rege rot. 2[illegible]. Cant. 7 H. 4. 27.

[b] A vicar, which inftructed an approver which could not reade, whileft he was in prifon, to reade, whereby he efcaped, was adjudged no acceffory to the felony.

Catlyn

Catlyn and Browne justices of assise in the county of Suffolke put this case to all the judges. [c] A man committed felony in the county of Suffolke, for which he was committed to the gaole; and R. an attorny advised the friends of the felon to perswade the witnesses not to appeare to give evidence against him, which was done accordingly. And it was resolved, that neither the friends nor the attorny were accessaries to the felony, but that it was a great contempt and misprision, for which they might be fined and imprisoned.

[c] Mic. 11 & 12 E [illegible] of Roberts the attorny.

[d] The accessory cannot be guilty of petit treason, where the principall is guilty but of murder. For *accessorius sequitur naturam sui principalis.*

[d] See before cap. Petit Treason.

[e] If divers commit any murder, or other felony, one man may be both principall and accessory to the other.

[e] 7 H. 4. 27.

See before cap. Clergie, that if the principall before attainder hath his clergie, the accessory is discharged. And note generally, where the principall before attainder is pardoned, or his life otherwise saved, the accessory is discharged.

[f] 2 H. 4. 16.

CAP. LXV.

Of Misprisions divers and severall: and first of Misprision of Felony, &c.

OF misprision of treason we have already spoken, and of the etymologie of the word. It remaineth now that we speak of other misprisions.

Misprision is twofold: one is *crimen omissionis*, of omission, as in concealement, or not discovery of treason or felony: another is *crimen commissionis*, of commission, as in committing some heynous offence under the degree of felony.

Or misprision is of two sorts, viz. passive and active: passive is of the nature of concealment, whereof some be by the common law, and some by statute. By the common law, as passive misprision, that is concealement of high treason whereof we have spoken; and passive misprision, that is concealement of felony, whereof we are now in this chapter to speak. Some by statute: as if any be moved to make commotion or unlawfull assembly, and do not within twenty four houres declare the same to a justice of peace, sheriffe, maior, or bailiffe, &c. concealement by juries, 3 H. 7. ca. 1. 33 H. 8. ca. 6, &c.

1 Mar. 1. Parl. ca. 12.
1 Eliz. cap. 17.

Now are we speak of concealement or not discovery of felony. As in case of high treason, whether the treason be by the common law, or statute, the concealment of it is misprision of treason. So in case of felony, whether the felony be by the common law, or by statute, the concealement of it is misprision of felony.

See the second part of the Institutes. W. 1. cap. 9.

If any be present when a man is slaine, and omit to apprehend the slayer, it is a misprision, and shall be punished by fine and imprisonment.

8 E. 2. cor. 395.

And as the concealment of high treason is higher by many degrees then the concealment of felony, so the punishment for the concealment of the greater is heavier then of the lesser, and yet the

W. 1. ca. 9. See the exposition thereof, ubi sup.

the concealment of felonies in fherifs, or bailiffs of liberties is more feverely punifhed then in others, viz. by imprifonment by one year, and ranfome at the will of the king. From which punifhment * if any will fave himfelf he muft follow the advice of Bracton, to difcover it to the king, or to fome judge or magiftrate, that for adminiftration of juftice fupplieth his place, with all fpeed that he can.

Bract. lib. 3. fo. 118. a.

Non enim debet morari in uno loco per duas noctes, vel per duos dies, nec debet ad aliqua negotia, quamvis urgentiffima, fe convertere, quia vix permittitur ei ut retrofpiciat.

And this is intended of a concealment, or not difcovery of his meer knowledge: for if in cafe of high treafon, he that knoweth it, before it be done, and affenteth to it, is *particeps criminis*, and guilty of treafon: and in cafe of felony, he that receiveth the thief, and affenteth to it, is acceffory.

See before the chapt. of Mifprifion of Treafon, fo. 36. and of Principall and Acceffory, fo. 138.
* Ecclefiaftes. ca. 10. v. 20.

See before in the chapter of mifprifion of treafon, that every treafon and felony doth include in it mifprifion of treafon and felony. See the ftatute of 23 El. ca. 1. of mifprifion, that is, *crimen commiffionis.*

Compaffings, or imaginations againft the king, by word, without an overt act, is an high mifprifion, as before is faid. * *In cogitatione tua ne detrahas regi, &c. quia aves cœli portabunt vocem tuam, et qui habet pennas annunciabit fententiam.*

a See the fecond part of the Inftitutes, W. 1. ca. 33.
25 E. 3. ca. 1. It is high treafon to kill any of them in their places.
b 22 E. 3. 13. 19 E. 3. Judgment 174. Mich. 6 E. 3. coram rege Rot. 55. Eborum.
41 E. 3. cor. 280. Nota the forfeiture of his lands is but during his life 41 E. 3. 25.
c Int. leges Alveredi, cap. 34. 3 El. Dier, 188. 2 Ja. Bellinghams cafe coram rege with his elbow and fhoulder.
d 33 H. 8. ca. 12.

[a] If any man in Weftminfter hall, or in any other place, fitting the courts of chancery, the exchequer, the kings bench, the common bench, or before juftices of affife, or juftices of oier and terminer, (which courts are mentioned in the ftatute of 25 E. 3. *De proditionibus*) fhall draw a weapon upon any judge, or juftice, though he ftrike not; this is a great mifprifion, [b] for the which he fhall lofe his right hand, and forfeit his lands and goods, and his body to perpetuall imprifonment: the reafon hereof is, becaufe it tendeth *ad impedimentum legis terræ.* [c] So it is, if in Weftminfter hal or any other place, fitting the faid courts there, or before juftices of affife, or oier and terminer, and within the view of the fame, a man doth ftrike a juror, or any other with weapon, hand, fhoulder, elbow, or foot, he fhall have the like punifhment; but in that cafe, if he make an affault, and ftrike not, the offender fhall not have the like punifhment.

[d] If any ftrike in the kings palace, where the kings royall perfon refideth, he fhall not lofe his right hand, unleffe he draw blood; but if he draw blood, then his right hand fhall be ftrucken off, he perpetually imprifoned, and fined and ranfomed.

Note the law makes a great difference between a ftroke or blow, in or before any of the faid courts of juftice, where the king is reprefentatively prefent, and the kings court, where his royall perfon refideth. For in the kings houfe (as hath been faid) blood muft be drawne, which needeth not in or before the courts of juftice, but a ftroke only fufficeth. Again, the punifhment is more fevere in the one cafe, then in the other: fuch honour the law attributeth to courts of juftice, when the judges or juftices are doing of that which to juftice appertaineth: and the reafon is, *Quia juftitia firmatur folium.*

But note that by the ancient laws of this realm, ftriking only in the kings court was punifhed by death. *Vide Lambard inter leges Inæ ca. 6. Si quis in regia pugnarit, rebus fuis omnibus mulctator, et fitne morte etiam plectendus, regis arbitrium et jus efto. Inter leges Canuti,*

nuti, cap. 56. *Si quis in regia dimicarit, capitale esto, &c. Inter leges Alvereai, cap.* 7. *Qui in regia dimicarit, ferrumve distrinxeret, capiter, et regem penes arbitrium vitæ necisque ejus esto, &c.*

[c] Peter Burchet prisoner in the tower, stroke within the tower John Longworth his keeper (who stood in a window reading of the Bible) with a billet on the head behind, whereby blood was shed, and death instantly ensued: this being without any provocation was adjudged murder, for which he was attainted, and before his execution (which was in the Strand over against Somerset house) his right hand was first strucken off, by force of the statute of 33 H. 8. for that the tower was one of the queens standing houses or palaces.

[c] Mich. 15 El. in the case of Peter Burchet esquire of the Middle Temple.

The kings palace at Westminster hath this liberty and priviledge, viz. *Nullæ citationes, aut sommonitiones, liceant fieri cuicunque infra palatium regis Westm.*

Pasch. 8. E. 2. Coram rege Rot. 28 Norff.

[141]

Like priviledge hath Westminster hall, or other place, where the kings justices, &c. sit, as by these following records appeareth.

[a] *Quia bedellus universitatis citari fecit Wil. de Wivelingham infra ostium aulæ Westm. justiciariis sedentibus, ad comparend' coram cancellario, &c. pro quo se posuit in gratiam regis, committitur gaolæ, et Henricus de Harwood, ad cujus sectam prosecutus fuit, committitur marischal. et finem fecit* 40. *s.*

[a] Mich. 12 E. 3. Coram rege Rot. 101. Cant.

[b] *Matilda de Nyerford, filia Willielmi de Nyerford militis defuncti,* did libell against John earl of Warren, and [c] Johan de Barro countes of Warren the kings niece *(in camitina dominæ reginæ consortis domini regis)* in a cause of matrimony and divorce, and the same Johan de Barro was cited in the kings palace at Westminster, &c. It was upon full examination of the cause, adjudged in parliament in these words, *Quòd prædictum palacium domini regis est locus exemptus ab omni jurisdictione ordinaria, tam regiæ dignitatis et coronæ suæ, quam libertatis ecclesiæ Westm', et maximè in præsentia ipsius domini regis tempore parliamenti sui ibidem: ita quòd nullus summonitiones, seu citationes ibidem faciat, et præcipuè illis, qui sunt de sanguine domini regis, quibus major reverentia, quam aliis fieri debet, &c. Consideratum est, quòd officiar' committatur turri London, et ibidem custodiatur ad voluntatem domini regis.*

[b] Placita coram domino rege in parliamento suo apud Westm' in præsentia domini regis, an. 21 E. 1.

[c] Ellanor daughter of E. 1. married with William earl of Barry alias Barro in France, and had issue the said Johan who married John earl Warren.

Here two things are principally to be observed: first, that this royall priviledge is not only appropriated to the palace of Westminster, but to all the kings palaces, where his royall person resides. Secondly, that this priviledge is to be exempted from all ecclesiasticall jurisdiction, *regiæ dignitatis et coronæ suæ ratione, &c.*

If any doe rescue a prisoner in or before any of the abovesaid courts committed by any of the aforesaid justices, it is a great misprision, for which he and the prisoner assenting to it, shall forfeit their lands and goods, and their bodies to perpetuall imprisonment, but shall not lose his hand, because no stroke or blow was given.

22 E. 3. 13.

But it was resolved by all the judges, that where Thomas Oldfield, sitting in the court of the dutchy of Lancaster, with a knife stabbed one Ferror a justice of peace in the view of the said court, that the court of the dutchy was none of the courts to make it a misprision to lose his right hand, &c. but the offender was to be indicted, and grievously fined.

Trin. 8 Jac. regis Oldfields case.

And in 9 El. one Guirling stroke another in the Whitehall, sitting

Pasch. 9 Eliz. Guirlings case.

sitting the masters of requests, and it was then resolved by the court of kings bench, that it was not any misprision, for the which he should lose his right hand, &c. but he was indicted and fined.

Hil 13 E. 3. Coram rege Rot. 104. Suff.

Quia Thomas de Holbroke manus violentas imposuit super Johannem de Loudham, &c. ad sessionem suam sedentem apud Gipwicum, et eum dementitus est, committitur in parliamento turri London, et finitur 20. li. et invenit sex milites manucaptores pro bono gestu suo.

And where some of the books abovesaid say, that the offender shall forfeit his lands, and some that he shall be disherited, yet the forfeiture of his lands is only for tearm of his life, (as before is said:) for being no felony, the blood is not corrupted, nor the heir disinabled to inherit. And this severe punishment is at the suit of the king, and the party may have his action, and it shall be tried by the officers and criers. And for such a stroke Thomas of Whittelley recovered five hundred pounds, Trin. 9 E. 3. Rot. 154. Midd.

Trin. 9 E. 3. Rot. 154. Midd.

Brit. ca. 25. fo. 47. * Nota for the dignity of knights.

Britton saith, *Ascuns trespasses sont nequedent pluis punishable, si come trespas fait en temps de peace a * chivaliers, ou auters gents honorables per ribaws, ou auters viles persons; en quel case nous volons, que si ribawe soit attaint al suit de chescun chivalier, que il eyt ferue per felony sans desart del chivalier que le ribawe perd son pome dont il trespassa:* so great a respect in those days was had of honour and order. Ribawe is taken here for a rascall ruffian. There is a great misprision when any revenge is sought against a judge, justice, officer, juror, serjeant, councellor, minister, or clerk, for that, which they doe in discharge of their severall duties, offices, and places, concerning the administration of justice.

[142]

Mich. 33 & 34 E. 1. Coram rege, Rot. 75.

Roger de Hegham and others being justices of oier and terminer, and sitting in the exchequer chamber, gave judgement for Mary late the wife of William Brewse plaintif, against William le Brewse defendant, which judgement was pronounced by Roger de Hegham. William de Brewse demanded of Roger de Hegham if he would avow the judgement, and said, Roger, Roger, now thou hast thy will which of long time thou hast sought: of whom Roger de Hegham demanded, What is that? to whom William de Brewse said, My shame, and my losse, and this I will reward or recompence, or I will think of it. Whereof he being indicted and arraigned, and confessing the offence, the record saith, *Et quia sicut honor, et reverentia, qui ministris domini regis ratione officii sui faciuntur, ipso regi attribuuntur; sic dedecus et contemptus ministris suis fact' eidem domino regi inferuntur; consideratum est quòd praed. Willielmus de Brewse, discinctus in corpore, capite nudo, tena deposita, eat e banco domini regis ubi placita teneritur in aula Westm', per medium aulae praedict', cum curia plena fuerit, usque ad scaccarium (ubi deliquit) et ibidem veniam petit a praefato Rogero, &c. et postea committitur turri London, ibidem moratur', ad voluntatem regis.*

Nota.

Bract. lib. 2. 105. These words were given to the treasurer of England by the procurement of Pierce of Gaveston.

Note this exemplary judgement against a gentleman of a great and honourable family. *Quaelibet poena corporalis, quamvis minima, major est qualibet poena pecuniaria.* And in that record it is said, *Quòd dominus rex filium suum primogenitum, et charissimum Edwardum principē Walliae, pro eo quòd quaedam verba grossa cuidam ministro suo dixerat, ab hospitio suo ferè per dimidium anni amovit, nec ipsum filium suum in conspectu suo venire permisit, quousque dicto ministro de dicta transgressione satisfecerat.*

Quia

Quia Petrus de Scales minatus fuit Ricūm de Worlingworth, qui fuit de conſilio Johannis de Moten, de vita et membris, dictus Petrus invenit plegios de bono geſtu ſuo. Hil. 20 E. 3. Coram rege Rot. 160.

There be many records for abuſing of jurours, viz. Paſch. 10 E. 3. Coram rege, rot. 87. Gilbertus Twiſt. Paſch. 26 E. 3 ibidem, rot. 22. Eſſex, Tho. Hubberd, Hil. 7 H. 5. ibidem, rot. 24. Ricūs Cheddre. Mich. 17 E. 2. Coram rege rot. 63.

Percuſſio clerici curiæ in veniendo verſus curiam, &c. Trin. 11 E. 2. Coram rege, rot. 42. London. Not only theſe particular revenges abovesaid, but all other of what kind ſoever are great miſpriſions.

Alſo when any revenge is ſought againſt any man for complaining in any of the kings courts, *ſuper gravaminibus, &c.* for grievances, &c. *Quia deterret homines à querelis ſuper gravaminibus in forma juris. De hiis qui vindictam fecerint, eo quod aliquo modo ſuper prædictis gravaminibus in curia domini regis conqueſti fuerunt.* Cap. Itineris §. ultimo.

Juſticiarii taxaverunt damna 2 marc' ſuper Willielmum Boteſford, eo quòd minabatur quandam Hawiſiam de vita et membris, eo quòd ipſa proſequebatur ipſum in placito tranſgreſſionis. Paſc. 10 E 3. Coram rege Rot. 86. Linc.

We will conclude this point for private revenge with an ancient law before the conqueſt. *Si quis privato conſilio illatam ſibi injuriam vindicarit, antequam jus æquum ſibi dari poſtulaverit, quod nomine vindictæ eripuit reddito, integrum rei pretium præſtato, et 30 ſolidos dependito.* Inter leges Inæ, cap. 9. Lamb. See the 4. part of the Inſtit. cap. Chancery., Artic. verſ. Cardinall Woolſey. Art. 4. 5, 6. 11. 41.

See in the fourth part of the Inſtitutes, cap. Of the chancery, in the articles againſt Cardinall Woolſey. Artic. 4, 5, 6. 11. 41.

[143]

C A P. LXVI.

Of CONSPIRACIE.

CONSPIRACIE [a] is a conſultation and agreement between two or more, to appeale, or indict an innocent falſely, and maliciouſly of felony, whom accordingly they cauſe to be indicted or appealed; and afterward the party is lawfully acquited by the verdict of twelve men: the party grieved may be relieved, and the offender puniſhed two wayes. Firſt, by a writ of conſpiracy, which is a civill or common action at the ſuit of the party, wherein the plaintife ſhall recover damages, and the defendant ſhall be impriſoned. Secondly, by indictment at the ſuit of the king, the judgement whereof is criminall: of which we are now to ſpeak.

Vide ſtatut. de conſpiratoribus, anno 21 E. 1. vet. Mag. Cart. part 1. fo 111. & definition conſpir. 33 E. 1. ibid. fo. 90. b. Artic. ſup. Cart. cap. 10. F. N. B. 114, 115. Stanf. pl. cor. 172, &c. Lib. 4. fo. 45. Lib. 9. fo. 16, 56, 57. 78.

[b] Upon this ſuit of the king, if the offenders be convicted, the judgement is grievous and terrible, viz. That they ſhal loſe the freedom or franchiſe of the law, to the intent that he ſhall not be put or had upon any jury or aſſiſe, or in any other teſtimony of truth: and if they have any thing to do in the kings courts, they ſhall come [c] *per ſolem, id eſt*, by broad day, and make their attorny, and

[b] 24 E. 3. 45. 27. aſſ. 43 E. 3. Conſpiracy, 11. 59. 4 H. 5. Judgment 120. the like judgement as in attaint. See the firſt part of the Inſtitutes. Sect.

[c] Trin. 18 E. 3. Coram rege, Rot. 148. Paſch. 32 E. 3. Coram rege. Rot. 58.

forthwith return by broad day: and their houſes, lands, and goods, ſhall be ſeiſed into the kings hands, and their houſes and lands eſtrepped and waſted, their trees rooted up and erraſed, and their bodies to priſon: all things retrograde, and againſt order and nature, in deſtroying all things that have pleaſured or nouriſhed them; for that by falſehood, malice, and perjury, they ſought to attaint and overthrow the innocent. Which judgement in our books is called, a villanous judgement. Firſt, in reſpect of the villainy and ſhame, which the party hath which receiveth it. Secondly, for that by the judgement he loſeth the freedom and franchiſe of the law, and therefore undergoeth a kinde of bondage and villany. And the reaſon of this heavy and terrible judgement is: 1. For that the offenders have conſpired and plotted the death and ſhedding of the blood of an innocent. 2. That they do it under faire pretence of juſtice and by courſe of law, which was inſtituted for the protection and defence of the innocent. 3. That if they had attainted the innocent, he ſhould have loſt his life, (by an infamous death) his lands, his goods, and his poſterity: for his blood thereby ſhould have been corrupted, &c. 4. All this falſhood, malice, and perjury is committed *in placito coronæ*, in a ſuit for the king, which aggravateth and increaſeth the offence; for that the king is the head of juſtice, and a protector of the innocent: and therefore at the kings ſuit, and not at the ſuit of the party, this villanous judgement ſhall be given. So as the law hath excellently diſtributed the remedies; the private action of the party to give him damages, &c. and the ſuit of the king for exemplary puniſhment. And it is to be obſerved, that this villanous judgement is given by the common law, (as in the caſe of attaint) and not by force of any ſtatute.

27 Lib. aſſ. p. 12. King E. 3. demanded of his juſtices and ſerjeants, whether divers men being indicted of conſpiracy for the indicting of R. of felony, were mainpernable or no? and they anſwered the king expreſly, that they were not, in reſpect of the odiouſneſſe of the offence.

[144]

CAP. LXVII.

Of Penſions, &c. received by Subjects, of Foraine Kings, &c.

See the fourth part of the Inſtitutes, cap. the Chancery Artic. againſt Cardinall Woolſey, art. 27. Vide parl. 7 R. 2. nu. 16. Mat. ca. 26. v. 24. *Nemo poteſt duobus dominis ſervire: aut enim unum odio habe-*

IT is not lawfull for any ſubject of the king of England to take a penſion, &c. of any foraine king, prince, or ſtate (without the kings licenſe) albeit they be in league with the king of England; both, for that they may become enemies, and for that alſo it is miſchievous and dangerous to the king himſelf and his ſtate, as it appeareth by this diſtichon,

Principe ab externo veniunt lethalia dona,
Quæ ſtudii ſpecie, fata, necemque ferunt.

And this was (ſay they) the caſe of the lord Haſtings chamberlaine to king E. 4. who in the fifteenth year of his raign, received a penſion a penſion of two thouſand crowns yearly from the French king: who being informed by juſt. Cateſbye his inward friend, and others learned in the law, that the receiving hereof was an offence againſt law, being deſired by Pierce Clerett a Frenchman (who paid the penſion) to make him an acquitance for receipt thereof for his diſcharge, utterly refuſed the ſame. This report I do the rather hold to be true, for that all our Engliſh hiſtorians, (who for the moſt part rehearſe but the carkaſſe or outſide of any point in law) give great credit hereunto. And what ill conſequence this and other like penſions, and others of the councell of king E. 4. had, you may reade in our hiſtories.

bit, et alterum diliget, aut unum ſuſtinebit, et alterum contemnet. 4 Regum, ca. 5. v. 26, &c. Geneſi. See 3 Jac. ca. 5. concerning the ſervice of a ſubject as a ſouldier or captain to a forain prince, hereafter cap. Fugitives. *Polydor. Hall. Hollingſhed. Stowe, &c.*

See the caſe in 7 R. 2. of [a] Spencer biſhop of Norwich; and there alſo the caſe of [b] Pierce Creſſingham, and others: and of [c] ſir William Ellingham and others, puniſhed for receiving of money, &c. of the French king, which drew them without the kings licenſe, to yeeld up caſtles and forts in France committed to their cuſtody, puniſhed by fine and impriſonment.

See the fourth part of the Inſtitutes, cap. of the Chancery, artic. 27. againſt Cardinall Woolſey.

[a] Rot. Parl. 7 R. 2. nu. 15. 18. 20. 21, 22, 23.
[b] Ibid. nu. 17.
[c] Ibid. nu. 24.

CAP. LXVIII.

[145]

Of Bribery, Extortion, Exaction, &c.

And firſt of Bribery.

BRIBERY is a great miſpriſion (1), when any man in judiciall place (2) takes any fee or penſion, robe, or livery, gift, reward (3) or brocage (4) of any perſon, that hath to do before him any way (5), for doing his office, or by colour of his office, but of the king only, unleſſe it be of meat and drink, and that of ſmall value, upon divers, and grievous puniſhments.

Forteſcue, ca. 51.

This word [bribery] commeth of the French word *briber*, which ſignifieth to devoure, or eat greedily, applyed to the devouring of a corrupt judge, of whom the Pſalmiſt ſpeaking in the perſon of God, ſaith, *Qui devorat plebem meam ſicut eſcam panis. Qui cognoſcit faciem in judicio, non bene facit: iſte pro buccella panis deſerit veritatem.*

Pſalm 13. 4. Prov. 28. 21.

But let us peruſe the branches of this deſcription.

(1) *A great miſpriſion.*] But it may be objected, that bribery in a judge was ſometime adjudged a higher offence. For whereas at the aſſizes holden at Lincolne in the 23 yeare of E. 3. an exigent was to have been awarded againſt Richard Saltley, Hildebrand Boreſward, Guilbert Holliland, Thomas Derby, and Robert Dalderby, who formerly had been indicted of divers felonies before ſir William Thorpe, chiefe juſtice of the kings bench, and one of the juſtices of aſſize of the ſaid county of Lincolne, he the ſaid ſir William

Rot. Pat. anno 24 E. 3. part 3. m. 2. and Rot. Pat. anno 25 E. 3. part 1. m. 17. Rot. Parl. 25 E. 3. nu. 10. 23 E. 3.

William Thorpe, to stay the said writ of exigent against them, *cepit munera contra juramentum suum*, viz. of Richard Saltly, 10 li. of Hildebrand, 20 li. of Holliand, 40 li. of Derby, 10 li. and of Dalderby, 10 li. King Edward the third appointed the earles of Arundell, Warwick, and Huntingdon, and two lords, the lord Grey and the lord Burghers' to examine this matter. Before whom sir William Thorpe being charged with the said bribery, *Non potuit*
Anno 24 E. 3. *dedicere, &c.* Now the record saith, *Consideratum est per dictos justiciarios assignatos ad judicand. secundum voluntatem domini regis, et secundum regale posse suum, quod quia praedictus Willielmus de Thorpe, qui sacramentum domini regis, quod erga populum suum habuit custodiendum, fregit maliciose, falsè, et rebelliter in quantum in ipso fuit, et ex causis supradictis per ipsum Willielmum, ut praedictum est, expresse cognitis, suspendatur, et quod omnia trae. et tenta., bona et catalla sua remaneant forisfacta.* This sentence seemeth to have his foundation as well upon the oath of the judges, (for the record saith) *contra juramentum suum*, and the conclusion of the oath, and in case ye
The oath of the justices anno 18 E. 3. be found in any default in any of the points aforesaid, ye shall be *ad voluntatem regis*, of body, lands, and goods, thereof to be done as pleaseth him: as also for that this last clause is enacted by au-
20 E. 3. cap. 1. thority of parliament (as they say) in *anno* 20 E. 3. And hereupon they the said lords were appointed to judge *secundum voluntatem domini regis, et regale posse suum*, according to the words of the oath and act of parliament. And this judgement was repeated in *anno* 25. to the lords, and affirmed by them.

This president is not to be followed at this day for divers causes. First, it seemeth by the violation of the kings oath, and of this word [*rebelliter*] and by the forfeiture of all his lands and tene-
[146] ments to the king, that this offence should be treason against the king, and then it being either high treason, or petit treason, it is taken away by the statute of 25 E. 3. *De proditionibus*, the same being none of them, that are there expressed. And in all the records this word [*felonice*] is not to be found, as it ought to have been, if it had been felony.

Neither by the words of the oath, or of the supposed act of 20 E. 3. can the judgement *(quod suspendatur)* be warranted: for these words [to be at the kings will for body, &c.] cannot be extended to losse of life, no more then the statute of Carlisle *(sub fo-*
Anno 35 E. 1. the stat. of Carlisle. *risfactura omnium, quae in potestate sua obtinet)* extendeth not to forfeiture of life, but to imprisonment, &c. viz losse of liberty, &c.
20 E. 3. cap. 4. But at this parliament, viz. in *anno* 20 E. 3. taking in hand of quarrels, other then their own, and maintenance of them is prohibited upon the paines aforesaid, viz. the paines contained in the said supposed act of 20 E. 3. cap. 1. upon paine to be at our will, body, lands, and goods, to do thereof as shall please us: which without question was never extended to losse of life, &c. but to imprisonment, as common experience daily teacheth. For *haec est*
2 R. 3. fo. 11. See 8 R. 2. cap. 3. Rot. Parl. 10 R. 2. nu. 24. *voluntas regis, viz. per justiciarios suos et per legem, &c.* Therefore as by the record appeareth, sir William Thorpe was pardoned and restored to all his lands. And we were desirous to see the record of the act of 20 E. 3 cap. 1. but there is no record of any such act in the parliament roll. And the very frame and composition of it seemeth to be but a rehearsall of a commandment from the king: for the letter of it beginneth. First, we have commanded all our justices,

justices, that they shall from thenceforth do equall law, &c. and therefore justly omitted out of the parliament roll of acts of parliaments: and yet the imprinting of it necessary, for that the fourth chapter of this parliament hath reference to the paynes contained in it.

It is enacted by Parliament *anno* 11 H. 4. in these words. Vid. 1 H. 4. nu. 99. & Nota.

Item, *Que nul chancelor, treasorer, garden del privie seal counselor le roy, sernts. a councell del roy, ne nul auter officer, judge ne minister le roy, pernants fees ou gages de roy pur lour ditz offices ou services, preigne en nul manner en temps à vener ascun manner de done ou brocage de ulluy pur lour ditz offices et services a faire, sur peine de responder au roy de la treble que issint preignont, et de satisfier la partie, et punys al volunt le roy, et soit discharges de son office, service, et councell pur touts jours, et que chescun que voiera pursuer en la dit matter, eyt la suite cibien pur le roy, come pur luy mesme, et eit la tierce part del somme, de que la partie est duement convict.* Rot. Parl. anno 11 H. 4. nu. 28. never imprinted.

By this act of parliament, which is the judgement of the whole parliament, it appeareth, that, if that which is imprinted as the first chapter of 20 E. 3. had been an act of parliament, then this statute of 11 H. 4. would never have inflicted this kinde of punishment, which is other, and farre lesse, then that which is mentioned in 20 E. 3. and where it is said in this act of 11 H. 4. *(et punis al volunt le roy)* that is, by fine and imprisoment by the court where the conviction shall be; for, as hath been said, *hæc est voluntas regis, viz. per justiciarios suos, et legem suam, et non per dominum regem in camera sua, vel aliter.* 2 R. 3. 11. a.

So as by warrant of this act of parliament we have said, that bribery is a misprision; for that it is neither treason, nor felony; and it is a great misprision, for that it is ever accompanied with perjury.

* True it is, that sir Thomas Weyland, chief justice of the court of common pleas, was attainted of felony, but it was not for bribery, but being guilty of † being accessary to murder, for the which by the common law he was abjured the realm. * Plac. de parl. apud Asherugg in Cro. Ep. anno 19 E. 1.

Likewise Adam de Stratton chief baron of the Exchequer a man of great possessions and riches was attainted of felony by him committed, all which I collect upon records of parliament the surest guides. For in the parliament holden in 18 E. 1. in the same year when he was attainted, I find two petitions, one preferred by himself in these words, *Adam de Stratton petit gratiam regis, quòd restituatur ad aliquam partem terrarum suarum, et de bonis suis quæ habuit tempore quo fuit.** viz. 26000 li. Et Hollingsh. Chron. pag. 284, 285. he confessed felony, and abjured.

[147]

Rot. Pari. 18 E. 1. fo. 5. nu. 61.

* There is a space left in the record.

The other by Margaret de Boteler in these words, *Margareta quæ fuit uxor Joh. de Boteler, de qua Adam de Stratton tenuit* 12 *li.* 10. *s. in London, clamat habere ut eschaet'. Responss. Rex non concessit; quia in civitate nulla est eschaeta nisi regis.* And at the same parliament, fo. 3. it is resolved, *non sunt nisi tres formæ brevis de eschaeta;* Et ibid. nu. 69.

eſchaeta; *quia utlagatus, vel ſuſpenſus, vel abjuravit regnum.* And by conſequence Adam de Stratton ſeeing his lands eſcheated, muſt have the judgement of one of theſe three. Which we have added to anſwer ſecret objections that might be made out of the miſtakings of our Chronicles.

Rot. Parl. 20 E. 1. fol. 5. The reſt of the juſtices were removed, fined, and impriſoned, ſaving Johannes de Mettingham, and Elias de Beckingham, who to their eternall memory and honour were found upright, and free from all bribery and corruption.

10 R. 2. nu. 24. It was petitioned in parliament, that the ſtatutes whereby the juſtices of the one bench or the other ſhould take no reward, ne be of any mans fee, may be obſerved. The kings anſwer was, [the king hath and will charge ſuch juſtices to miniſter right, and will puniſh the contrary, and therefore willeth that all ſtatutes made touching them and the barons of the exchequer, be made void.

(2) *When any man in judiciall place, &c.*] For the difference between bribery and extortion is, that bribery is only committed by him, that hath a judiciall place, and extortion may be committed both by him that hath a judiciall place, or by him that hath a miniſteriall office.

And this offence of bribery may be committed by any that hath Deut. 16. 19. any judiciall place either eccleſiaſticall or temporall. *Non accipies perſonam nec munera*, (and the reaſon is expreſſed by the Holy Ghoſt) *quia munera excæcant oculos ſapientum, et mutant verba juſtorum.*

If bribery hath ſo great force, as to blinde the eyes of the wiſe judge, and to change the words of the juſt, *Beatus ille, qui excutit manus ſuas ab omni munere. Judex debet habere duos ſales; ſalem ſapientiæ, ne ſit inſipidus, et ſalem conſcientiæ, ne ſit diabolus.*

Though the bribe be ſmall, yet the fault is great: and this appeareth by a record in the reign of E. 3. *Quia diverſi juſticiarii ad audiendum et terminandum aſſignat' ceperunt de Johanne Berners qui indictatus fuit, 4. li. pro favore habendo die deliberationis ſuæ, finem fecerunt domino regi per iiii M. marcas*, ſo as they paid for every pound a thouſand marks. See before ſir William Thorps caſe. Rot. Parl. 7 R. 2. the chancellour was accuſed of a bribe of ten pound, and his man four pound and certain fiſh, which, though the things were ſmall, yet it had been puniſhed, if it had been proved.

Paſch. 17 E. 3. Coram rege. Rot. 139. Eſſex. John Berners caſe. Rot. Parl. 7 R. 2. nu. 12, 13.

Anno 18 E. 3. (3) *Take any fee, robe, gift, or reward.*] This is warranted by the oath abovеſaid.

But admit the party * offereth a bribe to the judge, meaning to corrupt him in the cauſe depending before him, and the judge taketh it not, yet this is an offence puniſhable by law in the party that doth offer it.

* Since theſe Inſtitutes ſo was it reſolved in the Star-chamber, Trin. 6 Car. Reg. in an information againſt Bonham Norton and others.

(4) *Brocage.*] There is good warrant for this word by the ſaid act of 11 H. 4.

(5) *Of any perſon that hath to doe before him any way.*] This hath his ground upon the oath aforeſaid, ſo as bribery may be committed not only when a ſuit dependeth *in foro contentioſo* (as it was in the caſe of ſir Fr. Bacon lo. of S. Alban lo. chancellour of England, who for many exorbitant and ſordid briberies was ſentenced by the lords of parliament, which you may reade Rot. Parl. *anno* 19 *Jacobis regis)* but alſo when any in judiciall place doth any thing *virtute* or *colore officii*, though there be no ſuit at all. For example, if the

[148]

the lord treaſurer for any gift or brocage, ſhall make any cuſtomer, controller, or any officer or miniſter of the king, this is bribery, for he ought to take nothing in that caſe by the ſtatute of 12 R. 2. but that he make all ſuch officers and miniſters of the beſt, and moſt lawfull men, and ſufficient for their eſtimation and knowledge. (An excellent law tending greatly to his majeſties advantage, to the good uſage and encouragement of merchants, &c. and generally to the advancement of commerce, trade, and traffique, the life of this iſland.) Reade this ſtatute, for it is of a large extent, and the ſtatute of 5 E. 6. for they are laws made *contra ambitum*, and worthy to be put in execution, for they prevent bribery and extortion; for they that buy will ſell.

2 R. 2. ca. 2. See the ſtatute of 5 E. 6. ca. 16.

Vendit Alexander claves, altaria ſacra:
Vendere jure poteſt, emerat ille prius.

And that the ſtatute of 5 E. 6. doth extend as well to eccleſiaſticall offices, as temporall, which concern the adminiſtration and execution of juſtice. And it was reſolved in the caſe of doctor Trever chancellour of a biſhop in Wales, that both the office of chancellour and regiſter of the biſhop are within that ſtatute, becauſe they concern the adminiſtration of juſtice.

Hil. 8 Ja. in communi banco D. Trevers caſe. See hereafter ca. of Simony, and the 1. part. of the Inſtit. ſect. 378. fo. 234.

* L. Earl of M. lord treaſurer of England took *colore officii* divers bribes, &c. And namely where the farmers of the cuſtomes exhibited a petition to have certain juſt allowances, which his majeſty referred to the ſaid lord treaſurer, who long delayed the petitioners, untill they gave him ſeverall bribes, and then he gave way to relieve them. For this, and other his briberies, extortions, oppreſſions, and other grievous miſdemeanours in his ſeverall offices of the lord treaſurer, and maſter of the court of wards (no ſuit being in any of thoſe caſes depending) upon complaint, and charge of the commons in this parliament, and after evident proof and often hearing of the cauſe, the lords of parliament (the lord treaſurer being brought to the bar by the gentleman uſher and ſerjeant at arms, and kneeling till he was commanded to ſtand up) upon the petition of the commons by the ſpeaker gave this judgment againſt him by the mouth of the lord keeper in theſe words. This high court of parliament doth adjudge. Firſt, that you L. Earl of M. now lord Treaſurer of England ſhall loſe all your offices which you hold in this kingdome. 2. And ſhall be for ever uncapable of any office, place, or imployment in this ſtate and common-wealth. 3. And that you ſhall be impriſoned in the tower of London during the kings pleaſure. 4. And that you ſhall pay to our ſoveraign the king the fine of 50000. li. 5. And that you ſhall never ſit in parliament any more. 6. And that you ſhall never come within the verge of the kings court, as by the ſaid roll of the parliament appeareth, which is worthy of your reading at large.

* Rot. Parl. 21 Ja. regis.

In *anno* 21 H. 8. by articles under the hands of all the lords of the privy councell, (whereof ſir Thomas Moor then lord chancellour was one) and of the principall judges of the realm, which I have ſeene, cardinall Woolſey was charged with divers briberies, namely in the eighteenth article, in theſe words. Alſo the ſaid lord cardinall conſtrained all ordinaries in England, yearly to compound with him, or elſe he would uſurp half, or the whole of their juriſdiction by prevention, not for good order of the dioces, but to extort treaſure: for there is never a poor archdeacon

Anno 21 H. 8. Artic. 18.

in

in England but that he paid to him a yeerly portion of his living.

21 H. 8. ca. 5. Vide 2 R. 2. Rot. Parl. nu. 46.

If any ordinary, &c. having power by the act of 21 H. 8. to grant the administration of the goods of him that dieth intestate, or as intestate, to the widow or next of kin, &c. take any reward for preferring of any person, before another, to the administration, it is bribery.

[149] The law before the conquest. Inter leges Canuti, cap. 13.

Si quis contra fas et leges administrarit, vel pro odio, quod in alium habuerit, judicavit perperam, aut denique nummarium se judicem praebuerit, proprii capitis æstimatione Anglorum jure regi damnatur, nisi quidem legum id accidisse inscitia, &c.

CAP. LXIX.

Of Extortion, Exaction, &c.

[a] Lib. 10. fo. 101. & 102. Beawfages case. See the 1. part of the Institutes sect. 701. verb. [Extortioners] 2. part of the Instit. W. 1. ca. 26. The 4. part of the Institutes. ca. Chancery in the articles against Cardinall Woolsey, art. 3.
[b] Trin. 28 E. 3. Coram rege. Rot. 37 Eborum.
[c] Hil. 20 E. 3. Coram rege. Rot. 159. Norff.
[d] Ibidem in the same roll.
[e] 1 E. 3. stat. 2. ca. 15.
[f] Nota.

THIS is another great [a] misprision because it is accompanied with perjury. Hereof you may read in the first part of the Institutes, sect. 701. See also in the second part of the Institutes, W. 1. cap. 26. and cap. 10. And in the fourth part of the Institutes, cap. Chancery, in the articles against cardinall Woolsey, article 3. Extortion of Ordinaries. [b] *Ranusiatores hominum, extortionatores hominum:* a rancunnier, an extortioner of men.

[c] The collectors of the fifteens were committed to prison, for that they took of every town eighteen pence for an acquittance.

[d] A coroner was committed to prison, because he would not take the view of the dead body, before he had received for himself six shillings eight pence, and for his clerk two shillings, and was fined at forty shillings.

[e] If any of the kings councell or his ministers doe exact a bond of any of his subjects, to come to the king with force and arms, &c. when they should be sent for, such writings are to the kings dishonour; for that every man is bound to do to the king as to his liege lord, [f] al that appertaineth to him, without any manner of writing, (note the generality hereof) and such writings are to be cancelled, as by the act appeareth.

Hereupon (by authority of this parliament) these conclusions doe follow. First, whatsoever any subject is bound to doe to the king, as to his liege lord, no bond or writing is to be exacted of the subject for doing thereof. Secondly, whatsoever bonds or writings are to the kings dishonour, are against law. Thirdly, whether such bonds or writings be made to the king or any other, the bonds or writings be void.

[g] Int. Inquisit. apud Lanceston Coram Rogero Loveday, and Waltero de Wynburn, an. 6 E. 1. Cornub.

[g] If a bishop or other ecclesiasticall judge, or minister, doth exact a bond or oath of any person in any case ecclesiasticall, not warrantable by law, the bond is void, and this exaction is punishable by fine, &c. the record is very long, but worthy to be read. See Rot. Parl. *anno* 8 H. 4. nu. 15, 16, 17, 18, 19, 20. excellent matter

matter concerning fees in courts of juſtice, and in the kings houſhold.

[h] *Officialis indictatus de citando, et affligendo plurimos, non poteſt dedicere, et petit quod admittatur ad finem.*

[i] *Contra ſequeſtratores, commiſſarios, et alios offic' epiſcoporum pro captione feodorum, priuſquam debent pro teſtamentis probandis.*

[k] The extortion of the clergy, and of their miniſters to be enquired of by juſtices of peace.

Reſolutions upon the ſtatute of 21 H. 8. ca. 5.

[l] If a man makes his teſtament in paper, and dieth poſſeſſed of goods and chattels above the value of forty pound, and the executor cauſeth the teſtament to be tranſcribed in parchment, and bringeth both to the ordinary, &c. to be proved: it is at the election of the ordinary whether he will put the ſeal and probate to the originall in paper, or to the tranſcript in parchment: but whether he put them to the one or the other, there can be taken of the executor, &c. in the whole but five ſhillings, and not above, viz. two ſhillings ſix pence to the ordinary, &c. and his miniſters, and two ſhillings ſix pence to the ſcribe for * regiſtring the ſame: or elſe the ſaid ſcribe to be at his liberty, to refuſe thoſe two ſhillings and ſix pence, and to have for writing every ten lines of the ſame teſtament, whereof every line to contain ten inches, one penny.

If the executor deſire that the teſtament in paper may be tranſcripted in parchment, he muſt agree with the party for the tranſcripting; but the ordinary, &c. can take nothing for it, nor for the examination of the tranſcript with the originall, but only two ſhillings ſix pence for the whole duty belonging to him. Where the goods of the dead doe not exceed an hundred ſhillings, the ordinary, &c. ſhall take nothing, and the ſcribe to have only for writing of the probate ſix pence, ſo the ſaid teſtament be exhibited in writing with wax thereunto affixed ready to be ſealed. Where the goods of the dead doe amount to above the value of an hundred ſhillings, and doe not exceed the ſumme of forty pound, there ſhall be taken for the whole but three ſhillings ſix pence, whereof to the ordinary, &c. two ſhillings ſix pence, and twelve pence to the ſcribe for regiſtring the ſame. Where by cuſtome leſſe hath been taken in any of the caſes aforeſaid, there leſſe is to be taken. And where any perſon requires a copy, or copies of the teſtament ſo proved, or inventory ſo made, the ordinary, &c. ſhall take for the ſearch, and making of the copy of the teſtament or inventory, if the goods exceed not an hundred ſhillings, ſix pence, and if the goods exceed an hundred ſhillings, and exceed not forty pound, twelve pence. And if the goods exceed forty pound, two ſhillings ſix pence, or to take for every ten lines thereof of the proportion before rehearſed, a penny.

When the party dies inteſtate, the ordinary may diſpoſe ſomewhat in pious uſes, notwithſtanding the ſaid act of 31 E. 3. but with theſe cautions, 1. That it be after the adminiſtration granted, and inventory made, ſo as the ſtate of the inteſtate may be known, and thereby the ſum may appear to be competent. 2. The adminiſtrator muſt be called to it. 3. The uſe muſt be publique and godly. 4. It muſt be expreſſed in particular. And, 5. There muſt be a decree made of it, and entred of record: ſo in caſe of

4 commutation

[h] Mich. 22 E. 3. Coram rege Rot. 181. Eboum.

[i] Hil. 23 E. 3. Coram rege.

[k] Rot. Parl. 3 R. 2. nu. 38, 39. 1 H. 5. nu. 23, 24.

[l] Mich. 6. Jacobi Rot. 1301 in communi banco. int. Edm. Neale informer, &c. et Jacobū Rowſe official' infra Archidiaconat' de Huntindon defendant per le chief juſtice Walmeſly, Warburton, Daniell, and Foſter.

* [150]

For puniſhment of eccleſiaſticall judges for extortion. See Rot. de Inquiſit. in Com. Eborum, Somerſet, &c. anno 4 E. 1. in Theſauro. De judicibus eccleſiaſticis dicunt, &c. Rot. Parl. 8 E. 3. nu. 9. The ſtatute of 31 E. 3. cap. 4. Paſch. 32 E. 3. Coram rege. Rot. 27. Rot. Parl. 50 E. 3. nu. 9. 1 R. 2. nu. 109. 2 R. 2. nu. 40. 13 R. 2. nu. 38, 39. 7 R. 2. nu. 53. The ſtatute of 3 H. 5. ca. 4.

Mich. 20 Jacobi in Camera Stellata, in Sir Jo. Bennets caſe.

commutation of penance, it must be after sentence, and *mutatis mutandis, ut supra.*

2 H. 4. ca. 10. Whereas twenty, forty, or an hundred be indicted of one felony, or one trespasse, and all plead to an issue, as not guilty, the clerk of the crown of the kings bench, ought not to take for the *venire facias*, or for the entring of the plea, above two shillings, but the said clerk did take for every such name by extortion two shillings. It is ordained and established, that the said clerk of the crown, shall take no more then hath been duly used of old time. And moreover our soveraign lord the king hath charged the said justices of the kings bench, that no extortion be done in this behalf in the bench aforesaid.

2 H. 4. ca. 8. The chirographer of the king in the common bench for making and writing of every fine levied four shillings, and no more, upon pain (if he take more) to lose his office, be expelled the court, one years imprisonment, and to pay to the party grieved his treble damages.

2 H. 4. ca. 23. The fees to the marshall of the marshalsea of the kings house, you may read in the statute of 2 H. 4. Vide 9 R. 2. cap. 5.

33 H. 8. ca. 39. If any auditor of the exchequer, dutchy of Lanc', or court of wards take more then three shillings four pence, for the enrolment of any letters patents, decree, grant, or indenture of lease, he shall forfeit, for every penny so taken, six shillings eight pence.

Munera ne capias, uncus latet hamus in esca;
Nulla carent visco munera, virus habent.

[151]

CAP. LXX.

OF USURY.

37 H. 8. ca. 9. 13 Eliz. ca. 8. USURY is a contract upon the lone of money, or giving dayes for forbearing of money, debt, or duty, by way of lone, chivisance, shifts, sales of wares, or other doings whatsoever. *Usura dicitur ab usu et ære, quia datur pro usu æris:* or *usura dicitur, quasi ignis urens.*

Deut. cap. 21. Exo. 22. Levit. 25. Ezech. 2. Psal. 15. And first, usury is directly against the law of God. And the reason wherefore it was permitted by the law of God for an Hebrew to an infidell, was; because it was a mean either to exterminate, or to depauperate them, as they should not be able to invade, or injure Gods people.

c 13 Eliz. cap. 8. 21 Jac. cap. 17. [c] And it is adjudged by authority of parliament, that all usury being forbidden by the law of God, is sinne, and detestable. And it is also enacted by parliament, that all usury is unlawfull, that is to say, against the lawes of the realme. Let us therefore see what former laws have provided herein.

d See the Cust. de Norm. cap. 20. Int. leges S. Edw. [d] *Siquis de usura convictus fuerit, omnes res suas amittat.*

e Glanvil. lib. 7. cap. 16. [e] *Usurarii omnes res, sive testatus, sive intestatus decesserit, domini regis sunt: vivus autem non solet aliquis de crimine usuræ appellari, nec convinci, sed inter cæteras regias inquisitiones solet inquiri, et probari aliquē in tali crimine decessisse per 12 legales homines de vicencto et per*

eorum

corum sacramentum. Quo probato in curia, omnes res mobiles, et omnia catalla, quæ fuerunt ipsius usurarii mortui, ad usus domini regis capientur, penes quemcunq; inveniantur res illæ. Hæres quoq; ipsius, hac eadem de causa exhæredatur secundum jus regni; et ad dominum, vel dominos revertetur hæreditas. Sciendum tamen, quod si quis aliquo tempore usurarius fuerit in vita sua, et super hoc in patria publice desamatus, si tamen à delicto ipso ante mortem suam destiterit, et pœnitentiam egerit; post mortem ipsius, ille, vel res ejus lege usurarii minime censebuntur. Oportet ergo constare quòd usurarius decesserit aliquis ad hoc, ut de eo tanquam de usurario post mortem ipsius judicetur, et de rebus ipsius, tanquam de rebus usurarii disponatur.

Vide lestatute de Merton, cap. 5. *et Fleta, lib.* 2. *ca.* 50. [f] *Manifestus usurarius est intestabilis.*

[g] *Et inter les constitutions ordeins p. les viels royes Alfred, &c. ordeine fuit que les chattels des usurers fuissent al roy, et que les heritages des usurers remeissent escheats al seigniors des fees, et ne sert' interre in sanctuary.*

[h] *Item, atrox injuria est, quæ omnium mobilium amissionem confert et legem liberam aufert, quæ locum habet in usurariis Christianis.*

[i] *Ad* 16 *Artic. de usuris respondetur: quod licet episcopis pro peccato illo penitentiam usurario injungere salutarem. Sed quia committendo usuram, usurarius furtum committit, et super hoc est convictus, catalla et tre' usurarii, sicut catalla furis, sunt regis, et si qui-sequi voluerint contra hujusmodi usurarium, restituantur eis bona sua, quæ ipsi usurarii per usuram extorserunt.*

Merton cap. 5. [f] Fleta, lib 2. cap. 50. [g] Mirror, cap. 1. § 3. & cap. 5. §. 1. Parl. 50 E. 3. nu. 58. [h] Fleta, lib. 2. c. 1. [i] Rot. Parliam. 51 H. 3. Petitiones cleri.

[k] And it appeareth by Bracton, that it was an article of the charge of inquiry by justices in eire *de usurariis Christianis mortuis, qui fuerunt, et quæ catalla habuerunt, et quis ea habuerit. Et quòd nullus recipiet usuram arte vel ingenio.* And divers were indicted for taking of usury before justices in eire, and some were pardoned by the king, and others not.

In ancient time a great revenue by reason of the usury of the Jewes came to the crown: for between the 50 year of H. 3. and the 2 yeare of E. 1. which was not above seven yeares compleat, there was paid into the kings coffers four hundred and twenty thousand pounds of and for the usury of the Jews. And yet that excellent king for divers weighty reasons worthy to be written in letters of gold, did by authority of parliament utterly prohibit the same, in these words. Forasmuch as the king hath perceived that many evils and disherisons of the good men of his land had come to passe by the usuries which the Jews have done in times past, and that many sins and offences have risen thereupon: albeit he and his auncesters have had great profit thereby of the Jews; notwithstanding for the honour of God, and for the common profit of his people, the king hath ordained, and established, that no Jew shall take usury, &c. Before this time Jews were divers times banished this realm, but still they returned again. But this wise and worthy king by authority of parliament banishing their usury, put the Jews into perpetuall exile into forain countries, where usury was tolerated. By which act it appeareth that the suppression of usury tendeth to the honour of God, and the common profit of the people.

[k] Bract. lib. 3. fo. 116, 117. Fleta, lib. 2. ca. 1. Cap. itineris. vet. Mag. Cart. par. 1. fo. 151. Rot. pat. 3 E. 1. m. 10. 19, 20, 21, 22. 36 Rot. claus. 2 E. 1. m. 1. [l] Rot. pat. 3 E. 1. nu. 14. 17. 26. Willielm. Middleton reddit compotum.

[152]

Vet. Mag. Cart. 2. part, fo. 58. 59. Stat. de Judaismo. See the 2. part of the Institutes, stat. de Judaismo and the Exposition upon the same.

By which authorities and records, and by many others that might be remembred, it appeareth that by the ancient laws of this realm usury was unlawfull, and punishable, although the punishment

ment was not always one, but fometime greater, and fometime leffer: and therefore at the parliament holden in the fifteenth year
15 E. 3. ca. 5. of E. 3. It was enacted, and declared, according as it had been fometime holden, that the king and his heirs fhould have conufance of ufurers after their death, and that the ordinary of holy church fhould have conufance of ufurers alive, for as much as to them it appertains, to compell them by the cenfures of holy church, for the fin, to make reftitution of ufuries taken againft the law of holy church. But this ftatute was afterward repealed, as hereafter fhall appear.

Hil. 6 E. 3. Coram rege rot. 130. Norff. Vide 26 E. 3. fo. 71. Moignes cafe.

Johannes Hopd convictus per juratores pro ufura capiend' 11 *s.* 8 *d. pro* 20 *s. præftand', et fic de fimilibus.*

Many of the citizens of London giving over trade and traffick (which is the life of the common-wealth, and fpecially of an iland) and betaking themfelves to live upon ufury, Sir William Walworth being lord maior, by the advice of the aldermen his brethren, took fuch good and ftrict order for the execution of laws, and for fuppreffion of ufury within the city of London, as the commons in parliament put up a petition to the king in thefe words, [That the order that was made in London againft the horrible vice of ufury, might be obferved throughout the whole realm] whereunto the king anfwered; that the old law fhould continue.

Rot. Parl. 50 E. 3. nu. 158. Vide Rot. Parl. 6 R. 2. nu. 57. 14 R. 2. nu. 24.

After this Sir John Northampton, maior of the city of London, by the advice of the aldermen his brethren, took more ftrict order for the fuppreffion of unlawfull ufury within the city of London: which had fo good fucceffe, as the commons in parliament petitioned the king in thefe words. The commons pray, that againft the horrible vice of ufury (then tearmed fchefes) and practifed as well by the clergy as laity, the order made by John Northampton late maior of London, may be executed through the realm. Whereunto the king anfwered, The king willeth thofe ordinances to be viewed, and if they be found to be neceffary, that the fame be then affirmed. And here it is to be obferved, that of ancient time the notable merchants of London detefted ufury, and dry exchange.

Rot. Parl. 14 R. 2. nu. 14.

3 H. 7. ca. 5, 6. 11 H. 7. ca. 8. Vide 5 E. 6. c. 20.

By the ftatutes of 3 H. 7. and 11 H. 7. all ufury is damned and prohibited, and there it is called dry exchange. So as ufury is not only againft the law of God, and the laws of the realm, but againft the law of nature: *Ufura contra naturam eft, quia ufura fua natura eft fterilis, nec fructum habet.*

37 H. 8. ca. 9. 13 Eliz. ca. 8. 21 Jac. ca. 17.

But now by the ftatutes of 37 H. 8. and 13 Eliz. all former acts, ftatutes, and laws ordained and made, for the avoiding or punifhment of ufury are made void, and of none effect. So as at this day, neither the common law, nor any ftatute is in force, but only the ftatutes of 37 H. 8. 13 Eliz. and 21 Jac. And the ecclefiafticall jurifdiction is faved by the faid ftatute of 13 Eliz. as thereby it appeareth. For the expofition of which ftatutes of 37 H. 8. and 13 El. fee in my Reports, viz. lib. 3. fo. 80, 81. lib. 5. fo. 69, 70. lib. 9. 26.

CAP.

CAP. LXXI.

Of Simony and corrupt Presentations.

SIMONY. *Simonia est vox ecclesiastica, à Simone illo Mago deducta, qui donum Spiritus sancti pecuniis emi putavit.*

Against simony, &c. the statute of 31 Eliz. is made in these words.

Simony described by the act following.

Stat. de 31 Eliz. cap. 6.

See the 2. part of the Inst. in the exposition of the said act of 31 El. *Injustum est illa vendere quæ gratis distribui debent.* vide Matth. ca. 10. ver. 8.

Be it enacted that if any person or persons, bodies politique or corporate, shall or doe for any summ of mony, reward, gift, profit or benefit, directly, or indirectly, or for, or by reason of any promise, agreement, grant, bond, covenant, or other assurance, of or for any summ of money, reward, gift, profit or benefit whatsoever, directly, or indirectly, present, or collate (1) any person to any benefice with cure of soules, dignity, prebend, or living ecclesiasticall; or give, or bestow the same for, or in respect of any such cause or consideration: * That then every such presentment, collation, gift, and bestowing, and every admission, institution, investiture, and induction thereupon shall bee utterly voyde, frustrate, and of none effect (2) in law; and that it shall, and may be lawfull to and for the queenes majestie, her heires and successors, to present, collate unto, or give, or bestow every such benefice, dignity, prebend and living ecclesiasticall for that one time, or turne onely, and that all and every person and persons, bodies politique and corporate, that shall give or take any such summ of mony, reward, &c. shall forfeit and lose the double value of one yeares profit (3) of every such benefice, dignity, prebend and living ecclesiasticall. And the person so corruptly taking, procuring, seeking, or accepting any such benefice, dignity, prebend, or living, shall thereupon, and from thenceforth be adjudged a disabled person in law (4) to have, or enjoy the same benefice, dignity, prebend, or living ecclesiasticall.

* Nota, the statute doth not make the bond, promise, covenant, or other assurance void, but the presentment, &c. and so it was adjudged, Pasch. 40 Eliz. Rot. 1745, in communi banco, between Gregory plaintif and Oldbury defendant. Nota differentiam inter malum in se against the common law, et malum prohibitum by statute law; et malum in se against the common law, and malum prohibitum by the civill or canon law; whereof the judges of the common law in these cases take no notice.

This is the text of this part of the act, now let us proceed to the exposition hereof, being a necessary law to be put in execution.

(1) *Present or collate.*] This is not onely intended, where the person presenting or collating hath right to present, or collate; but also where any person or persons, bodies politique and corporate, doe usurp, and have no title to present or collate. And so it was adjudged in case where the usurpation was to a church of the king.

Mic. 13. Ja. in quare impeditit betweene the

 Sed

king and the b. of Norwich. Tho. Cole and Robert Secker, which began Pasch. 13 Jac. Rot. 21. for the vicarage of Haverell in Suffolk.

Sed quando præsentatio et jus patronatus sunt temporalia, quæritur quomodo sit simonia per donum pecuniæ pro illis: respondendum est quod jus patronatus et presentatio dicuntur spiritualia, respectu rei, ad quam præsentatur, quæ spiritualis est. Vide Linwood cap. de Jurejurando, fo. 80.

(2) *Shall be utterly voide and of none effect.*] But here is to be observed a diversity between a presentation, or collation made by a rightfull patron, and an usurper. For in case of a rightfull patron, which doth corruptly present, or collate, by the expresse letter of this act the king shall present: but where one doth usurp, and corruptly present or collate, there the king shall not present, [154] but the rightfull patron: for the branch that gives the king power to present, is onely intended, where the rightfull patron is in fault, but where the rightfull patron is in no fault, there the corrupt act, and wrong of the usurper maketh the benefice, &c. voide, but taketh not away the lawfull title to present from the rightfull patron, and so it was adjudged in the case abovesaid.

Mich. 13 Jac. ubi supra.

Also upon these words, [If any patron without the notice of the person so presented, or collated, doth take reward, &c.] yet by the expresse letter of this branch the church, &c. is voide, for both the letter and intention of this act is to make the admission, institution, and induction of any presentee, that commeth in by a corrupt patron voide. And so was it resolved in the case abovesaid, as it hath been formerly adjudged in the common place. But where the presentee is not privy, nor consenting to any such corrupt contract, as is prohibited by this act, because it is no simony in him, there the presentee shall not be adjudged a disabled person within this act: for the words of that branch be, And the person so corruptly giving, &c. so as he shall not be disabled, unlesse he be privy to the corrupt contract: and upon the severall penning of these several branches, the diversity abovesaid was resolved Mich. 13 Jac. *ubi supra.*

Mich. 41 & 42 El. in Communi banco between Baker and Rogers.

24 E. 3. fo. 35. 38 E. 3. 3. 7 Eliz. Dier 257.

(3) *Shall forfeit and lose the double value of one yeares profit.*] This double value shall be accounted according to the very, or true value, as the same may be letten, and shall be tryed by a jury, and not according to the extent, or taxation of the church: whereof one was made both of the spiritualties and temporalties in 20 E. 1. 1292. in the time of pope Nicholas: of that *vide* 11 H. 4. fo. 35. F. N. B. 176. and Polichron, lib. 7. cap. 38. Rot. Parl. 18 E. 3. nu. 44. sta. 2. 1 R. 2. nu. 102. 8 H. 6. nu. 15. And the other taxation was made in 26 H. 8.

(4) *Be adjudged a disabled person in law.*] It was resolved in the case of Mich. 13 Jac. *ubi supra*, that the king could not dispense with this disability by a *non obstante*: for when an act of parliament is made that disableth any person, or maketh any thing void, or tortious for the good of the church, or common-wealth, in this law all the kings subjects have an interest, and therefore the king cannot dispence therewith no more then with the common law: but where a statute prohibiteth any thing upon a penalty, and giveth the penalty to the king, or to the king and informer, there the king may dispense with the penalty, and this diversity is warranted by our books.

5 E. 3. 29. 11 H. 4. 76. 2 H. 7. 6 11 H. 7. 11. 13 H. 7. 8. b. 27 H. 8. F. N. B. 211. b. Placita com. 502.

King

* King James referred this case unto Sir Thomas Egerton lord chancellor of England, and to the chiefe justice of the kings bench. Sir Robert Vernon being coferer of the kings house, by reason of which office, he hath the receipt and payment of 40,000 li. of the kings treasure yearely, and payeth the wages beneath the stayres, &c. did bargaine and sell the said office for a great summ of money, and for certaine annuities to be paid, to Sir Arthur Ingram knight. The first question was whether the said office were void by force of the statute of 5 E. 6. ca 16. The second was, seeing the words of this act be [shall be adjudged a disabled person in law, to all intents and purposes to have and occupy any such office, &c.] whether the king might dispense with that [disabled] and upon mature deliberation and hearing of counsell learned, they resolved, and so certified the king, that the said office was void by the said bargaine and sale, and that the king could not dispense with the said disability, for the reason and cause above said; and thereupon Sir Marmaduke Darrell was preferred to that office. * Anno 12 Jac. regis Sir Arthur Ingrams case upon the statute of 5 E. 6. cap. 16.

Likewise by the statute of 5 Eliz. every person which shall be elected a knight, citizen, burges, or baron of the cinque ports for any parliament, before he shall enter into the parliament house, shall take the oath of supremacy appointed by the act of 1 Eliz. and that he that entreth into the parliament without taking the said oath, shall be deemed no knight, citizen, burges, or baron, nor shall have any voice, but shall be, as if he had been never returned, or elected. Here be words that amount to a disability, and therefore that according to the former resolutions the king cannot dispense with the same. 5 Eliz. cap. 1.

It is further enacted, that if any person shall for any sum of money, reward, &c. *(ut supra)* other then for usuall fees, admit, institute, install, induct, invest, or place any person in or to any benefice with cure of souls, dignity, prebend, or other living ecclesiasticall: that then every person so offending shall forfeit and lose double value, *ut supra*; and that thereupon immediately from and after the investing, installation, or induction thereof had, the same benefice, &c. shall be eftsoons meerely void, &c. [155]

The reason of this clause (for I was of this parliament, and observed the proceedings therein) was to avoid hasty and precipitate admissions, institutions, &c. to the prejudice of them that had right to present, by putting them to a *quare impedit*, and no such hast or precipitation is used, but for reward, &c. as it is to be presumed.

There be two great enemies to justice and right, viz. *praecipitatio, et morosa cunctatio.*

And albeit the church is full by the institution, &c. against all, but the king, yet the church becommeth not void by this branch of this act, untill after induction.

And that the patron, &c. shall and may present, &c.] This is intended of the rightfull patron, or of him that hath right to present.

Vid. 14 H. 4. 19.

And be it further enacted, that if any incumbent of any benefice with cure of soules shall corruptly resigne, or exchange the same, or corruptly take for or in respect of the resigning or exchanging of the same, directly or indirectly, any pension, sum of mony, or benefit whatsoever: That then as well the giver as the taker, &c. shall lose double the value of the money so given, and double the value of one years profit.

By another branch of this act it is provided,

That if any person or persons shall or doe receive, or take any money, reward, &c. *ut supra*, (ordinary and lawfull fees only excepted) for or to procure the ordaining or making of any minister, or giving any orders, or licence to preach, shall for every offence forfeit and lose the summe of forty pound, and the party so corruptly made minister, shall forfeit and lose the sum of ten pound, and if at any time within seven years after such corrupt entring into the ministry, he shall accept or take any benefice, living, or promotion ecclesiasticall, that then immediately, from and after the induction, investing, or installation thereof, or thereunto had, the same benefice, living, and promotion ecclesiasticall shall be estsoons meerly void, &c.

33 E. 1. tit. Annuity 51. Vid. Canon 40. 1 Jacobi 1603. the oath against simony, &c. * 9 E. 3. 22. 10 E. 3. 1. 29 E. 3. 44. Regist. 58. 21 H. 8 ca. 13. vers. finem.

Take a benefice.] This word *beneficium ecclesiasticum* extendeth not only to benefices of churches parochiall; but to dignities and other ecclesiasticall promotions; as to deaneries, archdeaconries, prebends, &c. And it appeareth in our * books that deaneries, archdeaconries, prebends, &c. are benefices with cure of souls; but they are not comprehended under the name of benefices with cure of souls within the statute of 21 H. 8. by reason of a speciall proviso; which they had been, if no such proviso had been added, viz. deans, archdeacons, chancellours, treasurers, chanters, prebend, or a parson where there is a vicar indowed.

[156]

If any person or persons, bodies politique or corporate, which have election, nomination, voice, or assent in the choice, election, presentation, or nomination of any scholar, fellow or any other person to have room, or place in any church collegiat or cathedrall, colleges, schools, hospitals, halls, or societies, shall take or receive any money, fee, or reward, &c. the place, room, office, &c. of the offender shall be void, &c.

Like cases in Pl. com. 176. upon the statute of 32 H. 8. of Cond. Dier, 20 Eliz. upon the statute of 27 H. 8. Of Uses.

Which have election, presentation, &c.] This act being a law perpetuall, these words extend not only to such person and persons, &c. as at that time had election, presentation, &c. but to all and every person and persons, that at any time hereafter should have election, presentation, &c. otherwise the law should be but temporary, which should be directly against the meaning of the makers of the act. And by the same reason this act extendeth not only to churches,

churches, colledges, ſchools, hoſpitals, hals, and ſocieties founded at the time of the making of the act, but to all ſuch as ſhould be erected or founded after.

And if any fellow, officer, or ſcholar in any of the churches, colleges, &c. *ut ſupra*, contract or agree for any money, reward, &c. for the leaving, or reſigning up of the ſame his room or place to any other, &c. ſhall forfeit and loſe double the ſum of money, &c. ſo received, and every perſon by whom or for whom any money, &c. ſhall be given, &c. ſhall be incapable of that place or room for that time or turn, &c. And it is further enacted, that at the time of every ſuch election, preſentation or nomination, as well this preſent act, as the orders, and ſtatutes of the ſame places concerning ſuch election, preſentation or nomination ſhall then and there be publiquely read, upon pain to forfeit and loſe the ſum of forty pound, &c. whereof, the one moiety to him that will ſue, and the other moiety to the church, colledge, &c.

I have read ancient verſes concerning ſimony, and other corrupt entries into churches, which are not unneceſſary, in deteſtation of them, to remember.

Quatuor eccleſias portis intratur in omnes,
Cæſaris et ſimonis, ſanguinis, atque Dei.
Prima patet magnis, nummo patet altera, charis
Tertia, ſed paucis quarta patere ſolet.

Four doors hath every church, and all but one forebod,
(Whereof unſeen ſome may be peradventure)
Of Ceſar, ſimonie, of kindred, and of God:
And each church man by one of theſe doth enter.
Great mens command doth open wide the firſt,
At next by money enter many one,
The third to weak allies, but (for the church the worſt),
Gods dore doth open to a few or none,

To conclude this chapter with this, that ſimony is odious in the eye of the common law: for a garden in ſocage of a mannor, whereunto an advowſon is appendant, ſhall not preſent to the church, becauſe he can take nothing for the preſentation, for the which he may account to the heir; and therefore the heir in that caſe ſhall preſent of what age ſoever. And if an heir of tenant *in capite*, hath livery *cum exitubus*, yet ſhall the heir not preſent to an advowſon, becauſe no iſſues or profit can be taken thereof.

7 E. 3. 39. a. 27 E. 3. 89. 29 E. 3. Preſent. al eglise. Fitz. 17. 8 E. 2. Preſent. 10. Fitz. N B. 33. S. 24 E. 3. 29.

* *Latro eſt qui aurum ex religione ſectatur.*

* *Jerome.*

And the common law would have the patron ſo far from ſimony, as it denied him to recover damages in a *quare impedit*, or aſſiſe of *darrein preſentment*, before the ſtatute of W. 2. cap. 5.

3 H. 6. tit. Damages. 17 adjudge. See the 2. pt. of the Inſtit. W. 2. ca. 5. Lib. 6. 10. 50. & 51. Lib. 5. 58, 59. Speccot.

[a] Simony is the more odious, becauſe it is ever accompanied with perjury, for the preſentee, &c. is ſworn to commit no ſimony.

[a] Vid. Linwood ubi ſupra.

CAP. LXXII.

Of Monomachia, Single Combate, Duell, Affrays, and Challenges, and of Private Revenge.

THIS single combat between any of the kings subjects, of their own heads, and for private malice, or displeasure is prohibited by the laws of this realm: for in a setled state governed by law, no man for any injury whatsoever, ought to use private revenge; for revenge belongeth to the magistrate, who is Gods lieutenant. And the law herein is grounded upon the law of God. *Vindicta est mihi, et ego retribuam, dicit Dominus.* Vengeance is mine, and I will repay it, saith the Lord. *Qui vindicari vult, inveniet vindictam à domino, et peccata illius servans servabit.* He that will revenge, shall finde vengeance from the lord, and he will surely keep his sins in remembrance.

Deut. 32. 35. Rom. 12. 19. Ecclesiasticus 28. 1. Gen. 34. ver. 25. & 30. of Simeon and Levi.

It is also against the law of nature and of nations, for a man to be judge in his own proper cause, *judex in propria causa*, especially *in duello*, where fury, wrath, malice, and revenge are the rulers of the judgement. See more of private revenge, cap. Misprision, in [*crimen commissionis.*]

Object. But it is objected, that this single combat may be undertaken for revenge, and preservation of the honour of the party grieved.

Respons. 1. The honour or estimation of the party may more justly and notoriously be revenged, and repaired by the magistrate in publique, then by the party in private. 2. There is nothing honourable, that is against the laws of his country, and the law of nature and nations. 3. Whatsoever is against the law of God is impious and dishonourable. 4. The eminent danger of the parties seeking private revenge. First, concerning the soules of both of them, as well of him that killeth (who is *vir sanguinis*) as of him that is slain, and dieth in his malice: and as to the world, he that slayeth is in worse case, then he that is slain. For the murderer loseth not only his lands and goods, but his life also and his honour, which he so much respected: for by his attainder his blood shall be corrupted, and if he were noble, or gentle before, he thereby becomes ignoble and base, and he that is slain by law loseth none of them: so as hereof it is truly said, *Infælix pugna, ubi majus periculum incumbit victori, quàm victo.* 5. Not only the soul of man, but the body also, was originally made to the image of God, *Quicunque effuderit humanum sanguinem, fundetur sanguis illius, ad imaginem quippe Die factus est homo.* Who so sheddeth mans blood, by man shall his blood be shed, for in the image of God made he man. *Solus Deus, qui vitam dat, vitæ est dominus; nec potest quisquam eam juste auferre nisi Deus, vel gerens authoritatem Dei, ut judex.* And this was the reason, that amongst Christians it was not lawfull for the lord to kill his villain.

Gen. 9. 6.

In ancient time so much the law did respect honour, and order, as hear what Britton saith, *Si trespas soit fait en temps de peace a chivaliers, ou a auters gents honorables per ribaudes ou auters viles persons, si le ferue soit per felony, &c. sauns desert del chivalier, que le ribaude perdra son poigne dount il trespassa.* Brit. c. 25. f. 49. b.

And many ordinances, laws, and acts of parliament, which doe prohibit the pardon of wilfull murder, are also grounded upon the law of God, to the end none should offend in hope of pardon. * *Non accipies precium ab eo qui reus est sanguinis, statim enim et ipse moritur. Ne polluatis terram habitationis vestræ, quæ cruore maculatur; nec aliter expiari potest, nisi per ejus sanguinem, qui alterius sanguinem effuderit.* Ye shall take no satisfaction for the life of a murtherer, which is guilty of death, but he shall be surely put to death: so ye shall not pollute the land wherein you are, for bloud defileth the land, and the land cannot be cleansed of the bloud that is shed therein, but by the bloud of him, that shed it. Glouc. 6 E. 1. c. 9. 2 E. 3. ca. 2. 4 E. 3. ca. 13. 14 E. 3. cap. 15. 13 R. 2. St. 2. c. 1. Read these stat. [158] * Num. 35. 31. 33. See before in chapter of murder.

And this law is confirmed by Christ himself in the Gospel, and by the last book of holy scripture. *Omnes qui acceperint gladium gladio peribunt. Qui in gladio occiderit, oportet eum gladio occidi.* Mat. 26. 52. Apocal. 13. 10.

But albeit upon the single combate no death ensue nor blood drawn, yet the very combate for revenge is an affray, and a great breach of the kings peace, an affright and terrour to the kings subjects, and is to be punished by fine and imprisonment, and to find sureties for their good behaviour; for it is *vi et armis, et contra pacem domini regis, &c.* and in respect of incrochment upon royall authority for revenge, it is *contra coronam et dignitatem.* Affray. Trin. 10 E. 3. Coram rege, Rot. 87. Northt.

An affray is a publique offence to the terrour of the kings subjects, and is an English word, and so called, because it affrighteth and maketh men afraid, and is enquirable in a leet as a common nusans. See the statute of 2 E. 3. c. 3. where it is; *(en effraier de la pais,)* and the writ grounded upon that statute saith, *In quorundam de populo terrorem,* as it appeareth in F. N. B. fo. 249. f. and the Register agreeth with the originall, and therefore the printed book *(en affray de la peace)* must be amended. 4 H. 6. fo. 10. 8 E. 4. fo. 5.

And if any subject by word, writing, or message challenge another to fight with him, this is also an offence before any combate be performed, and punishable by law, and it is *contra pacem, coronam, et dignitatem.* For *quando aliquid prohibetur, prohibetur et omne, per quod devenitur ad illud.* *Regula.* Or such offenders may be punished in the star-chamber, whereof there be many presidents. Now when an affray is made by single combat, any stander by, that is no officer, may endeavour to part them, and prevent further danger, and the law doth incourage them hereunto; for if they receive any harm by the affrayours, they shall have their remedy by law against them, and if the affrayours receive hurt by the endeavouring only to part them, the standers by may justifie the same, and the affrayours have no remedy by law. But if either of the parties be slain, or wounded, or so stricken, as he falleth down for dead, in that case the standers by ought to apprehend the party so slaying, wounding, or striking, or to endeavour the same by hue and cry, or else for his escape they shall be fined and imprisoned. But if the sherif, justice of peace, constable, or other conservatour of the peace doe not part the affrayers for the preservation of the kings peace, and apprehend them being within his view, or doe not his uttermost 8 E. 2. cor. 295. 22 Ass. pl. 56.

endeavour

endeavour to part and apprehend them, they may be fined and imprisoned for their neglect thereof, for they may command others to assist them, and therefore the rule holdeth in them, *idem est facere, et nolle prohibere cum possis: et qui non prohibet, cum prohibere possit, in culpa est.* And if any be commanded to assist them therein, and refuse or neglect the same, it is a contempt in them to be punished by fine and imprisonment.

3 H. 7. 10 b. Bedingfields case.

There is a *duellum* allowed by law depending a suit for the triall of truth, whereof we have spoken in another place, and as here it appeareth, there is a *duellum* against law: of both these an ancient authour saith thus, and first of the lawfull: *Duellum est singularis pugna inter duos ad probandum veritatem litis, et qui vicerit probasse intelligitur, et quamvis judicium Dei expectetur ibidem, quicunque tamen monomachiam,* i. e. *singularem pugnam sponte susceperit vel optulerit, homicida est, et contrahit mortale peccatum. Et eodem modo judex qui authoritate desert, vel præstat, omnesque accessores, et consulentes, faventes et auxiliantes, nec non et sacerdos qui dat benedictionem.*

Fleta, li. 1. c. 32. §. Duellum. 2. pt. of the Instit. W. 1. c. 40. Fleta ubi supra.

In a writ of right, if the tenant wage battail by his champion, and if the champion after become blind by infirmity, and not *ex stultitia,* he shall be discharged of the battail. And if a man be appealed of felony, and gage battaile, and after become blind, *ut supra,* he shall be discharged of the battail, because he becommeth so by the act of God. And if the appellant after battail waged become blinde upon any occasion, the appellee *in favorem vitæ* shall goe quit. When issue is joyned to be tried by battail, and the triall by battail is become impossible by the act of God, or by the default of the appellant, the appellee goeth free.

11 H. 3. tit. Droit. Fitz. 57.

[159]

And this kind of battail, in case of appeals and writ of right, is by publique authority and course of law, whereunto all the people by an implied consent are parties; and (as some hold) hath his warrant by the word of God by the single battail between David and Goliah, which was strucken by publique authority.

1 Regum, c. 17. ver. 4. 5, &c.

King E. 3. in the sixteenth year of his reign, having war with the French king for his right to the kingdome of France, out of the greatnesse of his minde, for love of his subjects, the saving of christian bloud, and a speedy tryall of the right, offered the single combate with the French king, but he refused it.

Afterwards also, after long and chargeable wars between the crowns of England and France, for the right of the kingdome of France, it was an honourable offer which king R. 2. made to Charles the French king for saving of Christians guiltlesse bloud, and to put an end to that bloudy and lingring war, which we will rehearse in the very words of the record it self.

[a] Rot. Franciæ 7 R. 2. m. 24. The offer of R. 2. to king Charles of France. 1. A single combat between the two kings. 2. Or a combat between the two kings and three of their uncles on either side. 3. Or that a fit day and place might be assigned when under the universall conflict of both their armies, an end might be put to the war.

[a] *Rex dedit potem. Johanni duci Lancast' avunculo suo de certis requestis seu oblationibus Carolo regi Franc' faciend', viz. quod negotium bellicum inter prædictos reges finiatur.* 1. *Per certamen personarum suarum.* 2. *Vel aliter inter personas suas cum tribus patruis ipsorum ipsis utrinque adjunctis.* 3. *Aut alioquin quod dies congruus assignaretur et locus, quibus sub universali certamine potentiarum suarum finis bello imponi valeat.* The duke of Lanc' according to his commission made these offers from the king of England to king Charles of France, but he was *auditus, sed non exauditus;* for king Charles liked none of these offers.

And

[b] And in *anno Domini* 1196. *anno regni Ricardi primi octavo*, Philip king of France ſent this challenge to Richard the firſt, that king R. would chooſe five for his part and he the king of France would appoint five for his part, which might fight in liſts for triall of all matters in controverſie between them for the avoiding of ſhedding of more guiltleſſe bloud. King Richard accepted the offer, with condition that either king might be of the number, but this condition would not be granted. [b] N. Trivet.

[c] Theſe, and the like offers, as they proceeded from high courage and greatnes of mind, ſo had they been lawfull, if they had been warranted by publique authority. [c] See the 2. part of the Inſtitutes W. 1. ca. 20.

CAP. LXXIII.

Againſt going or riding armed. [160]

Item, IT is enacted, that no man, great or ſmall, of what condition ſoever he be, (except the kings ſervants in his preſence and his miniſters in executing *des mandements le roy*, or of their office, and ſuch as be in their company aſſiſting them, and alſo upon a cry made for armes to keep the peace, and the ſame in ſuch places where ſuch things happen) be ſo hardy to come before the kings juſtices, or other the kings miniſters doing their office, with force and armes, nor bring force in affray of the people, nor to goe nor ride armed by night nor by day, &c. before the kings juſtices, or in any place whatſoever, upon paine to forfeit their armor to the king, and their bodies to priſon at the kings pleaſure, and to make fine, and ranſome to the king, &c.

2 E. 3. cap. 3. Paſch. 18 E. 3. Coram rege. Rot. 146. Midd. 8 R. 2. cap. 13. the printed book is 7. but it ought to be 8. and ſo recited in 20 R. 2. ca. 1. Lib. 5. fo. 72. St. Johns caſe.

20 R. 2. cap. 1.

Upon this ſtatute two things fall into conſideration. Firſt, what the common law was before the making of this ſtatute. Secondly, the true ſenſe and expoſition of this act. For it appeareth by a record in 29 E. 1. *quòd non liceat torneare, bordeare, juſtas facere, aventuras guerare, ſeu ad arma præſumere, ſine licentia regis.* See Britton, fo. 29. b. It was called *turneamentum decurſus*, of turning and winding, in reſpect of the agility, as well of the horſe, as of the man. For in thoſe daies this deed of chivalry was at randon, whereupon great perill enſued. Therefore in the reigne of E. 3. for ſafety the tilt was deviſed. See the ſtatute of 7 E. 2. *De defenſione portandi arma*, and the ſtatute of W. 1. cap. 9. & cap. 17. W. 2. cap. 39. and the expoſitions upon the ſame.

Paſch. 29 E. 1. coram rege. Rot. 101. Eſſex. Paſch. 18 E. 1. coram rege. Rot. 32. Glouc.

Vet. Mag. Cart. 2. part. fo. 40. b.

It is *lex et conſuetudo parliamenti*, that whereſoever the parliament is holden proclamation ſhould be made forbidding wearing of armor, and exerciſe of playes and games of men, women, or children, in or about the city, or place where the parliament is holden, leſt the proceedings in the high court of parliment *pro bono publico*, ſhould thereby be hindred or diſturbed.

Rot. Parl. 6 E. 3. nu. 2. & 3. 13 E. 3. nu. 2. 14 E. 3. nu. 2. 15 E. 3. nu. 2. 17 E. 3. nu. 2. 18 E. 3. nu. 2. 25 E. 3. nu. 50. Parl. 1 & 25 E. 3. Parl. 2. nu. 5.

If

a 11 H. 7. fo. 23. vide before cap. *Homicide.* Brook Coron 229. See 24 H. 8. cap. 13. Juſts, Turnies, Bariers, &c.

[a] If any by mutuall aſſent, do uſe juſts or turneaments, or to play at ſword and buckler, or any other deeds of armes, and the one killeth the other, this is felony, for that it is not lawfull to uſe them without the kings licence; which agreeth with the record abovefaid, of 29 E. 1.

b Paſch. 18 E. 3. Coram rege Rot. 145. Nota bene.

[b] *Willus Jordan inventus fuit vagans armatus de platis, attachiatus, &c. compertum eſt per juratores, quòd minatus fuit per quoſdam ignotos, et quòd pro ſalvatione vitæ ſuæ, platas prædictas oppoſuit ſuper corpus ſuum, tamen invenit ſecuritatem pro bono geſtu ſuo.*

c 25 E. 3. cap. 2.

[c] The clauſe of the ſtatute of 25 E. 3. concerning this matter, we have reſerved to this place, viz.

d See before cap. *High treaſon.* verb. *Ou ſi home levy guerre.* fo. 9.

[d] And if per caſe any man of this realm ride armed covertly or ſecretly, with men of arms, againſt any other to ſlay him, or rob him, or to take and keepe him, till he hath made fine or ranſome, it ſhall not be adjudged treaſon, but it ſhall be judged felony or treſpaſſe, according to the lawes of the realme of old time uſed, and according, as the caſe requires. And if in ſuch caſe, or other like, before this time any juſtices have judged treaſon, and for this cauſe the lands and tenements have come into the kings hands as forfeit, the chiefe lords of the fee ſhall have the eſcheats of the tenements holden of them, whether that the ſame tenements be in the kings hands, or in others, [161] by gift, or in other manner. Saving alwayes to our lord the king, the yeare, and the waſt, and the forfeitures of chattels, which pertain to him in the caſes above-named. And that writs of *ſcire facias* be granted in ſuch caſe againſt the land tenants without other originall, and without allowing any protection in the ſaid ſuit. And that of the lands which be in the kings hands, writs be granted to the ſherifs of the counties, where the lands be, to deliver them out of the kings hands without delay.

Vide cap. High treaſon, verb. *Fait compaſſer,* fo. 6.

Concerning the point of felony, it muſt be obſerved, that at the making of that ſtatute, and by the lawes of the realme of old time uſed in ſuch caſe, when any purpoſed to ſlay, and declare it by ſuch overt act, *voluntas reputabatur pro facto,* as hath been ſaid before; and ſo is this branch concerning that point to be underſtood.

Scire fac.

Note for reſtitution. See hereafter cap. Reſtitution.

And that writs of ſcire fac. be granted.] Here it may appeare what ſpeedy remedy by *ſcire fac.* the makers of this law gave for reſtitution to be made, where any of the juſtices had in any of the caſes mentioned in this branch judged it treaſon, which is declared by this law to be againſt law.

Now let us peruſe the words of the ſaid act of 2 E. 3.

W. 1. ca. 9. & 17. W. 2. cap. 39. 18 E. 2. execution, 251. 19 E. 2. ibid. 247. 3 H. 7. fo. 1 et 10. b. 14 H. 7. 8. Lib. 5. fo. 91. Semaynes caſe.

His miniſters in executing.] By the order of the common law and ſtatutes of the realme, the ſherif, or other miniſter of the king in execution of the kings writs, or proces of law, might after reſiſtance take *poſſe comitatus.* For, *ſequi debet potentia legem et not antecedere.*

Des mandements le roy.] That is, of the kings writs, and proces of law, *ſecundum legem et conſuetudinem Angliæ.* Though in this act there

there be three ſpeciall exceptions, yet the law doth make another exception, and that is, to aſſemble force to defend his houſe, as hereafter ſhall be ſaid.

To come before the kings juſtices, or other the kings miniſters doing their office, with force and armes.] Bracton doth notably write of the diverſity of forces, viz. that there is *vis expulſiva, perturbativa, inquietiva, ablativa, compulſiva, &c.* which you may read in him. And then (which is pertinent to our purpoſe) he ſaith: *Eſt etiam vis armata, (armis dejectum dico qualitercunque fuerit vis armata) non ſolum ſi quis venerit cum telis, verum etiam omnes illos dicimus armatos, qui habent cum quo nocere poſſunt. Telorum autem appellatione omnia, in quibus ſinguli homines nocere poſſunt, accipiuntur: ſed ſi quis venerit ſine armis, et ipſa concertatione ligna ſumpſerit, fuſtes, et lapides, talis dicetur vis armata; ſi quis autem venerit cum armis, armis tamen ad dejiciendum non uſus fuerit, et dejecerit, vis armata dicitur eſſe facta; ſufficit enim terror armorum ut videatur armis dejeciſſe.* Agreeing with that of the poet, Bracton, lib. 4. fo. 162.

Jamque faces et ſaxa volant, furor arma miniſtrat. Virgil.

Britton ſaith, *Nous volons, que touts gents pluis uſent judgement, que force.* Britton, 116. a.

Nor to bring force in affray of the (paiis, i.) country.] This act is notably expounded by the writ in the Regiſter, and F. N. B. for by that writ it appeareth, that if any doth enter into, or detaine with force any houſes, lands, or tenements, the party grieved may have a writ upon this ſtatute, directed to the ſherif, by force of which writ, if the ſherif find the force, then if any after proclamation made, (which proclamation is by reaſonable conſtruction to be made for avoiding of bloodſhed) ſhall diſobey, or if it be found by inquiſition, the ſherif is to ſeize their armes and weapons, and to arreſt and take the offenders and commit them to priſon, &c. But note the ſherif cannot reſtore the party grieved upon this writ to his poſſeſſion, [a] no more then he can upon the writ *de vi laica, removenda,* but reſtitution muſt be made by force of the ſtatutes of 8 H. 6. and 21 Jac. [b] And yet in ſome caſe a man may not onely uſe force and armes, but aſſemble company alſo. As any may aſſemble his friends and neighbours, to keep his houſe againſt thoſe that come to rob, or kill him, or to offer him violence in it, and is by conſtruction excepted out of this act: and the ſherif, &c. ought not to deal with him upon this act; for a mans houſe is his caſtle, *et domus ſua cuique eſt tutiſſimum refugium*; for where ſhall a man be ſafe, if it be not in his houſe? and in this ſenſe it is truly ſaid,

See the chapter next before. verb. *Affraye.* Regiſtrum. F. N. B. 249. f. Nota. Vide lib. 5. fo. 9. Semayes caſe F. N. B. 54. [a] 8 H. 6. cap. 9. 21 Jac. cap. 25. [b] 3. E. 3. cor. 303. 305. 26 Aſſ. p. 22. 21 H. 7. 39. [162] 21 H. 7. 39. Lib. 5. fo. 91. b. Semaynes caſe.

Armaque in armatos ſumere jura ſinunt.

But he cannot aſſemble force, though he be extreamly threatned, to goe with him to church, or market, or any other place, but that is prohibited by this act.

Nor to goe armed by night, or by day, &c. before the kings juſtices in any place whatſoever.] Sir Thomas Figett knight went armed under his garments, as well in the palace, as before the juſtice of the kings bench: for both which upon complaint made, he was arreſted by ſir William Shardſhill chiefe juſtice of the kings bench, and being charged therewith, he ſaid that there had been debate between him and ſir John Trevet knight in the ſame week, at Pauls in 24 E. 3. fo. 33.

in London, who menaced him, &c. and therefore for doubt of danger, and safeguard of his life, he went so armed. Notwithstanding the court upon their view awarded, that the armes were forfeited, and thereupon the same were seised, and he commanded to ward in the Marshalsea during the kings pleasure. Sir Thomas prayed to find mainprise, which was denied, untill the pleasure of the king was known, because he was imprisoned during the kings pleasure, according to this statute.

24 E. 3. ubi. supra. Vide the 4. part of the Institutes, cap. *Lect.* 20 R. 2. cap. 1. Vid. indorsf. clauf. 2 E. 2. 19 22.

Upon paine to forfeit their armor, &c.] It appeareth before by the case of sir Thomas Figett, that the offender was to bee punished according to this act, but by forfeiture of the armor and imprisonment; but the statute of 20 R. 2. cap. 1. doth add fine, and imprisonment.

And that the kings justices, in their presence, &c.] So did sir William Shardishill, as is abovesaid.

And other ministers in their baliwickes, &c.] That is to say, sherifs, bailifs of liberties, &c.

Lords of franchises.] And their bailifs, maiors, and bailifs of cities, and borowes within the same cities and borowes, and borowholders, constables, and wardens of the peace within their wards shall have power to execute this act. And the justices assigned at their comming down shall inquire how such officers, and lords have exercised their offices in this case, and to punish them whom they find that have not done that which pertaineth to their office. See 12 R. 2. cap. 6.

Registrum. F. N. B. 249. f. 24 E. 3. fo. 33.

It is to be observed, that upon this statute by the resolution of the judges a writ was framed, and inserted into the Register, when any with force and armes enter any lands and tenements, or detaine the same with force and armes, directed to the sherif, reciting the force, and our act, (and saith) *Nos statutum prædictum inviolabiliter observari, et idem infringentes juxta vim et effectum ejusdem statuti castigare facere volentes et punire, tibi præcipimus, &c. publice proclamari facias, &c.* as in the writ. And here is a secret in law, that upon any statute made for the common peace, or good of the realm, a writ may be devised for the better execution of the same, according to the force and effect of the act.

Vide 36 E. 3. ca. 9. simile.

Note, proclamations are of great force, which are grounded upon the laws of the realme.

[163]

CAP. LXXIV.

Of Perjury and Subornation of Perjury, and incidently of Oaths.

5 El. ca. 9.

EVERY person which shall unlawfully and corruptly procure any witnesse to commit any wilfull, and corrupt perjury in any matter or cause depending in suit, and variance, by any writ, action, bill, complaint, or information in any of the kings courts of chancery, star-chamber, or in any of the

the queens majesties courts of record, or in any leet, view of frankpledge, ancient demesne court, hundred court, court baron, or of the stannary, or elsewhere within any of the kings dominions of England or Wales, or the marches of the same: or shall unlawfully, and corruptly procure and suborn any witnesse to testify *in perpetuam rei memoriam.* That then every such offender shall forfeit the summe of forty pound, &c. And if any person either by subornation, or by their own act, consent or agreement, wilfully and corruptly commit any manner of wilfull perjury by their deposition in any of the courts abovementioned, or being examined *ad perpetuam rei memoriam*; then every person so offending shall lose and forfeit twenty pound, and to have imprisonment by the space of six moneths without bail or mainprise, &c. the one moiety of all which forfeitures to be to the queen, and the other moiety to such person or persons as shall be grieved, &c.

Albeit by the common law tryall of matters of fact are by the verdict of twelve men, &c. and deposition of witnesses is but evidence to them: yet, for that most commonly juries are led by deposition of witnesses, perjury of witnesses was severely punished by the ancient laws of this realm; perjury itself being forbidden by the law of God, [a] *Non perjurabis in nomine meo, nec pollues nomen Dei tui.* And again, *Non perjurabis, reddes domino juramenta tua.*

A false witnesse is called *perjurus, quia perperam jurat.* [b] Perjury before the conquest was punished sometime by death, sometime by banishment, and sometime by corporall punishment, &c.

[c] *Ascuns sont punies per cowper de langues, come soiloit estre de faux tesmoignes.* But too severe laws are never duly executed. Afterwards it came to be more milde, for [d] Fleta saith, *Atrox injuria est quæ omnium mobilium amissionem confert, &c. de perjurio convictis.*

Afterwards it came to fine and ransome, and never to bear testimony.

Et queux se voillont perjurer pur lower, ou par ascun doute de ascun, et ceux sont reints a nostre volunt, et mes ne soient crus per nul serement. And it appeareth in 7 H. 6. that he that is perjured shall be fined and imprisoned.

Thomas Vigrus, et duo alii sunt culpabiles, &c. perjurati pro fractione corbellorum Johannæ de Huntingfield in separali piscaria sua in aqua de Hadfeld.

Qui testes de perjurio convincere satagit, multo illis plures, producere necesse habet.

The punishment of perjury in jurors for a false verdict was so severe by the common law, as few or no juries were upon just cause convicted, for the judgement * against them was, 1. *Quod amodo amittant liberam legem imperpetuum.* 2. *Non trahantur in testimonium veritatis.* 3. *Bona et catalla sua forisfaciant regi.* 4. *Terræ et tenementa sua capiantur in manus regis.* 5. *Quod uxores et liberi sui amodo amoveantur.* 6. *Quod terræ et tenementa sua extirpentur, &c.*

[a] Exod. 20. 13. Levit. 19. 11. Mat. 5. 34.

[b] Leges Edw. c. 3. Ethelst. c. 10. 25 Edm. c. 6. Canuti, ca. 6. & 35. &c. Edw. and Gru. c. 11.

[c] Mir. ca. 4. § de paines. Int. Leg. Canuti, c. 15. Conviciatori lingua exciditor.

[d] Fleta, li. 2. ca. 1. § Item Atrox, &c.

Britton, fo. 38. 237, 238.

7 H. 6. fo. 25.

Hil. 8 E. 1. in Communi banco Rot. 38. Essex. Fortescue, ca. 32.

*[164]

Vide 1. pt. of the Institutes. Verb. Attaint. Sect. 514. Glanvill, lib. 2. ca. 19. 6 H. 3. Attaint. 72. Bract. li. 4. fo. 292. b. Fleta, lib. 5. cap. 21. Britton, fo. 245. 8 E. 2. Judgement. 196. 16 E. 3. ibidem 109. Mich. 3 H. 5. Coram rege Rot. 14 & 49. Fortescue ca, 29.

7. *Quod*

7. *Quod capiantur, et in gaolam detrudantur.* Which ſheweth how odious perjury was in the eye of the law: and this law doth yet remain in force; but a milder puniſhment is ſet down by the ſtatute of 23 H. 8. wherein the party grieved hath election to ground his writ of attaint upon this ſtatute, or to take his remedy at the common law.

23 H. 8. ca. 3.

2 H. 4. 10. 11 H. 4. 88. 20 E. 4. 10. b. 22 E. 4. 13 El. Dier, 302. Mich. 7 & 8 El. Dier, 242, 243.

For perjury concerning any temporall act, the eccleſiaſticall court hath no juriſdiction; and if it be concerning a ſpirituall matter, the party grieved may ſue for the ſame in the ſtar-chamber. See the ſtatutes of 3 H. 7. ca. 1. 11 H. 7. ca. 25. 32 H. 8. ca. 9. And when you have read the caſe in Mich. 7 & 8 Eliz. Dier 242, 243. you will confeſſe how neceſſary the reading of ancient authors and records is, and the continuall experience in the ſtar chamber is againſt the opinion conceived there.

Mich. 10. Ja. Rowl. Ap Elizaes caſe, in cam. ſtellat. See hereafter Verb. Information.

And Mich. 10. Jac. in the ſtar-chamber in the caſe of Rowland Ap Eliza, it was reſolved, that perjury in a witnes was puniſhable by the common law, as hereafter ſhall be ſhewed more at large. But now let us peruſe the words of the ſtatute.

Mich. 40 & 41 El. Lib. 5. fo. 99. in Flowers caſe.

By any writ, action, bill, complaint, or information.] Out of theſe words are perjury, and ſubornation of perjury upon an indictment for the king (for example of riot) as it was reſolved in Flowers caſe, becauſe that perjury upon an indictment is not within the ſtatute. But ſeeing perjury was an offence puniſhable by the common law, though the indictment of Flower grounded upon this ſtatute was overthrown, yet is ſuch perjury upon an indictment puniſhable, and moſt commonly puniſhed in the ſtar-chamber.

The caſe of Rowland ap Eliza in the ſtar-chamber ubi ſupra.

Information.] By this it appeareth, that perjury committed in an information exhibited by the kings attorny, or any other for the king, by any witnes produced on the behalf of the king, is puniſhable either by this act or by the common law. And ſo it was reſolved in the ſaid caſe of Rowl. Ap Eliza, which was this. The kings attorny preferred an information in the exchequer againſt Hugh Nanny eſquire the father, and Hugh Nanny the ſon, and others for intruſion and cutting down a great number of trees, &c. in Penroſe in the county of Merioneth. The defendant pleaded not guilty, and the tryall being at the bar, Rowl. Ap Eliza was a witneſſe produced for the king, who depoſed upon his oath to the jury, that Hugh the father and Hugh the ſon joyned in ſale of the ſaid trees, and commanded the vendees to cut them down: upon which teſtimony the jury found for the king, and aſſeſſed great damages, and thereupon judgement and execution was had. Hugh Nanny the father exhibited his bill in the ſtar-chamber at the common law, and charged Rowland Ap Eliza with perjury, and aſſigned the perjury, in that he the ſaid Hugh the father never joined in ſale, nor commanded the vendees to cut down the trees, &c. And it was reſolved, firſt, that perjury in a witneſſe was puniſhable by the common law. Secondly, that perjury in a witneſſe for the king was puniſhable by the common law, either upon an indictment, or in an information, or by this act in an information. And the ſaid Rowland Ap Eliza was by the ſentence of the court convicted of wilfull and corrupt perjury.

But for our more orderly proceeding, let us define, or deſcribe what perjury is in legall underſtanding, both upon this ſtatute, and at the common law.

Perjury

Perjury is a crime committed, when a lawfull oath is ministred by any that hath authority, to any person, in any judiciall proceeding, who sweareth absolutely, and falsly in a matter materiall to the issue, or cause in question, by their own act, or by the subornation of others. Now let us peruse the branches of this description. Perjury described.

[165]

A lawfull oath.] This word oath is derived of the Saxon word *eoth;* and is expressed by three severall names, viz. 1. *Sacramentum, à sacra, et mente,* because it ought to be performed with a sacred and religious mind. *Quia jurare, est Deum in testem vocare, et est actus divini cultus.* 2. *Juramentum à jure,* which signifieth law and right, because both are required and meant, or because it must be done with a just and rightfull mind. 3. *Jusjurandum,* compounded of two words, *à jure, et jurando.* In the common law *sacramentum* is most commonly used: in our books and ancient statutes published in French, *serement,* of the French word *serment,* is used. Serment or sarment. i. sacrement. i. sacramentum.

An oath is an affirmation or deniall by any Christian of any thing lawfull and honest, before one or more, that have authority to give the same for advancement of truth and right, calling Almighty God to witnesse, that his testimony is true. And it is twofold, either *assertorium ut de præterito, sicut testes, &c. seu promissorium de futuro, sicut judices, justiciarii, officiarii, &c.* So as an oath is so sacred, and so deeply concerneth the consciences of Christian men, as the same cannot be ministred to any, unlesse the same be allowed by the common law, or by some act of parliament; neither can any oath allowed by the common law or by act of parliament be altered, but by act of parliament. It is called a corporall oath, because he toucheth with his hand some part of the holy scripture. Fleta, li. 5. ca. 2. Brit. c. 97. fo. 237. 8. b. 19. 74. 134. 165. 236. b. Fleta, li. 5. ca. 21. So resolved an. 26 El. in the case of the under sherif.

The oath of the kings privy councell, the justices, the sherif, &c. was thought fit to be altered and enlarged, but that was done by authority of parliament. For further proof whereof, and of the matters abovesaid, see the statutes here quoted, and it shall evidently appear, that no old oath can be altered, or new oath raised without an act of parliament, or any oath ministred by any that have not allowance by the common law, or by an act of parliament. Magna Cart. c. 6. Stanf. Pr. 17. F. N. B. 264. W. 1. 3 E. 1. c. 40. 18 E. 3. ubi sup. 5 R. 2. cap. 12. 6 R. 2. ca. 12. 4 H. 4. ca. 18.

2 H. 5. ca. 7. 8 E 4. cap. 2. 1 R. 3. cap. 6. & 15. 19 H. 7. cap. 14. 14 H. 8. ca. 2. 23 H. 8. cap. 5. 32 H. 8. cap. 46. 2 E. 6. ca. 13. 27 El. cap. 12. See 3 Jac. c. 4.

And to conclude this point, it was resolved in parliament holden in *anno* 43 Eliz. that the commissioners concerning policies of assurances could not examine upon oath, because they had no warrant either by the common law, or by any act of parliament: and therefore it was enacted at that parliament, that it should be lawfull for the said commissioners to examine upon oath any witnesse, &c. At this parliament I attended, being then attorny generall. And oaths that have no warrant by law, are rather *nova tormenta, quam sacramenta,* and it is an high contempt to minister an oath without warrant of law, to be punished by fine and imprisonment. And therefore commissioners (that set by force of any commission that is not allowed by the common law, nor warranted by authority of parliament) that minister any oath whatsoever, are guilty of an 43 Eliz. ca. 12.

high contempt, and for the same are to be fined and imprisoned: * For commissions are legall, and are like the kings writs, and none are lawfull but such as are allowed by the common law, or warranted by some act of parliament: and therefore commissions of new inquiries or of novell invention, are against law, and ought not to be put in execution.

* Commissions. Regist. 1, 2, 3. 125, 126. 88. 128. 138. 161. F. N. B. 110, 111. 2 E. 3. 26. Pasch. 44 E. 3. Coram rege. Rot. 2. 24 E. 3. Com. Br. 3. 29 E. 3. 30, 31. 18 E. 3. ca. 1 & 4. 18 E. 3. Stat. 2. ca. 6. Rot. Parl. 18 E. 3. nu. 47. 28 E. 3. ca. 19. Rot. Parl. 50 E. 3. nu. 56. 61. 2 H. 4. nu. 22. optime. 4 H. 4. ca. 9. Rot. Parl. 9 H. 4. nu. 36. 42 Ass. p. 5. 12. 42 E. 3. ca. 3. Dier, 1 Eliz. 106. Scrogs case.

And albeit divers of the kings courts in England proceed not according to the course of the common law, yet are their proceedings allowed either by the common law or by some act of parliament.

Dorss. claus. an. 19 R. 2. nu. 17. * Exod. 20. 4. Deut. 5. 6. Psalme 86. 11. 96. 7. 115. 4. Levit. 26. 1. &c. Esay 44. 9. &c. Jeremy 10. 3. &c. Sapient. 13. 10. &c. August. Epist. 110. ad Jan. ca. 11. idem de fide & symbolo, ca. 7. idem in Psal. 113. con. 2. Gregor. lib. 9. Epist. 9.

Certain poor Christians that had spoken against the worshipping of images, were by the bishops sworn to worship images; * which oath was against the expresse law of God, and against the law of the land, for that they had no † warrant to minister the same. Let the children of the church be called and instructed by the testimonies of the holy scripture, that nothing made with hands may be worshipped. See the second part of the Institutes, Marlbridge, cap. 14. & 19. concerning oathes, and specially out of Glanvile, concerning the nobility of this realm, and W. 1. ca. 38.

†[166]

By any having authority.] For where the court hath no authority to hold plea of the cause, but it is *coram non judice*, there perjury cannot be committed. For as Bracton saith, *Sacramentum habet in se tres comites, veritatem, justitiam et judicium: veritas habenda est in jurato; justicia et judicium in judice.*

Bracton, lib. 4. fo. 186.

Jer. 4. 2.

And all this is grounded upon the law of God, *Jurabis vivit dominus, in veritate, et judicio, et in justitia.*

In any judiciall proceeding.] For though an oath be given by him that hath lawfull authority, and the same is broken, yet if it be not in a judiciall proceeding, it is not perjury punishable either by the common law, or by this act, because they are generall and extrajudiciall, but serve for aggravation of the offence, as general oathes given to officers or ministers of justice, citizens, burgesses, or the like, or for the breach of the oath of fealty or allegeance, &c. they shall not be charged in any court judiciall for the breach of them afterwards. As if an officer commit extortion, he is in truth perjured, because it is against his generall oath: and when he is charged with extortion, the breach of his oath may serve for aggravation.

Trin. 13 Ja. Li. 11. f. 98. Bagges case.

If a man calleth another perjured man, he may have his action upon his case, because it must be intended contrary to his oath in a judiciall proceeding: and so it is termed in our statute of 5 Eliz. but for calling him a forsworne man, no action doth lye: because the forswearing may be extrajudiciall. If the defendant perjureth himself in his answer in the chancery, exchequer chamber, &c. he is is not punishable by this statute, for it extendeth but to witnesses, but he may be punished in the star-chamber, &c.

Who sweareth absolutely.] For the deposition must be direct and absolute, and not *ut putat*, nor *sicut meminit*, nor *ut credit*, &c. Bract. lib. 4. fol. 289. Fleta, lib. 5. ca. 21.

And falsely.] Herein the law taketh a diversity between falsehood in expresse words, and that is only within this statute, and falsehood in knowledge or minde, which may be punished though the words be true. For example, damages were awarded to the plaintife in the star-chamber according to the value of his goods riotously taken away by the defendant: the plaintiffe caused two men to sweare the value of his goods, that never saw nor knew them; and though that which they sware was true, yet because they knew it not, it was a false oath in them, for the which both the procurer and the witnesses were sentenced in the star-chamber. Gurneis case in the star-chamber, Mic. 9 Jac.

For (as Fleta saith) *Ad rectum juramentum exiguntur tria, veritas, conscientia, et judicium:* truth and conscience in the witnesse, and judgement in the judge. And herewith agreeth Bracton, that a man may sweare the truth, and yet be perjured. *Dicunt quidam verum, et mentiuntur, et pejerant, eo quòd contra mentem vadunt. Ut si Judæus juraverit Christum natum ex virgine, perjurium committit, quia contra mentem vadit, quia non credit ita esse ut jurat.* Fleta, ubi supra. Bracton, lib. 4. fo. 289.

By the ancient law of England in all oathes equivocation is utterly condemned; for Britton saith, *Serement est honest, et leall, quant sa conscience demesne accord a chescun point a la bouche ne pluis, ne meins, et sil ad discord, donqs' est perillous.* And this is grounded upon the law of God. *Nunquid Deus indiget mendacio vestro, ut pro illo loquamini dolos, aut decipietur ut homo vestris fraudulentiis? Perjuri sunt qui servatis verbis juramenti decipiunt aures eorum qui accipiunt.* If equivocation should be permitted tending to the subversion of truth, it would shake the foundation of justice. Equivocation. Britton, fo. 237. Job 13. 7.

In a matter materiall to the issue, or cause in question.] For if it be not materiall, then though it be false, yet it is no perjury, because it concerneth not the point in suit, and therefore in effect it is extrajudiciall. Also this act giveth remedy to the party grieved, and if the deposition be not materiall, he cannot be grieved thereby. And Bracton saith, *si autem sacramentum fatuum fuerit, licet falsum, tamen non committit perjurium.* [167] Bracton, lib. 4. 188. Fleta, lib. 5. ca. 21. accord.

By their own act, &c.] This clause of the statute, although it be more generall then the clause of procurement, yet seeing the first clause concerning procurement, extendeth not to perjury upon an indictment: this clause by construction shall extend no further than the former. See Lib. Intr. Coke, fo. 164, 165, 362. Flowers case, ubi supra.

Or by the subornation of other.] Subornation is derived of *sub* and *orno*, and *ornare* in one of his significations is to prepare, so as *subornare* is as much to say, as to prepare secretly, or underhand. *Est autem subornare quasi subtus in aure ipsum male ornare, unde subornatio dicitur de falsi expressione, aut de veri suppressione.* And here is to be noted, that in the judgement of the parliament *plus peccat author quam actor;* for the suborner forfeits 40 li. and he that is suborned but 20 li. Fleta saith, *Si servus cogatur scienter à domino perjurare, uterque est perjurus; qui autem provocat eum ad jurandum quem scit* Fleta, lib. 5. ca. 21.

 falsum

falsum jurare, vel exigit, vel recipit juramentum, talis vincit homicidam, quia homicida solum corpus occidit, iste vero animam suam et alterius: et peccat, qui alium audit falsum jurare, scit, et tacet.

Mic 29 & 30 Eliz. coram rege.

In an action of perjury brought upon this statute, the plaintife counted, that the defendant *falso dixit et deposuit, &c.* and in what action, upon what issue, and in what court, &c. and concluded, *et sic commisit voluntarium et corruptum perjurium.* And it was ruled by the whole court, that the count was vicious and insufficient for two causes. First, for that in this act of 5 Eliz. as here it appeareth, there be two distinct clauses, one if he be perjured of his own proper act; the other if he be perjured by subornation, &c. and the plaintife ought to declare in certainty, within which of them the defendant is perjured. The second cause was, where the act saith [wilfully and corruptly commit any wilfull perjury, &c.] and the words of the count be *falso dixit et deposuit:* and saith not, *voluntarie et corrupte*; and the said clause, *et sic commisit voluntarium et corruptum perjurium*, salveth not the former insufficiency, because it is but a conclusion upon the former matter.

27 Eliz. Mellers case.

And the like judgement was given in this court, as to this latter point *anno* 27 Eliz. in the case of one Mellers of Lincolneshire.

Dier, 12 El. 288.

That as well the judge and judges of every such of the said courts.] If the perjury be committed by any witnesse deposed in the chancery, &c. and the party grieved commenceth his suit there upon this act, the same and all the proceedings thereupon must be in Latin according to the course of the common law, and the defendant shall not be sworn to his answer, nor examined upon interrogatories (unlesse the court of chancery had before this act used to examine perjuries, and to examine the defendant upon oath upon interrogatories before this act, for then such jurisdiction had been saved by a proviso in this act) and when issue is joined, it shall be tried in the kings bench, as by law it ought, *et sic de similibus.*

25 E. 3. 42. b. cor. 131.

If a man be taken for a suspect, and he is not indicted, nor is there any certaine cause to arraign him, the court may give him the oath of allegiance, viz. *Que il serra foial et loyal, &c.* Vide 45 E. 3. 17. b. simile devant, cap. 7. De Conjuration, &c. in fine. 22 E. 4. 36. 20 H. 6. 37. Attorney abjure.

See more of Perjury and of Witnesses in the fourth part of the Institutes, cap. Commissioners for examination of witnesses. See 21 Jac. cap. 20. a good act to prevent and reforme profane swearing.

CAP. LXXV.

Of Forging of Deeds, &c.

IF any perſon or perſons upon his or their own head or imagination, or by falſe conſpiracy or fraud with others, ſhall wittingly, ſubtilly, and falſely forge (1), or make (2), or ſubtilly cauſe or wittingly aſſent (3) to be forged or made any falſe deed, charter (4), or writing ſealed (5), court roll, or the will of any perſon or perſons, in writing (6), to the intent that the ſtate of freehold or inheritance of any perſon or perſons, of, in, or to any lands, tenements, or hereditaments free-hold or coppy-hold, or the right, title, or intereſt of any perſon or perſons of, in, or to the ſame (8), or any of them, ſhall or may be moleſted, troubled, defeated, recovered, or charged, &c. (7) Or ſhall pronounce, publiſh, or ſhew forth in evidence any ſuch falſe and forged deed, charter, writing, court-roll, or will, as true (9), knowing the ſame to be falſe and forged (10), as is aforeſaid, to the intent above remembered, and ſhall be thereof convicted, either upon action or actions of forger of falſe deeds to be founded upon this ſtatute, at the ſuit of the party grieved, or otherwiſe according to the order and due courſe of the lawes of this realme, or upon bill, or information, to be exhibited into the court of ſtar-chamber, &c. ſhall pay to the party grieved his double coſts and damages, &c. (11) And be it further enacted, that if any perſon or perſons, upon his or their owne head or imagination, or by falſe conſpiration or fraud had with any other, ſhall wittingly, ſubtilly, and falſely forge or make, or wittingly, ſubtilly, and falſely cauſe or aſſent to be made or forged, any falſe charter, deed (12), or writing, to the intent that any perſon, or perſons, ſhall or may have or claime any eſtate or intereſt for terme of yeares (13) of, in, or to any mannors, lands, tenements, or hereditaments, not being coppy-hold (14), or any annuitie (15) in fee-ſimple, fee-taile, or for term of life, lives, or years, or ſhall make or forge, as is aforeſaid, any obligation, or bill obligatory (16), acquittance, releaſe, or diſcharge (18), of any debt, account, action, ſuit, demand, or other thing perſonall, or ſhall pronounce, &c. *ut ſupra*. That then he ſhall pay, &c. (19) 5 Eliz. cap. 14.

And be it further enacted, that if any perſon or perſons being hereafter convicted or condemned of any of the offences aforeſaid, &c. ſhall after any ſuch his or their conviction or condemnation eftſoons commit or perpetrate any of the ſaid offences (20) in forme aforesaid, that then every such second offence or offences shall be adjudged felony, &c.

We have spoken of forgery or counterfeiting of the great seale of the kings coin, &c. which are declared by the statute of 25 E. 3. to be high treason: now we are to treat of forgeries of deeds, charters, and writings sealed, &c. in the case of subjects. And first, after our accustomed manner how these offences were punished of ancient time.

Mir. cap. 4. § Des paines. Et cap. 5. § 1.

The Mirror saith, *Ascuns peches sont punies p. pde. de poulce, come est de faulx notoires, &c.* peccans membrum puniebatur. *(Car pur fauxer de seale ne serr' judgement mortel.)*

[169]

Britton, fo. 16. a. & b.

Britton saith, *Judgement dée treyne, et de suffer mort doit encount' ceux coure, q. p. appeales de felony sont atteints, q. ilz eyent le seale lour seigniour, qui maintast ils sont, ou q. homes p. homage counterfait, ou autrement fause, &c. Et si tiels manners des faits soient atteints a nostre suit, si soient pur le seale fause juges a judgement de pillory, ou de perdre le oraile si le fait soit simple: et si le fait soit grand et leyde, sicome touchant disherison ou perpetuall domage, si soient juges à la mort.*

Fleta, lib. 1. ca. 22.

Fleta saith, *Crimen falsi dicitur, cum quis accusatus fuerit vel appellatus quòd sigillum regis, vel domini sui de cujus familia fuerat, falsaverit, et brevia inde consignaverit; vel cartam aliquam vel literam ad exhæredationem domini, &c. sigillaverit; in quibus causis si quis convictus fuerit, detractari meruit et suspendi. Et quod de hujusmodi falsariis dicitur, de sigilla adulterina cartis et literis apponentibus dicatur idem.*

Fleta, lib. 2. ca. 1.

And in another place he saith, *Est etiam atrox injuria quæ perpetuam inducit infamiam cum pœna pillorari vel tumbrelli, quæ quandoque fit per falsarios sigillorum (dum tamen non regis nec domini sui de cujus fuerit familia.)*

We have the more willingly repeated these ancient punishments, to shew how in part, (viz. concerning the eares and pillory,) this act for the first offence concurreth with the ancient punishment.

(1) *Forge.*] To forge is metaphorically taken from the smith, who beateth upon his anvill, and forgeth what fashion or shape he will: the offence (as it appeareth before) is called *crimen falsi*, and the offender *falsarius*, and the Latin word to forge is *falsare* or *fabricare*. And this is properly taken when the act is done in the name of another person.

26 H. 6. forger S. 27 H. 6. 3.

The statute of 1 H. 5. hath these words [forge of new any false deed.] And yet if A make a feoffement by deed to B, of certaine land, and after A maketh a feoffement by deed to C of the same land with an antedate before the feoffement to B; this was adjudged to be a forgery within that statute, and by like reason within this statute also: and the rather in respect of the words subsequent, [or make, &c.]

(2) *Or make, &c.*] These be larger words then to forge: for one may make a false writing within this act, though it be not forged in the name of another, nor his seale nor hand counterfeited. As if A make a true deed of feoffement under his hand and seale of the manner of Dale unto B, and B or some other rase out D the first letter of Dale, and put in S, and then where the true deed was of the mannor of Dale, now it is falsely altered and made

the

the mannor of Sale. This is a false writing under seale within the purview of this statute. And so it is if a rent charge of one hundred pounds by the year be granted out of land in fee or for life, &c. and the grantee or any other rase out one, and in stead thereof writeth two; this is a false writing within the danger of this statute.

(3) *Or subtilly cause, or wittingly assent.*] To cause, is to procure or counsell one to forge, &c. To assent, is to give his assent or agreement afterwards to the procurement or counsell of another: to consent, is to agree at the time of the procurement or counsell, and he in law is a procurer.

(4) *Deed, charter, or writing sealed.*] It is required, that the deed, charter, or writing must be sealed; that is, have some impression upon the wax, for *sigillum est cera impressa, quia cera sine impressione non est sigillum;* and no deed, charter, or writing, can have the force of a deed without a seale.

Pasch. 15 Eliz. Dier, 322 James Taverners case. In camera stellata.

(5) *Writing sealed.*] These are large words: for the making of a false customary of a mannor in writing under seale, containing divers false customes tending to the disherison of the lord of the mannor, and that the same had been allowed and permitted by the lords of the mannor, &c which was also false, was resolved to be within these words, [a false writing sealed.]

[170]

(6) *Court roll, or the will of any person or persons in writing.*] Here be two kind of muniments that need not be sealed, because they may take effect without any seal, for that they be deeds; as court rols concerning grants, surrenders, admittances, &c. of copy or customary lands: and the last will in writing. If any person which writeth the will of a sick man inserteth a clause in his last will, concerning the devise of any lands or tenements, which he had in fee-simple, falsly without any warrant, or direction of the divisor: albeit he did not forge, or falsly make the whole will, yet is he punishable by this statute, as it hath been often holden in the star chamber against the opinion reported by my lord Dier.

Dier 12 El. f. 288. Sir James Marvyns case.

(7) *To the intent that the state of freehold or inheritance, of or in any lands, tenements, or hereditaments, freehold or copyhold, shall or may be molested, troubled, defeated, recovered, or charged.*] The great doubt upon this branch, and of the branch hereafter ensuing, was, for that it is not expressed by this act, what estate, or interest should be mentioned to passe by the deed, charter, &c. whereby the estate of the freehold or inheritance should or might be molested, &c. or charged; whether if one did forge, &c. a deed, charter, &c. of an interest, or tearm of a hundred or a thousand years, &c. of lands, which are the freehold or inheritance of another, whereby the same shall or may be molested, &c. And the same question of a rent charge for years in the like case: and the doubt was the greater in respect of the clause hereafter ensuing, which is, To the intent that any person or persons shall or may have or claim any estate or interest for tearm of years of in or to any mannors, &c. And it was resolved, that a lease or charge for years of any lands being the freehold or inheritance of any person, was within this branch, for the clause is generall, not mentioning any estate or interest, &c. whereby the molestation, &c. should grow: and it was requisite it should extend to leases or charges for years, for otherwise mens estates of freehold or inheritance, &c. might be of little or no value:

Pafch. 38 Eliz. in camera ftellata the lady Grefhams cafe.

and accordingly it was refolved, Pafch. 38 Eliz. in the ftar-chamber between the lady Grefham plaintif, and Roger Booth fcrivener of London, Markham and others defendants, for the forging of a grant of a rent charge, by deed bearing date *anno* 21 Eliz. for ninety nine years to the faid Markham out of all fir Thomas Grefhams lands of inheritance, and for publication thereof; and fentence given upon the faid branch accordingly againft Roger Booth for publication of the fame.

And the faid branch after enfuing, is to be underftood when the forgery, &c. is to the moleftation of a termor. As if A. be poffeffed of a leafe of lands for years, and B. in his name doth forge an affignment to C. of his tearm, this is directly within the letter and meaning of this branch, and the rather in refpect of thofe things that be joyned therewith under the fame punifhment.

Vide 4 H. 6. 25. 8 H. 6. 33. 20 H. 6. 33 H. 6. 23. 15 E. 4. 24. Pl. com. 88.

(8) *Or the right, title, or intereft of any perfon or perfons in or to the fame.*] Thefe words were added, for that the ftatute of 1 H. 5. being to undoe, and trouble the poffeffion and title (in the conjunctive) of the faid kings liege people: doubt was made whether a forgery to bar one that had but a bare right or title, and no poffeffion, was within that ftatute: and therefore this claufe of 5 Eliz. added this claufe in the disjunctive, as here it appeareth. But now by a fpeciall branch of this act the ftatute of 1 H. 5. cap. 3. being doubtfully penned, is repealed by a claufe in this act, and greater punifhment inflicted by this ftatute.

[171]

(9) *Or fhall pronounce, publifh, or fhew forth in evidence any fuch falfe and forged deed, &c. as true knowing the fame to be forged.*] Here be two things to be explained: firft, what it is to pronounce, or publifh as true. Secondly, what knowledge is fufficient.

To pronounce or publifh is, when one by words or writing pronounceth or publifheth the deed, &c. to any other as true.

(10) *Knowing the fame to be forged.*] This knowledge may come by two means, either of his own knowledge, or by the relation of another. As if A. telleth B. that fuch deed is falfe and forged, and yet B. will after pronounce or publifh this to be a true deed, and afterwards it falleth out by proof that the relation of A. was true, and the deed in truth was forged, B. is in the danger of this ftatute: and fo was it refolved in the abovefaid cafe of the lady Grefham, againft Roger Booth, &c. *ubi fupra*, and fentence given accordingly.

Dier 15 Eliz. Taverners cafe, ubi fupra.

(11) *And that the defendant fhall fuffer upon the pillory the corporall penance, &c.*] And there is a claufe that the plaintif fhould not releafe nor difcontinue the punifhment, &c. but only cofts and damages: and yet it was refolved that the queen might pardon the corporall punifhment, which trencheth to common example.

Pafch. 34 E. 3. Coram rege, Rot. 30. Kanc' the cafe of Goditha Walfifh. Dier 7 El. 231.

And upon the ftatute of W. 2. ca. 25. which giveth two years imprifonment in the ravifhment of ward, the king may pardon the faid corporall punifhment of imprifonment. And the punifhment of finding of furety, and forjuring the realm, &c. upon the ftatute of W. 2. cap. 28. *De malefactoribus in parcis* may be pardoned by the king.

(12) *Any falfe charter or deed.*] This muft be intended to be fealed according to the former claufe, though it be not here fpecified.

Pl. com. 80, b.

(13) *To the intent that any perfon or perfons fhall or may have or claim* any

any estate or interest for tearm of years.] This branch hath been explained before in the former part of this statute

(14) *Not being copy hold.*] This needeth no explication.

(15) *Or annuity.*] This is evident.

(16) *Any obligation, or bill obligatory.*] These must be intended to be sealed: if a man forge a statute staple, or a recognisance in the nature of a statute staple, that is, acknowledge them, or either of them in the name of another; these are obligations within this act, for each of them hath the seal of the party. But otherwise it is of a statute merchant, or of a recognisance, because they have not the seal of the conusor. F. N.B. 96. b. c. & 10. a. 15 H. 7. 15, &c.

(17) *Or writing.*] This extends to a testament in writing, whereby the tearm for years or goods and chattels be devised, and the former branch extendeth to a will in writing, concerning freehold and inheritance. Dier, 13 Eliz. 302. b.

(18) *Acquitance, release or discharge.*] Lodowick Grevil esquire was bound by recognisance of two hundred pound, to Rowland Hinde of the Inner Temple, for payment of one hundred pound. Hinde wrote a letter to Grevil, and writ his name in the lowest part of the letter; (as many use when they write to men of great calling) Grevil caused the letter to be cut off, and a generall release in few words to be written above Hindes name, and took off Hindes seal, and fixed it under the release: so there was Hindes hand and seal to this release. Hinde being not paid his hundred pound, brought a *scire fac'* upon the recognisance, whereunto Grevill pleaded this release, Hinde pleaded *non est factum*, and tried his deed, whereupon judgement was given against him, whereby Hinde was barred of his debt. For this forged release Grevil was sentenced in the star-chamber upon this statute. Mich. 13 & 14 El. in camera stellata inter Hinde and Grevill. [172]

(19) *Shall pay to the party grieved, his double damages.*] Upon these words in the case aforesaid, between Hinde and Grevill, the question was, whether Hinde should have double damages in respect of the penalty, viz. the two hundred pound, or of the hundred pound, the due debt appearing in the condition of the recognisance. And it was resolved, that damages should be assessed by the court to double the penalty, for the penalty should be recovered by law if the forged release had not been: and this was reported by the lord Dier, and imprinted, and since omitted out of the print.

(20) *Being hereafter convicted or condemned of any of the offences aforesaid, shall, &c. estsoons commit, &c. any of the said offences.*] Here be four kind of offences; the first concerning molestation, &c. of freehold and inheritance. Secondly, the publication of the same knowing, &c. The third concerning a tearm for years, annuities, and demands personals. Fourthly, the publication thereof.

Now the question upon this branch concerning felony, was, that whereas the said Roger Booth was convicted in the star-chamber for the publishing of the forged grant by deed of a rent charge of a hundred pound *per annum*, as is aforesaid; afterwards the said Roger and others were charged in the star-chamber with the forging of a deed of feoffment in the name of sir Thomas Gresham bearing date 20 Eliz. but forged long after: whether this second forgery was felony, or no, within this branch; and the doubt did arise upon the said words [*estsoons*] commit any of the said offences. And it Pasch. 7 Ja. Inter sir Will. Reade pl. and Rogerum Booth et alios def. in camera stellata.

was

was objected, that by reason of this word [*estsoons*] *iterum*, the second offence must be of the same nature as the first offence was; as the first offence being for publication of a forged deed, &c. the second offence must be for the publication of another forged deed, &c. and upon that branch whereupon the first offence was grounded, or else it was said, it was not *iterum*, which word was in signification *quasi iter unum*, that is to say, *per idem iter*, and it is so taken for the second time. *Primo quidem decipi, incommodum est, iterum stultum, tertio turpe:* which doubt was referred to the considerations of the two chief justices, and chief baron, who upon hearing of councell learned of both sides, and upon conference, and consideration had of this act, resolved, that the second offence was felony within the words, and meaning of this act, for the words be expresly, being condemned of any of the said offences, estsoons commit any of the said offences. So as by reason of these words, any of the said offences, this word [*estsoons*] is well satisfied, if he commit the second time any of them: and so these words any of the said offences extend to any of the said four offences before mentioned. And it was also resolved by them, that by reason of this word [estsoons] the second forgery, &c. must be committed after the first conviction, or else it is no felony.

Cicero, lib. 1. de Invent.

Provided always, &c. that if any person, &c. hath of his own head, &c. forged or made, &c. or if any person, &c. hath heretofore published or shewed forth any false deed, &c.

Trin. 11 El. Dier in a manuscript not printed.

Hanford before this statute forged a lease for years of the land of the lord Williams of Tame, which lease after by Weynman (which hath married one of the daughters and heirs of the said lord Williams) was impeached, but not as forged, and by composition for two hundred pound was redeemed by Weynman, and the lease was cancelled. And after Weynman perceiving the lease to be forged, sued Hanford in the chancery to have restitution of the two hundred pound, and there Hanford after this statute of 5 Eliz. maintained the lease as good and true: whereupon Weynman sued Hanford in the star-chamber, where by the opinion of the chief justices it was holden, that it was not within this statute, because that the deed was cancelled, and Hanford made no title to the interest of the tearm.

[173]

Provided always, &c. that this act or any thing therein contained, shall not extend to any person that shall plead or shew forth any deed or writing exemplified under the great seal of England, or under the seal of any other authentique court of this realm, nor shall extend to any judge or justice, or other person that shall cause any seal of any court to be set to such deed, charter or writing enrolled, not knowing the same to be false or forged.

Mich. 10 Jacobi regis in communi banco in a prohibition between Tho. Read pl. and Avis Hide, and Rich. Hide defendants.

This must be intended of a deed or writing, which by law may be exemplified: for the knowledge whereof we will report a resolution of the whole court of the common pleas. The issue between the said parties to be tried at the bar was, whether the last abbot of Abbingdon, and all his predecessors, &c. held certain lands in the parish

parish of Saint Ellens, &c. discharged of the payment of tithes: and the plaintif offered to shew in evidence to prove the said land to be discharged of payment of tithes, a *vidimus*, or *innotescimus* under the great seal in these words: *Vidimus quendam antiquum librum in pergameno intitulatum volumen de copiis munimentorum seu diversorum gestorum, et actorum monasterii de Abbingdon.* In which book was a copy of a bull of the pope, for the discharge of the said land for payment of tithes, which was but part (amongst other things) of the said book. And by the opinion of the whole court, hearing of the counsell of both parties, it was resolved that the said exemplification ought not to be given in evidence to the jury for these causes: first, because that which was exemplified, was not of record; for neither deed, charter, or other writing, either sealed, or without seal, ought to be exemplified under the great seale, or any other seal in court of record, for seals of courts of record ought not to exemplifie any thing but that which is of record, because records be publique, whereunto every subject may have recourse to confer the exemplification with the record itself, and records be in the custody of sworn officers, and therefore no inconvenience can follow upon the exemplification of them. But a deed, charter, and other writings are private, and remain in the custody of the party, and may be rased, interlined, or corrupted in points materiall, and if they should be exemplified, the rasure, interlineation, and corruption shall not appear therein. Also the deed, charter, or other writing may be forged, and if they should be exemplified, then the exemplification might ever be shewed in evidence, and not the deed, &c. it self, and so the forgery, and falsity should never upon the view of the deed, or of the seal, or other things rising upon the view, be discovered. Moreover if a forged deed should be exemplified, then the effect of this statute concerning publication should be taken away; for then the forged deed, &c. it self might never be published, or given in evidence, but the exemplification, and so this statute in that point deluded: and therefore where this statute, or any other statute or book speaks of an exemplification, *vidimus* or *innotescimus* of a deed, &c. it must be intended of a deed inrolled, viz. the exemplification, *vidimus*, or *innotescimus* of the inrolment thereof, which is of record. It was further resolved that no record, or inrolment of any record, may be exemplified under the great seale, but of a record of the court of chancery, or other record duly removed thither by *certiorari*, *&c.* Furthermore it was resolved, that no exemplification ought to be of any part of a letters patents, or of any other record, or of the inrolment thereof, but the whole record or the inrolment thereof ought to be exemplified, so that the whole truth may appeare, and not of such part, as makes for the one party and nothing that make against him, or that manifesteth the truth. Lastly, in the case at the barre, the said book was intituled, *Volumen de copiis munimentorum, et diversorum gestorum.* So as seeing the bull itselfe (being no matter of record) could not be exemplified; *à fortiori*, no exemplification could be had of the copie of the same. And if bulls, &c. might be exemplified, then there might be an evasion to make the statute of 28 H. 8. cap. 16. of small force, which prohibiteth pleading, or alledging of bulls, &c. under paine of a premunire, as by that act appeareth.

Mich. 29 & 30 Eliz. lib. 5. fo. 54. in Pages case.

[174]

28 H. 8. cap. 16. 1 & 2 Ph. & Mar. cap. 8. 1 Eliz. cap. 1.

CAP.

CAP. LXXVI.

Of Libels and Libellers.

WHAT a libell is, how many kindes of libels there be, who are to be punished for the same, and in what manner, you may read in my reports, viz. Lib. 5. fo. 124, 125. Lib. 9. fo. 59. To these you may add two notable records. By the one it appeareth, that Adam de Ravensworth was indicted in the kings bench for the making of a libel in writing, in the French tongue, against Richard of Snowshall, calling him therein, *Roy de Raveners, &c.* Whereupon he being arraigned, pleaded thereunto not guilty, and was found guilty, as by the record appeareth. So as a libeller, or a publisher of a libell committeth a publick offence, and may be indicted therefore at the common law.

Mich. 10 E. 3. coram rege. Rot. 92. Eborum.

John de Northampton an attorney of the kings bench, wrote a letter to John Ferrers one of the kings councell, that neither Sir William Scot chiefe justice, nor his fellowes the kings justices, nor their clerks, any great thing would do by the commandement of our lord the king, nor of queen Philip, in that place, more then of any other of the realme; which said John being called, confessed the said letter by him to be written with his own proper hand. *Judicium Curiæ. Et quia prædictus Johannes cognovit dictam literam per se scriptam Roberto de Ferrers, qui est de concilio regis, quæ litera continet in se nullam veritatem: prætextu cujus dominus rex erga curiam et justiciarios suos hic in casu habere posset indignationem, quod esset in scandalum justic' et curiæ. Ideo dictus Johannes committitur maresc' et postea invenit 6 manucaptores pro bono gestu.*

Mic. 18 E. 3. coram rege Rot. 151. Libellum.

[175]

CAP. LXXVII.

Of Champerty, Imbracery, Maintenance, &c.

SEE the first part of the Instit. sect. 701. verb. Maintenance. And the second part of the Institutes, W. 1. cap. 8. 32. & W. 2. cap. 49. and the exposition upon the same. See also the statute of 32 H. 8. cap. 9. in the first part of the Institutes, *ubi supra.* Rot. Parl. 17 R. 2. nu. 10. John de Winsors case. And the fourth part of the Institutes, cap. Chancery. Whereunto you may adde, that where by the statute of 6 H. 6. cap. 2. it is recited, that divers in times past have been disherited, because that in speciall assises the tenant and defendant might not have knowledge nor copie of the pannel of them that be impannelled to passe in the said assises, to inform them of their right and title before the day of the session that the assises shall be demanded; which is a rehearsall of the com-

mon

mon law, but ſo to be underſtood, that both parties plaintiffe and tenant, &c. be preſent, when ſuch information is given, and conſenting thereunto: otherwiſe, if one of them informeth in the abſence of another, it is unlawfull, and a good cauſe of challenge of ſuch of the jury as ſhall be ſo on the one part informed: for every jury muſt be indifferent, as he ſtand unſworne.

CAP. LXXVIII.

Of Barretry.

SEE the firſt part of the Inſtitutes, ſect. 701. verb. Barretors. See the ſtatute of Ragman, temps E. 1. whereby the commiſſion of Trailebaſton is raiſed. It is thus provided. *Et pur ceo q. en tiels maners de quereles doit le court le roy eē favourable, voet le roy, et enjoint' les juſtices q. nul enquerelant, ne reſpoignant ne ſoit surpriſe nencheſon per hockettours, ou barrettours, pou. que le veritie ne ſoit enſue.* Vet. Mag. Cart. cap. 28. 2 part.

Hockettors or *hocquetours* is an ancient French word for a knight of the poſt, (worthy to be knit to a poſt) a decayed man, a baſket-carrier.

For barrettors, ſee the firſt part of the Inſtitutes, *ubi ſupra*.

CAP. LXXIX. [176]

Of Riots, Routs, Unlawful Aſſemblies, Forces, &c.

RIOTUM commeth of the French word, *rioter, i. rixari:* and in the common law ſignifieth, when three or more doe any unlawfull act, as to beat any man, or to hunt in his park, chaſe, or warren, or to enter or take poſſeſſion of another mans land, or to cut or deſtroy his corne, graſſe, or other profit, &c.

* *Routa* is derived of the French word *rout*, and properly in law ſignifieth, when three or more do any unlawfull act for their own, or the common quarrell, &c. As when commoners break down hedges or pales, or caſt down ditches, or inhabitants for a way claimed by them, or the like. * Latine Turba. —*comes eſt diſcordia vulgi; Namq; a turbando nomen ſibi turba recepit.*

An unlawfull aſſembly is when three or more aſſemble themſelves together to commit a riot or rout, and doe it not. *Praedones autem nominamus uſq; numerum ſeptem virorum; deinde (quouſq; numerus 35 coaluerit)* * *turmam (Saxonicè hloth) dicimus; numerus ſi excreverit, exercitum vocamus, hlothbota*, to be quit of unlawfull aſſemblies. Lamb. int. Leg. Inæ ca. 13, 14, 15. Vide Alvered. cap. 26. * Turma quaſi tordena.

One may commit a force. But of this, that I may not unprofitably repeat, you may reade at large Fitzherbert, and thoſe others that have written of this argument.

Intereſt

Regula. *Interest regi habere subditos pacatos. Vis legibus est inimica.* See Lib. 5. fo. 91. 115. Lib. 11. fo. 82. See the first part of the Institutes, sect. 431. 440. Custum. de Norm. cap. 52. fo. 66, 67.

C A P. LXXX.

Of Quarrelling, Chiding, or Brawling by Words in Church or Church-yard.

5 E. 6. cap. 4.

THE offender being a lay-man, is to be suspended by the ordinary *ab ingressu ecclesiæ*, and being a clerk from the ministration of his office, so long as the ordinary thinks meet according to the fault.

C A P. LXXXI.

[177]

Of Smiting, or laying violent Hands upon another in Church or Churchyard.

5 E. 6. ubi supra. V. lib. 6. fo. 29. b. Grenes case, sim.

THE offender shall be deemed *ipso facto* excommunicat, and excluded from the company of Christs congregation.

C A P. LXXXII.

Of malicious striking with any Weapon, or drawing of any Weapon in Church or Church-yard, to the intent to strike another, &c.

5 E. 6. ubi sup. * Note the disjunctive. Int. leg. Inæ. ca. 6. Qui in templo pugnaverit 120 soldis noxiam facito. Dier 23 Eliz. 177. case ultim.

THE offender being convict by the oath of twelve men, or by his own confession, * or by two lawfull witnesses, before justices of assise, justices of oier and terminer, or justices of peace in their sessions, shall lose one of his eares: and if he hath no eares, to be marked in the cheek with a hot iron with the letter F, and *ipso facto* be excommunicate.

CAP. LXXXIII.

For ſtriking, &c. in any of the Kings Courts of Juſtice: and for ſtriking, &c. in any of the Kings Houſes, &c.

SEE before in the ſixty fifth chapter of Miſpriſion, that is, *crimen commiſſionis*.

CAP. LXXXIV. [178]

Againſt Fugitives, or ſuch as depart out of the Realme without Licenſe, and ſuch as are beyond Sea, and returne not upon Command.

Omne ſolum forti patria eſt, ut piſcibus æquor, Ovidius.
Et volucri, vacuo quicquid in orbe patet.

IT is firſt to be ſeen of acts in parliament publiſhed in print, which of them are abrogated and repealed, and which of them ſtand in force. The ſtatute of 5 R. 2. cap. 2. is repealed by the ſtatute of 4 Jac. cap. 1. And the ſtatutes of 13 Eliz. cap. 3. & 14 Eliz. cap. 6. are expired. The ſtatute of 12 R. 2. ſuch as 12 R. 2. ca. 15. paſſe the ſea, or ſend out of the realme to provide or purchaſe any benefice of holy church, with cure or without cure, are in danger of a premunire. No perſon reſiant within any of the kings dominions, ſhall depart out of any of thoſe dominions, to any viſitation, congregation, or aſſembly for religion. 25 H. 8. cap. 19. 1 Eliz. c. 1. revive.

Anno 1 Jac. cap. 4. and 3 Jac. cap. 5. Againſt going or ſending of children to any ſeminary beyond ſea, and againſt the departure out of the realme (without licenſe) of any children not being ſouldiers, mariners, merchants, or other apprentiſes, or factors, for any cauſe whatſoever. And *anno* 3 Ja. ca. 4. againſt impoſing felony upon any ſubject that ſhall depart this realme, to ſerve any prince, ſtate, or potentate: or ſhall paſſe over the ſeas, and there ſhall voluntarily ſerve any ſuch foraine prince, ſtate, or potentate; not having before his or their going or paſſing, taken the oath mentioned in that act. And likewiſe impoſing felony upon any gentleman or perſon of higher degree, or any perſon which hath borne or ſhall beare any office, or place of captaine, lieutenant, or any other place, charge, or office in campe, army, or company of ſouldiers, or conducter of ſouldiers, that ſhall goe, or paſſe voluntarily out of this realme, to ſerve any ſuch foraine prince, ſtate, or potentate, 1 Jac. cap. 4. 3 Jac. cap. 5.

or

or ſhall voluntarily ſerve any ſuch foraine prince, ſtate, or potentate, before he be bound by obligation with two ſureties, as in that act is preſcribed. But it is provided that upon the attainder of any ſuch felony, no forfeiture of dower or corruption of blood ſhall enſue. Reade over theſe ſtatutes, for they are ſo plainly penned, as they need no expoſition.

Next unto this, two things fall into conſideration, firſt, what acts of parliament not publiſhed in print in our books of ſtatutes do prohibit men to paſſe the ſeas without licenſe. And ſecondly, what may be done therein by the common law of England.

At the parliament holden at Clarendon, *anno* 10 H. 2. called the aſſiſe of Clarendon, *Facta eſt recognitio cujuſdam partis conſuetudinum et libertatum anteceſſorum regis, et ca.* 4. *ſic recognitum eſt. Archiepiſcopis, epiſcopis, et perſonis regni non licet exire regnum abſque licentia domini regis, et ſi exiverint, ſi regi placuerit, ſecurum eum facient, quòd nec in eundo nec in redeundo, nec moram faciendo perquirent malum ſeu damnum domino regi vel regno.*

This appeareth in it ſelfe to be but a recognition, or declaration of the common law: and this is manifeſtly proved by the writ in the Regiſter at the common law, purſuing in effect the very words of the ſaid act of 10 H. 2. *Breve de ſecuritate invenienda, quod ſe non divertat ad partes exteras ſine licentia regis.*

Regiſt. fo. 89, 90. F.N.B. 85.

[179]

Vide ſimile Regiſt. 61, &c. Ad jura regia. Regiſt. *fo.* 193. De licentia transfretandi pro religioſis.

And hereupon there ariſeth a diverſity between one of the clergie, and one of the laity: for a man of the church may be compelled to put in ſurety, that he ſhould not depart the realme without the kings licenſe, nor ſhall there attempt any thing in contempt or prejudice of the king or of his people. And this writ is directed to the ſheriffe, and ſaith, *Quia datum eſt nobis intelligi, quòd A. B. clericus verſus partes exteras ad quam plura nobis et quam pluribus de populo noſtro præjudicialia et damnoſa ibid. proſequend.,* &c. Whereby it appeareth, that this writ lyeth only in the caſe of an eccleſiaſticall perſon, or a man of the church, and that for three reaſons. Firſt, for that they had the cure of ſoules, and therefore ought to be reſident. Secondly, for that they, maintaining foraine authority, impugned many of the kings lawes, to the great prejudice of the laity. Thirdly, they had no temporall lands, therefore they found ſureties.

[a] Regiſt. 89. 90. F. N. B. fo. 85.
[b] So as neither this writ, nor a proclamation in nature of this writ ought to be granted, but where the party intends to depart the realme for theſe ends.
[c] F. N. B. fo. 85. b. Vide Dier 1 Eliz. 165. b.

There is another writ in the [a] Regiſter, and that is to be directed to the party himſelfe, viz. either to the clerk, or to the layman, wherein the king reciting, *Quod datum eſt nobis intelligi, quod tu verſ. partes exteras abſque licentia noſtra clandeſtine te divertere, et* [b] *quamplurima nobis et coronæ noſtræ prejudicialia ibid. proſequi intendas,* &c. *ſub periculo quod incumbit prohibemus, ne verſ. partes exteras abſque licentia noſtra ſpeciali aliqualiter te divertas, nec quicquam ibid. proſequi,* &c. And upon this writ the party is not to finde any ſurety, for there is no word of ſurety in this writ. And if the [c] ſubject cannot be found, the king may make a proclamation under the great ſeale, to the effect of the writ laſt mentioned.

Now let us peruſe ſuch authorities as we finde in records or books of law *in ſerie temporis,* taking ſome few examples for many that might be cited.

[d] Rot. Finium 6 H. 3. Et Rot. clauſ. 7 H. 3. m. 5.

[d] *Willielmus Marmion clericus profectus eſt ad regem Franciæ ſine licentia domini regis, et propterea finem fecit,* &c. Note the going over without any prohibition precedent unlawfull.

Nul

[e] *Nul grand ſeignior ou chivalier de noſtra realm ne doit prender chemin (daler hors de realm) ſans noſtre conge, car iſſint purroit le realm remain diſgargne de fort gents.* And the [f] nobles and peers of the realm are of the kings great councel.

By this it appeareth, that theſe are prohibited to goe beyond ſea without licence: but others of the inferiour laity may go without licenſe, if they travell not to the abovesaid prohibited ends. But [g] thoſe of the laity and men of the church alſo being beyond ſea, may be commanded by the kings writ, either under the great ſeale, or privie ſeale, *in fide et ligeantia, &c.* to returne into the kingdome (though he be not there to any of the abovesaid prohibited ends;) and if he returne not, for his contempt his lands and goods ſhall be ſeiſed, *quouſque, &c.* [h] Commandement was given to an eccleſiaſticall perſon reſiding at Rome to returne into England.

[i] *Quamplurimæ literæ domini regis miſſæ Romæ, ad revocand' diverſos clericos ibid. commorantes, qui quamplurima attemptarunt in dedecus regni, præcipient' etiam, quòd redeant ad feſtum eis appunctuatum: et pro eo quòd non venerunt, præceptum fuit vicecomiti quod eos capiat. Et Rogerus de Holme præbendarius in eccleſia Sancti Pauli London captus per vic' London, et arrenatus, examinatus, et convictus mittitur priſonæ turris London ibid. moraturus, &c.*

[k] *Rex proclamari fecit in omnibus comitatibus Angliæ, quòd ne quis comes, baro, miles, religioſus, ſagittarius, aut operarius, &c. extra regnum ſe transferat, ſub pœna areſtationis, et incarcerationis.*

Herein it is to be obſerved, that ſeeing by law, no earle, baron, or knight (as Britton ſaith) nor religious, &c. ought to goe out of the realme, a generall proclamation declarative will ſerve to aggravate their offence: but otherwiſe it is of thoſe, that are not prohibited by law, they muſt have ſuch a particular writ or proclamation as is abovesaid.

[l] Sir Matthew Gourny knight was prohibited by the kings writ to depart the realm, and to ſerve in wars expreſly inhibited by the king: which notwithſtanding he did. Now the record ſaith, *Quia Mathæus Gourny miles contra defenſionem regis transfretavit, et ſe guerris ſibi per regem inhibitis immiſcuit, tam in corpore, quam in bonis* [m] *forisfecit regi manerium de Corimallet ſimul cum una carucat' terræ, &c.*

[a] *Rex* † *licentiam dedit abbati de E. quòd proficiſci poſſit ultra mare ad viſitandum caput Sancti Johannis Baptiſtæ Ambiani, corpora trium regum Coloniæ, feretrum Sancti Franciſci in et Sanctum Jacobum in Galicia, ita quod non proſequetur, aut procurabit quicquam in præjudicium regis, aut * legum ſuarum, ſicut idem abbas in præſentia cancellarii regis per juramentum promiſit.*

Note that eccleſiaſticall perſons could not goe beyond ſea on pilgrimage without licence, nor to doe any thing in prejudice of the king, or his laws.

[b] And it is to be obſerved that the king may grant licence to travail beyond the ſeas, either under the great ſeal, privy ſeal, or privy ſignet, but he cannot recall one that is beyond ſea, but by the great ſeale, or privy ſeal.

But for avoiding of tedioufneſſe, and heaping many to one end, let us deſcend to later times.

[c] The letters under the great ſeal, or privy ſeal to recall any from beyond ſea, ought to be ſerved by ſome [d] meſſenger, who upon his oath is to make a certificate thereof in the chancery, and from thence

[e] Britton temps E. 1. fo. 282, 283. Vide leſtatut. de 5 R. 2. ca. 2. Seigniours except out of that ſtatute.
[f] See the firſt part of the Inſtit. ſect. 164. f. 110. a. 27 Auguſt 5 H. 4. De ſon grand councell.
[g] An. 19 E. 2. in Scac. 2 & 3 Ph. & Mar. Dier, 128. pl. 61. Will. de Brittaine countee de Richmonds caſe.
[h] Rot. clauſ. 4 E. 3. m. 38.
[i] H l. 24 E. 3. coram rege, Rot. 13.
[k] Dorſ. clauſ. 25 E. 3. m. 18.
[l] Mic. 39 E. 3. coram rege. Rot. 97. Somerſ. Rot. Vaſc. 10 E. 3. m. 29.
[m] By ſeiſure and impriſonment.
[a] Rot. pat. 40 E. pt. 1. nu. 40. Mich. 41 E. 3. Coram rege Rot. 34. Prioriſſa Sancti Barth. et de novo caſtro quod mare non tranſiit, &c.
† [180]
* Nota (legum ſuarum) ut ſupra.
[b] F. N. B. 85. f.
[c] Dier Hil. 2 Eliz. 176. the caſe of Barteu and the dutches of Suffolk.
[d] See 10 H. 4. 5. Englefields caſe. Lib. 7. fo. 11. See the 1 part of the Inſtitutes ſect. 102.

thence a *mittimus* to be ſent into the exchequer, and thereupon a commiſſion to be granted to ſeiſe the lands and goods of the delinquent.

[e] Mich. 12 & 13 El. Dier, fo. 296. & Paſc. 23 Eliz. fo. 375.

[e] Mich. 12 & 13 Eliz. It was reſolved by all the juſtices (except two) that a merchant of London departing the realm, to the intent to live freely from the penalty of the law, and out of his due obedience to the queen, and not for any merchandiſe, that it was no contempt to the queen, for merchants were excepted out of the ſaid ſtatute of 5 R. 2. cap. 2. and by the common law merchants might paſſe the ſea without licence, though it were not to merchandize.

It is holden, and ſo it hath been reſolved, that divided kingdomes under ſeverall kings in league one with another are ſanctuaries for ſervants or ſubjects flying for ſafety from one kingdome to another, and upon demand made by them, are not by the laws and liberties of kingdomes to be delivered: and this (ſome hold) is grounded upon the law in Deuteronomy. *Non trades ſervum domino ſuo, qui ad te confugerit.*

Deut. c. 23. v. 15.

When queen Elizabeths ambaſſadour lieger in France, *anno* 34 of her reign, demanded of the French king Morgan and others of her ſubjects, that had committed treaſon againſt her; the anſwer of the French king to the queens ambaſſadour is truly related in theſe words. *Si quid in Gallia machinarentur, regem ex jure in illos animadverſurum; ſin in Anglia quid machinati fuerint, regem non poſſe de eiſdem cognoſcere, et ex jure agere. Omnia regna profugis eſſe libera, regum intereſſe, ut ſui quiſque regni libertates tueatur. Immo Elizabetham non ita pridem in ſuum regnum Mountgomerium, principem Condæum, et alios è gente Gallica admiſiſſe, &c.* and ſo it reſted.

Camden Elizab. pa. 355.

King H. 8. in the 28 year of his reign being in league with the French king, and in enmity with the pope, who was in league with the French king, ſent Cardinall Pool ambaſſadour to the French king, of whom king H. 8. demanded the ſaid Cardinall being his ſubject and attainted of treaſon, and to that end cauſed a treatiſe to be made (which I have ſeen) that ſo it ought to be done *jure gentium: ſed non prævaluit.* But Ferdinando king of Spain upon requeſt made by H. 7. to have Edmond de la Pool earl of Suffolk attainted of high treaſon by parliament, *anno* 19 H. 7. at the firſt intending to obſerve the privilege and liberty of kings, to protect ſuch as came to him for ſuccour, and protection, delivered him not, yet in the end upon the earneſt requeſt of H. 7. and promiſe that he would not put him to death, cauſed the ſaid earl to be delivered unto him, who kept him in priſon, and conſtruing his promiſe to be perſonall to himſelf, commanded his ſon Henry after his deceaſe to execute him, who in the fifth year of his reign upon cold blood performed the ſame.

An. 21 H. 7. Rot. parl. 19 H. 7.

We could add more examples of this kind, but (to ſpeak once for all) having purpoſed to give ſome taſte of every thing pertinent, or incident to ſuch things, as we have undertaken to treat of, theſe ſhall ſuffice.

[181]

See the ſtatute of 3 Car. an act to reſtrain the paſſing and ſending of any to be popiſhly bred beyond the ſeas.

3 Car. ca. 2.

* *Flemenesfreme, ſive flemenesfrenthe, interpretatur, catalla fugitivorum.*

* Mich. 10 H. 4. Coram rege, Rot. 59. Hertford.

CAP.

CAP. LXXXV.

Againſt Monopoliſts, Propounders, and Projectors.

IT appeareth [a] by the preamble of this act (as a judgement in parliament) that all grants of monopolies are againſt the ancient and fundamentall laws of this kingdome, and therefore it is neceſſary to define what a monopoly is.

[a] The ſtatute of 21 Jac. ca. 3. Rom. 1. 30. Inventores malorum.

[b] A monopoly is an inſtitution, or allowance by the king by his grant, commiſſion, or otherwiſe to any perſon or perſons, bodies politique, or corporate, of or for the ſole buying, ſelling, making, working, or uſing of any thing, whereby any perſon or perſons, bodies politique, or corporate, are ſought to be reſtrained of any freedome, or liberty that they had before, or hindred in their lawfull trade.

[b] A monopoly deſcribed. See the expoſition upon Magna Carta, c. 29. & 30. in the ſecond pt. of the Inſtit.

[c] For the word monopoly, *dicitur*, ἀπὸ τȣ̃ μόνȣ, i. *ſolo*, καὶ πωλέομαι, i. *vendere, quod eſt, cum unus ſolus aliquod genus mercaturæ univerſum vendit, ut ſolus vendat, pretium ad ſuum libitum ſtatuens:* hereof you may read more at large in that caſe. And the law of the realm in this point is grounded upon the law of God, which ſaith, *Non accipies loco pignoris inferiorem et ſuperiorem molam, quia animam ſuam appoſuit tibi.* Thou ſhalt not take the nether or upper milſtone to pledge, for he taketh a mans life to pledge: whereby it appeareth that a mans trade is accounted his life, becauſe it maintaineth his life; and therefore the monopoliſt that taketh away a mans trade, taketh away his life, and therefore is ſo much the more odious, becauſe he is *vir ſanguinis.* Againſt theſe inventers and propounders of evill things, the Holy Ghoſt hath ſpoken, *inventores malorum, &c. digni ſunt morte.*

[c] Trin. 44 Eliz. lib. 11. f. 84, 85. le caſe de Monopolies.

Deut. ca. 24. v. 6.

Rom. 1. 30.

That monopolies are againſt the ancient and fundamentall laws of the realm (as it is declared by this act) and that the monopoliſt was in times paſt, and is much more now puniſhable, for obtaining and procuring of them, we will demonſtrate it by reaſon, and prove it by authority.

Whatſoever offence is contrary to the ancient and fundamentall laws of the realm, is puniſhable by law: but the uſe of a monopoly is contrary to the ancient and fundamentall laws of the realme, therefore the uſe of a monopoly is puniſhable by law.

Commercium jure gentium commune eſſe debet, et non in monopolium, et privatum pauculorum queſtum convertendum. Iniquum eſt alios permittere, alios inhibere mercaturam.

That offence which is contrary to the ancient and fundamentall laws is *malum in ſe.* The minor is proved by this declaration in parliament.

11 H. 7. 11.

The liberty that the ſubject hath to goe to any clerk in the kings court cannot be reſtrained but by parliament.

W. 1. cap. 27.

In 50 E. 3. John Peachie of London was ſeverely puniſhed for procuring a licence under the great ſeal, that he only might ſell ſweet wines in London,

Rot. par. 50 E. 3. nu. 33.

See in the preambles of 9 E. 3. cap. 1. 25 E. 3. cap. 2. 27 E. 3. & 28 E. 3. Stat. Stap. 2 R. 2. ca. 1. See the ſtatute of Magna Cart. ca. 3. 31 E. 3. cap. 10. 7 H. 4. cap. 9. and 12 H. 7. ca. 6.

1 & 2 Ph. & Mar. ca. 14. Rot. Parl. 1 R. 2. nu. 20. 4 R. 2. nu. 39. 5 R. 2. nu. 89. Fortescue, cap. 35, 36. One of the articles wherewith William de la Pool duke of Suffolk was charged, was for procuring of divers liberties in derogation of the common law, and hindrance of justice: note this is an offence punishable.

Rot. Parl. 28 H. 6. nu. 30.

[182]

Mich. 2 & 3 El. Dier manuscript not printed.

King Philip and queen Mary by their letters patents granted to the maior, bailiffs and burgesses of Southampton and their successors, (for that king Philip first landed there) that no wines called malmsies, brought into this realm from the parts beyond the seas by any liege man or alien, should be discharged or landed in any other place of the realm, but only at the said town and port of Southampton, with a prohibition, that no person or persons shall doe otherwise, upon paine to pay treble custome: and it was resolved by all the judges of England that this grant made in restraint of the landing of the same wines was against the laws and statutes of this realme, viz. Magna Carta, 29, 30. 9 E. 3. cap. 1. 14 E. 3. 25 E. 3. ca. 2. 27 & 28 E. 3. statute of the staple. 2 R. 2. cap. 1. and others: and also that the assessment of treble custome was against law, and meerly void. And after at the parliament holden in *anno* 5 Eliz. the patent, as to aliens, was by a private act confirmed by parliament, and not for English.

Stat. de 5 Eliz.

Trin. 41 Eliz. coram rege, rot. 92. int. Davenant and Hurdys in trespasse. Trin. 44 Eliz. in Lib. 11. fo. 84, 85, &c. Edward Darcies case. Hil. 7 Jacobi in Lib. 8. fo. 121, 122. &c. the case of the City of London.

The judgement in the said case of monopolies cited before, Trin. 44 Eliz. was the principall motive of the publishing of the kings book mentioned in the preamble of this act, and that book was a great motive of obtaining the royall assent to this act of parliament, whereof we are now to speak. This act moved from the house of commons: the act is long and in print, and need not here to be rehearsed: yet will we peruse and explain the words in the severall branches of the act

By his grant, commission, or otherwise.] These words [or otherwise] are of a large extent, and are well warranted by this act, the words whereof extend not only to all proclamations, inhibitions, restraints, and warrants of assistance of the king, but all inhibitions, restraints and warrants of assistance of all or any of the privy councell or any other: and all other matters or things whatsoever either of the king, or of all or any of his privy councell to the instituting, erecting, strengthening, furthering, or countenancing of the sole buying, selling, &c. or any of them, are declared to be altogether contrary to the laws of this realm, &c. *ut in statuto.* This act herein, and in the residue thereof, is forcibly and vehemently penned for the suppression of all monopolies: for monopolies in times past were ever without law, but never without friends.

Sole.] This word [sole] is to be applied to five severall things, viz. buying, selling, making, working, and using; four of which are speciall, and the last, viz. (sole using) is so generall, as no monopoly can be raised, but shall be within the reach of this statute, and yet for more surety these words [or of any other monopolies] are

are added: and by reaſon of theſe words [ſole uſing] divers proviſions are made by this act, as hereafter ſhall appear.

Of any thing.] As the words before were generall, ſo theſe words [of any thing] are of a large extent. *Res enim generalem habet ſignificationem, quia tam corporea, quam incorporea, cujuſcunque ſunt generis, naturæ, ſive ſpeciei, comprehendit:* and this word cauſeth ſome exceptions hereafter to be made, whereof we ſhall ſpeak in their proper place.

Whereby any perſon or perſons, &c.] For this ſee the ſtatute of Magna Carta, *ubi ſupra:* and this clauſe is impliedly warranted by theſe words [or of any other monopolies] in the firſt clauſe of the purvien.

Shall be for ever hereafter examined, heard, tried, and determined by and according to the common laws of this realm, and not otherwiſe.] This act having declared all monopolies, &c. to be void by the common law, hath provided by this clauſe, that they ſhall be examined, heard, tried, and determined in the courts of the common law according to the common law, and not at the councell table, ſtar-chamber, chancery, exchequer chamber, or any other court of like nature, but only according to the common laws of this realm, with words negative, and not otherwiſe: for ſuch boldneſſe the monopoliſts took, that often at the councell table, ſtar-chamber, chancery, and exchequer chamber, petitions, informations, and bils were preferred in the ſtar-chamber, &c. pretending a contempt for not obeying the commandements and clauſes of the ſaid grants of monopolies, and of the proclamations, &c. concerning the ſame: for the preventing of which miſchief this branch was added. [183]

That all perſon and perſons, bodies politique, and corporate whatſoever, which now are, or hereafter ſhall be, ſhall ſtand, and be diſabled, and uncapable, &c.] This branch for further extirpation of all monopolies, diſableth all men, &c. to have, that is, to take any monopoly, or to uſe, exerciſe, or put in ure any monopoly, &c. whereby the wiſh and deſire of the poet is granted.

Funditus extirpa monopolas et nomopolas;
Hic labor, hoc opus eſt; Hercule major eris.
Paucorum nocuit ſcelerata licentia multis,
Argento mutat dum monopola piper.

If any perſon or perſons after the end of forty dayes next after the end of this preſent ſeſſion of parliament ſhal be hindred, grieved, diſturbed, or diſquieted, &c.]

By this branch ſix things are provided and enacted. 1. Remedy is given to the party grieved at the common law by action or actions to be grounded upon this ſtatute. 2. This remedy may be had in the court of the kings bench, common pleas, and exchequer, or any of them, at the election of the party grieved. 3. The party grieved ſhall recover treble damages, and double coſts. 4. No eſſoin, protection, wager of law, aid prayer, priviledge, injunction, or order of reſtraint to be allowed in any ſuch action. By (aid prayer) is intended as well the writ *de domino rege inconſulto*, as the uſuall form of aid prayer, for both are to one end, and (order of reſtraint) was added, for the councell table, ſtar-chamber, chancery, exchequer chamber, and the like.

5. If any perſon or perſons ſhall after notice given, &c. cauſe

or procure any ſuch action to be ſtayed or delayed before judgement, by colour or means of any order, warrant, power or authority, ſave onely of the court wherein ſuch action ſhall be brought and depending, the perſon or perſons ſo offending ſhall incur the danger of premunire, &c.

This clauſe extends to the privy councell, ſtar-chamber, chancery, exchequer chamber, and the like, and likewiſe to thoſe that ſhall procure any warrant, &c. from the king, &c. and ſo it was reſolved by a committee of both houſes before this bill paſſed; but it extendeth not to the judges of the court before whom any ſuch action ſhall be brought, for before judgements, days muſt be given by orders of court, &c.

6. Or after judgement had upon ſuch action ſhall cauſe or procure execution of or upon any ſuch judgement, to be ſtayed by colour or means of any order, warrant, power or authority, ſave only by writ of error and attaint, the perſon or perſons ſo offending ſhall incur the danger of premunire, &c.

This clauſe is more generall then the former, being the fifth clauſe, for this extendeth alſo to the judges of the court where the action is brought or depending, if any ſtay or delay be uſed by them after judgement, and ſo it was reſolved as is aforeſaid.

[184] There be in this act concerning monopolies or ſole buying, &c. many proviſoes. The firſt is, that this act ſhall not extend to any letters patents or grants of priviledge heretofore made of the ſole working or making of any manner of new manufacture: but that new manufacture muſt have ſeven properties. Firſt, it muſt be for twenty one years or under. Secondly, it muſt be granted to the firſt and true inventer. Thirdly, it muſt be of ſuch manufactures, which any other at the making of ſuch letters patents did not uſe: for albeit it were newly invented, yet if any other did uſe it at the making of the letters patents, or grant of the priviledge, it is declared and enacted to be void by this act. Fourthly, the priviledge muſt not be contrary to law: ſuch a priviledge, as is conſonant to law, muſt be ſubſtantially and eſſentially newly invented; but if the ſubſtance was in *eſſe* before, and a new addition thereunto, though that addition make the former more profitable, yet is it not a new manufacture in law: and ſo was it reſolved in the exchequer chamber, Paſch. 15 Eliz. in Bircots caſe for a priviledge concerning the preparing and melting, &c. of lead ore: for there it was ſaid, that that was to put but a new button to an old coat: and it is much eaſier to adde then to invent. And there it was alſo reſolved, that if the new manufacture be ſubſtantially invented according to law, yet no old manufacture in uſe before can be prohibited. Fifthly, nor miſchievous to the ſtate by raiſing of prices of commodities at home. In every ſuch new manufacture that deſerves a priviledge, there muſt be *urgens neceſſitas*, and *evidens utilitas*. Sixthly, nor to the hurt of trade. This is very materiall and evident. Seventhly, nor generally inconvenient. There was a new invention found out heretofore, that bonnets and caps might be thickned in a fulling mill, by which means more might be thickned and fulled in one day then by the labours of fourſcore men, who got their livings by it. It was ordained that bonnets and caps ſhould be thickned and fulled by the ſtrength of men, and not in a fulling mill,, for it was holden in-

Concerning new manufactures and heretofore granted, &c.

Paſch. 15 Eliz. in the exchequer chamber Bircots caſe.

Rot. parl. 21 E. 4. nu. 29. 22 E. 4. ca. 5. 7 E. 6. ca. 6. 1 Jacobi, ca. 5.

inconvenient to turn ſo many labouring men to idleneſſe. If any of theſe ſeven qualities fail, the priviledge is declared and enacted to be void by this act: and yet this act, if they have all theſe properties, ſet them in no better caſe, then they were before this act.

The ſecond proviſo concerneth the priviledge of new manufactures hereafter to be granted: and this alſo muſt have ſeven properties, firſt it muſt be for the tearm of fourteen years or under: the other ſix properties muſt be ſuch as are aforeſaid, and yet this act maketh them no better, then they ſhould have been, if this act had never been made, but only except and exempt them out of the purvien, and penalty of this law. Concerning new manufactures hereafter to be granted, &c.

The cauſe wherefore the priviledges of new manufactures either before this act granted, or which after this act ſhould be granted, having theſe ſeven properties, were not declared to be good, was, for that the reaſon wherefore ſuch a priviledge is good in law is, becauſe the inventor bringeth to and for the common wealth a new manufacture by his invention, coſt and charges, and therefore it is reaſon, that he ſhould have a priviledge for his reward (and the incouragement of others in the like) for a convenient time: but it was thought that the times limited by this act were too long for the private, before the common wealth ſhould be partaker thereof, and ſuch as ſerved ſuch priviledged perſons by the ſpace of ſeven years in making or working of the new manufacture (which is the time limited by law of apprenticehood) muſt be apprentices or ſervants ſtil during the reſidue of the priviledge, by means whereof ſuch numbers of men would not apply themſelves thereunto, as ſhould be requiſite for the common wealth, after the priviledge ended. And this was the true cauſe wherefore both for the time paſſed, and for the time to come, they were left of ſuch force, as they were before the making of this act.

The third proviſo is, that this act ſhall not extend or be prejudicial to any grant or priviledge, power or authority heretofore made, granted, allowed, or confirmed by any act of parliament now in force, ſo long as the ſame ſhall ſo continue in force. This was added for that the city of London and other cities and boroughs, &c. have ſome priviledges for buying, ſelling, &c. by acts of parliament. For example, the ſtatute of 1 & 2 Ph. and Mar. giveth a priviledge to cities, boroughs, towns corporate, and market towns, for the ſale by retale of certain wares and merchandizes, and ſome other acts of parliament in like caſe: all which do prove, that ſuch priviledge could not be granted by letters patents. But ſpecially this clauſe was added in reſpect of the generality of theſe words [ſole uſing.] [185] 1 & 2 Ph. and Mar. cap. 7.

The fourth proviſo. Provided alſo, and it is hereby further intended, declared, and inacted, that this act, &c. ſhall not in any wiſe extend, or be prejudiciall unto the city of London, &c.

By this proviſo, not only the grants, charters, and letters patents to any city or towne corporate, &c. but alſo the cuſtomes uſed within the ſame, are excepted out of this act: which ſeemeth to be more than need, becauſe the firſt clauſe of the purvien of this act doth extend but to commiſſions, grants, licences, charters, and letters patents.

The fifth proviſo doth except out of the purvien and penalty of this

this ſtatute four things, but leaveth them of the like force and effect, and no other, as this act had never been made. Firſt, the priviledge concerning printing made, or hereafter to be made. Secondly, commiſſions, grants, and letters patents made or hereafter to be made for or concerning the digging, making, or compounding of ſalt-petre or gunpowder. Thirdly, or the caſting or making of ordnance, or ſhot for ordnance. Fourthly, grants and letters patents heretofore made, or hereafter to be made of any office or offices heretofore erected, made, or ordained, and now in being, and put in execution, (other then ſuch offices as have been decried by any his majeſties proclamations.) So as to the thing by this branch excepted, four things are required. Firſt that it be an office. This extendeth only to lawfull offices for divers cauſes. 1. It was neceſſary to except lawfull offices in reſpect of theſe words [ſole uſing.] 2. Offices are duties, ſo called, to put the officer in minde of his duty. 3. That which is voide and againſt law, is no duty, unleſſe it be not to uſe them. 4. Such as are erected againſt law, are monopolies and oppreſſions of the people, and no offices. 5. In acts of parliament lawfull offices are intended, as in like caſes hath been often adjudged: therefore unlawfull offices are all taken away by this act, and lawfull offices remain and continue.

Lit. ſect. 731. Pl. com. 246. b. 11 H. 4. 80. 4 E. 4. 31. pl. 2.

Secondly, that it be an office heretofore erected. By this act the erection of all new offices, which were not erected before this act, are wholly taken away.

Thirdly, that it be now in being, and put in execution. Though the office were erected before this act, yet if it were not in being and put in execution the 19 day of February in the 21 year of the reigne of king James (at what time this parliament begun) it is cleerly taken away by this act.

See the proclamation bearing date 10 July, an. 19 Jac. regis, and another proclamation bearing date, 20 Martii an. 19 Ja. regis.

Fourthly, that it be ſuch an office, as hath not been decried (for ſo is the record of parliament, and not [decreed] as it is in the printed book) by any of his majeſties proclamations: for all ſuch offices as be decried, that is, either forbidden, or prohibited by any of his majeſties proclamations, or where the party grieved is left to his remedy at the common law by any proclamation, they be alſo decried; for being contrary to the lawes of this realme, as it is declared and enacted by this act, they are alſo decried with a witneſſe, and can never be granted hereafter.

The fift proviſo concerning the making of allom, or allome-wines, needed not, for they belong to the ſubject in whoſe ground ſoever the oare is: and therefore any priviledge thereof cannot be granted, but in the kings owne ground.

The ſixth proviſo concerns the hoſtmen of Newcaſtle, &c. This clauſe was inſerted in reſpect of theſe words [ſole uſing].

The reſt of the proviſoes concerne particular perſons, and do exempt and except certaine ſuppoſed priviledges out of the purvien and penalty of this law, but leaveth them of like force and effect, as they were before the making of it.

But it is to be obſerved, that all the proviſoes after the ſixth, extend only to the ſuppoſed priviledges therein particularly mentioned, already granted, and not to any to be granted hereafter.

CAP.

CAP. LXXXVI.

Againſt thoſe that obtaine Power to diſpenſe with penall Lawes, and Forfeitures thereof.

IT appeareth by the preamble of this act, that all grants of the benefit of any penall law, or of power to diſpence with the law, or to compound for the forfeiture, are contrary to the ancient fundamental lawes of this realm. The ſtatute of 21 Jac. cap. 3.

It was one of the articles wherefore the Spencers in the reigne of king E. 2. were ſentenced, that they procured the king to make many diſpenſations. *Per lour malveis counſell defeaſant ceo q. le roy ad grant p. parliament p. bone advice.* In Exilio Hugonis.

In 50 E. 3 Richard Lions a merchant of London, and the Lo. Latimer, were ſeverally ſentenced in parliament for procuring of licenſes and diſpenſations to tranſport wools, &c. Rot. parliam. 50 E. 3. nu. 17. & 28. See 28 H. 6. nu. 30. before.

It is declared and enacted, that all commiſſions, grants, licenſes, charters, and letters patents, heretofore made or granted, to any perſon or perſons, bodies politick, or corporate, of any power, liberty, or faculty, to diſpenſe with any others, or to give licenſe or toleration to doe, uſe, or exerciſe any thing againſt the tenure or purport of any law or ſtatute, or to give, or make any warrant for any ſuch diſpenſation, licenſe or toleration to be had, or made, or to agree, or compound with any others for any penaltie or forfeitures limited by any ſtatute, or of any grant or promiſe of the benefit, profit, or commoditie of any forfeiture, penalty or ſumme of money, that is or ſhall be due by any ſtatute before judgement thereupon had, and all proclamations, inhibitions, reſtraints, warrants of aſſiſtance, and all other matters and things whatſoever, any way tending to the inſtituting, erecting, ſtrengthening, furthering, or countenancing of the ſame or any of them, are altogether contrary to the lawes of this realme, in no wiſe to be put in execution. The purvien of the act of 21 Ja. cap. 3. The offence deſcribed.

And ſhall be for ever hereafter examined, heard, tried, and determined, by and according to the common lawes of this realme; and not otherwiſe, &c.

Provided alſo, that this act ſhall not extend to any warrant or privie ſeale made or directed, or to be made or directed by his majeſtie, his heirs or ſucceſſors to the juſtices of the courts of kings bench, common pleas, barons of the exchequer, &c. and other juſtices for the time being, having power to heare and determine, &c. to compound, &c.

This

This act moved from the house of commons. Now let us peruse, first, the words of the purvien of this act, and secondly, of this proviso.

In and by the purvien five things are declared and enacted to be void, and contrary to the ancient fundamentall lawes of this realme. First, all commissions, licenses, charters, and letters patents of any power, liberty, or faculty, or to give license or toleration to do, use, or exercise any thing against any law or statute. The reason hereof is notably expressed by the resolution of all the judges of England, in the case of penall statutes, whereunto we refer you,

Hil. 2 Jac. lib. 7. fo. 36. b. the case of penal statutes.

[187]

2. *Or to give or make any warrant for any such dispensation, license, or toleration.*] For this branch also, see the said case of penall statutes, *ut supra.*

3. *Or to agree or compound with any others for any penalty or forfeitures limited by any statute.*] By this branch, all commissions to agree or compound with any others for any penalty or forfeiture limited by any statute, are declared to be void, and against the ancient fundamentall lawes of the realme. The great inconvenience hereof appeared in the proceedings of Empson and Dudley, in the reigne of king H. 7. who had the office of masters of the forfeitures: and by colour of their commission and office, did most intolerably and unlawfully oppresse, burden, and depauperate the subjects. Let them which follow their steps be afraid of their fearfull end: *Qui eorum vestigia sequuntur, eorum exitus perhorrescant.* The like oppression was used by certain commissioners for compositions to be made for offences committed against penall statutes, in the reigne of queen Mary. This branch hath strucken at the root, and prevented this mischief for ever hereafter.

4. *Or of any grant or promise of the benefit, profit, or commodity of any forfeiture, penalty, or sum of money, that is or shall be due by any statute before judgement thereupon had.*] This branch declareth not only the grant to be void, and against the lawes of this realme, (for the which, see the resolution of all the judges in the said case of penall statutes, *ubi supra*,) but the promise thereof also. And the reason that the judges yeeld there, is notable in these words. For that in our experience it maketh the more violent and undue proceeding against the subject to the scandall of justice, and offence of many. So as the grant or promise of any forfeiture before judgement, is both against law, and inconvenient. And if it be so in case of a forfeiture or penalty; much more in case of life and death, for the forfeiture, &c. of any man to be begged, before he be duly and lawfully attainted. For, as the judges say, there is the more violent and undue proceeding against the subject to the scandall of justice, and the offence of many: and therefore such beggers are offenders worthy of severe punishment.

Micah 7. 2.

Against these hunters for blood the prophet speaketh thus, *Periit sanctus de terra, et rectus in hominibus non est, omnes in sanguine insidiantur, vir fratrem suum ad mortem venatur.* There is not a godly man upon earth, there is not one righteous amongst men, they all lye in wait for blood, and every man hunteth his brother to death.

5. *And all proclamations, inhibitions, restraints, warrants of assistance, and all other matters or things any way tending to the institut-*

ing,

ing, erecting, ſtrengthening, &c.] This is the like clauſe, and is ſo to be expounded, as before hath been in the chapter of Monopolies.

Concerning the ſaid proviſo, the judges before whom the cauſe dependeth, and that have power to hear and determine the ſame, who are preſumed to be indifferent between the king and the ſubject, may by warrant or privie ſeale, &c. compound, &c. for the king only, after plea pleaded by the defendant.

There is another proviſo concerning letters patents, or commiſſions for licenſing of keeping of any tavern, or ſelling, &c. of wines, &c. or for the making of any compoſitions for ſuch licenſes, ſo as the benefit of ſuch compoſitions be reſerved, and applyed to or for the uſe of his majeſtie, his heirs or ſucceſſors and not for the private uſe of any other perſon or perſons.

The report of the ſaid caſe of penall ſtatutes was a principall motive of the kings book, mentioned in the preamble of this act: and that book amongſt other juſt and weighty cauſes moved the king to give his royall aſſent to this act of parliament, &c. whereof we have ſpoken.

CAP. LXXXVII. [188]

Againſt Concealours (*turbidum Hominum Genus*) and all Pretences of Concealements whatſoever.

THAT the kings majeſtie, his heirs, or ſucceſſors, ſhall not at any time hereafter ſue, impeach, queſtion, or implead any perſon or perſons, bodies politick, or corporate, &c. Statut. de anno 21 Jac. cap. 2.

The act is long, and need not here be rehearſed. Yet will we peruſe and explain the ſeveral branches and parts of the act.

Before the making of this ſtatute, in reſpect of that ancient prerogative of the crowne, that *nullum tempus occurrit regi*, the titles of the king were not reſtrained to any limitation of time: for that no ſtatute of limitation that ever was made, did ever limit the title of the king to any mannors, lands, tenements, or hereditaments, to any certaine time. And where many records and other muniments, making good the eſtate and intereſt of the ſubject, either by abuſe or negligence of officers by devouring time were not to be found; by means whereof, certain indigne and indigent perſons prying into many ancient titles of the crown, and into ſome of later time concerning the poſſeſſions of divers and ſundry biſhopricks, dean and chapters, and the late monaſteries, chauntries, &c. of perſons attainted, and the like, have paſſed ſurreptitiouſly in letters patents, oftentimes under obſcure and generall words, the mannors, lands, tenements, and hereditaments of long time enjoyed by the ſubjects of this realm, as well eccleſiaſticall as temporall: now

now to limit the crown to ſome certaine time, to the end, that all the ſubjects of this realme, their heirs and ſucceſſors, may quietly have, hold, and enjoy, all and ſingular mannors, lands, tenements, and hereditaments, which they, their anceſtors, or predeceſſors, or any other, by, from, or under whom they claime, have of long time enjoyed; this act was made and moved from the houſe of commons, the body whereof conſiſteth of three parts. Firſt, that part which above is in part rehearſed, conſiſteth on three branches.

The firſt part.

Firſt, That the king, his heirs or ſucceſſors, ſhall not at any time hereafter, ſue, impeach, queſtion, or implead any perſon or perſons, bodies politick or corporate, for, or in any wiſe concerning any mannors, &c. *Secondly*, Or for or concerning the revenues, iſſues, or profits thereof. *Thirdly*, Or make any title, claime, challenge, or demand, &c.

This part is excluſive and negative: and herein ſix things are to be obſerved.

1. This clauſe extendeth to all maner of ſuits, &c. either in law, or in equity. 2. To all manner of courts whatſoever. 3. It extendeth not only to all manner of ſuits, but to all impeachments, queſtionings, impleadings, making of title, claimes, challenges, or demands. 4. Under theſe words [right, and title] not only bare rights and titles are comprehended, but reall eſtates alſo. 5. Not only ſuits, &c. for or concerning any mannors, &c. but for or concerning the revenues, iſſues, or profits, &c. and this extendeth to the ancient demeans of the crowne, which are mentioned to be reſtrained by an act of 11 H. 4. 6. So as all writs of *ſcire fac'* or other proces upon any record; all informations of intruſion, or charging any man as bayliffe: all finding of offices, either of intitling the king, or of information, are reſtrained, not only within theſe words [impeach or queſtion] but alſo within theſe words [or make any title, claime, challenge, or demand] which are large and beneficial words, and all other ſuits, &c. of what kind or nature ſoever. But this negative clauſe muſt have four incidents. 1. The kings right and title muſt accrew unto him above threeſcore years paſt before the nineteenth day of February, in the 21 year of king James, which was the day of the beginning of this parliament. The reaſon hereof was, that if any title of eſcheat, forfeiture, &c. accrewed within threeſcore years, then it ſhould be out of this act: for generally the time of limitation to bar the king was threeſcore years, but ſuch right or title muſt now be *in eſſe*. 2. Unleſſe the king or his progenitors, &c. or any under whom he or they claim, have been anſwered by force and vertue of any ſuch right or title to the ſame, the rents, revenues, iſſues, or profits thereof within threeſcore years, &c. In this branch theſe words [by force and vertue of any ſuch right or title] were materially added, for otherwiſe if the king had been anſwered the rents, revenues, &c, by reaſon or pretext of wardſhip, primer ſeiſon, extent, or the like, it might have made a doubt whether ſuch an anſwering of the revenues, &c. had been within this act; which doubt is cleared, that it muſt be by force or vertue of any ſuch right or title, whereby the king impeacheth the ſtate of the ſubject. 3. Or that

Rot. Par. 11 H. 4. nu. 23. not imprinted.

[189]

that the ſame have been duly in charge to his majeſty, or to the late queen Elizabeth within the ſpace of threeſcore years. Duly in charge in judgement of law, is the roll of the pipe: for although a note before the auditor or any other may be a mean to bring it in queſtion, and to be put in charge, yet that is not in judgement of law ſaid to be duly in charge, unleſſe it be in charge in the pipe. 4. Or have ſtood in ſuper of record within the ſaid ſpace of threeſcore years. It cannot ſtand in ſuper, unleſſe the thing in queſtion were before duly in charge.

But there is a good proviſo added towards the end of this act, viz. that no putting in charge, or ſuper, or anſwering of the farm rents, revenues, or profits, &c. in four caſes ſhall be within this act, viz. by force, colour or pretext of any letters patents of concealments: they were called letters patents of concealments, becauſe either they had a clauſe before the *habendum: quæ quidem maneria nuper fuerunt à nobis concelata, ſubtracta, vel injuſte detenta*, or to the like effect; or elſe a proviſo after the *habendum* to the like effect. Letters patents of concealment were granted in queen Maries time; and the firſt that I find, were granted to Sir George Howard: and in all ſucceeding acts of parliament of confirmation of letters patents, letters patents of concealments are excepted.

2. Or defective title. By letters patents paſſed by the warrant of certain commiſſioners under the great ſeal for compoſitions of defective titles, pretending the ſame to be for the kings benefit, and ſafety of the ſubject, in which letters patents no words of concealment, &c. are mentioned, but yet upon the matter, they were ſuppoſed to be concealed, &c. from the crown.

3. Or of lands tenements or hereditaments out of charge. This was a new device to have a certificate, that they were not in charge, and then to take a grant from the king, for a very ſmall compoſition, &c. And theſe were but inventions and ſubtill devices to deceive the king, to rob him of his tenures, and to the infinite vexation and trouble of the ſubject, all which miſchiefs are now remedied by this act.

4. Or by force, colour or pretext of any commiſſion or other authority to find out concealments, defective titles, or land, &c. out of charge. This was a neceſſary clauſe to be added, for of this kind there were infinite numbers.

Out of this firſt part all liberties and franchiſes be excepted.

And that every perſon and perſons, bodies politique and corporate, their heirs and ſucceſſors, and all claiming from, by, or under them, or any of them, for and according to their ſeverall eſtates and intereſts, which they have, or claim to have in the ſame reſpectively, ſhall hereafter quietly and freely have, hold and enjoy againſt his majeſty, his heirs and ſucceſſors, &c. The ſecond part.

This is the ſecond part of the body of the act, and as the firſt part is negative and excluſive of the right and title of the king, ſo this part is affirmative, and eſtabliſhing the eſtate of the ſubject. [190]

The

The miſchief before this ſtatute was in two ſorts, viz. either when the king had any eſtate veſted, or continued in him; or where the king had but a bare right. For example, the kings tenant ſeiſed of lands, &c. in fee is attainted of felony, and dieth, the king hath a real eſtate in him: but if before the felony the kings tenant were diſſeiſed, and after is attainted, and dieth, now hath the king but a bare right. In both theſe caſes, *et ſic in ſimilibus*, the ſubject is provided for by this act, both by the firſt part, and by this alſo: for where in this part it is ſaid, according to their and every of their ſeveral eſtates and intereſts which they have or claim. If they have an eſtate, and the king but a bare right or title, then are they within theſe words [which they have] and if the king hath a reall eſtate in him, then are they within theſe words [or claim] ſo as the remedy is applied to both the miſchiefs. Again, the words in this part are further, have held, or enjoyed. That is, where the ſubject hath an eſtate, and the king but a bare right or title.

Or taken the rents, iſſues, revenues, or profits thereof.] Theſe words extend to all caſes where the reall eſtate is in the king: hereby is underſtood the actuall taking of the rents, iſſues, revenues, or profits by one that claims an intereſt in the land: for albeit the king may in law charge him as bailif, yet without queſtion, *de facto*, he did take the rents, iſſues, revenues and profits, and that ſufficeth to anſwer the letter and meaning of this act.

Moreover, the words of this part are, [Againſt him, his heirs or ſucceſſors.] So admit in the caſe put before, the kings tenant being diſſeiſed, as is aforeſaid, before his attainder of felony, that that diſſeiſor had been diſſeiſed, or had morgaged the land before this ſtatute, this act in this caſe barreth the king of his right and title, and to that end worketh upon the eſtate of the diſſeiſor or morgagee: but yet the firſt diſſeiſor or the morgagee for the condition performed or broken may re-enter; for the words of this part be [againſt the king, his heirs, and ſucceſſors] ſo as the bar is only againſt them: and every ſubject ſhall take benefit of this act, for the kings right and title is thereby utterly barred: and there is a ſaving hereafter in this act to all perſons, &c. other then the king, &c. all ſuch right, &c. as they ought to have had before this act.

This part extendeth not to liberties and franchiſes.

Now followeth the third part of the purvieu of this act.

The third part.

And furthermore, that every perſon and perſons, bodies politique and corporate, their heirs and ſucceſſors, &c. ſhall quietly and freely have, hold, and enjoy all ſuch mannors, &c. as they now have, claim, and enjoy, &c. againſt all and every perſon and perſons, their heirs and aſſigns having, claiming, or pretending to have any eſtate, right, title, intereſt, claim or demand whatſoever, &c. by reaſon, or colour of any letters patents, or grants upon ſuggeſtion of concealment, or wrongfull detaining, or not being in charge, or defective titles, or by, from, or under any patentees, &c. of or for which mannors, &c. no verdict, &c.

This

This part ſecures the ſubject againſt the ſubject, viz. againſt patentees and grantees of concealments, defective titles, or lands not in charge, and all claiming under them. A beneficiall law both for the church and common wealth, in reſpect of the multitude of letters patents and grants of theſe natures and qualities, and many of them of large extents and in generall words, and had paſſed through the hands of many indigent and needy perſons, &c.

This part extendeth to liberties and franchiſes, which the former two parts did not.

The two firſt proviſoes are plain, and in effect are included in the body of the act. The ſecond proviſo was neceſſary to preſerve tenures: the ſaving needeth no explanation. The third proviſo is particular and evident. The fourth proviſo, Provided alſo, and be it enacted, that where any fee farm rent, &c. This was added for the preſerving of the kings fee farms and rents out of ſuch mannors, &c. which are eſtabliſhed and made ſure by this act. For example: king E. 6. did grant the mannor of D. which came to him by the ſtatute of Chanteries, to I. S. and his heirs, reſerving a fee farm, or any other rent, which grant for ſome imperfection was inſufficient in law to paſſe the ſaid mannor, and yet is eſtabliſhed and made ſure by this act. This proviſo maketh good the fee farm or rent to the king, if he hath been anſwered the ſame by the greater part of ſixty years laſt paſt. [191]

The laſt proviſo is particular and evident.

Of the benefit of this act the poor doe participate, as well as the rich, for hereby (amongſt other things) above an hundred lay hoſpitals having had prieſts within them in thoſe days to pray and ſing for ſouls, &c. (if need were) are eſtabliſhed againſt all vexations, and pretences of concealments.

See an excellent act made againſt theſe harpyes or heluones, that under obſcure words endeavoured ſurreptitiouſly in a patent of concealment to have ſwallowed up the greateſt part of the poſſeſſions of that ancient and famous biſhoprick of Norwich, which by the induſtry and proſecution of the then attorney generall was overthrown, and yet for more ſurety in a matter of ſo great weight preferred a bill in parliament for eſtabliſhing of the biſhoprick, which in the end paſſed as a law, *anno* 39 El. *ubi ſupra*.

See 39 El. ca. 22. which is worthy to be read. See this caſe at large in the fourth part of the Inſtitutes cap. Conſiſtory Courts, &c.

Triſtius haud illis monſtrum, nec ſævior ulla
Peſtis et ira Dei ſtygiis ſeſe extulit undis:
Virginei volucrum vultus, fœdiſſima ventris
Proluvies, uncæque manus, et pallida ſemper
Ora fame.

CAP.

CAP. LXXXVIII.

Againſt Vexatious Relators, Informers, and Promooters upon Penall Statutes.

Statutum de 21 Jac. reg. c. 4.

THAT all offences hereafter to be committed againſt any penall ſtatute, for which any common informer or promooter may lawfully ground any popular action, bill, plaint, ſuit or information, &c. ſhall be commenced, ſued, proſecuted, &c. before the juſtices of aſſiſe, juſtices of niſi prius, &c. in the counties where the offences were committed, and not elſewhere.

18 El. ca. 5.

Whereas a good and profitable law was made in the 18 year of queen El. for the eaſe and quiet of the ſubject, and for the regulating of informers upon penall ſtatutes, inflicting corporall puniſhments in certain caſes upon them. And whereas two other good

28 El. ca. 5.
31 El. ca. 10.

laws were made for the ſame ends, the one in the 28 year, and the other in the 31 year of the ſaid late queens reign, which yet ſtand and remain in force: yet theſe acts did not meet with all the miſchiefs and grievances offered to the ſubject by the relators, informers and promooters, (*turbidum hominum genus*) but theſe four miſchiefs and grievances remained ſtill.

[192]

Firſt, many penall laws obſolete, and in time grown apparently impoſſible, or inconvenient to be performed, remained as ſnares, whereupon the relator, informer or promooter did vex and entangle the ſubject: ſuch as were the ſtatutes made *anno* 37 E. 3. cap. 3. concerning the prices of poultry, and 34 E. 3. ca. 20. concerning tranſportation of corn, and 3 E. 4. cap. 2. concerning corn not to be brought into the realm, and 4 H. 7. ca. 9. concerning the prices of hats and caps, and 14 R. 2. cap. 7. concerning the paſſing of tyn out of the realm, and 15 R. 2. cap. 8. concerning the carriage of tyn to Calys, and 4 H. 5. cap. 3. concerning making of pattens of aſp, and 4 H. 7. ca. 8. concerning the prices of broadcloath, &c. and 11 H. 7. cap. 2. concerning vagabonds, unlawful games, and alehouſes, &c. and one other ſtatute in the 19 year of H. 7. ca. 12. concerning thoſe matters, and 11 H. 6. ca. 12. concerning waxchandlers, and the price of candles, and 34 H. 8. cap. 7. concerning the ſale of wines, and 28 H. 8. cap. 14. concerning the prices of wines, and 27 H. 8. ſtat. *de monaſteriis*, concerning keeping of houſe and houſholds upon ſcites of monaſteries, &c. and 4 H. 7. cap. 19. concerning houſes of huſbandry and tillage, and 7 H. 8. ca. 1. concerning letting down of towns, and 27 H. 8. cap. 22. concerning decay of houſes and incloſures, and 5 E. 6. ca. 5. for the maintenance of tillage, &c. and 5 Eliz. cap. 2. for maintenance and increaſe of tillage, and 14 R. 2. ca. 4. 8 H. 6. ca. 23. and 5 E. 6. cap. 7. concerning the buying of wooll, woollen yarn, &c. and 33 H. 8. cap. 5. concerning the keeping

keeping of great horſes, the ſtatute of Wincheſt. in the time of E. 1. concerning harneſſe and arms, Artic. ſuper Cart. ca. 20. concerning making of rings, croſſes, and locks, and 37 E. 3. cap. 7. that makers of white veſſell ſhould not guild, and 2 H. 5. ca. 4. ſtat. 2. that goldſmiths ſhould not take more then forty ſix ſhillings eight pence for a pound of troy ſilver guilt, and 2 H. 6. ca. 14. that no ſilver ſhall be bought for more then thirty ſhillings the pound of troy, and 2 H. 4. ca. 6. againſt the bringing in of coin of Flanders, Scotland, and other forain coin, and 13 R. 2. ca. 8. and 4 H. 4. cap. 25. concerning the prices of hay and oats ſold by hoſtlers, and 4 & 5 Ph. and Mar. ca. 5. concerning the putting to ſale of coloured cloth: and another part of the ſame ſtatute concerning the myſtery of making, weaving, or rowing of woollen cloth, &c. and 18 El. ca. 16. for toleration of certain clothiers to dwell out of towns corporate, and many other unneceſſary ſtatutes unfit for this time, about the number of threeſcore are repealed by an act made at this parliament in the 21 year of the reign of king James, as by that act appeareth: and many like acts are not continued, as by the conference between that act and other former acts of continuance may appear: ſo as theſe ſnares that might have lien heavy upon the ſubject, by this and other former ſtatutes either are repealed, or not continued. 13 E. 1. ſtat. de Winton.

The ſecond miſchief was, that common informers, and many times the kings attorny drew all informations for any offence, in any place within the realm of England againſt any penall law to ſome of the kings courts at Weſtminſter, to the intolerable charge, vexation, and trouble of the ſubject; and it was feared that Weſtminſter hall would labour of an apoplexy by drawing up all ſuits unto it, as the naturall body doth *tabeſcere*, when the humours of the body are drawn up unto the head, which in the end (if it be not prevented) turneth to an apoplexy.

The third miſchief was, that in informations, &c. the offence ſuppoſed to be againſt the penall law, and to be committed in one county, was at the pleaſure of the informer, &c. alledged in any county where he would, where neither party nor witneſſe was known, againſt the right inſtitution of the law, that the jury (for their better notice) ſhould come *de vicineto* of the place where the fact was committed.

The fourth miſchief was, that in divers caſes the party defendant in informations or actions upon the ſtatute, were driven to plead ſpecially, which was both chargeable and dangerous to him, if his plea were not both ſubſtantiall and formall alſo.

Theſe three miſchiefs laſt mentioned are expreſly and abſolutely provided for by this act, which moved from the houſe of commons. And ſo did the act of continuing and reviving of divers ſtatutes, and repeale of divers others. [193] 21 Jac. cap. 28.

The firſt part of the purvien beginning thus. For remedy whereof be it enacted by the authority of this preſent parliament, that all offences, &c. The firſt part of the act.

This clauſe conſiſteth upon three parts. Firſt, affirmative: and this is divided into two branches. 1. For the informations, &c. It is enacted, that where a common informer might before this act have informed upon any penall ſtatute before juſtices of aſſiſe, juſtices of *niſi prius*, or juſtices of gaole-delivery, juſtices of oier and terminer,

miner, or juſtices of peace in their generall or quarter ſeſſions; there a common informer may informe, &c. 2. Before what judges; this act appoints no new judges, but ſuch as former penall lawes appointed, viz. the juſtices before mentioned, or any of them according to the former act.

The ſecond part is reſtrictive, reſtraining any information, &c. to be commenced, ſued, &c. either by the attorny generall, or by any officer, common informer, or any other perſon whatſoever, in any of the kings courts at Weſtminſter. So as the kings bench, ſtar-chamber, chancery, common-pleas, exchequer, or exchequer-chamber, cannot receive or hold plea of any information, &c. upon any penall ſtatute, either by the kings attorny, any common informer, or any other perſon whatſoever: but the matter ſhall be heard and determined before ſuch juſtices as are foreſaid in the proper county where the offence was committed.

The third part giveth the like proces upon every popular action, bill, plaint, information, or ſuit to be commenced or proſecuted by force, of, or according to the purport of this act, as in an action of treſpaſſe, *vi et armis*, at the common law: but upon no other popular action, bill, &c. which is not ſued, &c. by force of this act.

The ſecond part of the act. The ſecond part of this act doth meet with the ſecond of the ſaid three miſchiefs, and ſtandeth upon three branches.

Firſt, that in all informations, exhibited, &c. either for the king or any other, &c. the offence ſhall be layed and alledged, &c. in the ſaid county where ſuch offence was in truth committed, and not elſewhere.

The ſecond branch is, that if the defendant pleadeth the generall iſſue, the plaintiffe or informer upon evidence to the jury muſt prove two things: firſt, the offence laid in the information, &c. Secondly, that the offence was committed in that county, otherwiſe the defendant ſhall be found not guilty.

The third branch is, that for more ſurety that the offence ſhall be alledged truly in the proper county where in truth it was committed, no information, &c. ſhall be received, filed, or entred of record, untill the informer, or relator hath firſt taken a corporall oath before ſome of the judges of that court, which conſiſteth on two parts: firſt, that the offence or offences laid in ſuch information, &c. were not committed in any other county, then where the ſame are alledged in the information, &c. Secondly that he believeth in his conſcience, that the offence was committed within a year before the information or ſuit. And this oath is to be entred of record. And all this is to be done before the information be received, filed, or entred of record.

The third part of the act. The third part of this act meeteth with the laſt miſchiefe: for by this part the defendant may plead the generall iſſue, and give any ſpeciall matter in evidence to the jury: which matter being pleaded, had been a good and ſufficient matter in law, to have diſcharged the defendant, &c.

27 H. 8. ſ. 21, &c. This is a very beneficiall clauſe, and cleereth many queſtions at the common law. And where it may be objected, that for want of ſufficient clerks, the proceeding according to this ſtatute will be erroneous, and to be reverſed by writ of errour, ſo as it will deter informers to informe, &c. and in effect, lay aſleep all penall lawes

To

To this it may be anſwered, Firſt, that it ſhall be the fault of the informer himſelfe; for if he informe before juſtices of aſſiſe or *niſi prius*, they * have ſufficient clerks. Secondly, I perſuade my ſelfe, that the other juſtices will in diſcharge of their conſcience and duty, provide ſufficient clerks. And laſtly, that few or no errours ſhall fall out in reſpect of the generall pleading.

The laſt clauſe of this act is this, Provided alwayes that this act or any thing therein contained, ſhall not extend to any information, &c.

By this clauſe this act extends not to penall ſtatutes of theſe ſorts: concerning 1. Popiſh recuſants for not comming to church. 2. Maintenance, champerty, or buying of titles. 3. The ſubſidie of tonnage and poundage, wooll, &c. 4. The defrauding the king of any cuſtome, tonnage, poundage, ſubſidie, impoſt, or priſage. 5. Tranſportation of gold, ſilver, powder, ſhot, munition of all ſorts, wooll, woolfels, or leather, but that every of theſe offences may be layed or alledged to be in any county at the pleaſure of any informer. But yet the informer cannot informe, &c. for any of theſe offences in any of the courts at Weſtminſter, but before the juſtices appointed by this act: for this clauſe extendeth only for the laying or alledging of any of theſe offences in any county that he will.

Inter Wideſton and Clark maior of Nottingham, the caſe was this. Wideſton being arreſted in Nottingham by precept in the nature of a capias, he was impriſoned in the cuſtody of the maior being keeper of the gaol within the ſame towne, and before the returne of the precept Wideſton offered to the maior ſufficient ſurety to appeare, &c. and he refuſed to accept the ſame: whereupon Wideſton brought his action by bill upon the ſtatute of 23 H. 6. cap. 10. whereunto the defendant pleaded the generall iſſue; and it is found by verdict againſt the defendant. In arreſt of judgement it was ſhewed, that by the ſaid ſtatute of 18 Eliz. cap. 5. it is provided, that none ſhall be admitted or received to purſue againſt any perſon upon any penall ſtatute, but by way of information or originall action, and not otherwiſe: in reſpect of the ſaid negative words it was adjudged, that, for that the ſaid action was brought by bill, and not by information or originall, *quod querens nihil capiat per billam*. See the reſt of the ſtatute of 18 Eliz. concerning informers.

Mic. 29. & 30 El. coram rege.

18 Eliz. cap. 5. Vi. lib. 6. fo. 19. b. Gregories caſe.

You have heard of four viperous vermin, which endeavoured to have eaten out the ſides of the church and common-wealth: three whereof, viz. the monopoliſt, the diſpencer with public and profitable penall lawes for a private, and the concealers are blowne up, and exterminated: and the fourth, viz. the vexatious informer well regulated and reſtrained, who under the reverend mantle of law and juſtice inſtituted for protection of the innocent, and the good of the common-wealth, did vex and depauperize the ſubject, and commonly the poorer ſort, for malice or private ends, and never for love of juſtice. And theſe are worthily placed amongſt the pleas of the crowne, becauſe it is for the honour and benefit of the crowne, when the church and common-wealth doe flouriſh in peace and plenty: for the king can never be poore, when his ſubjects are rich.

Hil. 36 Eliz. Rot. 135. int. plac. regis, coram rege. Hamonds caſe.

George Hamond informed upon a penall ſtatute concerning ſhipping of cloth in the name of another. *Qui tam, &c.* againſt Edw. Griffith defendant. Hamond the informer died and upon motion made by the attorney generall, it was the opinion of the whole court, that he the attorney generall might proceed for the queens moity after the death of the informer.

Trin. 31 Eliz. coram rege. Strettons caſe.

See hereafter, cap. 105. of Pardons. 37 H. 6. fo. 4. 5 E. 4. 3. 2 R. 3. fo. 12. 1 H. 7. 3 [195]

Between Stretton, *Qui tam, &c.* and Tayler defendant, that after a popular action commenced, although the attorney generall will enter an *ulterius non vult proſequi;* or if the defendant plead a ſpeciall plea, although the uſe be, that the attorney (to the end that there may be no jugling or covin between the informer and the defendant) reply only; notwithſtanding, if the attorney generall will not reply, the informer may proceed, and proſecute for his part; for the informer by his ſuit commenced hath made of a popular action his private, which the king cannot for the part of the informer pardon or releaſe. And notwithſtanding in all theſe caſes before any action or information commenced by the informer, but the ſuit remaining popular wherein the king only, and no ſubject hath any intereſt, the king may pardon and releaſe the ſame: for after that pardon, no informer can informe *tam pro domino rege, quam pro ſeipſo,* according to the ſtatute, &c. and for himſelfe only in a popular action he cannot informe.

CAP. LXXXIX.

See the firſt part of the Inſtitutes, ſect. 240. Domeſday. [a] Chent. Doverter. [b] Wirceſter. Scirropſcir Civitas. [c] Fleta, lib. 1. ca. 42. § Foreſtall, & lib. 4. cap. 11. Britton, fo. 33. a. 77. a. [d] Vi. Vet. M. C. part. 2. 24. b. 34 E. 1. de Piſtor. Braciatoribus et aliis Victuellariis, et de Foreſtellariis, hic infra. * 51 H. 3. Raſt. weights and meaſures. 4. 25 E. 3. c. 3. ſtat. 3. 27 E. 3. cap. 11. ſtat. Stap. 28 E. 3. cap. 13. 5 E. 6. cap. 14. 5 Eliz. cap. 12. 13 Eliz. cap. 25.

Of Foreſtalling, Ingroſſing, &c.

FORISTEL [a], *fariſtel* [b], *foriſtellum, et foriſtellarius,* derived of two Saxon words, viz. *far* or *fare (via* or *iter) unde fare* for a paſſage and farewell, to go or proceed well: we have turned *far,* to *for* and *ſtall,* which we retaine ſtill, and ſignifieth *interceptionem,* or [c] *impedimentum tranſitus,* hindrance or interception. And the offender is called *forſtellarius.* See of this offender in the ancient ſtatute: [d] *Nullus forſtellarius in villa patiatur morari, qui pauperum ſit depreſſor manifeſte, et totius communitatis, et patriæ publicus inimicus, qui bladum, piſces, allec, vel res quaſcunque venales per terram, vel per aquam venientes, quandoque per terram, quandoque per aquam obviando præ cæteris feſtinat, lucrum ſitiens vitioſum, pauperes opprimens, ditiores decipiens, qui ſic minus juſte illo qui eos apportaverit multo magis vendere machinatur. Qui mercatores exterraneos venalibus venientibus circumvenit, offerens ſe venditioni rerum ſuarum, et ſuggerit, quod bona ſua carius vendere poterunt, quam vendere proponebant, et ſic arte, vel ingenio vellam ſeducit et patriam. Primo convictus graviter amercietur, ſecundo ſubeat judicium pilloriæ, tertio incarceretur, et redimatur, quarto abjuret villam. Et hoc judicium fiet de forſtallariis univerſis, et ſimiliter de his qui * conſilium aut auxilium eiſdem præſtiterint vel favorem, &c.* And his deſcription ſee in a latter act. See before in the chapter of Monopoliſts.

Ingroſſator or *engroſſator,* of the Engliſh and French word, *groſſe,* that is, great or whole, *unde* merchant-groſſier, a merchant that ſelleth

leth by great or whole-ſale. We remember not that we have read of this word [ingroſſe] in any act of parliament, book-caſe, or record, but [e] rarely, before the ſaid act of 5 E. 6. And there is an ingroſſer by the common lawes, who is hereafter deſcribed. And there is an ingroſſer by act of parliament, and he is deſcribed by the ſtatute of 5 E. 6. And by that act a [f] regrator is alſo deſcribed, who is a kinde of ingroſſer. Regrator is derived of the French word *regratement*, for huckſtery. But in ancient time both the ingroſſor and regrator were comprehended under foreſtaller.

It was [g] reſolved by the juſtices and barons of the exchequer upon conference betwixt them, that ſalt is a victuall, and the buying and ſelling thereof was within the ſtatute of 5 E. 6. for it was not only of neceſſity of itſelfe for the food and health of man, but it ſeaſoneth and maketh wholeſome beefe, pork, &c. butter, cheeſe, &c. and other viands. And Peryam juſtice ſaid, [h] Hil. 26 Eliz. in communi banco, that ſo it had been lately adjudged.

[i] Mich. 6 Jac. in ſcaccario, in an information by Baron againſt Boy, upon the ſtatute of 5 E. 6. cap. 14. of ingroſſers for buying and ſelling of apples; the defendant pleaded not guilty, and was found guilty. But the barons gave judgement againſt the informer, and cauſed an entry to be made in the margent of the record, that the judgement was given upon matter apparent to them, that apples were not within the ſaid act, for that the act is to be intended of victuall neceſſary for the food of man, the words of the act being [corne, graine, butter, cheeſe, fiſh, or other dead victuall] which is as much as to ſay, (of other dead victuall of like quality: *id eſt*, of like neceſſary and common uſe.) And therefore apples being rather of pleaſure then neceſſity, are not within the ſaid ſtatute no more then plumbs, cherries, or other fruit; and no information hath ever been exhibited for ingroſſing of apples, plumbs, cherries, or other fruit: but the ſtatute of 2 E. 6. cap. 15. doth forbid conſpiracy of coſtermongers and fruterers, and maketh ſuch conſpiracie unlawfull. And the ſaid judgement of the barons was affirmed in a writ of errour in the exchequer chamber.

[196]

Venditio braſei non eſt venditio victualium, nec debet puniri ſicut venditio panis, vini, et cervisiæ, et hujuſmodi, contra formam ſtatuti. But the act of 5 E. 6. hath made corne, graine, &c. to be victuall within that act. *Vide* Vet. N. B. 2. part 23. b. ſtat. de piſtor., braceator., et aliis victelariis. 34 E. 1.

It was upon conference and mature deliberation reſolved by all the juſtices, that any merchant, ſubject, or ſtranger, bringing victuals or merchandize into this realme, may ſell them in groſſe: but that vendee cannot ſell them againe in groſſe, for then he is an * ingroſſer according to the nature of the word, for that he buy ingroſſe, and ſell ingroſſe, and may be indicted thereof at the common law, as for an offence that is *malum in ſe*. 2. That no merchant or any other may buy within the realme any victuall or other merchandize in groſſe, and ſell the ſame in groſſe againe, for then he is an ingroſſer, and puniſhable, *ut ſupra*: for by this means the prices of victuals and other merchandize ſhall be inhaunced, to the grievance of the ſubject; for the more hands they paſſe through, the dearer they grow, for every one thirſteth after gaine, *vitioſum ſitiunt lucrum*. And if theſe things were lawfull, a riche man might ingroſſe into his hands all a commodity, and ſell the ſame at what price

[e] For the word [*Ingroſſor*,] ſee 27 E. 3. c. 5. ſtat. 1. 37 E. 3. cap. 5.

[f] For this word [*Regrator*,] ſee 51 H. 3. weights and meaſures. 4. Raſtall. 14 R. 2. ca. 4. 8 H. 6. cap. 5. Regrators or choppers, and in ſome countries called jobbers.

[g] M. 44 & 45 El. at Serjeants Inne in Fleetſtreet.

[h] Hil. 26 Eliz. judgement cited p Peryam juſtice.

[i] M. 6. Jac. in Scac. Int. *Baron* and *Boy*.

P. 18 E. 2. Coram rege Rot. 76. Southt'.

Mich. 39 & 40. El. Reſolution de touts les juſtices.

* Dardanarius. An ingroſſer by the common law deſcribed.

—Lucrumq; acquirit eundo, Nivis utexiguus creſcit eundo globus.

price he will. And every practiſe or device by act, conſpiracy, words or newes, to inhaunce the price of victuals or other merchandize, was puniſhable by law; and they relied much upon the ſtatute aforeſaid, *nullus forſtallarius, &c.* which ſee before in this chapter: and that the name of an ingroſſer in the reigne of H. 3. and E. 1. was not known, but comprehended within this word [*forſtallarius*] *lucrum ſitiens vitioſum;* and ingroſſing is a branch of foreſtalling. And for that *forſtellarius* was *pauperum depreſſor, et totius communitatis et patriæ publicus inimicus*, he was puniſhable by the common law. They had alſo in conſideration the book in 43 Aſſ. where it was preſented, that a Lombard did procure to promote and inhaunce the price of merchandize, and ſhewed how: the Lombard demanded judgement of the preſentment for two cauſes. 1. That it did not ſound in foreſtalling. 2. That of his endeavour or attempt by words, no evill was put in ure, (that is) no price was inhaunced, *et non allocatur*, and thereupon he pleaded not guilty: whereby it appeareth, that the attempt by words to inhaunce the price of merchandize was puniſhable by law, and did ſound in foreſtalment: and it appeareth by the book that the puniſhment was by fine and ranſome. And in that caſe Knivet reported, that certaine people (and named their names) came to Coteſwold in Herefordſhire, and ſaid in deceipt of the people, that there were ſuch wars beyond the ſeas, as no wooll could paſſe or be carried beyond ſea, whereby the price of wools was abated: and upon preſentment hereof made, they appeared; and upon their confeſſion they were put to fine and ranſome. See the ſtatute of 25 H. 8. cap. 2. whereby the lords of the councell, juſtices, &c. or any ſeven of them, &c have power to ſet prices on victuals, and the ſame to be proclaimed under the great ſeale.

3 E. 2. Action ſur le ſtat. F.N.B. 250. I.

43 Aſſ. p. 38. tit. Aſſ. 354.

Nota, the abatement by undue means of the price of our native commodities, is puniſhable by fine and ranſome. See 23 E. 3. ca. 6. 13 R. 2. cap. 8. Inter leges Ethelſtani. cap. 12.

For preventing of all ingroſſing and foreſtalling, it was the ancient law before the conqueſt, *Decrevimus porro, ne quis extra oppidum quicquam 20 denariis carius æſtimatum emat, verum intra portum præſente oppidi præfecto, aliove viro fidele, aut. ipſo denique præpoſito regio, in celebri plebis concurſu, et hominum oculis quiſque mercator.*

Interdicimus etiam ut nullæ pecudes emantur niſi infra civitates, et hoc ante tres fideles teſtes nec alia neceſſaria ſine fideijuſſore et warranto, &c. Item, nullum mercatum vel feria ſit, nec fieri permittatur, niſi in civitatibus regni noſtri, et in burgis, &c.

Inter leges Will. Conqueſt. fo. 125.

*Commiſſio facta fuit Roberto Hadham ad vendend' blada et alia bona diverſarum abbathiarum alienigenarum, qui venit et cognovit, quod vendidit blada prioris de Tickford in garbis in duabus * taſſis exiſtent' pro 10 li. quæ venditio facta fuit contra legem et conſuetudinem regni Angliæ, vendend' in garbis, priuſquam triturat' fuerunt, quod fieri debuiſſet per menſuram poſt eorum triturationem: ideo committitur priſonæ, et adjudicatur, quòd ab omni officio domini regis amoveatur, et quòd finem faciat cum domino rege.*

Hil. 25 E. 3. coram rege. Rot. 13. Buck. Hadhams caſe.

* Of the French word *Taſer*, to heape in goves or ſtacks.

Obſerve well this judgement, that it is againſt the common law of England to ſell corne in ſheafes before it is threſhed and meaſured, and the reaſon thereof ſeemeth to be, for that by ſuch ſale the market in effect is foreſtalled.

See 5 E. 6 ca. 14. He is an ingroſſer that buyes (other then by grant or leaſe of land or tithe) any corne growing in the fields, &c.

CAP.

CAP. XC.

AGAINST ROBERDSMEN.

IT is an Engliſh proverbe; That many men talk of Robin Hood, that never ſhot in his bow: and becauſe the ſtatutes and records hereafter mentioned cannot well be underſtood, unleſſe it be known what this Robin Hoode was that hath raiſed a name to theſe kinde of men called Roberdſmen, his followers, we will deſcribe him.

This Robert Hood lived in the reigne of king R. 1. in the borders of England and Scotland, in woods and deſerts, by robbery, burning of houſes, felony, waſte and ſpoile, and principally by and with vagabonds, idle wanderers, night-walkers, and draw-latches: ſo as this notable thiefe gave not only a name to theſe kinde of men, but there is a bay, called Robin Hoods Bay, in the river of in Yorkſhire. And albeit he lived in Yorkſhire, yet men of his quality took their denomination of him, and were called Roberdſmen throughout all England. He was, ſaith Maior Scotus, prædonum princeps et prædo mitiſſimus.

Againſt theſe men was the ſtatute of Wincheſter made in 13 E. 1. for preventing of robbery, murders, burning of houſes, &c Alſo the ſtatute of 5 E. 3. which reciting the ſtatute of Wincheſter, and that there had been divers manſlaughters, felonies, and robberies done in times paſt, by people that he called roberdſmen, waſters, and drawlatches, and remedy provided by that act for the arreſting of them. 13 E. 1. ſtatut. de Wincheſt. ca. 1. 4. 5 H. 7. fo. 5. 5 E. 3. cap. 14.

At the parliament holden 50 E. 3. it was petitioned to the king that ribauds and ſturdy beggers might be baniſhed out of every towne. The anſwer of the king in parliament was touching ribauds: the ſtatute of Wincheſter and the declaration of the ſame with other * ſtatutes of roberdſmen, and for ſuch as make themſelves gentlemen, and men of armes, and archers, if they cannot ſo prove their ſelves, let them be driven to their occupation or ſervice, or to the place from whence they came. Rot. parl. 50 E. 3. nu. 61. * 5 E. 3. cap. 14. 2 H. 5. cap. 9. 8 H 6. cap. 14. Vid. 39 Eliz. ca. 4.

It is provided by the ſtatute of 7 R. 2. that the ſtatutes made in the time of king Edward, grandfather of the king, of roberdſmen, and drawlatches, be firmely holden and kept, and further proviſion againſt vagabonds wandring from place to place. See a law made in the ſixth parliament of queen Mary, *anno Dom.* 1555 in Scotland againſt Robert Hood, Little John, &c. 7 R. 2. cap. 5. Vid. 39 Eliz. ca. 4.

CAP. XCI.

OF BANKRUPTS.

VIDE in the fourth part of the Inſtitutes, cap. The Court of the Commiſſioners of Bankrupts.

CAP. XCII.

OF RECUSANTS.

1 Eliz. cap. 2. 23 Eliz. cap. 1. 28 Eliz. cap. 6. 35 Eliz. cap. 1, 2. 3 Jac. cap. 4. 7 Jac. cap. 6. Lib. 10. 54. the chancelour of Oxfords caſe. Lib. 11. 56, 57, &c. Dr. Foſters caſe. Lib. 5. fo 1. Caudries caſe. Dier 3 Eliz. fo. 203.

FIRST, the acts of parliament that are made againſt them are 1 Eliz. cap. 2. 23 Eliz. cap. 1. 28 Eliz. cap. 6. 35 Eliz. cap. 1, & 2. 3 Jac. cap. 4. 7 Jac. ca. 6. Theſe acts of parliament are interpreted and expounded by divers judgements and reſolutions heretofore given. Lib. 10. fo. 54. &c. Le caſe de Chancelour, &c. de Oxford, an expoſition of the ſtatute of 3 Jac. ca. 4. et lib. 11. fo. 56, 57, &c. Doctor Foſters caſe, an expoſition of all the ſaid ſtatutes. See lib. 5. fo. 1. &c. Caudries caſe. See Dier, 3 Eliz. fo. 203. an expoſition of the ſaid act of 1 El. concerning hearing of maſſe.

CAP. XCIII.

Of Newes, Rumours, &c.

SEE the ſecond part of the Inſtitutes, W. 1. cap. 34. Newes. See alſo in the fourth part of the Inſtitutes, cap. Chancery, in the articles againſt cardinall Woolſey, artic. 32. *Convicia, ſi iraſcaris, tua divulgas, ſpreta exoleſcunt;* if you ſeek to revenge ſlanders, you publiſh them as your own: if you deſpiſe them, they vaniſh.

Tacitus.

Int. leg. Alveredi, cap. 28.

The law before the conqueſt was, that the author and ſpreader of falſe rumours amongſt the people had his tongue cut out, if he redeemed it not by the eſtimation of his head.

CAP.

CAP. XCIV.

Of Weights and Meaſures.

SEE the ſecond part of the Inſtitutes, W. 1. cap. 4. and the expoſition upon the ſame.

CAP. XCV. [199]

OF APPARELL.

DIVERSE acts of parliament have been made againſt the exceſs of apparell in the reign of E. 3. as 11 E. 3. cap. 2. & 4. 37 E. 3. ca. 8, 9, 10, 11, 12, 13, 14. 38 E. 3. 3. cap. 2. In the reign of E. 4. 3 E. 4. cap. 5. 22 E. 4. cap. 1. In the reign of H. 8. 1 H. 8. cap. 14. 6 H. 8. ca. 1. 7 H. 8. cap. 7. 24 H. 8. cap. 13. 33 H. 8. cap. 5. 37 H. 8. ca. 7. 1 & 2 Ph. and Mar. ca. 2. 4 & 5 Ph. and Mar. c. 2. 5 El. ca. 6. 8 El. ca. 11. 13 El. ca. 19. Some of them fighting with, and cuffing one another, ſome of them expired. But foraſmuch as thoſe that ſtood in force were obſolete, and remained but as ſnares to catch or vex men at the pleaſure of the promooter; at the parliament holden *anno* 1 Ja. all acts of parliament before that time made concerning apparell are repealed and abrogated, and ſince that time no act hath been made concerning apparell, and ſo ſtandeth the law at this day. Three coſtly things there are that doe much impoveriſh the ſubjects of England, viz. coſtly apparell, coſtly diet, and coſtly building. The beſt mean to repreſſe coſtly apparell, and the exceſſe thereof, is by example: for if it would pleaſe great men to ſhew good example, and to weare apparell of the cloth and other commodities wrought within the realm, it would beſt cure this vain, and conſuming ill, which is a branch of prodigality, and herewith few wiſemen are taken. If you will looke into the parliament roll of 2 H. 6. you ſhall ſee what plain and frugall apparell that renowned king H. 5. after he was king did wear, his gown of leſſe value then 40 s.

[Margin: 1 Jac. R. ca. 25.]

[Margin: Exceſſe of apparell is beſt cured, exemplo et vituperio.]

[Margin: Rot. parl. 2. H. 6. nu. 30.]

Magna corporis cura, magna animi incuria.

Non induetur mulier veſte virili, nec vir utetur veſte fœminea: abominabilis apud Deum, qui facit hoc. Deut. 22. 5.

CAP. XCVI.

OF DIET.

[a] Rot. clauſ. 9 E. 2. m. 26 in dorſi. intitled *Ordinatio ſuper menſuration ferculorum.*
[b] 2 E. 6. cap. 19. 5 E. 6. ca. 3. 5 El. ca. 5. 27 El. ca. 11. 35 El. ca. 7.
* *Lent* 2. Saxon *Quinreſme Quadrageſima.*
[c] Hereof ſee the 4. part of the Inſtitutes, cap. The Court of Audience, &c. and Faculties.
* Vide Britton cap. 53. and other books make mention of theſe.

THERE was [a] an ordinance made by king E. 2. by advice of his councell againſt the exceſſe of diet, but becauſe it had not the ſtrength of an act of parliament, it wrought no effect.

[b] It is provided by ſtatutes made in the reigns of E. 6. and queen Elizabeth, that no fleſh ſhall be eaten on fiſh-days, viz. Friday, Saturday, embring days and vigils, and the time of * Lent; [c] and for licences to eat fleſh on fiſh-days, &c. See the preamble of the ſtatute of 2 E. 6. ca. 19.

Embring days, ſo called becauſe in former times when they faſted they put aſhes or embers on their heads. Job 2. 12. Jer. 6. 26. 2 Sam. 13. 19. And as the naturall converſion of the fleſh of the body is to duſt, ſo the ſins of the ſoul (unrepented) are turned to fire, and this was ſhadowed under embers that ever keep fire.

* Theſe embring days are the week next before Quadrageſima, ſo called, for that it is the fortieth day before Eaſter, and is the firſt Sunday in Lent. So Quinquageſima the Sunday fifty days before Eaſter, Sexageſima ſixty days before Eaſter, and Septuageſima ſeventy days before Eaſter.

Before theſe late acts the eating of fleſh on Fridays was puniſhable in the eccleſiaſticall court, as yet it is, the juriſdiction being ſaved by the ſaid acts.

[d] Luc. c. 21. v. 34. Rom. ca. 13. v. 13. Eccleſiaſticus, ca. 37. v. 30, 31.
[e] Eccleſiaſticus 31. 20.
[f] Cicero.

But there is no act of parliament againſt exceſſe of diet, for it is known to be ſo hurtfull for mans body, and ſo obſcureth the faculties of the mind, as the underſtanding, memory, &c. as to men, ſpecially to Chriſtian men, there needeth no law at all to be made, ever being mindfull of that caveat, [d] *Attendite autem vobis, ne forte graventur corda veſtra in crapula, et ebrictate, &c.*

[e] *Vigilia, et cholera, et tortura viro infrunito; ſomnus ſanitatis homini parco, dormiet uſque in mane, et anima illius cum ipſo delectabitur.* The morall heathen men by the light of nature agree hereunto. [f] *Tantum tibi et potus adhibendum eſt, ut reficiantur vires, non opprimantur.*

Horace, 2. Ser. 2.

Accipe tu, victus tenuis quæ, quantaque ſecum
Afferat, imprimis valeas bene: nam variæ res
Ut noceant homini, credas, memor illius eſcæ,
Quæ ſimplex olim tibi ſederit: at ſimul aſſis
Miſcueris elixa: ſimul conchylia turdis:
Dulcia ſe in bilem vertent, ſtomachoque tumultum
Lenta feret pituita: vides, ut pallidus omnis
Cœna deſurgat dubia? ————

Ex plenitudine generantur morbi, qui ſuperant medicorum artem.

King

King Edgar permitting many of the Danes to inhabite here ([g] who first brought into this realm excessive drinking) was in the end constrained to make a law against this excesse (which never commeth alone) driving certain nails into the sides of their cups, as limits, and bounds, which no man upon great pain should be so hardy as to transgresse.

William of Malmesbury, comparing Englishmen and Normans together, saith, that in his time, the English manner was to sit bibbing whole houres after dinner, [h] and that the Norman fashion was to walk the streets with great troops, with idle and loose serving-men following them, both which were causes of many disorders and outrages.

[i] If the excesse of drinking extend to the loathsome and odious vice of drunkennesse, it is punishable by act of parliament. And to say the truth the ancient Britains were free from this crime.

Ecce Britannorum mos est laudabilis iste,
Ut bibat arbitrio pocula quisque suo.

And the laws against drunkennesse are very new.

Nothing is here said against that great peacemaker, and branch of liberality, orderly hospitality, but against the dainty and disorderly excesse of meats and drinks, which is a species of prodigality: for it is provided by act of parliament that the grace of hospitality shall not be withdrawn from the needy.

See the statute of 37 E. 3. ca. 8. against excessive apparell and diet: but it was repealed in the next parliament, 38 E. 3. ca. 2.

[g] From whence excesse of drinking in England came.
[h] From whence troops of idle serving men came into England.
[i] 4 Jacobi, c. 5. See 1 Ja. ca. 9. 7 Ja. ca. 10. 21 Ja. c. 7. an excellent law. *Una salus sanis nullam potare salutem.*

[201]

W. 1. 3 E. 1. ca. 1.

CAP. XCVII.

OF BUILDINGS.

WE have not read of any act of parliament now in force made against the excesse of building, or touching the order or manner of building: but it is a wasting evill, whereunto some wise men are subject.

But the common law doth prohibit any subject to build any castle, or house of strength imbatteled, &c. without the kings licence, for the danger that might ensue. [a] Also the common law prohibiteth the building of any edifice to a common nusance, or to the nusance of any man in his house, as the stopping up of his light, or to any other prejudice or annoyance of him. *Ædificare in tuo proprio solo non licet, quod alteri noceat.*

[b] In Deuteronomy it is said, *Cum ædificaveris domum novam, facies* [c] *murum tecti per circuitum, ne effundatur sanguis in domo tua, et sis reus, labente alio, et in præceps ruente.*

[d] I like well the counsell to a nobleman, whosoever gave it. *Si vis (ait ille) ædificare domum, inducat te necessitas, non voluptas; cupiditas ædificandi ædificando non tollitur; nimia et inordinata cupiditas ædificandi expectat ædificii venditionem; turris completa, et arca evacuata faciunt tarde hominem sapientem.*

See the 1 part of the Institutes. sect. 1. fo. 5. a. Vet. Mag. Cart. 1. part, fo. 162. cap. Eschaetry, &c. 14 H. 6. nu. 7. licence to the D. of Gloc. to imbattel Greenwich.
[a] Li. 9. f. 54 & 58. Lib. 5. fo. 101. &c.
[b] Deut. 22. 8.
[c] Battlements. This was for safety only.
[d] Bernhard. consilium.

Ædificare

Euripides tranflated by Sir Th. Moor.

Ædificare domos multas, et pafcere multos,
Eft ad pauperiem femita laxa nimis.

To build many houfes, and many to feed,
To poverty that way doth readily lead.

Of thefe three it hath been truly faid: *Veftium, conviviorum, et ædificiorum luxuria ægre civitatis funt indicia, et fpecies prodigalitatis.*

Vide the like in the Regift. 36. b. Prohib. de decimis feperatis. In Epift. decret. Innocent. 3. l. 10. pag. 228.

But by the common law, and generall cuftome of the realm, it was lawfull for bifhops, earls, and barons to build churches, or chappels within their fees: and hereof king John informed pope Innocentius the Third (naming only, *honoris caufa*, the bifhops and baronage of England, albeit this liberty extended to all) with requeft that this liberty to the baronage might be confirmed. To thefe letters the pope made this anfwer, *Quod enim de confuetudine regni Anglorum procedere regia ferenitas per fuas liter s intimavit, ut liceat tam epifcopis, quam comitibus, et baronibus ecclefias in feudo fuo fundare, laicis quidem principibus id licere nullatenus denegamus, dummodo diocefani epifcopi eis fuffragetur affenfus, et per novam ftructuram veterum ecclefiarum juftitia non lædatur.* Whereas the baronage had abfolute liberty before, now the pope addeth the confent of the bifhop: but that addition bound not, feeing it was againft the liberty of the baronage warranted by the common law: and we would not have rehearfed this epiftle, but that it is a proof what the generall cuftome of the realm was concerning the building of churches by the baronage of England. And albeit they might build churches without the kings licence, yet could they not erect a fpirituall politique body to continue in fucceffion, and capable of indowment without the kings licence: but by the common law before the ftatutes of mortmain, they might have indowed this fpirituall body once incorporated, *perpetuis futuris temporibus*, without any licence from the king, or any other.

Tr. 20 E. 1. Rot. 13 in banco Rich. de Turnys cafe. Eborum.

[202]

* Lib. 10. fo. 27. Le cafe de Suttons hofpitall. See the ftatute of 39 El. cap. 4. whereby authority is given to juftices of peace to build and erect houfes of correction, &c.
[a] 39 El. ca. 5. 3 Car. ca. 1.
[b] *Tumba, tumulus, fepulchrum.*

And as the law is in cafes of devotion and religion, fo it is in cafes of charity: any man may erect and build a houfe for an * hofpitall, fchool, workinghoufe, or houfe of correction, or the like, without any licence, for that is but a preparation, and may be done as owner of the foyl; but by the common law could not incorporate any of them without licence, but now he may, and indow them with lands in certain cafes, [a] by the ftatutes of 39 Eliz cap. 5. and 3 Car. ca. 1. as in the fecond part of the Inftitutes in the expofition of thofe ftatutes it appeareth.

Concerning the building or erecting of [b] tombs, fepulchers or monuments for the deceafed in church, chancell, common chappell, or churchyard in convenient manner, it is lawfull, for it is the laft work of charity that can be done for the deceafed, who whiles he lived was a lively temple of the Holy Ghoft, with a reverend regard, and Chriftian hope of a joyfull refurrection. And the defacing of them is punifhable by the common law, as it appeareth in [c] the book of 9 E. 4. 14. a. And fo was it agreed by the whole court, Mich. 10 Jac. in the common place, between Corven and Pym. And for the defacing thereof, they that build or erect the fame fhall have the action during their lives, (as the lady Wiche had in the cafe of 9 E. 4.) and after their deceafes, the heir of the deceafed fhall have the action. But the building, or erecting of

[c] 9 E. 4. 14. the La Wiches cafe, wife of Sir Hugh Wiche. Mich. 10. Ja. in communi banco int' Corven & Pym.

of the ſepulcher, tomb, or other monument ought not to be to the hinderance of the celebration of divine ſervice. And in that caſe of Corven it was reſolved, that albeit the freehold of the church be in the parſon, yet if a lord of a mannor, or any other, that hath an houſe within the town or pariſh, and that he, and all thoſe whoſe eſtate he hath in the manſion houſe of the mannor, or other houſe, hath had a ſeat in an iſle of the church, for him and his family only, and have repaired it at his proper charges, it ſhall be intended that ſome of his aunceſtors, or of the parties whoſe eſtate he hath, did build and erect that iſle for him and his family only; and therefore if the ordinary endeavour to remove him, or place any other there, he may have a prohibition. [d] It was further reſolved, that if any man hath a houſe in a town or pariſh, and that he and thoſe whoſe eſtate he hath in the houſe, hath had time out of mind a certain pew, or ſeat in the church maintained by him and them, the ordinary cannot remove him, (for preſcription maketh certainty, the mother of quietneſſe) and if he doe, a prohibition lyeth againſt him. [e] But where there is no preſcription, there the ordinary that hath the cure, and charge of ſouls may for avoiding of contention in the church or chappel, and the more quiet, and better ſervice of God, and placing of men according to their qualities and degrees, take order for the placing of the pariſhioners in the church or chappell publique, which is dedicate and conſecrate to the ſervice of God.

Barth. Caſſaneus fo. 13. Concluſ. 29. Actio datur, [q]uis arma in aliquo loco poſita delevit, ſeu abraſit, &c.

[d] 8 H. 7. 12. a. per Huſſy accord. Paſch. 10 Jac. in curia Cam. Stellatæ, inter Huſſy plaintiff. & Kath. Layton, & al' Defendants iſſint reſolve per le court.

[e] 8 H. 7. 12. a. acc. 12 H. 7. 12. per Huſſye.

Nota, funerall expences according to the degree and quality of the deceaſed, are to be allowed of the goods of the deceaſed, before any debt or duty whatſoever, for that is *opus pium*, or *charitativum*.

Amongſt the people of Almighty God, as it appeareth in the holy hiſtory, ſepulture was ever had in great reverence, not only of kings, but of other men; as (amongſt many others) good old Barzillai, when he had excuſed himſelf for not going with the king to Jeruſalem, he concluded, *Obſecro ut revertar ſervus tuus, et moriar in civitate mea, et ſepeliar juxta ſepulchrum patris mei, et matris meæ, &c.*

2 Sam. 19. 37.

And alſo the morall heathens had building and erecting of ſepulchers, or monuments in great account, as it doth appear by the ſeven wonders of the world, which for memory may be expreſſed in theſe few verſes.

[203]

1. *Pyramides Memphis*, 2. *Babylonis mœnia celſæ*,
   3. *Templum ingens Epheſi virgo Diana tuum*,
4. *Mauſoli Cariæ monumentum*, 5. *Raraque Pharo*
   Turris, 6. *Olympiaci ſplendida imago Jovis*,
7. *Denique apud Rhodios ſplendentis ſtatua Phœbi:*
   Hæc ſeptem mundus mira, viator, habet.

Beſides the religious, and Chriſtian regard abovesaid, theſe monuments do ſerve for four good uſes and ends. Firſt, for evidence, and proof of deſcents, and pedegrees. Secondly, what time he that is there buried deceaſed. Thirdly, for example, to follow the good, or to eſchew the evill. Fourthly, to put the living in mind of their end, for all the ſons of Adam muſt die. *Statutum eſt hominibus ſemel mori.*

Monumentum

Monumentum ſervat alicujus rei memoriam aliter interituram, eamque nobis repræſentat: and therefore a monument is called a memoriall.

Monumentum dicitur à monendo; quicquid enim nos monet eſt monumentum, ut ſepulchrum, quòd nos ſumus mortales.

Cum tumulum cernis, tum tu mortalia ſpernis:
Eſto memor mortis, ſiſque ad cœleſtia fortis.

It is to be obſerved, that in every ſepulcher, that hath a monument, two things are to be conſidered, viz. the monument, and the ſepulture or buriall of the dead, * The buriall of the *cadaver* (that is *caro data vermibus*) is *nullius in bonis*, and belongs to eccleſiaſticall cogniſance, but as to the monument, action is given (as hath been ſaid) at the common law for defacing thereof.

* Britton, fo. 84. b.

In the year of our Lord 1586, and in the 28 year of the reign of that glorious queen Elizabeth, was the old gate called Ludgate in the city of London (as Stow ſaith) taken down to be new builded: there was found couched within the old wall thereof a ſtone, wherein was graven in the Hebrew tongue and characters, * an epitaph, ſignifying in Engliſh: This is the tomb of Rabbi Moſes ſon of the illuſtrious Rabbi Iſaac: which certainly was before the 23 year of the reign of H. 2. *anno Domini* 1177, for before that time all the Jews in England were buried within the city of London, and in that year, ſaith Hovenden, *Dominus rex pater dedit licentiam Judæis terræ ſuæ habendi cœmeterium in qualibet civitate Angliæ, extra muros civitatum, ubi poſſunt rationabiliter, et in competenti loco emere, ad ſepeliend' mortuos ſuos: prius enim omnes Judæi mortui Londoniâ ferebantur ſepeliendi.*

Stow in his Survey of London, fo. 19.
* For ſo is the truth.
Ro. Hovenden anno Dom. 1177.
Holl. eodem an. fo. 101. b. 20.

And albeit churches or chappels may be built by any of the kings ſubjects, (as hath been ſaid) without licence, yet before the law take knowledge of them to be churches or chappels, the biſhop is to conſecrate or dedicate the ſame: and this is the reaſon, that a church or not a church, a chappel, or not a chappel, ſhall be tryed, and certified by the biſhop.

8 H. 6. 32. 37.

See for this dedication or conſecration the 43 chapter of Ezechiel, the 23 chapter of Geneſis, the 90 Pſalme, the 24, 26, 27, 84, and 134 Pſalms, the 2 of Samuel 6. 10 of Saint John, verſ. 22. to the end.

Vide inter leges Edwardi Confeſſoris, cap. 3. Similiter ad dedicationes, ad ſynodos, et ad capitula venientibus, &c. in eundo, et redeundo ſit ſumma pax.

We find in ancient times that vaults, hollow places, or ſubſtructions under the ground were made by men for receits, or receptacles for keeping of their wives, children, money, and goods ſecret, to avoide violence, and rapine in time of hoſtility or rebellion, and we find no law againſt them.

De ſubterraneis, ſubſtructionibus, et cryptis.

Theſe kind of buildings we had from the Germans, as we find it in Tacitus, who treating of the old Germans ſaith, *Solent et ſubterraneos ſpecus aperire, et ſi quando hoſtis advenit, aperta populatur, abdita autem et defoſſa aut ignorantur, aut eo ipſo fallunt, quod quærenda ſunt.* They uſe to build vaults under the earth, and if the enemy come, he deſtroyeth all open and above ground, but ſuch things as lie hidden in the cave, either they lie unknown, or at leaſt they deceive him, in that he is enforced to find them out.

Tacitus.

Neither have we found any licence of the king to make them, nor puniſhment of any that made them without licence, and yet many have been made by many ſubjects, ſome whereof * we have ſeen.

* In the mannor of Minſter Lovel in com' Oxon' &c.

[a] We read of Alexander biſhop of Lincoln, in the reigns of H. 1. and king Stephen, a Norman born, who was, *inſanis ſubſtructionibus ad inſaniam delectatus.*

[a] Cambden Linc. pag. 4 6.

[b] No perſon can build or erect light-houſes, pharos, ſea-marks or beacons without lawfull warrant and authority.

[b] See the ſtatute of 8 El. ca. 13. and the letters patents of the Lord Admirall.

Lumina noctivagæ tollit pharus æmula lunæ.

In light-houſe top is rear'd the light,
As high as the moon that walkes by night.

[c] Proviſion was made by authority of parliament for building and erecting blockhouſes, bulwarks, piles, and the like, for without parliament ſubjects cannot be charged with building [d] or erecting of them, and that act is expired.

[c] 4 H. 8. ca. 1.

[d] De propugnaculis, munimentis, munitoriis, &c. of bulwarks, barbicans, blockhouſes, piles, &c.

[e] The lord of the ſoil may build a windmill, ſheepcote, dairy enlarging of a court neceſſary, or a curtilage in grounds, where men have common of paſture.

[e] 13 E. 1. ca. 46. 32 Aſſ. 5. 7 H. 4. 39.

[f] A man cannot erect any building upon his own ground in the kings foreſt, but it is a purpreſture, and may either be demoliſhed or arrented to the kings uſe, &c. at a juſtice ſeat.

[f] 7 El. Dier 240.

Concerning houſes of huſbandry and tillage, the ſtatutes of 4 H. 7. cap. 19. 7 H. 8. ca. 1. 27 H. 8. ca. 22. 5 E. 6. ca. 5. 5 El. cap. 2. are repealed by the ſtatute of 21 Jac. cap. 28. and the ſtatutes of 39 El. ca. 1. & 2. are expired, for that they were ſo like labyrinthes, with ſuch intricate windings and turnings, as little or no fruit proceeded of them.

[g] No man can erect an houſe or building to the nuſance of any other.

[g] See the 2. part of the Inſtitutes. W. 2. ca. 24. lib. 5. fo. 101. lib. 8. fo. 46. lib. 9. fo. 54. 55.

[h] See where a man hath any houſe or mill, &c. and having any priviledge or thing appurtenant thereunto, and pull it down and build a new, where the priviledge or appurtenant remain and where not.

[h] See lib. 4. f. 84. Lutterels caſe, and the authorities there cited.

[i] Concerning the erecting, &c. of cotages, ſee the ſtatute of 31 El. ca. 7. which could not be reſtrained in ſuch ſort as they are, but by authority of parliament.

[i] 31 Eliz. ca. 7.

There was a ſtatute made *anno* 35 El. (when I was ſpeaker) againſt buildings in the cities of London or Weſtminſter, or within three miles of the gates of the city of London, and againſt the dividing and converting of any dwelling houſe or building into divers habitations, and againſt inmates, but that endured but for ſeven years, and until the end of the next ſeſſion of parliament, which act, being holden dangerous, was not continued at the ſeſſion of parliament holden in 43 Eliz. being the next ſeſſion after the ſeven years, and therefore expired with the ſame. In the mean time there was a law made againſt new buildings, &c. which then was a warrant, and ſince hath been a colour for divers proceedings in courts of juſtice, not obſerving the expiration of that law; but now that law hath long ſince loſt his force, and the ancient and fundamentall common law is to be followed.

Sylliva, or *ſulliva* is a word derived from the Saxon *ſylle*, and ſignifieth a poſte, or plate fixed in the ground: the Saxon word

Lamb. perambulation of Kent. Theſe words, you ſhall read in records concerning priviledges.

word is not yet out of uſe, for every man knows what a groundſille is.

Pera, a peer, derived from the Latin word *petra: plance*, of the Engliſh word, planks, for boords or tables, in uſe alſo at this day.

Having ſpoken of erecting of houſes and buildings, &c. we will tell you what we find in our books and records of dilapidation, and decay of buildings.

k 29 E. 3. 16. 2 H. 4. f. 3. 9 E. 4. 34.

[k] Dilapidation of eccleſiaſtical palaces, houſes, and buildings is a good cauſe of deprivation.

l 4 H. 4. ca. 2. lib. 11. fo. 29. Alex. Poulters caſe.

[l] It appeareth by the ſtatute of 4 H. 4. cap. 2. that *depopulatores agrorum* were great offenders by the ancient law, and that the appeal or indictment thereof ought not to be generall, but in ſpecial manner; and provides, that the offenders therein might have their clergy. They are called *depopulatores agrorum*, for that by proſtrating or decaying of the houſes of habitation of the kings people, they depopulate, that is, diſpeople the towns.

[205]

Dorſ. Clauſ. an. 43 E. 3. m. 23.

Prohibitio regis quòd incolæ de villa de Southampton non proſternent domos ſuas in alias migraturi regiones.

Rot. Clauſ. anno 21 R. 2. m. 15.

Simile pro magna Jermenutha.

That which may lawfully be prohibited before it be done, may be juſtly puniſhed after it be done.

Firſt part of the Inſtitutes, f. 54. b. 56. b.

And herewith we will cloſe up this chapter: that the law doth favour the ſupportation of houſes of habitation, and uſe for mankinde.

C A P. XCVIII.

De Lupanaribus et Fornicibus, &c.

Brothel-houſes, Eſtuis, Bordelloes.

* Numb. 25. 9. Deut. 23. 18. Ezek. 16. 24. 31. 39. Joel 3. 3. 2. Mach. 4. 12. Hoſpes meritricum Lena. Leno, unde Lenocinium.

THE keeping of them is againſt the law of God, on which the common law of England in that caſe is grounded. * *Non offeres mercedem proſtibuli, nec precium canis in domo Dei tui, &c. Quia abominatio eſt utrumq; apud dominum Deum tuum.*

And the keeper, he or ſhe, of ſuch houſes is puniſhable by indictment at the common law by fine and impriſonment: for although adultery and fornication be puniſhable by the eccleſiaſticall law, yet the keeping of a houſe of bawdrie or ſtewes, or brothell-houſe, being as it were a common nuſance, is puniſhable by the common law, and is the cauſe of many miſchiefs, not only to the overthrow of the bodies, and waſting of their livelyhoods, but to the indangering of their ſoules. For the miſchiefs enſuing hereupon, ſee 11 H. 6. cap. 1. 1 H. 7. fo. 6. 12. 13 H. 7. 6. 27 H. 8. Rot. Parl. 14 R. 2. nu. 32.

By proclamation under the great ſeale 30 Martii. 37 H. 8.

King H. 8. ſuppreſſed all the ſtewes or brothel-houſes, which long had continued on the Bankſide in Southwark, for that they were (as hath been ſaid) prohibited by the law of God, and by the law of this land. And thoſe infamous women were not buried in Chriſtian

Christian buriall when they were dead, nor permitted to receive the rites of the church whilest they lived.

The word *estuis* or *stewes* is French, we having no English word for it.

Before the reigne of H. 7. there were eighteen of these infamous houses, and H. 7. for a time forbad them: but afterwards twelve only were permitted, and had signes painted on their wals; as a Boares Head, the Cross Keyes, the Gun, the Castle, the Crane, the Cardinals Hat, the Bell, the Swan, &c. Fabian Chron. Stowe.

Many wicked and common women had seated themselves in a lane called Water-lane, next to the house of the friers Carmelites in Fleet-street: this being an open and known wickednesse, king E. 3. to the end these friars might performe their vowes, one of which was, to live in perpetuall chastity, took order for removing of these women. The record saith, *Rex præcipit majori civitatis London quod amoveri faciat omnes mulieres meretrices in venella prope fratres Carmelitarum in Fletestreet inhabitantes.* In Dorf. Clauf. 21 E. 3. part 1. m. 6. Fratres beatæ Mariæ de Monte Carmeli, called White Fryers.

Read 3 Regum cap. 14. verse 24. eodem lib. cap. 15. verse 12. & 4 Regum cap. 23. verse 7.

And by the common law it appertaineth to the marshall of the kings house to free, or protect the court from *femes puteins*, which is more particularly explained by Fleta, who saith, *Mareschalli interest virgatam à meretricibus omnib' protegere et deliberare, et habet mareschallus ex consuetudine pro qualibet meretrice coi. infra metas hospitii inventa*, 4d *primo die; quæ si iterum in baliva sua inveniatur, capiatur et coram seneschallo inhibeatur ei hospitium regis, reginæ, et liberorum suorum, ne iterum ingrediatur, et nomina earum imbrevientur: quæ si iterum inventæ fuerint hospic' sequutrices, tunc aut remaneant in prisona in vinculis, aut sponte prædic' hospicia abjurentur; quæ si autem tertio inventæ fuerint, considerabitur quod amputetur eis tressoria, et tondeantur; quæ quidem si quarto inveniantur, amputentur eis superlabia, ne de cætero concupiscantur ad libidinem.* 7 E. 3. fo. 23, 24. Fleta lib. 2. cap. 5. lib. 10. Le case de Marshalsea, fo. 77. [206]

14 R. 2. It is enacted that no estews or brothel-houses should be kept in Southwark, but in the common places therefore appointed. Rot. par. 14 R. 2. nu. 32.

So odious and so dangerous was this infamous vice (the fairest end whereof is beggery) that men in making of leases of their houses, did adde an expresse condition, that the lessee, &c. should not suffer, harbour, or keep any *feme puteine* within the said houses, &c. 35 H. 6. Barre 162.

See the case of 1 H. 7. the custome of London for entring into an house, and arresting of an advowtrer, and carrying her to prison. In ancient times adultery and fornication were punished by fine and imprisonment, and inquirable in turnes and leets by the name of Letherwite. We find in Domesday *De adulterio vero per totum Chent, habet rex hominem*, (i. *amerciamentum hominis*) *et archiepiscopus mulierem*, (i. *amerciamentum mulieris*) *&c.* 1 H. 7. fo. 6. &c. Domesday. Chent. Dover. Ibid. Cestriæ civitas.

Vidua, si alicui se non legitime commisceb. 20 *s. emendabit, puella vero* 10 *s. pro consimili causa.* Ibid. Sudsex Lewes.

Adulterium faciens 8 *s.* & 4 *d. emendabit homo, et fœmina tantundem. Rex habet hominem adulterum, archiepiscopus fœminam.* Domesday. Huntedoiesc.

But now these offences belong to the ecclesiasticall court. Bracton. Fleta.

Legrewita, or *logrewita*, *legergeld*, or *logergeld*, of *legre* or *logre* for a bed, Rastall term. leg. Stat. de exposit. vocab.

a bed, and *wite amerciament*, by common ſpeech *letherwite*, or *laire-wite*, *lierwite*, *lotherwite*.

Childewite is for the lord to take a fine for his bondwoman defiled and begotten with childe.

Bawdry, *lenocinium*, *unde ribawdry et ribaude*. i. *Impudicus rabula*. See parliam. 50 E. 3. nu. 61. of ribauds and robertſmen.

[207]

CAP. XCIX.

De Aſſentatione, Fucologia, Pſeudologia, Flattery.

Int. leges Canuti, fo. 106. c. 7. Lam. Fatalis magnarum poteſtatum peſtis, adulatio. Semper aſſentor id, quod is ad cujus voluntatem dicitur, eſſe magnum; ut in Terentio: magnas vero agere gratias mihi, &c. ſatis erat reſpondiſſe magnas, ingentes inquit.

WE find a law before the conqueſt againſt flatterers in theſe words, Lıcceꞃaꞅ ⁊ Leoᵹoꞃaꞅ ꞃepeꞃaꞅ ⁊ ꞃeaꝼaꞃaꞅ ᵹoꝺeꞅ ᵹꞃaman habban, &c. which Dr. Lambard tranſlateth thus, *Aſſentatores, mendaces, prædones, et rapaces offenſionem Dei graviſſimam incurrant, &c.*

The ancient manuſcript tranſlateth it thus, *Seductores, mendaces, rapaces et raptores Dei gravamen habeant*. And both tranſlations do in effect agree, for a flatterer is a ſeducer for ſome private end, by fained praiſe and humouring of another, whereby he hath an *oultrecuidance* of himſelfe, his ſtate, and actions, *iſti ducunt et ſeducunt*.

The occaſion of making this law was, that king Canutus had been ſeduced by flatterers, who had ſhewed him his face and ſtate in a falſe glaſſe, making too great a ſhew of his own parts, actions, and ſtate, to the end to make him conceit himſelfe to be better and greater then he was, and his adverſaries leſſe, then in truth they were. Nay, this king by wicked flatterers aſſumed to him divine power and honour: for comming from ſea, he ſet his feet on the ſea ſtrond, as the ſea was flowing, and commanded the ſea not to riſe to wet his lordly and majeſtick feet nor clothes: the ſea keeping on his accuſtomed courſe, both wet his feet and thighs alſo: whereat being ſore amazed repented his preſumption (which he had undertaken by wicked flattery.)

And well is the flatterer marſhalled in this law with lyers, thieves, and raveners; for the divine deſcribed flatterers to be thoſe, *Qui colunt aliquem, et auferunt ab eo aliquid temporarii boni*. So as it is *peccatum viſcatum*, it getteth away much and giveth ſmoke.

And the Holy Ghoſt hath ſtyled flattery *oleum peccatoris*, that is, the oile of the ſinner, κατ' ἐξοχὴν, that is, of him that exceedeth others in ſinne, and doth affect greatneſſe, that is the head, making it greater and more proſperous then it is, as you may reade in the prophet David: *Corripiet me juſtus in miſericordia, et increpabit me, oleum autem peccatoris non impinguet caput meum*. Whereby he being both a king and a prophet, preferreth the reproofe, nay the ſharpe rebuke of the juſt and vertuous, before the ſmooth humouring of the

Pſal. 141. 5.

the flatterer *(per nomen)* of the finner. This *oleum peccatoris* is *mel venenatum, et venenum mellitum*, and commonly affecteth greatneffe, and is called lordbane.

And againe, David fpeaking of the flatterer faith, his words are fmoother then oile, and yet are they very fwords. *Hæc dicit Dominus Deus, Væ qui confuunt pulvillos fub omni cubito manus, et faciunt cervicalia fub capite univerfæ ætatis ad capiend' animas, &c.* Thus faith the Lord God, Woe to them that fow pillowes under all armeholes, and put kerchifes upon the heads of every age to hunt foules. They make the king glad with their wickedneffe, and the princes with their lyes. *In malitia fua lætificaverunt regem, et in mendaciis fuis principes.*

Pfal. 55. 22. Ezech. 13. 18. Ofee 7. 3.

The flattering mouth worketh ruine. And more kings and kingdomes have been overthrown by the means of flattery, then by publick hoftility. And this is the caufe that we have mentioned the faid ancient law for their punifhment, they be lawfully banifhed from princes courts, and fubjects houfes.

Prov. 26. 28. Qu. Curtius.

Ut videat, cæco fit fimia præda leoni:
Rex cæcus cernit, cum fycophanta perit.

[208]

What fearfull ends flattering favourites, corruptors of their foveraigne liege lords, abufing their favours in fubverfion of their lawes, have had, appeareth in our parliament rolls, records, and hiftories.

Nota, enemies to lawes punifhed by the lawes.

[a] King H. 3. had Hubert de Burgo chiefe juftice and earle of Kent, and many others: but this was his fafety, that upon juft occafion without any great grief he could forgoe a favourite. See in the preface to the fecond part of the Inftitutes, his counfell to H. 3. to burne Magna Carta.

E. 2. had [b] Pierce de Gavefton, the [c] Spencers, &c. and the Spencers proceedings againft *le grand charter* by name (amongft other things) tending to the fubverfion of law, &c.

R. 2. had [d] fir Robert Trefilian chiefe juftice, &c. and Robert earle of Oxford and duke of Ireland, &c.

H. 6 had [e] William de la Pole duke of Suffolk, &c. who endeavoured to have brought in the civill lawes, which was the occafion that the chiefe juftice Fortefcue wrote in the commendation of the lawes of England, preferring them for the government of this land before the civill lawes. This duke with others plotted the death and deftruction of Humfrey the good duke of Glouc. who ever ftood in his way.

E. 4. had [f] William lord Haftings the kings chamberlaine, and captaine of Callice. All thefe came to fearfull and untimely ends.

R. 3. had [g] Sir John Catefby one of the juftices of the common place, and Henry duke of Buck. &c. privy plotters and counfellors with R. 3. for the moft execrable murder of his nephews E. 5. and Richard duke of York. What a miferable end the duke had, you know: and juftice Catefby in his journey to London, in the kings high way had *fubitaneam et improvifam mortem.*

H. 7. had [h] Sir Richard Empfon, Edmond Dudley, &c. Sir

[a] Rot. pat. anno 17 H. 3. Nos integre et firmiter tenebimus judicium de Huberto de Burgo, per barones datum. Speed 18 H. 3. 520.

[b] Rot. parl. 7 E. 2. Ne quis occafionetur per mortem Pet. de Gavefton. Hil. 318. a. & ibid. 321. a.

[c] Vet. Mag. Cart. 2 part 44. ib. 50. exilium Hugonis, & 54. Ne quis occafionetur pro feloniis in profecutione d'Spencer patris & filii.

[d] Rot. par. 11 R. 2. nu. 8. &c.

[e] Rot. par. 28 H. 6. nu. 19. untill 47.

[f] Hollenfh. 713. a. 30.

[g] Hollenfh. 722. 748. 767. a. 2 H. 7. 10.

[h] Coram rege ap. 1 H. 8. In information verf. D. Peter & alios. The like indictment againft Edw. Dudley.

Richard Empson was indicted, *Quod ipse consiliarius excellentissimi princi is Henrici nuper regis Angliae septimi Deum prae oculis non habens, sed ut filius diabolicus subtiliter imaginans honorem, dignitatem, et prosperitatem dicti nuper regis, ac posteritatem regni sui Angliae minime valere, sed ut ipse magis singulares favores dicti nuper regis adhibere, unde magnat' fieri potuisset, ac totum regnum Angliae secundum ejus voluntatem gubernare, falso, deceptive, et proditorie legem Angliae subvertens, diversos ligeos ipsius nuper regis, ex sua falsa covina, et subtili ingenio, contra communē legē regni Angliae de diversis feloniis, &c. indictari fecit, &c. per quod plures et diversi populi dicti nuper regis hiis gravaminibus, et indebitis exactionib' multipliciter torquebantur, in tantum quòd populi dicti nuper regis versus ipsum nuper regem multipliciter murmurabant, et malignabant, in magnum periculum ipsius nuper regis regni sui Angliae, ac subversionem legum et consuetudinum ejusdem regni, &c.* And the like inditement was against Dudley.

Tr. 23 H. 8. coram rege. Rot. 14.

H. 8. had Thomas Woolsey cardinall. *Ipse intendens finaliter antiquissimas Angliae leges penitus subvertere, et enervare, universumq; hoc regnum Angliae et ejusdem regni populum legibus imperialibus, vulgo dict', legibus civilibus, et earundem legum canonibus subjugare et subducere, &c.*

We will for some causes descend no lower. *Qui eorum vestigiis insistunt, eorum exitus perhorrescant.*

But that right be done to him, who was a faithfull favorite and counseller to this king, we have seen a manuscript that relateth, that Charles Brandon duke of Suffolk a wise and warlike person, was for many years before his decease the greatest favourite the king had, upon whom he chiefly relied in all his weightiest affairs. This noble duke deceased in August in the 37 year of the reign of king H. 8. After whose death the next time the king sat with his councell, and missing the good duke, grievously lamented for him, and said, that when I was offended with any (as often I was) and acquainted him therewith, that he ever endeavoured to mitigate my displeasure, and never spake to me evill of any of them. And the king looking upon the lords of his councell one after another, said, and so (my lord) cannot you say, perusing them all throughout. A royall commendation of this great Duke, and a great argument of his piety

[209]

and honour, that no subject had ever the indignation or displeasure of his soveraign, by any private whispering of his.

Anno 5 R. 2. Th. Walf. p. 281.

We will conclude this chapter with one of our own histories. *Generaliter cunctorum habitatorum terrae peccatis inclusive ordines sumendo mendicantium ad cumulandum causas malorum, &c. isti possessionatis invidentes, procerum crimina approbantes, commune vulgus in errore foventes, et utrorumque peccata comedentes, pro possessionibus acquirendis, qui possessiones renunciaverant pro pecuniis congregandis: qui in paupertate perseverare juraverant, dicunt bonum malum, et malum bonum, seducentes principes adulationibus, plebem mendaciis, et utrosque secum in devium pertrahentes, &c.* Note what is said, that the full heap of the causes of Gods vengeance in those days, was made up by those flattering preaching friers. But parliaments, palaces of princes and pulpits should be free from adulation and flattery.

Read the story, and see the most lamentable estate of those times. Note these three PPP.

CAP.

CAP. C.

Of falſe Impriſonment.

SEE the ſecond part of the Inſtitutes, the ſtatute *de* 1 E. 2. *de frangentibus priſonam*, and the expoſition upon the ſame.

See the Petition of Right 3 Car. regis, and Mag. Cart. ca. 29. And it is to be obſerved that before the conqueſt it was thus provided. *Qui hominem paganum immerentem vinculis conſtrinxerit, 10 ſolidis noxiam ſarcito; eum ſi verberibus affecerit, 20 ſolidorum pœna eſto; ſi ſuſpenſum in ſublime rapuerit, 30 ſolidis culpa penſatur; ſi contumelioſe capillum ejus morionis in morem totonderit, 10 ſolid' præſtato; ſin caput in morem ſacerdotis raſerit, nec ipſum ligaverit, 30 ſolidos numerato; ſi barbam illi reſecarit, 20 ſolidorum compenſatio ſequitor; ſi denique ei vinculis conſtricto capillos in morem ſacerdotum abraſerit, 60 olidos pendito.*

Int. leges Alvredi cap. 31.

By way of addition, here it is neceſſary to be known, how and by what means one that is in priſon may be diſcharged. Every man that is in priſon, either is impriſoned without lawfull *mittimus* (whereof we have ſpoken before *ubi ſupra*, and how he may be freed from impriſonment in that caſe) or with lawfull *mittimus*. He, that is lawfully impriſoned, is either impriſoned by lawfull commandement, and order or warrant, or by the kings writ: by commandment and order of any court of record; and this commandment, warrant or writ is either for cauſes not being treaſon or felony, miſpriſion of the ſame, nor other publique offence or cauſe, or inferiour cauſes to theſe; as contempts, private actions or ſuits. If any court of record commit a man for a contempt done in court, they may diſcharge him by like order at their pleaſure: but if they having authority, doe commit him for treaſon, felony, or other crime, or for ſuſpition of the ſame, they cannot diſcharge him, untill he be inquired of, and either indicted and acquited, or an ignoramus found, and delivered by proclamation. [a] And ſo it is if any be taken and impriſoned by lawfull warrant, or the kings writ for treaſon, felony, or other crime, &c. he cannot be diſcharged by any without legall proceeding (but by the king only.)

[b] If a vagrant, refuſing to ſerve, had been committed to priſon upon the ſtatute of 23 E. 3. of labourers by the lord of the town, or juſtice of peace, they might have diſcharged him, even as the chancellour, &c. may commit a man for a contempt before him in court, and diſcharge him again at his pleaſure.

[c] If a man be taken by the kings writ in an action of debt or another private action, the plaintif may diſcharge the gaoler of him, and ſet him at liberty, though he be in execution: but if he be taken in an appeal of death, robbery, rape, * &c. the plaintif cannot diſcharge him, becauſe it is a publique offence, wherein the king hath an intereſt, and he may after nonſuit by the plaintif be arraigned at the kings ſuit.

[a] For bailment See the ſtatute of Mag. Cart. ca. 29. W. 2. ca. 15. and the expoſition thereof. 1 & 2 Ph. and Mar. ca. 13. 2 & 3 Ph. and Ma. cap. 10.

[b] 14 H. 6. 8. F. N. B. 167. b. See 12 H. 6. 3.

[c] Mich. 13 Jac. in banke le Roy. Int. Withers & Henry, adjudge accord. 27 H. 8. 28. b. 1 R. 2. ca. 12. 10 H. 7. 3. a. per Vavaſor. 13 E. 3. Bar. 253.

*[210]

There are two great adverſaries to the due execution of theſe laws (as (as before hath been touched) especially in criminall causes, viz. *præcipitatio, et morosa cunctatio.* Precipitation; as a man or woman to be committed to prison, and within so short a time to be indicted and arraigned, as it is not possible for them to send for, or procure their witnesses; this certainly is precipitation; for the law both in reall and personall actions doth give the party tenant or defendant a convenient time without respect of persons to answer, &c. much more it ought to be in case of life. *Nec unquam in judiciis tantum eminet periculum, quantum parit processus festinatus:* and again, *crebro in deliberationibus judicia maturescunt, in accelerat processu nunquam*, and specially in case of life. As for *morosa cunctatio*, froward or weyward delay; see the second part of the Institutes, Glouc. ca. 2. 9. And we will conclude this chapter with the rule of law, *Quòd in criminalibus, probationes debent esse luce clariores.*

Fortescue ca. 53. fo. 127. b.

CAP. CI.

Of Judgements and Execution.

JUDICIUM is derived *à jure, et dicto, et est quasi juris dictum* and therefore if the judgement be erroneous, both the judgement and execution thereupon, and all the former proceedings shall be reversed by writ of error: but if the former proceeding and judgement be good, if the execution be erroneous, the execution shall only be reversed: and because the judgement is the guide and direction of the execution, we shall treat principally of the judgement, and incidently of execution.

Of judgements, some be by the common law, and some by statute law, and some by custome.

Of judgements by the common law, some be in criminall causes, or pleas of the crown, concerning the life of man (whereof we are principally to intreat,) and of these some be expressed, and some implied. Other judgements at the common law be in actions reall and mixt, of which, some be *judicia interlocutoria*, and some *ultima seu principalia:* and again, *de principalibus, quædam sunt finalia, et quædam non sunt finalia.* Of judgements by statutes, some be in criminall causes, and some in common pleas: but judgements by custome are only in common pleas.

All pleas of the crown, concerning the life of man, are divided into treason and felony; and treason, into high treason, and petit treason; and felony into all the severall branches abovesaid. And as in the case of high treason, (as it hath before appeared) some be far more horrible and odious then other, yet (one case excepted, as before hath appeared) one and the same judgement is given for all. So in cases of petit treason, one judgement is given in all, nay in all the severall cases of felony, though some be far more hainous then other, yet all being but felony, one and the same judgement is given. See the judgement and forfeiture in cases of treason, felony, &c. in the severall titles thereof, these we will adde.

6 El. Dier 230. See before in the chapter of Treason.

Judgement

Judgement in High Treason.

Pl. Com. 387. b. See Stanford 182. d. e. lib. Int. Co. 361. * See the book of Judges cap. 19. ver. ult. Consider, consult, and give sentence. 19 H. 6. 47. Trahe, pende, et disclose. Bract.

*Et super hoc visis, et per curiam hic intellectis omnibus et singulis præmissis, * consideratum est, quòd prædictus R. usque furcas de T.* 1 *trahatur, et* 2 *ibidem suspendatur per collum, et vivus ad terram prosternatur, et* 3 *interiora sua extra ventrem ‡ suum capiantur,* 4 *ipsoque vivente comburantur, et* 5 *caput suum amputetur, quodque* 6 *corpus suum in quatuor partes dividatur; ac* 7 *quod caput et quarteria illa ponantur, ubi dominus rex ea assignare vult.*

li. 3. fo. 118, b. *Crimen læsæ majest. ut si contra personam ipsius regis sit præsumptum, quod quidem crimen omnia alia crimina excedit quoad pœnam.* Idem. l. 3. f. 104. b. maketh mention of execution, *laqueo et securi*, parliam. 21 R. 2. inter placita coron. nu. 50.

‡ [211]

35 H. 8. Br. Forfeiture, 99.

Implied in this judgement is, first, the forfeiture of all his mannors, lands, tenements, and hereditaments in fee-simple, or fee-tail of whomsoever they be holden. Secondly, his wife to lose her dower. Thirdly, he shall lose his children (for they become base and ignoble.) Fourthly, he shall lose his posterity, for his blood is stained and corrupted, and they cannot inherit to him or any other aunceftor. Fifthly, all his goods and chattels, &c. And reason is, that his body, lands, goods, posterity, &c. shall be torn, pulled asunder, and destroyed, that intended to tear, and destroy the majesty of government. And all these severall punishments are found for treason in holy scripture.

1 Reg. 2. 28. &c. *Joab tractus, &c.* — Drawing.

Esther, 2. 22, 23. *Bithan suspensus, &c.* — Hanging.

Acts, 1. 18. *Judas suspensus crepuit medius, et diffusa sunt viscera ejus.* — Bowelling.

2 Sam. 18. 14, 15. *Infixit tres lanceas in corde Absolon cum adhuc palpitaret, &c.* — The heart, &c. while he lived.

2 Sam. 20. 22. *Abscissum caput Sheba filii Bichri.* — Beheaded.

2 Sam. 4. 11, 12. *Interfecerunt Baanan et Rechab, et suspenderunt manus et pedes eorum super piscinam in Hebron.* — Quarters hanged up.

Corruption of blood, and that the children of a traitor should not inherite, appeareth also by holy scripture. — Damnatæ memoriæ.

Psal. 109. 9, 10, 11, 12, 13. *Mutantes transferantur filii ejus, et mendicent, et ejiciantur de habitationibus suis, et diripient alieni labores ejus, et dispereat de terra memoria ejus.*

[a] The judgement of a woman for high treason is to be drawn and burnt.

[b] Sir Andrew Harkley earl of Carlisle, convicted, degraded and attainted of treason.

[a] 25 E. 3. 42. b. Coron. 130. Brit. ca. 8. f. 16. b. accord. [b] *Degradation.* Hil. 18 E. 2. Coram rege rot. 34, 35. Walsing. p. 118.

Judgement in Petit Treason, where he is convicted thereof by Verdict or Confession.

19 H. 6. 47. Com. Cæsar. ante Christum natum 1600 annis, what the judgement was for petit treason 1 R. 3. f. 4. 25 E. 3. 42. 12 Ass. 30.

Super hoc visis, &c. ut supra, consideratum est, quod prædictus R. usque furcas de T. trahatur, et ibidem suspendatur per collum, quousque mortuus fuerit.

But a woman is to have judgement to be drawn and burnt, as well in case of petit treason as high treason, and ought not to be beheaded,

beheaded, or hanged. *De morte mariti si compertum est uxorem, &c. igne Britanni interficiunt.*

Bracton, li. 3 fo. 105. a. *Igne concremantur qui saluti dominorum suorum insidiaverint,* idem fo. 104. b.

Judgement in Felony, where he is convicted thereof by Verdict or Confession.

6 E. 4. 4. a. & b. See the Preface to the sixt part of Reports, what the law was before the conquest anno domino 995. in case of felony. * Pasch. 20 R. 2. coram rege, rot. 1. Lincoln.

Et super hoc visis, &c. ut supra, consideratum est quòd praedictus R. suspendatur per collum, quousque mortuus fuerit. Bracton, lib. 3 fo. 104. b. speaketh, *de laqueo.*

And it is a maxime in law, that execution must be according to the judgement, *Ea quae in curia nostra rite acta sunt, debit' executioni demandari debent:* * and for expresse authority, *non licet felonem pro felonia decollare;* and yet some examples are to the contrary.

See before cap. Murder.

True it is that the lord of Hungerford of Heytesbury was in 32 H. 8. attainted of buggery, and had judgement to be hanged by the neck, untill he was dead; and yet on the twenty eight day of July in the same year was beheaded at the Tower Hill. But as true it is, that Thomas Fines lord Dacres of the South, in *anno* 33 H. 8. was attainted of murder, and had judgement to be hanged by the neck, untill he was dead, and according to the judgement was hanged at Tiborn the twenty eight of June in the same year. And true it is, that Edward duke of Somerset was attainted of felony in *anno* 5 E. 6. and had judgement to be hanged by the neck untill he was dead, and on the twenty second of February in the same year was beheaded at the Tower Hill. And as true it is, that 3 & 4 Ph. and Mar. the lord Stourton was attainted of murder, and had judgement to be hanged by the neck untill he were dead, and according to the judgement, the sixth of March in the same year was hanged.

[212]

In case of high treason, beheading is part of the judgement, and therefore the king may pardon all the rest saving beheading, as is usually done in case of nobility. But if a man being attainted of felony, be beheaded, it is no execution of the judgement, because the judgement is, that he be hanged, untill he be dead. In this case the judgement doth belong to the judge, and he cannot alter it, the execution belongs to the sherif, &c. and he cannot alter it. And if the execution might be altered in this case, from hanging to beheading, by the same reason it might be altered to burning, stoning to death, &c. To conclude this point, *Judicandum est legibus, non exemplis,* and *judicium est juris dictum, et executio est executio juris secundum judicium.*

The forfeiture in case of petit treason and felony (which is implied in the judgement) is all one, which you may read in the first part of the Institutes. sect. 747.

Deut. 2. 13. Vide Hil. 1 H. 5. Rog. Actons case.

Quando peccaverit homo, quòd morte plectendus est, et adjudicatus morti appensus fuerit in patibulo, non permanebit ejus cadaver in ligno, sed in eadem die sepelietur. And the reason that divines yeeld hereof is, for that by the execution of the judgement by death, the law is satisfied, and abhorreth cruelty, and in that case, *mors dicitur ultimum supplicium.*

And herein this is observable, that in treason and felony, the judgement

ment is only of the fatall and corporall puniſhment, and nothing of the forfeiture, which is implied, but in common pleas the judgements are more particular.

Judgement in Appeal, when the Defendant joyning Battail is vanquiſhed in the Field, &c.

If the defendant in appeal be vanquiſhed in the field, the record reciteth the vanquiſhing in the field. *Ideo conſideratum eſt, quod ſuſ per col.* and ſo it is when the defendant is vanquiſhed and ſlain in the field, yet the judgement is *ut ſupra.* Otherwiſe there ſhould be no eſcheat: ſee the ſecond part of the Inſtitutes, W. 1. ca. 14. 8 E. 3. Judgement, 225.

Judgement in Treaſon or Felony, wherein neither any corporall Puniſhment or Forfeiture is expreſſed.

In caſe of treaſon or felony, if any perſon be outlawed, the judgement upon the exigent at the fift county court upon default of the party is, *Ideo, &c. per judicium coronatoris domini regis comitatus prædict, utlagatus eſt.* Which writ being duly returned of record by the ſheriff, the party ſhall have the like corporall puniſhment, and ſhall loſe and forfeit as much as if he had appeared, &c. and judgement had been given againſt him in caſe of treaſon or felony reſpectively. And note that in theſe words *(ideo utlagatur)* both the corporall puniſhments and forfeiture alſo are implied: and if the proceeding therein, or the judgement be erroneous, and upon his appearance upon the *capias utlagatum,* if it appear to the court (whereof any man, as *amicus curiæ,* may inform the court) that the party may either avoid the outlawry againſt him by writ of error, or by plea, the court ought not to award execution againſt the party, but aſſign him or her councell learned, and require him or her by their advice, either to bring a writ of error or plead: but if the party refuſe to bring his writ of error or plead after convenient time be given, if the utlawry be erroneous and not void, the court may award execution. And ſo it was reſolved, *termino Hil. anno 3 Jacobi regis,* by the whole court in the kings bench, and divers preſidents thereof ſhewed in the reigns of H. 6. E. 4. and one in the reign of queen Eliz. which we ſaw; for as long as the attainder by outlawry ſtandeth in force, the party outlawed cannot be drawn in queſtion by any new indictment or appeal for the treaſon, or felony, for the which he was outlawed: for *auterfoitz attaint* for the ſame offence is a good plea to free him from anſwer in that cauſe, albeit the record be erroneous. But if the attainder or outlawry be void againſt him, then may he be either arraigned upon the former indictment, or appeal, or newly indicted, &c. if there be cauſe. And therefore the judges are to take due conſideration of the whole record of the attainder or outlawry, that they may be truly informed of the true ſtate of the cauſe, before they award execution of death againſt him upon the outlawry. Read Bracton, lib. 3. tract. 2. cap. 14. and Britton, cap. 13. fo. 20, 21. excellently treating hereof, and Fleta, lib. 1. cap. 27.

Regiſt. 164. b. Fecit feloniam pro qua utlagatus fuit.

19 H. 6. 2. a. Error Fi. 26. 28 E. 3. 91. a. 6 H. 4. 6. 9 H. 7. 19. b.

Hil. 3. Ja. coram rege per curiam.

Auterfoits attaint de meſme le offence.

[213]

Vide 6 E. 3. 55. in Aiel. 12 E. 2. Eſch. 14. 19 E. 2. Cor. 387.

Bract. li. 3. f. 131. Britton. fo. 20, 21. Fleta li. 1. ca. 27.

And by the common law *auterfoitz attaint, &c.* of the ſame felony was a good plea as well in an indictment as in appeal by the common

mon law. See the ſtatute of 3 H. 7. cap. 1. concerning appeal of death: ſo as in an appeal of death, at the ſuit of the party, *auter foitz attaint de meſme le mort*, is no plea at this day, but in caſe of an indictment of death at the ſuit of the king, *auterfoitz attaint de meſme le mort* in appeal is a good plea. *Auterfoitz attaint de murder* is a good plea to an indictment, &c. of petit treaſon of the ſame death, for in effect it hath the ſame judgement, and the ſelf ſame forfeiture. So likewiſe if a man be attainted of manſlaughter, it is a good bar to an indictment of murder of the ſame death, *et è converſo*.

Auterfoitz attaint dun auter offence. 28 E. 3. 90. b. Dier 4 Eliz. Stones caſe. 6 H. 4. 6. 10 H. 4. coron. 237. 6 E. 3. cor. 394. 22 E. 3. cor. 471. Stanf. f. 107, 108. See 44 E. 3. 44. 7 H. 4. 31. 4 E. 4. 11. * 1 H. 6. fo. 5. Rot. Par. 3 R. 2. nu. 18. Jo. Imperials caſe.

By the common law if a man were attainted of a felony done by him, and admitting he were after pardoned, he cannot at the ſuit of the king be impeached for any felony whatſoever before his ſaid attainder by him committed, for by the attainder he was *mort in ley*; and in that caſe he had the judgement due for felony, viz. *ſuſ. per col.* But the party may have his appeal of robbery, for a robbery done before the felony, whereof he was attainted, becauſe in the appeal he is to have reſtitution of his goods, beſides judgment of death. * And if the party attainted of felony had committed high treaſon before his attainder, he ſhall anſwer to the treaſon notwithſtanding his attainder of felony, becauſe the king by the treaſon was intitled to have the forfeiture of all his lands, of whomſoever they were holden. Alſo for high treaſon there is another judgement being an offence of an higher nature: but being attainted of felony, if he commit treaſon afterwards, he ſhall anſwer thereunto, becauſe it is of higher nature then the felony, but it ſhall not deveſt the right of eſcheat, which lawfully was by the felony veſted in the lords, contrary to the opinion of juſtice Stanford in that caſe, for the act and offence of the party ſhall not deveſt the lawfull eſcheat of the lords: but if a man be attainted of treaſon, he cannot be after attainted of a former treaſon, *cauſa qua ſupra*.

Where a little before it is ſaid, that a felon by his attainder is *mort in ley*, it is to be underſtood of ſuch former offences as require *pœnam mortis*: for notwithſtanding the attainder, his body remains ſubject to arreſts and execution for debts, &c. *Vide hic paulo poſt*, Truſſels and Preſtals caſe *in margine*. Albeit for felony a man be adjudged to his penance, *pain fort et jure*, yet he may be impeached for any former felony, becauſe, the judgement is not given for the felony, but for his contumacy.

Dier 14 El. 308. Cobhams caſe.

If a man be attainted of petit larceny, he may be after attainted of a felony, for the which he ſhall have judgement of death, becauſe it is an higher offence, and is to have an other judgement.

Auterfoitz acquite, and the Judgement thereupon.

See Stanf. 105. a. & b. &c.

But *auterfoitz acquite*, muſt be of the ſame felony, and albeit he be acquit of the latter felony, yet may he be arraigned of any former felony: and ſo it is in caſe of treaſon, *auterfoitz acquite* of treaſon muſt be of the ſame treaſon, for it acquiteth no other, becauſe he ever remained a perſon able.

3 H. 7. ca. 1. 15 E. 3. tit. Coron. 116. 15 Aſſ. p. 7.

And albeit at this day in an appeal of death, *auterfoitz acquite*, upon an indictment of the ſame death is no bar, yet in an indictment

ment of death, *auterfoitz attaint de mesme le mort* in an appeal is a good bar.

In an indictment or appeal of death, if it be found that he killed him in his * own defence, he is acquited of the felony for ever.

It appeareth in Vauxes case, that if a man be erroneously acquited of felony by verdict and judgement thereupon given, yet if the indictment, &c. be insufficient, he may be indicted againe for the reasons and causes in that case reported, which you may reade there at large, and need not here be repeated: and thereunto this we wil adde, that the reason, wherefore upon an erroneous judgement of condemnation, the party as hath been said) is driven to his writ of error; and in the case of an erroneous judgement of acquitall, that no writ of error needeth to be brought by the king, but the offendor may be newly indicted, &c. is this, that in the case of condemnation the judgement is, *Quod suspendatur, &c.* which is the judgement of law due for the offence, and ought to be given therefore, and can have no other intendment: but in the case of acquitall the judgement is, *Quod eat sine die, &c.* which may be given as well for the insufficiency of the indictment, as for the parties innocency, or not guiltinesse of the offence. And the judges of the cause ought before judgement to look into the whole record, and upon due consideration thereof to cause it to be entred, *Ideo consideratum est quod eat sine die*; which upon that report, and this addition implied therein, we hold may satisfie the studious reader.

Lib. 4. fo. 44. 45.

And so it was adjudged Mich. 33 & 34 Eliz. coram rege, in an appeale of death between Katherine Wrote and Tho. Wigges. Vid. 19 E. 3. Barre 444.

Vi. 3 H. 4. fo. 3. 11.

Auter foitz convict de mesme le Felony devant Judgement.

For this division see Holcrofts case before in the chapter of Murder, and Lib. 4. fo. 45, 46. where the statute of 3 H. 7. cap. 1. is well expounded: and the second part of the Institutes artic. super Cart. cap. 3 & Lib. Intr. Co. fo. 53, 54, &c. and Lib. 4. fo. 40. Wetherels case. And Stanford, Lib. 2. cap. 37. in pl. coron.

Lib. 4. fo. 45, 46. Holcrofts case. Second part of the Institutes, art. super cart. cap. 3. Lib. Intr. Co. 53, 54, &c. Lib. fo. 40. Wetherels case. Stanf. lib. 2. ca. 37.

* Before the statutes of 8 Eliz. cap. 4. and 18 Eliz. ca. 6. If a man had committed divers felonies, if he had been indicted of the last, and had benefit of his clergy, he could not have been impeached for any of the former felonies, albeit for the same he could not have had his clergy: by that act it is provided, that notwithstanding the allowance of such clergy, he may be impeached for any former offence, for which he could not have had his clergy.

* *Auter foits convict. dun auter felony.* 25 E. 3. cap. 5. pro Clero.

Judgement to reverse an Outlawry for Treason or Felony.

The judgement to reverse an outlawry of A. B. in case of treason or felony in a writ of error is: *Ideo consideratum est quod utlagaria prædicta ob errorem prædict' et alios in recordo et process' prædict. compert', revocetur, adnulletur, et penitus pro nullo habeatur, et quod prædict. A. B. ad communem legem, et omnia quæ occasione utlagariæ prædict. amisit, restituatur, &c. et quod ipse eat sine die.*

Vid. Pasc. 39 E. 3. rot. 95. Scire fac. Dominis mediatis & immediatis

If the outlawrie be avoided by plea, then the judgement is, *Ideo consi-*

considerat um est quod prædictus A. B. de utlagaria prædicta exoneretur, et quod ipse ad communem legem, et omnia, quæ occasione utlagariæ prædict. amisit, restituatur, et ea occasione non molestetur in aliquo, nec gravetur, sed sit, et eat inde quietus.

If A. B. be indicted of treason or felony in the kings bench, or if he be indicted before commissioners of oier and terminer, or any other, and the indictment of treason or felony is removed into the kings bench: and by proces out of the kings bench he is erroneously outlawed and so returned, a writ of error may be brought in the kings bench for reversall thereof.

Stanf. pl. cor. 18. k. l.
33 H. 8. cap. 20.
‡ Nota, this act extends only to attainders of treasons before the act of 28 El. where the party hath been executed, and not to attainders of treasons afterwards.

And where it is holden by some, that if any person be attainted of high treason by the common law, that no writ of error should be brought for the reversall of that attainder by reason of these words of the statute of 33 H. 8. cap. 20. viz. And if any person or persons shall be attainted of high treason by the course of the common law, &c. that every such attainder by the common law shall be of as good strength, value, force, and effect, as if it had been done by authority of parliament. But the contrary hereof was resolved at a parliament holden *anno* 28 Eliz. that a writ of error should be maintained for the reversall of erroneous attainders of high treason by the common law: for that statute of 33 † H. 8. is to be intended of lawfull attainders by the due course of the common law, and not of erroneous or void attainders. And thereupon at that parliament holden *anno* 28 Eliz. an act was made, That no record of attainder of any person or persons, of or for any high treason, where the party so attainted ‡ is or hath been executed for the same treason, shall be, &c. in any wise hereafter reversed, undone, avoided, or impeached by any plea, or for any error whatsoever.

† [215]

* What interest the king hath in the body of the attainted before execution.
[a] 35 H. 6. 63.
[b] See Britton, ca. 122. Fleta, lib. 6. cap. 6. 7.
[c] Mich. 38 & 39 Eliz. in communi banco int. Banister and Trussel attaint de felony. Vide Mich. 33 & 34 Eliz. coram Rege rot. 532. int. Ognel and Trussel. Mich. 32 Eliz. inter Wade plaintife, and Prestal defendant attaint de haut treason, coram rege. Vid. sup.
[d] See the first part of the Institutes, sect. 1. §. Car. si home purchase.
[e] Ibid. sect. 199. 200. mort in ley
[f] First part Inst. sect. 405.
[g] 45 E. 3. 5. a. 18 E. 4. 25. 15 E. 4. 5. a. &c. Lit.

* And albeit judgement be given against a man in case of treason or felony, yet his body is not forfeited to the king, but untill execution remains his own. And therefore before execution, [a] if he be slain without authority of law, his wife shall have an appeal; for notwithstanding the attainder he remained her husband. And after such attainder his body may at the suit of a subject be taken in execution upon a judgement or statute, &c. And he may be executed for treason or felony, notwithstanding such execution had against him. And in an action of debt, or other action brought against a person attainted, he cannot plead the attainder, and demand judgement, if during the attainder he shall be put to answer: [b] for upon consideration had of the books in 11 Ass. 27. 2 E. 4. 1. 4 E. 4. 8. 6 E. 4. 4. 6 H. 4. 6. 8 Eliz. Dier 245, &c. [c] it was adjudged that the person attainted should not plead the said plea, but should be put to answer. And there is a great diversity between an attainder of treason or felony, and an entry into religion; for he that is attainted of treason or felony hath capacity, and [d] may purchase lands to him and his heirs, [e] but so cannot he that is entred into religion. And it is against a rule in law, that any man of full age should be received in any plea by the [f] law to disable his own person, [g] or take advantage of his own wrong. And if the person attainted be beaten or maimed, or a woman attainted be ravished, after pardon, they shall have an action of battery, appeale of mayme, or rape. See Lib. Intr. Co. 247, 248.

In

[h] In antient time a man indicted or appealed of life or member, or impriſoned, &c. ſhould not be compelled to anſwer at other mens ſuits, but (as before it appeareth) theſe opinions have been juſtly changed.

h Brit. ca. 122. a. § Encuſement de crime. Fleta, lib. 6. c. 6, 7. &c.

[i] There was a notable caſe adjudged in the kings bench Mic. 26 & 27 Eliz. wherewith I was well acquainted concerning the matters of outlawry and errors before ſpoken of, which was in effect as followeth.

i Mic. 26 & 27 El. Ninian Melvins caſe in the kings bench in bre. de errore.

Ninianus Menvile nuper de Stedwich in com' Dunelm. ar' anno 1 & 2 Ph. and Mar. was indicted in the kings bench of high treaſon, and upon proces he was outlawed, and ſo retorned, and his daughter and heire brought a writ of error in the kings bench, wherein two errors were aſſigned. 1. That before the exigent the 2 capias with a proclamation was awarded to the ſheriffe of the county palatine of Durham, where it ought to have been directed to the chancellour of that county. [k] For that point 30 H. 6. 6. 36 H. 6. 35. 1 E. 4. 10. the book of entries Raſt. fo. 52. Stanf. pl. cor. 68, 69. & 70. Vid. 19 H. 6. 2. 31 H. 6. 11. but the court gave no opinion concerning this error. The other error that was aſſigned, was that the ſheriffe retorned upon the ſaid capias, that at his court holden at the city of Durham the eight day of July in the ſecond and third yeares of the reigne of king Philip and queen Mary he made the proclamation, &c. and there were no ſuch years: for queen Mary began her reigne the 6 day of July, and the 25 day of July in the 2 year of her reign ſhe maried king Philip: ſo as between the 2 day of July, and the 25 day of July, the queen wrote two years before the king. And therefore there could be no ſuch years as 8 July *anno* 2 & 3, but ſhould have been 2 & 4. And ſo was the clear opinion of the whole court. But then it was objected, that by the ſaid act of 35 H. 8. and Stanfords opinion thereupon, that the attainder by outlawry being an attainder by the common law, it could not be reverſed by writ of error, for that the ſaid act of 35 H. 8. was to be intended of lawfull attainders: and after great deliberation the outlawry of treaſon was reverſed. And I take it, it ſhall not be altogether impertinent, ſure I am it ſhall not be unprofitable, to report the conſequent of this reverſall. In the next terme, ſc. term. Hil. *anno* 27 Eliz. for that queen Eliz. had the lands whereof the ſaid Ninian was ſeiſed in fee: his wife by petition of right, which comprehended the title of the wife, and the title of the queen, claimed her dower, which in effect was this: that her huſband was ſeiſed of certain lands in fee, and took her to wife; and before his treaſon committed *anno* 1 *Mariæ* levied a fine with proclamation to another, whoſe eſtate the queen had by lawfull conveyance therein expreſſed; and that afterward her ſaid huſband was attainted of high treaſon by outlawry, *ut ſupra*, and died in *anno* 4 Eliz. which outlawry was the laſt terme reverſed in a writ of error, as is aboveſaid: which petition being indorſed by the queen, *Soit droit fait al partie*, and delivered into the chancery, Sir Thomas Bromley a man of great gravity and judgement in law, then being lord chancellor of England, by advice of all the judges reſolved theſe four points following. Firſt, that the petitioner need not to have any office to finde her title, becauſe her title ſtandeth with the title of the queen, and the queen is not intitled by office (which ſhe might traverſe,

k See the ſtat. of 8 H. 6. cap. 10.

Hil. 27 Eliz. in filaciis cancellariæ.

[216]

traverse, or confesse and avoid) but by conveyance, which she affirmeth. Secondly, that a fine with proclamations, and five years past after the death of the husband doth bar the wife of her dower, and that the conusee shall take advantage thereof, and of the attainder also. Thirdly, that albeit five years and many more in this case were past since the death of her husband, yet the said fine with proclamations did not bar her; because as long as the said attainder of treason stood in force, she was barred of her dower, and could not have any remedy, or pursue her title, untill the outlawry were reversed, and then her title of dower did first grow due unto her, and therefore she might within five years after the reversall of the said outlawry, pursue her title by the expresse words of the saving of the act of 4 H. 7. Fourthly, albeit an attainder reversed by a writ of error, is as concerning restitution to the party by relation from the beginning become of no force, [a] and the record so annihilated thereby, as *nul tiel record* may be pleaded thereunto: yet this relation shall never work a bar, and consequently a wrong to a stranger, but that the truth of the matter may be shewed, viz. the record, and the reversall of the same: and the rather (as some said) because the wife could not have any writ of error to reverse the outlawry, [b] so as she had no mean to pursue her right so long as the outlawry remained in force, which it did, untill it was reversed by error. But admit the wife had been (in a remote degree of consanguinity) heir to her husband, so as she might within five years after the death of her husband have had her writ of error after the death of her husband to reverse the outlawry, and to enable herselfe to pursue for her dower, and reverseth not the outlawry within the five years: I hold in this case that she shall have five years after this reversall, and that within the said saving of the statute of 4 H. 7. for then did her title of dower (as hath been said) first grow unto her, * and it was not in her power to reverse the outlawry when she would. And in this term of S. Hillary, Popham attorny generall, according to the said resolution of the lord chancellor and judges, confessed the petition to be true; and thereupon judgement was given, that she should be indowed, and was indowed accordingly.

Vide Lib. 2. fo. 93. Binghams case. See the first part of the Institutes. sect. 55.

4 H. 7. cap. 24. the first saving.

[a] 26 E. 3. 75. 4 H. 7. fo. 22. & 11, 12. 38 H. 6. 4 & 12. 21 E. 4. 23. Dier 29 H. 8. fo. 32. pl. 8. idem. 6 Eliz. 228. pl. 45. 3 Eliz. fo. 188. pl. 8. a. Lib. 8. fo. 42. 43. b. Dr. Druryes case.

[b] 34 H. 6. fo. 2.

* Nota.

[c] By the statute of 26 H. 8. and 5 E. 6. it is enacted, that all proces of outlawry against any offenders in treason, being out of the realm, or beyond the seas, at the time of the outlawry pronounced, shall be as good and effectuall as if the offenders had been within the realme at the time of the outlawry pronounced. See the said statute of 5 E. 6. cap. 11. that, if the party outlawed shall within one year after the outlawry pronounced, yeild himselfe to the chief justice in England, and traverse the said indictment, &c. and thereupon be found not guilty by verdict, he shall be cleerly discharged of the said outlawry.

[c] 26 H. 8. cap. 13. 5 E. 6. cap. 11. These statutes not only extend to all treasons by the statute of 25 E. 3. by the common law, but by any other statute. Vi. Dier 12 Eliz. fo. 287. accord. First part of Institutes, sect. 479.

Judgement in case of Abjuration for Felony, whiles it was of Force.

After the flying of a felon for any kinde of felony whatsoever, sacriledge excepted, (but in case of high treason or petit treason a man could never abjure, because the coroner is not allowed by law

law to be a judge of thofe heynous crimes) into a church, &c. for fafegard of his life: and upon his prayer of a coroner [a], * and his voluntary and particular confeffion of the felony before the coroner, naming the certain time, the judgement was, *Idem A. petiit de præfato coronatore regnum dom. regis Angliæ abjurare: fuper quo tradito* [b] *ei libro p. præfat' coronatorē, idem A. regnum prædict. cora' præfato coronatore prædict' die, &c. in ecclefia prædicta abjuravit, in idem regnum nunquam rediturus abfque fpeciali licentia, et reconciliatione regis Angliæ, et affignatus eft eidem A. pro tranfitu fuo extra regnum prædictum portus de Yarmouth* [c] *cruce in manu fua dextra pofita, prout lex Angliæ eft et confuetudo.* Nothing is expreffed in this judgement but *abjuravit regnum*, but therein is implied, that all his lands, which he had at the time of the felony committed, [d] (and therefore the time of the felony was fet down in his confeffion particularly) or at any time after, efcheated to the lords of the fees, and forfeited to the king all his goods which he had at the time of his attainder, [e] the time whereof alfo was expreffed certainly, and his blood corrupted, and other incidents, as in other attainders of felony, only by his voluntary and particular confeffion. In this cafe for the offence of felony, he faved his life fo long as he kept himfelf *extra regnum*, but if he returned, then under this word [*abjuravit*] is implied *fuf. per collum*. Mich. 1 R. 2. rot. 1. Bedf. *rediit et fufpend.* See the firft part of the Inftitutes, fect. 200. fo. 132, 133. and the fecond part of the Inftitutes, W. 1. ca. 20. verbo, [f] *Fore jure le realm.*] artic. Cler. cap. 10. and 15. And the law was fo favourable for the prefervation of fanctuary, that if the felon had been in prifon for the felony, and before attainder or conviction, [g] had efcaped and taken fanctuary in church or church-yard, &c. and the gaolers or others had purfued him, and brought him again to prifon, upon his arraignment he might have pleaded the fame, and fhould have been reftored again to the fanctuary: fee more concerning abjuration, Mic. 9 E. 3, coram rege rot. 84. *extra legem pofitus, &c.* To conclude this judgment of abjuration, we take it, that for felony [h] abjuration is utterly taken away. For abjuration of recufants and of hunters in parks, &c. we have given but a light touch, becaufe they belong not to our treatife of the pleas of the crown, nor have we fpoken any thing of abjuration in cafe of herefy, *quia fpectat ad aliud forum.*

Thus have we fpoken of judgments, and attainders in cafes of high treafon, upon verdict, confeffion, or *nihil dicit*, and by outlawry: in cafe of petit treafon, upon verdict, confeffion, or by outlawry: and in cafe of felony, upon verdict, or confeffion, or by outlawry, or by abjuration; for none can be attainted of petit treafon or felony upon a *nihil dicit*, or refufal to anfwer, but in that cafe the delinquent is to have his punifhment of *peine fort et dure*, which next falleth to be handled.

[a] 6 E. 3. 53. in Ajell Malloms cafe. 12 E. 2. efche. 14. Tr. 21 E. 1. coram rege 42. fimile.

[b] Hereupon it was called abjuration, becaufe he was fworn to depart the kingdome. See the Oath Vet. Mag. Cart. 1. pte. f. 167. 168.

[c] That he might be known to be an abjured perfon, and not be let, or hindred in his journey. Et crux fuit fignum fervatæ vitæ per ecclefiam, and is fometimes called vexillum fanctæ ecclefiæ. Hil. 26. E. 3. coram rege rot. 20.

[d] Pl. com. f. 262. a. in Dame Hales cafe. Regifter, fo. 164. b. Fecit feloniam pro qua regnum noftrum abjuravit.

[e] Stanf. pl. cor. 117. E. 6 E. 3. 55. in Aiell Malloms cafe. 12 E. 2. Efch. 14. 6 E. 2. Forf. Br. 121. 6 H. 4. 6.

[f] Forejure in French is taken for abjure, in Latin abjurare. 1 E. 3. 17. lib. intr. Raft. fo. 246. b. pl. 6.

[g] Lib. int. Raft. 532. b. fanct. 2. Hil. 43 E. 3. rot. 115. Buck. William Attewels cafe.

[h] For all fanctuaries are taken away by 21 Jac. ca. 28. Note a fanctuary in the ftatute of 1 H. 7. cap. is called a hidel or hydle, becaufe it hideth and protecteth the party, &c. Vide Deut. cap. 19. 3. 9, 10. Numb. 35. 13. Jofhua 20. 8. See 2. part of the Inftitutes, Gloc. ca.

Peyne

i First part of the Instit. sect. 545. verb. attaint. 2 part of the Instit. W. 1. c. 12. Dier 3 El. 205. a. 13 El. 300. b. See before in the chap. of Treason. See after in the next chapter of Forfeiture fo. when the party arraigned challengeth peremptorily above the number of 36. viz. three whole juries.

k 35 H. 6. 57 58. Vide l. 9. fo. 124. the lord Zanchers case.

Peyne fort et dure.

In case of petit treason or felony, [i] when the offender standeth mute, and refuseth to be tried by the common law of the land; See *Paine fort et dure* in the second part of the Institutes, W. 1. ca. 2. but this holdeth but in case of petit treason and felony. In case of high treason, upon standing mute, or a *nihil dicit*, the judgement aforesaid shall be given against him, as if he had been convicted.

And in doing of execution, both in treason and felony, two things are to be observed. First, that it be done by the right officer, as the sherif, or marshall, for if any other execute the offender, it is felony. Secondly, execution must be made by him that is the right officer according to the judgement: for example, [k] where the judgement is, that the offender shall be hanged, he cannot behead him, &c. as before is said. Bracton, lib. 3. fo. 104. b. *Non alio modo puniatur quis, quam se habeat condemnatio.* P. 20 R. 2. coram rege rot. 58. Lincoln. *Non licet felonem pro felonia decollari.*

[218]

Judgement in case of Petit Larceny.

Bracton lib. 3. fo. 151. b. Britton. fo. 24. a. Fleta, li. 1. ca. 36. Bracton, lib. 3. fo. 104. b. maketh mention of punishment, verberibus et virgis.

* 18 Ass. p. 13. 8 E. Cor. 130. 41 E. 3. Cor. 451.

The judgement herein was in ancient time referred to the discretion of the judge, as in Bractons time, *Per fustigationem, et sic castigatus dimittitur* In Brittons time, sometime by the pillory, sometime by the losse of the ear: and Fleta saith, *Est enim furtum de re magna et parva, pro minimo tamen latrocinio 12 denariorum et infra, nullus morti condemnetur; pro hujusmodi modicis delictis inventa fuerunt judicialia pilloria, et deformitates corporum, ut scissio auricularum.*

* But in and since the reign of E. 3. no person lost any member for petit larceny, but were sometime punished by imprisonment, and sometime by other penance, as whipping, &c. If the delinquent flyeth for petit larceny, and so be found by the jury, he forfeiteth his goods.

Judgement in case of Misprision of High Treason.

That the offender by the common law shall for this concealment forfeit all his goods; and the profits of his lands during his life, and suffer imprisonment during his life. Vide Stanford pl. coron. fo. 38. 1 et 2 Mar. cap. 10.

Judgement for striking in Westminster Hall, &c. sitting the Courts.

Tr. 4. E. 4. coram rege rot. 3. 19 E. 3. Judgement. 174. 39 Ass. p. 1. 41 Ass. 25. 22 E. 3. 13. a. 41 E. 3. coron. 280. 42 Ass. 18. Stanf. pl. cor. 38. c. 3 Eliz. Dier 188.

That the offender shall be imprisoned during his life, forfeit all his lands, tenements, goods and chattels, *et quod manus sua dextra amputaretur (apud talem locum)* and this judgement is given by the common law. Bracton, lib. 3. 104. b. *Pœnarum quædam adimunt membrum, et corporis coercionem, sc. imprisonamentum, vel ad tempus, vel imperpetuum.*

Judgement

Judgement for ſtriking and drawing Blood in the Kings Court, &c.

The offender ſhall have his right hand ſtricken off, be impriſoned during his life, and be fined and ranſomed at the kings will: and this judgement is given by the ſtatute of 33 H. 8. cap. 12. 33 H. 8. Paine Br. 16.

We cannot omit to touch by the way an act made in 1 & 2 Ph. and Mar. intitled, an act againſt ſeditious words and rumours, by a branch of which act, he that ſhould ſend forth any booke, ryme, ballad, letter or writing containing any falſe, matter, clauſe or ſentence of ſlander or reproach, and diſhonour of the king and queens majeſty, or either of them, &c. ſhould have his or their right hand ſtricken off; which act being but a probationer, at the parliament in 4 & 5 Ph. and Mar. was continued untill the end of the next parliament. And by the act of 1 Eliz. (which was the next parliament) the ſaid act of 1 & 2 Ph. and Mar. was enacted to extend to queen Elizabeth, and to the heirs of her body kings and queens of this realm, ſo as by the demiſe of queen Eliz. that act hath loſt his force, as it was well worthy, being a dangerous act as ſome had felt in anno 23 Eliz.

1 & 2 Ph. and Ma. ca. 3. obtruncatio manus dextræ.

1 El. c. 6.

Judgement in a Premunire at the Suit of the King.

If the defendant be in priſon, *Quod prædictus R. ſit extra protectionem domini regis, et terras, et tenementa, bona et catalla domino regi forisfaciat, et quod corpus ejus remaneat in priſona ad voluntatem regis*, as in the book of entries, Raſt. Judgement 465. And this judgement is given by the ſtatutes of 25 E. 3. ca. 22. 25 E. 3. de Proviſoribus. 27 E. 3. ca. 1. 16 R. 2. ca. 5. and if he be not in priſon, *Quod præd. R. ſit extra protectionem domini regis, et terras et tenementa, bona et catalla domino regi forisfaciat, et quod capiatur.*

See the 1. pt. of the Inſtit. §. 159.

44 E. 3. 36.

Judgement in caſe of Theftbote.

That the offender be fined: and it is to be obſerved that whenſoever the delinquent, or defendant is to be fined, the judgement is *quod capiatur*, that is, to be impriſoned untill he doth pay his fine: but when the defendant is to be amerced, and not fined, then the defendant is *in miſericordia*, whereof you may read at large. Lib. 8. fo. 38, 39. &c. et 59, 60. et 120. lib. 11. 43, 44.

5 E. 3 Cor. 353. 29 E. 3. 9. 27 Aſſ. 69. 42 Aſſ. pl. 5. Stanf. fo. 40. b.

[219]

Pillory.

Pillory is a French word, and it is derived of the French word *pilaſtre* a pillar, *columna. Et eſt lignea columna, in qua collum inſertum premitur*, and thereupon in law it is called *colliſtrigium, quia in eo collum hominum conſtringitur:* this puniſhment is very ancient, for the Saxons called it *heals fang*, ſo called for ſtraining the neck. Britton, fo. 24. ſaith, that thoſe that have been adjudged to the pillory, or tumbrell, are ſo infamous, *Come ilz ne ſont receiv-*

Saxonicè *heals-fang*. Or *halſ-fang*, *hals* collum, *fang* preſſio. It is alſo called an amerciament for commutation of ſuch a puniſhment. 51 H. 3. Judicium colliſtrigii. Et pillorii,

Vet. N. B. 1. parte. 116, 117. Britton, fo. 24. Mirror, cap. 4. §. De paines en divers manners.

receivables al ferement faire in juries, enquefts ou en teftmoignants; and herewith agreeth Bracton. Vet. Mag. Cart. 2. parte, fo. 23, 24. 45.

Kelway temps E. 3. 145. b. Fleta, li. 2. cap. 8. By the ftatute of 51 H. 3. & 31 E. 1. Vet. Mag. Cart. 2. parte, fo. 23, 24. 45.

Bracton, lib. 3. fo. 104. b. 129. b. 151. b. 138. Mirror ubi fupra. Temps E. 3. Kelway 139, 140. b. 149. b. 152. Fleta li. 2. ca. 11. §. Item fi d'nus li. Intr. Raft. 494. a. in Quo warr. 7 E. 2. in eodem 260. b.

Tumbrell.

Tumbrell is a word in ufe at this day for a dungcart. Bracton calleth it *tymboralem*.

Infligitur pœna corporalis, fc. pilloralis vel tumberalis cum infamia. Secundum regni ftatuta, it is called tumberellum, there being no proper Latin word for a dungcart.

Furce pillor et tumbrel append al view de franckpledge And every one that hath a leet or market ought to have a pillory and tumbrell, &c. to punifh offenders, as brewers, bakers, foreftallers, &c.

Trebuchet.

Stat. de 51 H. 3. ubi fupra. Vet. Mag. Cart. part 2. fol. 44, 45. ftat. de pane & cervifia.

Or caftigatory, named in the ftatute of 51 H. 3. fignifieth a cucking ftool, and trebuchet properly is a pitfall or downfall, and in law fignifieth a ftool, that falleth down into a pit of water, for the punifhment of the party in it. And *cuck*, or *guck* in the Saxon tongue, fignifieth to fcould or brawl, (taken from the cuckhaw, or guckhaw, a bird, *qui odiofe jurgat et rixatur)* and *inge* in that language [water] becaufe fhe was for her punifhment fowfed in the water, and others fetch it from cuckquean, i. *pellex*.

Judgements to be given by juftices of affife, of oier and terminer, of gaol-delivery, of juftices of peace.

Now for that the judgement to the pillory or tumbrell (as it hath appeared before) doth make the delinquent infamous, and that the rule of law is, *Judicium de majore pœna quam quod legibus ftatutum eft non infamum facit, fed per breve de errore adnullare poteft*, and again, *pœna gravior ultra legem pofita æftimationem confervat*, that the juftices of affife, oier and terminer, gaol-delivery, and juftices of peace, would be well advifed before they give judgment of any perfon to the pillory or tumbrell, unleffe they have good warrant for their judgment therein. Fine and imprifonment for offences finable by the juftices abovefaid, is a fair and fure way.

* Vet. Mag. Cart. parte 2. fo. 24, 25.

And it is to be obferved that thofe kinds of punifhments of pillory, &c. have been given by acts of parliament in cafes of enormous and exorbitant offences, as by the ftatutes of 51 H. 3. 31 E. 1. De piftoribus, &c. 31 E. 1. De foreftallariis. 11 H. 7. ca. 4. 33 H. 8. ca. 1. 1 & 2 Ph. and Mar. cap. 10. 2 E. 6. ca. 15. 5 E. 6. ca. 6. & 14. 7 E. 6. ca. 7. 1 El. c. 7. 5 El. ca. 9. 16. 18 El. cap. And therefore the fafeft way for them is to follow thofe acts of parliament in cafes provided by the fame: but of the court of the kings bench, (the higheft court of ordinary juftice) in refpect of the multitude of the judicial prefidents (which we have feen) we fay with the poet. *Huic nec metas rerum, nec tempora pone*, (for judiciall prefidents of grave and reverend judges, are good guides to direct men in the right way) we will enumerate ſome of them.

21 E. 1. coram reg. rot. 2. Euſtachius de Porles Caſtel, for ſlandring of juſtice Beriſford, impriſonment in the tower, *ad voluntatem regis.*

Exemplary puniſhments adjudged in the kings bench.

Mich. 33 E. 1. coram rege. Rot. 75. William Brewces caſe, for ſlandering, &c. of Roger Hegham juſtice. Tr. 3 E. 2. int. mem. ſcaccarii for ſlandering of Foxley, a baron of the exchequer. Mich. 18 E. 3. coram rege, Rot. 151. for ſlandering of the juſtices of the kings bench, by a letter of Tho. Bulbroke a clerk of the ſame court. 30 Aſſ. p. 5. 19. 19 Aſſ. 1. Paſch. 10 E. 3. Rot. 87. *Thom. Twice Hazarder cois' ludens ad falſos talos adjudicatur quod per ſex dies in diverſis locis ponatur ſuper colliſtrigium.* Mich. 10 E. 3. Rot. 92. coram rege, Adam de Ravenſworth. Mich. 21 E. 3. coram rege, Warw. Verſs. Attornat' apparent' ſine warranto. Hil. 25 E. 3. coram rege, Rot. 13. *verſus Robert. Hadham commiſſionarium pro venditione bladi in garbis adjudicatur priſonæ, et quod ab omni officio domini regis amoveatur et finem faciat.* Tr. 2. H. 4. coram rege, Rot. 10. Suſſex. Mich. 4 & 5 Eliz. coram rege, Hugh Bakers caſe, for a libell againſt certain of the inhabitants of Cherſie, puniſhed by impriſonment, pillory, and good behaviour, &c.

[220]

See the fourth part of the Inſtitutes, cap. Star-Chamber, for puniſhment by pillory, &c. for enormious and exorbitant offences, which require more exemplary puniſhment then an ordinary courſe of the laws of the realm do inflict. *Nobiles magis plectuntur pecunia, plebei vero in corpore;* which is obſervable in all the ſaid ſtatutes. And Bracton ſaith, *Quælibet pœna corporalis, quamvis minima, major eſt qualibet pœna pecuniaria. Carcer ad continendos, non ad puniendos haberi debet, &c. Pœnæ potius molliendæ, quam exaſperandæ ſunt. Reſpiciendum eſt judicanti, ne quid aut durius, aut remiſſius conſtituatur, quam cauſa depoſcit; nec enim aut ſeveritatis, aut clementiæ gloria affectanda eſt. Aliter puniuntur ex eiſdem factionibus ſervi, quam liberi: et aliter qui quidem aliquid in dominum, parentemve commiſerit, quàm in extraneum; in magiſtratum, quam in privatum.*

Ancient rules of law in corporall puniſhments. Bracton, lib. 3. fo. 105. a. Ibid.

Ibid.

Death of a man per infortunium.

Of this miſchance there is no expreſſe judgement to be given, but the offender is to ſue out his pardon of courſe, as it appeareth in the ſecond part of the Inſtitutes, Gloc. cap. 9. And hereof Bracton ſaith, *Caſu, cum per infortunium, ut ſi aliquis venando per telum in feram miſſum, hominem interfecerit, et ſimilia perpetraverit, &c.* But albeit there be no expreſſe judgement given upon ſuch a verdict, yet the law giveth a judgement thereupon, viz. that he ſhall forfeit all his goods and chattels, debts and duties whatſoever, as in the ſecond part of the Inſtitutes, *ubi ſupra*, it appeareth.

Marlbr. cap. 25.

Bracton ubi ſup.

Judgement implyed, or in law. 24 H. 8. cap. 5.

Of Death of a Man, ſe defendendo.

Upon ſuch a verdict given the court giveth no expreſſe judgement, for he is alſo to be pardoned of courſe: but the law hath given a judgement, that he ſhall forfeit all his goods and chattels, debts and duties, as in the ſecond part of the Inſtitutes, *ubi ſupra*, it appeareth.

Judgement implyed, or in law. See ca. 7 fo. 95. b. 43. Aſſ. p. 31. Rot. parl. 3 R. 2. nu. 18. John Imperials caſe.

appeareth. But the jury cannot finde that the party killed him generally *se defendendo*: but they ought to finde the case specially, so as the court may judge whether in law it be *se defendendo*, or no. See Stanf. fol. 15.

Of the Death of a Man that offereth to rob, &c.

a 3 E. 3. cor. 305.

b 3 E. 3. cor. 330. 26 Ass. 23. Exod. 22. Si effringens vir domum sive suffodiens fuerit inventus, & accepto vulnere mortuus fuerit, percussor non erit reus sanguinis.

c Nota, declared, &c. and so was the common law, as by the books aforesaid it appeareth. 22 Ass. p. 55. 22 E. 3. cor. 261. 3 E. 3. cor. 328. 3 E. 3. ibid. 288. 289, 290.

If it be found by verdict, that the party (indicted or appealed for the death of A) A attempted to have murdered or [a] robbed him in or nigh any common high way, cart-way, horse-way, or foot-way, or in his [b] mansion or dwelling house; or for the killing of him which attempteth burglary to break his dwelling house in the night; the judgement upon such a verdict shall be, that he shall be acquited of the death of such a person paying his fees, and he shall forfeit nothing. And so it is [c] declared and enacted by the statute of 24 H. 8.

And if all the circumstances be proved to the jury in evidence required by this act in these cases, the jury may finde a generall verdict of not guilty. And where it is rehearsed in the said act of 24 H. 8. that before that act it was a question and ambiguity whether evill disposed persons so attempting, *ut supra*, should forfeit their goods and chattels: the reason of that question and ambiguity was in none * of those cases mentioned in that act, no robbery, murder, or burglary was done, but an attempt only to do it. But it was no question at the common law, that if a robbery, murder, burglary, or other felony was done, and pursuit made after the offender, who either by resistance or flight could not be apprehended without killing of him by inevitable necessity, the party so pursuing and killing should not forfeit his goods or chattels; for in those cases every man may arrest the felon by a warrant in law. But there is a diversity between a warrant in deed, and a warrant in law, in this, that if a man be indicted of murder, robbery, burglary, or other felony, and the sheriffe by vertue of a *capias* offer to arrest him, and he resisteth and flye, *ut supra*, the sheriffe may kill him, if otherwise he cannot arrest him, although in truth the party be not guilty, nor any felony done But in the case of the abovesaid warrant in law, there must be a felony done, and this diversity appeareth in our books. * And so it is, if after arrest for felony the party arrested resisteth or flyeth, and in pursuit is slaine by inevitable necessity, they so killing him forfeit nothing.

*[221]

* See in the cha. of Hue and Cry.

a Rot. par. 3 H. 4. part. 2. Duellum percussum. 13 H. 4. 4. 37 H. 6. 20, 21. See before in the chapter of Approver. Fleta, lib. 1. ca. 32.

b 4 E. 3. 41. 30 E. 3. 20. 29 E. 3. 12. 13 Eliz. Dier, 301. Mirror, cap. 3. § Combat, & § Juramentum duelli, & § Ordinatio pugnantium.

An approver that kils the party accused in battell, or a champion that killeth the other champion in a writ of right, or the plaintife or defendant in an appeale that killeth the other *in duello*, according to the common law, or in combat awarded by the [a] constable and marshall in the court of chivalry, the party killing shall forfeit nothing; for these combats or duels are such trials as the law appoints in such cases. For saith Fleta, *Duellum est singularis pugna inter duos ad probandum veritatem litis; et qui vicerit probasse intelligitur: et quamvis judicium Dei expectatur ibid. quicunque tamen monomachiam,* i. *singularem pugnam sponte susceperit, aut obtulerit, homicida est, et mortale contrahit peccatum.* But before we leave these champions, it is to be observed that whosoever taketh upon him to be a champion for another (the forme and [b] oath whereof you may reade in the second part of the Institutes, W. 1. cap. 40. and Glanvil.

Glanvil. lib. 2. cap. 3.) if he become recreant, that is, a crying coward or craven, he shall for his perjury [c] lose *liberam legem.* [d] Craven is derived from the Greek word κραυγη, *à vociferatione:* others nearer home, of crying and craving of mercy and forgivenesse. And *recreantia* is derived of the French word *recreance*, of giving back or cowardize. And sometime it is called *creantia* [e] *per antiphrasin*, because he that useth it is not faithfull, but breaketh his oath. And so if the appellant joyne battell, and cry craven, he shall also lose *liberam legem* for the cause aforesaid, but if the appellee cry craven he shall be hanged: * but if they combat untill night come, and starres appear, the defendant in the appeal goeth quit, and the plaintife in that case loseth not *liberam legem.* [f] *Amittere liberam legem* is to become infamous and of no credit, never to be witnesse, or juror: for when he is of fame and credit, he is called *liber et legalis homo:* and such men ought to be of juries and witnesses, because they do enjoy *liberam legem.* [g] And a champion ought to be *liber homo,* and so is the entry, *per corpus liberi hominis. Et quam infamiam victus incurrit,* see Glanvile, lib. 2. cap. 3. & lib. 14. cap. 1. And he further saith, *Talis debet campio petentis esse, qui sit, et esse possit inde testis idoneus.* So as no man by the ancient common law could be a champion, but he that knew the right, and was a witnesse thereof: and therewith agreeth the statute of W. 1. cap. 40. wherein observe what the oath was by the common law. *Aliquando patria stat pro campione et aliquando in bre. de recto campio stat pro patria. Campio* is derived *à campo*, because it is publickly stroken in the field, and is called camp-fight: and is taken in the common law for one that striketh a legal camp-fight or combat in another mans quarrel: in Latin he is called * *pugil à pugna.* But the defendant in an appeal that is to combat, is not called a champion, because he fighteth for himselfe. And these combats in cases whereof the conusance belongs to the common law, are to be directed by the judges of the common law *secundum legem et consuetudinem Angliæ*, and not by the constable and marshall by the civill law, as all our ancient authors and bookes abovesaid do agree, which also is apparant by the statute of 13 R. 2. ca. 2.

[c] Judgement in law against a recreant and craven champion is, *perdere liberam legem.* See a notable record hereof R. pa. 55 H. 3. m. 3. Glanvil, li. 2. ca. 3. lib. 14. cap. 1.

[d] Mirror cap. 3. § Ordinatio pugnantium, L'horrible mote de craven.

[e] 41 E. 3. cor. 98. *creant* for *recreant.*

Bract, lib. 3. f. 141. Brit. fo. 42. 81. Fleta lib. 1. ca. 32. 19 H. 6. fo. 35. 21 H. 6. 34.

* Mir. c. 3. §. ubi su.

[f] Glanvil, lib. 2. cap. 19. Legem terræ amittentes perpetuam infamiæ notam inde merito incurrunt. See the first part of the Inst. Sect. 514. 27 Ass. 59. liberam legem, qui, &c.

[g] 1 H. 6. 6. 3 H. 6. 55.

See the oath in appeal, Bracton, lib. 3. fo. 141. b. Britton, fo. 42. Fleta, lib. 1. ca. 32. Glanvil, lib. 2. c. 3. lib. 9. cap. 1. Et lib. 14. ca. 1. 9 H. 4. 3. 17 ass. 3. 17 E. 3. 2. 9 E. 4. 25. Fleta ubi sup. lib. Int. Co. fo. 182. 55 H. 3. ubi sup.

Judgement in an Indictment of Conspiracie, &c. where the Party indicted is legitimo modo acquietatus.

[222]

Nota, the judgement in this case is, as in case of attaint against a jury, (whereof we shall speak hereafter), viz. *Quòd committantur gaolæ domini regis, et quod omnia terræ et tenementa præd. R. & C. capiantur in manum domini regis, et devastentur, et extirpentur, et uxores et liberi eorum amoveantur, et omnia bona et catalla eorundem R. & C. forisfaciant domino regi, et amòdo amittant liberam legem imperpetuum.*

Nota in this judgement five severe punishments. 1. That their bodies shall be imprisoned in the common gaole. 2. Their wives and children amoved out of their house. 3. That all their houses and

4 H. 5. Indict. 220. Tr. 18 E. 3. coram rege Rot. 148. Walt. judicium reddit. contr. Conspiratores. Pasch. 32 E. 3. Rot. 58 Somers. 27 Ass. 59. 24 E. 3. 34. 43 E. 3. 33. b. Vid. Artic. super cart. cap. 10.

and lands ſhall be ſeiſed into the kings hands, and the houſes waſted and the trees extirpated. 4. All their goods and chattels forfeited to the king. 5. That they for ever ſhall loſe the freedome and franchiſe of the law. That is, firſt, they ſhall never be of any jury or recognitors of aſſiſe. Secondly, nor ever be received for a witneſſe in any caſe. Thirdly, that they ſhall never come into any of the kings courts, but make attornies, if they have any thing to do there. And this is called a * villanous judgement, becauſe of the villany and infamy which they deſerve againſt whom it is given: And all is inflicted by the common law, for that the offenders by falſe conſpiracy under the pretext of law, by indictment of treaſon or felony and legall proceeding thereupon, ſought to do the greateſt injuſtice by falſe conſpiracy to ſhed his blood, who afterwards is thereof *legitimo modo acquietatus*.

* 24 E. 3. fo. 33. 27 Aſſ. 53.

But in a writ of conſpiracy at the ſuit of the party grieved, the judgement is, damages to the party, fine to the king, and impriſonment. And the reaſon thereof is, firſt, for that when they are indicted at the ſuit of the king, the judgement is ſo ſevere, for that they falſely conſpired in the kings name, and at the kings ſuit by indictment, &c. to do ſo horrible injuſtice: therefore at the kings ſuit they ſhall be heavily puniſhed. Secondly, for that as it is ſaid in 15 E. 2. *De exilio Hugonis, &c.* the law which was inſtituted for the maintenance of peace and of good men, and the puniſhment of the evill, is turned to the diſheritance of the great men, and deſtruction of the people. Thirdly, for that the judgement at the kings ſuit is by the common law, and the action of the party is given by ſtatute, which giveth no ſuch puniſhment: but the party in his action, in reſpect of the danger of his life, is to recover anſwerable damages. Of conſpiracy ſee the Regiſter, fol. 134. a & b. & 188. F. N. B. 114, 115, &c. Stanf. pl. cor. fol. 172, 173, 174, 175, &c. and in the new Book of Entries, fol. 109. a preſident of a conſpiracy upon an indictment of felony.

4 H. 5. judg. 220. 24 E. 3. 34. 27 Aſſ. 59.

43 E. 3. 33 b. Tr. 32 E. 1. Rot. 15 Eborum.

It is enacted, that ſuch as be attainted of confederacy or conſpiracy, ſhall have no office of the grant of the king, queen, or other noble, neither ſhall be ſheriffe or eſcheator.

Parl. 17 E. 3. nu. 50.

Judgement in an Attaint.

1. That the plaintife ſhall be reſtored, &c. and the defendant party to the record ſhall be fined in reſpect the falſe verdict was given for him *(cui bono)* by the common law.

The judgement againſt the petit jury is, as it is in caſe of conſpiracy at the ſuit of the king, as is aboveſaid, and in no other, but in thoſe two caſes, that villainous judgement is given. See 8 E. 2. Aſſ. 396. and 42 E. 3. 26. b. judgements given in attaint, *et nota bene*. 16 E. 3. tit. Judgement, 109. 21 H. 7. 83. Kelway. a good preſident of a judgement given in an attaint. Forteſcue, cap. 26. Concerning Attaints, ſee the ſecond part of the Inſtitutes, Marlbr. cap. 14. W. 1. cap. 37, &c.

Lib. Intr. Raſtal. fo. 92. a. 9 E. 4. 51. 4 H. 5. ubi ſup. 15 Aſſ. 2. Kelway 130. b. Glanvil. lib. 2. cap. 19. Bracton, lib. 4. fo. 129. Brit. fo. 237, 238. Mirror, ca. 3. § de attaint. Flet. lib. 5. ca. 21. Apud. Northalverton in com. Eborum coram Hen. de Guildeford & aliis juſt. aſſignatis an. 35 E. 1. attincta. See the firſt part of the Inſtitutes, ſect. 514. verb. [en attaint.] Vide Mich. 3 H. 4. Rot. 149. Judgement en attaint. Kanc.

But

But now by the ſtatute of 23 H. 8. cap. 3. the ſeverity of the puniſhment is moderated, * if the writ of attaint be grounded upon that ſtatute: but the party grieved may at his election either bring his writ of attaint at the common law, or upon that ſtatute: but all attaints, either at the common law or upon the ſtatute are to be taken before the king in his bench, or before the juſtices of the common pleas, and in no other courts.

This act of 23 H. 8. provideth for divers miſchiefs which were at the common law, and giveth to thoſe of the pety jury divers pleas, which they could not have at the common law, and hath been well expounded. 7 E. 6. Dier, 81. b. Sir John Ailifs caſe. 3 & 4 Ph. and Mar. 129. b. Heydons caſe. 3 Eliz. 201. Clovils caſe. 3 Eliz. 202. Auſtens caſe. 7 Eliz. 23. b. Stephens caſe. See the record thereof upon the ſtatute of 23 H. 8. for it is an excellent preſident.

And generally of attaints, ſee Lib. fo. 111. 112. Lib. 3. fo. 4. Lib. 6. fo. 4. 14. 25. 26. 44. 80. Lib. 8. fo. 60. Lib. 9. fo. 12. Lib. 10. fo. 119. Lib. 11. fo. 6. 43. 62. See alſo the new book of Entries, 63. 66. 68. 70. 73. 76. 77. 81. 83. 85. 86, &c.

Judicium de corrupto Judice.

We could not paſſe over a ſtrange judgement of *ſuſpendatur, &c.* as in caſe of felony (which we have touched before in the chapter of Bribery given againſt Sir William Thorpe, lately before chief juſtice of England, which we finde of record in theſe words. *Proceſſus factus an.* 24 E. 3. *contra Willielmum Thorp chivalier nuper capitalem juſticiarium coram Rico. comite Arundel. T. de Bellocampo comite Warw. Willielmo de Clinton comite de Hunt. Joh. de Gray de Rothersfield ſeneſchallo hoſpitii regis, et Barthol. de Burgerſ. camerar. regis: pro eo quod idem Willielmus Thorp nuper capitalis juſticiarius domini regis ad placita coram ipſo rege tenenda, dum ſtetit in officio, cepit munera contra juramentum ſuum, viz. de Ricard. Saltley* 10 *li. de Hildebrando Boreſward* 20 *li. de Guilberto Hollyland* 40 *li. de Tho. Darby Sancti Botulphi, et de Roberto Dalderby* 10 *li. qui pro diverſis feloniis, falſitatibus, et trangreſſionibus coram ipſo Willielmo in ceſſione ſua apud Lincolne anno* 23 *fuerint indictati, et per ipſum Willielmum bre. de exigendo verſ. eos reſpect' fuit: quæ omnia et ſingula dedicere non potuit: ideo adjudicatum fuit prout ſequitur, viz. Conſideratum eſt per dictos juſticiarios aſſignatos ad judicandum* [a] *ſecundum voluntatem domini regis, et ſecundum regale poſſe ſuum, quòd quia prædictus Willielmus de Thorpe qui ſacramentum domini regis quod erga populum habuit cuſtodiendum fregit* [b] *malicioſe, falſe, et rebelliter in quantum in ipſo fuit, et ex cauſis ſupradictis per ipſum Willielmum, ut prædictum eſt, expreſſe cognitis, ſuſpendatur. Et quod omnia* [c] *terræ et tenementa, bona et catalla ſua domino regi remaneant forisfacta. Et poſtea dominus rex mandavit bre. ſuum ſub privato ſigillo,* all in French, and there entred *de verbo in verbum. Ideo conſideratum eſt quod executio judicii prædicti de ſuſpenſione ejuſdem Willielmi omnino ceſſet et ei pardonetur. Et quod idem Willielmus remittatur priſonæ turris prædict. ad gratiam domini regis expectandam, &c. Et non eſt intentio domini regis quod hujuſmodi judicium in conſimili caſu verſus quemcunque alium ex quacunq; cauſa ſe teneat*

Rot. pat. anno 24 E. 3. part 3. m. 2. in dorſ. & Rot. pat. anno 25 E. 3. part 1. m. 17.

In toto 80 li.

[a] The effect of the words of the oath hereafter mentioned.

[b] Nota, here is neither *felonice*, nor *proditorie* in this indictment, but *rebelliter*.

[c] According to the ſaid oath, for otherwiſe the king had no colour to have the forfeiture of all his lands for felony, but every lord of whom they were reſpectively holden, &c.

[d] Nota prædictum sacramentum.
[e] Rot. Parl. in Oct. Pur. an. 25 E. 3. nu. 10.

teneat vel extendat, sed solummodo versus eos qui prædictum [d] *sacramentum fecerunt, et fecerunt, et fregerunt et habent leges regales Angliæ ad custodiend'.*

[e] We have also found, that at a parliament holden at Westminster in *octabis purificationis beatæ Mariæ, anno* 25 E. 3. holden before Lionel duke of Clarence by force of the kings commission, &c. commandement was given, that the record of the said judgement against the said Sir William Thorp should be brought into the parliament, and there to be openly read before the nobles of the parliament to hear every of their advices, which was done accordingly, and there the nobles affirmed the judgement.

[224]

And these words in the said judgement, *Ad judicandum secundum voluntatem domini regis, et secundum regale posse suum*, and that his lands should be forfeit to the king, *et prædict. sacramentum*, were grounded upon the oath of the kings justices in *anno* 18 E. 3. the conclusion of which oath is, [upon pain to be at the kings will, body, lands, and goods, thereof to be done as pleaseth him.] We desirous to satisfie our self herein, searched for the record of this oath, and albeit there is a parliament roll of this parliament, and other acts, then passed by authority of parliament, be entred into the said roll, yet this is not; for that it had not the warrant of an act of parliament. It ought to have been printed amongst the statutes of the realm, and the title of them is, Here followeth the oath of the justices made in the same eighteenth year, but saith not at the parliament, &c. but after it became to be printed: and that which is printed in *anno* 20 E. 3. ca. 1. is but a recitall made by the king alone, and no act of parliament: for it appeareth by that which precedeth, and by the oath it self, that it was the act only and commandement of the king, for it beginneth: first, we have commanded all our justices, &c. which former part was but a recitall of some precedent act: and then followeth, we have ordained and caused our said justices to be sworn, &c. so as the oath was devised by the king, and the justices sworn before this parliament. Lastly, it is there said and concludeth: and for this cause we have encreased the fees of our said justices, &c. which the king of himself did before this act also.

And we have an ancient manuscript of the acts of parliament in *ann.* 18 E. 3. and the oath is not within it.

Fleta, li. 1. ca. 17. § Cum igitur non sit, &c.

And it appeareth by Fleta, that the punishment of a corrupt judge, that receiveth gift or reward was, *Si inde convictus fuerit, quod imperpetuum à concilio regis excludatur; terrasque, res, redditus, et proventus bonorum suorum amittat per unum annum: qui, si proventus non habuerit, puniatur per discretionem regni et consiliariorum regis.*

Vet. Mag. Cart. 1. parte fo. 165. Vide Bract. li. 3. fo. 109. Sacrament' Justic' itiner' and that then was the effect, de sacrament' Justic' residentium. Vid. Flet. l. 2. c. 7. § Item atrox est injuria, &c.

And that which Fleta calleth *sacramentum justic'*, in Vet. Magna Carta, is named, *juramentum consiliariorum regis:* for the judges of England are of the kings counsell (as elsewhere hath appeared) for, in, and concerning the laws of the realm, in which oath also the said fatall clause is omitted.

See the Mirror cap. 4. §. *de faux judges*, and ca. 5. §. 1. of the law in the time of king Alfred, how many justices were in one year hanged, as homicides, for their false judgements: but that law hath been long since deleat and antiquated, and yet may serve for a memoriall of the time past.

The offence of bribery was punished by fine, and ransome, and losse

losse in the reign of E. 1. as in the chapter of Extortion and Bribery before appears: only Sir Thomas Weyland chief justice of the common pleas, took sanctuary, and before a coroner confessed himself guilty of murder, and according to the course of the common law abjured the realm, so as indeed he was attainted of felony, (which case had been vehemently urged) but it was not for bribery, but for murder, as any other man might have been.

But to winde up the thred of this discourse with three acts of parliament. First, with the statute of 8 R. 2. wherein it is recited, that whereas in the time of king E. 3. it was ordained, that justices as long as they should be in office, should not take gift or reward, and so forth, as in Veteri Magna Carta (without the said fatall clause) that act provideth, that the oath without that fatall clause should extend as well to the barons of the exchequer, as to the justices, and expressed the penalty of all to be (according to the common law) viz. losse of office, fine and ransome. But at the next parliament, viz. 9 R. 2. the said act of 8 R. 2. for that it was [a] very hard, and needed declaration, was made of no force till it be declared in parliament. [b] Afterwards at the parliament holden 11 H. 4. it was debated what punishment great officers there named counsellors of the king, and judges, &c. should have, which should take any gift, reward, or brocage for doing of their offices or services: in the end it was declared and enacted by authority of parliament, in these words following. *Item que nul chancelor, treasorer, garden del privy seal, counsellier du roy servientes a counsiell du roy, ne nul autre officer,* * *jugge ne minister du roy pernont fees ou gages de roy pur lour dites offices ou service, preigne en nul manner, en temps avenir ascun manner de* [c] *done ou brocage de nulluy pur lour ditz offices et services affaire, sur peine de* 1 *responder a roy de la treble de ceo, que* † *issi preignont,* 2 *et de satisfier la party,* 3 *et punis al volunt le roy, et* 4 *soit discharges de son office, service, et counsell pur touts jours, et que chescun que verra pursuer en la dit mattier eit la sute sibien pur le roy come pur luy mesme, et eit la tierce part del summe de que la partie soit duement convict.* Respons. *Le roy le voet.*

8 R. 2. ca. 3. Vide Vet. Mag. Cart. fo. 165. a. ubi supra.
9 R. 2. cap. 1.
[a] In respect of the recitall.
[b] Ro. Par. 11 H. 4. nu. 28. not heretofore printed. Vid. 1 H. 4. nu. 99.
* Nota.
[c] This is agreeable to the law of God, Deut. 16. 19. Non accipies personam, nec munera, quia munera excæcant oculos sapientum, et mutant verba justorum. Exodus 23. 8.
† [225]
Nota four punishments.
1. By the court of justice where the matter shall depend (as hath been often observed) by fine and imprisonment.

[a] This act being by authority of parliament, hath limited the punishment (amongst others) of corrupt judges, of whom now we entreat, so as the former example of Sir William Thorp is not now to be followed, which we affirm not in favour of sordid bribery, (which we hate, as in the proper chapter thereof before appeareth) but in advancement of justice and right, which is the end of our labour in this and other of our works; [b] and therefore have caused that good act that hath lived so long in obscurity, for the better notice and observation thereof, to be put to the presse, which never was yet printed; and the cause thereof was, for that in the margent of the parliament roll of this act, it is written, *respectuatur per dominum principem et concilium:* a strange presumption without warrant of the king his father, and of the parliament, to cause such a *respectuatur* to be made to an act of parliament.

[a] In the oath of the justices in Wales, that fearful clause is omitted, neither is it in the oath of the barons of the exchequer of England.
[b] Veritas nihil veretur nisi abscondi.

The like he did to another act in the same parliament, nu. 63. concerning attorneys, the like whereof was never done in any former or latter parliaments. * This was that prince Henry, who keeping ill company, and led by ill counsell, about this time assaulted (some say) and stroke Gascoign chief justice sitting in the kings bench, for that the prince endeavouring with strong hand to rescue

* See Sir Tho. Eliot in his Governour, &c. Holl. Chron. 543. a.

rescue a prisoner, one of his unthrifty minions indicted and arraigned at the kings bench bar for felony, was prevented of his purpose by the perswasion and commandement of the chief justice, for which the chief justice committed the prince to the kings bench, whereof some of his followers instantly complained to the king his father: who informing himself of the true state of the case, gave God infinite thanks, that he had given him such a judge, as feared not to minister justice, and such a son, as could suffer semblably and obey justice. And this is that prince, who abandoning his former company and counsell, and following the advice of grave, wise, and expert men, whom he made choice of to be of his councel, became a victorious and vertuous king, and prosperous in all that he took in hand, at home and abroad.

For the duty of judges, it is truly said (as before hath been said) that *judex debet habere duos sales, viz. salem scientiæ, ne sit insipidus, et salem conscientiæ, ne sit diabolus.* And what persons should be judges, see Bracton, lib. 1. cap. 2. & lib. 3. fo. 106. & Fleta, lib. 1. cap. 17. § Caveat, and the Mirror, ca. 2. §. 2. de judges, and Rot. Parl. 17 E. 3. nu. 3. 10.

Anno 1 Mar. stat. 2. ca. 2. in print. See the Articles of Concord, 21 Maii anno Dom. 1420. et anno 8 H. 5. between king H. 5. and Charles the French king, whereby the crown of France after the death of the said Charles, was established to H. 5. and his heirs. Artic. 7, 8, &c.

To these we will add, that upon the conclusion of a marriage then to be had between Philip the son of the emperour, and prince of Spain, it was nobly and wisely provided by the queen, the lords spirituall and temporall, and the commons by authority of parliament (amongst many other excellent provisions worthy of observation) that the said prince should not promote, admit, or receive to any office, administration or benefice in the realm of England, and the dominions thereunto belonging, any stranger, or persons not born under the dominion and subjection of the most noble queen of England: and that the said most noble prince should doe nothing whereby any thing might be innovated in the state or right, either publique or private, or in the lawes and customes of England, or the dominions thereunto belonging, but shall contrariwise confirm and keep, to all estates and orders, their rights and priviledges.

And it is there further provided for the future, &c. that if the said prince should have issue male or female, the order of succession is there declared, but with this proviso. Provided neverthelesse, and expresly reserved in all and singular the above declared cases of succession, that whatsoever he or she be, that shall succeed in them, they shall leave to every of the said realms, lands and dominions whole and entire their priviledges, rights, and customes, and the same realms and dominions shall administer, and cause to be ad-

[226]

ministred by the naturall born of the said realms, dominions, and lands.

By this, Philip (after king of Spain) could not prefer any stranger born to any office of judicature, &c. within the realm of England, or dominions of the same, nor all the time he was within this realm, ever attempted the same.

Vide Camden. El. 322. Artic. inter reginam Eliz. et Franciscum ducem Alonson anno 23 El. populo super importune ut nuberet suadente in comitiis.

And in the articles, *De matrimonio prælocuto inter reginam Elizabetham et ducem de Alonson*, amongst others it was expresly provided, *Quod dux nullum extraneum ad aliquod officium in Anglia promovebit, et nihil in jure mutabit, &c.*

Also

[a] Alſo king James wiſely provided by authority of parliament, by the advice of the lords ſpirituall and temporall, and commons in that parliament aſſembled, that whereas in regard of ſome difference and unequality of the laws, trials, and proceedings * in caſe of life, between the juſtice of the realm of England, and that of the realm of Scotland, it appeareth to be moſt convenient for the contentment and ſatisfaction of all his majeſties ſubjects to proceed (with all poſſible ſeverity) againſt ſuch offenders in their own country according to the laws of the ſame, whereunto they are born and inheritable, and by and before the naturall born ſubjects of the ſame realm, if they be there apprehended. And by the next clauſe it is provided, that felonies committed by Engliſhmen in Scotland, ſhall be enquired of, heard, and determined before juſtices of aſſiſe, or commiſſioners of oier and terminer, and gaol-delivery, being naturall born ſubjects within the realm of England, and none other. And the like in another clauſe with an addition of juſtices of peace to be naturall born ſubjects within England; and God bleſſed and proſpered this act with happy and deſired ſucceſſe.

[a] 4 Ja. regis, ca. 1. about the midſt.

* That caſe being then in queſtion.

But contrariwiſe, *Petrus de Rupibus*, or of the Rocks, being a Gaſcoign born, preferred to be biſhop of Wincheſter by king John, and being a principall counſeller about king H. 2. both in his young years, did after in his riper age prefer to offices about the king, ſuch Gaſcoigns as were of his blood or alliance, (whereof one of his kindred, ſome ſay his ſon, Peter de Orival treaſurer of England) to the great grief and diſcontentment of the nobility of England to have a Gaſcoign born in place above them. And what heavy event enſued thereupon, let hiſtorians inform you, for it is grievous to me to remember it.

Math. Par. pag. 363. 380. 383, &c. Hol. Chron. pag. 231. & 1071. a. b.

If you deſire to ſee ſomewhat concerning eccleſiaſticall offices, promotions, and benefices, firſt what petitions have been made in parliament againſt aliens or ſtrangers; look in the parliament rolls of 50 E. 3. nu. 96, 97. 120. 13 E. 3. nu. 23. 17 E. 3. nu. 59, 60. 18 E. 3. nu. 38. 2 R. 2. nu. 6 H. 4. nu. 48. 4 H. 6. nu. 29, &c. And what laws have been made that aliens or ſtrangers ſhould not be advanced to the ſame; *Vide* 35 E. 1. Statut. de Carliſle. 3 R. 2. ca. 3. 7 R. 2. ca. 12. Rot. Parl. 13 R. 2. not in print. 1 H. 5. ca. 7. 4 & 5 Ph. and Mar. ca. 6.

Vide 50 E. 3. nu. 165. for the keeping of the caſtle of Nottingham. Vide 18 E. 1. Rot. Parl. nu. Solomon de Rolfes caſe.

CAP. CII. [227]

Forfeiture, Confiſcation, &c.

NOTA confiſcare et foriſfacere are *ſynonyma*, and *bona confiſcata* are *bona foriſfacta: Fiſcus* properly ſignifieth a panier or hamper of oſiers, wherein the Romanes kept their treaſure, and by the figure of *metonymia continens pro contento*, it is taken for the treaſure it ſelf, *unde confiſcare*, and *bona confiſcata*, and thereupon it is ſaid, *Quod non capit Chriſtus, capit fiſcus.*

For the derivation of *foriſfacere*, ſee the firſt part of the Inſtitutes, ſect. 74. fo. 59. a. 3 E. 3. forfeit 24.

Of forfeiture of lands and tenements, and other hereditaments for

for high treason, petit treason, felony, misprision of treason, premunire, and in some cases of misprision, * and what hereditaments which be not holden shall be forfeited for high treason, and shall not escheat for petit treason or felony, we have spoken before in their severall chapters, &c. now let us speak of forfeiture of goods and chattels in these and some other cases.

* See before cap. High treason, verbo [De t'res et tenements, &c.] fol. 18. & 19. Et cap. de Petit treason. Verb. [Et de tiel manner de treason,] &c. fo. 21.

[a] See the 1 part of the Institutes, of both these branches.

[a] Of these the forfeiture of some of them must appear, or be found of record, and therefore these cannot be claimed by proscription; of other some the forfeiture need not appear, or be found of record, and therefore these may be gained by prescription.

[b] See the 1 part of the Institutes, ubi supra, both the former and the latter sort.

[b] Of the former sort be *bona et catalla proditorum, felonum, utlagat', in exigend' positorum, fugitivorum, deodand' annus, dies, et vastum, &c.* and all other forfeitures which must appear or be found of record.

Of the latter sort be treasure trove, *bona et catalla waviat', extrahur' wreccum maris, &c'*

[c] 3 E. 3. Cor. 290. 312.

[c] If a traitor or felon either rescue himself, or will not submit him to be arrested, but resisteth, and in resistance is slain; upon presentment hereof he forfeiteth all his goods and chattels.

[d] 29 E. 3. 29. 45 E. 3. Cor. 100.

[d] If a felon in pursuit wave his own goods, they are forfeited, yet are they not *bona waviata.*

If in appeal of robbery the plaintif omit any of the goods stoln, they are forfeit to the king for the favour, which the law presumeth, the plaintif beareth to the felon: and for that he cannot have restitution for more then is in his appeal.

3 E. 2. Cor. 367, 368.

In appeal of robbery of goods, if the jury find that the defendant found them in the high way, in this case the plaintif for his false appeal, in seeking the blood of the innocent, shall forfeit his goods to the king.

3 H. 7. 12.

If one arraigned for treason or petit treason, challengeth peremptorily above thirty five, he forfeiteth his goods, and judgement of *paine fort et jure* shall be given against him, as one that refuseth the triall of law, by challenging three full juries, and like unto one that stands mute and will not put himself upon the triall of the law.

22 H. 8. c. 14. 32 H. 8. ca. 3. See before *Peine fort et dure* in the next preceding chapter. See before in the chapter of Petit treason, fo. 26.

By the statute of 22 H. 8. it was provided that no person arraigned for any petit treason, murder or felony, shall be admitted to any peremptory challenge above the number of twenty: but at this day in case of high treason, notwithstanding the statute of 33 H. 8. cap. 22, 23. and petit treason notwithstanding the act of 22 H. 8. he may challenge thirty five according to the common law, for it is enacted by the statute of 1 & 2 Ph. and Mar. cap. 10. that all trialls hereafter to be awarded, or made for any treason, shall be had and used only according to the due order and course of the common law, so as to petit treason the act of 22 H. 8. is abrogated, but in cases of murder and felony he cannot challenge peremptorily above the number of twenty, and if he challenge above twenty, and under thirty six, he forfeiteth not his goods and chattels, for no law giveth forfeiture for challenging above twenty; but the court ought to over-rule the challenge; neither is he convicted by the challenging above twenty, as he was by the common law by challenge of three juries, for the act of 22 H. 8. extendeth not to any conviction, but to the challenge only.

[228]

If

If the party defendant be attached or diftreyned by proces out of any court of record, county, by force of a jufticies, &c. hundred court, or other court baron, and make default, the goods or iffues are forfeited, and upon the attachment the fherif or other officer may take the goods with them: and this is the reafon that upon the attachment the fherif or other officer ought to return the certainty of the goods and the value, and it is not fufficient to return that he hath attached or diftrained the defendant by goods to fuch a value, and fo upon the diftreffe the iffues muft be returned in certain, becaufe they are upon default to be forfeited.

8 E. 2. Forfeit. 17. 23 E. contumac. 17. 7 H. 6. 9. 26 H. 6. Attachment 4. 28 H. 6. 9. 34 H. 6. 29. 49. 32 H. 6. ibidem 9 H. 7. 6. Broke tit. Forfeit. 4. 3 El. Dier, 199. pag. 54.

What a perfon convict of felony before attainder fhall forfeit: fee the firft part of the Inftitutes, fect. 745. verb. Attaint, fo. 391.

1. part of the Inftitutes. § 745.

See *fupra* in the chapter of Deodands, and in the chapter of Wreck, *vid.* Stanford Pl. Cor. fo. 183, 184. &c.

C A P. CIII.

Of the Seifure of Goods, &c. for Offences, &c. before Conviction.

REGULARLY the goods, &c. of any delinquent cannot be taken and feifed to the kings ufe, before the fame be forfeited. 1.

Vide 25 E. 3. ca. 14.

The fame cannot be inventoried, and the town charged therewith, before the owner be indicted of record. 2.

It is to be obferved, that there is two manner of feifures, one verball without taking, removing, or carrying away, only to make an inventory, and to charge the town: and the other an actuall feifure, and taking away the fame. 3.

26 Aff. p. 32. 43 E. 3. fo. 24. 44 Aff. p. 14. 7 H. 4. fo. ultimo.

As to the firft, the fame is manifeft by Bracton, and all our ancient authors: and let Bracton fpeak for them all.

Prifones imprifonati, antequam convicti fuerint, de terris fuis diffeifiri non debent, [a] *nec de rebus fuis quibufcunque fpoliari; fed dum fuerint in prifona debent de proprio in omnibus fuftentari, donec per judicium deliberati fuerint vel condemnati, &c.* And fo. 136. b. he faith thus, *Qui pro* [b] *crimine vel felonia magna, ficut pro* [c] *morte hominis, captus fuerit et imprifonatus, vel fub cuftodia detentus, non debet fpoliari bonis fuis, nec de terris fuis diffeifiri, fed debet inde fuftentari donec de crimine fibi impofito fe defenderit, vel convictus fuerit,* [d] *quia ante convictionem nihil forisfacit; et fi quis contra hoc fecerit, fiat vicecom' tale bre.* [e] *rex vic' falutem. Scias quòd* [f] *provifum eft in curia noftra coram nobis, quod nullus homo captus pro morte hominis, vel pro alia felonia pro qua debeat imprifonari, diffeifietur de terris, tenementis vel catallis fuis, quoufque convictus fuerit de felonia de qua* [g] *rectatus eft, fed quam cito*

Lib. 8. fo. 171. See the 1 part of the Inftitutes, fect. 745. f. 391. a. Bract. l. 3. f. 123. Brit. fo. 4. b. Fleta, li. 1. c. 25, 26.

[a] Nota the generality of thefe words. Hil. 29 E. 1. Coram rege in Aff. Campions cafe.

[b] In this word treafon is comprehended.

[c] Nota, Mort del home eft felonia magna. [d] Note this reafon extends as well to treafon, as to felony. [e] This writ is in the Regift. [f] That is, by Magna Cart. cap. 29. and that act extends to treafon as well as to felony, 5 E. 3. cap. 9. Fleta, li. 2. c. 26. accord. [g] Id eft, indictatus, for before indictment no verball feifure can be made, or inventory taken. Stat. de 4 E. 1. de offic. coronatoris, et aliquis culpabilis inveniatur, &c. Britton, f. 4. b. accord.

captus

captus fuerit per visum custodum placitorum coronæ nostræ, et per visum tuum et legalium hominum apprecientur catalla ipsius capti, et imbrevientur, et salvo custodiantur per [h] *balivos ipsius qui capitur, et qui bonam inveniant securitatem* * *de respondendo coram justiciariis nostris cum ab eis exigantur: salvo tamen eidem capto et familiæ suæ necessariæ, quandiu fuerit in prisona, rationabili estoverio suo, &c. i. rationabili victu et vestitu.* 3 E. 3. Coron. 366. 13 H. 4. 13.

[h] So it was in Bractons time, but afterwards the township was charged and answerable for the same. Britton, fo. 18. Mirror, c. 2. § 13. Fleta, li. 1. c. 25, 26. 43 E. 3. 18. a.

By the statute of 1 R. 3. cap. 3. it is enacted and declared, That neither sherif, escheator, bailife of franchise, [a] nor other person take or seise the goods of any person arrested, or imprisoned, before he be convicted or attaint of the felony, [b] according to the law of England, or before the goods be otherwise lawfully forfeited, upon pain to forfeit double the value of the goods so taken to the party grieved.

[a] Note the generality of these words.

[b] Mic. 18 E. 1. Coram rege Ro. 34. Norff. Nisi quis appellatus indictatus vel cum manu opere captus fuerit, non competit regi secta contra ipsum.

Begging of lands and goods before conviction, &c. unlawfull.

So as (*super toto materia*) these two conclusions are manifestly proved. First, that before indictment, the goods or other things of any offender cannot be searched, inventoried, or in any sort seised; nor after indictment seised, and removed, or taken away before conviction or attainder. Secondly, that the begging of the goods or state of any delinquent accused or indicted of any treason, felony, or other offence before he be convicted and attainted, is utterly unlawfull, because before conviction and attainder, as hath been said, nothing is forfeited to the king, nor grantable by him. And besides it either maketh the prosecution against the delinquent more precipitate, violent, and undue, then the quiet and equall proceeding of law and justice would permit, or else by some underhand composition and agreement stop or hinder the due course of justice for exemplary punishment of the offender. And lastly, when the delinquent is begged, it discourageth both judge, juror, and witnesse to doe their duty.

Cap. Itineris.

It was an article of inquiry, *de hiis qui aliquid agunt per quod veritas et justitia suffocantur.*

See Lib. 7. f. 36, & 37. the case of penall statutes, *et nota bene:* see also the statute of 21 Jac. ca. 3. *à fortiori* in case of life. *Placitum coronæ* ought not to become in effect *placitum privatum.* And if it fall out that the party accused be *legitimo modo acquietatus*, let such as begge him and prosecute against him be terrified by the villanous judgment against conspiratours, which you may read before cap. Judgements and Execution.

CAP. CIV.

[230]

Of Falsifying of Attainders.

Syers case, anno 32 Eliz.

AT twelfe sessions of the peace holden at Norwich for the county of Norfolk, *anno* 32 Eliz. one Syer was indicted of burglary, supposed to be committed 1 *Augusti anno* 31 Eliz. whereunto Syer pleaded not guilty. And upon the evidence it appeared that the burglary was committed 1 Septemb. *anno* 31 Eliz. so as at the time alledged in the indictment there was no burglary done:

done: and it was conceived that the very true day in the indictment was necessary to be set down in the indictment, for that the judgement doth relate to the day in the indictment, and so avoid feoffements, leases, &c. for that as it was also conceived) the feoffee, lessee, &c. when the attainder is upon a verdict, should not falsifie in the time of the felony: and thereupon the jury found Syer not guilty. And at the same sessions Syer was again indicted for the same burglary done 1 *Septembris anno* 31 Eliz. when in truth it was done. And he that gave the charge at that sessions doubted, whether upon this matter Syer might plead *auter foitz acquite* for the same burglary, (for seeing the offender is allowed no counsell, the court ought to do him justice and assigne him counsell *in favorem vitæ*, though he demand it not, to plead any matter in law appearing to the court for his discharge;) and thereupon he stayed the proceeding against him, and the assises being at hand he acquainted the justices of assize, Wray chief justice, and justice Peryam with this case, and with the doubts conceived thereupon; who answered him, that the like case had then been lately propounded by justice Peryam to all the justices of England; and by them three points were resolved. 1. That the crown was not bound to set down the very day when the treason, felony, &c. was done, but the day set down in the indictment being before or after the offence done, the jury ought to finde him guilty, if the truth of the case be so; and if it be alledged before the offence done, to finde the day when it was done in *rei veritate*, for they are sworn *ad veritatem dicendam*, and then the forfeiture shall relate but to the day in the verdict, which was the day of the offence done, and not to the day in the indictment. 2. That if the triers finde the offender guilty generally, yet the feoffee or lessee, &c. if the offence be alledged in the indictment before it was done to their prejudice, may falsifie in the time, but not for the offence. For seeing the crown is not bound to set down the very just day when the treason or felony, &c. is done, and that the triers have chief regard and respect of the offence it selfe, God forbid, but that the subject might falsifie as concerning the time of the offence. 3. If the offender be found not guilty, he in that case might plead upon a new indictment, *auterfoitz acquite:* and so Syer in the case aforesaid did, and was thereupon discharged according to the said resolutions. Nota three notable points resolved, that never were resolved in any book that we have read, and remember.

At the assises in Lent, 32 Eliz. in com. Norff.

Nota, The resolution of all the judges.

If a man infeoffeth another of his land, and after is indicted of a felony supposed to be committed before the feoffment, and thereupon he is outlawed; the party himself is bound hereby, and cannot traverse the felony, but the feoffee, &c. may; because he is an estranger thereunto: for a false indictment without any tryall by verdict shall not binde the feoffee, &c. but that he may falsifie, either by traverse of the felony it selfe, or of the time of the feoffement.

49 E. 3. 11. 7 E. 4. 1, 2.

[231]

And so it is if a man maketh a feoffement of his land, and after taketh sanctuary, and confesse the felony before the coroner by him to be done before the feoffement, and abjureth the realm; the feoffee shall falsifie the attainder by traversing of the felony. And so it is if a man be indicted of felony, and is attainted by his own confession, the feoffee shall falsifie the attainder by denying the felony.

11 H. 4. 94. 2 H. 5. Estop. 91. 7 E. 4. 1. 2. Vid. Rot. Parl. 23 H. 6. nu. 32.

felony. But otherwise it is if he be attainted upon a verdict given by twelve men, for then the feoffee shall not falsifie by traversing of the offence, but of the time only.

Pl. com. f. 390. Le Countee de Leic. case.

Where the case in effect is, that 19 *Januarii anno* 1 *Mariae*, a commission of oier and terminer in London was directed to Sir Thomas White the lord maior of London, and to divers others, reciting, that where Sir Robert Dudley knight, 9 *Januarii anno* 1 *Mariae* was indicted of high treason before Thomas duke of Norff. and 14 others commissioners of oier and terminer in the county of Norff. (where in truth that commission was directed to so many, but the indictment was taken but before 8 of them only) granting to them or any four of them, authority to receive the indictment taken before 15 commissioners, and to proceed thereupon as speciall justices of oier and terminer, &c. By pretext whereof they proceeded: and upon the confession of the said Sir Robert Dudley, gave judgement against him in case of high treason. [a] In this case it was adjudged, that Sir Robert Dudley, then earl of Leic. might falsifie the said attainder by plea, because it was void, and *coram non judice*; for that the said latter commissioners [b] had no power to proceed upon an indictment taken before 8, but before 15, and so the judgement was void, and *coram non judice*: for wheresoever the judgement is void or *coram non judice*, the party is not driven to his writ of error, but may falsifie the attainder by plea, shewing the speciall matter which proveth it void, or *coram non judice*. In which case the party forfeiteth neither lands nor goods. By which case it appeareth how necessary it is for judges, especially in cases of treason and felony, to look into the whole record, and the proceedings thereupon, before they give judgement, lest they give an unlawfull and unjust judgment, by means whereof the party may lose his life, &c.

[c] A and B were indicted, A as principall of felony, and B a accessory for receiving him. A fled and was attainted of the felony by outlawry. B the accessory (being seised of lands in fee holden of C) was arraigned upon the indictment and found guilty by verdict, and had judgement, and was hanged: C the lord entreth as lord by escheat: A the principall reverseth the outlawry, and to the felony pleaded not guilty, and by verdict was found not guilty, and thereupon was by judgement acquited. The heir of B, brought an assise of mordancestor against C the lord by escheat, who pleaded the outlawry of the principall, and the attainder of the accessory, his season in fee, and the execution, and his entry as lord by escheat. [d] The plaintife shewed the reversall of the outlawry by the principall, and his acquittall by verdict and judgement, whereupon the lord demurred in judgement. And it was adjudged that the plaintife in the writ of mordancestor should recover against the lord by escheat. Upon which judgement we observe these five conclusions. 1. [e] That the attainder of the accessory hath a kinde of dependancy upon the attainder of the principall. For it is a maxime in law, that the accessory ought not to be put to answer before the principall be attainted; and by the reversall and acquitall of the principall, the dependant judgement against the accessory cannot stand. 2. [f] That this attainder of the accessory may be falsified and avoided by the heir by plea, and is not driven to his writ of error; for that the attainder of the accessory is by matter in law avoided by record of as high nature as the

[a] Tri. 3 El.
[b] V. for this point 22 Ass. p. 64. 39 E. 3. 33, 34. 41 Ass. p. ult. 27 Ass. p. 55. 39 Ass. p. 6. 7 H. 4. 3. 9 H. 4. 1. 10 H. 6. 13. 36 H. 6. 32. 31 H. 6. 10. 4 H. 6. 24. 22 E. 4. 31. Colyns case. 2 H. 3. 10. 4 H. 7. 18. 2 H. 7. fo. Vide Rot. Parl. 18 E. 1. Rot. 11. Mountgom. Bogo de Knovil, &c.
[c] See this case temps E. 1. tit. Mordanc. 46. but not fully there reported. Vid. lib. 9. fo. 119. Lord Zanchers case.
[d] Where the ancestor of the accessory was lawfully and in due form attainted of felony and yet the heire shall inherit by matter *ex post facto*.
[e] Vi. li. 5. fo. 119. b. Lo. Zanchers case. Debili fundamento fallit opus. 2 R. 3. fo. 12.
[f] 26 E. 3. 57. 7 H. 6. 44. 43 E. 3. 3. 4 E. 3. 36. 11 H. 4. 4. 6. 9 H. 6. 38. b. 8 H. 4. 4. 10 H. 6. 6. 6 E. 4. 8. 8 H. 7. 10. 13 E. 4. 4.

the attainder of the principall was. For in this case it is impossible that there should be an accessory where there was no principall, of the same felony. 3. That the escheat of the land lawfully once vested shall by this matter *ex post facto*, be devested. 4. Though there were no immediate discent to the heir, yet upon the judgement of the acquitall of the principall the writ of mordancestor was maintainable. Lastly, that albeit the attainder of the accessory is avoided by judgement of law, yet the lord by escheat remain tenant of the land, until it be evicted from him by action or entry. And so it is if the principall be attainted of felony, and after the accessory is also attainted, if the principall reverseth his attainder by writ of error, the attainder of the accessory dependant thereupon is reversed. [232] 18 E. 4. 9. b.

A man commits treason or felony, and is thereof attainted in due form of law, and after this treason or felony is pardoned by a generall pardon; hereby the foundation it self, viz. the treason or felony being by authority of parliament discharged and pardoned, the attainder (being builded thereupon) cannot stand, but may be falsified and avoided by plea, for he hath no other remedy by writ of error or otherwise. Dier 20 Eliz. 135. lib. 6. fo. 13, 14. in Arundels case.

In the county of Warwick there were two brethren, the one having issue a daughter, and being seised of lands in fee devised the government of his daughter and his lands, untill she came to her age of sixteen years, to his brother, and died. The uncle brought up his niece very well both at her book and needle, &c. and she was about eight or nine years of age: her uncle for some offence correcting her, she was heard to say, Oh good uncle kill me not. After which time the childe after much inquiry, could not be heard of: whereupon the uncle being suspected of the murder of her, the rather for that he was her next heir, was upon examination *anno* 8 *Jac. regis* committed to the gaol for suspicion of murder, and was admonished by the justices of assise to find out the childe, and thereupon bailed him untill the next assises. Against which time, for that he could not finde her, and fearing what would fall out against him, took another childe as like unto her both in person and years as he could find, and apparelled her like unto the true child, and brought her to the next assises, but upon view and examination, she was found not to be the true child; and upon these presumptions he was indicted and found guilty, had judgement, and was hanged. But the truth of the case was, that the child being beaten over night, the next morning when she should go to schoole, ran away into the next county: and being well educated was received and entertained of a stranger: and when she was sixteen years old, at what time she should come to her land, she came to demand it, and was directly proved to be the true child. Which case we have reported for a double caveat: first to judges, that they in case of life judge not too hastily upon bare presumption: and secondly, to the innocent and true man, that he never seek to excuse himself by false or undue means, lest thereby he offending God (the author of truth) overthrow himself, as the uncle did.

Falsifying concerning Goods.

Bract. lib. 3. f. 128, 129. a. Brit. ca. 12. fol. 20. 3 E. 3. Forfeit 25. 22 Ass. 96. 13 H. 4. 13. [a] 4 H. 7. 18. [b] 3 E. 3. cor. 296. & 344.

If A be indicted before the coroner for the death of another, and that A fled for the same; hereby are all the goods and chattels of A forfeited which he had at the time of the verdict given; and this cannot be falsified by traverse. For if the party be arraigned upon the same indictment before justices of gaole delivery, and is by verdict acquitted of the felony, and that he did not flee for the same; yet he shal forfeit his goods and chattels, but yet, [a] such a *fugam fecit* may be falsified by matter in law; for if the indictment be void or insufficient, there is no forfeiture. [b] But if a man be indicted before justices of oier and terminer, and is acquited by verdict, and they finde further that he fled for the same, his goods are forfeited which he had at the time of the verdict given; [c] and it being also found in particular what goods he then had, that may be traversed by any that had property in those goods.

[c] 47 E. 3. 26. 13 E. 4. fo. 8. a. Travers de chattell al common ley.

[d] 27 Ass. p. 50. 41 Ass. p. 13. 44 Ass. p. 16. Lib. 5. fo. 111. Foxleyes case. [e] Bra. li. 3. f. 129. a. 43 E. 3. 18. 7 E. 4. 17. a. per Cheke. 45 Ass. p. 9. Stanf. pl. cor. 284. d. 30 H. 6. tit. forfeit. 31. 19 E. 3. ibid. 19.223. 45 E. 3. Ass. 9.

There is also a *fugam fecit* in law. [d] As if a man be indicted or appealed of felony and proces continued against him, upon his default of appearance, and an exigent awarded against him, whereupon he appeareth, albeit he be after acquited of the felony, yet all his goods and chattels are forfeited by the awarding of the exigent upon this *fugam fecit* in law. [e] But this may be falsified by matter in law: for if the indictment or writ of appeal be insufficient, or error be in the proces or exigent the same may be avoided by exception, and no forfeiture of goods. And there is no book to warrant the opinion of justice Stanford * in this case: for in 43 E. 3. the originall writ was good, *quod adnoto, non ut arguam, sed ne ipse arguar.* And also by matter in deed or record he may excuse his absence, as if he were in prison or beyond the sea, at the time of the exigent awarded, or if the king before the exigent doth pardon him.

*[233]

8 E. 2. cor. 406.

A is indicted of petit larceny, and upon his triall is found not guilty, and that he did flye for the same, he shall forfeit his goods. And so it is if an exigent be upon such an indictment awarded against him: but he may falsifie the same to free him of the forfeiture of his goods by such means as is aforesaid. See the first part of the Institutes, sect. 745. fol. 391. a.

Hæ leges vitam vestram (generosa juventus)
Instituunt, quæ sunt fugienda, sequendaq; monstrant.

CAP.

CAP. CV.

OF PARDONS.

WE have ſpoken of the royall and eſtabliſhing vertue of
juſtice: royall and eſtabliſhing I ſay, becauſe *juſtitia fir-* Prov. 16. 12.
matur ſolium, by juſtice the royall throne is eſtabliſhed.
We are now to ſpeak of his mercy: for the ſame Holy Spirit
ſaith, *Miſericordia et veritas cuſtodiunt regem, et roboratur clementia* Prov. 20. 28.
thronus ejus. Mercy and truth preſerve the king, and by clemency
is his throne ſtrengthened. And hereupon is the law of England
grounded. *Non ſolum ſapiens debet eſſe rex, ſed et miſericors, ut cum* Bract. lib. 2. fo.
ſapientia miſericorditer ſit juſtus, &c. Quibus tamen et qualiter eſt mi-
ſerendum, doceant eum merita vel immerita perſonarum, &c. Of this
royall vertue we ſhall ſpeak the more willingly, for that (as it hath
appeared before in the chapter of Sanctuary) all ſanctuaries and
places of refuge for ſafegard of life are taken away. And where
Bracton in the ſame place ſpeaking of the kings mercy ſaith, *Nihil*
tam proprium eſt imperii quam legibus vivere, it is to be obſerved, that
the lawes of this realm have in ſome ſort limited and bounded
the kings mercy, as ſhall appear hereafter. And for as much
as his mercy is conveyed unto his ſubjects by his pardons, we
ſhall now ſpeak thereof, being led thereunto by the book in
9 E. 4. where it is holden *a cheſcun roy appent per reaſon de ſon office* 9 E. 4. 2. a.
a faire juſtice et grace; juſtice in execution des leyes, &c. et grace de
granter pardons, &c. [a] Seneca, lib. de

[a] A pardon is a work of mercy, whereby the king either before Clementia, ca.
attainder, ſentence, or conviction, or after, forgiveth any crime, 24. Remiſſius
offence, puniſhment, execution, right, title, debt or duty, temporall imperanti me-
or eccleſiaſticall: [b] all that is forfeited to the king by any attain- lius paretur.
der, &c. he may reſtore by his charter: but if by the attainder the [b] See the firſt
blood be corrupted, that muſt be reſtored by authority of parlia- part of the Inſt.
ment. ſect. 1. fo. 8. and ſect. 646, 647. See after cap. Reſtitution.

We call it in Latin *perdonatio*, and derive it *à per et dono: per* is
a prepoſition, and in the Saxon tongue is *for*, or *vor*: as to forgive
is throughly to remit, and * forethink is to repent, and forbear is * Rot. par. 17 R. 2. nu. 11. &c.
to bear with patience, as it is ſaid, *leve eſt ferre, perferre grave.*

[c] All pardons of treaſon or felony are to be made by the king, [c] 27 H. 8. cap.
and in his name only, and are either generall or ſpeciall. All par- 4. Hil. 29 E. 1.
dons either generall or ſpeciall, are either by act of parliament coram rege Heref. Jo. fil. Phi-
(whereof the court in ſome caſes ſhall take notice) or by the char- lippi Perpoint.
ter of the king, (which muſt always be pleaded.) And theſe 1 H. 4. fo. 37.
againe are either abſolute, or under condition, exception, or qualifi- 17 H. 6. pro-
cation: for ſome of thoſe pardons laſt mentioned the party may tect. 57.
have a writ of allowance, or take an averment in certain caſes, in [234]
others the party may be aided by averment only, where no writ of
allowance doth lie.

And firſt of generall pardons. Generall pardons are by act of 11 H. 4. fo. 41.
parliament, if any of theſe pardons be generall and abſolute, the 28 H. 8. Dier 28. 3 Mar. ibid. 200. 26 H. 8.

 court

fo. 7. There is a very generall and abſolute pardon. Ro. par. 15 H. 6. nu. 31. 33 H. 6. nu. 29. &c.

court muſt take notice of them, though the party plead it not, but would wave the ſame. But in theſe dayes the generall pardons have ſo many qualifications and exceptions of offences and things, and of perſons alſo, that the court cannot take notice of them, neither can the party take benefit or advantage thereof, unleſſe he plead it: and for that it may concern the ſafety and quiet of many a ſubject, we have expreſſed the form of the pleading of a generall pardon, and have it ſet down here in Latin: but if the offence be objected in the ſtar-chamber, or any other Engliſh court, then it muſt be pleaded in Engliſh.

* This is put but for an example, but care muſt be taken, that what generall pardon ſoever be pleaded the firſt clauſe of the pardon of diſcharge, &c. be truly alledged. For the expoſition of generall words, ſee L. 5. fo. 47. Littletons caſe. Ibid. fo. 46. Franklyns caſe. Ibid. fo. 48. Drywoods caſe. Ibidem 49. b. Wirrals caſe. Li. 6. fo. 79, 80. Sir Edw. Fittons caſe. Li. 6. f. 13. b. Li. Keylw. 8 H. 8. 187. ibid. 10 H. 8. fo. 198. a. ter.

Et præd. A. per B. attornatum ſuum venit, &c. (or *in propria perſona) et dicit quod dominus Jacobus rex nunc ipſum A. occaſione præmiſſa impetere ſeu occaſionare non debet: quia dicit, quòd per quendam actum in parliamento dicti domini regis nunc tent' apud Weſtm' in com' Midd' nono die Februarii anno regni ſui ſeptimo, inter alia, inactitat' et ſtabilitum exiſtit authoritate ejuſdem parliamenti, * quòd omnes et ſinguli ſubditi dicti domini regis tam ſpirituales, quam temporales hujus regni Angliæ, Walliæ, inſularum Jernſey, et Garnſey, et villæ Barwic, hæredes, ſucceſſores, executores, et adminiſtratores ſui, et eorum quilibet, ac omnia et ſingula corpora aliquo modo corporata, civitat', burgi, comitat', riding, hundred, lath, rape, wapentag', vil', villat', hamlet' et tithing, et eorum quilibet, ac ſucceſſor, et ſucceſſores eorum, et cujuſlibet eorum authoritate ejuſdem parliamenti acquietarentur, perdonarentur, relaxarentur, et exonerarentur verſus dictum dominum regem, hæredes et ſucceſſores ſuos et quemlibet eorum de omnibus proditionibus, feloniis, offenſis, contempt', tranſgreſſ', intrationibus, injuriis, deceptionibus, malegeſturis, forisfacturis, penalitatibus, et ſummis pecuniæ, pœnis mortis, pœnis corporalibus, et pecuniariis, et generaliter de omnibus aliis rebus, cauſis, querelis, ſectis, judiciis et executionibus in prædicto actu non exceptis, neque forpris', quæ per ipſum dominum regem aliquo modo, ſeu per aliquem modum perdonari potuerunt ante et uſque nonum diem Novembris tunc ultim' præterit' ante editionem actus prædicti, cuilibet, aut alicui ſuorum ſubditorum, corporum corporat', civitat', burgorum, comitat', riding, hundred, lath, raparum, wapentag', villæ, villat', et tithing, vel aliquorum aliorum prout in actu prædicto plenius continetur. Et idem A. dicit quòd * offenſa prædicta verſus ipſum in forma prædicta objecta non eſt in actu prædicto excepta, neque forpriſata. Et quòd ipſe eſt et tempore editionis actus prædicti fuit ſubditus et ligeus dicti domini regis nunc natus ſub obedientia ſua, videlicet apud Weſtm' prædict', quodque ipſe non eſt aliqua perſona in actu prædict' except' neque forpriſat'. Et hoc paratus eſt verificare, unde non intendit quòd dictus dominus rex nunc ipſum A. occaſione præmiſſa impetere ſeu occaſionare velit, unde petit judicium. Et quòd ipſe de præmiſſis prædict' exoneraretur, et quòd generalis pardonatio prædicta ei allocatur, &c.* See before cap. of Falſifying of Attainders.

* Theſe averments (as you perceive) may be taken without any writ of allowance. 8 E. 4. 3. 4 H. 7. 8. Li. 8. fo. 68. Trollops caſe. Vid. l. 6. fo. 13, 14. in Arundels caſe. A caſe of Burton.

Hil. 29 El. the reſolution of all the juſtices.

By the generall pardon of 28 El. all felonies are pardoned, burglary excepted. Hil. 29 El. it was reſolved by all the juſtices, that a man being attainted of burglary was excepted, for the burglary remains, and is made more apparant by the attainder, and the offence of burglary is the foundation.

The moſt beneficiall generall pardons for the ſubject were thoſe of the fift, and thirteenth years of the reign of queen Elizabeth, as by compariſon of thoſe with others, will to the judicious reader eaſily appear. The beſt generall pardon in all king James time, was that of the 21 year of his reign, as by compariſon of that

with

with any of his former, will evidently appear, and were too long here to be rehearsed.

And now of particular pardons. No particular pardon, be it at the coronation, or any other, of any offence or offences whatsoever, that is absolute without any * condition, &c. need any writ of allowance, but when the pardon is conditional by force of the act of 10 E. 3. cap. 2. there a writ of allowance out of the chancery testifying that the condition is performed, viz. surety found according to that act may be had, or the party may plead the finding of surety, &c. and vouch the record.

Hil. 26 E. 3. Coram rege rot. 21. Wiltes. 3 H. 7. 7. a. this statute expounded, and this act extend to felony, and not to treason.

The most large and beneficiall pardons by letters patents, that we have read, and doe remember, were that to William Wickham bishop of Winchester (for good men will never refuse God and the kings pardon, because every man doth often offend both of them) and that other to Thomas Woolsey cardinall, which are learnedly and largely penned.

Rot. pat. 21 Julii anno 1 R. 2. Rot. pat. 12 Feb. 21 H. 8. great offences need great pardons, little offences are soon forgiven.

But let us turn our eye to ancient charters of pardon, and consider well of them.

Hil. 29 E. 1. Coram rege Hereford. Johannes fil. Ph. Perpoint, &c.

*Edwardus Dei gratia rex Angliæ, dominus Hiberniæ, et dux Aquit', omnibus balivis et fidelibus suis, ad quos presentes lræ. pervenerint, salutem. Sciatis quod pro bono servitio quod Johannes Chaumprona de Thornton in Pickerings, in partibus Scotiæ nobis impendit, perdonavimus ei sectam pacis nostræ, quæ ad nos pertinet * pro morte Isabellæ, quondam uxoris suæ, unde indictatus est, et firmam pacem nostram ei inde concedimus. Ita tamen quod stet recto, si quis versus eum inde loqui voluerit. In cuius rei testimonium has literas nostras fieri fecimus patentes. Teste me ipso apud Roukesburge, nono die Febr. anno regni nostri tricesimo.*

* It appeareth by the record that he killed her per infortunium.

Edwardus Dei gratia rex Angliæ, dominus Hiberniæ, et dux Aquitan', omnibus balivis et fidelibus suis, ad quos præsentes literæ pervenerint, salutem. Sciatis quod pro bono servitio quod Galf. filius Warnum in partibus Scotiæ impendit, perdonavimus eidem Galfro. sectam pacis nostræ quæ ad nos pertinet, de homicidiis, roberiis, latrociniis, fractionibus domorum, feloniis et aliis transgressionibus contra pacem nram. in regno nro. factis, unde indictatus est, et similiter transgressionem quam fecit ab ecclesia de Watford, in quia aliquamdiu pro timore inimicorum suorum se tenuit fugiendo, et se secundum legem et consuetudinem regni nostri justiciar' non permittendo, et etiam utlagariam, si qua in ipsum ea occasione fuerit promulgata, et firmam pacem nostram ei inde concedimus. Ita tamen quod stet recto in curia nostra, si quis versus eum loqui voluerit de homicidiis, roberiis, latrociniis, fractionibus, feloniis et transgressionibus prædictis. In cujus rei testimonium has literas nostras fieri fecimus patentes. Teste me ipso apud Linlijcu vicesimo secundo die Januarii anno regni nostri tricesimo, per breve de privato sigillo.

Delib. gaolæ de Windesfore, coram Hugone de Braund, et Johanne Neprunt die Jovis proxim' post clausf. Pasc. anno 25 E. 1.

It appeareth by this record, that the said Jeffry was indicted for the death of a man, and of divers burglaries and felonies, and being thereupon arraigned prayed his clergy, *sed salvo sibi privilegio clericali posuit se super patriam*, and was found not guilty, &c. in the proceeding whereof there was manifest error, and obtained the said pardon. Herein divers things are observable: first, that the pardon is *de * homicidiis*, and not *de murdris*, neither have we seen any pardon of murder by any king of England by expresse name. Secondly, by these ancient words the king doth pardon *sectam pacis nostræ, quæ ad nos pertinet de homicidiis, &c. et firmam pacem nostram ei*

* For this word homicide, see in the chapter of Murder. See Hil. 31 E. 3. Coram rege rot. 7. Northumb. 9 E. 4. 28.

ei inde concedimus. This *ſecta pacis* is by indictment, which is the kings ſuit, and, as it were, his declaration. Thirdly, that the king of ancient time did not pardon *homicidium, &c.* but *ſectam pacis noſtræ quæ ad nos pertinet de homicidiis, &c.* yet when he pardoned, and releaſed the ſuit or mean, viz. *ſectam pacis, &c.* the offender was diſcharged of the homicide it ſelf, *in diebus illis,* but at this day the offence it ſelf is pardoned, which is the ſureſt way.

8 H. 4. fo. 22. Li. 6. fo. 13. b.

The king brought an action of debt upon an obligation, the defendant pleaded *non eſt factum,* and at a *niſi prius* it was found the deed of the defendant; and before the day in bank, the king pardoned the defendant all debts, querels, &c. and after the king had judgement, and ſued out execution, and the defendant came and pleaded the pardon, and it was adjudged that in the kings caſe, he might plead the ſame, though he had no day in court, becauſe he could not have an *audita querela,* or a *ſcire fac'* againſt the king, and therefore if he could not plead it, he ſhould be without remedy, but againſt a common perſon he could not plead it, becauſe he ought to have an *audita querela,* or a *ſcire fac'.* And in this caſe it is obſervable, that albeit by the judgement a new title to the ſaid debt is accrewed to the king of record after the pardon, the obligation at the time of the pardon being but a matter in fact, yet for that the obligation was the * foundation of the debt, and the matter whereupon judgement was given, and by the pardon the debt due by the obligation was extinct, the judgement thereupon cannot bind, but is to be avoided by pleading the pardon.

34 H. 6. 3. a. 35 H. 6. 1. a. 11 H. 7. 10. Li. 6. f. 79. l. 8. 68. Lib. Keylw. 8 H. 8. fo. 187. 2 R. 2. 4. b. ſimile.

[236]

* Pl. com. f. 401. Coles caſe. 37 H. 6. fo. 21. Quatermains caſe. Li. 5. fo. 49. Vaughans caſe. Li. 6. fo. 13. *Caſes de pardon.*

What things the king may pardon, and in what manner, and what he cannot pardon, falleth now to be treated of.

[a] In caſe of death of man, robberies, and felonies againſt the peace, divers acts of parliament have reſtrained the power of granting charters of pardons. Firſt, that no ſuch charters ſhall be granted but in caſe where the king may doe it by his oath. [b] Secondly, that no man ſhall obtain charters out of parliament, and accordingly in a parliament roll it is ſaid; [for the peace of the land it would much help, if good juſtices were appointed in every county, if ſuch be let to mainpriſe doe put in good ſureties, as eſquires or gent. and that no pardon were granted but by parliament.] Thirdly, for that the king hath granted pardons of felonies upon falſe ſuggeſtions, [c] it is provided, that every charter of felony which ſhall be granted at the ſuggeſtion of any, the name of him that maketh the ſuggeſtion ſhall be compriſed in the charter, and if the ſuggeſtion be found untrue, the charter ſhall be diſallowed. And the like proviſion is made by the ſtatute of 5 H. 4. cap. 2. for the pardon of an approver.

20 El. Dier 135. Exod. 21. 12, 13, 14. Deut. 19. 13. *Non miſereberis ejus, &c.*
[a] 2 E. 3. c. 2. 14 E. 3. ca. 14. 10 E. 3. ca. 2.
[b] 2 E 3. c. 2. 4 E. 3 ca. 13. Rot. Par. 13 E. 3. nu. 10.
[c] 27 E. 3. c. 2. Trin. 30 E. 1. Rot. 2. coram rege London, anno 29 E. 1. A pardon of death, ad inſtantiam Johan. Butecourt. Mich. 33 E. 1. coram rege Ro. 65. a pardon ad requiſitionem H. de Bohun, count. Heref. & Eſſex.

[d] Fourthly, it is provided that no charter of pardon for murder, treaſon, or rape, ſhall be allowed, &c. if they be not ſpecified in the ſame charter.

[d] 13 R. 2. ſta. 2. c. 1. 16 R. 2. ca. 6. 9 E. 4. fo. 26. b.

Before this ſtatute of 13 R. 2. by the pardon [e] of all felonies, treaſon was pardoned, and ſo was murder, &c. [f] At this day by the pardon of all felonies, the death of man is not pardoned. Theſe be excellent laws for direction, and for the peace of the realm. [g] But it hath been conceived, (which we will not queſtion) that the king may diſpenſe with theſe laws by a *non obſtante,* be it generall or ſpeciall, (albeit we find not any ſuch clauſes of *non obſtante,* to diſpenſe with any of theſe ſtatutes, but of late times) theſe

[e] 1 E. 3. f. 24.
[f] 8 H. 6. 20. 4 E. 4. fo. 10.
[g] Li. 6. fo. 15. 9 E. 4. 26. b. per Billing chief juſtice.

theſe ſtatutes are excellent inſtructions for a religious and prudent king to follow, for in theſe caſes, *ut ſummæ poteſtatis regis eſt poſſe quantum velit, ſic magnitudinis eſt velle quantum poſſit.* Hereof you may read more in juſtice Stanford, lib. 2. cap. 35. in divers places of that chapter, of his grave advice in that behalf. Moſt certain it is, that the word of God hath ſet down this undiſputable generall rule, [h] *Quia non profertur cito contra malos ſententia, filii hominum ſine timore ullo perpetrant mala.* And thereupon the rule of law is grounded. [i] *Spes impunitatis continuum affectum tribuit delinquendi. Et veniæ facilitas incentivum eſt delinquendi.* This is to be added, that the intention of the ſaid act of 13 R. 2. was not that the king ſhould grant a pardon of murder by expreſſe name in the charter, but becauſe the whole parliament conceived, that he would never pardon murder by ſpeciall name for the cauſes aforeſaid, therefore was that proviſion made, which was (as in other caſes I have obſerved) grounded upon the law of God, *Quicunque effuderit humanum ſanguinem, fundetur ſanguis illius; ad imaginem quippe Dei creatus eſt homo. Nec aliter expiari poteſt, niſi per ejus ſanguinem, qui alterius ſanguinem effuderit.* And the words of every pardon is after the recitall of the offence, *Nos pietate moti, &c.* See before in the chapter of Murder, and in the ſecond part of the Inſtitutes, ſtat. de Glouc. ca. 9. and the Regiſter, fo. 309. pardon of the king, *de morte per infortunium, ſe defendendo, vel per lunaticum, vel per furioſum.*

[h] Eccleſ. 8. 11.

[i] Regulæ. Maledictus eſt qui peccat ſub ſpe.

Geneſ. 9. 6. Num. 35. 33.

By the ancient and conſtant rule of law, *Non potuerit rex gratiam facere cum injuria et damno aliorum; quod autem alienum eſt, dare non poteſt per ſuam gratiam.* Bract. l. 3. f. 132.

[237]

In an appeal of death, robbery, rape, &c. the king cannot pardon the defendant, for the appeal is the ſuit of the party, to have revenge by death: and whether the defendant be attainted by judgment, &c. or by outlawry, the pardon of the king ſhall not diſcharge the defendant. * In an appeal, the defendant wages battail, the plaintif counterpleads, for that the defendant brake priſon, if the king pardon the breaking of priſon, the counterplea fails: note the breaking priſon is a collateral act: and yet in divers caſes at the only ſuit of the party, when the defendant either by the common law, or by any ſtatute (beſides the reſtitution, or dammage of the plaintif) is thereby alſo to have an exemplary puniſhment, the king may pardon the ſame. For example, in an attaint by A. againſt the party, and the petit jury; againſt the party to have reſtitution, this the king cannot pardon: againſt the petit jury, by the common law that they ſhould loſe *liberam legem*, their wives and children caſt out of their houſes, their houſes waſted, their trees proſtrated, their meadows ploughed up, their goods and chattels ſeiſed, and their bodies taken, this the king may pardon, becauſe it is a puniſhment exemplary to deter others, and tendeth not to the reſtitution or ſatisfaction of the plaintif.

11 R. 2. Chre. 17. 2 R. 3. fo. 8. See 4 Mariæ Dier 133.

* 2 E. 3. Cor. 134.

13 E. 4. 5. a.

Now to take an example upon a ſtatute: *De pueris maſculis ſive fœmellis (quorum maritagium ad aliquem pertineat) raptis et abductis, ſi ille qui rapuit non habens jus in maritagio, licet poſtmodum reſtituat puerum non maritatum, vel de maritagio, ſatisfecerit, puniatur tamen pro tranſgreſſione per priſonam duorum annorum.* In this caſe the party being ſatisfied, the king may pardon the impriſonment by two

W. 2. ca. 35. anno 13 E. 1.

years, for that was added as a punishment exemplary, *puniatur, &c.* And this doth notably appear by a charter of pardon which king E. 2. made after this statute. *Rex de gratia sua speciali perdonavit Godithæ, quæ fuit uxor Roberti de Waldisch, id quod ad ipsum pertinet, de transgressione quam ipsa Goditha fecit Agathæ, quæ fuit uxor Johannis de Waldisch de Ellam, rapiendo et abducendo Johannem fil' et hæredem Johannis de Waldisch infra ætatem existentem, cujus maritag' ad ipsam Agatham pertin', unde ipsa Goditha coram domino E. quondam rege Angliæ patre ipsius regis convicta fuit, et per considerationem cur' dicti patris prisonæ adjudicata per biennium ibidem moratura, et etiam tempus imprisonamenti quod adhuc restat de biennio prædicto. Ideo vult idem rex quod præfata Goditha * de eo quod ad ipsum pertinet pro transgressione prædicta sit quieta, et quòd à prisona prædicta, si pro eo quod ad ipsum regem inde pertinet, et non alia de causa detineatur in eadem, deliberetur. Teste rege apud Westm' 8. die Maii anno regni sui primo. Ideo ipsa Goditha inde quieta quoad hoc, quod ad dominum regem inde pertinet, &c.*

Pasch. 34 E. 1. Coram rege Rot. 30 Kanc. in Ravishment de gard. See the first part of the Institutes. W. 2. ca. 35.

* Nota de eo quod ad regem pertinet.

Anno 1 E. 2.

See more of this matter, 3 El. Dier 201, 202. 9 El. Dier 261, Musgraves case. 16 El. Dier 323, Taverners case.

Trin. 40 El. Coram rege in appeal de murdro. Inter Shugborough & Buggins. Li. 5. fo. 50. & 110. b. 15 H. 7. 9. 4 H. 7. ca. 13.

The defendant in an appeal of murder upon not guilty pleaded, was found guilty of manslaughter: and it was resolved by the justices upon conference between them, that the queen might pardon the burning of the hand, for that is no part of the judgement at the suit of the party plaintif in the appeal, but it is a collaterall, and exemplary punishment inflicted by the statute of 4 H. 7. cap. 13.

In some actions wherein the subject is sole party (as appeareth by that which hath been said) some things the king may pardon: so on the other side, where the king is sole party, yet some things there be, that he cannot pardon. As for example; for all common nusances, as for not repairing of bridges, high-ways, &c. the suit (for avoiding of multiplicity of suits, which the laws abhorre, and that *nulli magis tueri rempublicam creditum est quam regi*) is given to the king only, for redresse, and reformation thereof, but the king cannot pardon, or discharge either the nusance, or the suit for the same; for, as Bracton saith, *Non poterit rex gratiam facere cum injuria et damno aliorum.* See Glanvill li. 7. cap. 17. vers. finem.

3 E. 3. Ass. 445. 16 E. 3. Grant. 53. 35 H. 6. 29. per Fortescue. 37 H. 6. 4. b. Pl. com. 487. in Nichols case.

[238]

4 E. 4. fo. 4. 12.

The customer albeit the bond and surety be made to him for the importing of bullion according to the statute of 14 E. 3. cap. 1. yet cannot he release it, *quia pro bono publico.* If one be bound in a recognisance, &c. to the king to keep the peace against another by name, and generally all other lieges of the king; in this case, before the peace be broken, the king cannot pardon or release the recognisance, although it be made onely to him, because it is for the benefit and safety of his subjects.

11 H. 4. 43. 37 H. 6. 4. b. 1 H. 7. 10. b.

After an action popular be brought, *tam pro domino rege, quàm pro seipso,* according to any statute, the king cannot discharge but his own part, and cannot discharge the informers part, because by the bringing of the action he hath an interest therein: but before action brought, the king may discharge the whole, (* unlesse it be provided to the contrary by the act) because the informer cannot bring an action or information originally for his part only, but must pursue

1 H. 7. 3. 37 H. 6. 4. See before ca. 88. Against vexatious relators, &c. in fine. * 3 H. 8. c. 12. &c.

ſue the ſtatute: and if the action be given to the party grieved, the king cannot diſcharge the ſame.

All ſuits in the ſtar-chamber, though exhibited by the party, are informations for the king, and the king may pardon them, but after judgement (and dammages, if any be given) and coſts taxed, the king cannot pardon them. Lib. 5. fo. 50. Buggins caſe. Eodem li. fo. 51. Hals caſe.

[a] And that party which informeth not the king truly, is not worthy of his grace and forgiveneſſe, and therefore either *ſuppreſſio veri*, or *expreſſio falſi* doth avoid the pardon. [a] Prov. 20. 28. Miſericordia et veritas cuſtodiunt regem.

[b] A man commits felony, and is attainted thereof, or is abjured for the ſame, the king pardoneth him the felony without any mention of the attainder, or abjuration, the pardon is void. [c] But if a man be attainted of burglary, and by the generall pardon all felonies, &c. are pardoned (except all burglaries) the attainder and burglary be excepted, as before is ſaid. [b] 9 E. 4. 28. 19 E. 3. Cor. 124. 6 E. 4. 4. per Cheke. 11 H. 4. 16. [c] Lib. 6. fo. 13.

The king pardoneth to A. a felony whereof he ſtandeth indicted, or indicted and attainted, &c. and in truth he is not indicted, nor attainted, &c. this is *expreſſio falſi*, and maketh the pardon void. A is outlawed, and the king pardons him the outlawry, and all his goods; it is void for the goods, for he muſt have a grant of them. F. N. B. 225. c. 9 H. 5. 14, 15.

If a man be indicted of felony, and the king reciteth the ſame, and pardoneth the felony contained in the indictment, and all outlawries thereupon, if any be, this is a good pardon of the outlawry, though it be doubtfully alledged, and the king not certainly informed.

The king may pardon one convict of hereſie, or of any other offence puniſhable by the eccleſiaſticall law. In all proceedings in the eccleſiaſtical court *ex officio*, the king may pardon the offence. The king may alſo pardon piracy upon the ſea; but by what word, and in what manner, ſee before in the chapter of piracy. F. N. B. 269. 20 El. Dier, 135. Li. 6. fo. 13, 14. Li. 5. fo. 51. Hals caſe. Regiſt. 67.

All the juſtices of England being aſſembled at Serjeants Inne in Fleetſtreet, when I ſerved queen Eliz. as her attorney generall, I moved this caſe unto them. A man ſeiſed in fee of two mannors, the one holden of the queen by knight ſervice *in capite*, and the other holden of a common perſon, alieneth both, and the alienee ſueth out a pardon for both, in which pardon the words are, *quæ de nobis tenentur in capite per ſervic' militare*, *ut dicitur*, and after this pardon being tranſcripted into the exchequer, proceſſe goeth out againſt the alienee, who pleadeth the pardon, beginning his plea thus, *Quibus lectis et auditis idem A. queritur ſe colore præmiſſorum graviter vexatum et inquietat' fore, et hoc minus juſte: quia dicit quoa eadem domina regina per literas ſuas patentes, &c.* and plead the letters patents of pardon, as they be with the ſaid clauſe of *ut dicitur*, and after he alieneth the manor which *in rei veritate*, was not holden; the queſtion was, whether the ſecond alienee may plead the truth of the matter or ought to be concluded by the pardon and plea of the firſt alienee. And firſt the juſtices had conſideration of the books in 29 Aſſ. pl. 38. 46 E. 3. 33. Pl. com. 398. 7 E. 6. tit. Eſtoppel. Br. 222. And in the end it was reſolved by all the juſtices, that the pleading of the pardon or of a licenſe, as it is, is no concluſion for no more then the pardon or licenſe being not poſitive or affirmative, but (*ut dicitur*) is a concluſion; no more is the Mic. 37 & 40 El. Reſolution of the juſtices concerning pardons and licences of alienation and the pleading of them, &c. 29 Aſſ. pl. 38. 46 E. 3. 33. Pl. com. 398. 7 E. 6. tit. Eſtop. Br. 222. [239]

the pleading of them with the clause of *(ut dicitur)* any conclusion. And conclusions shall not be wrought by inference or implication of a thing that is not directly alledged. But if the pardon or license had been affirmative and direct without the clause, *ut dicitur*, it had been a conclusion, and so had the pleading thereof been also. Lastly, it was resolved, that in case of the pardon or license with the clause, *ut dicitur;* if the party confesse the tenure that plead the same: as to say, *bene et verum est*, that the land is holden by knights service *in capite*, and plead the pardon or license, this shall conclude: and some of the barons said, that according to these resolutions it hath been used in the exchequer, and many presidents be there accordingly: and by these resolutions the books abovesaid shall the better be understood.

34 H. 6. 3. 21 E. 4. 46. 2 R. 3. 4. lib. 5. fo. 56.

If the king release to A all debts, and in truth A and B be indebted, this shall not discharge B: but otherwise it is in the case of a subject, for in that case the release to one dischargeth both.

If one be indebted to the king, if the king pardon or release the debt, the action and suit for the debt is discharged, and if he pardon or release the action and suit, the debt is discharged: and so it is in both these cases in the case of a subject.

22 Ass. pl. 37.

A man is indicted of trespasse and outlawed at the suit of the king. *Rex pardonavit utlegatiam in eum promulgat', et quicquid ad eum pertinet*, and notwithstanding the defendant shall make fine, for it seemeth that these words, *quicquid ad eum pertinet*, without any reference, are too generall to dispense with the fine.

We finde also a discharge of further proceeding directed to the judges of the court, &c. (not by any pardon of the offence) but by the kings acknowledgement under the great seale of the parties innocency, with commandement to the judges, that in the former proceedings and proces, &c. they shall altogether surcease: whereupon the court will award that the party shall go *sine die*, and that there shall be no further proceeding against him: as taking one example for many. William de Melton archbishop of York was accused in the kings bench *coram rege et concilio suo*, in *anno* 3 E. 3. for adherency to Edmond earle of Kent in his treasons, whereunto the archbishop pleaded not guilty; and after two writs of *venire fac.* awarded, the king directed his writ under the great seal to the judges of the kings bench, to this effect. *Licet venerabilis pater Willielmus archiepiscopus Eborum, et Stephanus London episcopus, per diversa br'ia n'stra coram nobis ad sectam nostram implacitentur de eo quod ipsi Edmundo nuper comiti Kantiæ adhæsisse debuerant: quia tamen prædict. archiepiscopus et episcopus de adhæsione predict. omnino immunes reputamus: vobis mandamus, quod placitis prædictis coram nobis ulterius tenen' omnino supersedeatis. Teste me ipso apud Westm.* 12 *die Decembr. anno regni nostri* 4. The award of the court that is given thereupon, is very observable, *viz. Cujus brevis prætextu, consideratum est, quod prædict. archiepiscopus eat inde sine die, &c. Et ulterius non procedatur versus eum.*

Pasch. 4 E. 3. Coram rege. rot. 38.

Stephen Gravesend bishop of London was charged with the same offence in parliament, *anno* 3 E. 3. whence by order of parliament the matter was referred to the kings bench to be tried, where he pleaded not guilty, and after was discharged *ut supra*, by the same writ. These men (it may be) thought that the taking of the pardon should

Pasch. 4 E. 3. Coram rege. rot. 53.

ſhould be an implyed confeſſion of the fault, and therefore went a new way: but no man that is wiſe and well adviſed will refuſe God and the kings pardon how often ſo ever he may have it; for there is no man but offendeth God and the king almoſt every day, and the pardon is the ſafeſt and ſureſt way.

If a man be indicted of felony, and found guilty, and being in priſon the king may under the great ſeale reciting the offence, &c. retain him to ſerve in his wars on this ſide or beyond the ſeas: this charter he may plead, and the court ought to allow it. As for example: *Quidam indictatus de felonia, et inde culp. dicit quòd rex eum conduxit, et inde producit cartam, quòd rex eum conduxit in vaſc. in exercitu, et dicta carta allocata fuit per curiam.* But a protection lyeth not in that caſe: becauſe a protection is a formed writ, and cannot have ſuch a recitall of the truth of the caſe: and [a] writs of protection lye not in caſe of felony, nor is it to be allowed to any that is priſoner to the court.

Paſch. 22 E. 3. tit. cor. 239. Coram rege.

[240]

[a] 7 E. 4. 29. a acc' 30 H. 6. 3. See the firſt part of the Inſtitutes. ſect. 199.

[b] One indicted of felony, without any learned councell, ſhewed forth a charter of pardon which was diſcordant to the indictment, and alſo to his name; and becauſe the court perceived that it was the kings meaning he ſhould be pardoned, he was remanded to get a better pardon.

[c] What things be requiſite to a pardon of outlawry, ſee the ſtatute of 5 E. 3. cap. 12.

[d] When the parties defendants appeared to the court to be poore, and were to be amerced or fined, the entry of ancient time was, *perdonantur per juſtic' quia pauperes.*

[e] It is obſerved that repeals by parliament of pardons lawfully and duly obtained, have been ſeeds of great diſcontentment, and of evill event.

[f] Generall pardons have been often granted at the petition of the commons, for they know beſt, where the ſhooe wringeth them, and wherein, and how they are to be eaſed.

[b] 26 Aſſ. p. 46.
[c] 5 E. 3. cap. 12.
[d] Paſch. 8 E. 1. in banco Rot. 79. Abbas de Burton, &c.
[e] Vid. Rot. Parl. 21 R. 2. nu. 12, 13, &c.
[f] 36 E. 3. ca. ult. 4 R. 2. nu. 30, 31, 32. 1 H. 4. ca. 20. 2 H. 4. ca. 13. 5 H. 4 ca. 15. 4 H. 5. cap. 8. a ſhort and effectuall pardon, and many others.

So odious was perjury, that by the law of God it was not to be pardoned: *Non miſereberis ejus, &c.*

Deut. 9. 21.

CAP. CVI.

OF RESTITUTIONS.

THERE is another work of grace and mercy, that is, when any man or woman being attainted of high treaſon, petit treaſon, or felony, (whereby the blood is corrupted, &c.) or his or her heir is reſtored.

And ſeeing we have formerly ſpoken how far, and to what intent in thoſe caſes, the king of his grace may by his charter of pardon reſtore the party: we ſhall now treat of the reſtitution of the delinquent, or of his or her heirs by parliament. Attainders ought to be had upon plain and direct evidence, (as before is ſaid) for if the party be executed, reſtitution may be had of his lands, &c.

See the firſt part of the Inſtitutes, ſect. 1. fo. 8. a. & 646, 647. 745. Vid. cap. Pardon. fol. 233.

&c. but not of his life. Generally, *Reſtituere nihil aliud eſt, quam* * *in priſtinum ſtatum reducere.*

* Gen. 40. 13. Job 12. 23. 42. 10. Reſtitutio ſecundum quid, ſeu in partem. Reſtitutio in integrum.

Of reſtitutions by parliament ſome be in blood only, (that is to make his reſort as heir in blood to the party attainted and other his anceſtors, and not to any dignity, inheritance of lands, &c.) and this is a reſtitution *ſecundum quid*, or in part. And ſome be generall reſtitutions, to blood, honours, dignities, inheritance, and all that was loſt by the attainder: and that is *reſtitutio in integrum*, with an addition ſometimes, that it ſhall be lawfull for the party reſtored and his heirs, to enter, &c. Of the firſt you may reade in Dier 10 Eliz. fo. 274. in Petition: and Rot. Par. 23 Eliz. of the earl of Arundel, &c. Of the ſecond you may reade 15 E. 3. tit. Petition 2. 3 H. 7. fo. 15. a. 10 H. 7. 22, 23. pl. com. fo. 175. Rot. Par. 13 H. 4. nu. 20, &c. Of both of them you may reade plentifully in our books, and parliament rolls, and in divers of them with addition of entry. See 1 H. 8. Kelw. 154. Sir William Oldehalls caſe, 4 H. 7. 7. Lo. Ormonds caſe. Rot. Parl. 11 H. 4. nu. 42. Rich. de Haſtings caſe, and Rot. Parl. 14 E. 4. nu. 4. Sir Joh. Forteſcues caſe, attainted of treaſon in 1 E. 4. &c.

Brit. ca. 13. fo. 23. 10 Eliz. Dier 274.

*[241]

3 E. 6. tit. Reſtitution. Br. 37. See the firſt part of the Inſtitutes. ſect. 646, 647. 745. fo. 392. verb. *Le ſank eſt corrupt, &c.*

And the reaſon wherefore the king may by his charter pardon the execution, and reſtore the party or his heirs to the lands forfeited by the attainder, and remaining in the crown is, for that no perſon hath thereby any prejudice; but to make * reſtitution of his blood he cannot do it, but by act of parliament, becauſe it ſhould be to the prejudice of others.

[a] See 10 El. Dier ubi ſup. 41 E. 3. 5. b. 27 Aſſ. p. 48. 17 E. 3. 40. 5 E. 3. 66. 29 E. 3. 7. 20 Eliz. Dier 360. Pl. Com. 252. a. 16 E. 3. Livery 30. 44 E. 3. 45. 18 E. 3. 21, 22. 24 E. 3. 29. 40 E. 3. grant 50.

In cartis benigna facienda eſt interpretatio, in fundationibus domuum religioſarum, hoſpitalium, et aliorum operum charitatis benignior, in teſtamentis magis benigna, in reſtitutionibus benigniſſima. [a] For it is holden in our books, that in reſtitutions the king himſelf hath no favour, nor his prerogative any exemption, but the party reſtored is favoured.

[b] Mich. 8 E. 1. in Banco. Rot. 62. Norff.

[b] king H. 3. was intitled, &c. to the lands of William de Albo Monaſterio by his attainder, and granted the ſame to Robert de Mares and his heirs, *donec eas reddiderit rectis hæredibus per voluntatem ſuam, vel per pacem.* And albeit at the making of this grant William de Albo Monaſterio (being dead) could have in reſpect of the attainder and corruption of blood no right heir; yet becauſe it was to make reſtitution, it had a moſt benigne interpretation.

[c] Rot. Par. anno 4 E. 3. nu. 18. on the backſide of the roll.

[c] William Lo. Zouche of Mortimer and Elianor his wife prayed to be reſtored to their land of Glannor and Morgannon in Wales, the mannor of Haveley in the county of Worceſter, the mannor of Teukeſbury in the county of Gloceſter, being the inheritance of the ſaid Elianor: who by the extort means of Roger late earle of March, were inforced to paſſe the ſame to the king by fine, in conſideration of ten thouſand pounds the king reſtored them thereto as in their former eſtate.

* An example of reſtitution in blood only. 11 H. 4. nu. 42. 13 H. 4. nu. 19, 20.

* Henry Courtney marquiſſe of Exeter and earl of Devon, having iſſue Edward Courtney, his only ſonne, was attainted of high treaſon by the courſe of the common law in *anno* 31 H. 8. and in the ſame year was alſo attainted by act of parliament. Queen Mary by her letters patents bearing date 18th Sept. *anno* 1. *regni ſui* granted the mannors of P and O, &c. in the county of Devon, &c. to the

the ſaid Edward Courtney and his heirs: and afterwards 5 *Octobris* in the ſame year, at a parliament then holden, the ſaid Edward and his heires were from thenceforth by authority of that act reſtored and inabled only in blood, as well as ſonne and heir of the ſaid lord marquiſſe his father, as to all and every other collaterall and lineall anceſtor and anceſtors of the ſaid Edward. And that the ſeverall attainders againſt the ſaid lord marquiſſe for the attainder of the ſaid lord marquiſſe be not in any wiſe prejudiciall or hurtfull to the ſaid Edward or his heirs for the corruption of the blood only of the ſaid Edward, but that the ſeverall attainders and either of them be againſt him and his heirs for the corruption of blood only, utterly void. Provided always that the ſaid act, ne any thing therein contained, ſhould not in any wiſe extend to give any benefit or advantage to the ſaid Edward, ne to his heirs, to demand, claime, or challenge any honors, caſtles, &c. ne any other hereditaments whatſoever whereunto H. 8. and E. 6. or either of them was entituled, or ought to have and enjoy by reaſon of the ſaid ſeveral attainders of the ſaid late lord marquiſſe, or of either of them. Edward Courtney died ſeiſed of the ſaid mannors without iſſue, 18 Septemb. annis 3 and 4 Ph. & Mar. and Reinold Mohun, Alexander Arundell, John Vivian the younger, John Trelawny Eſq. and Margaret Buller widow, were his collateral couſins and heirs: and whether the ſaid reſtitution extended to the heirs collaterall of the ſaid Edward, was by the queens commandment referred to the conſideration of the two chief juſtices Popham and Anderſon, Peryam chief baron, and to Egerton attorny, and to the ſolicitor generall. And it was reſolved, that by reaſon of the attainder of the lord marquiſſe, if there had been no act of reſtitution, the heirs collaterall of the ſaid Edward could not have inherited to the ſaid Edward, in reſpect of the corruption of the blood wrought by the ſaid attainder only: hereupon it was objected, that when it was enacted by the ſaid act of reſtitution, that the ſaid Edward and his heirs ſhould be reſtored and inabled in blood only as ſonne and heir to his ſaid father, as all his anceſtors lineall and collaterall, that the ſaid reſtitution extended only to his heirs lineall, for other heirs he could not have as long as the ſaid attainders of the marquiſſe ſtood in force, and the words of the act of reſtitution to Edward and his heirs, might be ſatisfied with the heirs lineall. And upon due conſideration had of the caſe, it was *(una voce)* reſolved by them all, that corruption of blood is a diſtinct penalty inflicted by law; and that the ſaid act of reſtitution did extend to the heirs collaterall of the ſaid Edward, (having no heirs lineall) as to the cleering and reſtoring of the blood, and avoiding of the corruption thereof: and that it had been ſufficient if the act had reſtored and enabled him in blood only as heir to his father, thereby he and his heirs, as well collaterall as lineall, might make their deſcent or reſort from the marquiſſe (for there was the ſtop and corruption) and from all other the anceſtors of the ſaid Edward, lineall or collaterall, and *ex abundanti* the other clauſe alſo is added, for the more manifeſtation hereof.

Mic. 35 & 36 El.

[242]

Margaret Plantagenet was daughter to George duke of Clarence attainted of high treaſon by act of parliament 17 E. 4. and ſiſter of Edward earl of Warwick, only ſonne of the ſaid George, and Iſabel eldeſt daughter of Richard Nevil earle of Warwick and Saliſbury: which

which Edward was attainted of high treaſon in *anno* 15 H. 7. before John Earle of Oxford then being high ſteward of England. The

Statute de 5 H. 8. not in print.

ſaid Margaret was by act of parliament *anno* 5 H. 8. reſtored to the ſtyle, ſtate, name, title, honour, and dignity of the counteſſe of Saliſbury, (ſhe was the laſt of the firname of Plantagenet) which act is very well penned, and worthy the reading for many reſpects, and the preamble thereof, *inter alia.*

14 R. 2. nu. 36.

Bils of reſtitution may begin in the parliament, either in the houſe of commons, or in the lords houſe.

a Rot. par. 18 E. 1. nu. 11. of Liberties. Stanf. pl. cor. fo. 165, 166, 167. 186. 66. 105. 107. F. N. B. 66. a.

[a] There be alſo other kinds of reſtitutions to be treated of amongſt the pleas of the crown, as reſtitution of goods upon an appeal, whereof you ſhall reade in Stanford with this addition. Vide lib. 5. fo. 110. a. 21 E. 4. 10.

b 21 H. 8. cap. 11. 22 E. 3. cor. 460.

[b] And by the ſtatute of 21 H. 8. cap. 11. reſtitution is to be granted upon an indictment, &c. For by the common law the party ſhould not be reſtored to his goods upon an indictment (becauſe it is the ſuit of the king) albeit the enqueſt found that the party had made freſh ſuit. But reſtitution was to be made upon an appeal which is the ſuit of the party.

Stanf. 167. a. b. Lib. 5. fo. 110. Lib. 6. fo. 80.

See Stanford alſo fo. 167. a. b. whereunto you may adde Lib. 5. fo. 110. a. & Lib. 6. fo. 80. where you ſhall finde, that though this ſtatute of 21 H. 8. ſpeak only of the party robbed, yet his executors are within the ſtatute, and ſo are his adminiſtrators. For it is a beneficiall law, and giveth a more ſpeedy remedy to the party robbed, &c. then the common law gave by way of appeale, and therefore ought to be conſtrued beneficially.

F. N. B. 66. a. 8 E. 2. tit. Forfeiture 34. 3 E. 3. cor. 365. Vid. 40 E. 3. 42. lib. 5. fo. 110. Hoſtons caſe.

Vide the Regiſter, 68. b. that in ſome caſes when the king ought *ex merito juſtitiæ* to make reſtitution to the party: yet for the honour of the king the writ ſaith, *Sine dilatione, reſtituas de gratia noſtra ſpeciali*, which derogate nothing from the right of the ſubject, when right is accompanied with grace.

c 8 H. 6. cap. 9. See the ſecond part of the Inſtit. cap. 8. H. 6. cap. 9. d 31 Eliz. cap. 11. Vide 4 Mariæ, e Dier 141.

Laſtly, there are other lawes concerning reſtitutions of another kind. [c] As by the ſtatute of 8 H. 6. reſtitution is to be made, when he that hath any eſtate of inheritance or freehold is diſſeiſed by forcible entry or forcible deteyner. [d] By the ſtatute of 31 Eliz. there ſhall be no reſtitution by the ſtatute of 8 H. 6. upon an indictment of forcible entry or forcible deteyner, where the defendant hath been three whole years together before the day of ſuch indictment [e] in quiet poſſeſſion, and his eſtate not ended, according to the true meaning of a proviſo in the ſaid ſtatute of 8 H. 6. as it is declared by the ſaid act of 31 Elizabeth.

21 Jac. cap. 15. By the ſtatute of 8 H. 6. cap. 9.

By the ſtatute of 21 Jac. regis, ſuch judges, juſtices, or juſtice, as are enabled to give reſtitution of poſſeſſion unto tenants of any eſtate * of freehold, &c. ſhall by reaſon of this act of 21 Jac. have the like and the ſame authority upon indictment of ſuch forcible entries or forcible with-holdings before them duly found, to give like poſſeſſion unto tenant for years, tenant by copie of court roll, guardens by knights ſervice, tenants by elegit, ſtatute merchant, or by ſtatute ſtaple.

[243]

And for as much (as it hath been ſaid) no reſtitution ought to be made where the defendant or party indicted in caſe of freehold hath been in poſſeſſion by the ſpace of three whole years, &c. they having the like and ſame authority in caſe of tenant for years, tenant by copie of court-roll, and other the tenants above named,

cannot

cannot give reftitution or poffeffion, where the party indicted hath been in quiet poffeffion by the fpace of three whole years. *Nota*, this act of 21 Jac. extends not to a garden in foccage, nor to a garden or keeper of a park: neither (as fome hold) doth it extend to him, that by a laft will hath an intereft in lands or tenements untill debts and legacies be paid, becaufe certain tenants be particularly nominated, and this is *cafus omiffus*. But this being a beneficiall law to reftore him, that right hath, to his poffeffion of lands, &c. whereof he was wrongfully by force difpoffeft, or by force withholden, &c. and being in like cafe in equall mifchief, others do hold, that this act extendeth to this cafe of fuch a devifee, &c. and fo it is for a tenant for a year, or for an halfe, or three quarters of a year.

See the ftatute of 32 H. 8. cap. 3. where the particular tenant charged with more then the land is worth, may after his term expired hold over untill he be fatisfied, &c. in equall cafe with fuch a devifee.

* *Nota*, there be divers prefidents in the chancery for reftitution by writ to be made after execution upon a ftatute ftaple. * Reftitution of another kinde, whereof we remember no book cafe.

Anno 25 H. 6. Execution was fued upon a ftatute ftaple, and for that no certificat of the ftatute, &c. appeared of record, the conufor had a writ of *fuperfedeas* out of the chancery with reftitution to be made; and the forme of this writ appeareth in a Regifter M. S. in the chancery.

In the cafe of Sir Robert Gardner in the time of Sir Thomas Bromley lord chancellor, after a *fuperfedeas* granted, execution was done upon a ftatute ftaple, whereupon a *fuperfedeas* was granted with reftitution reciting the fpeciall matter.

There is another prefident in 33 Eliz. in the cafe of one Carrant, (but there the writ recited no fpeciall caufe, but *pro diverfis caufis et confiderationibus*,) a *fuperfedeas* with reftitution was awarded.

THE EPILOGUE.

THUS have we by the great goodneffe of Almighty God, *per varios cafus, per tot difcrimina rerum*, brought this work concerning high treafon, and other pleas of the crowne, or criminall caufes, and of pardons, and reftitutions, to a conclufion: wherein (as we are verily perfwaded) we have made it apparent from the lively voice of the lawes themfelves, that no country in the Chriftian world have in criminall cafes, of higheft nature, laws of fuch expreffe and defined certainty, and fo equall between the king and all his fubjects, as this famous kingdome of England hath, being rightly underftood, and duly executed, to the great honour of the king, and of the laws, and the happy fafety of all his loving and loyall fubjects.

Now feeing *juftitia eft duplex*, viz. *fevere puniens, et vere præveniens*; that is, juftice feverely punifhing, whereof we have fpoken, and truly Juftice divided.

truly preventing, or preventing justice, *(quæ adhuc desideratur)* for we have spoken onely of the former; wee will therefore at this place (for a conclusion) point at the other with a direction how it may be effected.

True it is, that we have found by wofull experience, that it is not frequent and often punishment that doth prevent like offences, *Melior est enim justitia verè præveniens, quam severè puniens*, agreeing with the rule of the physitian for the safety of the body, *Præstat cautela, quam medela:* and it is a certain rule, that *Videbis ea sæpe committi quæ sæpe vindicantur;* those offences are often committed, that are often punished: for the frequency of the punishment makes it so familiar as it is not feared. For example, what a lamentable case it is so see so many Christian men and women strangled on that cursed tree of the gallows, insomuch as if in a large field a man might see together all the Christians, that but in one year, throughout England, come to that untimely and ignominious death, if there were any spark of grace, or charity in him, it would make his heart to bleed for pity and compassion. (But here I leave to divines to inform the inward man, who being well informed, *verbo informante*, the outward man will be the easilier reformed, *virga reformante.)*

Regula.

Sta, perlege, plora.

Seneca li. 1. De Clem. cap. 24. *Non minus principi turpia sunt multa supplicia, quam medico multa funera.*

Regula.

Non morbus plerisque, sed morbi neglecti curatio corpus interficit.

This preventing justice consisteth in three things. First, in the good education of youth, and that both by good instruction of them in the grounds of the true religion of Almighty God, and by learning some knowledge or trade in their tender years, so as there should not be an idle person, or a * begger, but that every childe, male or female, whose parents are poor, might at the age of seaven years earn their own living: for *ars fit quod à teneris primum conjungitur annis:* and this, for the time to come, would undoubtedly by preventing justice avoid idlenesse in all, (one of the foul and fatall channels that lead into *mare mortuum)* and by honest trades cause them to become good members in the common-wealth.

* Deut. 15. 4. *Non erit omnino indigens & mendicus inter vos, ut benedicat tibi Dominus.*

Otiosus nihil cogitat nisi de ventre, et venere.

Secondly, in the execution of good laws: True it is that there be good laws already to punish idlenesse, but none of sufficient force or effect to set youth, or the idle on work.

Thirdly, that forasmuch as many doe offend in hope of pardon, that pardons be very rarely granted, for the reasons in the chapter of pardons expressed.

See before ca. of Pardons fo. 236.

But the consideration of this preventing justice were worthy of the wisdome of a parliament, and in the mean time expert and wise men to make preparation for the same, as the text saith, *ut benedicat eis dominus.* Blessed shall he be that layeth the first stone of this building, more blessed that proceeds in it, most of all that finisheth it, to the glory of God, and the honour of our king and nation.

Psal. 58. 11. *Misericordia domini præveniet me.* 1 Maccab. 6. 27. *Nisi præveneris illis, majora quam hæc facient et non poteris eos obtinere.* 3 & 4 E. 6. ca. 5. in the preamble. *Imprimis interest reipublicæ, ut pax in regno conservetur, & quæcunque paci adversentur, provide declinentur.* 1 Mar. cap. 12. 32 H. 8. ca. 9. See the fourth part of the Institutes, fo. 312. b.

Et pergrata Deus nobis hæc otia fecit,
Optimus est patriæ jura referre labor.

Deo gloria, et gratia.

F I N I S.

A
T A B L E
TO THE
Third Part *of the* Inſtitutes of the Laws of England.

Buggery.

Buildings.

Bulls.

Burglary.

Burning of Houfes.

Challenge.

Chancery and Chancellour.

Childwite, *quid?* 206

Church.

Clergy.

Commiffions.

Divorce.

Exigent.

Extortion and Exaction.

Falſifying of Attainders.

Felo de ſe.

Felony.

Fines.

Fines. *vide* Amercements.

Flattery.

Flememsfreme, *quid?* 181

Force, and Forcible Entry.

The

Gentlemen.

Gaoler and Prifoner.

Guns.

Habiliment.

Hawks.

Heir.

Herefie.

Hobelarius; quid? 79

Hockettors or *Hocquetours*; quid? 175

Homicide.

Hue and Cry.

Indictment.

The

The

Jurors.

Larceny.

Law.

Letherwite, *quid?* 206

Libels.

London.

What

What

News.

Non compos mentis.

Non obstante.

Nusance.

Oath.

Office.

Ordnance. *vide* Guns.

Ordinary.

Outlawry.

Pagans.

Pain fort & dure.

Pardon.

Parliament.

Peers.

Penfions.

Pera, quid? 204

Perjury.

The

Where

Quare

Quare Impedit.

Rack. *vide* Torture.

Rape.

Records.

Redoubbons and Addoubbors.

Regrator; *unde?* 195

Relation.

Religion.

Restitution.

Riots, Routs, and unlawful Assemblies.

Roberdsmen.

Robbery.

Rogues.

Roy.

Sacriledge.

Sakebere.

Saving.

Treafure and Treafury.

Treafure Trove.

Trebuchet.

Trials.

Tumbrel. *vide* Pillory.

Turneaments.

Value.

Value.

Verdict.

Uſury.

Witchcraft.

Witneſſes.

Women.

Wooll.

Writs.

FINIS.